D0904883

The Legend *of the*

Wandering Jew

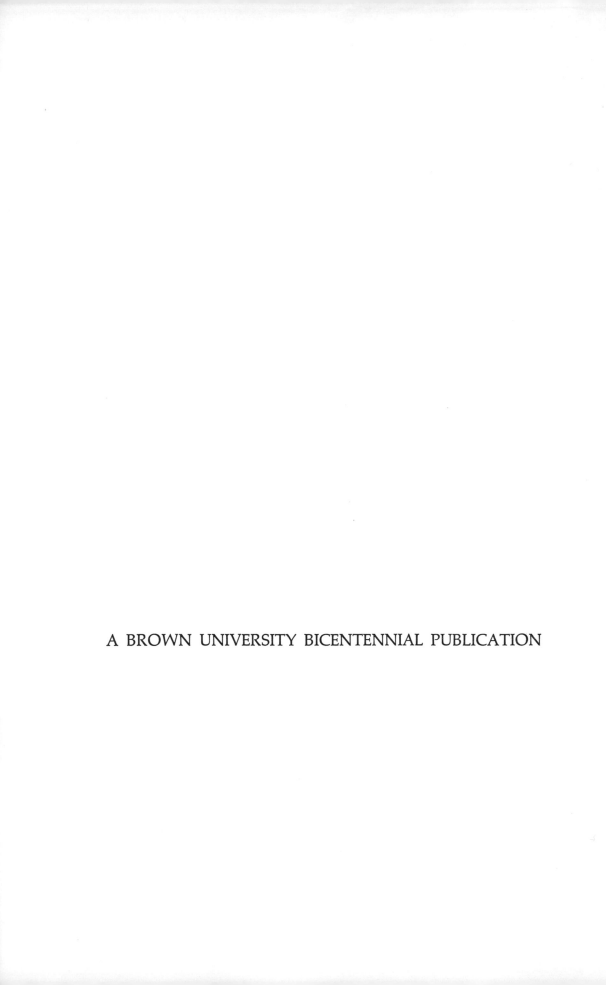

A BROWN UNIVERSITY BICENTENNIAL PUBLICATION

The Legend *of the* Wandering Jew

GEORGE K. ANDERSON

———

Providence

Brown University Press

1965

The lines from "The Wandering Jew" used as an
epigraph are reprinted with the permission of
The Macmillan Company from *The Three Taverns* by
Edwin Arlington Robinson (copyright 1920 by
E. A. Robinson, renewed 1948 by Ruth Nivison).
We also acknowledge with thanks the permission
granted us to reprint excerpts from the following
publications: Curtis Brown, Ltd., and The Viking
Press: *Jew Süss* (*Power*) by Lion Feuchtwanger,
translated by Willa and Edwin Muir —— E. P.
Dutton & Co., Inc.: *Jesus* by Edmond Fleg, translated
by Phyllis Mégroz —— John H. Bennett: *The Doctor
to the Dead: Grotesque Legends and Folk Tales of
Old Charleston* by John Bennett —— Houghton
Mifflin Co.: *The Complete Works of Geoffrey
Chaucer* edited by F. N. Robinson —— Random
House, Inc.: *The Sibyl* by Pär Lagerkvist, translated
by Naomi Walford (copyright 1958 by Random
House); *The Death of Ahasuerus* by Pär Lagerkvist,
translated by Naomi Walford (copyright 1962 by
Random House).

Designed by Asher T. Applegate

Type set in Palatino by Connecticut Printers, Incorporated

Printed by Connecticut Printers, Incorporated

On University Text

Bound by Russell-Rutter Company, Inc.

Preface

There is a card game, apparently a kind of whist, called the Wandering Jew, as well as a dice game resembling backgammon or pachisi; there are Wandering Jew dolls, puppets, and coins. Various plants and birds have at one time or another been designated as Wandering Jews. The fine arts and music have dealt with the Wandering Jew in sufficient degree to require a separate book. In collections of folk tales he has stalked all over western Europe, even sometimes America. Some two thousand written testimonials to his influence are extant, to say nothing of his continuing existence through oral tradition. His is certainly one of the most extensive and pervasive of all migratory legends, and one of the most famous. Under such circumstances, a definitive work on him is probably impossible, yet each generation should bring him up to date, if it can be done. This has been the objective of the present work.

In preparing this account of my formidable protagonist, I have been fortunate enough to have had the help of many of my colleagues, whose suggestions have often thrown clear light on a forbidding subject. Previous to this present work, I have had published the following articles on the Wandering Jew: "The Wandering Jew Returns to England," *Journal of English and Germanic Philology*, XLV (1946), 237-50; " 'The History of Israel Jobson,' " *Philological Quarterly*, XXV (1947), 303-20; "Joseph Krantz, Twin of Ahasverus," *Germanic Review*, XXII (1947), 188-201; "Popular Survivals of the Wandering Jew in England," *Journal of English and Germanic Philology*, XLVI (1948), 367-82; "The Neo-Classical Chronicle of the Wandering Jew," *Publications of the Modern Language Association*, LXIII (1948), 199-213; "*Die Silberlinge des Judas* and the Accursed Treasure," *Studies in Philology*, XLVIII (1951), 77-86; and "The Legend of the Wandering Jew," *Books at Brown*, XIX (1963), 143-59. I am indebted to the journals in which my works appeared for use of my previous research in this effort.

I am grateful also for the assistance rendered by the Harvard University Library, the Yale University Library, the New York Public Library, the Library of Congress, the British Museum, and the National and University Library of Prague. Mr. Grant Dugdale and Mrs. Barbara Dickinson have been of inestimable service through their painstaking and perceptive editorial work. Most of all, however, I am obligated to Mr. W. Easton Louttit, Jr., of Providence, Rhode Island, whose private library of material pertaining to the Wandering Jew, now a special collection in the Brown University Library, is unmatched. Without the resources of this collection my study would be seriously incomplete. I owe in addition my deepest personal thanks to Mr. Louttit, for without his enthusiasm for his library, his zeal in adding to it, and his unfailing kindness in making everything immediately available to me, I could hardly have completed the task.

G.K.A.

Contents

	Page
I. PUNISHMENT BY WANDERING	1
The Tedious Punishment	2
Some Illustrations	2
II. THE BEGINNINGS OF THE LEGEND	11
The Legend of Malchus	12
The Legend of St. John	13
Two Parallels	15
The Thirteenth-Century Chronicles	16
Other Thirteenth-Century Allusions	21
Into the Early Renaissance	23
III. THE ADVENT OF AHASUERUS	38
The *Kurtze Beschreibung*	42
Further Consideration of Details	48
The Forming of the Ahasuerus-book	51
The Development of the French *Volksbuch*	53
Minor Versions in French and Flemish	59
The English Version of the Ahasuerus-book	60
The *Volksbuch* in Scandinavia	66
The *Volksbuch* in Slavic Territory	67
The *Volksbuch* in Hungary	68
Ahasuerus in Southern Europe	68
The *Wunderbare Erzehlung*	69
IV. THE WANDERING JEW IN FOLK TALES	71
The Eastern Folk Tale	71
The Western Folk Tale	75
Germany	76
Austria	80
Switzerland	82
France, Flanders, and Luxembourg	85
Italy	87
Britain	90
Slavic Countries	95
Hungary	99
America	99
Miscellaneous	102

V. IMPOSTORS REAL AND FICTITIOUS 106
 Mortal Claimants 107
 Mythical Claimants 113
 The Scholars Attack the Problem 120

VI. AHASUERUS THE EIGHTEENTH-CENTURY TRAVELER 128
 The History of Israel Jobson 133
 Ahasuerus as Historian: The Beginnings 141
 The Neoclassical Chronicle in Summation 144
 The Romantic Chronicle 148
 Hoffman's Contribution to the Chronicle 153

VII. EARLY EXAMPLES OF THE ART FORM OF THE LEGEND 161
 The *Complaintes* 162
 Neoclassical Elements Persisting 166
 Goethe and Schubart 168

VIII. AHASUERUS IN THE ROMANTIC HEYDAY 174
 Schiller's *Geisterseher* 175
 Monk Lewis, Godwin, and Southey 177
 The Major English Romanticists' Treatment of the Legend 181
 The Art Form in Germany at the Death of Goethe 190
 Caigniez and Quinet 200
 Minor Romantics 207

IX. EARLY VARIATIONS ON ROMANTIC THEMES 212
 Ahasuerus as Romantic Sinner 214
 Mosen 218
 Ahasuerus Begins to Mix with Humanity 220
 The Beginnings of Ahasuerus as Representative of Mankind 222

X. MID-CENTURY SATIRISTS AND EUGÈNE SUE 228
 A Note on Ahasuerus in the Boulevard Theater 231
 Sue and His Influence 231
 Miscellaneous Satirical Writings 239

XI. VARIATIONS ON PRECEDING THEMES: 1850-1890 243
 On the Fringes of the Folk Tale 244
 The Purely Romantic Ahasuerus Continued 247
 From Sinning Jew to Agent of God 248
 In Kindness and Remorse 258
 Revivals of the Chronicle of the Wandering Jew 261
 Ahasuerus as a Vehicle for Satire 265
 Composites and Contaminations 268
 Ahasuerus the Emerging Modern Man 273
 Ahasuerus and the *Judenfrage* 275
 Central European Romantic Survivals 278
 Ahasuerus Amid Suffering Humanity 280
 Mark Twain and Van Nievelt 288

XII. TRADITIONAL TREATMENTS OF THE LEGEND: 1890-1920 ... 290
    Some Borderline Analogues 291
    Ahasuerus and the Jewish People 293
    Ahasuerus and the Promethean Complex 302
    Ahasuerus the Defiant and Destructive 312
    Ahasuerus the Repentant but Unredeemed 317
    Ahasuerus the Complex Sinner 323
    Buchanan and Makeever 328

XIII. THE DECLINE OF THE ROMANTIC: 1890-1920 334
    Further Imitations of Folk Tale and Chronicle 334
    The Skeptic Becomes the Jokester 338
    The Initial Impact of World War I 344
    Hints of Redemption 348
    Ahasuerus Considered for Redemption 350

XIV. WITHIN THIS GENERATION 355
    Recent Examples of the Chronicle of the Wandering Jew 358
    Latter-Day Ironists 365
    Folk-Tale Variants 368
    Ahasuerus in Passivity 371
    Ahasuerus Identified Anew with Humanity 374
    Conclusion 391

APPENDIX A. NOTES ON THE STUDY OF THE LEGEND 399
    Nineteenth-Century Beginnings 399
    Critical Works from 1850 to about 1875 400
    From 1875 to about 1900 402
    Other Minor Studies around the Turn of the Century 407
    Major Studies from Neubaur to Gielen 409
    Miscellaneous Special Studies 411

APPENDIX B. NOTES ON THE WANDERING JEWESS 414

APPENDIX C. A NOTE ON MODERN HUNGARIAN TREATMENTS
    OF THE LEGEND 416

NOTES 421

INDEX 463

The Legend *of the*

Wandering Jew

I saw by looking in his eyes
That they remembered everything;
And this was how I came to know
That he was there, still wandering.

EDWIN ARLINGTON ROBINSON
"The Wandering Jew"

CHAPTER ONE

Punishment by Wandering

What man has done to man is the saddest chapter in the history of the world. The story of the peoples of the earth is in large measure the tale of how the world whipped the nonconformist with its displeasure and visited upon him dishonor and ignominy, torture and death. The history of punishment has written its own commentary.

Since the beginnings of time billions of men and women have been punished for one reason or another and perhaps for none. All too often the powerful individual or the barbarous society of a given era has wreaked this punishment with sadistic severity. It is impossible even to attempt to describe all the methods by which an individual has been punished. Many a book or pamphlet has contributed to the general indictment of mankind on the charge of common brutality in its vengeance. The ingenious and complicated ways of killing a human being, for instance, have been studied and applied well enough in the cradle of our Western civilization, and if we should include the tropical luxuriance of Oriental and African methods of happy dispatch, we may well decide that the human mind has almost exhausted itself on this subject. It becomes a relief to consider mere beheading, hanging, shooting, or the relatively humane instruments of physics and chemistry in the present age.

Even among barbarians, no doubt, an offender would usually be knocked in the head quickly or strangled efficiently, and so an end to the business. But under all the smoke of folklore and legend there is always some fire of fact, and folklore, as it happens, has a way of being right in the long run. Many of the strange and fantastic executions, mutilations, imprisonments, and exiles recorded in story are based upon actual punishments inflicted upon real human beings. Even if these were rare—and it is obvious that only the unusual would be likely to attract enough attention to assume the stature of a legend—still they probably happened once upon a time. Moreover, many a cruel magistrate or fanatical high priest would possess the imagination to decree mental as well as physical torture, although this would be infrequent enough to interest a professional bard, minstrel, or communal storyteller. In this way a refinement of punishment would be perpetuated in legend, for that is the way folk tales come about—they are begotten by the unusual. Most stepmothers are well-intentioned and kindly; the occasional wicked one, however, is worth talking about. If all stepmothers were intrinsically evil, it is doubtful whether much would be made of them in legend. They would be accepted and tolerated as any natural cross is to be borne. Since few sons kill their fathers, or fathers their sons, it is entirely fitting that there should be the folk tale of the father and son combat, in which one or the other is killed. This is an affair about which one can enjoy hearty gossip.[1]

The Tedious Punishment

The direst of punishments would necessarily be that which lasted the longest. Thus the eternal, tedious punishment is common in the folklore of most peoples and races. The long-enduring punishment, physical or mental or both, is most impressive; it challenges the imagination of poet and peasant alike. The punishments of hell, conjured up by the prophets of wild infernos, are all of this type. Classical mythology abounds in such examples—Prometheus torn by an eagle, Sisyphus eternally rolling a huge rock uphill, Ixion revolving endlessly on a wheel, Tantalus suffering forever from hunger and thirst.

Cruel and unusual punishment, inflicted upon a real physical being, must naturally be limited by the endurance of the body. A Chinese coolie of mandarin days slowly strangled as he stood upon bricks within a wooden frame which constricted his throat (one brick was removed each day); another coolie tied to the ground while bamboo shoots grew through him; a victim impaled upon the fumbling bayonets of the Iron Maiden of medieval German notoriety—these can inspire little more than morbid horror. We should probably agree that the fiery tombs in Dante's *Inferno* do not represent the best of the great poet's vision.[2] The ghastly spectacle of the Crucifixion has been re-enacted for centuries in Christian fetishism and pageantry. For the fact remains that it is the painful, tedious punishment which challenges the man of imagination, the poet, and the prophet, because they can see clearly, in the protracted suffering of the victim, a symbol of man's struggle against overmastering principalities and powers, a vague but poignant allegory of life itself.

Oriental and Occidental legendry alike yield examples of one form of tedious punishment—eternal wandering. About a hundred instances of wandering, for various reasons, could be cited.[3] But the penalty is usually exacted for blaspheming or some other offense against a deity, notably for pride and presumption, personal arrogance directed against a god. Thus Sisyphus defied the gods and put Death in fetters; Ixion slew his father-in-law and was pardoned by Zeus, but then was so rash as to abuse his pardon by making advances to Hera; Prometheus had the audacity to bring fire down from heaven for the use of man and compounded his offense by devising men from clay. And the unfortunate mortal women who were the not unwilling vessels of Jove's lust were set to wandering by jealous Hera, goddess of marriage. Io, turned into a heifer and harried by a gadfly, fled all over the world in a fruitless effort to escape it. Callisto, transformed into a bear, is now Ursa Major, whirling constantly around the polar star and never setting in Mediterranean latitudes. Doubtless many of these myths are celestial (solar or lunar) to begin with; but most, by the time we hear of them, are so far removed from their archetype that we should treat them as folk tales.

Some Illustrations

Such offenses against gods being unforgivable, without forgiveness punishment must remain. Classical mythology holds no monopoly on the eternal tedious punishment; the three great religions of the world—Christianity, Mohammedanism, and Buddhism—all furnish examples in their legendry of an Eternal Wanderer. In fact, Christianity has more than one. The Wandering Jew, Cain, Al-Sameri, Pindola, the Wild Huntsman, the Flying Dutchman, and the peculiar American contribution, Peter Rugg, all blasphemed, or were at least disobedient to God. The Man without a Country blasphemed against the demigod Patriotism. The punishment of these sinners in each case was to remove them from the normality of mankind, usually to mark them apart from the society which they had flouted and to make them realize their predicament while realizing also that the conformists were prospering.

Before we meet the Wandering Jew, the Eternal Wanderer about whom the most has been said and written, it is important to have before us at least the outlines of his most celebrated competitors in wandering. In the scriptures, the classic story of wandering is the account of Cain as it appears in the Book of Genesis (4:1-15). Cain, son of Adam, obviously a short-tempered man, is piqued by the Lord's preference for the offerings of his younger brother Abel, which favoritism would be inexplicable were it not that Jehovah preferred animal sacrifices to vegetable ones, and Cain was a tiller of the soil, whereas Abel was a keeper of sheep. At the end of a spirited interchange, in which Cain "talked" to his brother—one of the best examples of understatement in all literature—Cain slew Abel. But of more significance than the mere murder is Cain's unrepentant spirit and insolent reply to the Lord's "Where is Abel thy brother?": "I know not: Am I my brother's keeper?" Cain has placed himself in the hopeless position of a man whose pride has violated, without qualms, the law of One greater than he. And so the eternal tedious punishment is imposed, with the addition of a blighting power and a stigma: "When thou tillest the ground, it shall not henceforth yield unto thee her strength; a fugitive and a vagabond shalt thou be in the earth. . . . And the Lord set a mark upon Cain, lest any finding him should kill him." This desolating power of blight and this stigma, or rather what interpreters subsequently conceived this mark to be, will reappear later on, because in them one can detect a borrowing from the Cain Legend by the shapers of the Legend of the Wandering Jew.

From the Koran comes the Legend of Al-Sameri, probably a transference of the Hebrew Legend of Cain to the holy book of Islam. The incident is told in the twentieth chapter of the Koran and parallels the thirty-second chapter of Exodus. In the Old Testament version the temporarily corrupted Aaron made a golden calf for the Israelites to worship, an act of disaffection which caused Moses to break in anger the tablets of the Lord. Aaron managed to squirm out of his predicament by shifting the responsibility, in weasel words, to the Israelites themselves. The Lord plagued the people because they had worshipped the calf, but Aaron himself slipped into the background. Al-Sameri replaces Aaron in the Koran, at least as far as the golden calf is concerned. Al-Sameri confesses to Moses: "I took a handful of dust from the footsteps of the messenger of God, and I cast it into the molten calf, for so did my mind direct me." And the golden calf proceeded to low in convincing fashion. Therefore Al-Sameri becomes a wanderer under the curse of Moses; his punishment is to be, moreover, that he must say to those who meet him: "Touch me not!" Again the blight and the wandering, x and now the addition of untouchability, which we will see occasionally in the progress of the Wandering Jew. But Al-Sameri's punishment seems implicit rather than explicit. Still, the formula is sound. Not only did Al-Sameri violate the first commandment in setting up another god before the true God; like Prometheus, he also brought life to an inanimate object—not only life but also voice.

A minor analogue, perhaps, but sufficient to show the universal nature of the sentence of eternal wandering visited upon sinners who affront the dignity of a god, is the instance of Pindola in his disobedience to Buddha. The story is very old, of course, but it has been known to the Western world only since the nineteenth century. In the Divyavadana, a collection of Buddhistic rules, is a special section known as the Açoka Avadana which gives a version. The same tale appears in the Far East in the Samyuktagama Sutra of about the same date (ca.450). King Açoka, having been converted to Buddhism, desires to glorify all the places once sanctified by the presence of Buddha. He calls about him all his sages and priests:

> Three hundred thousand religious folk were gathered together in his presence. But among these hundreds of thousands of the elect, including disciples of Buddha and ordinary men of virtue, not one had the presumption to occupy the place of honor. "How comes it," said the king, "that the seat of the Elder is not filled?" Then old Yaças, who possessed the six supernatural senses, answered him as follows: "Great King, that is the seat of the Elder." "O Sthavira," replied the king, "is there any man of faith older than thee?" "Yea," said the Sthavira, "there is one who has been designated by the most eloquent of the wise men as the chief of those who make the roaring of the lion heard in the land; it is Pindola, descendant of Bharadvaja; and the Seat, the first of them all, is his." Immediately the king, on whose body all the hairs were standing on end like the stems of the kadamba flower, asked this question: "Is there still some religious man in the world who has seen the Buddha?" "Yes," answered the Sthavira, "there is one who has seen the Buddha; it is Pindola, descendant of Bharadvaja, and he is still alive . . ."

Pindola, being sent for, makes a spectacular entrance:

> . . . Straightway the Elder, Pindola . . . surrounded by several thousand of the elect, who then deployed to the right and to the left like the tips of the crescent moon . . . came and sat in the Seat of Honor . . . The king saw Pindola, whose head was white, and whose forehead was covered by long and bristling eyebrows which hid his eyelids . . .

Questioned by the King, Pindola tells him how he had seen Buddha and for what reason the Master had condemned him to immortality on earth. For Pindola had, in addition to the six supernatural senses, the ability to fly, though it was not in man's province to fly:

> But when the Master, invited by Sumagadha, daughter of Anatha Pindika, came to visit her at Pundravarddhana, escorted by five hundred of the elect, I, seizing the opportunity offered me by my supernatural power, reached the summit of a mountain and hurled myself into the air in order to reach Pundravarddhana. And at that moment the Master gave me the command: "You will not enter fully into Nirvana as long as my Law shall not have disappeared."[4]

This tale was current not only in Buddhist India but also in Armenia, a territory which, as we shall see on a later page, has a peculiar importance in the genesis of the Legend of the Wandering Jew. Pindola's punishment, however, is imposed upon him with Oriental obliqueness and vagueness; he is granted immortality but does not necessarily have to wander. His doom renders him akin to the Wandering Jew, but only in an earlier phase.[5]

Cain and Al-Sameri must wander indefinitely, but for others the wandering may be for a definite term only. If the term is sufficiently long, it will be enough as an ordeal. For example, there is an Italian folk tale, preserved in Basile's *Pentamerone*, about a woman who, in order to recover a lover who had been bewitched, was obliged to wander until the pair of iron shoes which she must wear had worn out completely.[6] This, however, involved a task covering only seven years. Perhaps the wandering will be for the duration of the victim's life, and death will be his release. But since in folklore the sinful dead may not be able to rest, the penal wandering may continue after death and therefore eternally until Judgment Day.

As an excellent example of the growth of a legend of wandering, consider the Legend of the Wild Huntsman, the ghostly hunter who, with his retinue, continues the chase after he has departed from the mortal scene. This legend has certain analogues which can be traced all over the continent of Europe, but it has become concentrated principally in Germany and France. The gods of Germanic mythology were great hunters, as might be expected of deities created by people to whom hunting was a necessary means of livelihood. The elaborate deified chase which Woden, king of the gods, was wont to indulge in, along with his lesser divinities, afforded an opportunity for certain privileged mortals to see the gods in procession. Then, later, a prominent king, nobleman, historic or romantic hero, commoner, forest ranger, or even saint could slip into Woden's place and appear as huntsman under wondrous circumstances. In this manner was kept alive the tradition of the renowned mortal, such as King Arthur or Frederick Barbarossa, who would return to the sight of special members of the human race.[7]

Such awesome manifestations of folkways, of course, would scarcely be pleasing to the workers in the medieval Church. Besides, at least as old as Woden or Thor or King Arthur was the belief that the sinful dead cannot rest. Why should not some wandering ghost spend his time, since he can never come to rest, in some futile chase? Thus the leader of the hunt might be the fey King Herla, who was once immured in a supernatural castle while three centuries passed in the twinkling of an eye.[8] Or it might be the king of the Ostrogoths, Theodoric the Great.[9] In more piquant guise, it might be a woman, such as Herodias, the notorious sister-in-law of King Herod, an evil woman whose name subsequently turns up in the Legend of the Wandering Jew.[10] Or it might be the goddess Diana, or the infernal otherworldly creature Hecate, or a mysterious embodiment of carnal sin whom the Germans call Frau Holle.[11]

Sometime in the Middle Ages—we cannot tell exactly when, for the topic has not yet been fully studied—there grew up the story, analogous in many respects to the Legend of the Wandering Jew, and no doubt constructed in the same manner, of a Jew who would not allow Jesus to drink from a nearby horse trough during the agonizing march to Calvary, but pointed instead to some water in a hoofprint and observed that it was good enough for such an enemy of Moses. In punishment for this obvious indignity to Christ, the Jew was condemned to become the Wild Huntsman.

Le chasseur maudit had for his favorite haunts the Black Forest in Germany and the forest of Fontainebleau in France. In England he appeared in debased form as Herne the Hunter, once a keeper of game in Windsor Forest, who moved about, particularly on winter nights, blasting trees and cattle, wearing horns, rattling chains, and comporting himself generally in "a most hideous manner."[12] In France he seems to have been sometimes identified with St. Hubert, the traditional patron saint of the hunt. Hubert assumed this patronship as a penance assigned by the Lord, who once caught him hunting on a Good Friday. On this occasion the Lord revealed himself between the antlers of a stag; and the stag's head is, appropriately enough, an occasional attribute of the Wild Huntsman.

The many details associated with this Legend of the Wild Huntsman are typical of all such sagas and will prepare us for the ramifications of the Legend of the Wandering Jew. For instance, the Huntsman may appear in the shape of a man with a stag's head. Or he may have a normal human head clothed grotesquely, on cold winter nights, in a strange cap of fur. Or he may be headless, carrying his skull about with him under his arm. He may ride about in a disembowelled state, with his entrails rolling along ahead of him. He may be luminous, or breathing fire; he may, on the other hand, be altogether human in appearance, with rich and costly garments, equipped with a staff of white or of any given color, with only the extremely long hair of the Huntsman to suggest his supernatural nature. His favorite time of hunting is at night, usually between midnight and the first cockcrow at one o'clock in the morning; but he can be seen in daylight, and in fact no season of the year passes without his being seen, under proper circumstances. His retinue is usually a motley one. There may be knights and ladies in his train, but he is more commonly followed by witches and warlocks, courtesans, renegade churchmen, mercenaries, and other ranks of the beautiful and damned, including even unbaptized children. He is accompanied also by an assortment of animals— some, such as dogs and horses, natural accessories of the chase; others, such as bears, sows (especially sows about to litter), ravens, and owls, not so often associated with the hunt as pursuers but rather as pursued. These animals may often be altogether lurid in their appearance, for they are frequently returning spirits of the dead, or revenants, portrayed amid a stampeding mass of hellhounds with fiery tongues, glowing heads, blazing eyes which may protrude over the snout; maimed dogs; three-legged quadrupeds of various species; winged hounds (often proceeding in strict single file) baying in devilish fashion and held in check with a fiery leash. The horses, of many colors, likewise exhale fire and are anatomically unconventional, being often headless or two-legged.

The quarry of the Wild Huntsman is of similarly infernal attributes. It may consist entirely of revenants; even if it is an innocuous hare or deer, it may be the reincarnation of some damned soul. Women are often the victims; if so, they are naked, and are being perpetually cut in two by the Huntsman or torn to pieces by his hounds. Their status is that of a quondam lecherous mortal, a prostitute, a witch, or some minor pagan deity, such as a fairy or a wood sprite. Infants who have never been baptized may offer up their pathetic little bodies to the pursuers.

In effect, though, there seems to be little difference between the pursuers and the pursued; it is all a horrid, nightmarish kind of phantasmagoria.[13]

As to occasion, the hunt may take place at any time and at any place. The more romantic treatments of the legend, however, set the hunt at night and in some wooded place, although hills, mountains, deserts, old battlefields, and even the courtyards of deserted castles are possible. One strange tendency of the hunt is to move in an approximate circle about a given locality. Near a settlement of moderate size, or near a city, the hunt is likely to take to the air, skimming the tops of trees. It may be heralded in many ways by curious noises and odors of various kinds. Sudden clankings of chains, unwonted clashings of swords, unaccustomed ringing of church bells, unearthly music, unexpected trampings of horses' hoofs or bayings of hounds, shouts of huntsmen, and vague menacing reports of storm and fire are all proper warnings that the hunt is afoot.

This infernal chase may, indeed, be turned loose upon anyone. It may be sufficient to frighten the spectator out of his wits; or, failing that, the hellhounds will attack normal dogs, driving them mad and thus inflicting upon a community the dread scourge of rabies. Fortunately there are certain things that can be done to avert disaster if one should be so unlucky as to witness the mad progress of the Wild Huntsman. For, as in certain treatments of the Legend of the Wandering Jew, the presence of the supernatural creature is most deleterious to the mortal who happens to encounter him. But, as to the Wild Huntsman, standing on a grave is one kind of protection, because hellhounds cannot pass over a human grave. They will, furthermore, respect the inviolability of the magic circle. Prayers, charms, even silent communion with God will prove to be helpful. A variety of local devices is efficacious, provided one is acquainted with the necessary protocol. One may be saved by standing in the middle, or at the side, of a road— whichever is more convenient; by staying at home, surely one of the safest of all remedies; by throwing oneself to the ground; by holding a magic plant or magic food in one's hand; by sticking one's fingers in one's ears; by offering food as a sacrifice to the hellhounds; even by scolding the otherworldly intruders—but this last is probably useful only if it comes from a notorious female shrew.

The total effect of the apparition of the Wild Huntsman upon the viewer is not easily determined. Mockers and scoffers at the Church, thieves, and the unnecessarily inquisitive are especially susceptible to the ravages of the hunt. If the Huntsman or one of his retinue should throw human flesh or carrion at a mortal and hit him with this unsavory tidbit, it will stick to him for life. The decayed hoofs of dead horses may also be hurled at random; they too will adhere permanently. The sight of the hunt may throw the spectator to the ground so violently that by mere impact he will be rendered unconscious; it may drive him mad; it may blind him; it may make him drive a knife or an ax into his foot. It may actually kill him and snatch away his soul. Or it may be that he will be kidnapped to lead a death-in-life amid this fiendish company. Happily, such extreme eventualities are rare. On the other hand, the hunt may have the bathetic effect of making one's head swell. It can only be concluded that to see the hunt is not a good thing.

If some of these effects appear ridiculous, there is comfort in the thought that equally ridiculous remedies can be resorted to for counteracting them. If it can be arranged somehow that one may see the hunt in exactly the same spot a second time, all previous injuries will be cured. The difficulty is, however, that the Wild Huntsman cannot be casually summoned as a spirit from the vasty deep. A pinch of mold from Christ's grave, which can scarcely be had for the mere asking, when thrown at the Huntsman can blast the whole hunt. Or the Huntsman may be turned away by boldly asking him for some salt or some parsley or a share of his quarry. Throwing back at him the carrion which has been thrown at you will prove effective; the still more heroic expedient of eating a portion of the human flesh cast upon you will work even better. The surest recourse in any such crisis is of course earnest prayer.

As to the significance of the appearance of the hunt, it may or may not have punitive value; more likely it serves simply as an omen, warning about almost anything of importance—good or bad crops, storm and tempest, war, pestilence, and ultimate disaster. The vagaries of folklore know no rules. The important thing is to see all the possibilities in such a legend as that of the Wild Huntsman, for the Wandering Jew could be of similar portents, especially when the romantic imagination of the ages got a grip on him.

Of more recent date are three other legends of wandering. One of these, the story of the Ancient Mariner, in many ways Coleridge's poetic masterpiece, is so intimately connected with an important milestone in the history of the Legend of the Wandering Jew that it should not be considered until later. But this parallel should be noted: Just as Coleridge based his impressive creation upon the age-old theme of the wanderer in general and yet gave his Mariner a story all his own, thereby making available a Legend of the Ancient Mariner for posterity to perpetuate if it cared to do so—just so, some unknown author or authors based the Legend of the Wandering Jew upon the same age-old theme of wandering and shaped the story, drawing upon other legends for the ingredients when they were needed, and passed the new Legend along to subsequent generations for them to continue it. The difference is, of course, that no one has given the world another version of the Ancient Mariner, whereas the perpetuators of the Wandering Jew's saga have been numbered in the many hundreds.

Another legend of wandering is the tale of the Flying Dutchman, which has achieved a certain degree of deathlessness through the fact that it was turned into a grand opera by Richard Wagner. To English-speaking readers the Dutchman is known also through Frederick Marryat's novel, *The Phantom Ship* (1839). A sea captain makes an oath that he will round the Cape of Good Hope if he has to try until Doomsday, and this precise task of futile attempt is imposed upon him for eternity. Other accounts testify as to his great brutality toward his crew, who rise in mutiny against their commander. This is the version in Sir Walter Scott's *Rokeby* (1813): the ship becomes a hellship and is doomed to sail the seas until Judgment Day. It is evident that the Marryat version, which introduces the blasphemy motif, is closer to the customary pattern of the Eternal Wanderer. In Wagner's opera (1843), on the other hand, the blaspheming Dutchman is ultimately redeemed through the self-sacrificing love of a pure maiden. This romantic conclusion, suggesting a medieval legend of martyrdom, marks a decline in the vitality of the legend and requires no further comment. The same kind of degradation, attained by falling in love, sometimes befalls the Wandering Jew.

Although this business of blasphemy and wandering obviously relates the Legend of the Flying Dutchman to that of the Wandering Jew, it is clear, on closer examination, that, like the Legend of the Wandering Jew, the Flying Dutchman is a tale comprising more than one older tale or folk motif. The spectral ship, for example, is one motif that goes back as far as the time of the invention of ships. The wandering motif is another. The gory violence and the romantic, sentimental woman-love are cultural refinements of the early nineteenth century. The wandering of the Dutchman, as fits the formula, was imposed because he swore a rash and insolent oath and, in so doing, offended God. The time limits of the legend—at least the *terminus a quo*—are indicated by the presence in the legend of the Cape of Good Hope. In other words, the tale had its beginnings some time during the Age of Discovery or the Renaissance. The fact that the leading figure is a Dutchman, rather than a Portuguese or Spaniard, restricts the legend still further. The seventeenth century may be taken as the great period of Dutch maritime activity. At any rate, whatever his origins, the Flying Dutchman follows the Wandering Jew and the Wild Huntsman among those who seek eternally and find not.

Another such wanderer, who seems to have sprung up in highly original fashion on native American soil, is Peter Rugg, the Missing Man. He is the creature of the lively imagination of William Austin (1778-1841), whose melancholy tale of Rugg was published in the *New England Galaxy* for September 10, 1824.[14] Peter Rugg, who lived in Middle Street, Boston, in the days when George III was still sovereign in Massachusetts, was a man of violent and profane temper. On one occasion he and his little daughter Jenny were visiting in Concord. A storm was coming up, and his friends tried to dissuade him from the journey back to Boston. But Peter vowed, amid oaths, that he would make the trip home in his horse and buggy or never see his house again. This is exactly what happened; for the next fifty years and more Peter Rugg was seen on the Boston Post Road, or near Hartford, or in Delaware, or even in Virginia, where he committed the tactless social indiscretion of breaking up a horse race. He could never make an appearance without a thunderstorm to herald his approach. His old buggy was always drawn by a horse which had certainly become a steed of hell. With his little daughter beside him, the ever-distraught man kept asking each person he met whether he was on the road to Boston. Clearly he had become one of the damned. When at last his house in Middle Street was about to be auctioned off by the sheriff for nonpayment of taxes, Peter finally penetrated into the immediate neighborhood, only to be greeted by a mysterious voice which announced that he, Peter Rugg, must keep traveling forever on his frustrated quest.

Austin's novelette is an impressive little piece of quasi-realistic, imaginative writing. Its author seems to have influenced both Poe and Hawthorne, and it is obvious enough that he in turn was influenced by the Legend of the Wandering Jew, which, as we shall see, enjoyed a heyday during the 1820's. Not only were there Wandering Jews in profusion then, but also many other mysterious mortals and immortals of unhappy lot—Fausts, Ancient Mariners, Frankensteins, and Peter Schlemihls. One other writer of nineteenth-century America evidently thought that the theme of the wanderer who blasphemed was inspiration for an effective fictional creation, this time for political propaganda. Edward Everett

Hale's *The Man without a Country* (1863) had its protagonist, Philip Nolan, conveyed over the seven seas without ever returning to the United States because he had in his youth cursed his native land. Not that cursing the United States is in theory so heinous an offense as blaspheming God, except in the mind of a chauvinist, but Hale was writing during the depressing and militarily critical days of the American Civil War. His story is a piece of American legendry which is not easily forgotten.

Austin and Hale, and, before them, Coleridge, fathered the legends of Peter Rugg and the Man without a Country and the Ancient Mariner out of their own romantic imaginations. Legends do not just happen; they must have someone to bring them into being. The original creator who set in motion the Legend of the Wandering Jew will never be known to us, nor when and where he lived; but it is very likely that he was from in or near the city of Jerusalem, at a time when Christian belief was widespread enough to support him, and his motive in creating the Legend was to create a story of vengeance for the killing of Christ and to propagandize the power of His word. In any event, he is the reference point to be designated as the Originator.

Whatever the circumstances, the Legend of the Wandering Jew is never, throughout the many centuries of its existence, without symbolic value; in even some of the most trivial, literary representations of the Legend, the Wandering Jew can point a moral. The Originator made clear, if only by inference, that his creation was an object lesson for mankind: Do not blaspheme; advantage rarely comes of it. For if you do, you may suffer the most monotonous and soul-piercing of punishments. Blasphemy comes from overweening pride, and by that sin fell the angels. And when the moderns inherited the Legend, their message seemed to be: *Ecce homo!* Behold the man who sinned and is being punished for it amid all these terrors; but look again, see how he represents the spirit of revolt, of unconquered courage, of the very Jewish race itself, and "what else is not to be overcome."

The Beginnings of the Legend

Throughout the Near East and the shores of the eastern Mediterranean, during the first half-dozen centuries after the Crucifixion, many legends of extrascriptural nature circulated in oral tradition. Examples would be the legends of the Holy Cross (St. Helena), of St. Veronica, of Judas, of the Antichrist, and many others.[1] Many of these, of course, had their origins much later than even the year 500. Some of them did not have currency, in fact, until well along in the Middle Ages. The Legend of the Wandering Jew is one of these extrascriptural legends, and like every legend, does not arise spontaneously from nowhere, any more than a river can grow without the contributions of its headwaters.

For that matter, there is more than one legend from the regions of Asia Minor in which a Jew possesses immortality. Thus in the Old Testament Enoch "walked with God" and was translated to heaven, no doubt for his godliness. Better known is the case of Elijah, who not only was carried up to heaven in a fiery chariot as a reward for his courageous and untiring efforts in behalf of Jehovah, but also became identified in Semitic mythology with Al-Khadir (Chidar, Khidar, Childher, etc.), who was at once a vegetation god and a healer of the sick. But neither of these, not even Al-Khadir, is our Wandering Jew.

The true Legend of the Wandering Jew, at the point where it becomes molded into recognizable shape, and without reference to the multitudinous variations of detail which it came to assume in posterity, is the tale of a man in Jerusalem who, when Christ was carrying his Cross to Calvary and paused to rest for a moment on this man's doorstep, drove the Saviour away (with or without physical contact, depending on the variants), crying aloud, "Walk faster!" And Christ replied, "I go, but you will walk until I come again!"

In this capsule of the Legend, two things must be emphasized: first, the phrase "until I come again," which means that there must be a waiting for an indefinite period, during which the victim will know no rest; and second, the indignity offered to the Saviour. These two motifs point to two legends, which may be called the headwaters of the Legend of the Wandering Jew. Such a metaphor, however, is a mere convenience, for these two contributing legends continue to exist independently. They are the Legend of Malchus, which emphasizes the suffering and anguish brought down upon the offender in punishment for an insult, either physical or mental, or both; and the Legend of St. John, which stresses waiting and doing the will of Christ. The detail of wandering seems to derive more from the Legend of Malchus than from the Legend of St. John. Although it is probable that the Legend of St. John is the older of the two—this, however, is obscure— there is no doubt that the Legend of Malchus plays a much more essential part in the genesis of the Legend of the Wandering Jew. It is, moreover, fed by the general tradition of the eternal punishment visited upon those who offend a god.

The Legend of Malchus

The Legend of Malchus has its ultimate origins in the Gospel of John. While Jesus was in the garden on the night before the Crucifixion, Judas, knowing the place, led thither "a band of men and officers from the chief priests and Pharisees," fully equipped with lanterns, torches, and weapons:

> Jesus therefore, knowing all things that should come upon him, went forth, and said unto them, Whom seek ye? They answered him, Jesus of Nazareth. Jesus saith unto them, I am he. And Judas also, which betrayed him, stood with them. As soon then as he had said unto them, I am he, they went backward, and fell to the ground. Then asked he them again, Whom seek ye? And they said, Jesus of Nazareth. Jesus answered, I have told you that I am he: if therefore ye seek me, let these go their way . . . Then Simon Peter having a sword drew it, and smote the high priest's servant, and cut off his right ear. The servant's name was Malchus.　　　　—John 18:4-10.

In the corresponding accounts in the other Gospels (Matthew 26:51; Mark 14:47; Luke 22:50-51), the wounded man is merely "a servant of the high priest," and the aggressor "one of them"—that is, one of Christ's followers. The Gospel of John specifies that it was Peter who made this rather ineffective attack. The Gospel of Luke takes note that Jesus restored the amputated ear, for Luke had been a physician. Thanks to the version in John, we have the name of the wounded man—Malchus.

Later, when Jesus had been brought before the high priest, he is asked about his doctrine:

> Jesus answered him, I spake openly to the world; I ever taught in the synagogue, and in the temple, whither the Jews always resort; and in secret have I said nothing. Why askest thou me? ask them which heard me, what I have said unto them: behold, they know what I said. And when he had thus spoken, one of the officers which stood by struck Jesus with the palm of his hand, saying, Answerest thou the high priest so?　　　　—John 18:20-22

Is the officer who struck Jesus the same as the servant of the high priest named in the preceding passage?[2] Perhaps so; perhaps not. Even though his ear had been restored, he might still have harbored resentment. Or he may have been over-anxious not to be identified with Christ's faction. Be all that as it may, legend has it that he was henceforth to bear the name of Malchus. The inscrutable process, known to folklorists as the law of transposition, decreed that the two men should be identified as one. The important fact remains that here the Saviour was offered violence—a physical blow, in this instance. But whether the violence is physical or only mental, this particular detail, which I shall call Malchean, is of supreme importance in the Legend of the Wandering Jew.

It is, as usual, impossible to say when or where the Legend of Malchus took root. Sooner or later, however, it became a tale of punishment visited upon the offender of Christ. It may therefore be inferred that the origin of the Legend is

Christian. Perhaps it first developed when Christianity was in a position to exact punishment for such an offense, possibly in the fourth century, when it became the official religion of the Roman Empire, West and East. But this can be only a supposition. The first *written* version to survive is to be found in the *Leimonarion* of Johannes Moschos (Eucrates), a monk born at Damascus about 550. The story he tells must therefore date from some time in the latter part of the sixth century or the beginning of the seventh. The *Leimonarion* ("spiritual meadow") is a collection of pious tales of miscellaneous nature. Some of them are no more than moral anecdotes. The scene of this particular story is Cyprus:

> [At the monastery of Philoxenes] . . . we met a monk named Isidor, whom we saw continually weeping and lamenting. Although we all begged him to lessen his woe, he would not, saying to us all: "I am a great sinner; there has not been one so great since the time of Adam." And when we said to him, "Truly, friend abbot, no one is without sin save God himself," he replied, "Believe me, brethren . . . if you think that I blame myself unduly, listen to my offense and then pray for me.
> "When I was in secular life, I had a wife. We were both Severians [a Unitarian sect]. One day, when I entered my house, I could not find my wife, but I heard that she had gone out to visit a neighbor. This neighbor was a communicant of the Holy Catholic Church, and so I rushed out to intercept my wife. Entering my neighbor's house, I found my wife partaking of the holy wafer. Seizing her by the throat, I made her spit out the wafer, which I took and threw to the ground, where it fell in the mud. At the same time, I saw something shining on the spot where the wafer had fallen. Two days later I saw an Ethiopian, clad in rags, who said to me, 'You and I are condemned to the same punishment.' I said to him, 'Who are you?' And the Ethiopian who had appeared to me replied, 'I am he who struck on the cheek the creator of the universe, our Lord Jesus Christ, at the time of the Passion.' That is why," said Isidor, "I cannot stop weeping."[3]

Although Malchus, in this case an Ethiopian, is not named, this is clearly his story. In the Gospel of John, the blow was merely one delivered by the palm of the hand; here it is a blow on the cheek, a more ignominious kind of assault. A blow it remains, in any event, upon the person of the Saviour. The offender is therefore being punished, and has survived under rather mysterious circumstances for some five hundred years since the Crucifixion. To be sure, he does not explicitly express regret, but he is in rags, presumably miserable; and if he has been condemned to the same punishment as Isidor, who weeps incessantly, then we are justified in supposing that the story contributes not only the act of violence but also indefinite survival, with the potentialities of wandering and suffering irremediable woe for having committed the act. The subsequent versions all stress suffering, often of a most cruel kind, as well as the harrowing details of indefinite life and an infinite regret.

The Legend of St. John

For the Legend of St. John, we return to the Gospels. One source is Matthew 16:28: "Verily I say unto you, There be some standing here, which shall not taste of death, till they see the Son of man coming in his kingdom." Christ's statement seems to indicate his belief that the kingdom of God is to come within the lifetime of many in Christ's audience; it is not to be some divine, far-off event, but something to take place in the not distant future. If we leave aside this theological point, however, the actual interpretation of this remark by certain followers of Christ made it possible to read into the verse a promise of immortality, although this immortality might mean only a continuance on earth until such time as Christ returned with God's kingdom.

At the same time, a most vital supplement to this verse in Matthew is the passage in John 21:20-22. Jesus has shown himself after the Resurrection to the disciples at the Sea of Tiberias. "The disciple whom Jesus loved," always taken to be John himself, recognizes the Master. After dining, Jesus asks Simon Peter three times whether he loves him, and is answered in the affirmative each time, whereupon the Saviour prophesies the passing of the disciple from the mortal scene for the glory of God. He asks them all to follow him. "Then Peter, turning about, seeth the disciple whom Jesus loved following; which also leaned on his breast at supper, and said, Lord, which is he that betrayeth thee? Peter seeing him saith to Jesus, Lord, and what shall this man do? Jesus saith unto him, If I will that he tarry till I come, what is that to thee? follow thou me."

This tart little speech of Christ seems to contain a rebuke. Peter is being told to mind his own business. But legend-mongers are never satisfied by a simple explanation. In this case they disregarded the conditional *if* and assumed that Jesus was saying in effect that John was to tarry—on earth, of course—until Christ returned; and the rest were to follow without asking questions which did not concern them. Ironically enough, the Gospel hastens to add in the very next verse (John 21:23): "Then went this saying abroad among the brethren, that that disciple should not die: yet Jesus said not unto him, He shall not die; but, If I will that he tarry till I come, what is that to thee?" And so the last bit of direct discourse in the Gospel of John takes cognizance of the possibility that precisely such a legend might arise, or had already arisen, and tried to counteract it specifically.

From the first of these quotations from John 21 it is to be inferred that some of the disciples are not to taste death until the Saviour returns; from the second, it would appear that John is the only one thus to be honored. Here is the genesis of the Legend of St. John. According to this, St. John the Apostle, the fiery son of thunder ("Boanerges"), the dearly beloved disciple, never died, neither at Ephesus, where he was said to have labored after the departure of Christ, nor yet at Patmos, whither he was exiled. Tradition insisted that the apostle, as a hoary, benevolent patriarch, passed from men's view at an advanced age in an unknown place; but his grave could not be still, for after he was buried it quivered as a blanket under which a body is moving. When the grave was eventually opened, the apostle was no longer there.[4] No, John has never yet died, but is somewhere, a true vicar of the Lord, waiting for the day of the Second Coming. In the meantime he is a traveler in Asia Minor and parts east and, most important of all, an awaiter and a wanderer.

This Legend of St. John was of course given a particular stimulus by the general ignorance of posterity about the facts of John's life after the Crucifixion and the Resurrection. For his death there are hypothetical dates which cover most of the later first century. Moreover, there is confusion about the identity of the author of the First Epistle of John on the one hand and the Second and Third Epistles of John on the other, to say nothing of the vexed problems concerning the writing of the Gospel of John and of the Apocalypse. It was Papias, bishop of Hieropolis, writing about 125, who first indicated that there were two contemporary Johns—John the Apostle and John Presbyteros, or the Elder.[5]

All such biographical guesswork is bound to beget legendry. Where there is any slightest doubt about fact, and even where there is none, legend may step in, as with Nero, or Czar Alexander I of Russia, or Theodosia Burr Alston, or even Adolf Hitler. Why should not John, therefore, still be in infidel parts, preaching the word of God, combating heresies, rescuing the oppressed and afflicted, and ever waiting until Christ returns to save mankind? He was one of the three or four disciples particularly close to Christ and came to have the prestige of a prophet. In most respects he remains the most mysterious of the twelve. But when and where the Legend of St. John began, who was first responsible for it and its dissemination, is all lost to us now. There are evidences of its existence in the writings of Papias in the second century, of Tertullian in the third, and of Sulpicius Severus in the fifth.[6]

Two Parallels

Two other tales have been cited as related to the Legend of the Wandering Jew in its early stages, and yet it is apparent that they are at best only possible analogues, and I am inclined to reject them both as of only secondary importance. The first of these is the Mohammedan Legend of Fadhila:

In the sixteenth year of the Hegira [638], a captain named Fadhila, who was in command of 300 warriors, having arrived with his band at the end of a day at a place between two mountains, and having called aloud in evening prayer in these words, "Allah is great!" heard a voice repeating these very words, which continued to pronounce with him the words of the prayer. Fadhila supposed at first that it was an echo; but having observed that the voice repeated distinctly and completely each word, he said: "O thou who answerest me, if thou art of the order of angels, God be with thee: but if thou art of the race of other spirits, well and good; but if thou art a man like me, show thyself before mine eyes." He had hardly said these words, when an old man with a bald head, holding a staff in his hand and having the appearance of a dervish, appeared straightway before him.

When they had greeted each other civilly, Fadhila asked the old man who he was. He replied that his name was Zerib, son of the son of Elijah, and added: "I am here by order of the Lord Jesus, who has left me alive in this world, until he shall come a second time on earth. So I await the Lord, who is the source of all my bliss: and according to His commands I dwell behind the mountain." Fadhila asked him when the Lord Jesus was to appear. He answered: "At the end of the world: at the Last Judgment."[7]

After describing to Fadhila some of the signs which will indicate that the end of the world is at hand, the old man disappeared. Zerib is a Hebrew, but he is not a wanderer. He is an awaiter, like Pindola in the Buddhist tradition and St. John in the Christian.

The second tale is a curious one. In the Byzantine *Chronicle of Ahimaaz (ca.*

1055), it is told how the great Hebrew schoolman Aaron ben Samuel ha-Nasi was teaching among the communities of southern Italy:

> When he reached Beneventum, the entire community came out as one man to welcome him. On the Sabbath, an esteemed young man arose to read the prayers before Him who dwelleth on high. He chanted with pleasing voice. When he reached the words *Barechu et adonai hammevoroch,* his voice lingered on the sound, but he did not pronounce God's name. The master at once realized that the reader was actually a dead man, and it is known that the dead do not praise God. "Stop," he at once commanded in a loud voice. "Do not give praise."

The master questioned the young man, who replied that he had once sinned and would now confess it. He said that he was once taken by a rabbi named Ahimaaz on a pilgrimage to Jerusalem. Ahimaaz had promised the boy's father and mother, "I will bring him back to you; if I do not, I shall have sinned before God." They went on their way, and on one occasion, when they were seated in a company of scholars, ". . . the teachers of the Law exclaimed, 'Let us give praise . . . to Him that is adored by myriads.' The head turned to them and said, 'Let the young man in our midst who has come with our colleague Ahimaaz cheer us and delight our heart.' " The boy proceeded to give praise to God, but in the midst of his song it was noticed that an elder sat apart weeping sadly. When asked why, he replied that God had decreed that in a little while the young man would die. Ahimaaz was shocked because of his responsibility to the boy's parents, and cried out:

> " 'I have no place among the living . . . how can I return to my house if the lad is not with me?' Seeing his affliction, they wrote the Holy Name that was written in the Sanctuary; they made an incision in the flesh of my right arm, and inserted the Name where the flesh had been cut. So I came away in peace and returned to my mother. When Ahimaaz was alive, I wandered from land to land. Living since that time, I can live forever if I so desire, for no man can know the place of the Name unless I reveal it. But I will show you; I am in your hands; deal with me as seems right in your eyes."
> And so they brought the grave-clothes; he approached and put them on; he then showed where the master had made the incision, and took the Name out of it. His body became lifeless; the corpse crumbled in decay as from the dissolution of many years; the flesh returned to the dust.[8]

Here is a Jew who wanders. But he is not the Wandering Jew of the Legend. Possibly this story was known to the originator or originators of the Legend of the Wandering Jew, but there are other considerations much more important in the study of the genesis of the Legend.

The Thirteenth-Century Chronicles

Now, while the Legend of Malchus and the Legend of St. John both contribute to the formation of the Legend of the Wandering Jew, it becomes increasingly apparent, as one continues to study the problem, that the Legend of Malchus is the main source. There remains, however, the enormous gap of six hundred years and more between the first written version of ascertainable date in Johannes Moschos (a rudimentary version, in any event) and the first recognized outline of the Legend of the Wandering Jew. We may safely assume, though, that oral tradition during those six hundred years eventually brought about the blending of the two legends to produce our Legend. From all that may be ascertained, both the Legend of Malchus and the Legend of St. John originated in the Near East and the eastern Mediterranean; one is tempted to think that they both came from Jerusalem, but this can hardly be proved, and it is much too simple. Unfortunately our knowledge of the oral traditions of the Levantine and eastern Mediterranean areas between 200 and 1200 must be pieced together in fragmentary fashion and only with the greatest difficulty. Experience with the spread of folk tales or any other kind of myth or legend persuades us that some versions of these tales, either pure or adulterated, stayed at home, so to speak, and others moved abroad. In consequence the pure, original form of the tale is impossible to determine, and its exact point of origin is equally obscure. Thus it seems likely that there is a kind of eastern and western division of the Legend of the Wandering Jew in its folkloristic aspects. There are varying versions of the Legend in folk tales around the Aegean Sea, in Asia Minor, and in contiguous parts, which may have been spread later into Slavic regions by migrants and travelers through the Balkans.[9]

Westward, a similar spread was made possible by contacts between the East and West through the Crusades, through the exploitation of trade routes and the increase of travel, through increased missionary activity in the Church, and through other things which would improve communication among peoples. It has long been a cliché that the Crusades were of enormous importance in the transmission of Eastern story and legend to western Europe. Cliché or not, it remains a fact. The natural port of entry for such Oriental material was the peninsula of Italy. Here we find the next reference, after Johannes Moschos, to the Legend, most of the allusions to the Wandering Jew before 1500, and the first extended account of some of his adventures, from a manuscript which is to be dated only a few years after 1500.[10] To put it in another way, Italy seems to be a distribution point for the movement of the Legend westward and northward.

In speaking of the Crusades, one tends to think chiefly of the first one (1095-99), which was successful; but there were two others within the next century, which, less successful, nevertheless continued the necessary contacts. As to the Fourth Crusade (1202-4), however deplorable its achievement, it is particularly interesting to the students of our Legend, because in the conquest of Byzantium and adjacent parts and in the establishment of a Latin empire in Byzantium, there were special opportunities for the importation of legendry belonging to an alien civilization.

Another historical event also may be of more than passing significance. The Fourth Lateran Council of 1215, held under the presiding genius of Pope Innocent III, most feudal and splendid of medieval popes—if such superlatives can be bestowed upon only one of many—condemned the heresies of the Albigenses and all other heresies, resolved to give emphasis to the singleness and inviolability of the Christian faith, and encouraged belief in any legend, however un-Christlike in nature, as long as the legend glorified the wonders of God's works and his miracles. Thus the Jews, who had killed Christ, were nevertheless to be tolerated because their continued and continuing existence demonstrated the greatness of God's mercy. And the conferring of eternal life upon a mortal, sinner or not, wanderer or not, would obviously come under the head of a miracle. Indeed, this motive is apparent in the very first references to the Wandering Jew.

Whatever the precise determining factors, shortly after 1200 the Legend of the Wandering Jew reappears. How old it was by that time is impossible to determine; it may well have been in existence for a thousand years. But now it is evident that the Legend of St. John has merged to some extent with that of Malchus; to put it another way, if the Legend of Malchus was the original, it has, in technical language, become contaminated with the Legend of St. John. The first written account since Moschos is in a Latin chronicle, *Ignoti Monachi Cisterciensis S. Mariae de Ferraria Chronica et Ryccardi de Sancto Germano Chronica priora*, of Bolognese origins, which rather remarkably covers the years all the way from 781 to 1228. The passage is found in an entry for the year 1223, eight years after the Fourth Lateran Council and about twenty years after the Fourth Crusade:

In that same year, when Frederick II was visiting the Pope Honorius III and met in the monastery of Ferraria with King John of Jerusalem, the Bishop of Tarento, and other noblemen, there came some pilgrims from adjacent regions on the other side of the mountains [*ex ultramontanis partibus*] and told the abbot and the brothers of this place that they had seen a certain Jew in Armenia, who had been present at the Passion of the Lord and, as He was going to His martyrdom, drove Him along wickedly with these words: "Go, go, thou tempter and seducer, to receive what you have earned." The Lord is said to have answered him: "I go, and you will await me till I come again." This Jew is said, every hundred years, to be made young to the age of thirty, and he cannot die until the Lord returns.[11]

Five years later, the English chronicler Roger of Wendover, writing his *Flores Historiarum*, or "Flowers of History," at the monastery of St. Albans, told much the same story but with embellishments not found in the earlier Italian version. The added details are most interesting, and since this was considered for generations to be the first appearance of the Legend in writing, it should be quoted entire. In the year 1228, according to Roger, an Armenian archbishop, neither identified nor even identifiable, visited St. Albans. During his entertainment:

. . . he was asked whether he had ever seen or heard anything of Joseph, a man of whom there was much talk in the world, who, when our Lord suffered, was present and spoke to Him, and who is still alive in evidence of the Christian faith; in reply to which a knight of his retinue, who was interpreter, replied, speaking in French: "My lord well knows that man, and a little before he took his way to the western countries, the said Joseph ate at the table of my lord the archbishop in Armenia, and he was often seen and held converse with him."

He was asked then what had passed between Christ and this same Joseph, to which he replied, "At the time of the suffering of Jesus Christ, He was seized by the Jews and led into the Hall of Judgment, before Pilate the governor, that He might be judged by him on the accusation of the Jews, and Pilate finding no cause for adjudging Him to death, said to them: 'Take Him and judge Him according to your law.' The shouts of the Jews, however, increasing, he, at their request, released unto them Barabbas, and delivered Jesus to them to be crucified. When therefore the Jews were dragging Jesus forth, and had reached the door, Cartaphilus, a porter of the hall in Pilate's service, as Jesus was going out of the door, impiously struck Him on the back with his hand, and said in mockery: 'Go quicker, Jesus, go quicker; why do you loiter?' And Jesus looking back on him with a severe countenance said to him, 'I am going, and you will wait till I return.'

"And according as our Lord said, this Cartaphilus is still awaiting His return; at the time of our Lord's Passion he was 30 years old; and when he attains the age of 100 years, he always returns to the same age as when our Lord suffered. After Christ's death, when the Catholic faith gained ground, this Cartaphilus was baptized by Ananias (who also baptized the apostle Paul), and was called Joseph. He often dwells in both divisions of Armenia, and other eastern countries, passing his time amidst the bishops and other prelates of the Church; he is a man of holy conversation and religious, a man of few words and circumspect in his behavior, for he does not speak at all unless when questioned by the bishops and religious men; and then he tells of the events of old times, and of the events which occurred at the suffering and resurrection of our Lord, and of the witnesses of the Resurrection, namely those who rose with Christ, and went into the holy city, and appeared unto men; he also tells of the creed of the apostles, and of their separation and conversation; and all this he relates without smiling or levity of countenance, as one who is well practised in sorrow and the fear of God, always looking forward with fear to the coming of Jesus Christ, lest at the Last Judgment he should find Him in anger, whom, on His way to death, he had provoked to just vengeance. Numbers come to him from different parts of the world, enjoying his society and conversation; and to them, if they are men of authority, he explains all doubts on the matter on which he is questioned. He refuses all gifts that are offered to him, being content with slight food and clothing. He places his hope of salvation on the fact that he sinned through ignorance, for the Lord, when suffering, prayed for His enemies in these words, 'Father, forgive them, for they know not what they do.' "[12]

Obviously this account is fuller, more dramatic, and more given to scriptural reflection than the Italian entry. In both accounts, however, it would seem that a blow was struck.[13] Here it is before the high priest rather than in the *Via Crucis*. The central incident in both is Malchean. Yet in Roger's story the protagonist is fulfilling many of the missionary functions of St. John and is an awaiter rather more than a wanderer, although he moves about through Armenia Major and Armenia Minor and other parts of the Near East. (In fact, the name of Armenia is applied most loosely during the Middle Ages to almost any region in Asia Minor except Palestine.) In the Italian version he was an unnamed Jew (*quendam Iudaeum*); here he has a name, and nothing is said about his being a Jew. Instead he bears a name, Joseph, honored in the scriptures. Before baptism he was called Cartaphilus, an appellation generally broken down into *kartos* and *philos*, roughly to be translated as "strongly" or "dearly" and "loved"—the relationship of which to the dearly beloved disciple John needs no further comment.[14] Clearly, then, we are dealing here with the characteristic blending of the Malchus and St. John motifs which defines the Legend of the Wandering Jew.

Roger's account further stresses Cartaphilus' preternatural gravity of conduct, his taciturn nature, his austere living, and by inference his contrition. We shall meet all these characteristics, from time to time, in later treatments; here is the starting point.

However, as duly noted, "there was much talk in the world" of the 1220's about this amazing survivor, "in evidence of the Christian faith"—a phrase which should be remembered whenever we consider the motive for the Legend. There is no real evidence to show that Roger of Wendover knew the entry in the Italian chronicle. As is usually the case, both accounts probably derive from an anterior source current in oral tradition. It is possible that Roger made up some of these details out of whole cloth, but he does not give elsewhere the impression that he is a sheer romance-monger. Certainly the narrative is in his own words. At the same time, one must remember that in all medieval chronicle-writing there is a very thin line between fact and fiction, between chronicle and romance; and such is the weakness for a good story or a moral tale among all these chroniclers that the line was crossed all too often. No doubt the archbishop from Armenia was telling a tale that was current, adding the natural decoration proper to the entertainment of strangers in a remote part of his world. The "knight" (*miles*) who served as interpreter also challenges particular interest. Was he transmitting the story directly from the mouth of the archbishop, or was he doing some narrating of his own, adding material as he went along? Either is possible; that is the way folk tales develop. More significant, it seems to me, is the fact that the story was told because someone of the St. Albans group had asked for it; in other words, the Legend, or the important part of it, had already penetrated into thirteenth-century England. Also, it is evident, from the remark that Joseph "is still alive in evidence of the Christian faith," that the tale already had value as Christian propaganda.

Roger of Wendover's successor as chronicler at St. Albans, Matthew Paris (*ca.* 1200-1259), saw fit to follow the customary procedure—he took Roger's history bodily, adding a few notes here and there, until it was necessary for him to launch out on his own. His *Chronica Majora*, which runs through the year 1259, is not independent until the entry for the year 1236. The author was much more of a cosmopolitan than Roger, and his history has a larger international canvas. For 1228, however, he adds little to Roger's account of Joseph Cartaphilus. He has the archbishop answer at first directly before relying on his interpreter, who is here given the name of Antichenius. The ensuing sentence passed on the offender is more specific—Cartaphilus is to await the Second Coming. The blow was delivered *impie* in Roger; *contemptibiliter* in Matthew. One notable addition, picked up by many a later narrator, is that when thereafter Cartaphilus attained the age of one hundred years, he was seized with an apparently incurable affliction and fell, as it were, into a trance, whereupon he eventually convalesced and returned to the age he had been when his indiscretion took place, "that it may truly be said with the psalmist, 'My youth is renewed as the eagle's' " (Psalms 103:5). As in Roger's account, the subsequent behavior of Cartaphilus is extremely serious; in addition, he is "given to reproof and argument . . . looking to the coming of Christ in fire to judge the world." This eschatological detail is new. At the conclusion of the story, Matthew comments that Cartaphilus' expectation of forgiveness has ample parallel in the grace bestowed upon Peter and Paul, for all three sinned either *per fragilitatem* or *per ignorantiam*, whereas Judas, who knew full well what he was doing, ended with a violent death.

Evidently Matthew believed that his readers might have reservations about his story, for he adds an important passage: he cites as witness one Ricardus de Argentomio, whom he leaves otherwise without identification, a *miles* or knight who once visited Armenia as a pilgrim. There he saw evidence of the truth of the archbishop's statement—evidence, however, which Matthew does not give to us —not only concerning Cartaphilus but also concerning the ark, "which is still to be found in the mountains of Armenia," in a place so remote and so infested with venomous serpents that no man dares to visit it. Bishop Gualerannus of Beirut, he says, is also a living witness.

Furthermore, in Matthew's entry for the year 1252 he tells how certain Armenians arrived at the Abbey of St. Albans. They were an austere and outlandish lot, with pale faces, severe and ascetic, but with much to talk about. They asserted that they had clear and unshakable knowledge of the fact that Joseph Cartaphilus, "who saw Christ crucified," was still alive, as was his wont. "And he is one of the wonders of the world and a great argument for the Christian faith."[15]

The archbishop who had regaled the monks of St. Albans with his marvelous story spread the Legend elsewhere. At least Philippe Mouskes, or Mousket, archbishop of Tournai, was sufficiently impressed to record the incident in his *Chronique rimée*, written about 1243.[16] In some forty short couplets he notes that the Armenian archbishop visited the shrine of St. Thomas of Canterbury and then speaks of a man who, when the Jews were leading Christ to crucifixion, expressed interest in seeing the "false prophet" nailed to the Cross; Christ then told him that he must await him, and must do so until Judgment Day. The offender is not called a Jew, and his insult is mental rather than physical. Mouskes's version is not remarkable otherwise but serves as further confirmation of the currency of the Legend at the time. The fact is that Matthew Paris is an important transmitter of many aspects of the Legend to posterity, as we shall see; a curious instance to be mentioned here is the case of the *Svatovítský rukopis*, a fourteenth-century Czech manuscript which contains a translation from the Latin *Dialogos beatae Mariae et Anselmi de passione Domini*.[17] Interpolated in this text is an account of the Wandering Jew obviously based upon Matthew Paris' version. The *Chronica Majora* was later (1586-87) translated into German at Zurich, where it became a basic consideration in the history of all German folk tales concerning the protagonist of the Legend.

Other Thirteenth-Century Allusions

The Wandering Jew, then, has emerged as a distinct entity in the thirteenth century, but he soon drops the name Cartaphilus in the lands around the Mediterranean. His new name, Buttadeus, is oriented toward the Malchus rather than the St. John aspect of the Legend. The derivation of *Buttadeus* remains a somewhat obscure matter, but the most plausible and probably the correct explanation has it that it comes from a Vulgar Latin variant of the classical Latin *batuere*, "to beat or strike or shove," plus the word for God, *deus;* and although it makes rather bad grammar, it can be translated as "God-pusher" or "God-beater."[18] The Italian version of the name is *Botadeo* and the French *Boutedieu*. But to complicate matters a bit, *Botadeo* was occasionally garbled into *Votadeo* ("devoted or dedicated to God"), which brings us back to the concept of Cartaphilus, the dearly beloved. It is an easy step to "trusting or placing one's hope in God," or "serving God," which produces the Spanish *Juan Espera en Dios*, the Portuguese *João Espera em Dios*, and the rare Italian *Giovanni Servo di Dio*. All of these names may be applied to the same legendary figure that we call the Wandering Jew. And the name of John, frequently given to legendary figures who live a long time (because of the Legend of St. John), speaks for itself.

It is impossible to determine when the name of Buttadeus was first used. The Spanish and Portuguese references come from a later date. It is clear, however, that Buttadeus was known in this same thirteenth century that we have been concerned with, and of course it may have been known before. One can only surmise. But the next reference to the Legend after Philippe Mouskes is clear enough. It comes from the writings of the eminent Italian astrologer Guido Bonatti of Forli, who died about 1300. He had once taught at Paris, become a Franciscan, and passed away in either Bologna or Ancona at the age of seventy. He attracted the attention of Dante sufficiently to be given immortal sepulture in the *Inferno* (XX, 118), where he appears to foretell the future and thus merits the punishment of having his face turned about, so that he must walk ever backwards —another illustration of the tedious punishment inflicted on those guilty of blasphemous presumption. It is said that Bonatti's lord, Guido de Montefeltro, never went into battle except when advised by his astrologer.

In his *De Astronomia Tractatus X*, first printed at Augsburg in 1491, Bonatti comments on longevity:

> Many men have reached a very advanced age: of these I have seen in my time only a certain Ricardus, who said that he had been at the court of Charlemagne and was 400 years old. And it is said also that there was another, who lived at the time of Jesus Christ and was called Johannes Buttadeus. Because he had driven the Lord along when he was being led to the Crucifixion, the Master made clear to him: "You shall await me, until I come again." This Ricardus I saw at Ravenna in the year 1223; Johannes, on a pilgrimage to Santiago, passed through Forli in the year of our Lord 1267.[19]

As to the very old man who had come from the time of Charlemagne, four hundred and more years before, he represents the medieval Legend of Juan de los Tiempos, or Jan van den Tyden.[20] Charlemagne, like Frederick Barbarossa, was the subject of a tradition of immortality—the legendary recognition of an unwillingness to accept a physical death. Is Ricardus to be identified with Ricardus de Argentomio, whom Matthew Paris named as a witness to the authenticity of the Armenian archbishop's story of 1228? As Bonatti died about 1300 at the age of seventy, even if one allows several years one way or another, he could have been at the most only a mewling infant when he saw Ricardus at Ravenna in 1223. It is possible, though perhaps fanciful, to think that Bonatti had heard about Ricardus from Matthew Paris. He is much more likely to have heard about him from the "much talk that was in the world." As for the passing of Buttadeus through Forli in 1267—if Bonatti saw that, he is entitled to his opinion. Many others since his time have thought that they saw the Wandering Jew.

The reference by Bonatti marks the first appearance of the name Buttadeus in print. More important is the fact that Bonatti made this reference as of the year 1267, for it continues the tradition of the Wandering Jew in the thirteenth century.

Then dour Cecco d'Angiolieri of Siena (1250?-1319), in dedicating a sonnet to his detested father, remarks that his hate for his progenitor will live longer than Botadeo.[21] Similarly, Nicolo de Rossi of Bologna, from near 1300, speaking also in an exasperated moment, says of the governors of his city that they will survive Botadeo.[22] A fourteenth-century description of a wedding feast, attributed to Francesco Vannozzo, observes that a certain indigestible dish will torture you at the stake for as long as the age of "Saint" Botadeo—as extreme a case of chronic indigestion as could well be found in medical annals.[23] It is to be presumed that the sainthood of Buttadeus here is ironical. At about the same time that Bonatti saw Johannes Buttadeus at Forli in 1267, Filippo de Novara, an Italian writing in France, mentions in his *Assises de Jérusalem* the name of Jehan Boutedieu as a prime instance of longevity.[24] The allusions by these Italian writers seem merely to exemplify a popular saying about long life, much as English-speaking people referred, in those ancient days when the Bible was a matter of common knowledge, to someone who is "as old as Methuselah." Clearly the Legend of the Wandering Jew was so well known and so widely current in at least the Italian peninsula before 1300 that a writer could make a reference to the protagonist and expect to be understood. It is interesting, furthermore, that all of these allusions just mentioned call attention to Buttadeus' longevity rather than his Malchean aspects.

An anonymous Italian poem of 1274 recognizes the Legend and brings with it a new note. Here two Breton noblemen, who had been visiting the court of King Arthur, are on their way back from England. They are met by a pilgrim who explains that he has been on a journey to Palestine to see the holy places, "and the man who is awaiting Christ, from that hour when He was being scourged and beaten by those Jews who struck Him and treated Him as if he were a robber. Then spoke this man to Him in sympathy: 'Go faster, so that you will not receive so many blows.' And Christ looked at him and said: 'I shall go, and you will await me until I come again.' He was then nailed to the Cross amid the cries and shrieks of the crowd, while the whole earth shook." The point to be made here is that the man himself offered no violence to Jesus, nor even insult, so far as we can see. He was actually urging Him to hurry in order to save Himself unnecessary pain. It may be true that he laid hands on Him to propel Him forward and shorten His ordeal, but this detail is not specifically stated. His punishment remains the same, whatever his motive, no matter if he did speak *pietosamente*. The St. John motif is strong.[25]

None of these references has much to say about the wanderings of the protagonist, except for that kind of moving about which can be expected of a perpetual pilgrim or itinerant missionary.

Into the Early Renaissance

The Malchean elements, however, must assert themselves sooner or later. The fourteenth century represents something of a hiatus in the written records of the Legend, yet one must assume a continuing and inventive circulation by word of mouth. Near the end of the century the written references begin once more. Several works from near 1400 treat of the holy places of Jerusalem and give some attention to the legends accruing to them.[26] From such writings as these, and their progeny, were developed the descriptions of the *Via Crucis* or the Stations of the Cross. Perhaps I should note as an exception the Evreux MS description, which is dated as early as 1325.[27] Here the author explains that along the *Via Crucis* there was a certain unnamed place where Johannes Buttadeus pushed Christ, with the resulting interchange of words which forms the core of the Legend. So far, so good; but the narrator then makes a mess of things by confusing Johannes Buttadeus, "called in temperate language Johannes Devotus Dio" (the Botadeo-Votadeo substitution already mentioned) with the long-lived shield-bearer of Charlemagne to whom Bonatti referred, Juan de los Tiempos or Jan van den Tyden, the protagonist of a distinct legend. Yet this very confusion is valuable in that it shows that there had been contaminations of the Legend of the Wandering Jew as early as the first part of the fourteenth century, just about a hundred years after the first written references to the Legend.

Again, in the fifteenth century, Mariano da Siena, in *Del Viaggio in Terra Santa, fatto e descritto da Ser Mariano da Siena* (1431), speaks of a certain gate in Jerusalem, where "the sweet and humble Jesus was going out, with the Cross on His shoulder, on His way to Mount Calvary . . . and it is said that there was one called Johannes Botadeo. . . ."[28] The now familiar story is told here in an uncomplicated version. It indicates that the culprit has never been pardoned. Combined with this reference in Mariano's work is an extended allusion in a chronicle by Sigismondo Tizio, a Florentine living in Siena (1459-*ca.*1538), who, in his entry for the year 1400, calls attention to Johannes Buttadeus, a man who once brutally pushed Christ while he was being led through the gate, only to hear the Saviour call out: "You will await me until I come" ("Expectabis me dum venero"). And Tizio remarks also that there is a painting by Andrea di Vanni of Siena (1369-1414) showing this scene with Christ bearing the Cross; he observes that it is a good likeness of the Saviour. No Wandering Jew, however, is identifiable in any of Andrea di Vanni's surviving paintings.[29]

All these allusions have been detailed here to illustrate how, in their many little variations, they exemplify the development of a legend. They are also straws in the wind; they testify to the continued circulation of the Legend of the Wandering Jew. But when we reach a date near 1500, we seem to have come to a temporary stopping place in the growth of the Legend. Actually this pause is more apparent than real, for it is clear that these seemingly fallow decades were years of slow and steady development of the Legend in oral tradition, as we find many new details added when next we hear of it. One final note here—it is curious how often these early allusions bring us to the Florence-Forli-Siena triangle in Italy. If there is any one focal spot for the transmission of the Legend from its cradle in the Near East to western Europe, we have here at least some ground for believing that this triangle was the area of importance.

This theory is strengthened by the fact that the most complete account of the Wandering Jew before 1500 is to be found in some papers in the Strozzi Palace in

Florence. The author of this manuscript is Antonio di Francesco di Andrea, who flourished not long after 1400; the manuscript itself is clearly from the fifteenth century, probably close to 1450.[30]

In spite of the fabulous material in this manuscript, there is no reason to doubt the historicity not only of Antonio but also of others named in the work. The author informs us that he lived in two houses, one in Borgho a San Lorenzo, in the mountains northeast of Florence, and the other in Florence itself. With the customary seriousness of the credulous storyteller, he begins with protestations of the truth of his narrative. He says that a man, "Giovanni Votaddio, or Giovanni Servo di Dio"—he prefers that latter name throughout, although the variants Botaddio and the peculiar Batte-Iddio also appear—was seen in Italy between 1310 and 1320. Many aged citizens have testified to the truth of this; and one in particular, Bartolo di Iacopo da Faena, reported that the said Giovanni had been in his house in Borgho a San Lorenzo. With this shaky authority before us, we may proceed.

Because of its length, Antonio's tale—to be known henceforth as the Antonio version—can be only summarized here. In 1411, a certain Giano di Duccio and his two little sons, on a journey in the company of Antonio's brother Andrea di Francesco di Andrea, were overtaken in the mountains by a raging snowstorm. Things were going badly, and the younger of the sons was in danger of perishing. Then appeared this Giovanni Votaddio, in the habit of a Franciscan friar of the third order, with cowl but no sandals; he took the boy up on his back and whisked him away toward the inn whither the storm-beset travelers were bound. So quick was the rescue that the travelers completely lost sight of Giovanni. Yet when they arrived at the inn in Scaricalasino, the rescuer and the rescued were there. During the evening at the inn, while the thankful father was conversing with Giovanni, the innkeeper made the remark that he was poor, too poor to endow his daughter for marriage. Whereupon this Votaddio laughed, in such a tone as one may imagine, and when asked why, replied that the innkeeper was a miserable liar: he had 240 florins tucked away. To silence the travelers' disbelief he told them just where the money would be found, and his directions proved to be accurate.

All in all, Giovanni proved a good friend in need but still a most difficult companion. He could never stay long in his friends' homes, lest he make trouble for them. Three days represented the limit. On one occasion he was seized by the authorities at Vicenza and sentenced to hang as a spy. Try as they would, however, they could find no rope to carry out the execution: as soon as Giovanni was to be launched into eternity, the rope would break, until the authorities gave up in disgust and superstitious fear. Moreover, he had the ability to foretell, in often embarrassing ways, the fortune of those whom he met, whether or not it was solicited. His fame as a seer evidently preceded him; but although he dismayed some, to the point of attempted retaliation, by observing that they would be hanged or shot in battle or would die mysterious deaths, he was always able to escape violence. The renowned humanist Leonardo Bruni (Aretino), having met him, pronounced him either an angel of God or a devil, for he knew all languages. He was able to cure a woman of a loathsome disease by giving her husband a chain to put around her neck; with this chain he healed others as well. He eventually disappeared as suddenly as he had come.

Considering the spectacular behavior of Giovanni Votaddio, it was an unconscionably long time before anyone questioned him as to his identity and origins. Of course, since Giovanni always talked with the inhabitants of a town as if he had long been a native of that town, perhaps it was taken for granted that he was one of them. Once the *vicario* at Florence tried to find out his identity through a subordinate but got no satisfaction whatever. Finally Antonio, in his own house, asked Giovanni outright if he was perchance Giovanni Bottadio. He answered, "You mean to say Giovanni Batte-Iddio, that is Giovanni who struck Christ. When He was ascending the hill where the Cross was, and His mother with other women went beside Him amid great sorrow, lamentation, and grief . . . then this Giovanni struck Him over the reins, and said, 'Go faster!' And Jesus turned to him: 'And you will go faster and await me!' And this is the Giovanni whom you mean?" "Are you the one?" "Antonio, ask me no more questions." Having said this, he shed a tear but spoke no more. His admission was nonetheless implicit. This Giovanni, says Antonio, is the third great witness to the power of God, along with Elijah and Enoch. Those were transported to heaven; Giovanni, however, must remain on earth, and so goes about ceaselessly, never staying more than three days in any one place. He can be visible or invisible at will. He has ample, even inexhaustible means at his disposal, but he never produces more money than is needed at any given time. He is to be distinguished from an ordinary pilgrim by his habit—a plain friar's garb, no scrip or flagon, cowled but unshod most of the time, girded with a cord. There is no suggestion that he is mortifying the flesh; on the contrary, he eats and drinks and laughs heartily; his hands are always full of good things; and he is learned to the point of omniscience. His command of the staple classical languages—Greek, Latin, and Hebrew—is absolute, and he can always converse fluently in the language or dialect of any given region on earth. He cannot be confined and he cannot die.

Compared with all the accounts and allusions which preceded it, the tale of Antonio di Francesco di Andrea is almost a full-blown version of the proper Legend of the Wandering Jew, although it has already some obvious contamination with other legendary material. The pilgrimage to which Guido Bonatti referred has now become a perpetual wandering toward no particular destination; it is, in fact, wandering and little else, except that Giovanni's purpose, wherever he goes, seems to be to do as much good as possible, to expose evil, to obstruct the autocratic actions of mere human officers, and so to confirm the greatness of God.

To support the story of Antonio's experience with Giovanni, there is a brief report, discovered in the state archives of Florence, as told in the diary of Salvestro di Giovanni Mannini, who lived near the city. On June 23, 1416, Giovanni Servo di Dio discussed Florentine affairs with Mannini, who was impressed by what he considered the "impious tone" of the said Giovanni—something that had not occurred to Antonio di Francesco di Andrea. Impious or not, the stranger possessed an exhaustive knowledge of the present and an equal assurance about the future, foretelling plague and famine and armed revolt—not too rash a prophecy to make in a city of early Renaissance Italy. He was neither reticent nor modest, as Cartaphilus had been before him.[31]

It seems clear that this Giovanni, who left his mark upon Antonio and Mannini, was a notably effective charlatan who must have become a local tradition around Florence, so that it was easy for someone about a century later to pick up the details and tell his version of what befell a fellow Florentine back in 1411. In any event, the manuscript identified with Antonio is a most important milestone in the development of the Legend of the Wandering Jew, and one that has been strangely neglected. Its author combined various motifs current in oral tradition, and, whether or not they had to do with Buttadeus, fused them into a coherent picaresque tale of the blow struck, the sentence of wandering, the repentance, the sudden appearances and disappearances, and the impossibility of killing the protagonist. No other version before 1500 and none until after 1600 show all these details.

The accretions shown here, however, call for a little more comment. The three-day maximum respite from wandering parallels the three-day period of Christ's Passion, Death, and Resurrection, to be sure; but a three-day stretch is common throughout folklore, and some have pointed out a tradition that all those descended from Cain could stay no longer than this period in any country without becoming either vermin-ridden or moribund.[32] Since Cain was himself a famous wanderer, the parallel here challenges interest. There is also the motif of invisibility. When combined with the motif of the inexhaustible purse and that of a miraculous means of transportation, this forms the arresting figure of Fortunatus, the hero of a popular folk tale in late-medieval and early-modern Europe.[33] Yet each of the three motifs associated with Fortunatus reaches back through antiquity to outer darkness. Any reader of Oriental tales will recognize them.

Since it is not Christ's intention that the man who struck him should die before his return, the detail of the breaking rope on the gallows is not so much a matter of folklore as a kind of miraculous intervention in an awkward situation, analogous to the last-minute rescue of saints who are about to be put to death. Thus, when St. Juliana was cast into a vat of boiling oil, the formidable liquid was cooled by divine intervention to a tolerable, even lukewarm temperature. When the Israelites were in the fiery furnace, they were not consumed, nor even scorched. In all attempted torments of chosen followers or those who have received the special attention of a deity, it is contrary to that deity's will that they should suffer. Then, to descend to a realistic plane, it undoubtedly happened sometimes that an inefficient hangman allowed the rope to break, and such rare incidents would be seized upon immediately, to be passed down in story for those who seek examples of divine intervention.

Still another detail, first mentioned in the Antonio manuscript, reappears from time to time. That is the ability of the Wandering Jew to smell out treasure, as he did with the innkeeper's florins. This is, as it should be, an intuitive gift. Giovanni needs no divining rod; he merely states positively that the treasure will be found in a certain place, and it is. Forever afterward the Wandering Jew may reveal this particular talent, sometimes for the benefit of mankind, sometimes for its harm. Again, he may, at any time after the Antonio manuscript, exercise the preternatural ability to foretell the future. The miraculous curing of a desperate illness, on the other hand, is comparatively rare, although the Wandering Jew can always become a god from the machine.

All in all, Antonio di Francesco di Andrea, gullible Florentine, has put us a long step forward along the path of the Wandering Jew. Although the protagonist of his story has not yet been called that, he is Buttadeus, and most important of all, he is a wanderer and a restless three-day sojourner at best. His comings and goings are sudden; he has superhuman attributes, and he tacitly admits his unfortunate association with the events of Good Friday.

Now about this time, that is between 1400 and 1600, the Wandering Jew is at large also in Spain and Portugal. The version of the Legend in these countries is distinctive, but curiously passive; little is made of his wandering and much of his age, experience, and wisdom. Here in the Iberian peninsula he outlives Methuselah and Nestor; he is a miraculous traveler with seven-league boots—a new detail; he is a magician and necromancer who is all-knowing; he is a missionary of the Christian faith. As early as the first quarter of the 1500's his name in Spain is Juan (de) Espera en Dios; later he may be referred to as Juan de Voto a Dios and, in one instance, by the Spanish Jesuit man of letters, Baltasar Gracian (1584-1658), as Juan de Para Siempre.[34] The corresponding Portuguese name is João Espera em Dios. Once more we see the association of the name John with fabulous men of immortal potentialities—Johannes Buttadeus or Giovanni Bottadio or Jehan Boutedieu, Juan de los Tiempos or Jan van den Tyden, and Don Juan—all striking testimonials to the vitality of the Legend of St. John.

The identity of Juan de Voto a Dios with Giovanni Votaddio, derived from Bottadio or Botadeo, as in Antonio di Francesco di Andrea's tale, is obvious. If, as is most likely, Italy is the distribution center for the Legend in western Europe, and since Bottadio or Botadeo is by far the most common appellation for the Wanderer, it seems plausible that both the Italian *Votaddio* and the Spanish *de Voto* are misunderstood forms or instances of popular etymology. Be that as it may, the older and more common Spanish name, Juan Espera en Dios, is explained by an old Andalusian folk tale, which seems to have been some version of the Legend of St. John. The Wanderer is here a God-baiter who offered insolence to Christ and is set to walking. But on each Good Friday at three o'clock in the afternoon (the "ninth hour" of the Gospels) he sees a vision of Calvary and the three crosses, at the foot of the largest of which a woman stands and comforts his repentant despair by saying to him, "Juan, espera en Dios" ("John, put your hope in God").[35]

This tale may be as old as the later fifteenth century but hardly older. Juan Espera en Dios is known in Spain, however, as early as 1528, when Francisco Delicado, in his *Retrato de la Lozana Andaluza*, alludes to Juan's formidable wisdom, which comes from his advanced age.[39] In the next generation and later the Portuguese writers Francisco de Sá de Miranda (in his comedy *Vilhalpandos*), Jorge Ferreira de Vasconcellos (in his *Eufrosina*), Antonio Prestos (in his *Auto dos Dous Irmaos*), and Rodrigues Lobo (in his *Corte ne Aldea*) all pay similar tribute to João's venerable sagacity.[40] Such references, however, are of a generally "literary" nature; moreover, all of these writers were thoroughly acquainted with classical, Italian, and Spanish literature, and so their allusions are derivative. On the other hand, both Eugenio de Salazar in 1560 and Cervantes in his *Galatea* (*ca.*1583) have picked up the detail first mentioned in Cristobal de Villalón's *Viaje de Turquia* (*ca.*1540?)—that of the inexhaustible purse, which had already appeared in Antonio di Francesco di Andrea. The three coins specified in Salazar and Cervantes later become five, to correspond to the five wounds of Christ. Villalón's detail is particularly noteworthy, because he was very much interested in folklore. The contamination with the Legend of Fortunatus, already noted, may or may not be a Spanish contribution. Taken in conjunction with the seven-league boots, however, it is suggestive, for there has been much discussion whether or not the Fortunatus Legend, in the form in which we have it, may have been molded in Spain.[38]

At the same time, it must be admitted that, while these Spanish and Portuguese allusions indicate that the Legend was current in southwestern Europe before 1600, they do not indicate much else.[39] Juan Espera en Dios remains a rather shadowy version of the protagonist, a pale reflection of an individual who stands up in more substantial form elsewhere. For one thing, the St. John aspect is too prominent, and is even recognized as such. Thus Alexo Vanegas, in his *Agonía del Tránsito de la Muerte* (1537), identifies the Wandering Jew with St. John. A second and more important reference in the same work, however, illustrates a Spanish tendency to bring together Juan Espera en Dios and the legendary Juan de los Tiempos, the now familiar ageless soldier in the army of Charlemagne. This belief, it will be recalled, dates back at least as far as the allusion by Guido Bonatti of 1267; and the fourteenth-century guidebook to Jerusalem in the Evreux MS, a book written quite possibly by a Spaniard, insists on the identity.[40] The belief is perpetuated in Pero Mexia's *Silva de Varia Leccion* (1541), where the doughty warrior's life is extended from 250 to 360 years. It is not until the seventeenth century that Spanish writers come to be skeptical about the identification of the two.

We may conclude, for the moment, the account of the Legend in Spain and Portugal with the important reference in Villalón's *Crotalon* (*ca.*1557). In this satirical piece, done in the manner of Lucian, an omniscient cock tells his master, Miçilo, who Juan de Voto a Dios was:

> Superstitious rascals and vagabonds make out that there was a shoemaker who stood in the "Street of Bitterness" in Jerusalem, and when Christ passed through the street, laden with the Cross, he appeared and gave Him a blow with his shoe last, saying: "Go, go, thou son of Mary!" And then Christ answered: "I go, and thou wilt stay here forever to give testimony of me."[41]

Three points emerge from this passage: the incredulity of the narrator, a disbelief which later becomes so marked as to make the Wandering Jew an object of low comedy, synonymous with deceit, imposture, and low life; the fact that he was a shoemaker; and the fact that he is to be a witness, a piece of testimony, of Christ. The last point we can dispose of first: This was a particular argument of Roger of Wendover and Matthew Paris, and may be assumed as basic to any medieval aspect of the Legend. The first point—that the Wanderer should become a subject for comic treatment—is probably inevitable, for seldom can any serious matter be treated seriously for an indefinite time. The second point—that he is a shoemaker—is new; at least this is the first appearance of the detail in written literature. It is tempting to take Spain as the country of origin of this important detail, but since it turns up elsewhere in old folk tales of indeterminate date, its source can never be proved. I will bring up the matter again in reference to the German *Volksbuch* of 1602 (pp. 42-48 below). Hitting the Saviour with a shoe last instead of the hand, appropriate for a cobbler, represents the usual increment of cruel violence to be expected in oral tradition when it deals with an already cruel story. Villalón, incidentally, repeats the detail of Juan's rejuvenation at the age of one hundred.

None of these early Spanish writers, however, can think of the Wandering Jew as more than a character out of some old wives' tale. Even the expulsion of the Jews from Spain by Ferdinand and Isabella in 1492 does not seem to have produced any special stimulation of the Legend in Spanish or Portuguese folklore or popular tradition. When the Legend is now found among Spanish-speaking people—faint echoes of it have reached as far as South America—it is generally something once heard from afar and no more, something to be read about in a book and usually a foreign one at that.

Meanwhile, in other parts of Europe evidence of the currency of the Legend has survived from the later Middle Ages. We have seen the report of Philippe Mouskes of Tournai in the thirteenth century and the allusion to Jehan Boute-dieu by Filippo de Novara, the Italian living in France in the same century. Both Botadeo and Malchus appear in some medieval miracle plays of the fourteenth to sixteenth century, if not earlier, in Provence and Italy and elsewhere. Perhaps, however, the Malchus here may be only the soldier mentioned in the account of the Passion. The difficulty lies in the fact that neither Boutedieu nor Malc, as they are called, is more than a name in the *dramatis personae*, with two exceptions.[42] In a French Passion play, published at Valenciennes in 1547, Malchus, although Christ has beneficently cured him of his wound, conspires to fashion the nails of the Cross. The wife of the local smith forges them and asks for payment, where-upon Malc tells her that the devil will pay for them. In the sole surviving example from Germany, Malchus, in the *Donauschinger Passionsspiel* of the fifteenth century, pulls the stool out from under Christ at the hearing before the high priest.[43] But, aside from these rather tantalizing appearances in medieval drama, there is no further glimpse of the Wandering Jew in France until after the historically important German pamphlet of 1602, to be described later, gave the Legend a new lease on life. The only good explanation for this rather surprising silence about the Legend on French soil during the later Middle Ages seems to be the lack of written evidence, but it may be simply that at this time the tale of Buttadeus-Malchus had no particular appeal in France.

The same thing is more or less true of England, and yet the English show that in the generations following Roger of Wendover and Matthew Paris they continued to have knowledge of the Legend. In the Middle English religious poem of instruction known as the *Northern Passion*, there are references to the protagonist in two of the surviving manuscripts.[44] This poem was originally written about 1300 and is heavily obligated to a French poem of similar content. One of the manuscripts of the English poem (Rawlinson C. 655), from about 1350, speaks of a John Puttedieu, who was present at the Crucifixion and is still alive. But in the other manuscript (British Museum Additional 31042), of about 1450, some circumstantial detail has been included, for now we learn that John Putte-Dieu pushed Jesus with his hand, crying: "Traytour, ga forthe; here sall thou not stande!" And Jesus answered that Putte-Dieu must stay amid snow and rain and cold until he comes again. Here, then, is the Cartaphilus-Buttadeus combination as late as 1450 in England—the God-pusher but also the awaiter. *Putte-Dieu* is an obvious variant of *Boutedieu;* its source is clearly French. Another allusion, from about 1506, is in William Dunbar's *The Flyting of Dunbar and Kennedy,* perhaps the most conspicuous piece of personal satire in English literature before Dryden. Here, in a catalogue of notorious villains, appears the name of Puttidew. Probably Dunbar picked this up from the French, for he spent some time in France, although he could of course have heard it in Britain. For that matter, he could have known the *Northern Passion,* especially the later and more northerly version of the two manuscripts just mentioned.[45]

These few English references to the Legend bring us sooner or later back to France. The magnificent passage in Chaucer's *Pardoner's Tale,* however, if valid, disturbs the order of things. It will be recalled that the three "riotoures," in their search for the villain Death, who has been killing so many in the neighborhood, come upon a mysterious old man, whom they accost rudely and from whom they receive a dignified reproof when they ask why his face is so completely covered and why he lives so long:

> This olde man gan looke in his visage,
> And seyde thus: "For I ne kan nat fynde
> A man, though that I walked into Ynde,
> Neither in citee ne in no village,
> That wolde chaunge his youthe for myn age;
> And therfore moot I han myn age stille,
> As longe tyme as it is Goddes wille.
> Ne Deeth, allas! ne wol nat han my lyf
> Thus walke I, lyk a restelees kaityf,
> And on the ground, which is my moodres gate,
> I knokke with my staf, bothe erly and late,
> And seye 'Leeve mooder, leet me in!
> Lo how I vanysshe, flessh, and blood, and skyn!
> Allas! whan shul my bones been at reste?
> Mooder, with yow wolde I chaunge my cheste
> That in my chambre longe tyme hath be,
> Ye, for an heyre clowt to wrappe in me!'
> But yet to me she wol nat do that grace,
> For which ful pale and welked is my face."[46]

Leaving aside the most unlikely hypothesis that the old man is Death himself, or the more acceptable one that he represents Old Age or Experience or Wisdom, or the like, one must realize that this is the first statement of the theme not found elsewhere for a long time to come, so far as the Legend of the Wandering Jew is concerned, of the man seeking someone with whom to exchange his fate, someone seeking Death but unable to find him. Moreover, the frail aged form, the piercing look, and the pale and withered countenance are romantic attachments to the Legend not to be heard of again for centuries. Chaucer certainly could have known some form of the Legend. But, if he heard of it in England, there is no evidence that it was sufficiently developed in that country by 1400 to give such a brilliant picture of an old man who cannot die. Did Chaucer hear of the Legend on one of his Italian journeys, and was he so impressed by it that he stored it up in his mind for use some twenty years later when an artistic need presented itself? Stranger things have happened. For what we have here, no matter what the source, are details associated centuries later with the Wandering Jew—the vain quest for death; the ascetic, lean, withered countenance and wasted figure. There is no such corresponding figure anywhere else in contemporaneous medieval literature. I am inclined to answer the question which I have just raised in the affirmative. I believe that Chaucer heard, somehow, of the Legend, and that his transmuting genius did the rest, to give us prophetically a portrait of the Wandering Jew of four hundred or five hundred years later, just as in *The Wife of Bath's Prologue* he created a powerful dramatic monologue five hundred years before Browning. But then Chaucer always had the gift of being generations in advance of his contemporaries.

It is a rather perverse fact that there is no true sign of the Wandering Jew in medieval Celtic literature; indeed, the Legend seems never to have taken root in Celtic soil.[47] The only clear manifestations of the Legend in Scotland, Wales, Ireland, and Brittany all date from more or less modern times. In point of fact, Brittany appears to be the first Celtic region to take note of the Wanderer, probably because of its close relationship to France. Nevertheless, one would have expected more of the Legend, when one considers the natural aptitude of the Celtic creative imagination in the realm of the supernatural, particularly where the timeless and the dateless are concerned.

Something of the same peculiar restraint, not to say inhospitality, with respect to the Legend is apparent in Slavic lands. Here the cause is a little easier to find and may perhaps account also for the Celtic reticence about which I have just complained: Slavic and Celtic written literatures are from too late a date. But, unlike the Celtic, the Slavic writings did have some folk tales which are relevant, and they will be considered in chapter iv. Still it seems worth recording here that the Slavic tales about a certain Phanjas (Phalas, Kalos), servant of the high priest Caiaphas, analogous to Malchus, who dies thrice a day, are in reality examples of a separate extrascriptural legend.[48] In old Bohemia we have already heard of the tale told by the Armenian archbishop, which appeared in *Svatovitský rukopis,* out of Philippe Mouskes of Tournai, Roger of Wendover, and Matthew Paris. A Bohemian folk tale concerning one Kokot, a linen weaver, who was enabled to find a treasure belonging to his deceased father through the peculiar gift possessed by the Wandering Jew for such discoveries, mentions the date

1505.[49] It would seem to be clearly a sixteenth-century product; perhaps it and the corresponding incident told in Antonio di Francesco di Andrea go back to a common folk-tale source.

As for Scandinavia, there is an analogue to certain aspects of the Legend in the case of the Icelandic *Bragda Magus Saga*, a late adaptation of near 1500 of a subromance in the great Charlemagne cycle of medieval romances, a type which is the pride of medieval French literature. The basic point of the analogue is the motif of rejuvenation. Vidförull comes before Charlemagne and explains to the incredulous Frankish court that he can cast off his skin and become younger than before. But, whereas in Roger of Wendover's narrative the protagonist changed from the age of one hundred to the age he had been at the time of the Crucifixion, Vidförull has no such periodicity. The first time he shed his skin he was three hundred and thirty years old; the second time, only two hundred and fifteen. When the time came for his transformation, he was afflicted with a lassitude and then a fainting fit; when he revived he found himself young again. Charlemagne was assured that the preternatural visitor was about to undergo a change for the third time. This was accomplished when Vidförull dragged himself through a solid beam of wood and sprang up, holding his old skin "rolled up from off his head . . . and they say that he was no other than a beardless youth and fair-faced, with age unspecified."[50]

An analogue this remains, and no more. After all, another superhumanly long-lived individual whom we have met before, Juan de los Tiempos (Jan van den Tyden, Jean des Temps), was a shield-bearer in Charlemagne's army; and Ogier the Dane, a knight in that monarch's retinue, could pass through centuries in the twinkling of an eye. Vidförull and the others may be immortals, but not all immortals, even when they are rejuvenated, are the Wandering Jew.

Now while it is clear that by 1600 expectant Cartaphilus, suffering Malchus, and restless Buttadeus had been fairly well blended, it would seem that there was still more expectation than suffering in the then picture of the Wandering Jew. This may be true in western Europe, but there is a real difference in the East. As I have said, there seems to be a division possible into eastern and western versions of the folk tale of the Wandering Jew, and these will be considered in the gross in a subsequent chapter. Then, as now, one must insist that it is impossible to date the great bulk of folk tales; some of them may be extremely old, and others may be as recent as the eighteenth and even the nineteenth century.

Evidently, however, about the time of the Antonio version—that is, during the later fifteenth century—there was a revivifying of the Malchus aspect in the East. The most striking instances are those from the Holy Land itself, as might be expected. It will be recalled (p. 24) that a fourteenth-century French manuscript indicated a place along the Via Dolorosa where the Wandering Jew had committed his blasphemous offense, and Ser Mariano da Siena pointed out a notable gate along the Way of the Cross. Certain travelers to Jerusalem during the fifteenth century, such as Giovanni Zuallardo, Pietro della Valle, and Ludovico degli Agostino—Italians all—did much to establish the traditions of the holy places in the city, especially those of the *Via Crucis*. These travelers speak vaguely of Malchus but consider him for the most part a figment of rumor. For that matter, they do not give any indication that the Legend of Malchus originated in the Holy Land.[51]

Then we unexpectedly come upon the curious narrative of the Fleming, Jan Aerts van Mecheln, who, as a factor for the King of Portugal, made a voyage to Jerusalem in 1484. The account of this voyage was not printed until 1652, but one may assume that the story he told dates from near 1500.[52] According to the narrative, while Jan Aerts was in Jerusalem, he met a mysterious Jew, who bears the Flemish name of Jan Baudewyn. This Jew is carefully guarded behind eight wooden doors, and one of iron. Only with the consent of the Sultan can he be seen. He is not allowed to show himself to an unbeliever, for the glance of the prisoner can compel with supernatural power every one to accept the Christian faith. Jan Baudewyn was once the occupant of a house outside Jerusalem. He was standing on his threshold as Christ came by, laden with the Cross. At the sight of the Saviour, Jan's heart flamed in anger; he chided the Man of God, crying out to him meanwhile: "On your way, on your way! For a long time you should have been taking this road!" Jesus turned to him and said: "I shall go, and you will stay here; and each year you will ask whether I have returned." Truly each year now he asks whether the Man with the Cross has returned yet—only once a year, however, on Good Friday—otherwise he never speaks. His appearance awakens terror, as does that of Marcus (Malchus). He is completely naked; his body is covered with long hair. He continues in the same state, motionless. But his eyes roll, and one can hear plainly the breaths drawn in his chest. The room in which this Jew waits for the end of the world lies right on the spot where he jeered at the Saviour.

This Jan Baudewyn in his waiting and his power to convert to Christianity through a mesmeric eye—an interesting detail out of which the romantic writers of the eighteenth and nineteenth centuries made much—is Cartaphilus; in his God-baiting he is Buttadeus; in his suffering he is Malchean, but curiously he does not seem to be Malchus himself, according to Jan Aerts, for Aerts later saw the hand that struck Christ hanging from a pillar in Solomon's Temple. Of course this last detail is probably mere garbling, because in Jan Baudewyn we have an excellent example of the Eastern aspect of Malchus. Of particular importance here as a characteristic detail is the question: "Has he returned yet?" or, as some folk tales put it, "What day is it?"

At about the same time, in the 1480's, Felix Fabri, a visitor in Jerusalem, discovered that the offender who struck Christ had never been allowed to leave the scene of his offense (the house of the high priest), but occupied a subterranean chamber in that house, where he paced about and lamented his sins perpetually. Fabri does not mention the sinner's name.[53] Strangely enough, other stories of this sort, all of which seem to be of one piece, do not give Malchus' name until after 1500.

Still other travelers had something to tell about Malchus and the soldiers who scourged Christ. Fabri's story bobs up in the account of a French soldier who later served under the Marshal of Anjou, who in turn passed the tale on to the French cleric Michel Menot. Menot died about 1518; his sermons, which contain the story, appeared in 1525. The soldier had undertaken a journey to Jerusalem to fulfill a vow. Here he won the love of one of the sultan's wives—a good French touch. She begged him to stay, and he agreed, provided he might keep his Christian faith. On one occasion, a slave of the sultan's wife came to him and offered to show him a great mystery which pertained to the Christian faith. He led the soldier to a subterranean chamber enclosed by an iron door; here there was a vast pool. In the middle of the pool was a man suffering perpetual torment. His hands and arms flailed about like the blades of a windmill. The slave said to the soldier: "There is that accursed Malchus, who in the house of Hanna gave Christ a blow on the back. From that time on, the earth has swallowed him up, and here he is paying for his deed."[54]

Similarly, Carlo Ranzo, or Soranzo, a noble Venetian, once was a pilgrim in Jerusalem. His account was not written down until the seventeenth century, but his pilgrimage probably took place during the previous century.[55] Once, he says, he was stopped in the streets of Jerusalem by a Turk, who, under the cloak of secrecy and for the inevitable monetary return, showed him one of the unofficial sights of the city—a prisoner under his charge. This prisoner was a powerful man, armed and in armor, confined in a room behind several iron doors. He had been condemned to stay there without food or drink until Doomsday. He was constantly walking up and down the room, beating his breast and declaiming in typical Malchean despair. Although he is not named, one may assume that he was Malchus.

The tale told here appears in several other versions, but the substance of all is the same. The most detailed account is attributed to the pilgrim Peter Brantius Pannalius, who had visited Jerusalem at the end of the sixteenth century. On his return to Italy he told how in Jerusalem he had been accosted by a Turk who revealed himself to be a former slave of Pannalius' uncle in Turin and now captain of the police in Jerusalem. Pannalius was entertained in secret at the Turk's house and was led through mysterious darkness across a drawbridge into a chamber behind five iron doors, where he saw the armed man pacing about. After pledging his word to remain silent he is told that this is the man who struck Christ. "See, his right arm which struck your Christ is twitching!"[56] Pannalius is of most doubtful historicity. But the same story is told of Charles de Rancis of Vercelli in Father Quaresmi's *Terrae Sanctae Elucidatio* (1616-26)[57] and of a certain Charles Carini in D. Laffi's *Viaggio in Levante* (1683).[58] Both Quaresmi and Laffi say that it happened also to John Francis Alcarotto, canon of the Cathedral of Novara, but Alcarotto, in his *Del Viaggio in Terra Santa* (1595), is silent on the subject; it is possible that Quaresmi and Laffi have mistaken some pamphlet material for Alcarotto's work.

Related to this is the analogous report of Father Bonifatius Stefani of Ragusa, bishop of Stagno, who was guardian of the Franciscan monastery in Jerusalem from 1552 to 1564. It is recorded in his *Liber de Perenni Cultu Terrae Sanctae*, published in Venice in 1875. In his description of the Chapel of the Flagellation, then in Moslem hands, he observes:

Only in 1558, my seventh year as Guardian, was I able to enter and see and adore in the place where such abundant Blood was shed. An old woman took me there one day when the bad man [the Governor] was away worshipping in Hebron. Shortly after we arrived at the place, I heard a noise as if Christ were again being scourged. I asked the old woman and the other Friars, and they too heard it. The old woman said she had heard it day and night for sixty years—the whole time she had been with this family. I asked her what caused it, and she said, "The Jews! They are confined in that dark prison over there, and after the final judgment they will be flung headlong into Hell, for they flogged your Christ." I remarked that it was the Roman soldiers who scourged Christ. But she replied with animation: "Those soldiers are the accursed Jews!" Nor could we persuade her otherwise, so I gave her the promised money and we left.[59]

But this little ghost story is apparently a minor local legend; we hear no more of it. At the same time, it is obvious that this Malchus redivivus is a persistent customer, even if he represents only one aspect of the Wandering Jew and is eventually submerged in the more common and familiar conception of the protagonist as an eternal wanderer at large, not a pacer about a subterranean chamber. Still another account which seems to have had some audience is that of the Dominican friar, Auberton, who asserted in a Paris pamphlet of 1623 that he had been in Jerusalem in 1507; there he saw Malchus immured in a subterranean room behind the house of the high priest Hanna, or that of Pontius Pilate—it is the former place in Auberton and the latter in a later version of the same tale by one Dauterlin, who saw the same thing in 1547. It is most likely that Dauterlin is Auberton, for the two accounts are otherwise virtually identical. In whichever house it might be, there was a red-headed man, about thirty-five or forty years of age, who knew all languages but tended to answer questions with the rather irrelevant "Answerest thou the high priest thus?" The spectacle of extreme anguish in a human being, which the writer nevertheless fails to describe, was the most harrowing sight the traveler had ever seen.[60] Another Frenchman, the Franciscan friar Leonard of Clou, who had been a councilor in the Holy Land, repeated the tale about 1670.[61] But the credulity of the Christian listener seems to have evaporated after about 1700; thenceforth any references to the tale indicate both disbelief and condemnation of such crass falsehood. In spite of which, the nineteenth-century traveler was often told of the abode of the Wandering Jew. Mark Twain, in *Innocents Abroad*, wrote a rather neat summary of the Legend.[62]

In referring to these various Jerusalem stories, it is advisable to look ahead for a moment to the fact that there are several Italian folk tales, first brought together in the nineteenth century but certainly very old, perhaps medieval, in which a Jew by the name of Malchus (Marcus, Marco, Malco) gives Jesus a blow with an iron glove. The hand has been brutally strengthened and the blow is necessarily more violent. For this offense Malchus is condemned to a subterranean chamber, where he paces incessantly about a pillar. In at least one tale he has worn a path a mile deep about the pillar. According to the Scriptures, Christ was scourged before the Crucifixion. It was the tradition in Jerusalem that he was first bound to a column in the hall of the high priest. Evidently this pillar and the pillar about which Malchus moves were identified at the time when the Legend of Malchus developed. In some versions Malchus stops from time to time and beats his head against the pillar. He knows all visitors and their names, homes, and languages. He can never find death, for it is his traditional sentence that he must walk around the pillar until Judgment Day. (Perhaps the pillar in the Temple of Solomon, where Jan Aerts saw the hand that struck Christ, is a reminiscence imperfectly remembered.) Sometimes these Italian tales put Malchus, like Jonah, in the belly of a whale; sometimes at the bottom of the sea. Sometimes, instead of pacing around a pillar, he strides endlessly about the floor of a narrow cell. Wherever he may be, he is inconsolable.[63]

It seems likely that the Italian tales, which are found chiefly in Sicily, were brought there from Jerusalem by travelers such as those whom we have just met. The differences between this folk tale and that told by Johannes Moschos about A.D. 600 are the differences accumulating inevitably after the lapse of many centuries of oral tradition. As usual, contamination with other tales is extremely common, for that is the way folk tales develop.

CHAPTER THREE

The Advent of Ahasuerus

Medieval theologians divided the world into two realms, the kingdom of God and the kingdom of Satan. Those who were not for God in Christ were against him. As God performed his works in the world through the Son of God, Jesus Christ, so Satan performed his works in the world through the Son of Satan, Antichrist. Christ and Antichrist therefore confronted each other in irreconcilable conflict. The power of Antichrist was great, and his final desperate attacks upon mankind would be terrible. The eventual battle would engulf and destroy the world; and, although Christ would of course triumph in the end and bring the millennial era of peace under the banner of his Church, no man could dare be so hardy as to take too lightly the woes and miseries that must first befall man through the operations of Antichrist before this ultimate triumph. False prophets and false Messiahs would seduce multitudes of the human race, as the scriptures had long foretold, and all that man could do was to keep vigil and resist as best he could with the help of God.

This division and this doctrine of inevitable warfare with the Devil had been an essential part of Christian doctrine from the very beginning. The authority for the existence of Antichrist was to be found in Matthew 24:5 ("For many shall come in my name, saying, I am Christ; and shall deceive man"); in Matthew 24:24 ("For there shall arise false Christs, and false prophets . . . they shall deceive the very elect"); and particularly in I John 2:18 ("Little children, it is the last time: and as ye have heard that antichrist shall come, even now are there many antichrists; whereby we know that it is the last time"). It was not until the later Middle Ages, however, that the Legend of Antichrist came into full bloom. In the writings of the two greatest medieval theologians, Thomas Aquinas and Albertus Magnus, in the thirteenth century, there was much discussion of the matter. According to them, Antichrist would be born in Babylon ("Mother of Harlots and Abominations of the Earth") of the Jewish tribe of Dan. This particular tribe was chosen presumably because of Genesis 49:17 ("Dan shall be a serpent by the way"), a reference which bestowed upon Dan enough obloquy to lead to the belief that Judas was a Danite. Antichrist, having been brought into the world, would proceed to Jerusalem, adopt the Jewish religion, and persuade the people that he was a Messiah. His power would grow prodigiously, although it would last only three and a half years. Enoch and Elijah would be sent against him and would fail. Eventually the archangel Michael would destroy him on the Mount of Olives. The scholars differed as to when this would happen: some believed that it was imminent, others thought there might be a little time left for man to repent, but all agreed it must happen sooner or later.

The medieval clerical mind soon began to elaborate this already spectacular legend.[1] A good illustration is the medieval Antichrist play, beginning with the Latin original (*Ludus paschalis de adventu et interitu Antichristi*) of the thirteenth century.[2] This play does not immediately associate Antichrist with the Jews, but the French and German Antichrist plays following shortly thereafter certainly do. These Continental plays are very much concerned that Antichrist should be numbered among the Jews. They are, in short, another of the many indications of the strong wave of anti-Semitism which came to a peak during the fourteenth and fifteenth centuries. These dramatic representations conclude with the destruction of both Jews and Antichrist, and the coming of the millennium tends to be hailed as much because the Jews are forever damned as because God and his holy kingdom have triumphed.

Following the early symptoms of disunity and rebellion within the medieval Church such as the Great Schism of the fourteenth century, the activities of the Albigenses in southern France around 1200, of the Wycliffites in England in the fourteenth century, and of the Hussites in Bohemia in the fifteenth, the tension engendered by the concept of Antichrist increased to a most sinister degree. For example, the German Lenten play, *Herzog von Burgund*, written by a certain Hans Polz some time in the middle of the fifteenth century, concentrates chiefly upon the allegiance that the Jews pledge to Antichrist. Here the program of the Son of Satan calls explicitly for the liquidation of all Christendom. In this play, to be sure, Antichrist is as usual confounded, but in a remarkable speech he explains that he and the Jews have been persecuted by Christians for fourteen hundred years and in return have resorted to all the traditional alleged revenges of the Jews which had been given credence during the Middle Ages—poisonings, blood baths, ritual murders (especially of Christian children), sorcery, and witchcraft. And although he has failed this time, Antichrist announces that he will return in another person and again and again until his ultimate purpose has been achieved. The Duke of Burgundy's men then torture and kill the Jews, every one of them, following up the massacre with a dance of joy around the mutilated corpses. The effect of this play upon a superheated Christian citizenry must have been pernicious in the extreme. It is a relief to hear that the city council of Frankfurt, in 1469, passed a special ordinance to protect the Jewish inhabitants during the performance of the Antichrist play. In view of the fact that the infidel Turks had already captured Constantinople sixteen years before and were to press on into the Balkans and threaten Central Europe intermittently during the next two centuries, the action of the city fathers of Frankfurt is remarkably restrained.[3]

The leaders of the Protestant Reformation in the sixteenth century subscribed to the belief that Antichrist would soon come. Although Calvin once remarked, rather too smugly, that the approach of Antichrist was evidently a matter of much concern among Catholics, the great Martin Luther had been willing to admit the possibility of such a disaster and had even looked for the signs of Antichrist's coming.[4] As usual, however, the opinions of the leaders were not so dangerous as the reaction to them of the people as a whole. By the time the great events of the early Reformation had rumbled past, a large segment of Christendom was convinced that something more real than intangible, dogmatic abstractions and legends was confronting the world. The contemporaneous invasion of Europe by the Turks, to say nothing of the tales of the fabulous depredations of earlier times by Genghis Khan and Tamerlane, was, in popular estimation, only the first faint sign of far more terrible incursions by heathens and hostile principalities and powers from the Orient. Specifically, there arose a widely circulated rumor that a vast, uncountable horde of Jews, headed by Antichrist, the son of Satan and a Jewish whore—in some versions a misguided Jewish virgin instead of a whore—was to debouch in hellish violence all over Europe.[5] Well may we refer to this report as the Great Rumor.

A German tract of the times, printed some time after 1550, announced the birth of Antichrist in Babylon.[6] This same rumor or news item, as you will, appearing in France, was recorded in Pierre de l'Estoile's *Mémoires-Journaux* in the entries for December, 1601, and August, 1609.[7] The news had been brought to King Henry IV of France by the Grand Master of the Knights of Malta. The newborn child was abnormally large, had cat's teeth, spoke after eight days, and could make manna fall from heaven. De l'Estoile is as appropriately scornful as a sophisticated Parisian should be. The earliest contemporary printed warning of this invasion by the innumerable hosts of Antichrist was another German pamphlet, *Newe Zeytung von den newgeborenen Antichrist* (1579), which places the birth of Antichrist in the preceding year.[8] A score of years later came a more circumstantial account, *Warhafftige erschreckliche newe Zeitung und Geschicht*, which reports blood and fire raining down from heaven on St. Mary's Church in Stralsund—a stern, minatory document which stresses the imminence of Judgment Day, when Christ will appear to judge the living and the dead. It discusses the many signs of doom—a throwback to the old medieval belief that the world was to come to an end at the conclusion of the first millennium. We learn of the progressively more sinister omens on the days preceding the cataclysm and of the dreadful confusion on earth until Doomsday clears all away.[9] Another alarming publication, *Chronologische Gewisse* (1605), which was probably written in Prague some ten years earlier, computes in elaborate fashion that the Day of Judgment is to take place within sixty-seven years. The Holy Scriptures say so, insists the author; it is not his own claim.[10]

In all those unhappy decades of religious warfare and intolerance, superstition, rumor, and credulity were rife—Antichrists, Fausts, astrologers, charlatans, and soothsayers of all kinds flooded Europe with their magical, diabolical, infernal merchandise. The peak of anxiety concerning these sad times seems to have been reached by the Breton chronicler, Canon Moreau, in his *Histoire de ce qui s'est passé en Bretagne durant les guerres de la Ligue* (1609?). Moreau adds little new to the story, except to fix the year of the Great Rumor as 1599, ten years before De l'Estoile appears to have heard about it, and to observe that the matter was so generally talked about and with such emotional disquiet that King Henry IV forbade any discussion of the news.[11] When, in 1610, Henry fell under an assassin's dagger, there was much shaking of heads at the fulfillment of the gloomy prophecy that, when Antichrist was near, kings and potentates would be destroyed to make way for the final perilous battle at Armageddon. Moreau, of course, knew nothing of the assassination to come, but contemporaneous ballads after 1610 are only too happy to link prophecy and deed.

No wonder, therefore, that at such a time of rumors and counterrumors there should be a new cycle of popular literature concerning the Wandering Jew and particularly an attempt to relate him, as well as his fellow Jews, to Antichrist, thus to call attention to the Christ-baiting, Christ-killing Jew. Now Buttadeus could appropriately continue his restless march, but with more ominous steps. The sorcery which the Jew of the Middle Ages was supposed to practice could now assist the infernal necromancy of the wizard of all wizards, Satan himself. The impetus for this new cycle came from the fresh, urgent forces of the Protestant Reformation rather than from the now decaying medieval Church. Yet in their polemical writings and their more militant popular ballads and tracts, the extremists of both sides were explicit. The Protestant called the pope Antichrist; the Catholic returned the compliment and bestowed it upon Martin Luther. Both kinds of partisans agreed that the Wandering Jew, whoever or whatever he might be, belonged to Antichrist.

Into this seething stew we should throw in a few ingredients drawn from the history of the literature of the period. Some old accounts of the Wandering Jew were published. The first was the chronicle of Sigismondo Tizio, the Florentine living in Siena. His chronicle, it will be remembered, emphasized the awaiting by the protagonist (*Expectabis me dum venero*). It was first printed in Basel in 1550, with a German translation from the same city in 1572. The second was a reprinting of Guido Bonatti of Forli's *De Astronomia Tractatus X*, which contained one of the more striking passing references to the Jew's having been seen in 1267. This had been first printed at Augsburg in 1491; the reprinting was done at Basel in 1550, and a German translation, once more from Basel, appeared in 1572. The identity of dates in the publication of these two works and the fact that they were both printed at Basel may be a coincidence, but a striking one, for it links these two for future reference. Yet the significance remains somewhat obscure.

More important than either of these, for they were, after all, rather minor allusions to the Legend, was the printing of Matthew Paris' *Chronica Majora* in London (1571) and in Zurich (1582), for it should be recalled that this is the fullest account before the Antonio version (pp. 25-26 above). Now it was in print for the first time. This, as we have seen, was virtually identical with the account in Roger of Wendover's *Flores Historiarum*. And, finally, there was the publication of the Faust-book at Frankfurt in 1587. Here was the testimony of a Protestant as to the activities of the "widely renowned sorcerer and practitioner of the black arts," a horrible example and a warning to all devout men. It outlined the career of Johannes Faustus—another John—the great sixteenth-century scholar and magician, and gave him marked anti-Catholic proclivities, although his adventures in the pursuit of such proclivities were too often slapstick, undignified antics, such as the boxing of the pope's ears, the tantalizing and deluding of monks, the wringing from them of a malediction, the net effects of which could only be ironical. Faustus was himself a wanderer, but his travels were for the limited period of twenty-four years and for reasons altogether different from those which sent the Wandering Jew along his endless road. Faustus crosses the path of the Wandering Jew in later years, although it is evident that the two legends should be kept separate.

The Kurtze Beschreibung

Fifteen years after the appearance of the Faust-book and twenty after the Zurich edition of the *Chronica Majora*, there was published a pamphlet which is perhaps the most important single milestone in the progress of the Legend of the Wandering Jew. Had it not been for this pamphlet, it is altogether likely that the Legend, like many another legend of extrascriptural origins, would have trickled out into a sandy desert and have been known only to the antiquarian and the specialist in folklore. This is *Kurtze Beschreibung und Erzehlung von einem Juden mit Namen Ahasverus,* to be known henceforth as the *Kurtze Beschreibung*.[12] It came out in 1602 under different imprints: by Christoff Creutzer of Leyden, by Wolffgang Suchnach of Bautzen, by Jakob Rothen of Danzig. There are nine printings of this pamphlet under the same title, with varying subtitles: six have the Bautzen imprint, one the Leyden, one the Danzig, and one does not give the name of publisher or place of publication. One of the Bautzen imprints gives 1502 instead of 1602—an obvious typographical error—and the one without name of place or printer gives 1603 instead of 1602 but is believed, nonetheless, to have been printed in 1602. The contents of all nine, however, are identical except for the title page. All are four-page quartos. They have a vignette portraying the Wandering Jew in crude outline, a bearded individual with a kind of turban on his head, clothed in a long mantle; his hands are held before him in an attitude of prayer. An indication of the rarity of this original 1602 edition is the fact that only some twenty copies are known to have survived to the present day.

The problem of these various imprints is a complicated and obscure business. Leyden, Bautzen, and Danzig are widely separated localities. Most of the copies bear the Bautzen imprint, and Bautzen is not far from Dresden, in Saxony; yet the story tells of what happened in Hamburg on a particular occasion. The only important character in the narrative, apart from the Wandering Jew himself, is Paulus von Eitzen (1521-1598), a prominent theologian of Hamburg, where he spent most of his life. In a word, the setting and the characters call for a north German, more particularly a Schleswigian, origin for the pamphlet. For this reason, Neubaur, by far the most expert bibliographer in this problem, insists that the pamphlet came from Schleswig, or at least had for its author one who came from Schleswig.[13]

On the other hand, the pamphlet calls attention, rather gratuitously, to the fact that the Wandering Jew had visited Danzig in 1599. Neither Leyden nor Bautzen comes into the substance of the work; they are merely given as places of publication, and there is no way now of ascertaining their validity. In fact, it has been suggested that all nine of these copies came from the press of Johannes Schröter of Basel, for he seems to have been notorious as a publisher, much given to the mystification of his readers. And Basel, be it remembered, was the city where Tizio's chronicle and Bonatti's treatise had been published thirty years before.

The recurrence of Danzig, however, as the city named and said to have been visited by the Wanderer only three years earlier, throws the spotlight on that locality, where an attractive possibility immediately springs into view.

One of the nine copies bears the imprint of Danzig, giving the name of the publisher as Jakob Rothen. This copy differs from the others in that its subtitle makes reference to Buttadeus and more particularly to the fact that the protagonist was called Buttadeus by Guido Bonatti of Forli. As for the printer, he was most probably Jakob Rhode, one of a distinguished line of Danzig printers bearing that surname. He began printing in 1573 and died during an epidemic of the plague in Danzig in 1602. The place of his press and bookshop was the Danzig Gymnasium, formerly a Franciscan monastery, which was the center of the artistic and intellectual life of the city.

Also in Danzig at this time was living a remarkable individual, Giovanni Bernardini Bonifacio, marquis d'Oria (1517-1597). He had been a religious and political refugee from Naples, whence he had fled the Inquisition and traveled northward into Switzerland, Austria, Poland, and various German cities, settling finally in Danzig. He was by nature something of a traveler, and the exigencies of the time hastened his footsteps, for he was an avowed Protestant and a great admirer of Melanchthon. At Wittenberg he had become acquainted with Paulus von Eitzen of Hamburg, already mentioned. The marquis was noted in Danzig for his cultured mind and his remarkable library, which he had been able to collect and—what is rather astonishing—to transport all over Central Europe. Throughout the 1570's and 1580's he kept a kind of intellectual court in Danzig. Among his friends were the painter Anton Moller, an Italophile with a special love for Venice and Siena (where Buttadeus had certainly been known for some time); Dr. Welsius, professor of rhetoric and homiletics at the Hochschule of Danzig; and the printer Jakob Rhode. Welsius wrote a memorial to the marquis on the occasion of the latter's death, and it was printed, of course, by Rhode.

We may therefore build up a theory about the composition of the *Kurtze Beschreibung.* This was first suggested by Arno Schmidt in 1927;[14] it is a useful and valid enough theory, although one should not follow it all the way. After the deaths of the marquis in 1597 and of his friend Paulus von Eitzen in 1598, a certain Danziger from the circle of the marquis wrote the pamphlet. The time was ripe for the circulation of the wondrous tale of Ahasuerus. Antichrist was near, and for Danzig at least there was a further indication of the imminence of doom in the fearful presence of the plague, which in 1601 and 1602 virtually paralyzed the city. It is possible that the author was the painter Moller or Dr. Welsius or, even more probably, Valentin Schreck, director of the church school in Danzig. It could have been, for that matter, any other member of the coterie. But we should, in all justice, refer to the author as "learned," in the sense that he knew of Buttadeus and of Guido Bonatti, of whom he may have been made aware by the marquis himself or by items in the marquis' library. The portrait of the Wandering Jew in the vignette has been thought by some to derive from the figure of Jürgen, a legendary character of Lithuanian folklore, but any educated man in Danzig would probably know something about Lithuanian folklore. The author would almost certainly have known the contents of a chapbook printed by Rhode in 1589, describing a weird-looking prophet of the latter day, *aus*

Gallien, bareheaded, barefoot, heavily bearded, lean and hungry, disheveled, and carrying a staff. He need not have known about Jürgen at all.[15] He could well have known the new Zurich edition of Matthew Paris' *Chronica Majora*. He would be a Protestant. The rest would depend on his imagination, which would most likely be influenced by folk tales about the Wandering Jew or others like him, which might be in the air at the time but whose impact upon the author can hardly be measured at this distance.

The advantage of this theory, besides its harmonizing with certain known facts, is that it affords an easy link between Italy, the distribution point of the Legend in western Europe, and Germany, where the Legend does not seem to have been hitherto known.[16] At least there are no medieval references to it from there. The link would be the Marquis d'Oria himself, straight from Italy. Moreover, we can thus account for the Protestant nature of the *Kurtze Beschreibung*. We must now assume, however, that the imprints other than the Danzig imprint are forgeries. So they have been accepted by some. But why the forgeries? The only explanations that seem likely are: (1) that Rhode, like Schröter of Basel, wished to mystify his public and thus enhance the credibility of his supernatural tale; or (2) that he wished to impress upon his readers the currency and the popularity of the Legend and thereby increase the sale of the pamphlet. Beyond these the purpose of such faked imprints remains obscure.

Nor, indeed, should anyone feel bound to the theory of Danzig origins for the *Kurtze Beschreibung*, although it is the only theory to shed much light on the matter. Neubaur, for example, sees too much Schleswig influence in the pamphlet to be satisfied that it could have come from any other place: (1) the presence of Von Eitzen himself; (2) the fact that there were no Jews in Schleswig in 1602, so that Ahasuerus becomes a much more unusual phenomenon; (3) the pamphlet's reference to an authentic embassy to Spain from Adolph of Schleswig and Holstein; and (4) the identification in the next "edition" of the author as a Westphalian. No one so far has chosen Bautzen, in far-off Silesia, as the real place of publication.

In 1603 a new printing of the *Kurtze Beschreibung* appeared, with a different title—*Wunderbarlicher Bericht von einem Juden Ahasverus*—and some additional material, to be described later, including some minor alterations of text and sixteen lines of verse summarizing the contents. This was issued under the imprint of Christoff Creutzer, with the same place (Leyden) and date (1602), and there are a half-dozen subsequent printings during the next decade, all but one ostensibly published in Leyden. The odd member purports to come from Revel, Estonia, as late as 1613. The putative author is named here as Chrysostom Dudulaeus Westphalus, and the "Westphalus" is snapped up by those who place the original pamphlet in the neighborhood of Hamburg. These printings will be referred to hereafter as the Dudulaeus pamphlets. This ridiculous name is most likely a pseudonym, and the identity of the author remains unknown. If one can believe in the Danzig origin for the *Kurtze Beschreibung*, the name may have taken its origin from the word *Dudler* ("one who mumbles"), and the historical evidence indicates that this would be a most appropriate nickname for Dr. Welsius, who, although a teacher of speech and rhetoric, was inclined to splutter.

More intriguing, and also more difficult to believe, is the possibility that the name is a Latinization of *Dudley*, the family name of Lord Leicester, the quondam favorite of Queen Elizabeth I of England. The explanation offered is that the author, a man from Westphalia, assumed the pseudonym because it was the name of a famous courtier of the age, whose character had been represented in a Franco-Latin tragedy of Mary Stuart written by Adrianus Rulerius of Douai as early as 1593.[17] The whole explanation seems illogical and far-fetched, and yet it remains possible that the glamorous Leicester's name could have appealed to someone as an attractive pseudonym.

Since we seem to be dealing with falsifications of names, dates, and places throughout this particular subject—although there is no reason to doubt the date 1602—it is not fruitful to speculate further. Be his identity what it may—and I for one favor that of Valentin Schreck—the obscure author of the *Kurtze Beschreibung* was most successful in the long run. He initiated the *Volksbuch* of the Legend of the Wandering Jew. With its numerous progeny, it seems to have been better known during the next two centuries than the more celebrated Faust-book.

Therefore, since the *Kurtze Beschreibung* underlies nearly all the treatments of the Wandering Jew during the seventeenth and eighteenth centuries, the following translation of the "Leyden" copy of 1602 in the British Museum is offered. A few irrelevant phrases have been omitted.

Since these times have contributed little that is news to us, I will relate to you something old which is still considered with awe by many as something new . . .

Paulus von Eitzen, doctor and Bishop of Schleswig . . . told me and other students more than once, that when he was a student in his youth at Wittenberg, he once went to Hamburg in the winter of the year 1542, to visit his parents. On the following Sunday in church, during the sermon, he saw a man who was a very tall person, with long hair reaching down over his shoulders; he was standing barefoot close by the chancel. He paid such close attention to the sermon that one could detect no movement in his body, except that when the name of Jesus Christ was pronounced he bowed his head, beat on his breast, and sighed very deeply. He wore no other clothing, in that very hard winter, than a pair of trousers badly worn at the bottom, a cloak reaching to the knees, and over that a mantle reaching to the feet. Otherwise he appeared to be a man of about fifty years. Since he attracted attention to himself because of his tallness, clothing, and behavior, he was asked who he was and what his business was. And it was reported that . . . he was born a Jew in Jerusalem with the name of *Ahasuerus*. His vocation was that of shoemaker; he had been present in person at the Crucifixion of Christ, and since that time had remained alive and had traveled through many lands, and for proof of the truth of his assertions he had knowledge of many circumstances concerning Christ after he had been taken and led before Pilate and Herod and finally crucified. He could tell more of such things than either the evangelists or the historians. He told further of many changes of government, especially in Eastern countries, as they had occurred throughout these many centuries. Then he told with great minuteness the lives, sufferings, and deaths of the holy apostles.

Now when Paulus von Eitzen heard such things, he wondered about them greatly and sought an opportunity to speak directly with this man. When he finally succeeded in bringing this about, the Jew told him all these things in detail. He had been living at the time of Christ in Jerusalem. He had been stirred against the Lord

5

10

15

20

25

Christ, whom he considered a heretic and seducer of the people (because he knew no better), as did the high priests and the scribes. And all the time he did his best to have this seducer of the people (as he considered Him) put out of this world. And finally, when they had seized Him, and He had been led before Pilate by the high priests, he took part in the cry "Crucify Him!" and called for the deliverance of Barabbas, and helped to bring it about that the sentence of death was passed on Him. And when the sentence had been pronounced, this Jew hurried to his house, since the Lord Christ must be led that way, so that he could see Him. He took his little child in his arms and stood before his door, that they might see the Lord Christ go by. Then, when the Lord Christ under his Cross was led by, he leaned for a moment against the Jew's house. The anger of the Jew rose up more than ever, and with curses he ordered Him to pack and be off to where it was fitting for Him to go. Then Christ looked sternly at him, and spoke to him with meaning, "I WILL STAND HERE AND REST, BUT YOU MUST WALK!"

Immediately the Jew put down his child; he could stay no longer in the house. Rather he had to follow along and see, as it had been ordained him. Afterwards everything came to pass; it was impossible for him to return to the city of Jerusalem and to enter it. His wife, his child, and his relatives he never saw again. Forthwith he went into foreign lands, one after another, until the present time. When, after many centuries, he came back to his land, he found it all laid waste and Jerusalem destroyed, so that he could no longer recognize it. What God now intended to do with him, in leading him about so long in this wretched life, he could not explain otherwise than that perhaps he should be on Judgment Day a living witness of the Passion of Christ, to the greater confusion of the godless and the infidels. But he must endure his portion until it pleased God to call him forth from this vale of sorrow to eternal peace.

Whereupon Paulus von Eitzen, along with the rector of the schools in Hamburg, who was a learned man expert in history, asked him for the true account of all kinds of things which had occurred in the countries of the East after Christ's birth and times. He gave a satisfactory and circumstantial account of that, so that they could scarcely wonder enough. In his own life, the Jew said, he was quiet and withdrawn within himself. He did not talk much, except when asked a question. If invited into a house, he did not eat or drink much. If anyone should offer him money, he would take not more than two shillings, which he would straightway give to the poor, with the remark that he did not need money and that God would provide well for him. None ever saw him laugh during the time he was in Hamburg. In whatever land he came he spoke the language; he could at that time speak Saxon as well as if he had been born a Saxon.

Many people, as Von Eitzen observed, came from many lands and widely separated regions of the earth to see and listen to him while he was in Hamburg, and many came to judge him. Most of these thought that he had with him an errant spirit that could reveal such things to him as those whereof he spoke. But he [Von Eitzen] did not think so, for the Jew not only was attentive to God's word and spoke of it, but also showed great reverence and named God's name with deep sighs. Moreover, he could not tolerate a curse. When anyone cursed in the name of God's sufferings and wounds, he would tremble at it and reproach that man with fierce zeal, saying "Miserable man! miserable creature! Wilt thou then take in vain the name of God and His martyrdom? If thou hadst seen and heard how sorely the Lord Christ was wounded and tortured for thee and me, as I saw it, thou wouldst rather torture thyself than name thus His name!"

All these things Paulus von Eitzen told me truthfully and with many other further circumstances, which also I have heard from several old burghers throughout   80
Schleswig, who themselves saw this man and talked with him.

In the year [15]75, the Secretary Christoph Ehringer and Magistrate Jacobus who . . . had been sent as ambassadors to the King of Spain and afterwards to the Duke of Alba in the Netherlands . . . when they returned home and came to Schleswig . . . reported that they had seen at Malduit [Madrid] a man with the same   85
build, clothes, behavior, and age; that they had talked with him; and that other people had understood him, and that he talked good Spanish.

What are we to think of this man? One may be free in his judgment. The works of God are wonderful and inscrutable, and as time goes on they will be more so, and more things hitherto hidden will be revealed, particularly . . . on the ap-   90
proaching Day of Judgment and end of the world . . .

Dated Schleswig, June 9, 1564

This man or Jew is said to have soles on his feet so thick that one can measure them with the thickness of two fingers across. They are as hard as horn because of his long walking and traveling. He is said to have been seen in Danzig in the   95
year 1599.

When one compares this account with that furnished by the servant of the Armenian archbishop to Roger of Wendover, thence to be transmitted to Matthew Paris, one is drawn to the conclusion that the author of the *Kurtze Beschreibung* must have been acquainted with the *Chronica Majora*, probably in the Zurich translation. In both accounts the source of the tale is a bishop. The sinner is contrite, patiently abiding the time when his sentence may be lifted. He is a man of grave demeanor and few words. He shrinks from oaths and blasphemy. He is charitably inclined; certainly there is nothing of the sinister about him. Instead, he seems to have the temperament of a missionary, to be a living witness to the greatness of God and the Passion. Indeed, the same phrase appears here and in Matthew Paris.

To be sure, Ahasuerus is more ascetic than the *bon vivant* whom Antonio di Francesco di Andrea knew. He is more the German Reformationist than the gay, arresting Latin. He is shabby where Votaddio was not. But he is nonetheless a wanderer, though not limited, apparently, to the three-day sojourn which was the lot of Votaddio. The differences are partly those between an Italian of 1500 and a German of 1600, with the possibility that intervening folk tales have influenced the later of the two.

Yet there are so many details in the *Kurtze Beschreibung* which survive for the next three hundred years, to be picked up by this and that author, that the student of the Legend should virtually memorize the entire pamphlet. Since this is rather impractical for the casual reader, he might well concentrate on these seventeen articles of faith:

1. The physical appearance of the protagonist is typical—he is tall and eye-catching, barefoot, with threadbare clothes, ragged, and shabby. He may or may not be bearded; he may or may not have any head covering. But his hair is long, and he is lean, wiry, gaunt, and conspicuous (ll.6-7, 11-14). If he is barefoot, the thickness of his soles is remarkable (ll.93-94).

2. He is about fifty years old, or at least of indeterminate middle age (l.13).

3. He is called Ahasuerus (Ahasverus, Ahasver). Buttadeus, Malchus, Cartaphilus, and other names which appear from time to time are usually displaced by the new name (l.16).

4. He is or was a shoemaker (l.16).

5. His knowledge of what has taken place since the Crucifixion is profound; hence he is ready at any time to step into the role of world-chronicler (ll.19-24).

6. He was opposed to Christ on both political and emotional or personal grounds —a motive, not supplied before, which adds dimensions to the Legend with its capacity for refinement and manipulation (ll.28-31).

7. He has a wife and child (or children), whom he must abandon because of the curse (ll.36-37, 46).

8. He cannot stay in his house after the curse, but must follow the Saviour to witness the Crucifixion, after which he must wander. Here the wanderings begin technically with his going to watch the martyrdom of Christ (ll.43-47).

9. He does not see his home again (ll.45-49).

10. When, after many centuries, he manages to return to Jerusalem, he finds the site of his home desolate and the city destroyed. This is a favorite detail of the romantic novels of the early nineteenth century and is part of the folk tradition which links Ahasuerus with Cain and destruction (ll.48-49).

11. He is a living witness to the Crucifixion, with all the implications to be derived from this (ll.51-52).

12. He must endure his fate, no matter how terrible his lot; therefore he is seldom seen to laugh or even to smile (ll.54-55, 64).

13. He is questioned by scholars and always shows more knowledge than they can hope to possess (ll.55-59).

14. He is quiet and withdrawn in manner and taciturn in speech, seldom speaking at all unless spoken to (ll.59-60).

15. He accepts little or no money and is primarily charitable and abstemious. There is no suggestion here of the inexhaustible purse, nor of the presence of a definite amount of money on his person (three coins, five sous, etc.) (ll. 61-63).

16. Into whatever country he may go, he is able to speak the language of that country fluently (ll.65-66, 84-85). This talent has been recognized, also, in earlier references to the Legend and is obvious enough in the Antonio version.

17. He cannot tolerate cursing or swearing in the name of the Lord (ll.73-78).

Of course, a given writer in a given land at a given time may and will depart from such a formula as that indicated by these seventeen points, yet, by and large, these points set up a satisfactory basic pattern for the treatment of the Wandering Jew from the time of the *Kurtze Beschreibung* of 1602 to the present.

Further Consideration of Details

It may be suggested, then, that the Legend, transmitted by the Marquis d'Oria and his library (what a pity that we do not know the contents of that library!), reached Germany in the later years of the sixteenth century for what appears to be the first time. Since it lent itself to the purposes of religious propaganda at a time when such propaganda was considered most important, it spread in this hitherto untouched territory with great rapidity and wide currency. The *Kurtze Beschreibung*, with its many adaptations and translations, produced a large progeny, which survived well into the nineteenth century. It was rendered or paraphrased in Swedish, French, English, Flemish, and, eventually, in Italian and Spanish and even Russian. Neubaur, who seems to have spent much of his scholarly life in the pursuit of this *Volksbuch*, had knowledge of between seventy-five and eighty variants of the original *Kurtze Beschreibung*. Before giving attention, however, to the major examples of such translations and adaptations, we should pause over some of the details thrust into the foreground by the *Kurtze Beschreibung*.

The picture presented by this Ahasuerus—his flowing hair, lank form, and ragged clothing—is now distinctive and will remain so. Perhaps the author of the *Kurtze Beschreibung*, as I have noted, drew some details from the portrayal of Jürgen in Lithuanian legendry. But I should call attention again to the pamphlet printed by Jakob Rhode in 1589, *Newe Zeytung—ein alter Prophet*, which contains close parallels to the description of the Jew in the *Kurtze Beschreibung*. The length of hair suggests age in any land, as well as a certain antisocial, or at least nonconformist, attitude; the lank form suggests self-denial and privation. The ragged clothing is not likely to be only a realistic detail in the picture of a travel-stained wanderer and his worldly poverty; it has a symbolic value, representing the Wanderer's tattered spiritual status.

Then, as to the occupation of shoemaker: We may consider, first, the fact that the Wandering Jew (Juan de Voto a Dios) was a *çapatero*, or cobbler, in the reference to him found in Villalón's *Crotalon* of about 1557.[18] This alone demolishes the strained theory of Arno Schmidt that the author of the *Kurtze Beschreibung* in Danzig made Ahasuerus a shoemaker, as a play on the name of his friend and fellow townsman, the magistrate Simon Schuhmacher. Yet just when the Jew was first associated with the gentle craft of St. Crispin, and where and why, are questions not easily answered. There is no confirmation of his trade of shoemaker before the sixteenth century, and undoubtedly the most famous shoemaker in this age, the German poet and playwright Hans Sachs (1494-1576), seems to know nothing of the Wandering Jew, who would be precisely the kind of character Sachs would have enjoyed. This detail hardly seems to belong to northern Europe. My surmise is that the detail of the shoemaker came from an unknown contributor who lived in southern Europe during the sixteenth century, if only because Villalón's allusion, from Spain, is the first of such allusions. To be sure, the Wanderer is a shoemaker also in an eastern Mediterranean folk tale (p. 72), but this tale is impossible to date definitely. In any event, it sounds rather too sophisticated and therefore probably too recent to aid us. Besides, the *when* and the *where* are perhaps not so important as the *why*.

Classical tradition, as expressed in the works of Aristophanes, Plato, Martial, Juvenal, and others, indicates that the shoemaker was considered among the lowest of workers. One of Burkhard Waldis' sixteenth-century fables tells of a tench that fled from the company of other fishes because he had been called a shoemaker. Another German squib, in Janus Gruter's *Florilegium politicum*

(1612), brackets shoemakers, linen weavers, and tailors as the world's greatest liars.[19] Moreover, shoemakers have by tradition been considered notoriously independent and improvident.[20] One is reminded of the old Hebrew proverb: a shoemaker's children always go barefoot. The shoemaker is often the village skeptic or atheist. Hans Sachs was a celebrated man of independence; so also was the Englishman Simon Eyre.[21] Finally, would it not be a matter of ironical interest to assign to the occupation of shoemaker one who must wander perpetually and so wear out an infinite number of shoes—more, in fact, than the victim could possibly make, considering his ambulatory predicament? Such a subtly imaginative twist seems more southern European than northern, although the refined ways by which one human being can make himself objectionable to another know no special geographical boundaries. This is about as far as one can go with speculation. But there is certainly nothing in the history of shoemaking which would make the introduction of this detail more appropriate in the sixteenth century than at any other time.

The new name, Ahasuerus, would be chosen in the Germany of about 1600 for a likely enough reason. The Jewish festival of Purim celebrates each spring the defeat of the machinations of Haman in his desire to massacre the Jews, a defeat in which Ahasuerus (the Biblical form of the name of the Persian Emperor Xerxes) was chiefly instrumental. The story, of course, takes up the Book of Esther. The celebration of this festival was the occasion for demonstrations of feeling against all who were not Jews. One of the features of the celebration was the reading aloud of the Book of Esther, accompanied by loud cries and curses against the gentiles. There was also a dramatic presentation, an Ahasuerus play, equally vociferous and equally inciting to racial and religious hatred.[22] *Ahasuerus*, in consequence, became, during the sixteenth century, a cant-name for a Jew, although Xerxes had not been Jewish. It would naturally suggest itself to the author of the *Kurtze Beschreibung* as a suitable name for the protagonist in his story. Other hypotheses all seem to me stretched too thin, and inadmissible on general principles: (1) that it is a garbling of *Cartaphilus*; (2) that it was chosen as appropriate to a great sinner because the historical Xerxes had sworn to destroy Western civilization in the persons of the Greeks; (3) that it is derived from the name of the Norse god Vidar with the great shoes; or (4) that it is a corruption of *Ariya Buddha deva*, or the great God Buddha.[23]

Why was a historical personage, Paulus von Eitzen, chosen to have hung on him this fantastic tale? For one thing, according to biographical records, he had in his possession a picture of the Crucifixion in which Malchus, or a soldier of Pilate, was portrayed.[24] This would bring him into the periphery of the Legend if one cared to place him there. The connection with Melanchthon has been definitely established, and this would bring him into contact with the Danzig group described above. It should be observed that the *Kurtze Beschreibung* came out after his death, when he could not very well repudiate the tale. If the author of the pamphlet was one of the Danzig group, he could have told Von Eitzen the tale as he got it from the Marquis d'Oria. Or Paulus von Eitzen could have known already about Cartaphilus. The discussion of such suppositions is not fruitful. No matter who the author might have been, or from where—from Danzig or Schleswig, as some would have it—he could have used the name of Von Eitzen as a sell-ing point, because the real Von Eitzen was a prominent figure in the Lutheran Church, and his words, however unauthentic they may have been, would as-suredly carry weight.

As a final note, the fact is that the author of the *Kurtze Beschreibung* mentions the distrust Ahasuerus felt for Christ, which caused him to turn violently against the Saviour. Later on, in more romantic treatments of the Legend, this point is offered as a justification for the Jew's action, but in 1602 it would be interpreted as an admission of guilt. Ahasuerus would be considered a sinner, however re-pentant he might be. The animus directed against him in the *Kurtze Beschreibung* is not remarkable, although his race and his offense have been made definite. Malice comes to the surface in unmistakable fashion only after the successors to the author of the *Kurtze Beschreibung* have had their say.

The Forming of the Ahasuerus-book

The animus starts in the Dudulaeus pamphlets.[25] There are nine versions of these, beginning with three which are dated 1602, although they were almost certainly printed a year later. These make no important changes in the narrative of the *Kurtze Beschreibung*, but the date of the alleged visit of Ahasuerus to Hamburg, 1542, tends to slip farther along in the sixteenth century—an inevitable variation. They include some verses in Latin and German giving the "argument" of the tale.[26] They have also a kind of postscript or appendix which is a most significant increment, if rather obscure. This is an *Erinnerung* or "Reminder to the Chris-tian Reader" about this Jew. The racial and religious drawbridge has now been pulled up about halfway. The "Reminder" observes that Christ's mercy has ac-tually been demonstrated even in the case of Ahasuerus, who had been an arch-persecutor of Christ "in the full fury of a lion, but who turned from a Saul into a Paul, from a haughty scornful man to a humble one, from an extreme enemy to a loyal acknowledger of the Saviour. . . ." The old point, that the immortality of the Wandering Jew is testimony to God's word, is covered over in rather con-fused language, with acid comments upon those few stiff-necked ones who per-sist in disbelief. At the same time, the author of the "Reminder" is vaguely trou-bled by the discrepancy between the tedious eternal punishment inflicted and the avowed mercy of God; he strives to reconcile the discrepancy by citing the stric-tures of Jesus on the Pharisees and Sadducees. The forgiveness invoked by Christ for the sake of his fellow sufferers on Calvary applied, it is said, only to the repentant, not to those for whom the dire portents attending the Crucifixion —the breaking of rocks in an earthquake, the rending of the veil of the Temple, and other things—were meant as a horrendous lesson. It is left to the reader to study the screed and get from it whatever grains of salvation there are to gather. It is easy to see how this insertion swells the pamphlet from the four pages of the *Kurtze Beschreibung* to twelve.

Some of the Dudulaeus pamphlets bear no date; some appeared as late as 1613, 1614, and 1617. Three of these pamphlets, issued between 1614 and 1619, are en-titled *Warhafftige Contrafactur . . . von einem Juden, etc.;* these were ostensibly printed at Revel, Estonia. They differ in no important respect from either the *Kurtze Beschreibung* or the Dudulaeus pamphlets, except that there has been inserted, just before the account of how the ambassadors saw Ahasuerus in Spain, a report that he appeared to a burgher of Augsburg and a pastor in Wittenberg, as well as to sundry folk in Wolfenbüttel. The statement is made, furthermore, that he has been among the Belgians and other people. The snowball of Ahasuerian travels has begun to roll. The author is sure of his facts because this Ahasuerus bore a startling likeness to the copperplate vignette of the original pamphlet. Hence the title of these pamphlets, which are now extremely rare.[27]

Two important descendants of the *Kurtze Beschreibung* remain to be considered. These are the *Gründliche und Warhafftige Relation von einem Juden, etc.* and the *Unruhiger Wall-Bruder aus dem Jüdenthumb* ("Restless Pilgrim from Jewry").

The *Relation* also bears the name of Chrysostom Dudulaeus, but since it appears with dates of 1634, 1644, 1645, and perhaps later, it should be classed as a separate pamphlet. One copy unashamedly claims the date 1584—this may be a misprint for 1684 or simply a matter of mendacity.[28] The *Relation,* indeed, adds nothing new to the narrative, and retains the postscript of the Dudulaeus pamphlets, but then inserts a notice concerning the Twelve Tribes of Israel. It offers further a suggestion, in the form of a learned opinion, to the effect that the story it tells in no way represents a tenet of Christianity and has no scriptural authority. Most of the copies are sixteen pages in length; but the most elaborate, the "1584" copy, runs to twenty pages because, after the notice of the Twelve Tribes, it adds a treatise on the blood-judgment undergone by Christ and a woodcut showing Ahasuerus, with his child, repulsing the Saviour from his door.

As for the *Wall-Bruder,* it takes its narrative from the *Relation,* repeating the additional material found there, but including more increments of its own in the form of a discourse on longevity; various epistles, such as that of Lentulus to the Roman Senate or of Pontius Pilate to Tiberius; and an account of the punishments which the various tribes of Israel have undergone because of the Crucifixion of Christ. The pamphlet, which now bulks large with thirty-two pages, what with all this extraneous material, first appeared without name of place or publisher in 1660; the last copy was issued as late as 1694. Obviously we have come a long way from the *Kurtze Beschreibung* of 1602. The farther we come, the more accrues to the original narrative; one of the versions of the Dudulaeus pamphlets, dated 1793, is swollen up to forty-six pages.

To summarize, these four pamphlets—the *Kurtze Beschreibung,* the Dudulaeus, the *Relation,* and the *Wall-Bruder*—taken together, constitute what I shall refer to hereafter as the German *Volksbuch* on the Wandering Jew. On the analogy of the Faust-book, let us designate it as the Ahasuerus-book. (Perhaps the *Warhafftige Contrafactur* might be given a certain independence of contribution, but it actually is too close to the Dudulaeus pamphlets to warrant the distinction.) But where the Faust-book can be referred to one year—1587—the Ahasuerus-book covers a whole century and more. Each one of these four pamphlets has its special points of value: the *Kurtze Beschreibung* is the archetype; the Dudulaeus pamphlets add the "Reminder to the Christian Reader"; the *Relation* inserts material concerning the Jews; and the *Wall-Bruder* illustrates the later tendency of the narrative to become imbedded in information or moralizing reflections of an extraneous nature. Still, it is obvious that the *Kurtze Beschreibung* is historically the most important in its impact and in the general simplicity of its outlines.

To put the matter in another way, we may say that the German references to the Wandering Jew during the seventeenth century are many, but, after the *Kurtze Beschreibung* gets the story started, little is added to the tale until the end of the century, except for a gradual heightening of anti-Jewish tension. The significant years are those from 1602 to 1620. It is then that we begin to get written notices of the visits of Ahasuerus to France, England, and the Scandinavian and Slavic countries, where the seeds of the Legend, once planted, proceeded to grow with varying degrees of hardiness.

Later we shall see how the educated writers of the seventeenth century were inclined to view the Legend. Here it need only be said that they were not much amused by it and were inclined to approach Ahasuerus with skepticism, although hardly with the contemptuous disbelief of a modern investigator. Thus Libavius, a physician of Rothenburg, Germany, observed in 1604 that the surmise the Renaissance scholar Paracelsus (1493-1541) had never died but was merely sleeping under magical influence was the kind of story that might lend credibility to the Legend of the Wandering Jew—Ahasuerus or Buttadeus or whoever he might be—even if the scriptures themselves gave no express authority for the story.[29] In other words, one explains the presence of one legend by the presence of another. Similarly, the old tale of the Seven Sleepers of Ephesus was used to account for the legend of a man of preternatural age.[30]

Yet there was always someone to add something which was, as Pooh-Bah in *The Mikado* puts it, "merely corroborative detail, intended to give artistic verisimilitude to a bald and unconvincing narrative." J. Nicolaus Heldvader, in his *Sylva Chronologica circuli Baltici* (Hamburg, 1624), reports that in 1604 a legend had public circulation about "a Jew in Jerusalem who in the time of Jesus Christ is said to have been a shoemaker, and therefore on Good Friday struck the Saviour with a shoe last as he was on his way to his martyrdom. The Jew can never die but must wander about the world until the Last Judgment."[31] This is the tale told in Villalón's *Crotalon*, some seventy years earlier; there the tone of the narrative was scoffing; here the tale is merely recorded.

The Development of the French Volksbuch

The Legend was now receiving fitting notice in France. A parliamentary advocate in Paris, Raoul Boutrays (Boterius), in his *De Rebus in Gallia et pene toto orbe gestis, commentarii* (Paris, 1610), observes with the diffident condescension of a "doctor":

I fear that it will be imputed to me that I am reporting stale fairy tales if I should embark upon the story of a Jew contemporary with Christ, which is spread all over Europe, and is even told in the chronicle written in our own vernacular, as I have as witnesses the compilers of our old annals. . . . They tell how this man, who wanders all over the whole earth and never has any fixed abode, belongs to those dregs of humanity who wished to have Barabbas freed instead of Christ; beyond which this Jew committed another crime, by driving away Christ from his lodgings when he, on his way to Golgotha, wished to rest for a moment before the door of this commoner. (He was said to be a laborer.) Whereupon the punishment of eternal wandering came upon him. This same person has been seen in more than one century in Spain, Italy, Germany, and even in this particular year [1604] he was recognized as the one who was seen in Hamburg in 1564. The people can tell even more about him; I have not been willing to speak of more than half the circumstances.[32]

It is not clear who "the compilers of our old annals" may be (l.4). It seems most likely that Boutrays has as a source for this statement the *Chronica Majora* of Matthew Paris. The appearance of the Jew in Hamburg in 1564 is further vouched for by the French Jesuit, Julius Caesar Boulenger, who in his *Historiarum sui temporis,* written early in the seventeenth century, marvels at the ability of the Jew to subsist for a thousand years without food and drink.[33]

There may have been French popular ballads or chapbooks current in the first decade of the seventeenth century which were derived from some part or parts of the Ahasuerus-book, presumably the *Kurtze Beschreibung,* but this must remain conjecture. There certainly was an early French translation of the *Kurtze Beschreibung,* however. This appeared first in P. V. P. Cayet's *Chronologie Septenaire* (Paris, 1605) and was reprinted as a separate text at Bordeaux in 1603.[34] A 1609 issue of the Bordeaux pamphlet is now more commonly seen. The separate work was entitled *Discours véritable d'un juif errant.* Both it and the Cayet version are close translations of the *Kurtze Beschreibung* and so need no comment. Pierre de l'Estoile, acid-tongued and scornful, may have condescended to report the rumored birth of Antichrist in 1609, but as to the *Discours véritable,* he dismisses it as *sot et fabuleux.*[35] Yet this French translation has one point of distinction: it is the first printed reference to the Jew as "wandering," for the Germans have customarily spoken of him to this day as "the eternal Jew" (*der ewige Jude*). And another bit of distinction: It contains some verses of a ballad on the subject, which tell how two noblemen met the Wandering Jew in Champagne. This ballad emerges in fuller form and with variants a few years later. The meeting with the noblemen, in fact, is a minor commonplace in the French folk treatment.

Interviews with people of lesser social rank seem to have been reported. Thus the jurist Louvet, in his history of the city of Beauvais (1615):

Several people, including the author, saw him [the Jew] in Beauvais in October, 1604. It was on a Sunday during Mass, and he was standing within a circle of small children in the neighborhood of the cathedral. To them he was giving a talk and speaking about the Passion of Christ. People said, indeed, that it was the Wandering Jew; in spite of that, however, they had little to do with him because he was plainly dressed, and they considered him a retailer of tall tales. For it seemed unlikely that he should have lived in the world since the time of Christ. The author was very curious and anxious to talk with him, and would have been glad to question him all about it, but the contempt with which people spoke of the Jew caused the author to miss his opportunity, which he has very much regretted. Nevertheless, he talked with several men and women of Beauvais about the Jew, but these gave him the reputation of being untrustworthy.[63]

Later the Jew was seen near Fontainebleau, one of the favorite haunts of the Wild Huntsman; again at Châlons-sur-Marne. The soldiers of the Prince of Condé met him once near Paris. All this according to the tale told in the pamphlet, *Les rencontres faist ces jours passez du Juif-Errant* (1615). The end product of these various references—plus the undoubted influence of the Ahasuerus-book, plus the inevitable individual increments going along with them, traceable to folk tales and popular imagination—is the *Histoire admirable du juif errant*, originally from about 1650, a pamphlet which went through many and many a printing until well into the nineteenth century and which may appropriately be called the French *Volksbuch* of the Wandering Jew.[37]

The original place of publication of this influential chapbook is uncertain, for it appeared at one time or another in Bruges, Limoges, Epinal, Namur, and Paris. That part of the work which treats the Legend is obviously based on the *Kurtze Beschreibung,* with some material from both the Dudulaeus pamphlets and the *Relation.* On the whole, however, the author of the French pamphlet was more ambitious than any of his sources and had besides a wide-ranging imagination. The captions at the head of each of its five sections indicate its general scope: (1) "How the Wandering Jew Was Recognized in the Neighborhood of Hamburg"; (2) "The Birth of the Wandering Jew"; (3) "Of the Three Kings and of the Flight to Egypt"; (4) "Jesus Preaching in the Temple; How He Worked with Joseph on the Trees Which Grew from the Three Seeds . . . and Which Had Been Placed near the Temple; of the Carving of These Trees in the Form of Blocks Which Were To Serve as Foundations for the Temple; of the Death of St. John the Baptist"; and (5) "Of the Sufferings of Jesus, the Life of Judas, and the Punishment of the Wandering Jew."

Despite the sprawling nature of its narrative, the *Histoire admirable* has a beginning and an end worthy of study. It is at once apparent that it is a throwback to the homilies of the Middle Ages, to medieval tales of the life of Christ, and to the famous medieval extrascriptural Legend of the Holy Cross. Much of its material, in short, is irrelevant in respect to the Legend of the Wandering Jew. It was evidently written by one so removed in time from the *Kurtze Beschreibung* or so carelessly and ignorantly informed about the substance of that pamphlet that he was often badly confused. Thus he makes two individuals out of Paulus von Eitzen, who is now the Bishop of Schleswig and now a certain Franz Eyssen. The meeting of Von Eitzen and Ahasuerus took place, he says, as late as 1633, a generation after Von Eitzen's death. He gets Protestant Wittenberg mixed up with Catholic Württemberg in southern Germany—although one may suppose that to the Wandering Jew such confusion would mean nothing at all.

The information which Ahasuerus gives the Bishop is new:

My name is Ahasuerus and I was born of the tribe of Naphtali in the year 3992 after the creation of the world. My father was a carpenter, my mother a seamstress, who worked on the clothes of the Levites. They taught me to read and write; later they put in my hands the laws of the prophets. Moreover, my father possessed a very old book, inherited from his forefathers, in which were marvelous stories, of which I will share with you some which bear upon my further tale.

This leads us to the life and career of Jesus, which has only incidental bearing upon the Legend. Of particular interest, however, is the fact that the *Histoire admirable* is the first work to bring together the legends of the Wandering Jew and of Judas, whose paths cross more than once in later literary treatment. An attempt has been made also to present Ahasuerus as one of good and honest background; his parents have honorable trades; they have tried to educate him, and they come from the more attractive part of Palestine, the lands of the tribe of Naphtali.

Consider next the circumstances of the curse:

When the time drew near that Christ was to be crucified, the whole city was in turmoil; people ran about hither and thither in the streets. Inasmuch as the great paschal feast was approaching, there was no time to lose. Workmen in the city had been ordered to make a cross, the sentence having been imposed that Christ should be crucified. They took the three . . . trees which had grown from the seeds placed under Adam's tongue after his death. When the cross was finished, they placed it on the shoulders of Jesus for him to carry to the Mount of Calvary, which was the place where malefactors were put to death. As for me, I was at my door, and saw the people running, saying that Jesus was going to be crucified. I took my child in my arms to let him see; I saw Jesus coming along, laden with a heavy, burdensome cross; He was staggering and wished to rest a bit in front of my door. But I took this as a great insult and said to Jesus Christ these most bitter words: "Go, go, get away from my door; I don't want a criminal to rest there." Jesus immediately looked at me sadly, and said: "I shall go and I shall rest; but you will walk and will not rest; you will walk as long as the world is the world, and that will be the final Day of Doom. Then you will see me seated at the right hand of my Father to judge the Twelve Tribes of Israel who have crucified me." Forthwith I set down my child and followed Jesus. The first person whom I saw was St. Veronica, who had just wiped the face of Jesus with a cloth on which his face remained imprinted. A little farther along I saw Mary and other women who were weeping, and I saw a laborer passing with a hammer and nails. He took one of the nails and thrust it into Mary's face, saying: "Behold, woman, it is with these nails that your son was nailed."

Some idea of the subsequent wandering of Ahasuerus will be gathered from these details of his endless march. Although there were suggestions of this program in the German Ahasuerus-book, we have not yet seen so full an itinerary:

After having traversed many countries, I came to Europe, and I came to Lithuania, where I saw a young man hang himself, the reason being that he had committed a murder, and for that he was supposed to hang himself—it was the common custom of the country. Thence I came to Italy, and thence to Rome, where I saw many Christians suffering martyrdom for the faith. . . . After having seen all that, I came to Hungary; they were burning dead bodies; at the same spot where a body was burned, they brought each day food and drink to give refreshment to the soul of the deceased. Thence I crossed a river which is called the Rhine, and I saw a little town which is called Cologne; there I saw the statue of a great man which was of solid silver; he had been one of their principal divines. Pilgrims came hither from all countries, and by the thousands. They call the statue Tentis. Thence I crossed the Meuse, and I saw a big town that is called Rongres; it is three leagues around it, and in it there were four kings who governed each a part of the town; and these kings paid tribute to the Emperor. Thence I went to Bavay, which is also a very big town, in which there is one of the most beautiful palaces in

Europe; that is the place where the Emperor Tiberius had a dwelling. This town is a dozen leagues in circumference and is full of various people. There was a great trafficking in the market place of all sorts of things. I passed through France and came to Marseille; there I embarked on a ship and came to Asia; and following my road I came again to Judaea, and I found no more either parents or friends, for it had been already a hundred years that I had been traveling.[38]

The victim does not seem to be suffering much here; rather he is a world traveler, offering as it were a guidebook to Europe, at least in germ. This portion of the *Histoire admirable,* in fact, belongs to the literary tradition of marvelous journeys. It is a short step from this to the typical neoclassical concept of the Wandering Jew as primarily an observer and commentator. For this general concept the French are chiefly responsible.

That France responded quickly to the Legend in the form given it in the *Histoire admirable* is evident from the many later editions of the pamphlet, in which details are added from time to time, keeping up with the course of history, so to speak; and the date of the meeting of Ahasuerus and Von Eitzen (Eyssen, Eisen, etc.) comes farther and farther down into the present. The last edition that I have seen brings into the audience some veterans of the Napoleonic Wars. Translations into Flemish and Dutch were many. Yet these later versions, in spite of incidental and sometimes gratuitous embellishments, do not depart from the established lines of the story as told in the first edition of about 1650.

We should therefore pause for a moment over some of the contributions which can legitimately be credited to the *Histoire admirable.* We learn that Ahasuerus, of the tribe of Naphtali, was the son of a carpenter and a seamstress. In some of the later versions he was himself a carpenter instead of a shoemaker. Sometimes he is reputed to have been a doorkeeper for Pontius Pilate. He saw the infant Jesus in His mother's arms. He saw a nail held up for the Virgin Mary to see. His itinerary is explicit, extensive, and completely factual in the telling. In some of the later versions he includes America in his travels, but with no details of his sojourn there; he simply remarks, "Je m'en allai en Amérique," and the very next sentence takes us with bewildering speed to Crete. But all this gadding about has nothing to do with repentance or contrition or the preaching of God's word; rather we have ostentatious sight-seeing with a penchant for the sensational. The Reformation has yielded to the *grand siècle.* Some of the concluding portions of the work are reminiscent of the fabulous stuff in the fourteenth-century *Travels of Sir John Mandeville,* which may possibly have suggested some details to the author. His chief indebtedness, however, is to scriptural and extrascriptural narrative, his own power to conjure up a yarn, and of course the German Ahasuerus-book.

Seventeenth-century France made another contribution to the Legend in the form of a lyric lament, or *complainte,* of the Wandering Jew. Just when the first of these *complaintes* appeared is doubtful, but the type must go back at least to the opening decade of the century, for the *Discours véritable* of 1609, which Pierre de l'Estoile found so vapid, had one of them subjoined to it. The genesis of this sort of lyrical effusion is the inspiration of some popular singer, the utterance even of some more sophisticated bard, who saw in the pedestrian telling of the tale in the *Kurtze Beschreibung* or its adaptations and translations (of which the *Discours véritable* was one) a need for songful expression. These *complaintes* continue to come out intermittently as late as the early nineteenth century, when they merge in imperceptible fashion with more "literary" efforts; nevertheless, they may properly be considered early art forms of the Legend. They will therefore be considered later.

There is also a quickening of interest in the Legend in the folklore of seventeenth-century France. It is almost as if the French were making amends for time lost during the growth of the Legend in the later Middle Ages. The Bretons in particular—the only Celtic people to pay any special attention to the Legend—have left two anonymous songs of indeterminate age, neither of which probably came into existence before 1650.

The first of these is a type of ballad, a Breton *guerz*.[39] Here the career of the Wandering Jew, now once more called Buttadeus (Boudedeo)—although on one occasion Absarius (Ahasuerus)—is outlined in some detail, and the piece is topped off by a passage lamenting the misery which has come to the Jew for his heartlessness and beseeching all Christians to pray for him. He was born of the tribe of Naphtali, in the city of Jerusalem at the time of the Slaughter of the Innocents. He married a girl from the tribe of Benjamin. He refused to be baptized by St. John the Baptist and was not impressed even when he saw Christ working his miracles. After the curse was pronounced, he forthwith began his travels, most of which follow the same course as itemized in the *Histoire admirable*, which the author of the *guerz* must have known. He has always with him in his pocket five sous; his shoes and clothes never wear out. He has made four complete circuits of the world and is now about to start on his fifth. Two new items: In Turkey he came upon the city of Vesopa, where the army consists entirely of dogs and women; and in Estopet, also in Turkey, he saw snakes forty feet long.

The second of these Breton pieces may be from as late as 1700. It has a peculiar significance in that it represents the meeting of two separate legends, that of the Wandering Jew and that of the French folk character Bonhomme Misère. Concerning the latter it must be explained that he had once given lodging to Peter and Paul and received from Paul in recompense the gift of having a wish fulfilled. Accordingly he made the wish that no one who climbed his precious pear tree after the fruit, unless invited to do so, could come down until Bonhomme Misère was willing. On one occasion Death himself, about to claim the old man, acceded to his prospective victim's last wish for a pear, got up into the tree, and was allowed to come down only on condition that he never again would try to claim Bonhomme Misère until the end of the world. That is how the old man achieved immortality.

The piece is in reality a disputation or controversy between the Wandering Jew and Bonhomme Misère as to which is the elder. The opening speeches will suffice:

Listen, comrades, to the talk which two old men once had with each other. Two older men do not exist in this world; they are to live until the Last Judgment. One is called Isaac, the hastening wanderer; the other Misère, the dour companion, and wherever he goes over land and sea, woe follows behind him. If he were dead, truly man would be free of all his troubles.

At Orléans they met and greeted each other as brotherly friends. And Misère said first to Isaac: "Say, Wandering Jew, whither goest thou? And say, what dost thou in this world? I see that thou art sad at heart!"

THE WANDERING JEW: I wander by day and I wander by night. So God wills it, to whom I brought pain. I wander by night and I wander by day and I suffer more than a man can endure. O I live—and I cannot die! I must live until the Last Judgment! I thought myself the oldest on earth; now I see that thou bearest still older tribulation.

OLD MISÈRE: Thou mere child, who wast born but yesterday! I have lived now already many thousand years! When Adam broke God's commands, I came into this world under His roof. . .[40]

The name Isaac given the Wandering Jew here is part of the name that he often bears in France and Flanders—Isaac Laquedem (Lakedem). Some rather wild explanations of this name have been offered; the most sensible one is that it is bad Hebrew for "the one who goes to the east," a regular expression for "traveler."[41]

The learned men and court-dwellers in France, meanwhile, continued to condescend to the Legend. Just as the pamphleteers began to suggest that Ahasuerus was a world traveler primarily, so there are early signs that he may someday play comic or satirical roles. For the moment we need trouble ourselves only with the preliminary symptoms. We have already heard the comments of Raoul Boutrays and Pierre de l'Estoile. There survives a curious little ballet, the *Mariage de Pierre de Provence et de la belle Maguelone*, which was performed at Tours in 1638. Here the Wandering Jew is in the disreputable and humorous company of a fool, a physician, a buffoon, and a muleteer, and holds his own against all four. Further allusions to Ahasuerus in France—such as the amusing stanza in Claude d'Esternod's *L'Espadon satyrique* (Cologne, 1680), which has him leering pawkily among nuns—are so self-conscious in their literary pretensions that they fall into the category of the art form rather than the *Volksbuch* tradition.[42]

Minor Versions in French and Flemish

In the interim Ahasuerus has been hopscotching his way all over Germany. At times, indeed, he seems to be on a grand tour of the Continent. Several towns see him within the period of a year or two—even, perhaps, in the same year. At other times nothing is heard about him for a decade or more. In 1604, as we have seen, he was in France. The year before he was in Lübeck, Germany, according to Heinrich Bangert's *Commentatio de ortu vita et excessu coleri juris consulti Lubecensis* (1644).[43] The theologian and historian Johann Cluverius, in his *Historiarum totius mundi epitome* (1637), says he visited Saxony in 1603-4.[44] Later, in Naumburg, where he was seen in 1630, he comported himself in the usual contrite manner, according to J. S. Mitternacht's *Dissertationes de Johannis XXI* (Naumburg, 1665).[45] In Leipzig, if we are to believe the *Annales Lipsienses*, he made a typical appearance in 1642.[46] Since all of these visits are characterized by the same set of circumstances as those related in the *Kurtze Beschreibung*, their origins are not far to seek. Once begun, his visits all over the Continent and elsewhere are an integral part of European folklore.

At the same time the revivified Legend was spreading through the Low Countries. Willem Baudaert of Zutphen, in his *Memoryen*, a chronicle of remarkable events taking place in Holland between 1603 and 1624, picks up the Dudulaeus versions and notes that the Jew had been the subject of rumors both before and after 1616, but he assigns the meeting of Von Eitzen and Ahasuerus to 1598, and expresses gross disbelief in the tale.[47] And, whereas Philippe Mouskes had told of Cartaphilus nearly four hundred years before, Canon Cousin of Tournai says that the Jew appeared in a picture dating from 1616. He also considers him to be a purely fictitious personage; especially does he doubt the statement that he was still alive in 1613.[48]

Granted that the folk tradition is there. Still, the chief medium for the spread of the Legend in this area would seem to be the Flemish translations and adaptations of the *Kurtze Beschreibung* and Dudulaeus pamphlets. The standard example is the *Afbeeldinghe ende corte beschrijvinghe van den dolenden Jode* (the *Afbeeldinghe*), printed at Antwerp in 1620; its author is the local licenser of publications, or censor, L. Beyerlinck. But a rare earlier version, *Corte en de waerachtighe beschrijvinge van eenen Jode*, printed at Ghent and bearing the spurious date of 1599—three years before the original German pamphlet from which it was derived—must take precedence, if only in time.[49] Presumably it was printed, however, about 1610 or 1612; in other words, even this pitiful precedence must be denied. Neither translation is very good. It is apparent that both had only an indirect obligation to their German source, and that they owe more to the French version of Cayet or the *Discours véritable* than to the German Ahasuerus-book. That is to say, the Flemish and Dutch versions come from Germany only through France. Eighteen or twenty later versions of this Flemish pamphlet, including some directly obligated to the *Histoire admirable*, appear in Belgium and the Netherlands until about 1875. Some of the copies contained ballad matter analogous to the French *complaintes*, and one of these songs, the so-called Brabantine ballad (pp. 165-66 below) became very well known. The name, Isaac Laquedem, appears commonly. I have already attempted to explain Laquedem (p. 59), and Isaac is another generic name for a Jew. In Flanders, the protagonist has one hitherto unmentioned gift: he can make old women young.

Once Ahasuerus, or Isaac Laquedem, or whoever he may have been, met two citizens of Brussels in a forest reputed to be the haunt of the Wild Huntsman, just as in France he appeared in the forest of Fontainebleau, another place frequented by *le chasseur maudit*. Once he regaled a citizen of Dunkirk with an account of his life, in the manner of the Ancient Mariner, but this is in a ballad which belongs to the very late eighteenth or early nineteenth century. For that matter, he often met people and told his tale. His conduct on these stated occasions, however, continued to be the conventional conduct already described in the Ahasuerus-book, and the incidents are remarkable only for their setting and for the fact that they caught suffcient hold of the popular fancy for the scene to be perpetuated in several woodcuts entitled "Les bourgeois de la ville parlant au juif-errant."[50]

The English Version of the Ahasuerus-book

It was also from the Ahasuerus-book, and via the French translations of Cayet and the *Discours véritable*, that the Wandering Jew returned to England nearly four centuries after Roger of Wendover and Matthew Paris, and three centuries after the *Northern Passion* and Chaucer. Licenses were issued in London in 1612 to print a prose piece and a ballad on the subject of the Wandering Jew.[51] No trace of the prose piece of 1612 has been found, as such; it may never have been printed. There is a ballad, however, entered in the Stationers' register for August 21, 1612, and assigned to Edward Marchant, *A Ballad Called "Wonderful Strange News out of Germanye of a Jewe that Hath Lyued Wandering ever Since Our Saviour Christ."* So far as is known, there is no copy of this extant either, but what may possibly be the same ballad was later assigned to John Marriott and John Grisman (Grismond) under the date of October 6, 1620. This was reprinted in 1635 under the auspices of Edward Wright. It is the ballad to be found in the noted seventeenth-century ballad collections, *The Roxburghe Ballads* and *The Bagford Ballads.*[52] Almost unchanged it turns up in a black-letter ballad of about 1690 found in the Pepys Collection. With a few minor changes it was printed in Bishop Percy's famous *Reliques of Ancient English Poetry* (1765).[53] The early edition of F. J. Child's *English and Scottish Popular Ballads* (1861) gives the Percy version, but the editor omitted it from his later definitive edition (1883-1898). This ballad, *The Wandering Jew: Or the Shooemaker of Jerusalem,* tells its story in all essentials and proceeds to narrate in rather sententious language how the Jew passed from land to land, unable to find either rest or death, never smiling but rather lamenting in Malchean fashion. He will accept alms only a groat at a time.

THE WANDERING JEW
Or
The Shooemaker of Jerusalem. Who lived when our Lord and
Saviour JESUS CHRIST was Crucified, and by him [was] appointed to
Live till his Coming again.

When as in fair *Jerusalem* our Saviour Christ did live,
And for the Sins of all the World his own dear Life did give;
The wicked Jews, with scoffs and scorns, did daily him molest,
That never, till he left this life, our Saviour could have rest.
    Repent therefore, O England! *Repent while you have space;*
    And do not (like the wicked Jews) despise God's proffered Grace.

When they had crown'd his head with thorns, and scourg'd him with disgrace;
In scornful sort they led him forth unto his dying place;
Where thousand thousands in the street did him all pass along;
Yet not one gentle heart was there that pity'd this his Wrong.
    Repent, etc.

Both old and young reviled him, as thro' the streets he went;
And nothing found but churlish taunts, by every one's consent.
His own dear Cross he bore him self (a burden far too great!)
Which made him in the street to faint, with blood and water-sweat.

Being weary, thus, he sought for rest, to ease his burthen'd Soul
Upon a stone; the which a Wretch did churlishly controul.
And said, *"Away, thou King of Jews, thou shalt not rest thee here;*
Pass on; thy Execution-place, thou seest, now draweth near."

And thereupon he thrust him thence, at which our Saviour said,
"I sure will rest, but thou shalt Walk, and have no journey stayed."
With that this cursed Shoemaker, for offering Christ this wrong,
Left wife and children, house and all, and went from thence along.

Where after he had seen the Blood of Jesus Christ thus shed,
And to the Cross his Body nail'd, away with speed he fled,
Without returning back again unto his dwelling-place;
And wandereth up and down the world, a Runagate most base.

No resting could he find at all, no ease, or heart's content;
No house, nor home, nor dwelling-place, but wandering forth he went.
From town to town, in foreign lands, with grieved Conscience still,
Repenting for the hanious Guilt of his fore-passed Ill.

Thus, after some few Ages past, in wandering up and down,
He once again desired to see *Jerusalem's* fair town.
But finding it all quite destroy'd, he wander'd thence with woe;
Our Saviour's words which he had spoke to verify and show:

"I'll rest," said he, *"but thou shalt walk!"* so doth this Wandering Jew
From place to place, but cannot stay for seeing countries new,
Declaring still the Power of Him, where'er he comes or goes;
And of all things done in the East, since Christ his death, he shows.

The World he still doth compass round, and see those nations strange,
That, hearing of the Name of Christ, their Idol Gods do change.
To whom he hath told wondrous things, of times fore-past and gone;
And to the Princes of the World declar'd his cause of moan.

Desiring still to be dissolv'd, and yield his mortal breath;
But as the Lord had thus decreed, he shall not yet see Death.
For neither looks he Old [n]or Young, but as he did those times
When Christ did suffer on the Cross, for mortal sinners' crimes.

He passed many foreign lands, *Arabia, Egypt, Africa,*
Grecia, Syria, and Great *Thrace,* and through all *Hungaria,*
Where *Paul* and *Peter* preached Christ, those blest Apostles dear,
Where he hath told our Saviour's words, in countries far and near.

And lately in *Bohemia,* with many a German Town;
And now in *Flanders,* as 'tis thought, he wandereth up and down.
Where learned Men with him confer, of those his lingering days,
And wonder much to hear him tell his journeys and his ways.

If people give this Jew an alms, the most that he will take
Is not above a groat a time; which he for *Jesus'* sake
Doth kindly give unto the poor, and therefore makes no spare,
Affirming still that Jesus Christ of him hath daily care.

He was not seen to laugh or smile, but weep and make great moan,
Lamenting still his miseries, and days fore spent and gone.
If he hears any one Blaspheme, or take God's name in vain;
He tells them that they crucify Our Saviour Christ again.

"If thou had'st seen grim Death," said he, *"as these mine eyes have done,*
Ten thousand thousand times, would ye his Torments think upon;
And suffer for His sake all pains, all torments, and all woes."
These are his words, and this his Life, where'er he comes and goes.[54]

The editors of *The Roxburghe Ballads*, in their introduction to this ballad, speak of the possibility that the Elizabethan song writer and general pamphleteer, Thomas Deloney (?1543-?1600), was its author, but their only evidence for this is the dubious point that the refrain in the ballad (*"Repent therefore*, O England!") echoes that of a song accepted as Deloney's. There were, as it happened, many exhortations to England to repent at this time, when perils from France and Spain and Antichrist, as well as from factions within, were constantly threatening. Besides, Deloney seems to have died a little too soon to have been the author of this particular ballad or to have known the German Ahasuerus-book in even its earliest phases, to say nothing of French translations thereof. One may at least assume, however, to judge by its frequent reprinting, that it was a rather well-known ballad, if unfortunately rather pedestrian.[55]

Now it is virtually certain that the missing prose piece for which the license was issued in 1612 was a translation or adaptation of some part of the Ahasuerus-book, direct from the German or—as would be more likely in the England of 1612—through an intervening French version.[56] Here I must report a real find—an English prose version of the Legend dated 1620, which may or may not be a written copy of the missing pamphlet. It is to be found in a commonplace book now in the British Museum (Add. 38599) which belonged to the Shann family of Methley, Yorkshire. Most of this manuscript is in the handwriting of Richard Shann (1561-1627). Its contents comprise a survey of the local manor, the assignment of pews in the local church, chronicles of local weather, comments on the livestock of the surrounding countryside, and a record of events of general interest between 1617 and 1620. The entry for 1620 consists entirely of the following:

THE HISTORIE of a WANDRINGE JEWE
much spoken of this yeere

LOVINGE READER, if novelties and wonders please the, thou maiyst here fynde admiration in the historie of a wandringe Jewe, confirmed by many good and authentique authours which have maide mention of him in divers ages. For GUIDO BONATUS, who lived about foure hundred yeares since, in a Booke which he maide of Judiciall astrologie of the fixed stars, in the firste parte tract. 5.   5
consid. 1401, affirmes confidentlie that he had seene in the towne of Forlive, a Jewe called John Butadeus, whom others have since called AHASUERIUS, who went to CAMPOSTELLA a place dedicated to ST. JAMES. And the life of the saide Jewe was at that tyme manifested to all, even in the same manner as it shalbe now sett
downe. That is to saie, whenas JESUS CHRIST, oppressed with the heavie bur-   10
then of his Crosse, woulde have rested him selfe against his house, he churlishlie thrust him away, so as our Saviour looking mildlie upon him, saide, I WILL REST, BUT THOU SHALT WALKE. They allso make mention of the same Jewe, in the seaventh Booke of the historie of peace, betwixt the kinge of FRANCE, and
SPAINE, printed at Paris in the yeare 1605, under the inscription of these letters,   15

P.V.P.C.: that of late yeares havinge past by STEA[X?]NSBOURGE [probably Strasbourg] he had left an acte with the maistrait thereof, declaring that he had passed there two hundreth yeares before, and for proofe thereof, he sent them to their regester booke, which being searcht and found true, filled all mens myndes with amazement. The same is verified in an Epistle, printed at LEIDEN, in the yeare, 1602, as allso in the yeare, 1608. The same man was seene about PARIS in FRANCE. He came to PRAGUE the metropolitaine Cittie of BOHEMIA in the yeare 1602, and then into HUNGARIA in the yeare 1613. And in the yeare 1614 two French gentlemen mett him neare unto CHALLONS, to whom he related manie thinges. And finallie the last yeare he came into the cuntrie of FLAUNDERS, being 1619, and in ANTWARPE, he was seene and questioned by manie judicious and learned men, whom he satisfied in everie pointe. He is a man of fewe wordes, drie and leene, and continent in all his actions. His picture was drawne from a towne called MALDUVIE, and afterwards from the cabonet of a verie curious gentleman, to whom CHRISTOPHER EYSINGER, secretarie to ADOLPH duke of HOLSTEIN had given it in the yeare 1571. And since it was brought unto PARIS, 1615, so as one called PAULE of EITSEN, a doctor of Divinitie, and BISH-OPE of SLESWING, a man of creditt and commendable for his worthie writinges, reportes that in the yeare 1542, being at HAMBROUGH at a sermon, he sawe a tall man right against the pulpitt, with long haire, bare footed, mariners breeches, and a long cloake to his ancles, which seemed to be of the age of fiftie yeares. And in this manner, he harde a sermon with great devotion, kneelinge downe and beat-inge his brest at the holie name of Jesus. In the ende, being demanded what he was, he answered that he was a JEWE, borne at JERUSALEM, a showmaker by profession, and that he had beene present at the death of CHRIST. And since that tyme had ever remained in life wandringe through the worlde, for a pennance im-posed upon him for insolence he had committed against our SAVIOUR. For he had no sooner pronounced these scandalous wordes, sayinge to ouwr Lorde, who beinge loaden with his Crosse leaned against his house, passe on, shewinge our SAVIOUR the place of his execution, but CHRIST saide unto him, I WILL REST, BUT THOU SHALT WALKE. So that at the same instante, leavinge a childe, which he had in his armes, and followinge JESUS CHRIST unto the death of the Crosse, he underwent his decree; for he coulde never returne to the place where whence he parted, to see his wyfe and children, but had alwaise beene a vagabond. Yet after some ages, he had returned to JERUSALEM, and findinge it cleane channged, and ruined, he still continued a wanderer, not knowinge (as he saide) how God woulde dispose of him, unless it weare to reserve him unto the day of judgment, to serve as a witnesse against infidels. But he desired that it would please God to call him. The Bishopp beinge much amazed sent for the rectorie of the schoole of HAMBURGE, and other men well redd in histories, who conferred with him of what had past in the Easte, from the death of JESUS CHRIST unto that daie, whereof he satisfied them in such sorte as they were all amazed. If they gave him any almes he never took above iii d. or a groat, the which he gave to the pore, saying that God had care of him. He was never seen to laugh, but still la-mented his miserie and was much grieved when he harde anie man blaspheame the name of God, cryinge out who dares, O miserable creature, how dares thou thus abuse the sacred name of God, thy lord and maister, whom if thou haddest seene suffer for the, as I have doone, thou woulds oft rather suffer a thousand tymes for his glorie, then blaspheame his holie name.

Wheresoever he went, he alwaies spake the vulgar tongue, he then spake the

Saxon, as if he had bene borne in the cuntrie. We may hereunto applie the sayinge
of our SAVIOUR, in St. marke, and St. Luke, chap. 9: There be some which shall
not tast of death, before he come into his kingdome. And in the Apocalipps it is
written, that some shall seeke death and shall not fynde it. In all probabilitie this is
one, seinge he hath lived so manie Ages. We may also observe and probalie inferr,   70
that as St. John, Enock, and Elie, shall encounter Antichrist, as we read in St.
Hypolita in the booke of Antichrist, so in like manner there shall be three, which
shall convince the Impietie of the Jewes, that is to saye, Pilate, Malchus, and this
man. By all these reasons we may inferre, that he is a true man, and that it seemes,
he hath beene condemned to this punnishment untill the daie of judgment. How-   75
soever it be we leave the beliefe unto those that have seene him as for the event,
not onelie in this, but in all other worldlie things we must referr our selves to God,
to whome be all honour, and glorie both now and for ever. AMEN.

THIS is drawne out of the printed storie worde for worde. There was allso his
picture livelie drawne, and all the cuntrie was full of Ballads, expressinge the   80
same.[57]

We may begin comment on this valuable prose account with the final short
paragraph. Mention of ballads (l.80), of which England was "full," has some
bearing on the ballads of the Wandering Jew just mentioned, even if none was
printed before this same year of 1620. The "printed storie" (l.79) from which
Shann's version is drawn "worde for worde," as I have said above, may be the
missing prose piece for which the license was issued in 1612. It might, of course,
refer to the *Kurtze Beschreibung* or Dudulaeus pamphlets directly, but it is more
likely that it does not. It could be, and probably is, a French version of the *Kurtze
Beschreibung*, unless it is the missing English work itself. In any event the *Kurtze
Beschreibung* underlies Shann's version, "The Historie of a Wandring Jewe." For
one thing, it is actually mentioned—the "Epistle, printed at LEIDEN, in the yeare,
1602" (ll.20-21). A reprint of the *Kurtze Beschreibung* in 1608 is actually not
extant, but there were many reprints of this pamphlet, as we have seen, and two
of these bear no date. The fact that Shann gives 1542 as the date of the appearance of Ahasuerus in Hamburg clinches the point, for that is the date mentioned
in the "Leyden" print and not in the reprints, where there is a considerable variation in the date specified. On the other hand, only in the Danzig print of 1602 is
there the introductory reference to Guido Bonatti.

But would Richard Shann of Methley have known enough German to read a
German pamphlet? It would not have been necessary for him to have had that
knowledge, however, in view of the fact that the *Kurtze Beschreibung* was
first translated into French in 1605 in Pierre Victor Palma Cayet's *Chronologie
Septenaire*—"the seaventh Booke of the historie of peace, betwixt the kinge of
FRANCE, and SPAINE, printed . . . under the inscription of these letters,
P.V.P.C." (ll.14-16).

It appears, in effect, that most of Shann's account is derived from Cayet, who
speaks of the Leyden pamphlet in the same words as Shann, and who makes a
direct reference to St. Hippolytus' *De Antichristo* (ll.71-72). At the same time, it
is just as clear that Shann knew some other writings on the subject. True, the
Guido Bonatti reference (ll.4-7) appears in the Danzig print of the *Kurtze Beschreibung*, but this allusion does not give chapter and verse, as does Shann

(ll.5-6). The pamphlet already mentioned, *Les rencontres faist ces jours passez du Juif-Errant* (p. 55), is the only surviving authority for the Châlons reference (l.24), but this was not printed until 1650. There must have been an earlier printing. The same pamphlet notes the Wanderer's presence in Paris (l.21). Ahasuerus was placed in Hungary (l.23) and Flanders (l.25) in the Dudulaeus pamphlet, but the French versions pick up these details at once. Beyerlinck's *Afbeeldinghe* (1620) throws light upon the references to Prague (l.23) and to Antwerp (l.26) in the year 1619. The Flemish piece may have had a French translation, although this is far from certain; things would more likely go in the opposite direction.

There was once an actual mission to Madrid in 1574-75 to raise money for the campaign of the Duke of Alba in the Low Countries; it began with Adolph of Schleswig and Holstein, and the envoys were named Jacob Berglin and Christoph Erich. Such garbling of names as Eysinger (l.30) or Ehringer, as Cayet gives it, can be expected whenever one deals with a popular pamphlet in which historical accuracy is a feeble consideration. The allusion, however, to the picture "drawne . . . from the cabonet of a verie curious gentleman" (ll.28-30) remains altogether obscure. It is reasonable to suppose that there must be here in Shann's account a reference to some increment of the Legend now unfortunately lost, for it does not appear elsewhere. All in all, certain things intervene between even Cayet and Shann—lost ballad material, lost versions of the Ahasuerus-book, perhaps a lost English prose account.

As matters now stand, however, the Shann version and the 1620 ballad still represent the earliest surviving accounts of the Wandering Jew in England after the Reformation and they close the yawning gap, as far as any serious reception of the Legend in England is concerned, between the Middle English period and the Renaissance.

The Volksbuch *in Scandinavia*

After the alleged appearances of Ahasuerus in Hamburg and Danzig, according to the Ahasuerus-book, some knowledge of him would naturally spread among the Scandinavian peoples. Denmark, at least, knew the Dudulaeus pamphlet, which was translated at Copenhagen in 1621 (the *Sandru Beskriffuelse*) and reprinted in 1631 and 1695, with increments.[58] Sweden got a similar translation in 1643 (*Jerusalems Skomager*). As far as I can determine, there were no translations in Norway, although it is evident that the Legend had become known throughout the northland.

Prior to 1830 there are only two other important Danish works on the subject. One is a rather effective literary ballad. The other is a "chronicle" of the Wandering Jew, a common eighteenth-century form of the Legend, which is also entitled *Jerusalems Skomager* (1828).[59] The Swedish translations of portions of the Ahasuerus-book continue into the nineteenth century. Between 1800 and 1830 there were at least three good examples: (1) *Trenne Trowärdiga Relationer* (1805),[60] which is a translation of the *Relation*, with some help from the *Histoire admirable*, and divisible into three parts—the story of Ahasuerus, the punishments of the Twelve Tribes of Israel, and the judgment of Pilate; (2) *Berättelser om en Jude* (Stockholm, 1823); and (3) *Trenne nya och mycket märkwärdige Berättelser* (1826).[61] There is little to be said about these chapbooks; they are crudely and carelessly printed, and if they represent the state of knowledge concerning Ahasuerus current in Sweden during the early nineteenth century, then the Legend had made little headway in that country behond the stage of folk tales, for none of these pamphlets can compare in any way with contemporary works on the subject in Germany, France, or England.

A Finnish broadside ballad, *Jerusalemin suutari* (1822), is testimony to the appearance of the Legend in Finland.[62] There is some evidence that there was an older ballad from as far back as 1695, but this is impossible to substantiate. At any rate, the substance of this ballad tallies almost exactly with that of the Swedish chapbooks of comparable date, and so there can be little doubt that the Legend spread into Finland from Scandinavia.

The Volksbuch *in Slavic Territory*

We are handicapped by a lack of material relating to the Legend of the Wandering Jew in Slavic regions. We know that he is there in folk tales, to be described in a moment, and in certain later literary treatments, but we could profitably know more than we do. I have already mentioned (p. 21) a Czech version of the story of Cartaphilus, as Roger of Wendover and Matthew Paris told it in England in the thirteenth century. This Czech version, in *Svatovítský rukopis*, is about a century younger. Near 1500 there grew up a Czech folk tale which told how the Wandering Jew helped the linen weaver Kokot to find some treasure (p. 115 below). This tale is reminiscent of an incident in the Antonio version (pp. 25-26 above), where the beneficent Giovanni Votaddio pointed out treasure to give two girls a dowry. The Legend could well have entered Bohemia from Italy via Austria as early as the sixteenth century; Bohemia is so far west that at that time it constituted a veritable Slavic island surrounded by non-Slavic people, and it would be simple for an Italian folk tale to slip in there unostentatiously.

The first written version of the Legend in Pan-Slavonia, however, is from Russia in the mid-seventeenth century. It is to be found in *Kuranty*, or *Vestovyia pisma*, a newssheet compiled from foreign sources for the use of the Czar. It is a version of the Legend, dated 1663, obviously an offshoot of the Ahasuerus-book. Some additional material has been added, concerning which the date is significant, for the end of the world and the coming of Antichrist were expected by the Muscovites in 1666.[63]

There are also a half-dozen Estonian pamphlets concerning Ahasuerus, all printed during the latter half of the nineteenth century or the beginning decade of the twentieth, all heavily indebted to one or another part of the Ahasuerus-book. There is no possible argument about the way the Legend got into Estonia via the printed word; it will be recalled that one of the Dudulaeus pamphlets bears the imprint of "Revel, 1613." Whether this is authentic is dubious, but there is no doubt about the influence of the Ahasuerus-book. The Estonian folk tales on the subject are curious variants, though, and due attention should be paid them at the proper time.

To put it as succinctly as possible, the written versions of the Legend reached Slavic lands through Germany. The relevant folk tales, on the other hand, pose a different problem.

The Volksbuch *in Hungary*

Again, in Hungary, one may conclude that the Legend was spread about by translations and adaptations of the Ahasuerus-book. None of these appears before the 1840's, after which almost a dozen have come to light. Unlike some of the other late reworkings of the Ahasuerus-book, however, some of the Hungarian chapbooks show the influence of some nineteenth-century writers whose treatment of the Legend was notable. Thus Varga Lajos' *Ahasvérus vagy a Jézus által megátkozott örökké élö zsidó* ("Ahasuerus or the Ever-Living Jew Cursed by Jesus," 1894) owes nearly everything to Eugène Sue's novel. One chapbook, by Karakoi Pista (1873), is a narrative poem so original that it must be considered a piece of belles-lettres, however unworthy its achievement. The one closest in manner to the true *Volksbuch* is the *Az örökké való zsidó* (Debreczen, 1861), which contains material found also in the *Histoire admirable* in its late (eighteenth-century) version; the closest in language is the earliest, *Az örökké való zsidó*—the title of both pamphlets signifies "the eternal Jew"—which must have been printed before 1848 (and not too long before), since it was suppressed as leading to "the propagation of fanaticism."[64]

Ahasuerus in Southern Europe

As Ahasuerus was going on his weary way over the mountains, valleys, and plains of Germany and adjacent countries, one may assume that at the same time Buttadeus and Malchus were either wandering about Italy and southern Europe or suffering in prison as a damned soul is supposed to suffer, depending upon whether one thought of him as Buttadeus or Malchus. The allusions to the Wandering Jew in Spain and Portugal, dating from the sixteenth and seventeenth centuries, give him a different name—Juan Espera en Dios—and a different appearance perhaps from that presented by Ahasuerus, although that is not clear; and yet it is evident that the personalities are all beginning to blend. And, after all, the *Kurtze Beschreibung* reported an appearance of Ahasuerus in Madrid.

Therefore, as we approach 1700, we may say that the merging of Ahasuerus, Cartaphilus, Buttadeus, Malchus, Juan Espera en Dios, Isaac Laquedem, or however else he may be addressed, into one legendary character—the Wandering or Eternal Jew—is rapidly approaching completeness, if not already complete. On the other hand, it should be no surprise that Ahasuerus, the creature of German Protestantism, should never find much favor in Italy or Spain, although there may be a sporadic mention in Italy of one Assuero. In this guise he came to Italy about 1650, as it is told in the *Narrazione d'un Giudeo errante*, which is a close translation of one of the Dudulaeus versions. But much more characteristic are two lively Italian chapbooks, the *Narrazione dello Stato* (Naples, 1849) and the *Narrazione di quel servo* (Turin, 1650?), both of which are more or less independent of the Ahasuerus-book and devote their attention to the "scellerato ed ingratis-simo Malco," the "servo che diede le schiaffe a . . . Jesu Christo." The latter of these includes as a separate item, or "un altro racconto," the *Narrazione d'un Giudeo errante* just mentioned. In other words, even a translation of the German pamphlet is not allowed to stand alone but must be incorporated into an original Italian text on the subject of Malchus. After all, the Italians could learn little from the Germans about the Wandering Jew. They had known him too long already.[65]

The Wunderbare Erzehlung

To illustrate how the *Volksbuch* put forth branches during the seventeenth cen-tury and later, let me describe, in conclusion, one of the prize exhibits of the popular literature of the age. This is a pamphlet ostensibly printed in 1660—ac-tually, I think, about 1662—now in the ducal library at Wolfenbüttel.[66] Its full title is *Wunderbare Erzehlung von einen Juden Ahasverus genannt/wie derselbe bey der Creutzigung Christi gewesen/was seinet wegen darbey/vorgangen/und wie von den HERRN CHRISTO ihm angedeutet worden/dasz Er als ein leben-diger Zeuge dessen/so sich bey der Creutzigung Christi zugetragen/bisz an der Welt Ende herumb wallen solle.* Its material comprises:

1. A discussion of longevity among men.
2. Various epistles directed toward the authorities at Rome, including a message from Pilate to the Emperor Tiberius.
3. An enumeration of various punishments visited upon each of the Twelve Tribes of Israel for its part in the Crucifixion.
4. The text of the *Relation* with several additions. In the usual "Reminder to the Christian Reader" there is further exemplification of long life from rather eso-teric sources, drawing upon Spanish and Portuguese material, German *exempla*, and even Wendish folklore.
5. The sentence pronounced upon Christ.
6. The history of the rocks cast down during the earthquake which took place at the time Christ was crucified.
7. The punishment of Pilate.
8. The pre-Christian *Historia Suidae*.
9. A copy of a letter written by King Abgarus (Toparcha) to Jesus, sent to Jeru-salem by the messenger Ananias. This is from the fourth-century Church father Eusebius Pamphili.
10. The story of a young man first corrupted and then led back into the straight path of righteousness.
11. Some verses warning of the frailty of mankind.
12. Finally, an epilogue addressed to the reader—

Honored Reader, to issue this pamphlet necessitated my dealing in many languages. So many kinds of people have been led astray by this Jew, and sometimes have main-tained foolish opinions about him. And so I have brought as much as I could before you to make it commensurate with truth in sharing it with the reader. Doubt not that he should be satisfied with it, realizing, however, that it is no necessary article of faith in itself. If it should please him, he can expect from me in the near future (1) a complete description of Palestine, of the great wars between Christians and Turks from the seeking of the Holy Sepulchre until our own times, and (2) a *Compendium Historicum* of the most noteworthy affairs which took place between the years 1617 to 1661 and which are not to be found in the histories. Farewell!

We have indeed come a long way from the comparatively simple account of Ahasuerus in the *Kurtze Beschreibung*. Any one of the dozen topics listed here would be worth a monograph in itself. The original Legend is about to be lost in a sea of extraneous additions. All this, moreover, has been accomplished within two or three generations after the *Kurtze Beschreibung*. When one adds to this all other adventitious matter often included—such as accounts of the Tribes of Israel; the story of Judas; the Legend of Adam, Seth, and the Holy Pips to be found in the *Histoire admirable*; the grand itinerary of the Wandering Jew found in this same work and elsewhere; to say nothing of other later additions—one gets a dizzying impression that the Legend has assumed the nature of the classical Hydra, for when one goes to examine and fix a particular aspect of the story, two different aspects spring up in its place.

In retrospect, the complicated evolution of the Ahasuerus-book, which took place mainly in the seventeenth century, suggests that the Germans gave the Legend a very powerful new impulse, one which spread it over northern and western Europe and across the water into England. Most important of all, they established for good the tradition that Ahasuerus must wander ceaselessly. From now on it is less than accurate to call him only the Eternal Jew (*der ewige Jude*), as the Germans have ever since paradoxically done; rather he should be called the Wandering Jew, a term which seems to have originated in France. Nevertheless, ever since the seventeenth century the Germans, an essentially romantic-minded people in their literature, have worked tirelessly on the Legend and have produced far more writings on the subject than the rest of Europe combined. This of course does not establish them as the inventors of the Legend, as some of them have considered themselves. That is an eminence which history must deny them. But it indicates that they have become the most faithful sponsors of the Legend in its modern form. What manifold shapes this modern form may take will occupy the remainder of this study. The miscellanea of the versions allegedly told to Paulus von Eitzen are many and varied, traveling the whole road through reverence to ridicule and back again. Now for about the first time it will be possible to get some adequate idea of the great scope of the Legend. I shall begin by listing and commenting on the main types of folk tale in which Ahasuerus is the arresting central figure. This means, of course, leaving aside chronological considerations for the moment and observing these tales as timeless and dateless phenomena.

CHAPTER FOUR

The Wandering Jew In Folk Tales

We are probably right in distinguishing between an eastern and western branch of the folk tale of the Wandering Jew. Not very many examples of the eastern branch, however, have been collected, and one gets the impression that the Legend was never particularly attractive in the eastern parts, save in the vicinity of Jerusalem and the seaboard of Asia Minor. There are enough survivals, nonetheless, to fix in rather vague terms the features of the eastern branch.

Assuming that the original Legend of Malchus originated in the Jerusalem sector, as I believe most likely, the scholars have theorized that it then spread along the islands off the coast of Syria and Asiatic Turkey, into Cyprus, Rhodes, Crete, and the Dodecanese and Aegean Islands, thence to the mainland of Greece, and thence up the eastern side of the Balkan peninsula into ultimately Slavic territory. Such a theory accounts for the fact that in general the Russian examples of the folk tale of the Wandering Jew follow the eastern rather than the western pattern. But in Russia the Legend undergoes a considerable amount of contamination with the western branch, thanks in large measure, I believe, to the influence of the Ahasuerus-book.

At the outset, however, it should be clear that the Ahasuerus-book did not create all these folk tales. Many of them very likely came into existence long before the *Kurtze Beschreibung*, which, in its turn, has some basis in folk tale. There is between the *Volksbücher*—like the *Kurtze Beschreibung* or the *Histoire admirable* —and the folk tale a kind of mutual interplay. Sometimes the influence of the one is clearly discernible upon the other; sometimes the two genres merely parallel each other in obscure fashion. And there is always the possibility of contamination with other legends or folk tales. Even in the earliest phase of a folk tale there may be admixture with something else. Thus the tale told by Johannes Moschos (p. 13 above), considered the first surviving version of the Legend in point of time (*ca.*600), is actually a kind of oblique reference, since the protagonist is to be only *like* Malchus, not Malchus himself, and actually he is another figure altogether who has unfortunately interfered with Christian ritual and in this way has blasphemed.

The Eastern Folk Tale

A summary of the best examples of the eastern branch is necessary to define its salient motifs. Three points are characteristic: (1) the tales represent the phase of Malchus rather than of Cartaphilus; (2) the wandering is limited in range, often confined to a particular locality; and (3) the protagonist will ask the questions: "What day is it? Does Christ still live?"—and on being answered in the second case with a confident affirmative will sigh or weep or otherwise indicate distress of soul. Moreover, the eastern branch is especially susceptible to contamination with other tales, and the essential motive for the curse—the insult, physical or otherwise, to the Saviour—is often blurred to the point where it can no longer be perceived.

1. From Syme, an island near Rhodes, comes the folk tale of Kutendes, an extremely hairy immortal who lives under the burden of a curse. He dwells on the Mount of Fools (Lollobouni) but wanders about the mountain ceaselessly. At night he lights a lantern and kindles a fire. Whenever he meets someone he asks, "How long is it since the Son of Mary died?" When he has received an answer, he groans and cries out: "How old am I, miserable one that I am?" He strikes himself in torment and flees, calling out again, "How old am I, miserable one that I am?"[1]

2. At Myra, near present-day Dembre, in southwest Asiatic Turkey, on the top of a mountain near Kastellorizo, there lived in ancient times the Jew Kutris. He was a shoemaker, who chased away the foreigner (*sic*) Jesus from in front of his house and refused him a drink. He then grasped a stick with which to beat Jesus. The latter, sighing, turned to him and said, "I go, but the curse of my Father will fall on your head. The hill whereon we stand shall be the place of your abiding condemnation. At daybreak you shall roll down from the top to the foot of this hill, and in the evening fire shall burn your body, which shall vainly defend itself against the flame." And so it has been to the present day.[2]

3. In Attalia (Adalia) in Asiatic Turkey, Kutendes runs around the mountains because he had given Christ a blow on the cheek. He is burdened with the curse of immortality. The inhabitants of Kastellorizo still see him. When they build a fire at night, Kutendes comes and throws a block of wood on it, but when he sees that they fear him, he hurries away, crying: "Hu! hu! hu!" Sometimes he turns himself into a horse or sheep, or what he will.[3]

4. From the island of Lesbos, it is reported that when a woman is angry with her child, she says to it, "May you become like the Short One!" They say that the Short One, Koutetes or Koulotes, who lived at the time of Jesus Christ, was chiefly responsible for the Passion. Jesus Christ cursed him and condemned him never to die. Since that time he wanders from one country to the other. He is small and deformed. Vainly he seeks death; it will not receive him. Many think they have seen him.[4]

5. From the European Turkish province of Ioannina in the nineteenth century (now on the borders of Greece and Yugoslavia), they tell of a tough old man, who is said to live (or have lived) as Photo Des. He was a Jew who struck Jesus with a stick when He was on the Way of the Cross. The curse was that he should live solitary and not die until he had eaten the stick. Since that time he has chewed on it, reliving the moment when he did his cruel deed. Each year on Maundy Thursday he is glad, because the stick is nearly eaten up. But on the Day (Good Friday) it grows again to its former size. When a ship passes by the shore, he asks: "Does

Christ still live?" And to his great anguish he must always hear: "He lives and reigns."[5]

6. A Greek topography of Jerusalem, dating from the fifteenth century, tells the story of Phalas, who was cured of lameness by Christ, yet still gave the Saviour a blow on the cheek while He was carrying the Cross. Therefore he was condemned to be torn to pieces three times a day by a wild animal, yet always to remain alive. This will continue until Doomsday.[6]

Now it is evident that in all save Tale 4 above, where the motive has been hopelessly eroded, the Legend of Malchus, of the man who struck Christ, lies at the core. As to Tale 4, its statement that the Short One wanders from one country to another, whereas in the others his wandering is generally only local, suggests that it is of more recent vintage than the others and has become westernized.

The contaminations in these tales are even more interesting. The names of the protagonist are new. *Koutentes* (*Kutendes, Koutetes, Koutris, Koulotes,* etc.) in its various garbled forms, seems to be a dialectal Greek word for "blockhead" or "baldy" and is an opprobrious term for an old man. *Photo Des* in Tale 5, not previously explained in satisfactory manner, I suspect to be a mispronunciation of *Buttadeus;* but then Tale 5 as a tale clearly belongs to some legend other than that of Malchus, which nevertheless gives the tale its impetus. *Phalas* in Tale 6, which appears in some Russian tales with the variant form *Phanyas,* has been transferred from the name of the protagonist of an entirely separate legend. The punishments in Tale 2 and Tale 6 are certainly not the usual ones; they belong in the category of tedious punishments, of course, but that in Tale 6 in particular reminds one of the torments visited upon Prometheus or Tyteus in Hades, just as the punishment in Tale 2 recalls vaguely the rock which Sisyphus had to roll uphill, only to have it roll down. Such matters are easily explained, in view of the locale of the tales, as pertaining to Greek folklore—local contamination, in other words.

Nevertheless, four of the above tales (2, 4, 5, and 6) indicate either implicitly or explicitly that the protagonist was a Jew or at least lived in Jerusalem; and one of them, Tale 2, specifies that he was a shoemaker. I wish it were possible to fix the date of Tale 2 accurately, because, as we have seen, the Wandering Jew does not appear as a shoemaker in the West until the sixteenth century, and then in Spain (p. 30). In this, we should not give much thought to the likelihood that Tale 2 was the source of this detail, because in its present form it would seem to be rather too romantic to be a good old folk tale, what with Christ's sighing and referring to the curse as coming from his father and not from himself. It is too apologetic and too humanitarian. Whoever made it up probably knew already that the Jew had been a shoemaker.

The possibilities of variation in folk tales are of course innumerable. The fact that they circulate for generations by word of mouth is sufficient reason for this state of affairs. When, in addition, one must deal with a region where illiteracy is the rule and particularly where there has been no codifying of folk tales into some written version—no *Volksbuch,* in short—the variants are even more frequent, so that unless one is sure of the archetype one is forced into the belief that there is no such thing as an uncontaminated folk tale. And so, when the type represented by these Greco-Levantine folk tales spreads into Russia, for example, a greater degree of contamination is the result. In fact, the only tales collected thus far in Russia which can be assigned with any logic to the eastern branch of the Legend derive from southern Russia—the Ukraine, Podolia, and Little Russia.[7] Thus:

7. *Question:* Who dies three times a day? *Answer:* Phanjas or Phalas or Kalos, servant of Caiphas, who gave Christ a blow on the cheek while He was being judged. For this reason the Lord has decided that he must be devoured three times a day by a wild beast and always be brought back to life, and so on until Judgment Day.[8] (This is analogous to Tale 6, with the same name for the protagonist.)

A curious subsidiary legend seems to have grown up, which associates the Jews and the Crucifixion without bringing the Wandering Jew into the picture. According to this, the Jews who crucified Jesus remain sitting at the Holy Sepulcher in Jerusalem, always in the same position. When men ask them, "When were you born?" they answer, "Yesterday." "When will you die?" "Tomorrow."[9] This is closely related to a tale which Father Bonifacius Stefani of Ragusa, bishop of Stagno, brought back from Jerusalem in the sixteenth century (pp. 35-36 above), but no similar stories since that time have appeared except in Russia.[10] It merges with the Legend of the Wandering Jew, however, in a Ukrainian folk tale:

8. There are Jews who will wander till the end of the world. These are the Jews who never gave Jesus any peace. When the moon is young, the Jew is young; and when it is old, he too is old. If you ask him, "When did you come?" he answers, "Yesterday." "When will you go?" "Tomorrow.' (Here the motive of the Crucifixion has been almost obscured, and the tale introduces the comparatively rare motif of lunar correspondence, which appears in the Slavic versions only and which led some Slavic folklorists to insist that the whole Legend of the Wandering Jew is a lunar myth. It is clear that at one time lunar or solar phenomena may have influenced the legends of wanderers—witness the tradition of the constellations associated by the Greeks with wandering figures—but that the Legend of the Wandering Jew came from anything more than a revenge motif in the form of a tedious punishment is not to be proved. Two or three more instances of this tendency to contaminate with lunar myth, however, are worth noting.)

9. In old times, peasants in Podolia believed that the watch set at the Lord's tomb is still there. It consists of two Jews, and they are both still alive; and when the moon is old they are so very old that they shake; and when the moon is young, they too are young, looking as though they were going on twenty. When asked, "When did you come?" they answer, "Yesterday." "And when will you go?" "Tomorrow." That is the fate that God imposed upon them: to live till the Last Judgment. (The connection with the Legend of Malchus has to all intents been severed. We are dealing here, basically, with another legend, one connected with the watchers at the tomb. In this case the outlines are a little clearer than in Tale 8, but the folk tales are closely related.)[11]

The last two examples I would quote are much more characteristic of the western than the eastern branch, but I mention them because of their contaminations. In the Ukraine it is said that:

10. There was once a Jew; when they were torturing Christ and were already

taking him to be crucified, he came up with his Cross and wanted to lean awhile against the Jew's house and to rest, but the Jew cried: "Go hence! go hence!" Christ turned around and said to him: "I shall go, but you too must go and roam the earth until the Last Judgment." So he is still wandering. He has recently been seen, people say, up our way. But it is hard to recognize him, because when the moon is old, he is very, very old; and when the moon is young, he turns young again. (Except for the increment of the lunar parallel, this could be a simple example of the western branch. The tale is basically one that could have been introduced from Germany and then contaminated with the moon-myth. In the western branch, as we have seen, the rejuvenation of Cartaphilus was accomplished miraculously every hundred years; here it is in a lunar cycle. In Western medieval Christendom one thought more in terms of centuries; in Eastern primitive culture, as in most primitive cultures, one calculated by months.)[12]

Finally in this group, there is the noteworthy example from the Ukraine of a further contamination with the ancient folk motif of the Unquiet Grave, according to which the tears of a loved one upon a grave will disturb the rest of the dead person:

11. When the Jews were torturing Jesus Christ and were already taking him to be crucified on the Cross, he passed by the house of a Jew and wanted to rest there. The Jew ran out of the house, pushed Jesus aside, and said: "Go, go! Why do you stand beside my house?" And Jesus replied: "From now on you shall wander to the end of time!" The Jew immediately went to the grave of his daughter Estya, and she arose from her coffin and said: "Faithless father! You are faithless toward God and faithless toward me; you do not deserve to weep on my grave." But he wept on her grave and lamented that God had taken away his daughter so young. Ever since then he has been wandering without rest. When the moon is in its last quarter, his hair turns gray, and he gets old, very old; but when the moon is young, he is young again and strong, and his hair is blond and short. People say that some years ago he was in our part of the country.[13]

These eleven tales, plus the more sophisticated accounts from fifteenth- and sixteenth-century travelers to Jerusalem (pp. 34-37 above), represent all that is available of the eastern branch of the Legend, at least at the time. It is unfortunate that so many of these should be rather weak. They have historical interest to some degree, but little else, and are actually irregular versions. It is a further misfortune that the collecting and recording of these tales did not begin sooner. Much has been lost that would have been most useful to the student of the Legend. The curious conclusion which suggests itself is that the farther the eastern branch traveled away from Jerusalem and contiguous parts, the more shadowy it became; whereas the western branch, transplanted to Italy and the adjacent islands of the central Mediterranean, throve mightily and even tended to encroach upon eastern territory. Some of the Russian versions, for example, such as Tale 10 and Tale 11 just cited, are in effect representative of the western branch.

The Western Folk Tale

The distinguishing characteristic of the western branch, quite apart from the absence of such individual details as the restricted wandering, the repeated question and inevitable answer, and the Malchean core of the eastern branch, is the fact that Buttadeus and Cartaphilus (under whatever name) tend to dominate. We are already more than familiar with it. At the same time, however, the ramifications of the folk tale of the Wandering Jew are certainly more numerous in the west than in the east. Moreover, collectors have been far more active; there have been more printed accounts because the western countries have a better record for literacy. The point is that the Legend received almost from the beginning a greater stimulation in western than in eastern Europe.

More than a hundred folk tales of the Wandering Jew have been assembled from central and western Europe, and this takes no account of the printed accounts such as those considered in the preceding chapter. Comparatively few of these folk tales, interestingly enough, come from Italy, which we may take to be the distribution point of the western branch. There are many from the German-speaking peoples in Germany, Austria, and Switzerland; some from France and England; some from the Low Countries. The Legend seems foreign to Celtic lands, with the exception of Brittany. A few Scandinavian folk tales have been salvaged, but most of the versions in Scandinavia are derived pretty directly from the Ahasuerus-book. The English and Germans apparently took a few seedlings of the Legend to America, but the American "folk tales" are so sophisticated or so localized, and certainly so rare, that they are most easily handled as literary rather than folkloristic forms.

It is not my purpose to discuss all of these hundred and more folk tales in detail, but to comment on the significant ones. These pieces of folkloristic evidence of the Legend can be found all along the road through the seventeenth, eighteenth, and nineteenth centuries. No specific time or place of birth for the tales can be given, for we are dealing here with a migratory legend which has traveled for a long time. Naturally there are many instances in which the Legend in its pure form collides with a local legend in such a way as to produce a considerable deviation from the norm. If a specific date should be given in a tale, it suggests that there is a real person in the role of the Wandering Jew—an impostor or charlatan, of which more later (see chap. iv).

Germany

The German folk tales are numerous; some of them are of major influence in the development of the Legend, while others are of only passing importance.

12. In Buchenberg, Württemberg, Ahasuerus wore either a simple jacket and gray coarse cotton stockings, or a dark cowl, almost like a monk's, and an old dirty kerchief. But he rejected any offered shoes or stockings, explaining to the people that if he kept all the pieces of clothing offered him, four horses could not carry the stuff away. He had spent the night with the local pastor.[14]

13. In Röthenberg, Silesia, they say that Ahasuerus always has a groschen in his sack, which, as soon as he empties it, is always filled anew.[15]

14. Between Münster and Paderborn in Westphalia, the Wandering Jew has been seen going about from one place to another. He can rest only for as long as it

takes him to devour a morsel of white bread. Moreover, it is permitted him, as in many other instances, to sit only on two oak stumps whose roots have so grown together that they form a natural seat.[16] (This is one of the more important German folk tales; there are several variants of it. Sometimes the stumps will grow together in the form of a cross. Or perhaps there may be two harrows, tied together in an open field, which can serve as a seat for the Jew; otherwise he must keep moving his feet continuously. The use of a harrow or harrows is apparently unique among German-speaking people. It may reflect the symbolism of the harrow in the medieval Legend of the Harrowing of Hell—the purging by Christ, during the three days between the Crucifixion and the Resurrection, of worthy souls who had been condemned to the abode of perpetual pain because they had been born and had died before Christ. Or it may symbolize the fact that Ahasuerus, as a repentant sinner, can rely upon—that is, rest upon—the harrow, which is an implement for leveling and hence the instrument of Christ. Or it may be that, as an unrepentant sinner or one expiating his sin, he must sit on a very uncomfortable seat. Or the harrow may have no special significance at all. Sometimes a plough is used instead of a harrow. In any farm community a farm implement would occur to anyone as an important accessory to the landscape. As a matter of academic interest, it may be added that Ahasuerus never did any good to the implement by resting upon it, for the points of the harrow or the edge of the plowshare would be blunted forever after.)

15. Around the Jade Bay of Oldenburg, the Wandering Jew is a habitué of the region, but in this instance the punishment is said to represent a suspended sentence, as it were.[17] The original sentence may therefore have been much more severe than that of perpetual wandering, but no specific details are given.

16, 17, 18. Indeed, many of the German folk tales amount to vague, unremarkable statements of superstitious belief and nothing more. Thus on the Jaberg on the Rhine, near Hilden (Tale 16), Ahasuerus sits alone, which is most unusual for him.[18] Or at Bretten in Baden (Tale 17), he was once seen in the woods.[19] At both Bamberg and Würzburg in Bavaria (Tale 18), he was seen some time during the eighteenth century—no one knows when—and whenever anyone addressed him, he vanished forthwith.[20]

19. Once the Wandering Jew went into a farmer's house at Ertingen, Württemberg, and, as elsewhere, kept walking about a table in the middle of the room. This time, however, he lay down between midnight and one o'clock, and rested on the bench by the fire. The next morning he had disappeared before anyone else in the house was up and about.[21] (In instances of this sort, the impossibility of seeing him depart is something of a commonplace, but his ability to seize rest during the witching hour from midnight to one o'clock is most unusual.)

20. At a market in Frankfurt am Main the Wanderer once made a rather original appearance. All nations and races were represented at the fair: Christians, Jews, and Moslems. To sell dear, to buy cheap—that was the whole thought of the crowd. Profit, a devil armed with a yardstick and a pair of scales, was squeezing all those souls between his crooked fingers. A man with gray beard, half-clothed in a torn tunic, covered to the eyes with a dirty turban, evidently exhausted by

long travel, came up to a secondhand dealer. After turning the whole shop up-side down, he chose a samite robe, furred with miniver, and peered at it in the daylight. He at once gave it back, then picked it up again, returned it again, and once more picked it up and began bargaining for it. The dealer, who recognized the man as a Jew by his avariciousness and persistence, swore to him by the eyes of the Saviour that he would not give any discount. The old man sighed in anguish, turned his head away, took up the robe, and presented the dealer with a gold coin bearing the image of the Emperor Tiberius, saying to him: "There's your money." "This money has no currency in the Empire," protested the dealer. "Well, it's fourteen hundred years since it was struck at Rome," replied the Jew, "and it was then that I came by it." The dealer, in his fright, made the sign of the cross. "O tell me," he cried, "aren't you the Wandering Jew?" The stranger, however, had disappeared.[22] (This tale, to judge by the alleged date of the coin, would have been a late medieval tale. Since there is no evidence that the Legend was known in Germany in the fifteenth century, the authenticity of the date immediately becomes suspect. Besides, the moralizing tone of the whole indicates that it is in essence more a literary effort than a true folk tale. Genuine or not, however, it is often repeated. The protagonist has about him a distinct Oriental aura, notably the dirty turban, and he is presented as exhibiting the less lovely aspects of certain Jews. Plainly this anti-Semitic picture of him is relished by the teller; the Jew possesses devilish overtones, and the sign of the cross is sufficient to get rid of him. Considering all this and bearing in mind the Orientalistic tendency of the late seventeenth and eighteenth centuries in fiction and travel books, it is most likely that this particular tale is no older than perhaps 1675 and maybe as late as 1800.)

21. Ahasuerus comes back to the vicinity of Hannover every seven years and always follows the same path. His beard reaches to the ground. Each day he is offered, and accepts, eighteen pfennigs for his sustenance.[23] (Sometimes he will receive no alms whatsoever; at other times he will accept a limited number of coins or a limited amount of money.)

22. At Heidthausen, as in many other places in Germany, Austria, and Switzerland, the Wandering Jew stated on one occasion, very definitely, that he had made seven circuits of the world.[24]

23. One persistent tale, evidently a variant of Tale 14, found also in Denmark and Sweden but having its probable focal point in Schleswig, has it that on Christmas night Ahasuerus, wherever he may be, must rest upon a plowshare. After that the farmer will always plow too deep. He has been seen in many places; he is never hungry or thirsty and never sleeps under a roof. On his mantle moss sometimes grows.[25]

24. A peculiar variant of the classic version of the Legend appears at Deilbach, according to which the Wandering Jew met Christ on his way to Calvary, carrying a load (sic) on his back. When Christ asked appealingly for help, the Jew answered: "I am on a journey." Thereupon he was cursed by Christ and doomed to wander until he should find a harrow upright with its two points against each other.[26] (This is also an obvious variant of Tale 14.)

25. Still another variant, this time from Elberfeld, has it that Ahasuerus did business on Christmas Day, saying: "I must close out my wares; I must always do business." And from that time on he must do it; at the Christmas feast one can always see him moving around doing business.[27] (This tale is so far removed from the chief outlines of the Legend that one must suspect that it has an independent source.)

26. From the Schleswig area also comes this unusual tale, told this time by a woman and contributed to Müllenhof's collection by a man from Uetersen:

When I was a girl of thirteen, I went with my parents to Lübeck. When we arrived there, we went to a tavern where my father ordered schnapps. As he was about to drink, a very old man got up and came and sat down beside us and said, "I can drink up that schnapps. Prosit!" . . . He then said, "I am the Eternal Jew [the usual German designation], and this afternoon I was at your house in Seedorp, where I called on your daughter." Then he went away. We asked the innkeeper if he knew the man. He said, "Yes, I know the man quite well; that is the Eternal Jew; he is everywhere and nowhere and has no rest. He is never older than he is now; I have known him for many years. He never works and is never hungry or thirsty!"

When we got home about midnight, I asked my sister if a man had been there. She said, "Yes, this afternoon near dusk a man was here who told me that he had spoken with my father and sister an hour before in Lübeck, and that I must not be surprised if my father took sick and died within twenty-four hours. Whereupon he went away." My father had hardly returned from Lübeck before he died, on the very same day. I have never seen the man since that time.[28]

(Although, as we shall see, the Wandering Jew is often a herald of disaster and desolation, it is very seldom that he puts the mark of death directly upon an individual, particularly by the simple means of drinking schnapps at the same table. Moreover, it is most unusual to have him drink hard liquor under any circumstances.)

A few miscellaneous notes, dealing chiefly with the Algäu region of southwestern Germany (Bavaria and Württemberg in particular), are worthy of record:

27. In Nosbach the Wandering Jew is to be identified directly with the Wild Huntsman: when he passes by you, you can clearly hear the baying of hounds.[29]

28. In Unterjoch he performed the remarkable feat of sleeping briefly on a cooper's spike.[30] (Still another variant, apparently, of Tale 14.)

29. The same incident, with rather more detail, is told at Oberdorf in Bavaria, where Ahasuerus reportedly spent the night with the town's cooper—without significant incident.[31]

30. From Hinterstein, it has been reported that the Wandering Jew will enter a house only if it is made all of wood or, at the least, of wood and plaster. Since wood in folklore is generally construed as a beneficent, protective kind of agency, the stranger is evidently relying upon the mercy of the Lord.[32]

31. At Faulenbach, in the Algäu region, the stranger spent a short time at the local inn, and it was noticed that he kept walking restlessly around a table in the middle of the room and never sat down.[33] (This may be compared with Tale 19 above. The table in the middle of the room becomes commonplace before long.)

32. From Marieney in Saxony we have a detailed description of this awesome apparition. He is portrayed as a man of middle age, with dark complexion and stern and resolute glance. He is clothed in a long traveling cloak and wears a broad-brimmed hat, never stained by weather or dust. Once a credulous shepherd tried to speak to him. He was convinced that it must be the Wandering Jew, because the stranger expressed surprise that here, where a thousand years before he had seen nothing but forests, there was now a thriving community.[34] (This last detail is interesting as the reverse of a common theme to be found, in particular, farther south in Switzerland and the Tyrol—namely, that the visit of the Wandering Jew brings decay and desolation.)

The German folk tales given here may be called typical. They describe the Wandering Jew as to clothing and general appearance; they emphasize his wandering (he is everywhere and nowhere); they describe certain taboos concerning his ability to rest, and here, except for the assertion that he rests only upon a plow or a harrow or an oak stump, there is very little in the way of a pattern. The part Ahasuerus plays as a prophet of death, as in the Schleswig story (Tale 26), is a rare performance. Most of his visits, it may have been noticed, are in small settlements, hardly to be found on an ordinary map, and usually in the mountainous regions of southern Germany. A crossroads, a church, a few farmhouses or hillmen's huts—these furnish an apt setting for a wonder of wonders.

Austria

The resemblances between the German and Austrian folk tales of the Wandering Jew are striking, as might be expected. The political boundary between the two countries is naturally of no significance. The Algäu tales move easily into the Tyrol in one direction and into Switzerland in another. There is an undeniable tendency, however, for the more southerly tales to stress the emotional and even the sinister aspects of Ahasuerus. In number the Austrian tales are fewer, but this may be only a matter of fortuitous collecting.

33. Sometimes the references to the appearance of the Wanderer are altogether casual, such as the brief note that at St. Andräa, in Carinthia (Austria), the officer in charge of the local prince's linen once spoke with Ahasuerus. Nothing seems to have come of the conversation.[35] (The Wandering Jew, according to report, was often in Carinthia, yet satisfactory specimens of folk tales from this province have been hard to come by.)

34. At old Grandfather Jokub's house in Lustenau, near the Lake of Constance, the Wandering Jew noticed a crucifix hanging in a corner of the room, the sight of which threw him into fear and anger, so that the people of the town were glad when he went outdoors and finally left.[36] (There seem to be many variants of the motif of Ahasuerus' reaction to crucifixes and other holy symbols; sometimes, as here, he is perturbed and at other times he assumes a very judicious, not to say critical, attitude.)

35. Throughout the Vorarlberg district, for that matter, it is a tradition that

Ahasuerus has only one groschen in his bag, which, whenever he offers it to pay for something, returns to him as soon as he runs three times around a table.[37] (Although we have seen that his predilection for moving about a table has been noted in Germany, as in Tale 31 above, such an absurd corruption of the motif of the inexhaustible purse is unique.)

36. At Brennbichl, a village not far from Imst in the Austrian Tyrol, the Wanderer once arrived in a sad condition of great hunger. To allay the pangs in his stomach, the kindly villagers set in front of him a large bowl of pap or mush, on a wooden table in front of a house, and he fell to gorging on it as if he had been empty for days. It was easy to tell that he was the "mysterious" Jew, for he kept walking about the table all the time that he was eating.[38] (In this tale Ahasuerus is referred to as the *umgehadi Schuachta,* the shoemaker who keeps moving. It is notable that none of the German tales designates him as a cobbler or anything else; if then some subsequent German reference makes him a shoemaker, it is an imported commodity.)

37. Again, at Dellach the *ewige Schuster,* or eternal shoemaker, paid his bill at the inn with seven new coins which no one recognized.[39] (This is one of the more distinctive of Carinthian tales.)

38. An interesting example of the contamination of two separate legends is the tale told of the witch Langtüttin, who sits on the Oetzthaler Glacier. It appears that she once drew lots with the Wandering Jew to see which of the two should go wandering over the world and which should sit on the glacier. The old witch drew the sedentary lot.[40] (It was therefore the fortune of the Jew to wander, although the motive for his wandering is far different from that given within the classic confines of the true Legend of the Wandering Jew. Moreover, in this perpetual sitting on a glacier there is at least a faint reminiscence of a detail from the medieval Legend of St. Brandan, who discovered an individual freed on stated occasions for a day from the tortures of Hell. He spent that day sitting on an iceberg to get a real change.)

39. At Töll, Ahasuerus pronounced a crucifix which he saw floating, rather incongruously, in the River Etsch (Adige) to be the best likeness of Christ that he had seen in a long time. This high praise, however, he bestowed rather too impartially on other crucifixes in other villages. On this occasion at Töll there was a peculiarity in his gait: he had to take two steps backward for every three steps forward. Truly the progress of the sinner in this world is laborious! The only spot where he could find rest was the stump of a fallen tree whose roots formed five little crosses into one big cross. It was the common belief in the neighborhood that if you sat on a stump of this sort, nothing evil could touch you, and you would be safe from all accidents.[41] (We have here a good example of the implanting of a local legend into the widespread migratory Legend.)

40. When the Wanderer was once given shelter at Schönebergle, he expressed his gratitude by leaving a wedding present for the son and daughter of the house.[42] (This tale is also found across the border in Italy; we may recall also the analogous tale in the version of Antonio di Francesco di Andrea [pp. 25-26

above], in which the visitor revealed the presence of money which could serve as a dowry for the innkeeper's daughter.)

41. As at several places in Germany, it was a tradition at Flattach that the Wandering Jew never can eat without walking constantly around the table; and in a few instances he carries a little table with him.[43]

42. At Schilsbach a fowler once recognized the Wandering Jew by the five nails in the soles of his shoes, which printed a cross on the ground.[44] (This detail, of considerable importance in certain literary treatments of the Legend, is by no means common in the folk tales. Perhaps it is because we do not happen to have collected instances. But the five nails, corresponding to the five wounds of Christ, seem to be the imposition of an old medieval folk tradition upon the Legend and could have come best from a learned source.)

43. The compassionate inhabitants of Münnichkirchen kept a store of old shoes for Ahasuerus, because he already has had to go for nine centuries—in some versions, for nine thousand years—over thistles and thorns.[45]

44. The final item from Austria, centering around Villach, is actually part of a Swiss folk-tale tradition, and will serve as a good transition to what follows. According to this, the Wanderer has already visited the locality twice; if he should come a third time, the whole settlement will disappear.[46]

Switzerland

Most of the Swiss folk tales concerning the Wandering Jew are more distinctive than either the German or Austrian ones. Many of them go to shape a pattern in which the protagonist of the Legend is a figure of sinister, even disastrous, portent. This formula is so striking and so seldom met elsewhere that it seems a reasonable supposition that it derived from the Alpine regions in general and probably from the Swiss Alps in particular. I shall therefore designate it as the Swiss sublegend.

45. In a rather elementary form, the pattern is illustrated by the tradition at Entlebuch, near Lucerne, that Ahasuerus came to this town and told how there used to be a vineyard on the summit of a nearby hill where there were now only green uplands.[47]

46. The pattern then develops into a form represented by a tale from Blumenstein in Bern canton. The church in the village is said to have belonged once to a city. When the Wanderer first traveled through this region, it was blessed; the second time he cursed the city because of its wickedness, and it became a sterile wind; and when he comes by the third time, the whole region will become a glacier.[48]

47. Similarly, when the Wandering Jew first climbed to the Maienwang above the Rhone Glacier, he found a vineyard; the second time a fir tree; and the third time a snowy, rocky wilderness. Tears started from his eyes, so copious that the lake by Hospiz was thus formed.[49]

48. About the Furka Pass the same story is told, except that there were first fruitful fields instead of a vineyard.[50]

49. The most influential and widely known of these local variants of the Swiss sublegend hovers about the Grimsel. First there was a city here which once refused Ahasuerus shelter. The second time that he came he found only open fields. The third time he found only snow and ice. He wept bitterly, and the Grimselmeer was the result.[51] (There are several adaptations of the Grimsel Legend in German poetry of the nineteenth century in which the essential nature of the tale does not deviate from the norm given in the last few examples.)

50, 51. The Grimsel tale is soon transferred to the not too distant Thunermeer (Tale 50), and the Wanderer had the same experience at the little village of Leissingen (Tale 51), where he had already made his disastrous third visit, but he likes to go there at Christmas time and walk hither and yon.[52]

52. As for probably the most celebrated of all Swiss mountains, the Matterhorn, there was once a city here which received the Wandering Jew hospitably enough on one occasion, but when he came back a thousand years later, he found only the great mountain. In his sorrow he wept bitter tears, from which arose a lake down in the valley.[53] (It seems to make little difference whether or not the original community treated Ahasuerus well or badly.)

53. At Gsteig, near the Wildhorn, the Wanderer prophesied that on his second appearance in these parts, it would be as desolate as it is now on the Santesch Pass. But while he was on the Gsteigberg, he gazed at and prayed before a crucifix. When he was asked about this, he answered that this was a correct likeness of the Saviour, a remark which was construed as a great compliment to the maker of the crucifix, Gabriel Luidl, court sculptor at Munich.[54] (Here the customary three visits have been cut to two, and there has been an interesting contamination with Tale 39, as well as some adventitious advertising for an identifiable mortal, the court sculptor. Such localizing can be expected at any time.)

54. A curious inversion of the sublegend turned up near Basel. On his first visit there, the Wandering Jew found a forest of fir trees; on his second, a single fir tree; and on the third, a large city, presumably without fir trees.[55] (That the city should become the climactic desolation in the usual formula might be explained simply by the fact that the inventor of the tale did not like cities. A better explanation, however, is to be inferred from a variant, Tale 55.)

55. When Ahasuerus travels through the Frick Valley, a region whose inhabitants are chiefly Catholic, as well as in the neighborhood of Basel itself, he always spends the night at the same inn, although he is out of his bed and moving about all night long until it is time to resume his journey at dawn. He will explain to all who will listen that when he first came to this little corner of the Rhine Valley where Basel is situated, he found only a dark pine forest; the second time, there were only extensive fields of bramble bushes; the third time, he saw the ruins of a large city thrown down by an earthquake; the last time he came that way, he had to look all over the neighborhood before he could find so much as a broomstick.[56] (The inference to be drawn is that Basel had better look to its morals, lest the old story of the destruction of Sodom and Gomorrah be repeated.)

56, 57, 58, 59, 60. There are several instances where the folk tale of the Wanderer has penetrated into Switzerland without taking the form of the sublegend. Thus there are vague references to him from Lengnau (Tale 56), Endingen (Tale 57), and the Frick Valley again (Tale 58) with no circumstantial detail to lend interest to the references.[57] At Gaiserwald (Tale 59) he was reported as a very old man, a beggar who walks hither and thither while he eats. The same tale comes from Anwill (Tale 60).[58]

61. The Swiss novelist Gottfried Keller (1819-1890), in his *Der grüne Heinrich* (1853), includes a short account by the shopkeeper Margret of how the Wandering Jew visited her town of Zurich: "Twelve years ago he spent the night at the Black Bear; I spent two hours in front of the house to see him leave; but in vain, for he left before the break of day."[59] (Although a literary reference of this sort may be technically out of place here, the fact remains that Margret's experience is characteristic of the sort of vague folk tale in which the whole German-speaking area abounds.)

62. Because of the difficult traveling in old Switzerland, Ahasuerus often found it convenient to wear shoes. (Some accounts will have it that he was habitually barefoot.) But he was prone to discard his shoes on a glacier because they were then an irksome burden. He once left a pair behind, along with his staff, in Bern, where Pastor Ulrich of Zurich saw them, the shoes uncommonly large and sewed together with a hundred stitches.[60] (Such a pair of shoes was actually on exhibition in the Bern library during part of the eighteenth century until they disappeared between 1773 and 1775, when the library underwent repairs and enlargement. Another pair of shoes, however, appeared in the Gewerbemuseum in Ulm, Germany, in 1856, the ultimate gift of a credulous female sheep dealer named Bässwenger. They had been left behind by a strange wanderer and penitent who had once had quarters for a night in the suburbs of the city. The contact with the Legend here is, of course, too tenuous to deserve more than passing note. Alleged relics of the Jew are an authentic part of his folklore, however obvious the kind of charlatanry which creates them.)

63. As further evidence that the Swiss are inclined to think of the Wanderer as a prophet of evil, his supernatural character is frequently emphasized. Thus at Niederbüren he casts a shadow a half-hour long—that is, a half-hour's walk long.[61]

64. On the lofty pass from Zermatt to Breil, the Wandering Jew once left a curse, and that curse lingers on, a malediction bringing desolation and danger to all passers-by. It is said, however, that St. Theodolus dispelled the curse, at least for a time, when he walked through the pass following exactly the footsteps of the Jew, conjuring away many venomous serpents before he had completed his journey. The mountain has therefore been named after him.[62]

Throughout the Alpine ranges, on both sides of both the Italo-Swiss and Franco-Swiss borders, the appearance of Ahasuerus foretells some sort of calamity. We may find other places where this sinister quality shows itself, but not to the same degree. It is not, to repeat, a common attribute of our Wanderer, who is just as likely to be benevolent as not. Yet why should not a magnificent yet barren land of ice, snow, glaciers, storms, and avalanches breed this ominous concept of the Wandering Jew? From mountains are spawned devils, giants, gnomes, trolls, and other infernal agents of greater or less power; within mountains are caves occupied by fabulous sleepers or legendary heroes who may return again. Mountains have beauty and grandeur, but they are also obstacles, sometimes deadly enemies of man. It is natural enough that Ahasuerus, who came to represent to many the followers of Antichrist, should become identified in the Alps with the legions of the unholy.

France, Flanders, and Luxembourg

There are very few allusions to the Wandering Jew in France before 1600. Such as they are, they appear to be imports from southern Europe in general and from Italy in particular (pp. 87-90 below). Flemish and Dutch tales seem to be derived from the Ahasuerus-book and material adapted from it. The Swiss sublegend may be found along the southeastern French frontier, and some of it penetrated farther into France.

65. At the boundary between France and Italy it is explained why the Wanderer no longer comes from Italy into France: the first time he came, there were fertile wheat fields; the second time God had placed there a fir forest because the Jew had passed through. When he came for the third time, he found that God had covered the place with perpetual ice and snow. "Bah," said the Jew, "when He sees his houses and fir trees treated in this way, the snow and ice will melt. I shall come back next year." But God heard him and said, "Nothing will melt, and until the day of the Last Judgment, the snow will stay there." That is why the Wandering Jew no longer travels from Italy to France.[63] (The inference to be drawn here is that the Jew came from Italy to France, not in the opposite direction; in short, it is recognized early that Italy is the distribution point. The Swiss sublegend had here been given a slightly French touch in the airy reaction of Ahasuerus to his disconcerting discovery.)

66. Coming over into the Brittany area we find that the Wanderer told the inhabitants near the forest of Haute-Sève that there, where were standing hundred-year-old oaks, he had once seen fields of grain.[64]

67, 68. An extension of this tale is told in La Chapelle, near St. Brieuc in Brittany (Tale 67), as well as in Chateauneuf, in the department of Sarthe (Tale 68). In these villages they have seen the Wandering Jew standing on spots which a dozen years before had been wastelands.[65] (This and the preceding are pale versions of Tale 65, but they remain recognizable as belonging to the Swiss sublegend, which has spread sufficiently through France to receive an implantation here and there, particularly where there is a sufficiently wild landscape, as in parts of Brittany.)

69. Thus one of the better examples of this particular type comes also from St. Brieuc. A fisherman's daughter told about a visit of Ahasuerus:

He was a tall, thin old man with a long white beard. He came to our home and we invited him in to rest; but he stood in the doorway and said, "I cannot sit but must always wander. This little village has changed greatly." "Then you have been here before?" I asked him. "Oh yes," he said, "a thousand years ago. All the land here was a huge forest, of which I now see no trace. Farewell!" And he departed.[66]

(This tale has its modern-sounding touches, no doubt, but the first part of it is almost a perfect example of the folk tale of the Wandering Jew: he seeks or is invited to shelter but cannot tarry. We may be sure that this tale is much older than the nineteenth-century setting which its collector gave it. But then a similar discounting must be made in most of the tales printed by collectors of the past century.)

70. In another Breton tale the fourteen-year-old son of a road worker near Chateaubriant in Loire-Inférieure reported that a few years before Ahasuerus had actually passed through the locality and found that the region had very greatly changed. For more than a thousand years, he said, there had been a forest here, in which wild animals and bandits went their lawless ways and threw the whole neighborhood into spasms of terror. While the inhabitants were idly lamenting this sorry state of things, the authorities decided to construct a large dam, the purpose of which was to shut off the sea water. All their endeavors, however, were useless; the water broke through the dam so violently that the forest and everything that it sheltered were destroyed. At the same time, the Wanderer did not assume credit for the disaster. He merely noted it in passing.[67] (It is likely that we have here a contamination with the Breton Legend of Ys, the submerged city punished thus for its sins. Actually it is a historical rationalization of the Legend—what the folklorists would call an etiological local tale.)

71. The Wandering Jew is sometimes, however, held responsible for the calamity of Ys in that he is made God's agent to bring about the disaster.[68]

72. Also associated with Ys, or Koz-Guedot, is the tale of how Boudedeo (*sic*) once met a peasant on the road and led him away to a market place; when the peasant returned home, he found that seven years had passed away.[69] (This is obviously a noteworthy contamination with an old folk motif of definitely Celtic currency—the miraculous passage of a long time, sometimes centuries, in an apparently short period.[70] The most noted example in literature is probably the Breton *lai* of *Guingamor*, attributed to Marie de France [*ca.*1200].)[71]

These Breton tales are of special interest because they seem to be among the few representatives of the Legend in any Celtic region before the appearance of sophisticated literary treatments of the protagonist. It is proper, I think, to credit the Breton *guerz* (p. 58 above) with being more sophisticated than otherwise, especially since it was indebted to the *Histoire admirable*. At the same time, there is nothing to suggest that the Legend was anything more than a foreign tale imported into Brittany: the frequency with which the Swiss sublegend appears is indication enough that Ahasuerus as harbinger and reporter of wastelands is not a native Breton.

Elsewhere among French-speaking people, there are no good accounts of the Wandering Jew until after the appearance of the *Kurtze Beschreibung* of 1602, with its progeny both domestic and foreign. One or two minor allusions only remain to be filed in this pigeonhole.

73. In the Maximein Forest near Hünsdorf in Luxembourg, a forester met an old man who had his hair growing down to his shoulders. The woodsman asked this venerable stranger where he was going and was told to mind his business, whereupon Ahasuerus, or Isaac Laquedem, for so the forester considered him, kept on his way.[72] (If this is to be included as an authentic folk tale of the Wanderer, it is certainly not a striking example, but it may be mentioned as illustrating the characteristic credulity of the peasant mind which helped to keep the Legend in circulation. The stranger here was neither benevolent nor evil, merely churlish.)

74. And at Jaunais an enormous stone lies in the woods, which is believed to be nothing less than a grain of sand which the Wandering Jew got out of his shoe.[73] (Obviously this is a contamination with the tradition of Gargantua, for Ahasuerus, apart from his occasional half-hour-long beard and a few other minor manifestations of such kind, is not ordinarily described in terms gigantic.)

Yet there is certainly in the treatment of the Wanderer in the folklore of France more than a hint of the monstrous as well as the sinister, which sometimes goes over into the outright evil, for there is an old saying when a storm wind howls without, "C'est le juif errant qui passe!" In epidemics and famines, the saying is, "The Wandering Jew has been here!"

Italy

The Italian folk tales concerning the Wandering Jew, as we might expect, remain Malchean in tendency, although Buttadeus has his innings. Some of them are closer to the eastern than the western type. Many were doubtless brought to Italy from the eastern Mediterranean, reported by Italian travelers such as those we have already heard of, and developed on their own. Some of them very likely contribute to, or are influenced by, the Antonio version. All who remember the accounts of Jan Aerts, Michel Menot, Carlo Ranzo (Soranzo), and others mentioned above (pp. 34-37), will recognize the relationship with such a folk tale as the following:

75. They say that the accursed Malchus lives chained at the bottom of the sea. All who approach him on the sea are drawn down to the depths. He is known to some also as Buttadeu and to others as Arributa-Diu. (The last of these names may still be heard in Partinico and Palermo and a few other places in Sicily; indeed it is peculiar to the island. The usual translation of it is something like "rebuffed by God.")[74]

76. In a version from Randazzo the narrator reports:

I have heard say that he is an old graybeard who constantly wanders about through the world. He bears a sack on his back and wears a turban and a shirt for covering, colored like dragon's blood. But still more ominous, a wooden club is in his hand. They call him Arributa-Diu, that is "repudiated by God" or "rejected by Christ," whom he himself rejected on the way to the Cross, when He wished to rest in his house. Everybody who meets him hears him tell, always moving along as he does so, of the Passion of Christ and of the hard buffets and torture which He endured. Then he begins to weep bloody tears.[75]

(The Orientalism of the turban is an eighteenth- or possibly late seventeenth-century detail; we saw this kind of head covering on the Jew's head in the market place at Frankfurt [Tale 20 above].)

77. Typical also is the tale, once told in the vicinity of Siena, of how the Wandering Jew lives under the earth, where he makes a great deal of noise digging a pit, which will reach into hell. They say that he is shut up in a chamber, where he continually moves about even while digging. Next to this chamber he has dug a sort of trench, in which he can now stand up to his nose. When he can get completely into the pit, the end of the world will be near.[76] (This tale might be compared with profit to such a Jerusalem tale as that told by Menot or Carlo Ranzo [pp. 34-35 above]. What is notable here is the subterranean activity.)

78. In popular parlance, an ugly person is said to have a "face like the Jew Marco (Malco, Malchus)."[77]

79. A person who cannot stand still for a moment "is a Buttadeo"; "is like Buttadeo"; "isn't still any more than Buttadeo"; "is always running around like Buttadeo."[78] (These expressions, and the one in Tale 78 above, are current in Sicily. Interestingly enough, there is an identical saying in Poland.)

80. The Wandering Jew wears a dirty hat with a broad brim, has very long hair and beard; both are white as snow. His expression is one of great suffering. His body is covered with a long, broad topcoat of deep red; his boots are badly torn.[79] (The wearing of a hat in contrast to his common bareheaded state in the north of Europe is probably imposed upon the Wanderer by the torrid Mediterranean sun, but Antichrist is often pictured traditionally wearing a foul kind of headpiece. The redness of the coat tends to suggest sinfulness and hell-fire. The torn condition of his footgear is hardly to be wondered at, since he is here not barefoot as he often is elsewhere.)

81, 82. At Borgofranco (Tale 81) it is said that the Wandering Jew gave Christ a blow on the cheek. His beard is so long that it must be fastened around his body. He always has five coins. He calls himself Il Balarin de Padova, or the Dancer of Padua.[80] (No explanation is forthcoming for this curious and unique nickname, but there must be contamination with some other tale. The same details appear in Tale 82 from Strambino.)

83, 84. Once he stopped at Donnaz, near the Swiss border, for oil—one may presume that it was olive oil (Tale 83). Across the frontier in Chiasso (Tale 84) he once bought a loaf of bread. And so it goes—pieces of trivia from various little places, small and isolated communities where few strangers ever appeared.[81]

85. The number of coins immediately available to the Wanderer on any given occasion is not necessarily restricted to five. In Salaparuta in Sicily the Wanderer is said to have appeared before the farmer Antonio Cascio and his youngest daughter while the two were staying in a hut in order to keep warm during a severe spell of winter weather. The daughter later testified that the hat and shoes worn by the strange visitor were striped yellow, red, and black. Antonio Cascio was greatly frightened by the sight of the intruder, but the latter calmed him, saying: "Don't be scared; my name is Buttadeo." Cascio immediately remembered

the Legend and invited the Jew to come in and sit by the fire and tell them the marvelous story of his wanderings. Buttadeo complied, but since he could not sit still, he kept moving constantly about the room, excited and restless, while he told his history. Before he left he taught them five prayers on the right hand as well as one on the left hand of Jesus.[82] (In short, we can add to the five coins in the Wanderer's inexhaustible purse and the five-studded print of his shoe the five prayers for the five fingers on the hand of Jesus—all symbolizing the five wounds of Christ. The color symbolism of the hat and shoes, if it has the conventional significance [though unfortunately the interpretation may be quite arbitrary in a given case], tallies in general with the circumstances of the tale—red for wrath or violence or sin; yellow for jealousy or presumption; black for evil portent, sin, or death.)

86. There are further variants from Sicily. In Borgetto, as well as in Palermo and Portinico, where the Malchean aspect is a favorite, it is told that the wicked *Abreu*—note that the Jew is here designated specifically as "wicked"—was sitting on a bench in front of the door of his house; and when Jesus, going by with the Cross on his shoulder, asked if he might rest, the Jew drove him away with words of abuse. "And so you will never have rest your life long," replied the Saviour; "you will wander forever and ever." And so it came to pass. Now he is old, yea, very old; but he can never die, this Jew who received the name Buttadeo, because he pushed Jesus away (*arribatau*). And many have seen him passing through Borgetto (or Palermo or Portinico), at midnight in the pouring rain, with thunder and lightning attending him. No one, however, has ever seen him standing still or accepting even a morsel of bread, because, as he himself says, it is forbidden for him to do so until the Last Judgment has been spoken.[83]

87. And furthermore the Sicilians explain that whoever meets the Wandering Jew must listen to him tell with relish the torments of Jesus, the pain and torture which he endured. In the meantime the God-pusher himself weeps bloody tears. (This emphasis on the violence and agony is evidently to the liking of the Sicilian folk imagination, as are the tears, which appeared sometimes, it will be recalled, in the Swiss sublegend—a detail very likely derived from the Italian folk tale.) In some quarters it is said that Marcus (Marco, Malco) gave Christ such a blow on the mouth with an iron glove that all his teeth were dashed out.[84]

88. But not all the tales from southern Italy and the neighboring islands are so definitely Malchean. One of the best simple examples from this region is Maltese, and for the sake of geographical convenience I am considering it along with the Italian:

Christ wished to take a rest in the house of the Kumbu. But the latter said, while he twirled a cinquina between his fingers: "This little house which belongs to me, Kumbu, is old and rickety. The very least shaking could bring it down, and this cross is much too heavy to find room in Kumbu's house. So clear out!" Then Christ said: "From this hour you are never to find rest anywhere, neither on earth nor at the bottom of the sea. But the money which you are twirling in your hand will always find its way back to you, so that you will know that no man can participate with you." And so it came to pass. The nails on his toes become like hoofs, his beard reaches to the ground, his nose and mouth are awry, and he has long black teeth. He made faces at our Lord. Every forty or fifty years he goes to Jerusalem to look at his house, but he cannot find it, for at the moment when the Cross was put into the ground, the house collapsed.[85]

(We have here an explanation, however belated, of the purse that cannot be exhausted: the Jew's money returns to him so that no human being can share in even an economic communion with him. Although the house is never seen again by its owner, it is unique to have it disappear at the particular time specified in this tale. As for the various deformities or anomalies of appearance suffered by the protagonist, they are often matched elsewhere, although it is rare to find so many detailed in one folk tale.)

89. As might be expected, as one travels north into Alpine Italy, one may note appearances of the Swiss sublegend, although it is not too common. One such tale, however, centers about the Valley of Aosta. Where now rises the great peak of Monte Cervino (the Matterhorn), there was once a prosperous city, in which the Wandering Jew had once received friendly treatment, so that he was able to rest his weary limbs for a time. But when he returned a thousand years later, he found in place of the city this monstrous mountain. Deeply distressed over the fate of the city and its people, he wept for so long a time that his tears formed the black lake across the Swiss frontier not far from Zermatt.[86] (This is essentially the same tale as Tale 52.)

90. Finally, there is a Venetian tale of more facetious nature. Here the Wandering Jew, again as Malchus, wheels about a pillar or column standing on a hill. He keeps beating his head and ears, as he once gave a box on the ears—not to Jesus, but to his mother Mary! Here also he stamps out a ditch beneath him in the course of his circumambulations, and he is moving at present up to his neck in the ditch. As in the Siena tale (Tale 77), when he sinks below his head in the ditch, the end of the world will be at hand. But to God alone is left the disposition of the fate which will overtake Malchus after the end of the world. In the meantime, he has no prospect of any early relief from pain. If anyone comes along the way over the hill where the Wanderer is beating his head against the pillar, the Jew will ask him, "Excuse me, how late is it in the day? Are women still being beaten?" The passerby must say Yes, as if it were taken for granted. Thereupon Malchus or Buttadeus will sigh deeply and say, "Then it still isn't time, for before the world comes to an end, women won't have been beaten with a club for seven years!"[87] (The misogynistic twist of this tale, which, with its Siena counterpart, is a version of the Jerusalem tales of Malchus [p. 35 above], begins with the deviation that the original insult was to Mary rather than to Jesus. All it seems to tell us is that it owes its existence to someone who must have had a poor opinion of women. The core of the tale, however, was undoubtedly imported by some Venetian returning from the Holy Land.)

Britain

None of the English popular versions of the Legend has the same vitality as characterized the folk tales of the Wandering Jew on the Continent. Yet it is clear that the saga of Ahasuerus had currency in England, and even some degree of popularity, but this currency and popularity alike seem to have spent themselves under the surface, so to speak. Apart from the versions derived from the Ahasuerus-book (pp. 60-61 above), many of the so-called folk tales of the Wandering Jew in England may not be concerned with him directly at all, although they may well have been suggested by his tradition.[88]

91. The celebrated collector of curious biographical lore, not to say gossiper, John Aubrey (1626-1697), notes in his *Miscellanies* (1696) that a poor man in the moorlands of Staffordshire, back in the 1650's, heard a stranger knock on his door one day and ask for some beer. Since the aged man had been ill for some time, it was an effort to satisfy the request, and yet he did so, and was rewarded by the stranger's recommendation of certain therapeutic procedures to cope with the illness. The old man followed his advice and recovered fully. The stranger left almost immediately and was never seen again; the distinctive purple shag gown which he wore had made him conspicuous.[89]

92. Virtually the same story, in greater detail, is told in Francis Peck's *Academia Tertia Anglicana: Or the Antiquarian Annals of Stamford in Lincoln, Rutland, and Northampton Shires* (London, 1727):

Upon Whitsunday, in the year of our Lord 1658, about six of the clock, just after even song, one Samuel Wallis of Stamford, who had been long wasted with a lingering consumption, was sitting by the fire, reading in that delectable book called *Abraham's Suit for Sodom*. He heard a knock at the door; and as his nurse was absent, he crawled to open it himself. What he saw there, Samuel shall say in his own style:

"I beheld a proper, tall, grave old man. Thus he said: 'Friend, I pray thee, give an old pilgrim a cup of small beere!' And I said: 'Sir, I pray you, come in and welcome.' And he said: 'I am no Sir, therefore call me not *Sir*; but come in I must, for I cannot pass by thy door.'

"After finishing the beere, 'Friend,' he said, 'thou art not well.' I said, 'No, truly, Sir, I have not been well this many years.' He said, 'What is thy disease?' I said, 'A deep consumption, Sir; our doctors say, past cure; for, truly, I am a very poor man, and not able to follow doctors' counsel.' 'Then,' said he, 'I will tell thee what thou shalt do; and, by the help and power of Almighty God above, thou shalt be well. Tomorrow, when thou risest up, go into thy garden, and get there two leaves of red sage, and one of bloodwort, and put them into a cup of thy small beere. Drink as often as need require, and when the cup is empty fill it again, and put in fresh leaves every fourth day, and before twelve days shall be past, thy disease shall be cured and thy body altered.' " After this simple prescription, Wallis pressed him to eat. "But he said, 'No, friend, I will not eat; the Lord Jesus is sufficient for me. Very seldom do I drink any beere, neither, but that which comes from the rock. So, friend, the Lord God be with thee.' "

So saying he departed, and was never more heard of; but the patient got well within the given time, and for many a long day there was war hot and fierce among the divines of Stamford, as to whether the stranger was an angel or a devil. His dress has been minutely described by honest Sam. His coat was purple, and buttoned down to the waist: "his britches of white, but whether linen or jersey, deponent knoweth not; his beard and head were white, and he had a white stick in his hand. The day was rainy from morning to night, but he had not one spot of dirt upon his clothes."

It is a question whether we have any right to call either Tale 91 or 92 a folk tale of the Wandering Jew. It is true that they both present a mysterious stranger of beneficent purpose; and his dress and general appearance correspond well enough to some of the descriptions of Ahasuerus in unmistakable tales of the Wanderer. But not every mysterious stranger is the Wandering Jew, and not every Jew who wanders is necessarily he. Yet these two tales may well have been suggested by the Legend of the Wandering Jew, even if there is nothing to connect the stranger with the basic legendary event on the day of the Crucifixion. There are one or two points for comment, even so. If we take the stranger to be Ahasuerus, we should then note his thirst here. In respect to drinking, the Wanderer is *usually* abstemious in the folk tales, although we have seen that in the account of the Antonio version and in the German tale from Lübeck (Tale 26), he could partake of wine or schnapps without urging.[90] In the later literary treatments of the Legend, of course, he may be a debauchee. Most unusual here, also, is the white raiment, the symbolism of which, indicating immortality, is obvious but nevertheless rarely encountered in the Legend. For the rest, Peck's account is a remarkably fine example of the sophistication of a folk tale, when it is compared to the version told by Aubrey.

93. Equally ambiguous is the story told by V. T. Sternberg in 1855. It is true, to be sure, that the description of the protagonist here is the one traditionally given, but again there is no direct linkage with the classic form of the Legend:

. . . Sometimes, during the cold winter nights, the lonely cottager will be awoke [*sic*] by a plaintive demand for "Water, good Christians! Water, for the love of God!" And if he looks out into the moonlight, he will see a venerable old man in antique raiment, with gray flowing beard and a tall staff, who beseeches his charity with the most earnest gesture. Woe to the churl who refuses him water or shelter! My old nurse, who was a Warwickshire woman, knew a man who boldly cried out: "All very fine, Mr. Ferguson, but you can't lodge here." And it was decidedly the worst thing he ever did in all his life, for his best mare fell dead lame, and corn went down, I am afraid to say how much, per quarter. If, on the contrary, you treat him well, and refrain from indelicate inquiries respecting his age—on which point he is very touchy—his visit is sure to bring you good luck. Perhaps years afterwards, when you are on your deathbed, he may happen to be passing; and if he should, you are safe, for three knocks with his staff will make you hale, and he never forgets any kindnesses. Many stories are current of his wonderful cures [But if there were such stories, they have evaporated before they ever got into print.][91]

(This narrative immediately suggests contamination with another legend. The motivating great thirst of the visitant is appropriate enough in a land fond of its ale and tea, but there is a strong likelihood that there has been here a transference of the thirst of Christ on the Cross to the man who traditionally insulted him. To be noted also is the fact that one of the headwaters of the Legend of the Wild Huntsman is an obscure tale of a Jew who, when Christ wished a drink on his way to the Cross, referred him to a puddle in the street.)

In the seventeenth-century tales told by Aubrey and Peck, the attitude of the stranger is benevolent. He seems to be devoting his indefinite stay on earth to the accomplishment of good deeds. This praiseworthy existence is in contrast to that in Tale 93, for there the Wanderer is kind only if he is not crossed and is willing to bring down misfortune on those who rebuff him, as he does in some of the tales on the Continent. Nevertheless, all three of these English tales (91, 92, and 93) seem to be on the fringe of the Legend only, and are tantalizing in what they imply but do not tell of the Legend in England. It is amusing for the stranger, if he is the Wandering Jew, to be addressed as "Mr. Ferguson"—certainly a unique name, but one which reminds the reader irresistibly and irrelevantly of the fictitious name imposed upon the unfortunate Italian guide by the unregenerate Mark Twain and his doctor friend in *Innocents Abroad*.

94. A more definite indication of the furtive survival of the Legend in British oral tradition appears in the following incident told first by Moncure D. Conway. This particular recognition of the Wandering Jew in England, however, is more characteristic of the Celt than of the Saxon. One James Pearson reported from the Lancashire moors that one evening in 1866 he was in the company of an "intelligent old man" when they suddenly heard above their heads the cry of the dotterel, a bird of the plover family. The old man observed that in his youth old people considered such a happening a bad omen, for the person who heard "the Wandering Jew," as he called the dotterel, would certainly be overtaken by some misfortune. In reference to the name which had been given the birds, he explained that there was a tradition according to which they were the souls of those Jews who had participated in the Crucifixion of Christ, and as a consequence had been condemned to fly about forever in the air.[92] (There is something of a resemblance between this and Tales 7 and 8; these Russian tales in turn probably derive from the Jerusalem tale [pp. 35-36 above] which dealt with the Jews participating in the Crucifixion. The likelihood is great that this particular version came to England from travelers to the Holy Land—that, in other words, the English and Russian tales derive from the common source in Jerusalem.)

95. And as a certain kind of bird may be thus associated with the Wandering Jew, so with the flora as well as the fauna. A few plants are known as the "Wandering Jew," particularly *Zebrina pendula,* a fast-growing leafy plant of special hardiness, which will grow in either sun or shade. The name is applied also to a kind of spiderwort (*Tradescantia fluminensis*), to the beefsteak or strawberry geranium (*Saxifraga sarmentosa*), and to the Kenilworth ivy (*Cymbalaria muralis*). I can find no record of this name applied to any one of these four plants, however, before the middle of the nineteenth century. The creeping habits of the ivy and the quasi-perennial nature of all four evidently appealed to some imaginative popular naturalists, living in an age when romantic names were fashionable, whose fortune it was to give them names which stuck.

Yet when it comes to tracing the original christener of the birds or the plants, of course, it is always a case of the oldest inhabitant who remembers his grandfather's having said something once about his own grandfather's friend who had heard somewhere why this bird or this plant was called the "Wandering Jew," and so the real facts are never forthcoming.[93]

96. A Glamorganshire tale, material for a bad Gothic novel, has it that a farmer had an unmarried daughter. One day a stranger came to the farm and asked for lodgings. He stayed with the family for two months and was accepted as one of them. He was so popular in the vicinity and so well liked at the farm that he tar-

ried through the winter, devoting himself to study, contemplation, and the unmarried daughter. The rumor spread that he was paying court to the squire's
daughter also. The sons of the farmer protested for their sister's sake, but this
only served to drive the stranger away: "It is my fate to win love; it is my doom
never to marry." The daughters of the farmer and of the squire became fast
friends after this, but the farmer's daughter pined away and died two years later.
After twenty years had gone by, the squire's daughter, her baronet husband,
and the farmer were visiting the girl's grave when the mysterious stranger suddenly appeared, moved over the grave, and disappeared. The consensus was that
he could be none other than the Wandering Jew.[94]

97. Beside this sickly romantic yarn, a Carmarthenshire tale from the nineteenth century is much tauter as narrative and far closer to a true folk tale, although the telling of it is expressed melodramatically to the point of bathos. The
narrator is a squire:

It seems that when his father was a youth, he met a remarkably clever stranger, who
appeared to have studied all that was possible in the world. Languages, art, science, music, and a host of other things were at his fingers' ends. He had traveled all over the
world and was a most interesting companion. For six months they traveled together and
then parted. Before parting, the stranger told his companion that they would meet and
be together on three separate occasions of their lives. "After our third meeting and
parting," said the stranger, "you will die, but I shall continue to wander until the day of
doom." The younger man in due course became squire, was married and had children.
When he was about fifty, the stranger reappeared in Carmarthenshire, and was as interesting as ever. The squire invited him to his seat, and when alone, laughingly reminded
the stranger of his prophecy. "It will be verified to the letter," said his guest. Later on
the visitor took his leave. The squire lived until he was 86, and then revealed the story
to his son. The latter thought it was an old man's fancy, and humored it but little. A
year later, the stranger appeared again, and visited the old squire, who was delighted to
see his former friend. Two days he stayed, and when taking leave of the squire he said:
"Good-bye, my dear old friend. You will never see me again." The next night the squire
died, murmuring as he peacefully passed away: "The Wandering Jew! the Wandering
Jew!"[95]

These British folk tales are admittedly poor specimens; they may some of them
even be spurious. Perhaps they were once more numerous and more characteristic, but they have become shadowy and untrustworthy by the time they have
been recorded. We may concede that the British knew the Legend; they have done
virtually nothing, however, to develop it. Why this stunted growth of the Legend
in Britain? Perhaps one answer lies in the temperament of the British country-
man of the seventeenth and eighteenth centuries, who would of all Britons be
most likely to accept the Legend. Perhaps, indeed, the Puritan tradition is too
discouraging to the dissemination, on any wide scale, of such a fantastic and essentially unchristian legend as that of the Wandering Jew. Perhaps the small proportion of Jews in the British population has tended to render the Legend somewhat remote; but a similar situation in Italy did not discourage the Legend. Or
perhaps the trueborn Englishman considered the Legend a secondhand kind of
"foreign," even popish, tale. Whatever the reason, the English Puritan and the

Scottish Covenanter drew a sharper line than most between the didactically imaginative and the fantastically incredible—they might create a *Pilgrim's Progress* but would frown upon a pamphleteer's *Volksbuch*. Still, British folklore is remarkably rich in local traditions and legends. Perhaps the true answer lies just there—they prefer the local native legend to the migratory imported one.

Slavic Countries

I have already cited some Russian examples of the folk tale of the Wandering Jew to illustrate the eastern version of the Legend (Tales 7-11). A few others, however, are representative of the more common western version. The likelihood is that most, if not all, of the following came over into Russia from German-speaking people in eastern Germany and Poland.

98. Thus we have a good example in a Ukrainian tale, first written down in Galicia:

. . . when Christ was going to be crucified, carrying the Cross on his back, he grew tired and stopped to rest beside a Jew's house. The Jew came out of his house and said to Jesus, "Go, go, don't stand beside my house!" The Saviour looked at him and said, "From this day forth, Jew, you shall wander forever till the Last Judgment." Then the Jew's wife came out of the house and said to Christ, "Well, why have you stopped here? Go on!" (*Jdi dali buk*). And Christ said to her, too, "You shall wander here on earth forever," and went on toward Calvary. Since then people have used *Jdi dali buk* as an oath, but it is a sin to say it. Immediately after Christ's Resurrection, the Jew and the Jewess began roaming the earth, and they are still wandering, unable to find any rest. As soon as they come to a village, they must go to another. They do not travel together; rather each goes alone. Every hundred years they meet again and talk a while; then they must part again.

The Wandering Jewess' appearance bespeaks a fairly late date for this tale, certainly not before the nineteenth century. This unwonted mate for the Wandering Jew must be considered later [Appendix B]. *Jdi dali buk* means more than "Go on," because the Ukrainian word for God (*buk*) is sooner or later involved, hence no doubt the taboo on the expression as blasphemous. The general idea of the phrase is "God, get out!")[96]

99. A White Russian version, first gathered in Poland, asks: "Why does the Jew wander on earth?" "When Christ was carrying the Cross up Mount Calvary, he grew weary and leaned his cross against the house of a certain Jew. When the Jew noticed this, he ran out and said in a sing-song: 'You will knock over my house!' To which Christ retorted: 'You shall wander till the end of the world!' So from that day on the Jew has wandered and wandered, and he has already gone around the world twice."[97] (Note here the resemblance to the first part of the Maltese folk tale, Tale 88. It is to be presumed that the reference here is only to the guilty Jew, not to all Jews; we have not reached the point of sophistication which sees the Wandering Jew as symbolic of the whole Jewish race.)

100. Throughout Poland, but particularly in the region near East Prussia and the Masurian Lakes, the saying "He is as restless as the Wandering Jew" is com-

mon, applied especially to children.[98] (This was noted also in Italy, as in Tale 79, but the widespread nature of the saying is such that it may be regarded as a commonplace wherever the Legend is known.)

101. Some of the Baltic versions are rather elaborate, being mixed with all kinds of other traditional material and therefore often rather remote from the true Legend. Thus in Lithuania it is said that once upon a time, during the Passion of Jesus in Jerusalem, there lived a Jew named Ahasuerus. He was a miser, uncharitably envious, altogether a very bad man. He exploited the poor, deceived and swindled them so as to gather ever more riches to himself. When Jesus was going to the place of judgment and was weary along the way, he wanted to rest on the threshold of the house of Ahasuerus, but the malicious Jew ran out and drove Jesus away, saying: "If you could make me live forever, you could stay here." He said this because he did not want his property to go to someone else. Jesus granted him this wish. At first the Jew was happy to think he would never die and leave his property to someone else, but gradually he lost his possessions and became a poor wanderer. Now others paid him back for the evil he had done before. So one year after another went by; the Jew became older, but death did not come to him. He survived many and many a generation; all his friends and relatives had died, and it was tedious and sad for him to be left in the world. He had ceaselessly longed for death, but death has never come. He has tried many times to kill himself, in vain.[99] (This, too, with its melancholy conclusion, is probably of late vintage. The original motive for wandering has been altered. There is here in capsule form, however, the central idea of most of the romantic treatments of the Legend in belles-lettres, although the various motives for the conduct of the protagonist can take many different forms. In all such cases, though, the point is that the Wanderer discovers sooner or later that his immortality puts him in a desolate and hopeless human situation.)

102. A mutilated version of the foregoing is also Lithuanian. The Wandering Jew lived in Palestine. There he wandered about in all the houses and bought all kinds of wares. One evening Jesus came to him. He asked shelter with him for the night. The Jew refused him. Jesus, on his departure, cursed him with these words: "May you, dying, never die!" From this time on he has been the Wandering Jew.[100] (The departures from the norm here are too obvious for comment.)

103. It is apparent from the following Lithuanian tale that it also is pretty well romanticized and over-sententious for an honest folk tale:

While Jesus was being led to Golgotha, a Jew laughed at Him and asked whether such a one could have eternal life on earth. Then Jesus cursed him and said: "You will live until the whole earth turns to dust and ashes!" At first the Jew was very happy about the fact that he had achieved so long a life. When he was one hundred years old, he became somewhat rejuvenated; and this was repeated every hundred years. After a while, however, he became bored with life and longed for death; he flung himself into abysses, into rivers and oceans to drown himself, but always some lucky circumstance made it necessary for him to continue to live. In his unending life he wandered about in all lands, and wherever he was led to settle down, misfortune and disaster happened. So he still wanders about today and tries at every opportunity to kill himself, but he never succeeds. At the end of every hundred years he gets young again; and while posting about through the world, he constantly regrets the folly of having wished for eternal life.[101]

(The sinister effect that Ahasuerus has wherever he settles down is the familiar contamination with the Legend of Cain.)

104. Another kind of contamination comes at the conclusion of the preceding Lithuanian tale:

A Jew had lived for a long time and had prayed that he might never die. Then God decided that he should live. Now he had become so old that all who saw him were afraid. He himself had become tired of life and wanted to die but could not. So whenever he heard of mortal illnesses he went to see the dying. But he still could not die. Once a little cloud, like a thimble, appeared in the heavens. This carried him away, so that no one saw what had happened to him.

(The Legend of Enoch, in somewhat fanciful form, may be present at the end, although the resemblance is rather vague. But the little cloud reminds us of the cloud in I Kings 18:44, "like a man's hand," which is associated with Elijah's bringing rain. Whether Enoch or Elijah—both were translated to heaven—the influence of the scriptural tradition seems apparent here. Even more important is the fact that the original circumstances of the Legend of the Wandering Jew have faded completely out of the tale.)

105. Thus far the rejection of the Saviour in these Slavic folk tales, when it is actually stated, is limited to the verbal rebuff or refusal of the Lord's request. In this Estonian folk tale, which is otherwise undistinguished, the rejection may be more physical, more Malchean. Here the Wandering Jew, along with other Jews, was driving Jesus along while he was carrying his Cross to Golgotha. Jesus became very weary and wished to rest himself, but this particular Jew granted him no rest; then Jesus said to him: "You too will never have any rest." And now this Wandering Jew lives forever; he has wanted to put an end to his life many times and in many ways, but he has never succeeded, and he goes through the world as the Wandering Jew, until the Last Judgment.[102] (The frustrated desire of Ahasuerus to kill himself is not a prominent detail of the Legend until the late seventeenth century and is always something of a refinement.)

106. In another Estonian tale, Jesus throws himself down in exhaustion across the threshold of a certain house. This house belongs to a Jew, who comes and pushes the Cross away from the threshold with his foot. When the curse of Jesus sets him wandering, he goes out of one town into another, from one land to another, seeking death. He casts himself into a volcano, expecting death, but the lava throws him far away from there. He seeks death in battle but does not find it. Finally he throws himself into the sea, but the waves cast him back on shore. So the curse of Jesus never lets him taste death. His children and grandchildren all die from one generation to the next, but Ahasuerus still wanders in this world, seeking oblivion.[103] (This tale in outline bears a striking resemblance to the gist of Schubart's poem of 1783, which, as we shall see [pp. 171-73], breaks the path for a whole succession of treatments of the Legend written in the Byronic vein.)

107. Much the same story, with a few touches of would-be verisimilitude, is the

Estonian tale of the immortal Jew who leaped into a fire-spitting mountain but could not perish. His hair is so long that it trails the ground. At the end of every hundred years he is rejuvenated. Forty years before, he visited the monastery of Arensburg on the island of Ösel. He will not die before the Saviour comes again.[104]

108. Often the race of the protagonist is never specified in a given tale, so that we have the same quality as in the early medieval references to the Legend. The temptation is to regard such tales as older than others, but this is not provable, however likely it may be. Thus from Wesenberg, in Estonia, the story is that when Jesus was carrying his Cross to the hill of Golgotha and grew weary, he leaned it against the edge of the roof of a shoemaker's house. The shoemaker began to quarrel with him and drove him away. Jesus said, "Your tribe shall never have its own place." Since that time the tribe of shoemakers has been vagabonding around the world.[105] (The evidence for antiquity in the non-Hebraic troublemaker is somewhat canceled out by the fact that he is a shoemaker. As we have seen, it is difficult to spot the origin of this detail: we have seen it in Spain in the sixteenth century; we have it in a folk tale from the Near East [Tale 2]; and here it is in Estonia, collected late in the nineteenth century. I suspect that there has been contamination with a separate legend about shoemakers, which is a bit of migratory folklore—the Germans have an old saying that the shoemaker is the *Urvater der Zigeuner*, "the ancestor of the gypsies," although this saying is not widespread. If, however, we note the existence of a tradition that shoemakers must wander about, then we have a plausible explanation of how the Wandering Jew became a shoemaker. For if shoemakers wander, and the Wandering Jew wanders, then the Wandering Jew is a shoemaker.)

109. A variant of the preceding, however, emerges also from the area of Wesenberg. Here the occupant of the house is said to be a Jew. Otherwise the two tales are virtually the same, except for the comment in this second tale that this Jew, who now still "lives in this world," cannot be wounded—even a cannon ball will make no impression upon him. He can recall only his long life-history and knows nothing of what has happened in the world since he began wandering, in this respect differing from the general conception of the Wandering Jew in later literary treatments.[106]

110. A most curious tale, which must be a local legend that has somehow been connected with the Wandering Jew, derives also from Estonia:

One summer, early in the morning, came two young men, Mart and Mihkel, out of a thicket in Sillu and started home. They had things to do in Sillu; for that reason they had gone there the day before and spent the night; now, early in the morning, a little after sunrise, they started on the way home.

They had gone a couple of versts, when they saw a huge man coming their way. He was so tall that his head was as high as the forest; the stick that he carried in his hand was of juniper-wood, and so thick that one could have used it for a narrow beam. He wore peasant's shoes, with two black sacks on his back, and his gait was so slow that he could hardly place one foot halfway ahead of the other.

When the men saw him, they were at first very much afraid, but when they came up to him, they had recovered to such an extent that they ventured to greet him.

But as the huge man raised his head to see who had greeted him, his eyes lit up the wood so much that the men once more became altogether frightened, and as he responded to their greeting, the men stood still with stiff limbs and gawked at him, for his voice rumbled like thunder, so that the woods echoed. Then, when the huge man passed by them, Mart came to himself sufficiently to realize that he had gone, and Mihkel also. But they fled. Some four versts they ran thus, one after the other, without saying a word. Then Mart said: "What a monster that was!" Mihkel had neither time nor wish to answer, but tried to hurry past Mart. Mart, seeing this, was silent and ran farther, lest he have to stay behind Mihkel. Mihkel, on his part, came near Mart, although he was still running behind him.

So they ran for another verst; Mihkel recovered the power of speech and began to talk to Mart, who had recovered earlier.

When they told about this in the village, people who, they said, had also seen the same sight, believed it to have been the Wandering Jew, who moves restlessly in the world and awaits the Last Judgment.

Some said that they also had seen him before.

When Mart, a year later, came to Mihkel again on some sort of business, Mihkel asked him, "Do you remember what happened when we came out of the woods at Sillu?" "Yes, as if it were only yesterday," replied Mart.

These men are still alive [in 1902] and have told this tale many times, and their accounts tally.[107]

(A sinister-looking stranger is met in an ominous landscape in a country in which deep woods are believed to harbor all kinds of gnomes, spooks, and lesser bogies. The incident is magnified by fright and the helpful imagination of a sympathetic audience, and the stranger is identified as the Wandering Jew. This is a good example of the factors, starting with an ordinary incident, which can combine to produce a folk tale referable to the true Legend of the Wandering Jew only by extension.)

Hungary

Apart from the chapbooks already mentioned (p. 68), there appears to have been a rather vague knowledge of the Legend in Hungary, but everything which has thus far come to light seems to be derivative and unoriginal, and the German *Volksbuch* is still the leading source of whatever acquaintance there may be with the Legend. The saying, "He is as restless as the Wandering Jew," which we have recognized already as a commonplace, has been known in Hungary for several generations, and an entry in an almanac for 1924 shows that the Legend was circulating among the Hungarian people, as it was then circulating all over Europe. A ballad was transcribed by A. Scheiber in Mezőkövesd as late as 1954; it contains all the essential features of the classic account and treats them in most orthodox fashion.[108] Much more will undoubtedly be found if the digging is done soon enough, but at present the Hungarian contribution is not in any way remarkable.

America

The same is hardly true of those few American contributions to the library of folk tales concerning the Wandering Jew, and yet it is admitted that all such tales in America must be derivative, imported from that particular segment of European population where the local legend may have sprung. For all folk tales in the Western Hemisphere are local, unless it can be shown that they originate among the inhabitants who were here before the advent of the white man.

111. We may ignore the ambitious title of Phoebe Dey Jackson's *The History of the Wandering Jew*, for it is by no means a study of the Legend nor even an example of the Chronicle of the Wandering Jew (pp. 141-60), but a bit of folklore from the Finger Lakes region of New York. It was published at Geneva, New York, in 1898. The author explains that the story of the Wandering Jew of Lake Seneca had been known to the older inhabitants of Geneva, but only a few thereabouts knew of the great Legend itself. In other words, this is to be a strictly local legend:

As a child, she was one of a party of some 150 Genevans invited by Captain Joseph Lewis of the steamboat "Geneva" to visit a spot on the shores of Lake Seneca reputed to be haunted by the mysterious Wandering Jew. She suffered much childish disappointment when she saw only a tree floating upright in the water, its branches and roots blackened by age and worn by the waves. A few hours later, however, the tree was seen floating with its roots instead of its top sticking up in the air. Then, to her surprise, the tree disappeared entirely. It has not been seen since, and that was fifty years ago, although one still hears vague and discredited rumors to the contrary, rumors which invariably speak of a strange white log.

In the meantime, however, while the group was on this excursion, the child's teacher, Miss Martha Tillinghast, sympathizing with her little charge's evident disappointment, offered to tell her why the floating tree was called the Wandering Jew. It had come originally from historical Hector Falls, near the town of Watkins. Once the local Indians, of a tribe ruled by the semi-legendary Queen Katharene, discovered that a mysterious being often traveled among the ravines and woodlands of the lake country and was seen only at night. Supposing it to be a spirit doomed to wander over the face of the earth for at least a thousand years, they avoided it with great care, hiding away in terror whenever there was a hint of its presence. At last some unnamed hardy soul discovered that the visitor was a Jew, but this fact could not dispel the superstition that he should be left strictly alone, for any violence directed against him would undoubtedly bring calamity to the tribe and its queen. But the suspense created by his visits proved too great. A council was held to decide how to get rid of him without violence. It was concluded that he must be lurking about for the purpose of assassinating Queen Katharene, and that it would be necessary to drive him to earth and then expel him from the neighborhood. After a long watch he was discovered, pursued, and cornered by the warriors. Escaping suddenly, he darted away in the direction of Hector Falls. In his terror he leaped over a precipice in the darkness, grasping as he did so the branches of a small tree, to which he clung until it was torn from the edge of the cliff by his weight. The site of his plunge was marked by the Indians, who painted a white spot on the face of the rock, to this day called "the painted rock." The Indians searched for years to find the body of the visitor. But in vain; they found only the tree to which he had clung, floating at the foot of Hector Falls, as it has continued to float off and on for over a century. Supposing that the tree was also searching for the corpse of the victim, the would-be assassin of their queen (as they believed), they named it the Wandering Jew.

(It would seem that this is a legitimate local Indian folk tale—there are many sinister strangers and death leaps in Indian legendry—which has been contaminated in a curious manner with the Legend of the Wandering Jew. Evidently, in spite of the author's statement about the rarity of the true Legend, there were enough local inhabitants familiar with it to perpetuate it, if only indirectly. To judge by the history of the settlement of the colony and state of New York, these would probably be British rather than Dutch, because the Dutch official occupation of New York comes a little too early for a folk tale to have been imported by them from the Continent. The probability is that this local tale is post-Revolutionary.)

112. An item in the *Deseret News* of Salt Lake City for September 23, 1868, reports that two little boys in Hart's Corners, New York (no longer identifiable as such), "a few miles from New York, discovered a grotesquely aged man in a cave; he had with him extracts from the Talmud and what purported to be credentials to prove that he was the Wandering Jew." (Although this event is reported from Utah, it is still said to have happened in the state of New York, where a few memories of the Legend doubtless lingered in the nineteenth century. For this reason the authenticity of the foregoing becomes entirely suspect when we learn that its source is a newspaper in Utah, for the Mormon settlers of Utah, many of whom, like the founder of their religion, had roots deep in the state of New York, seemed to have a natural predilection for an outcropping of the Legend.)

113. There originated in Utah, spreading out wherever the Mormons and their missionaries went, the Legend of the Three Nephites,[109] which gives every sign of being a derivative of the Legend of the Wandering Jew—a kind of three-way split of the Legend, so to speak—made possible by the presence of the original Legend in the background of Mormonism.

It is essential to bear in mind that Mormon theology arose from the Judaeo-Christian tradition. According to the Book of Mormon, there was once in Jerusalem, at the time of Zedekiah (*ca.*600 B.C.), a faithful soul named Lehi, who, disgusted with the iniquities of the children of Israel, migrated with his family and eventually settled in South America, where one son, Nephi, begat the white inhabitants of that continent, and another, Laman, begat the redskins. After the Resurrection, Christ himself went to South America and established there his Church, as told in the Book of Nephi, and he had twelve disciples there as he had had twelve in Galilee. When he left, he took with him nine of the twelve. The remaining three, at their own request, were left to await his second coming, in the meantime preaching his word and doing his works. This is an obvious version in triplicate of the Legend of St. John, as we saw it represented in Cartaphilus; indeed, the wording of the Book of Nephi (p. 28) is strongly reminiscent of that in John 21, for the three Nephites are not to taste of death until they see Him again and are transformed from mortals to immortals. They were once caught up to heaven for a brief visit. There they saw ineffable things. Later they returned to fulfill their missions, wandering as emissaries of the Lord all over the face of the earth, doing all good in so far as it was their fortune to accomplish, miraculously untouched by dangers of any and all types. And thus they are still wandering.

When the Nephites are seen by men, usually only by Mormons, they appear as individuals, never as a trio. The Nephite is poor and simple in speech and behavior; his clothing is ragged and untidy; he has white hair and a long white beard, and is tall and lean of build; but although he is obviously very old, he is always in vigorous health. There survive some sixty accounts of a Nephite visitation, some oral and some written. In most instances the Nephite will be approachable and may even ask for bread or clothing, but he has a trick of disappearing suddenly. In fact, this vanishing act is typical, and in many of the tales the mysterious appearance and disappearance of the stranger is the chief point of the story. In others, the stranger is important as the bearer of a message—in defense of Mormonism or on the significance of events of the past two thousand years. Again, he may be a healer, either moral or physical; he will counsel patience in distress; he will furnish missing genealogical information to those seeking it; he will guide lost wayfarers; he will tactfully notify of death; he will prophesy war or peace, sickness or recovery from sickness; he is especially helpful in bringing food and wished-for messages to those who are in want. At other times he appears for no very good reason, unless it be to illustrate the wonders which God can perform; and here he ranges far and wide, from Vancouver to Georgia, and from Mexico to West Virginia. (Otherwise the Legend in America, if not the business of some consciously artistic writer, survives only in the memories of settlers of English or German extraction.)

Miscellaneous

It is always an untidy matter to consider the miscellaneous, but there is a great convenience in doing so when we observe some folk tales which are not in themselves particularly important but which are interesting as deviants, in this way or that, from the norm of the Legend.

114. We have virtually nothing in the way of Spanish or Portuguese folk tales in printed collections, but the following indicates that there is still life in the old Legend in those parts. This is the diverting incident reported by an anonymous contributor to the London *Academy* in 1884:

Two friends of his, with unusually long beards, were greeted in Burgos by a crowd of children with the cry: "Look, see the sons of the Wandering Jew!" Stones were thrown at them, which so upset one of them that he gave up the exploration of a land in which he found the memory of this Legend a little too alive.[110]

(The detail of the long beard has already been met with so often that it is now a mere commonplace.)

115. In the province of Jutland in Denmark, a long-bearded man with a staff in his hand and a bag on his back was once wandering over the countryside; when he came to water, he did not stop, but waded in so that the sea covered him, yet he came out dry on the other shore. By that one knew that he was the shoemaker of Jerusalem.[111] (The peripatetic Wandering Jew going over his head in water

and walking over a sea-, lake-, or river-bottom reminds us of the submarine Malchus from the Sicilian tale [Tale 75]. On the other hand, the name of Ahasuerus, which he bears here, bespeaks some bearing on the Ahasuerus-book.)

116. A folk tale from Guingamp in Brittany drags the Wandering Jew into an identification with the Man in the Moon. It seems that Ahasuerus once found himself, in the course of his wanderings, on the moon, where he spends his time heaping up faggots in order to set fire to the earth on the Day of Doom.[112] (The Man in the Moon has long been a universal figure in folklore; he means all kinds of things in different parts of the world, but in Europe he is usually associated either with Judas or with the unfortunate disobedient man in Numbers 15:32-36, who collected sticks on the Sabbath and therefore was stoned to death. Two such sinners could easily be joined by a third, in this case Ahasuerus. The contamination of legends here is self-evident.)

117. Curious analogues, for that matter, constantly present themselves, yet in justice to the Legend, one must harden one's heart and refuse to admit as a version of the Legend such a narrative as the following from Finland:

God wished to slay Väinämörner, because he had lived long and wished to be better than the Creator and higher than the Lord. Old Väinämörner fell to his knees, then threw himself to the ground under the lap of the great Lord: "Don't kill me yet, my Creator, don't annihilate me. Forge for me three pairs of shoes, iron foot-coverings; bless me with life until I have used them up."

The Creator wrought for him and finished in haste three pairs of iron shoes. "Now you may live until you have used up these shoes, have worn out these iron shoes." Then he went home, kept his own shoes, and saved the iron ones.

The Creator sent his messenger to kill Väinämörner, for He thought that he must by now have used up his shoes. Väinämörner said that he still had not used up the first pair, and should live still. The messenger came a second time. Väinämörner still had not used up the shoes. The great Creator was angry, good God was in wrath: "May you keep your old soul as long as the world lasts."

God drove Sampoliet into the sea. Väinämörner wept and was driven to Nordheim [or Potrjola]. The hostess in Nordheim sent her maidservant to look after him. She then came herself and said: "Now you are under a curse for your misdeeds, which you tried to hide. Get out now and go where I bid you." [There follows a song about Väinämörner's departure.] "In the gulf of the ocean's eddy, in the vengeance of the ocean's rocks, to the eternal seats, the age-old steps, you will never be released from there, in your lifetime you will never be purified."[113]

(Here is a deity offended, a curse of tedious punishment as long as the world lasts. There are shoes, which suggest walking. But this is not the Wandering Jew.)

118. More directly connected with the Legend, in that it at least mentions the Wandering Jew, is a tale from Lithuania. Yet it is clearly a different legend, perhaps merely a local one, for it has no currency in other lands:

The Wandering Jew was the grandson of Jacob. Jacob had twelve sons, among them Joseph and Reuben. When the brothers sold Joseph into Egypt, they did not tell their father. Later, when the brothers found Joseph alive, they did not dare tell their father that they had sold him. And so they gave the son of Reuben, Joseph's brother, a pipe or flute of cedarwood, with which the boy, dancing around Joseph's father blew: "Joseph still lives!" Jacob said to the boy: "If Joseph is still alive, may you live forever." From this statement of Jacob came the fact that the boy lived forever. From the Hebrew books he got magic words which he wrote in the palm of his hand, and then he did as he wished. Once he was a war leader; he went into the army of the enemy when no one suspected it and killed the leader. There followed a tremendous victory under the command of the Wandering Jew. He opposed the customs of the other Jews and is therefore hated by all the others. Later he became avaricious. He knew where the old rabbis were buried, and knew that in their graves much gold had been buried with them. So he went and tried to get all this gold out of their graves. But when he went to take the gold, it all turned into coal. At the same time the life of the Wandering Jew ended.[114]

(This appears to be some sort of rabbinical rationalization of the Legend to give it a pre-Christian status. Of course the revenge motif of the original would then be cast aside; in its place is an appendage to the new story which exacts vengeance for a wrong to the dead rabbis. It is interesting, nevertheless, to note that this Jew is associated with treasure; even more interesting is the fact that he is killed off at the end—something which never happens except in a few highly romanticized literary treatments in the nineteenth century and later.)

119. In a Flemish tale, an old peasant, in order to gain wealth, sold his soul to the devil for twenty years. When the time was up, he was punished, not by an eternal sojourn in hell, but by being doomed to wander the earth forever, doing good to humanity.[115] (This is primarily a folk tale in the Faust tradition which has become contaminated with the Legend of the Wandering Jew; it needs no further elaboration, except to say that the two legends later became crossbred with some frequency, particularly in the nineteenth century.)

120. Or perhaps a more sporting motive for the wandering may be proposed. A belief expressed in Oldenburg, Germany, has it that Ahasuerus bet Christ that he could be idle, and the Jew lost the bet.[116] (This is an obverse of the old saying that Satan finds mischief for idle hands to do.)

At times the folk tale of the Wandering Jew, as we may see from these manifold examples, is simple and unadorned and close to the original outlines of the Legend. At other times it is widely divergent; other legends will mix with it until it becomes distorted almost beyond recognition. The Jew wanders over the world many times—seven, nine—or perhaps only two. The Jew is seen only on a certain island or on a certain mountain and then but rarely. He comes down into the market place to mix with humanity; he may flee from the sight of man. He is tall and thin; he is short and fat. His beard is thin and scraggly, or it may extend the distance of a half-hour's walk. Sometimes, as in some of the eastern versions, he seems to be somebody else or linked with the corresponding protagonist of some totally different legend. He may be hard to see; he may almost force himself upon your attention. He may be benevolent; he may be a spiteful herald of disaster. It all depends, of course, upon how, when, and where the tale about him came into being. The plasticity of these tales is striking. There are some who insist that such tales are polygenetic—that is, they arise spontaneously in different parts of the world, independently of any central legend. This is probably true of tales of wandering in general, but will hardly apply to anything as specific as the Legend of the Wandering Jew.

These variations in the many individual tales can be traced to the imagination of the individual teller, who has carried the tale in his memory for a long time—as, no doubt, had his ancestors before him. Does he ever tell the same tale the same way twice in succession—in other words, is his narrative a matter of formula told by rote? Hardly in this case, or, at most, very seldom. Under the circumstances of oral tradition, the teller would see nothing wrong in the contamination of one legend with another, if indeed he was even aware of any contamination. If we had been able to collect the folk tales of the Wandering Jew from the time of their inception, we should now be overwhelmed by the mass of variant details; as it is, we have more than enough to see how the true core of the Legend has become encrusted with much that is merely peripheral.

Folk tales, however, like folk music, have an appeal to serious writers and composers. One cannot therefore approach the art form of the Legend of the Wandering Jew without keeping alert to the possibility that a given writer may, can, and will borrow from such folklore. There is still no formula for such borrowing, of course, but many a detail in the romantic treatment of Ahasuerus, for example, comes straight out of some folk tale. The same certainly holds true even for the Ahasuerus-book, which is, after all, an elementary phase of the art form of the Legend and should be so considered.

Impostors Real and Fictitious

How many of these reported appearances of the Wandering Jew were actual visits by a true, flesh-and-blood impostor, and how many were figments of the popular imagination, based partly on the traditional Legend and partly on some forgotten encounter with such an impostor? We may take the position that whenever or wherever Ahasuerus was actually seen and spoken to by a witness to any degree credible, or whenever or wherever it is a matter of actual legal record, then the visitor was an impostor making claims on the gullible.

On such terms Cartaphilus, as described by the archbishop in Roger of Wendover's and Matthew Paris' accounts (pp. 18-21 above), would be defined as a charlatan, as would Malchus in Jerusalem and Ahasuerus in Hamburg. These three, however, being the earliest definable prefigurations of the Legend, had to be treated early in the game because without them we should have no clear idea of the Legend itself. The combination of these characters, the alleged Wandering Jew, remains a legendary figure. To put it in another way, the Legend came first, after which men exploited it—and themselves—by claiming to be the protagonist of the Legend.

We must remember, too, that these terms are dangerously oversimplified. Thus we know that Paulus von Eitzen was a real person, of presumably unimpeachable credibility. If he spoke with Ahasuerus, then the stranger who identified himself as Ahasuerus was an impostor. But did Paulus von Eitzen ever speak to such a man? Could not his name, that of a reputable theologian, be attached after his death to a story in order to give it credibility and thus enhance its sales value in a printed version? The Armenian archbishop, who has thus far eluded identification, was not telling his story for publication, yet his very position would lend some weight to his narrative and at least make it more credible.

If a tale haunts a given locality, without specifying date or time or identifying names, we are justified in considering it a local folk tale. But when we are given names, dates, and a specific place, I should call it an instance of charlatanism. The border line is very hard to draw, and there is a neutral zone which defies exact definition. For that matter, any folk tale treating of the Wandering Jew may be a case of charlatanism long since faded, but not every case of such charlatanism is necessarily a folk tale of the Wandering Jew. Of course, when a legend is widely circulated and popularly received, many who want to believe it—who find it attractive—try very hard to believe and can usually come to believe implicitly in the legend. If subconsciously they wish to be gulled, they will be gulled. And although the evidence in the great majority of folk tales—all of those examined in the preceding chapter, for example—is too slender to bear any weight of historical authenticity, there are instances on record of men who for one reason or another openly professed to be the Wandering Jew. Moreover, we may be sure that there were undoubtedly many other cases of such impostors who never got into the record book.

Most of the obvious cases of charlatanism occurred in the seventeenth and eighteenth centuries. I suppose that the case of the visitors to Staffordshire and Northamptonshire, as recorded by Aubrey and Peck (Tales 91 and 92 of the foregoing chapter), are instances of charlatanism, although, because they have such frail bonds with the true Legend, it matters little what we consider them. Others, more specific, are listed below. The more we consider the credulousness of the decades from 1600 to 1800 and the way in which all kinds of swindlers, confidence men, quacks, and soothsayers—good, bad, and indifferent—made inroads over the whole of Europe, the more remarkable it is that there were not more flagrant instances of a rascal's posing as the Wandering Jew and cheating an entire countryside. Perhaps there were, and we do not know about them now. But no century is immune from such infection, and it would be tedious to show how the years from 1800 to 1965 were but little different. Besides, this charlatanism may be at times quite harmless, a matter of foolery and little else. Ahasuerus was twice seen in the men's room of the main branch of the New York Public Library in 1948. I have known a New Yorker who, until his death in 1957, seriously considered himself to be the living incarnation of the Wandering Jew. He believed that there would and should always be such an incarnation; but he did not know, or neglected to say, who would be his successor. There have been countless such eccentrics, one may be sure, who did not happen to be recognized.

Mortal Claimants

1. Leaving aside Cartaphilus, Malchus, and Ahasuerus himself, I suppose the first recorded impostor, in point of time, must have been the stranger who discussed Florentine politics with Salvestro di Giovanni Mannini and who presumably revealed himself as Giovanni Votaddio to Antonio di Francesco di Andrea in the early fifteenth century (p. 25 above).

2. The next case, one of the most clean-cut examples of charlatanry in the history of the Legend, is a matter of judicial record. In March, 1547, one Antonio Ruiz (Rodriguez) was, among other things, sentenced to a hundred lashes for proclaiming himself to be Juan de Espera en Dios among the hardy mountaineers near Toledo in Spain. Testimony had it that he was a youth of twenty, of rather modest family background, a Christian without either Jewish or Moorish blood. On a pilgrimage to Notre Dame de Guadeloupe, he fell in with Pierre, a French pilgrim of disreputable character, who seems to have led him to assume his deception and swindle the people. At his trial it was brought out that he had put on his arms certain marks in the form of a Catherine wheel. These he represented as divine stigmata which he had borne since his birth. His deception of the populace was easy because it was alleged in the neighborhood that the Wandering Jew had passed by in the preceding year (1546). In consequence he was able to go from village to village, hearing confessions and getting in return money, rings,

and silver gewgaws. The case has two particular points of interest: first, the fact that Ruiz was apprehended and punished—a not too common outcome; and second, that his success bespeaks a general knowledge of the Wandering Jew in Spanish folklore at a relatively early date—several years, for instance, before the allusion to him in Villalón's *Crotalon* (p. 129 above), the earliest of the literary references in a country where such literary references were actually more in evidence than folk tales on the subject.[1]

3. There was a case at Liège in Flanders in 1616 which may be the basis of a curious ramification of the Legend to be looked at later (pp. 120-21). A fugitive tract printed in that year and at that place, later translated into German, gives an account of *two* such persons—not mentioned by name, however—who together made a visit to the town in peculiar garb, with bare head and bare feet, preaching in the streets that if the inhabitants did not repent, the town would be destroyed. They complained of the serious sin of idolatry, which they found rampant in Liège, and they declared that the prebends of the monastery of St. Lambert and the members of the local courts of justice were all damned. Having been constrained by the not unnatural resentment of both the clergy and the courts, these prophets received visits in prison from several Jesuits and others who were monks and scholars. Disputations followed, conducted in various languages—Latin, Greek, Hebrew, Arabic, and, of all things, Chaldean. The Jesuits were utterly confounded. When asked about their religion, the prophets declared that they belonged to the Apostolic Catholic faith. They prayed night and day and finally announced categorically that the Last Judgment was at hand, and that the world would be destroyed in 1630. They asserted that they had come from Greece and had been sent by God; between them they counted nine hundred years of age. When the magistrates heard this astounding statement, the prophets were kept in prison while the authorities pondered the case. No sentence was ultimately pronounced, for the tale does not go beyond that point. Perhaps they are there yet. (Of course these two were not, strictly speaking, Wandering Jews. Neither of them was old enough. The special importance of this weak pamphlet—*Een Waerachtight Bescrijvinghe van twee nieue Propheten*[2]—is that it presents impostors in a pair. As we shall see, there arose later a serious discussion as to whether or not there was a double aspect of the modern Wandering Jew. Otherwise the pamphlet is routine: the strangers are sensationally versed in dispute and confound the learned men around them, they are clad in general conformity with the descriptions offered in the Ahasuerus-book, and they are not conclusively prosecuted.)

One peculiar fact about such suspicious individuals of historical or semihistorical validity is that gossip about them may come from sources far removed from the territory in which they actually appeared. Thus there are cases in which a man purporting to be the Wandering Jew imposes himself upon the English—according to tales told on the Continent. The English themselves, however, seem not to have known anything about the matter. At least they made no report of a visit at the time.

4. A typical instance of such moonshine is that noted in the ponderous *Nachdenkliche Prophezeyungen, Visionen, und Träume*, an extremely rare German

book of the early eighteenth century.[3] The prophet with whom this incident is concerned stopped in London. He did not know about his parents, but boasted that his kin had been known before Adam and Eve. He wore on his head a bloody crown; his clothing was neither sewn nor patched, neither of linen, wool, silk, nor net; he drank no wine, only water; he satisfied himself with little food, cared nothing for money, wore neither girdle nor sword, but went about boldly under the very noses of his enemies. He argued with none; left a man's religion to himself; complained about the Protestants, preferring the Catholics because of their fasting; rested little by day or night; found fault with the various Roman bishops who had expressed no faith in him; cared nothing for beds, but slept on hard wood; called out with loud voice and outstretched arms about this naughty world, keeping doors and windows open as if he were about to announce the Latter Day of the Lord. He was expert in all tongues, so that he could be understood everywhere. He especially loved beautiful gardens. The most distinguished people often had him to visit them; he greeted no one and conversed with very few. Many, however, believed that his tribe would endure until the end of the world. He said that he had been in the Ark with Noah; he prophesied concerning himself that he would die no natural death, but that this wicked world would try to destroy him. He had been present at the Crucifixion, yet he did not believe in the resurrection of the flesh nor in eternal life.

It is reported that a similar visitant was later seen in Newcastle; perhaps he was the same as the man just described, perhaps he was the one mentioned in John Brand's *Popular Antiquities* (see Case 25), or perhaps still another individual altogether. At any rate, the editor of *Nachdenkliche Prophezeyungen* is irritatingly vague as to date, although from the tone of his account it may be inferred that the stranger was in London not long before, perhaps about 1700. Another incident (that reported in Case 6) places the Wandering Jew in England in 1694. It is almost unnecessary, however, to point out how this prophet differs from the usual picture of Ahasuerus. Is it indeed he? This stranger seems rather to be in a class by himself, for he is ignorant of his parentage; his clothing is peculiar, not to say supernatural; and his bent toward the Catholics, even if he did not care for their bishops, would not get him very far socially in eighteenth-century English society. His English love of gardens is touching but hardly in character. No doubt he is an impostor of some originality, but it strikes me that he owes his existence to a writer of chapbooks on the Continent who slapped him into England because it seemed a remote and unknown country.

5. The alleged journey of Ahasuerus to England late in the seventeenth century, however, receives more than one notice, even if the English themselves appear to have known nothing about it. Dom Augustin Calmet, author of a *Dictionnaire . . . de la Bible* (1722), included in this encyclopedic work a "Dissertation sur le juif errant," from which we have the following:

I have a letter . . . written from London by Madame de Mazarin to Madame de Bouillon, in which we read that in that country there was a man who pretended to have lived more than 1700 years. He claimed also to be an officer of the Divan of Jerusalem at the time when Jesus Christ was sentenced by Pontius Pilate; that he harshly pushed the

Saviour outside the Praetorium, saying to Him: "Go, get out! Why are you lingering here?" And Jesus Christ answered him: "I shall go, but you will walk until my return." He remembers having seen the Apostles, the features of their countenances, their hair, their clothing. He has traveled through all the countries of the world, and must wander until the end of time; he boasts of having cured the sick by touching them; he speaks many languages; he has given an account of all that has happened during the ages, so accurate that those who hear him do not know what to think of it. The two universities have sent their learned men to converse with him; but with all their learning they have not been able to surprise or confute him.

After quoting a little more of the letter, in which Madame de Mazarin insists that the individual referred to is believed in only by the stupid, Calmet dismisses the Wandering Jew as "un personnage de théâtre." His subsequent remarks are a fitting requiem to be chanted over all impostors who have said that they were the Wandering Jew:

Those who have appeared at different times and in different regions of the world were swindlers who, exploiting the credulity of ignorant and gullible people, were anxious to make a spectacle of themselves before the world, to gather in alms or to bask in the inane flatteries of a beguiled community. . . . Certainly nothing seems more opposed to the spirit of mercy, patience, kindness, or grace, which the Saviour showed throughout His passion, than this vengeance which they say He showed against this Wandering Jew. He prayed for those who blasphemed against Him on the Cross; He let Himself be led to agony as a sheep before its shearers; would He have struck with such a curse this shoemaker who refused to let Him rest before his shop? All the circumstances and the fitness of things should suffice to have these fables rejected as utterly false.[4]

Calmet, in short, is one of the few people to put his finger upon the moral weakness of the whole Legend, yet it continued to roll on its unchristian way.

No date is given by Calmet to the letter of Madame de Mazarin, but she is known to have lived in London during the last quarter of the seventeenth century.[5]

6. As it happens, however, another account of the same "incident" is forthcoming in the *Theatrum Europaeum* (Frankfurt, 1702), which specifies the year 1694 as that in which Ahasuerus appeared in London. Otherwise the account is to all intents and purposes the same as that in Calmet's *Dictionnaire,* except that it is stated explicitly here that Oxford and Cambridge sent down a delegation of scholars, as in the *Nachdenkliche Prophezeyungen* account (Case 4).[6]

7. Even more circumstantial is the statement in Johann Jakob Schudt's account, which sketches the career of Ahasuerus, refers to the London visit, and then cites the statement of the Frankfurt jurist Konrad von Uffenbach, who visited England in 1710, that at Cambridge Ahasuerus interviewed the "famous" scholars Covet, Bentley, and Baker.[7] On second thoughts, however, Von Uffenbach decided that because of the subsequent ignorance of everybody about this incident, it must have been a fabrication. Now there is no difficulty in identifying Bentley: he would be the decidedly famous scholar Richard Bentley (1662-1742), who in 1694 was librarian of the King's Library at St. James and a distinguished

classicist. The Baker referred to is presumably Thomas Baker (1656-1740), called by Schudt the librarian of St. John's College, Cambridge. But Thomas Baker was a writer *manqué*, a graduate of St. John's, not, so far as is known, a librarian. The identity of "Covet" eludes us. The whole episode is characteristic of the slipshod methods of an inventor of such tales. I am sure that any biographer of Richard Bentley will look in vain for any material which portrays the scholar as combating Ahasuerus in learned debate. But the use of a celebrated name adds value to a publication.

Meanwhile three strange affairs, if that is indeed the word for them, had taken place on the Continent.

8. First there is the affair of Gualdo. A manuscript from Tübingen, Germany, reports that a certain individual named Friderico Gualdo claimed to be four hundred years old. On the face of it, this age hardly qualifies him as the Wandering Jew; yet to prove his antiquity, if not the exact truth of the assertion, he carried about with him a picture of himself which, he said, had been painted by none other than the renowned master Titian, who had been dead for one hundred thirty years. This would place the incident in 1706, or about that time, and would indicate that Gualdo was assuredly possessed of an elixir of youth. As always, there was a sensation-seeking populace who accepted Gualdo's claims as true and passed the news about the vicinity, thereby assisting greatly in whatever success the imposter may have had. It is inconceivable that he had none. In dispassionate retrospect, however, it is obvious that Gualdo belongs not in the category of the Wandering Jew but rather in that of the celebrated Comte de Saint-Germain, whose alleged possession of an elixir of life aided him in countless kinds of intrigue at the court of Louis XV of France.[8]

9. Gualdo's assertions, for what they may have been worth, affected a community as a whole. With the luckless individual the case is different. A striking example is the Ypres incident of 1623.[9] Here a man appeared, dressed in more or less "Turkish" fashion, without trousers or stockings, bald-headed, with an extremely long gray beard, and carrying in his hand a pilgrim's staff, on which hung a flask—bearing, in short, quite a resemblance to the Ahasuerus of the woodcuts in the Ahasuerus-book. The watchman at the city gate asked him in Flemish about his origins and the purpose of his visit. When he did not answer, the same questions were directed to him in Spanish.

Thereupon he answered, "I am the Wandering Jew." The astonished watchman, De Breyne, led him to the knight Van de Casteel, who gave him audience in Spanish. The alleged Jew told his familiar story. He asked only for permission to beg his bread in town, as he had been doing in other places. This was allowed him, and he collected alms with much success. At the table of the archbishop, who had invited him to come and see him, he spoke fluently in Italian, Latin, Spanish, French, English, and other languages; but he did not understand Flemish, for he had never before been in Flanders. (A lame excuse for the Wandering Jew!) In brief, he presented some of the attributes of Ahasuerus, but was far behind him in at least one important capability.

One day he was brought before an Italian officer, who had for a servant an old soldier. The servant identified the mysterious stranger as a former comrade-in-arms named Leopold Delporte, an erstwhile acquaintance who had fought in his regiment in Spain, which regiment was now stationed in Ghent. The officer wrote to the commander of the regiment, asking for information and instructions.

Meanwhile the alleged Wandering Jew approached the daughter of his land-lady. He courted her and eventually promised her marriage. He told her that he had always been married, and that Wife 123 had died three months before. His former wives had always been with him in his wanderings, sometimes on foot, sometimes in a cart, sometimes in a boat. They had always had money and nothing to fear. The girl, Christine Verschuere, accepted the proposal. One day, while the stranger was visiting in a nearby village, a young woman arrived in Ypres and asked for the so-called Wandering Jew. At the inn, whither they directed her, she told the landlady that she was the wife of this stranger, who had married her in Arras three months before. When the stranger returned to Ypres before the gates were closed for the night, she confronted him with, "Now, my dear husband, when did you intend to come home? You left me alone in Saint-Omer without any money." When the stranger denied that he knew her, she went to the magistrate, to whom she told her sad story and remarked also that the stranger was indeed named Pol Delporte.

The magistrate ordered her to appear next day before the town council. Meanwhile a letter had arrived from Ghent, from the commanding officer of the regiment stationed there, which made clear that the stranger was in fact a deserter. A quickly convened court-martial ascertained that Pol, or Leopold, Delporte, the "Wandering Jew," had left the Walloon regiment three years before. The sentence of death was executed on him in Ghent. A son of Christine Verschuere, who received the name of Leopold, came to be known also as Pol Joodts (the Jew's Pol). He was the ancestor of the family of Joodts of Ypres.

10. There was at least one such impostor, however, who was more dangerous than a bigamous deceiver of weak-willed women. His connection with the Legend admittedly hangs by a gossamer thread. He was the self-styled New King of the Jews, Oliger Paulli, a learned merchant born in Copenhagen in the year 1644. Although a Lutheran by birth, he showed himself to be more and more the enemy of the Evangelical Church, seeking his followers among the Separatists and the Jews. He made efforts through his agents to plunder first Denmark, then France, England, and Palestine, and finally to lead his Jews to the Holy Land. He was, in short, a megalomaniac of the first magnitude. But when he approached men of power and wealth he found them—as was Leopold I of Austria, to whom he promised the spoils of Constantinople—in no agreement with his plans. Through his *Bericht an alle Puisancen von Europaea* (1704) he and a small but loyal group tried to win Peter the Great of Russia and Frederick I of Prussia to support their adventure. In his last years he lived in Amsterdam, where he was confined for a short time in a madhouse. After 1705 all trace of him was lost.[10]

Such a fantastic personality, who among other things was persuaded that God had revealed himself to him within the pages of his Bible, was attracted to the concept of the Wandering Jew in order to confirm his dreams of a thousand-year realm. We are reminded at once of a twentieth-century dictator, whose beginnings were scarcely more frightening, and his dream of a thousand-year realm. In a document addressed to the Oberleutnant Neubaur in Bremen and the priest Hosmann in Zelle, Hannover, Paulli declared that those who opposed him were so stupid that they could not believe the tale of Ahasuerus. In other words, he and Ahasuerus were mighty realities; thus he, Paulli, and the Cartaphilus of Matthew Paris (*sic*) could both serve to give testimony as to the greatness of God.

Mythical Claimants

We can see, then, that some of what I have called impostors are a matter of historical record, while others lack some of this historicity, even though they may be vouched for by presumably reliable people. The visitors mentioned next are in a kind of misty mid-region between folk tale and fact. Many of them undoubtedly find their excuse for being in the pages of the Ahasuerus-book, but most of them continue to be made "authentic" by dates and other circumstantial factors. This is especially true in the long series of visits made by Ahasuerus to various places during the seventeenth century, some of which we have heard about already.

11. For example, an Ahasuerus came at least once more to Hamburg after the historic interview with Paulus von Eitzen described first in the *Kurtze Beschreibung*. There was uncertainty, it will be remembered, about the actual date of this interview, although the various printings of the *Kurtze Beschreibung* agree on 1542. But the later versions differed, and in the Ahasuerus-book as a whole we find 1547, 1572, 1599—in the French *Histoire admirable* the dates come down into the seventeenth century. So far as Hamburg is concerned, however, a seventeenth-century German pamphlet certifies, according to its author, the preacher Christian Solinus of Holstein, that in the year 1606 "a certain man appeared . . . who is considered to be a wanderer who can never die and must wander about till Judgment Day; whether or not it is a fable is a matter of dispute."[11]

12. On his rather well-known visit to Naumburg in 1630, Ahasuerus was seen in church during divine services; he kept beating himself on the breast and inclining his head on his right shoulder. He could not stand long in one place but frequently stepped, now forwards, now backwards, and wept many tears, so that those present took him to be insane. After the sermon he gave answers to those who wished to question him and said that he had been condemned by Christ, to whom he had not been willing to grant the favor of a brief rest before his door, to eternal wandering; and so far he had had no repose, day or night. Many local merchants bestowed gifts upon the man; others considered him a mere fraud. When he was summoned to appear next day before the magistrates, to submit himself to examination, he disappeared.[12] (The indebtedness of the reporter of this incident, whoever he was, to the *Kurtze Beschreibung* is too obvious for comment. At the same time, the appearance of such a man and the things that happened later are all possible.)

The same kind of witnessing is the rule at many other places: at Prague (1602), Lübeck (1603), Paris (1604), Leipzig (1642), Hamburg again (1633), Brussels (1640), Frankenstein (1676), Munich (1721), etc.[13] Are all these instances mere fiction? Or was there a living impostor in each case? It is impossible to say with any prospect of certainty, but the close parallel usually found with the Ahasuerus-book, plus the minor increments added here and there, suggest that a wily charlatan, familiar with the Ahasuerus-book, was exploiting the credulous and making the most of his opportunities in his own way.

13. For example, when Ahasuerus came to Leipzig in 1642, he was an aged man with ice-gray hair and beard, who asked the people for bread and maintained that he had been born a Jew and had been present at the Passion of Christ and must wander about until the Last Judgment. This is all according to formula, save for the demand for bread. This was, I think, a real charlatan enacting the role of Ahasuerus as beggar for obvious reasons. So, in all likelihood, were the others. And when, as at Oberstdorf, he persisted in coming to church to listen to a sermon whenever the occasion offered, clad in a dress and behaving in a manner similar to the descriptions in the Ahasuerus-book, and then begged when the services were over, he was, in modern parlance, pressing his luck.[14]

14. Nor does this kind of Ahasuerus hesitate to adopt the part of a prophet of evil, like many a religious crackpot before and after him. At Füssen in 1642, in the Church of the Franciscans, he cried out, to the great disgust of the preacher in the pulpit, that the living faith was vanishing everywhere and had now become so little—"indeed, so little has it become that it can be contained under my small hat." When he left, he made a tremendous leap over the Lech River and disappeared between two rocks. This last detail, however, was probably added by some heated bystander.[15]

15. The last two or three cases are, of course, on the border line. But there is little doubt about the following, as reported from Breslau. Here, in 1646, an impostor who proclaimed himself to be the Wandering Jew is recorded in the diary of the rector of the Breslau Elisabeth Gymnasium, one Dr. Elias Major. On the visitor's hat were chalked inscriptions which the pastor at St. Bernardin, Dr. Schlegel, to whom they were shown, could recognize as neither Hebrew, Greek, Latin, nor German. He stayed for a while on the Schweidnitz Meadows. His deception was "ill-rewarded"; the details are not given. In November of that same year the same man was observed at Fürstenstein; he had a little bag of kindling wood and was girded with an iron chain.[16] The last detail suggests a folk tale derived from the actual visit of the stranger to Breslau, with a touch of contamination with the tale of the Man in the Moon.

16. A stranger, ostensibly the Wandering Jew, appeared before the Isarthor in Munich on July 22, 1721, but was not admitted to the city, for which reason he left for Heidthausen and there told how he had gone around the world seven times already.[17] The pattern here is similar to that of Case 15 above: the impostor makes a definite appearance on a definite date at a definite place, and then a local folk tale concerning him springs up—in this instance the same as Tale 22 of the preceding chapter. Or perhaps the folk tale is already in existence and is grafted on to the account of the actual happening.

17. A similar kind of specific dating indicates that some one calling himself the Wandering Jew visited Frankenstein in Silesia on November 2, 1676.[18]

18. At Altbach-am-Neckar, Württemberg, where the Wandering Jew appeared in 1766, the innkeeper, at Ahasuerus' request, showed him to lodgings in a sheepfold. The next morning they found written on the wall: "I, Ahasuerus of Jerusalem, have now been given lodging twice in this sheepfold; may God reward you for it. January 1, 1766."[19] The inscription is said to have been still in existence ten years later.

19. A picture by Pierre Leloup (1769-1844) is entitled "Le vrai portrait du juif errant tel qu'on l'a vu passer en Avignon le 22 Avril 1784."[20]

20. There is a rather unusual incident told of Bartholomaeus Anhorn (1616-1700), a preacher at Elsau, near Zurich, Switzerland, who issued among many other works a comprehensive *Theatrum concionum sacrarum topicum.* He went to England to deliver to King William III (d.1702) a copy of this work, perhaps his last. "The lively appearance of this nearly eighty-year-old man, which because of his gray hair and snow-white long beard was extremely dignified, brought Englishmen to the mad idea that they should engrave the likeness of this old Swiss (*sic*) in copper and pass it about under the title, 'The Wandering Jew of the World.' "[21]

21. More difficult to classify as charlatanism is the old tale of how the Wandering Jew came to Bohemia in 1505, during the reign of Ladislas I, and helped the weaver Kokot to find the treasure belonging to his great-grandfather, who had buried it in the royal palace some sixty years before. At first blush this seems a true folk tale, but the details of the story as reported by its collector and the definiteness of the date are suspicious. At least it is more than likely that it was founded upon some factual occurrence more authentic than is true of most folk tales.[22]

22. An exceptional incident is the visit of Ahasuerus to Brussels on April 22, 1774. This is notable chiefly because it inspired a Belgian *complainte,* a work often referred to as the Brabantine ballad, composed by some writer who had in his poetic system enough native wood-notes wild to kindle in turn some lyrical fire in the popular French poet Pierre de Béranger (1780-1857). Both poems will be considered below (pp. 165-66, 207-8). The combined achievement of the Brabantine ballad and Béranger's poem served as material for the remarkable engravings on the subject of the Wandering Jew created by Gustave Doré, although the direct inspiration for these pictures came from a poem by Pierre Dupont (p. 260 below). Furthermore, the visit to Brussels made the date noteworthy in the calendar of *dies curiosi* compiled in the nineteenth century, Robert Chambers' *Book of Days.*[23] All of which is rather strange, since the Brussels visit seems to have been so unspectacular and devoid of interest that it passed unnoticed in the city.

The coincidence of the twenty-second day of the month in the Munich, Avignon, and Brussels visitations cited above is curious, and can best be explained by the fact that the earliest one—that at Munich in 1721—came to be a part of the folkloristic aura of the incident. I strongly suspect that the Brussels and Avignon incidents derived their dates from that of the Munich visit, as far as the day of the month is concerned; indeed, since the Avignon and Brussels incidents are exactly ten years apart, with that of Brussels first, one might suppose that the tale of Avignon is simply a garbling of that of Brussels, with 1784 read for 1774. Such a point, of course, cannot be proved. It is enough to file for future reference the importance of the Brussels visit and of the ensuing Brabantine ballad.

23. On July 1, 1606, Peter Knudtszön, a burgher of Oslo, testified that not more than two years had passed since the death of a man who had been born before the birth of Christ and had seen Christ in the living flesh and had lived in this sinful world until 1604.[24] Apparently this witness had been reading some version of the *Kurtze Beschreibung*, yet he recognizes that this stranger is mortal, and that detail is certainly not in the Ahasuerus-book.

24. In a late version of the Swedish translation (1643) of the German Ahasuerus-book, which was printed in 1818, it is reported that on June 12, 1759, an unknown man of tall and powerful build, with a long beard and very aged features, came through Jönköping. He bore on his back a bag full of shoes, such as shoemakers are in the habit of carrying. He was clothed in a long coat flecked with horsehair, with stockings and vest of camelskin; his head covering resembled a winter cap; his girdle was of tigerskin. He looked very sad, and when he was asked who he might be, he replied that he obviously was the unfortunate shoemaker of Jerusalem. After delivering to the people a friendly warning that they should look to their souls, he disappeared.[25]

25. A well-known instance in England is reported in the fascinating *Observations on Popular Antiquities* (1777) by John Brand (1744-1806):

> I remember to have seen one of these impostors some years ago in the North of England, who made a very hermit-like appearance, and went up and down the streets of Newcastle, with a long train of boys at his heels, muttering: "Poor John, alone, alone!" I thought he pronounced his name in a manner singularly plaintive.[26]

We see that Brand notes the hermit to be an impostor. He adds, moreover, that "Poor John!" sometimes came out as "Poor Joe!" "John" as applied to the Wandering Jew, no longer calls for comment. The Cartaphilus who comes to us in Roger of Wendover's or Matthew Paris' chronicle was named Joseph, though this name, on the whole, is an uncommon one for the protagonist. As a matter of fact, it seems to me that Brand's "Poor Joe!" is rather an amusing corruption of "Poor Jew!" The incident is nevertheless significant: here is a clear-cut example of a cracked individual who voluntarily or involuntarily receives an association with the Wandering Jew.

26. Newcastle, in fact, apparently harbored another "Wandering Jew" at about the same time that Brand saw his "impostor." Perhaps, indeed, he is the same man. But, when compared with the more spectacular examples we have seen on the Continent, this one is hardly an impostor at all, merely a recluse of more than eccentric nature. It is reported further that he had a son, of whom it was said that he was living in Hull as late as 1881, in a miserable tumble-down shack of a house encrusted in filth and squalor. So much for the unclean, obscure, and altogether passive son of a supposedly illustrious father, a drab and dirty publican who never wandered at all, but took his place merely in the undistinguished gallery of a city's eccentrics.[27]

27. It remained for Hull to furnish the most remarkable account of a visit of the Wandering Jew to England—or, if not actually the Wanderer, at least a fair facsimile thereof. The report is contained in a chapbook bearing the completely unoriginal title, *The Wandering Jew, or the Shoemaker of Jerusalem*,[28] the same as that of the popular English ballad on the subject, to which reference has already been made (pp. 61-63). The pamphlet was printed by J. Pitts at a place unspecified, without date, not before 1769. It has been hailed by some as the true English Ahasuerus-book, but I should prefer to bestow that honor upon the Shann version of 1620 (pp. 63-66 above). I must concede that this 1769 pamphlet, as we may call it to distinguish it from the ballad, is indebted to the seventeenth-century Ahasuerus-book in no small measure. The opening of the pamphlet will suffice here for illustration:

This Jew was born at Jerusalem, and was by trade a shoemaker; when our Saviour was going to the place of crucifixion, being weary and faint, he would have sat down to rest at the shoemaker's stall, but the shoemaker came to the door and spitting in our Lord's face buffeted him from the door, saying that was no place of abode for Him. On which Christ said, "For this thing, thou shalt never rest, but wander till I come again upon the earth."

From this he is called the Wandering Jew of Jerusalem.

Now according to this saying of [our] Saviour who was crucified, this man has no power to return home, but went abroad wandering from place to place ever since, even unto this day.

After traveling through Asia and Africa, he roamed to America, and is now on his journey to visit every town in Europe.

Some time since he landed at Hull, in Yorkshire, where Dr. Hall, taking him for a cheat, caused him to be locked up in a room all night, but next morning they found the door opened, though their prisoner had not attempted to escape. Dr. Hall sent for Dr. Harrisons, in order to assist in the examination of so remarkable a personage, that they might be sure whether he was impostor or not.

They asked him concerning the breaking of the locks in the room in which he had been shut up. He told them if they would attempt to confine him with chains, it would avail nothing—human force cannot confine him whom the Almighty had sentenced to want a resting place.

They being like Thomas a Dindimus, hard of belief, sent for a smith to put strong chains on him, but they instantly burst asunder to the surprise of a thousand spectators. Not being able to doubt any longer, they sent for a painter and had his picture drawn, in which he looked neither old nor young, but just as he did 1769 years ago, when he first began his journey.[29]

The King of France, hearing of this, wrote for his picture, which Dr. Hall accordingly sent him.

If he hears any one curse or swear, or take the name of God in vain, he tells him that they crucify their God again. If any one offers him money, though it were the richest Lord or Lady in all the land, he will take no more than one groat and that he says he takes for Christ's sake, and gives it to the next poor person he meets. He is always crying and praying, and wishing to see death, but that ease from his labouring pilgrimage, he says, that can never happen until Christ comes again upon the earth . . .

These first few paragraphs of the chapbook give the traditional picture of the Wandering Jew, as already described in the Ahasuerus-book and in the popular ballad already mentioned. But now the assembled clergymen proceed to ask the stranger a series of hard questions, some of which have a Talmudic or even cabalistic ring. How long, according to Moses and the prophets, will the world last? Within six thousand years, comes the answer, the world will be destroyed twice— once by water and once by fire. According to the visitor's calculations, this sinful world has scarcely more than two hundred years left. What was the mark which God set upon Cain's head? The mark was black; from Cain sprang the race of blacks. Why did God hide the body of Moses? To keep the Devil from persuading the children of Israel that there was no God. Why do men and women live a shorter time now than in the days of the Old Testament folk? Because they eat too much meat and drink not enough water.

And so the inquisitive clergymen who signed the report of this interview—Dr. Hall, Dr. Harrisons, Mr. Reubens, and Mr. Crouch—were convinced. Theirs were good Yorkshire names all, but not names which can be connected with any church in Hull during the 1760's and 1770's. Nor is it likely that the aged and ailing Louis XV of France or otiose Louis XVI would have bothered to send for the picture of a suspicious stranger in Hull.

28. This impression of the generally fictitious nature of the business in Hull is strengthened by the appearance of another pamphlet in 1780, printed in Dover, printer unknown.[30] The first portion of this is virtually identical with the 1769 pamphlet. The indefatigable Dr. Hall is this time interviewing the stranger on the Holy Island of Lindisfarne, near Berwick. His companion is Dr. Harris, not Harrisons. The stranger again submits to chains, which he promptly breaks, in the presence this time of *thousands* of witnesses. His portrait is again painted and sent off to the king of France, who now is Louis XVI. The questioning to which the stranger is subjected is the same as it was at Hull, but when it comes to the interrogation concerning Cain, there is a break in the proceedings (is a page of copy missing?), and we get instead some gibberish about Adam and Eve. Eventually returning to coherence, however, the visitor passes the remainder of his examination. Four clergymen sign an attestation; in addition to Hall and Harris (instead of Harrisons), there are two new signatories, Gough and Davis—all good English names and again not in the records as ministers in any church of Dover, Berwick, or their vicinity. And after the attestation comes a further note signed by three ministers and an attorney:

This Wandering Jew left Dover the last month, after wandering above forty-two miles up the country; his stay is always short and [he] is possessed of many different languages; when learned men put questions to him, he desires them to go to the sacred records, and there they will be fully satisfied; as to his pilgrimage in this world, when he receives fourpence (which he calls a groat) he will have no more until he distribute what he has got to a pious use. He is still in a mourning and praying posture, he sleeps little in any bed, chusing rather more hardships than Christian people can give him. He drinks water and eats very sparingly; and has a great delight in little children, because, says he, his great master loved them.

He arrived in a fishing smack at Blyth, on the southward of Berwick; and is on his way to the Holy Island, within a few miles of the town of Berwick. If he returns northward, or southward, or goes to sea, it is not yet known.

Three ministers near Blyth was with him, and several men of repute, who all agree, that he makes the tears fall from their eyes that hears him talk, which is attested by

> Mr. Jos. Burton ⎫
> Mr. Geo. Naperlin ⎬ Ministers
> Mr. Chris. Ewbank ⎭
> Mr. Jo. Stanton, Attorney

The postscript is dated January 25, 1780, from "Overtown." The name of the place is almost certainly fictitious.[31]

The obvious conclusion is, of course, that the Dover chapbook is a crude re-working of the 1769 pamphlet, to which has been added some new material in the form of a change of locale and the touching detail of the stranger's love of children. Not often does Ahasuerus say, "Suffer little children to come unto me!" As a matter of fact, a comparison of the two pamphlets is an excellent study of how a folk tale can be varied with incremental detail and invention. The narrative in both chapbooks comes in great part from the seventeenth-century English ballad. The authors could have got this from Percy's *Reliques* if not from general oral tradition. The stranger has the characteristic ability, for example, to break locks and chains, and he refuses to accept more than one groat at a time for alms.

29. But the great Age of Enlightenment has no monopoly on such mysterious visitants, in spite of the paradoxical credulity which allowed it to accept on a most disconcerting scale Cagliostro, Casanova, Saint-Germain, and the querulous visitor to Dover, Hull, and parts north. As we shall see, the nineteenth century, being inclined toward the romantic, could absorb the Legend with fascination. Thus the staid *London Athenaeum*, in its issue of November 3, 1866, records another visitation, not this time from the rural moorlands or the provincial city, but from the heart of teeming London:

From the year 1818 (perhaps earlier) to about 1830, a handsomely featured Jew, in semi-eastern costume, fair-haired, bareheaded, his eyes intently fixed on a little ancient book he held in both hands, might be seen gliding through the streets of London, but was never seen to issue from or enter a house or to pause upon his way. He was popularly known as "the Wandering Jew," but there was something so dignified and anxious in his look that he was never known to suffer the slightest molestation. Young and old looked silently on him as he passed, and shook their heads pitifully when he had gone by. He disappeared, was seen again in London some ten years later, still young, still fair-haired, bareheaded, his eyes bent on his book, his feet going steadily forward as he went straight on; and men again whispered as he glided through our streets for the last time, "the Wandering Jew!" There were many who believed that he was the very man to whom had been uttered the awful words, "Tarry thou till I come!"[32]

The picture of a young, studious, peripatetic Ahasuerus is certainly novel; but in his dignity, his gliding gait, his ability to enter and leave a house undetected, a few shreds of the Legend still cling to him in the comparatively modern streets of Regency London. Thus he flits, shadow-like, through the City; none molests him; none addresses him. He speaks to none—only the furtive ghost of the hero of a great legend, nothing more, in fact, than an innocuous Levantine student more at home in the British Museum than elsewhere. Moreover, the early nineteenth-century sentimentality clothing this account of his sojourn in London savors too much of the art form of the Legend.

Now any one of these visitors, or impostors, or what you will, may owe his participation in the Legend to the Ahasuerus-book or to the folkloristic tradition, fished up from below the surface of the waters and given a habitation, a name, and more or less identifiable witnesses. Any one of these may also be thrown back into the fish pool of folklore, as it were; and any one of the stories told in the preceding chapter may be concerned with an erstwhile impostor whose identity has faded out. Those who chose to believe have done so, and the skeptics have remained skeptical to a degree which now commands attention.

The Scholars Attack the Problem

Meanwhile, if the ignorant, the superstitious, and the credulous received these reports of the visits of the Wandering Jew with awe and perpetuated the Legend as best they could, even to the extent of being hospitable to the impostors who came in the name of Ahasuerus, the same is not true of the academicians, theologians, and professional men in general. Witness the manner in which Calmet dismissed the Legend (p. 110 above). Long before Calmet, we saw how, in the flurries during the Reformation and Counter Reformation, hard-headed men like De l'Estoile and Boulenger and Boutrays (Boterius) poured out either skepticism or outright scorn. In fact, the scholars of the seventeenth and eighteenth centuries who investigated the Legend were many; their conclusions are almost uniformly in denunciation, for it was in their minds a fable, an improbability, a fantasy. Although they admitted that all things were possible with God, still it was unlikely that his infinite mercy, about which so much had always been preached, would permit such a barbarity as the punishment inflicted on unfortunate Ahasuerus. At the same time, there were a few stern moralists or Jew-baiters, or those with a mentality best described as Old Testament perverted, to whom the fate of eternal wandering must be a just reward for a blasphemer. After all, the seventeenth century, at least, had not yet cleared up the matter of witchcraft in Europe. Especially in Protestant countries, where there was a tendency to interpret the scriptures literally, the presence of such a supernatural being as Ahasuerus was not altogether unthinkable.

One little problem which received passing attention arose from the possibility of splitting the Wandering Jew into two individuals. One will recall that the Liège pamphlet of 1616 (p. 108 above) mentioned two "prophets." I have not found any such dichotomy at an earlier date, and so I gather that the idea of a gemination of the Wandering Jew occurred to someone who knew something about the Liège incident or perhaps to the author of the pamphlet himself. Yet the tendency of legendary characters to travel about in pairs (Dioscurism) is a well-recognized by-product of the creative processes of folklore. There are Castor and Pollux in Homeric tradition, Hengest and Horsa in early English history or story (one cannot tell which), the ridiculous knights Harold and Barold in the Middle English romance *King Horn*, Balin and Balan in the Arthurian sagas—perhaps even the strange pair, Rosencrantz and Guildenstern in *Hamlet*. In the Gospels, for example, there are the two thieves crucified with Jesus, one penitent and the other not.

At any rate, two Wandering Jews make their appearance in the second known edition of the *Relation*. This Ahasuerus-book pamphlet was printed in Amsterdam in 1647, and in Hamburg and Frankfurt in 1660. Its authorship or editorship may be tentatively ascribed to a certain Abraham von Franckenberg, who attributes his authority for the twin Ahasueri to a 1645 edition of the Dudulaeus pamphlet, which is now unfortunately no longer extant. He is of the opinion "that the histories tell us of two different wonder-men, a heathen and a Jew, who both were present at the Passion and Crucifixion of Christ and still today are to be found alive in the world as a testimony against the blind heathen and the unrepentant Jews, and proclaim the crucified Christ with great sobriety and zeal unto the end."[33] Having called attention to the "Reminder to the Christian Reader," printed in all later editions of the Dudulaeus pamphlet, he continues: "For our part, we have something more to say on the matter. Did not God have His own face hidden from the eyes of the world? Did He not hold back seven thousand who did not bow their knees before Baal? Of whom even the man of God, Elijah, had no knowledge? Can this not be a continuing mighty force? When the unbeliever says, 'I do not believe it,' and the ignorant, 'I do not understand it'; *ergo*, 'It cannot be'? For truly, all things are possible."

This separation of Ahasuerus into two actually came about, in all probability, from a natural differentiation between Cartaphilus (who became the "heathen" member of the duality) and Ahasuerus. Indeed, the Frenchman Jacques Basnage, in his *Histoire des Juifs* (1706-7), distinguished not only between Cartaphilus and Ahasuerus but brought into the picture Al-Sameri, who will be recalled (pp. 3-4 above) as the wanderer set going in the Koran by the wrathful Moses.[34] This trinity appears also in a Spanish study of the Legend as late as 1781.[35]

The concept of three Wandering Jews, however, was not greeted with enthusiasm even by the believers, for it was too much of a good thing. But two Wanderers can be traced well into the eighteenth century. Sometime near 1750 was written a rare German broadside, the *Wahre eigentliche Abildung desz unsterblichen Heydens Joseph Krantz von dessen Wandel Ursachen und neuester Eräugnis im Norden von Engelland seinem Altherthum Vorgehen und gantzer Natur aus allen glaubhafften AUTHORIBUS nebst noch andern Denckwürdigkeiten zusammen gezogen und erläutert auch darbey den Unterschied zwischen ihn und den unsterblichen Juden gar deutlich gewiesen wie folgt: etc.*[36] Note the mention of the North of England, where the 1769 pamphlet and its Dover successor tell us that Ahasuerus was. This German broadside by no means makes good its ambitious plan. It is a rough compilation of a highly condensed summary of material from Marana's *Turkish Spy* (pp. 128-32 below), the Ahasuerus-book in general, and a tasty detail first mentioned in J. Nicolaus Heldvader's *Sylva Chronologica* (1624) which has it that Christ was struck by the cobbler's shoe last, losing thereby all his teeth. As for the difference between Joseph Krantz (representing Cartaphilus) and the immortal (*unsterbliche*) Jew (representing Ahasuerus), it is certainly not made entirely clear (*gar deutlich*). The main fact is established, however, that Joseph Krantz (Cartaphilus) does not have to be an incessant wanderer, but is merely an awaiter and a preacher. Thus Krantz is the medieval, and Ahasuerus the Renaissance, aspect of the Wandering Jew.

This use of the name Joseph Krantz, instead of Joseph Cartaphilus, is unique. What is its origin? In medieval Christian symbolism, the *Krantz*, or wreath, signified a sanctified person, a king, or a divinity.[37] The Jew has, of course, been "touched" by Christ in the sense that he has been cursed by the Saviour, but it is only a painful immortality which crowns him. Does the name symbolize the crown of immortality suggested by the crown of thorns pressed upon the head of Jesus? Is it a corruption of Cartaphilus? One can only conjecture, but I should call attention to the perhaps incidental fact that in John Donne's "Third Satire," printed in 1633, the name "Crantz" seems to be a generic term for a Calvinist, presumably German, Dutch, or Swiss.[38]

To return for a moment to the 1647 edition of the *Relation*. The author, having allowed that all such things are possible, remarks anent the rejuvenation of Cartaphilus as soon as he has reached the age of one hundred: "By the analogy of the pelican of the waste and the glorious phoenix-bird in her mystery, these are both old and true witnesses." He concludes his explanation or apologia by observing: "People believe many things that never happened, and many things happen that none believes, for each man judges as he understands things. Yet that can often happen in nature which often enough seems to be against sense or belief, except for the truths of actual experience. Therefore we on our part are satisfied that it is true and trust that the kind reader will accept this evidence of mercy, divine wisdom, and omnipotence, with faithful notice." This old defense of the Legend is naïve—too naïve to satisfy some of the scholars who considered the matter—but the author of the pamphlet wanted to sell his wares.

It is a monotonous business to listen to all of the scholarly guns fired against the Legend and the few small arms fired in its behalf during the years before 1800, but a few illustrations are necessary. One of the first of the rebuttals will be found in J. Sebastian Mitternacht's treatise on John 21:22 ("Jesus saith unto him, If I will that he tarry till I come, what is that to thee? follow thou me").[39] The discharge of ordnance here is ponderous. In the same year, 1655, the Dutch theologian Hoornbeek, in a pamphlet printed at Leyden, *De convincendis et convertendis Judaeis*, speaks most scornfully of the "empty rumor," "the mere trifles" which have created unrest between Christians and Jews and implies that the Catholics have been especially gullible.

More specifically, the 1647 edition of the *Relation* evoked two very erudite counterblasts, two dissertations from Wittenberg and Jena, respectively. In the Wittenberg monograph, coming ironically from the city so intimately associated with the beginnings of the Ahasuerus-book, Gottfried Thilo makes sport of the credulousness of the author of the *Relation* by pointing out the defective nature of the evidence adduced to prove the existence of Ahasuerus, particularly because of internal contradictions (*Meletma historicum de Judaeo immortali*, 1668). A German vernacular translation of this work, entitled *Der unsterbliche Jude*, was printed at Leipzig in 1702. Also in 1668 came the attack on the Legend from Jena in Martinus Dröscher's *Dissertatio theologica de duobus testibus vivis Passionis dominicae*, which considers the dual theory of the Wandering Jew just mentioned,

weighs in heavy-footed, pedantic fashion all the evidence of the possible existence of such a Jew or Jews, and concludes that the opponents of the Legend are
right.

On the other hand, there was a stouthearted dissenter from the majority in the
person of Pastor Georg Hadeck from the Palatinate. His opinion, expressed in the
anonymously published *Nathanelis Christiani Relation eines Wallbruders mit
Nahmen Ahasverus, etc.* (1681),[40] was that since Christ, according to John 20:31
and 21:25, often did things about which his disciples had not been told, the ad-
missibility of such a marvel as the Wandering Jew was not impossible. By and
large, we may take Hadeck's attitude as typical of all those who would believe the
Legend. But Hadeck was in turn overwhelmed by the dissertation of Christopher
Schultz, *Dissertatio historica de Judaeo non mortali.* Schultz's work was a popular tract (judging by the fact that it went through several reprints), in which, with
much display of learning, the credibility of the Legend is denied. The first edition
of Schultz's work is from Königsberg in 1689; the latest from Jena in 1734. It
was reprinted in 1693, 1698, and 1711.

However, the first statement of an important idea which comes to full flower in
the later nineteenth century—that Ahasuerus is symbolic of the Jewish people as a
whole—comes from Johann Jacob Schudt. In his massive *Jüdische Merckwürdigkeiten* (1714-18),[41] he devotes himself to the Legend and reaches the conclusion that Ahasuerus is not a single person but rather all Jewry, scattered about in
the world after the Crucifixion and awaiting the Last Judgment according to the
testimony of Christ. His attitude toward the Legend is one of disbelief, based
upon three main arguments: (1) Christ forgave all and prayed for his enemies,
hence the impossibility of imposing such a harsh sentence or curse; (2) neither in
the Gospels nor the Epistles can anything be found concerning the Legend, nor
in the secular writers of ecclesiastical history; and (3) there is no agreement about
the Legend—now Ahasuerus is a heathen, now a Jew; now he is called Joseph,
now Ahasuerus or Cartaphilus; sometimes they say he was a shoemaker, at others
that he was a porter in the palace of Pilate; according to one version he is wandering, according to another he is living in Armenia or in Jerusalem. In an earlier
work, *Compendium historiae judaicae* (Frankfurt, 1700), Schudt had already referred to the Legend, with specific allusion to the use of the shoe last in the offense against Christ.[42]

The roll call of scholars dismissing the Legend is striking. As early as 1604, the
German Libavius, in *Praxis Alchymiae*, fires an oblique shot.[43] In discussing Paracelsus' use of charms, he remarks: "I would sooner believe that the old Jew Ahasuerus has been living on earth since the birth of Christ than this: although there
is no single acceptable argument for the story of the Jew—even the book contra-
dicts itself!" It will be recalled that the Parisian advocate Raoul Boutrays (Boterius), in the year 1610, dubbed the Legend a fairy tale. Jean Cousin, in his *Histoire de Tournay* (1619), in speaking of a broadside picture of Ahasuerus issued
in a printing of a *complainte* calls both the Jew and his wanderings *fabuleux*.[44]
Similarly, Boulenger, in *Historia sui temporis* (1619), an account quoted by
Schultz, washes his hands of the Legend. "Believe it who will! Since I was not in
Paris at the time [of Ahasuerus' visit], I neither have seen anyone of this sort nor

have had any dealings with anyone who did."[45] M. C. Lundorpius, in his *Joannis Sleidani de Statu religionis ac reipublicae continuatio* (1615-19), agrees with Boutrays.[46]

Occasionally a more cautious note enters the discussion. J. Cluverius' *Historiarum totius mundi, etc.* of 1637 admits that the story is a somewhat remarkable matter, worthy of remembrance and, if true, a great testimonial of the power of Christianity against infidels.[47] Two works by Thomas Bartholinus are similarly indecisive in judgment, although the author clearly does not wish to believe the Legend. The first of these, *De Latere Christi aperto dissertatio* (Leyden, 1646), mentions it, but observes: "Concerning the credibility of the Wandering Jew I cannot decide, although he has been reported in certain public appearances and acts. I should attach more belief to the truth of the Legend than to its tellers! . . . He seems to be a remarkable man, of supernatural or otherworldly traits. It is best for him to remain, over all these years, as a character in a good story than not."[48] No doubt Bartholinus is waxing ironical here, for later, in his *Historiarum anatomicarum et medicarum rariorum centuria V et VI* (Dresden, 1654-61), he brackets Ahasuerus and the fabulous Thomas Parr, the "old, old, very old man," who died in London in 1635 at the reputed age of one hundred fifty two—an age which cannot be substantiated in fact, although it may be conceded that Parr was a centenarian. In this instance, Bartholinus, having cited the two as remarkable cases of longevity, insists that the Legend is incredible because the Church fathers never made mention of it.[49] "At best a deceiver," so say Heinrich Nicolai, in *Passionalia* (1648); Johann H. Hottinger, in *Historiae Ecclesiasticae* (1653); the Dutch university professor Hoornbeek, already noted; and Erasmus Schmid, in *Opus sacrum posthumum* (1658).[50] But whereas these reject the Legend in passing as merely incredible, others are more impressed by the lack of authority justifying it; such is the attitude in Johannes Lyserus' *Aphtharsia* (1662).[51]

Fabulous or not, the Legend receives occasional recognition for its value as Christian propaganda. This is particularly well expressed in Carl Scharschmidt's *Europaeischer Staats- und Kriegs-Saal* (1686):[52] here the Legend is considered one of the most notable witnesses "against the Jews." Miscellaneous minor comments are numerous throughout the two centuries. Erasmus Francisci, in *Der lustigen Schau-Bühne vielerhand Curiositäten* (1698), wonders whether the printer is printing this legend pure and undefiled simply for the sake of profits, for certainly there is no moral purpose that he can see in it.[53] The eighteenth century followed its predecessor in condemning Ahasuerus as a fiction of imagination, an interesting fable. So it is in the interesting and important *Physico-Theology* of William Derham, delivered as Boyle Lectures in London in 1711-12, published in 1713, translated into German in 1750.[54] This is seconded in J. C. Koch's *Observationes miscellaneae* (1715)[55] and also in J. T. Jablonski's *Allgemeine Lexikon* (1748).[56] Perhaps the disbelief is implicit in the title, as in the *Schau-platz vieler ungereimter Meynungen und Erzehlungen* (Berlin, 1735-42) by Tharsander or *Der sogenannte unsterbliche Jude, etc.* (Havelberg, 1706) by Gottlieb (or Gottlob) Rothen.

Sometimes, for reasons that are no longer apparent and probably no longer ascertainable, there is a violent reaction to the Legend, as if it offended the nostrils of the commentator. Caspar Kildgaard's *De Judaeo non mortali* (1733) cannot accept the truth of the Legend and indicates that anyone who does is a benighted fool.[57] A reference, expressed with considerable acerbity, appears in Gotthard Heidegger's *Acerra philologica nova* (1735).[58] It likens the Legend to something attached by turpentine to better material; where it touches it clings so hard that it cannot be torn away. Obviously, then, turpentine was used for adhesive purposes in the eighteenth century. Johann Friedrich Pfeffinger's *Merckwürdigkeiten des XVII. Jahrhunderts* (1706) labels the Wandering Jew as a *Narro* (obviously more than a mere *Narr*, or fool) of idle, frivolous, empty-headed and useless people.[59] But the roughest rejection comes from Johann Moller's *Cimbria Literata* (1744). In an article on Paulus von Eitzen it describes the Legend as a "fabula putidissima" (*putidissima* can be translated only as "most rotten and stinking") and asserts that any one who tells of a meeting between Von Eitzen and Ahasuerus is an unmitigated liar.[60] More temperate, but condemnatory for another reason, are the strictures in F. Albrecht Christiani's *Der Juden Glaube und Aberglaube* (Leipzig, 1705). The author, a Jew converted to Christianity (who later reverted to the faith of his fathers), cannot believe in the Legend: it is baseless and similar to too many worthless Jewish legends. What these Jewish legends may have been we are not told; it would help a great deal to know about them, but they are simply not forthcoming.

Among these many carping critics, the two who seem to have attracted the largest following are J. S. Mitternacht and Christopher Schultz. The latter is the main source of the treatment of the Legend in Hermann Suden's *Der Gelehrte Criticus über 247 curieuse Dubia, etc.*, which relies completely on Schultz's rejection.[61] P. Laurenberg's *Neue und vermehrte Acerra Philologica, etc.* (Frankfurt-Leipzig, 1708) sides with Mitternacht, agreeing on reasons for an utterly skeptical attitude, but going out of its way to inject an anti-Semitic drug. Any survey of the whole material, however, would give to Schudt's *Jüdische Merckwürdigkeiten* the honor of being the most carefully worked-out discussion of the Legend.

In short, as the eighteenth century rolled along, the weight of general disbelief among the scholars grew more and more oppressive. Their attitude is summed up as well as anywhere in the anonymous *Historische Nachricht von dem ewigen Juden* (Frankfurt-Leipzig, 1723). The position taken here is simply one which denies the authenticity of the entire Legend; all the available evidence is examined, and attention is called in a calm, objective style to the essential absurdity, the uncertain tradition, the silence of all reliable contemporary authorities, and so on. Any wider interpretation is, for the moment, suppressed. Thus J. G. Heinsius' *Kurtze Fragen aus der Kirchen Historia des Neuen Testaments* (Jena, 1725), which follows Schudt's theory that the Wandering Jew is symbolic of the whole Jewish race, fails to make any particular subsequent impression. But it is doubtful whether the Age of Reason, at its peak in 1725, would admit such an esoteric kind of interpretation. Perhaps it is also significant that in none of these early eighteenth-century works is scriptural authority invoked to any marked degree, as it had been in the seventeenth century. The curious twist, however, lies in the fact that the *Historische Nachricht* of 1723 had some influence upon Carl Anton, professor of philosophy at Helmstedt, who supported its conclusions in his *Lepidam fabulam de Judaeo immortali, etc.* (1755).[62]

The monograph by Anton would have been of no consequence, since it adds nothing of importance to the discussion, if it had not provoked an amusing and delightfully ingenuous document from Maria Krüger, wife of a professor of mathematics at Helmstedt. There seems to have been an energetic and acrimonious intellectual civil war within the walls of this university on the subject of Ahasuerus. Frau Krüger's pamphlet is excessively rare. It rejoices in the somewhat formidable title, *Marien Reginen Krügerin gebohrnen Ruhlemannin an den Herrn Professor Carl Anton darinnen bewiesen wird dass es einen ewigen Juden gabe;* let it be known simply as the *Schreiben der Krügerin* (Halle-Helmstedt, 1756). She wrote the tract and directed it against Anton without the knowledge of her husband, "because I did not think it necessary to let him know anything about it." She insists that the Wandering Jew was alive as late as 1743; at least she would believe so, and she thinks that all true Christians should likewise believe it. Indeed, she saw him; therefore she can support the stories of the blessed Paulus von Eitzen and the Armenian archbishop. Since Anton himself had admitted that he had traveled extensively, he *must* have met the Jew; and if he failed to recognize him, all the more stupid he. To be sure, Paulus von Eitzen had described Ahasuerus as a tall man, and the man she saw was short. But she explains this embarrassing detail by the fact that as people grow older their vertebrae shrink, and in two hundred years or so, the Wandering Jew would have become appreciably shorter. A brief footnote to Frau Krüger's story is the fact that she clothes her Jew in the conventional manner, clearly as she remembered it from the German Ahasuerus-book, except that she gives him cuffs to his sleeves which were so long that they reached far beyond the tips of his longest fingers. The ingenious explanation of the discrepancy in height is worth remembering. Her pamphlet is a fascinating combination of female emotionalism in argumentative exposition and specious explanations emanating from a not too well understood application of academic and pseudoacademic information. One might characterize the lady thus: fine woman, no mind.[63]

She was not, however, satisfied with her original contribution. In the same year (1756) she issued a supplement, even more rare than the first pamphlet and far more important.[64] It gives the first extended mention of the Wandering Jewess (see Appendix B). Ahasuerus, of course, once had a wife. She is not absent from any full account of the Wandering Jew after 1602. But Frau Krüger makes her more than a word or phrase or the mother of a child whom Ahasuerus held in his arms when he received the curse of Christ. As the author explains:

The Wandering Jewess [*ewige Jüdin*], who in these days has proved the existence of herself and her husband, will be well disposed toward me inasmuch as I have added to her testimony my information about the Wandering Jew. I am one of the most credible instruments for disseminating the whole business; for not only have I seen the Wandering Jew with his Jewess, but I was also in the village of Helfte when he came and married Schmul Ner Ruhlmann's daughter. He was dressed as his wife describes it in her writing in this pamphlet. In body he was rather thickset and fat; he spoke in a high treble and was as gallant as a young gentleman. However, I wish to say nothing about him except to make known the facts and the documents as befits a true historian. These documents I have in my possession; they pertain to the Wandering Jew and the Wandering Jewess and will continue to do so, as long as the marvelous couple themselves . . .

She concludes with some execrable verses concerning the sinister habits of the domestic life of the Wandering Jew and his Jewess and the necessarily disturbing effect which their existence must have on Christian morality and the peace and quiet of a Christian community.

These verses attracted the attention of an anonymous writer in the *Hannover-ische Beyträge zum Nütze und Vergnügen* for September 7, 1761. This observer comments that the Legend seems to have originated at the time of the Crusade of Frederick Barbarossa (the Third Crusade, which began in 1189), but gives no useful evidence for such an opinion, which we can see is incorrect. But the noteworthy thing about this Hannoverian is the smugness of his tone: the world is certainly more intelligent than it was; surely we are better than our fathers, to say nothing of our grandfathers; and the whole Legend is the most utter foolishness and should be repudiated forthwith.[65] The learned and the sophisticated of the eighteenth century are ready to nail down the coffin lid. Indeed, such an attitude had been prevalent for decades: the anonymous author of *Historische Nachricht von dem ewigen Juden*—a pamphlet that descended directly from the Dudulaeus pamphlet—was willing to cap his narrative by demonstrating fundamentally (*gründlich*) the impossibility that Ahasuerus could ever have been *in rerum natura*; an article in the *Dresdener gelehrte Anzeiger* for 1788 refers to the "warmed-over coal" of the Legend; and A. du Lignon, a French pastor of Doornik, Belgium, wrote rather plaintively in 1769 that a misinterpretation of a passage in the Gospels "a causé ce désordre."[66]

Yet only a few years after the egregious bit of self-praise in the *Hannoverische Beyträge*, just mentioned, the Wandering Jew paid a visit to Brussels and, as we have already seen, set in train a series of lyric *complaintes*. Indeed, if the author of that article could have foreseen the part which Ahasuerus was to play in the literature of the coming Romantic Age, he would have eaten his words in shame. True, it may be that we know more than our grandfathers, but the Wandering Jew marches on. The condemnation of scholars throughout the seventeenth and eighteenth centuries seems to have had little effect upon the vitality of the Legend on popular soil, which was ever ready to nourish it. That was all that was needed; let the pundits rave.

CHAPTER SIX

Ahasuerus the Eighteenth-Century Traveler

It was inevitable that Ahasuerus, now in the early 1700's the most celebrated *parcoureur du monde,* should sooner or later come to be regarded as omniscient as well as ubiquitous. He had been alive since the beginnings of the Christian era, and there was supposedly no land in the generally known world of the Occident where he had not at one time or another allegedly passed by or spent his allotted stay—one night, three days, until the next midnight hour, a fortnight, five minutes. In his privileged state of one who had seen everything, it would be easy for him, if he were so disposed, to assume the mantle of teacher and prophet, with a particular liking for history and geography, although he need not confine himself to those two subjects.

The neoclassical age, from about 1650 to about 1750, sometimes called upon Ahasuerus for social comment, criticism, and satirical observation. The concept of him as teacher was fostered in part by the inclination toward instruction always associated with the literature of that age. It was nourished, at the same time, by the image of the Wandering Jew in the German and French *Volksbuch* treatments of the seventeenth century. Even in the *Kurtze Beschreibung* of 1602 he showed not only a pious and zealous spirit of proselytism but also the ability to pass, with flying colors, an examination in Oriental history since the Crucifixion.

Some of the later derivatives—such as the *Relation,* the French *Histoire admirable,* and the *Wunderbare Erzehlung*—developed an itinerary for Ahasuerus. The *Histoire admirable,* for example, conducted our protagonist all over western Europe, where he saw many strange sights, and across to America and back again. It is with the addition of such details that the outline of the Wandering Jew as a chronicler of world history begins to take shape, if only in a perfunctory way.

A chief architect in the construction of this Chronicle of the Wandering Jew,[1] as I shall call it hereafter, is the identifiable author of a celebrated work of the century. He was Giovanni Marana, a Genoese who died in Paris in either 1692 or 1693. The work is a series of essays in epistolary form, an honorable predecessor both in satirical spirit and in style to Montesquieu's *Lettres persanes* or Goldsmith's *Citizen of the World.* The original of this work was supposedly written in Italian, but if it ever existed in this form, it is now lost. A French translation, probably by Marana himself, appeared in Paris in 1684 under the title, *L'Espion du Grand-Seigneur et ses relations secrètes envoyées au divan de Constantinople.*[2] An English version by William Bradshaw was published in 1686 as *Letters Writ by a Turkish Spy, Who Lived Five and Forty Years Undiscover'd at Paris,* and before 1748 there had been twelve English editions. In fact, Bradshaw was for a long time believed to be the original author.

As to Marana, he was a man of imagination, or at least happy invention, and the turn he gave to the course of the Legend is important. The chief reference comes in a letter addressed to "Ibrahim Haly Cheik, a Man of the Law," and deserves to be quoted in full:

Here is a Man come to this City, if he may be called a Man, who pretends to have lived about these Sixteen Hundred Years. They call him the Wandering Jew. But some say, he is an Impostor. He says of himself, That he was Usher of the Divan in Jerusalem, (the Jews call it the Court of Judgment) where all Criminal Causes were try'd, at the Time when Jesus, the Son of Mary, the Christian's Messias, was condemned by Pontius Pilate, the Roman President: That his Name was Michob Ader; and, that, For thrusting Jesus out of the Hall, with these Words, Go, why tarriest thou? The Messias answered him again; I go, but tarry thou till I come; thereby condemning him to live till the Day of Judgment. He pretends to remember the Apostles that lived in those Days, and, That he himself was Baptized by one of them: That he has travelled through all the Regions of the World, and so must continue to be a Vagabond till the Messias shall return again. They say, That he heals Diseases, by touching the Party affected. Divers other Miracles are ascribed to him by the Ignorant and Superstitious; but the Learned, the Noble, and the Great, censure him as a Counterfeit, or a Madman. Yet there are, who affirm, That 'tis one convincing Argument of the Reality of his Pretence, That he has hitherto escaped a Prison, especially in these Countries, where the Authors of all Innovations are severely punish'd. He has escaped the Inquisition at Rome, in Spain, and in Portugal, which the Vulgar will have to be an evident Miracle.

One Day I had the Curiosity to discourse with him in several Languages; and I found him Master of all those that I could speak. I conversed with him five or six Hours together in Arabick. He told me, That there was scarce a true History to be found. I asked him, What he thought of Mahomet, the Prophet and Lawgiver of the Mussulmans? He answered, That he knew his Father very well, and had been often in his Company at Ormus in Persia; That Mahomet was a Man full of Light and a Divine Spirit, but had his Errors as well as other Mortals; and that his chiefest was, in denying the Crucifixion of the Messias; for, said he, I was then present, and saw Him hang on the Cross, with these Eyes of mine. He accused the Mussulmans of Imposture, in making the World believe, That the Tomb of their Prophet hangs miraculously between Heaven and Earth, saying, That he himself had seen it, and that it was built after the Manner of other Sepulchres. Thou who has been in the Holy Place, knowest whether this be false or true. He upbraids the Persian Mahometans with Luxury, the Ottomans with Tyranny, the Arabians with Robbery, the Moors with Cruelty, and the Mussulmans of the Indies with Atheism: Nor does he spare to reproach the Christian Churches: he taxes the Roman and Grecian with the pompous Idolatry of the Heathens. He accuses the Aethiopian with Judaism, the Armenian with Heresies; and says, That the Protestants, if they would live according to their Profession, would be the best Christians.

He told me, He was in Rome when Nero set Fire to the City, and stood triumphing on the Top of a Hill to behold its Flames. That he saw Saladine's Return from his Conquests in the East, when he caused his Shirt to be carried on the Top of a Spear, with this Proclamation; Saladine, Lord of many rich Countries, Conqueror of the East, ever victorious and happy, when he dies, shall have no other Memorial left of all his Glories, but only this poor Shirt.

He relates many remarkable Passages of Solyman the Magnificent, whereof of Histories are silent; and says, He was in Constantinople, when Solyman built that Royal Mosque, which goes by his Name. He knew Tamerlane the Scythian, and told me, That he was so call'd, because he halted with one Leg. He pretends also to have been acquainted with Scanderbeg, the Valiant and Fortunate Prince of Epirus. He seem'd to pity the insupportable Calamity of Bajazet, whom he had seen carried about in a Cage by Tamerlane's Order. He accuses the Scythian, of too barbarous an Insult on the Unfortunate Sultan. He remembers the ancient Caliphs of Babylon and Egypt; the Empire of the Saracens, and, the Wars in the Holy Land. He highly extols the Valour and Conduct of the Renowned Godfrey of Bulloign. He gives an accurate Account of the Rise, Progress, Establishment, and Subversion of the Mamalukes in Egypt. He says, he has wash'd himself in the two head Springs of the River Nile, which arise in the most Southern Part of Aethiopia. That its Increase is occasion'd by the great Rains in Aethiopia, which swell all the Rivers that fall into the Nile, and cause that vast Inundation, which has so much puzzled Philosophy to find out the Origin. He says, That the River Ganges in India, is broader and deeper than the Nile; That the River Nigor in Africa is longer by some Hundreds of Miles; and, That he can remember a Time, when the River Nile overflowed not till three Months after the usual Season.

Having professed himself an universal Traveller, and that there was no Corner of the Earth where he had not been present, I began to comfort myself with the Hopes of some News from the Ten Tribes of Israel, that were carried into Captivity by Salmanassar, King of Assyria, and could never be heard of since. I ask'd him several Questions, concerning them, but found no satisfactory Answer. Once he told me, That both in Asia, Africa and Europe, he had taken notice of a Sort of People, who (though not Jews in Profession) yet retained some Characteristicks, whereby one might discover them to be descended of that Nation.

In Livonia, Russia, and Finland, he had met with People of distinct Languages from that of the Country, having a great Mixture of Hebrew Words; That these abstained from Swines Flesh, Blood, and Things strangled. That in their Lamentations for the Dead, they always used these Words, [Jeru-Jeru Masco Salem.] By which he thought, they called to Remembrance Jerusalem and Damascus, those two famous Cities of Palestine and Syria. In the Circassians also he had traced some Footsteps of Judaism; their Customs, Manner of Life, Feasts, Marriages, and Sacrifices, being not far removed from the Institutions of the Mosaick Law. But, what is most remarkable, he said, That he had conversed with professed Jews in the North Parts of Asia, who never so much as heard of Jesus, the Son of Mary, or of the Revolutions in Judaea after his Death, the Siege and Destruction of Jerusalem, or any other Matters wherewith all Histories abound, concerning that Nation. He said moreover, That these Jews had only the Pentateuch, not having heard of the rest of those Books which compose the greatest Part of the Old Testament; and, That this Pentateuch was written in a Sort of Hebrew, far different from that which is now commonly spoken by the rest of the dispersed Jews throughout the World. That the Number of these Jews was infinite. And finally, he thought, That these, (if any) were the true Posterity of those Ten Captive Tribes.

Having mentioned the Destruction of Jerusalem, I ask'd him, Where he was at that Time? He told me in the Court of Vespasian at Rome, and that he had heard the Emperor say, when he understood the Temple of Solomon was burnt to Ashes, He had rather all Rome had been set on Fire. Here the old Man fell a weeping himself, lamenting the Ruins of the noble Structure, which he described to me as familiarly, as if he had seen it but Yesterday. He says, That Josephus wrote partially of the Seditious in the City, being related to one of the Chief Ringleaders, whom therefore he spar'd, being loth to stain the Reputation of his own Family to all Posterity.

I tell thee, Sage Cheik, if this Man's Pretences be true, he is so full of choice 100
Memoirs, and has been Witness to so many grand Transactions for the Space of sixteen Centuries of Years, That he may not unfitly be call'd, A Living Chronology, the Proto-Notary of the Christian Hegira, or Principal Recorder of that which they esteem the Last Epocha of the World's duration.

By his Looks one would take him for a Relick of the Old World, or one of the 105
Long-liv'd Fathers before the Flood. To speak modestly, he may pass for the
Younger Brother of Time.

It would be endless, to tell thee how many other discourses we had of his Travels and Memoirs, till tired with his Company, and judging all to be a Cheat, I took my leave. 110

I tell thee, he seems to be a Man well vers'd in all Histories, a great Traveller, and one that affects to be counted an extrardinary Person. The common People are ready to adore him; and the very Fear of the Multitude restrains the Magistrates from offering any Violence to this Impostor.

Live thou in the Exercise of thy Reason, which will not permit thee to be se- 115
duced into Errors, by the subtle Insinuation of Men. Continue to love Mahmut, who honours thee without a Fiction.

—Paris, 4th of the 1st Moon, of the Year 1644.[3]

We now have a new name for the Wanderer, Michob Ader (l.7), and an entirely new occupation, that of "Usher of the Divan" or doorkeeper in the Court of Judgment (ll.4-5). Both the name and the occupation, when found in later tellings of the tale, are to be acknowledged as Marana's. We meet for the first time direct allusions to Saladin (ll.40-44), Nero (ll.39-40), Suleiman the Magnificent (ll.45-47), Tamerlane (ll.47-48), Bajazet (ll.50-52), and Scanderbeg (l.49). Subsequent references to these in connection with the Legend are to be traced to the *Turkish Spy*. Of particular importance is the appearance of Nero in this roll call of personages, for the nineteenth-century writers make a good deal of him as a participant in the Legend. This is what may be termed the Ahasuerus-in-Rome motif.[4] At times one meets again the encounter with Mahommed's father in Ormuz, the appearance of Suleiman the Magnificent (ll.45-47). The destruction of Jerusalem (l.91) under Titus and Vespasian inspired several works in the nineteenth century which used Ahasuerus as a secondary character. For the most part Marana seems to have invented these matters, as far as the Legend of the Wandering Jew is concerned. There is, of course, much material in this essay in the *Turkish Spy* which is indebted to the German Ahasuerus-book and the French *Histoire admirable*, but Marana's net achievement was to put the Chronicle of the Wandering Jew on its feet.

There are two other references to the Wanderer in the *Turkish Spy*. In the first of these, addressed to the learned Ben Saddi in 1666, the narrator goes to some pains to explain what the Jew told him of the Jews he found living in North Africa and Asia and of the lost Ten Tribes of Israel. As for these Ten Tribes, it will be recalled that they went to form part of the adventitious material which had already been added in profusion to the Ahasuerus-book during the seventeenth century.[5]

Then again in a letter written, he says, in 1672, it appears that the Wandering Jew came to a city as remote as Astrakhan, Russia, and there preached that all Christendom was due for an overhauling in the year 1700. A "famous voyager," one Fousi, had an interesting map of the wanderings of Ahasuerus (Michob Ader), although nothing is said as to how this came into his possession. But it is apparent, reports the Turkish Spy, that all Christendom would be overwhelmed by the Ottoman Turks in 1700; that the continent of Europe, having been inundated by this wave of the future, would be lost, while all surviving Christians would flee to England for refuge. At about this same time a great personage would arise to fight for the Christians; he would begin by reconquering Jerusalem and making good his claims to the abashed infidels that he was the true Messiah. Of course, the Turkish Spy hastens to add, he takes no great stock in such a prophecy. How can one be sure of such things? (Did he realize that Prince Eugene would defeat the Turks in 1697, not far from Vienna?) However, he admits the matter to be discussed by others, and since those who receive his letters are Moslems, it is natural that he should flatter them to the extent that he considers it possible that Christians may suffer disaster while Islam is triumphant, if only for a short time.[6]

Marana's contribution is the ultimate source of the account of the Wandering Jew in Dom Augustin Calmet's *Dictionnaire . . . de la Bible*, within which a letter from Madame de Mazarin is cited (pp. 109-10 above). It is responsible also for the story told in the *Theatrum Europaeum* (p. 110 above) and for a large part of the German broadside concerning Joseph Krantz, twin of Ahasuerus (pp. 121-22 above). Both the *Theatrum Europaeum* and the Joseph Krantz accounts are obvious condensations of the first letter of Marana's quoted above, although they add the information, not given elsewhere, that the Jew was closely questioned by scholars from Oxford and Cambridge, who could not bring him to contradict himself in any way.

Another work, written not much later, is highly indebted not only to Marana but also to Matthew Paris. This is *Voyages et Aventures de Jacques Massé*, printed at Bordeaux in 1710. Its author is Simon Tyssot de Patot, a Huguenot refugee, professor of mathematics at Deventer in the Netherlands, and writer as well of deistic pamphlets. There is an English translation, *The Travels and Adventures of James Massey*, by Stephen Whately (London, 1733). The Jew Michod—close enough to Michob Ader—is, in effect, an eighteenth-century Cartaphilus. The telling of the Legend here is in no way remarkable, except that the story of the Crucifixion receives this curious elaboration:

. . . All Jerusalem was in an uproar, when the rumor spread that those who were in the graveyards had seen the ground moving in many places, the sepulchres opening without anyone's putting his hand to them, and nude corpses appearing and making a thousand different movements. The fear . . . that such a sight, so little expected, produced in the bystanders, caused a fever and even in some cases death. The more hardy of them, however, were determined to see the end of this wonder; they were amazed indeed when, some time later, they saw human creatures leaving their tombs altogether and fleeing in great haste among the crowd, which opened up a way for them by falling to the ground as if each one of them were about to go and take the places of the specters. No one could see . . . however attentive he might be, of what sex these resurrected creatures were; they all seemed of the same size, the same age, the same degree of fleshiness; and they bore no mark to distinguish one from another. They had no hair on their bodies; their abdomens were flat and seemed as if loosely attached to their loins; several kept their mouths open, but no teeth were visible; and their fingers, rounded and joined together, seemed to be entirely devoid of nails. This made all the people conclude that all of the organs of elimination and those which serve to receive, digest, and absorb our food while we are subject to death do not accompany us into the next world, where they would be of no use to us. In short, to judge by what we heard, we never knew positively what became of these creatures; however, the rumor circulated some days later that they had gone into Galilee, where they were said to have met Jesus Christ with joy; and thence they were transported to the Abode of the Blessed.[7]

A work of minor importance illustrates the versatility of Ahasuerus as a teacher—an ability not always attributed to him. This is an anonymous French pamphlet of 1722, bearing the pretentious title, *Les grandes prophéties du Sieur de Montague, autrement nommé le juif errant.*[8] The name for the Jew is unique. Here we have some prophecies concerning the weather to be expected for the next seven years, with special mention of its effect upon certain crops—in fact, an early *Farmer's Almanac*—to which is added a series of verses in execrable doggerel summarizing the prophecies and seasoning them with some platitudinous observations.

The History of Israel Jobson

Thus we have, so far, the beginnings of Ahasuerus in the role of historian, of philosopher speculating upon the effects of the Crucifixion on corpses, and of weather prophet. One of the most remarkable eighteenth-century documents, in which he serves as teacher of astronomy and cosmology, is a long-buried pamphlet of extreme rarity which combines the contemporary interest in travel upon and above the earth (where it is an interest in space fiction) with pious deistic reflection, and with a certain amount of the Orientalism that marked the literature of the age.[9] This is the work with the following elaborate title page:

The/HISTORY/of/ISRAEL JOBSON,/the/WANDERING JEW./Giving a Description of his Pedigree, Tra-/vels in this lower World, and his As-/sumption thro' the Starry Regions, con-/ducted by a Guardian Angel, exhibiting/in a curious Manner the Shapes, Lives,/and Customs of the Inhabitants of the/Moon and Planets; touching upon the/ great and memorable Comet in 1758, and/interwoven all along with the Solution/of the Phaenomena of the true Solar/System, and Principles of Natural Philo-/sophy, concording with the latest Dis-/coveries of the most able Astronomers./Translated from the Original Chinese/by M. W./Haec scripta sunt novitatis gratia Non ad/augendam fidem, nec diminuendam:/LONDON:/Printed for J. Nickolson, Bookseller, in/Cambridge. 1757.

M. W. is Miles Wilson, curate in the tiny Yorkshire village of Halton Gill from 1737 to 1777. He is probably the Miles Wilson who matriculated at Queen's College, Oxford, December 3, 1728 (aged eighteen), whose home is given as Beralls, Westmoreland.[10] He does not seem to have taken any degree while at

Oxford; and his occasional lapses into northerly habits of speech, as well as his frequent errors in grammar, indicate that his training was far from complete. In most respects, then, he must have been a self-educated man. His charge in the little chapel at Halton Gill would hardly be important enough or large enough to require a university graduate in the eighteenth century, provided the incumbent had other ministerial qualifications. Certainly Wilson seems to have been a colorful individual given to much free and easy unlocking of his word hoard.

He was the author of another pamphlet, *The Man in the Moon*.[11] So far as I can determine, there is no longer a copy of this work in existence, for it was spoken of in 1831 as extremely rare. Its substance, however, has fortunately been preserved:

Old Israel Jobson, a thrifty cobbler, who lived down at Horton,[12] seems to have been imbued with a strange life-long desire to visit some of the planets, and in order to gratify (as he thought) this peculiar whim, managed by his industry and frugality to save enough to purchase an enormous quantity of rope and timber. With these materials, and after many years of patient labour devoted to its construction, he made and erected on Penyghent an immense ladder that enabled him, after a long and fatiguing journey, to reach the moon. But at length, entering the strange planet, and having shaken hands and had a little explanatory conversation with the Man-in-Charge, the Horton cobbler began to feel uncommonly hungry; but perceiving the inhabitants around him were made of a kind of pot-metal, and were feeding off common clay, which they scooped out of the ground, Israel seems to have manifested some uneasiness at the spectacle; and ascertaining that that would be his only provision if he remained, he politely declined, not without a feeling of disappointment, and lost no time in descending to mother Earth, and to a more appetizing fare of his wife's home-made bread and good old-fashioned Yorkshire ham and eggs.[13]

There is no way of dating this missing *The Man in the Moon*, but from its facetious nature, I should gather that it probably antedates *The History of Israel Jobson*, which is a much more ambitious work of ninety-five pages, a true pamphleteer's magnum opus. Besides, in the latter work Jobson has become the Wandering Jew, an honor not usually bestowed upon the neophyte. There were two well-known accounts of imaginary voyages through the heavens which Miles Wilson had conceivably read, *The Life and Astonishing Adventures of John Daniel* by Ralph Morris (London, 1751)[14] and Robert Paltock's *The Life and Adventures of Peter Wilkins*, published in the same year. Both of these works are interesting for their contribution to the popular history of aeronautics. *The Life and Astonishing Adventures of John Daniel* carries the protagonist to the moon, where he meets and talks with the inhabitants, who are of a copper-colored complexion (*sic*) and partake of a tasteless, savorless food. If Wilson was influenced by the adventures of John Daniel, as seems very likely, we may assign *The Man in the Moon* a date not long after 1752.

The Man in the Moon has little to do with the Legend of the Wandering Jew, except that it introduces the name of Israel Jobson, a cobbler; the cognomen itself is unique among the various appellations bestowed upon the famous Wanderer. Where did Wilson find such a name? Presumably he was reminded of the boisterous wife-beater Jobson, the shoemaker in Charles Coffey's perennially popular

The Devil To Pay (1731), a diverting dramatic afterpiece, which held the stage periodically until the early 1800's. In this musical play, Jobson is a cobbler. Zekel, not Israel, is his given name in the drama, but Wilson would be safe in using Israel on his own. Of course he may also have known the current English ballad, *The Shooemaker of Jerusalem* (pp. 61-63 above).

Having, then, given Jobson a grotesque and entertaining experience in *The Man in the Moon*, Wilson settled down to business in *The History of Israel Jobson*. In a brief preface, he explains that he found the document in the Chinese language and has taken pains to translate it. And so it becomes another in the long line of eighteenth-century works clothed in synthetic, hypothetical Orientalism. "I employ'd my leisure Hours this last Winter in Translating by the Fire, this most delightful History into English. . . ." (The glimpse into the life of a little village in a remote and inaccessible part of the West Riding, in the dead of an eighteenth-century winter, needs no embellishment.) As for the composition of the pamphlet, its author observes, "indeed, the Stile is some Times too sublime for a Cobler, and at other Times too low for an Angel." The preface is dated March 7, 1756, "at H-lt-g-ll in Yorkshire."

The main purpose of *The History of Israel Jobson*, curious and enjoyable performance that it is, remains the dissemination, in a popular vein, of astronomical information, with a certain amount of other scientific fact thrown in. It is a rough equivalent of our modern popular science and space fiction literature. In view of the personal whimsicality which Wilson appears to have possessed in abundance, we should expect to find some facetious and farcical effects, and we find them; but the pamphlet was meant to be taken seriously as a whole. It is garnished with a modicum of rational deism, in the approved manner of an eighteenth-century philosopher, but there is not enough of this to disturb the author's Anglicanism. Wilson was an eccentric, but he was obviously an able and amusing one. Nor are his literary powers to be despised; he may have been an uncultivated individual, and his rhetorical capabilities often fell behind his emotional promptings, yet some of his phrases are happily conceived and forcefully expressed.[15]

According to Wilson, the Wandering Jew, one Israel Jobson, was the son of a cordwainer "in Sychem, between Mount Gerizim on the South, and Ebal on the North." (This is the only account of the Wandering Jew to give him so definite a birthplace.) He was given a "tolerable Proficiency" in writing and arithmetic. At the age of nineteen he was left an orphan; "after a decent Time for Mourning, I married into a reputable Family, and had for my Partner a Lady of Beauty and Merit, and in Process of Time was blessed with an Issue of hopeful Children." His wife's relatives, however, thought his occupation of shoemaker beneath the dignity required and prevailed upon him to sell his shop and merchandise on the occasion of the fair "held on the Seventeenth Day of the Month Abib, or Harvest Month."[16] At this fair—the Crucifixion is never mentioned—the Saviour came passing by, asked to rest (although no reason for his weariness is forthcoming), was rebuffed, and pronounced his curse. And so Jobson wandered until "the Soles of my Feet became hard and callous as a Stag's Horn."[17]

He would spare us a full account of all the regions of the earth which it was his lot to visit. He saw everything and was everywhere, but he does not care to talk about his experiences. He cannot avoid pausing briefly, however, to consider the wonderful state of the Great Mogul, the emperor of Hindustan, whose lavish resources in the year 1710 were the wonder of the world.[18] "But what?" asks Jobson, "What signifies the Pomp and Pageantry of Terrestrial Monarchs, when put in the Balance with the Inhabitants of the Coelestial Mansions? . . . My Soul swells at the Idea of them, and disdains the Relation of such inferior Transactions."

Although he had never been dismayed by the burning sands of Libya or the terrors of the Alps, Jobson was finally brought down to the depths of despair by "the haggard Mountains, dismal Chasms, and deep Vales" of the West Riding. The horrid view of desolation from the summit of Penyghent Hill, where the former Israel Jobson of *The Man in the Moon* had built his pathway to the moon, was altogether too much for him. He knelt down and prayed to "that Awful Being who Rules and Presides over all Things" to mitigate his sentence:

My prayer was heard, the Mountain was immediately cover'd with a Cloud of Mist, and an Ethereal Chariot descended with a Messenger from the Regions of Bliss. No Language can describe the Port and Glory of an Angel. He commanded me to Erect a small Pile of Stones as a Monument of Antiquity, and ascend the Chariot: I gladly obey'd, but as I was making the pile more grand, Enough, enough, says he, those few Stones shall stand till Time be outdated and swallow'd up in Eternity. Well, Jobson, says he, Chear up, and give Attention while I relate some Matters that surpass the Knowledge of Finite Creatures.

The chariot is the same kind of chariot that took Elijah away to dwell in bliss. Jobson's curse will be lightened to the extent that he may now wander for a while in celestial regions and get away from barren earth. The angel will be his guide.[19] Let him not worry longer about the desolation of the Yorkshire moors, for all such sterilities of nature are only the scars left when angels and devils fought for supremacy. Off they go, therefore, into the heavenly blue, amid the dancing rays of the aurora borealis ("nothing but Thunder immature, a Composition of Sulphur and Nitre").

They move effortlessly upon the surface of the air, as Christ once walked upon the waves. Jobson is terrified, but the angel tells him not to fear; soon he will be out in pure "Aether." He raps Jobson over his metaphorical knuckles with some statistics. It seems that neither Jobson nor the angel now have any weight in their bodies; Sir Isaac Newton knows why.

The first heavenly body to be visited is the moon. In both the seventeenth and the eighteenth centuries there were accounts of voyages to the moon.[20] Most of these lunar voyages were romantic yarns in which the moon appeared as a fair and fertile field with interesting creatures, or Lunarians, of a recognizable human stamp. The better textbooks of 1750 admitted the probable lack of atmosphere on the moon and therefore the impossibility of life there. Still, the earlier romantic fervor, with some rather grotesque symptoms, had laid hold of Miles Wilson. I have found few parallels to his particular lunar world in antecedent literature, except that in his adventures John Daniel met strange creatures of a copper color who subsisted on unsubstantial food. Wilson had already touched on this matter in *The Man in the Moon*, but now he draws upon his own imagination, which is by no means inconsiderable. His moon is inhabited by strange individuals of "Pan Metal."

Jobson's ears are assailed by a terrific clangor of metal, as coppersmiths—the moonmen's surgeons—minister to those who have been wounded in battle. (The inhabitants of the moon are mortal, "For if an Hole be made either in the Head or Body to let out the vital heat, which their Life consists of, they immediately die.") Jobson cannot understand why there should be war on the moon as on earth:

Pray inform me, said I, since these Men of Metal have no occasion for Meat, Drink, or Cloaths, what can be the Reason of their Wars? Well, I must tell you, said the Angel, that the Progeny of Pan Metal, are Propagated in your Way by Mutual Embraces, which in the Coition become so Hot as to Melt and Dissolve a little of their virile Substances; which in the Space of Nine Weeks, commonly produce a Metallick Youth of the same Species, either Male or Female; but sometimes it happens to be what they call a Lunarian, which, having Rent it's Parent comes gingling into the World like a Kettle Drum; this is one of the greatest Rarities in the Lunar World, and peculiar to it, which is constantly sought for by Ten Thousand Men of the Two Neighbouring Principalities; the Lunar World has it's Follies as well as your Planetary People.

But what this peculiarity of Wilson's Lunarians may be is never more than darkly hinted at. Here as elsewhere, however, we are reminded of Swift's *Gulliver's Travels*. Thus the war between two neighboring principalities brings to mind the conflict between Lilliputians and Blefuscans in Book I. The rare birth of a "Lunarian," though not explained, suggests that the Lunarian was of preternatural quality, perhaps like the Struldbrugs in Book III of *Gulliver's Travels*.

For the first time on record the Wandering Jew is to be seen fawning over a lady's hand in the manner of an eighteenth-century beau:

But do you not observe some more shining and more beautiful than the rest of the Croud? I answered yes, they seem to be made of burnish'd Brass, and almost dazzle my Eyes: These Jobson, are the Females, who use all Arts to inveigle and ensnare unwary Youth, but they only Flourish a while, for sometimes they Scour their Copper Noses plain with their Faces, or their Bodies so thin, that the vital Heat evaporates: Those that die a Natural Death hold out nigh Two Hundred Years, but are still wasting away into Verdegrease, as all your Brazen Vessels, if not well tin'd commonly do.

Jobson, as you have been a Man of Gallantry, take this fine Lady by the Hand, and give her a gentle Salute. In obeying his Commands I had not only my Beard taken off without a Razor, but my Hand all blister'd: The Angel perceiving how I was chagrin'd, told me, this was a slight Penance for some of my former Amours; and at the same Time bid me take Notice here how the intemperate Youths of both Sexes are melted down, and thereby render'd incapable of Procreation; and like luxurious Mortals, diminish their own Life, by giving Life to others.

The final glimpse of the moon shows some little moonboys leaping from rock to rock and breaking an occasional arm or two, in order to make business for the coppersmiths, and a great troop of metal folk asleep, snoring away "like so many Organ Pipes or Brazen Trumpeters."

At the next heavenly body to which Jobson is conducted by the angel, he finds that the Martians, nine million in number, have been placed on Mars merely to glorify the Creator. They live only for themselves in the present and will infallibly be annihilated "at the final Dissolution of your Solar System, which will be Executed by breaking the Laws of Attraction and Centrifugal Motion, and then your Six Planets with their Satellites or Moons, will of course fall into the Sun, and be consum'd in a Moment by that formal fiery Body." "How wonderful is the Handiwork of God!" Jobson comments piously. True enough, agrees the angel; and here is a new illustration of that handiwork—on Mars the inhabitants "are of the Neuter Gender, that is, they are of no Sex: They never remove from their Station, and are as fix'd as Trees, and so will remain to the End of Time." How miserable they must be. Well, not exactly; they know no better. They are little more than stone images; but they have two sets of eyes. With one set they can sleep; with the other, they can gaze with rapture on the beauties of creation. For they are, in their dull way, capable of rapture.

"Oh! Divine Intelligencer!" exclaims the now deistic Jobson. "I am still more sensible of the infinite Power of the Supreme Being and the Weakness and Imperfection of our own."

When Jobson expresses surprise that they can reach distant Jupiter in such a comparatively short time, he is once more treated to statistics, this time inaccurate. Light travels about 186,000 miles a second, not 2,103,475; and this fact had been discovered by Römer almost a century before Wilson wrote. Our author's remarkable figure is purely imaginary. Yet the general force of these untrustworthy statistics is still obvious: angelic spirits, like light, are beyond human comprehension or power to imitate. At the same time we are offered an explanation, this time correct, of the use of Jupiter's moons to ascertain terrestrial longitude.[21]

Jobson has the temerity to defend human understanding, but the angel, with awful severity, puts the Wanderer in his place:

I gave thee Liberty to ask Questions without Reserve, but not to make Satirical Repartees, thou begins[22] to grow vain and insolent with the Freedom I have indulg'd thee in, and I have also assumed thy Shape to take away all Terror, but learn to know thy Distance, Shoemaker, for I wou'd have thee to know (if Heaven permits) I am able to Kick your largest Globes like so many Foot-Balls, and play with your Moons at Racket-Court. In the most Suppliant Manner I crav'd Ten Thousand Pardons for my Presumption, and at last obtained a Reconciliation; Now in the Angel's Face milder Beams of Mercy play'd, and with a gracious Smile, [he] told me, Envy dwells not in Heavenly Breasts.

Fortunately, too, the awe-inspiring spectacle of Jupiter, with its bands and moons, tends to ease the situation. Jobson is astonished at the great weight he feels himself to be, and is given therefore a lecture on the relation of weight to density.

The Jovians are in some respects as remarkable as the Brobdingnagians of Book II of *Gulliver's Travels:*

Jobson, says he, your Lady's Hoop-Petticoats are an extraordinary Piece of Vanity, and the Subject of Ridicule among our Heavenly Essences. Scarlet Stockings hide the lean Shank Bone, while the jaunty Whale-Bone shew[23] both them and the naked Thigh; Temptation strong enough to break the Heart of a Potter's Vessel, the Ingredient of your frail Composition: But these Females are not so Extravagant, for as all Things are but great and little by Comparison, so these Petticoats are proportion'd to their Corporeal Substances, and that you would find if you durst attempt such a Discovery, but let me Caution you not to be guilty of such Rashness and Indecency, lest you get a box on the Ear sufficient to fell an European Troop of Horse.[24]

Jobson questions the angel as to how the Jovians fit into the Creator's scheme of things and is assured in a manner characteristic of the rationalism of the age, when the influence of the microscope and telescope had begun to operate on the thoughts of men:

There is in this World as well as in all the other of your System, an infinite Swarm of Animalculae, of which many Thousands may Dance on the Point of a Needle, there is scarce an Atom that is not peopled with Life, every Green Leaf, every single Humour in the Body of Man, abounds with Myriads of living Creatures, and the Surface of one Animal is the Basis of another that live upon it, and as there is a Succession of these and other Animals from the Minutest to the largest Monster, so there is a Gradation of Reason from the vilest Animalculae, to the Lord of the Planet.

Jobson is once again struck into rapturous comment, but the angel grimly reminds him that men on earth are vile, which makes him think in turn of the curious structure of the human body.

While the angel explains to Jobson that he, a mere mortal, has had to receive special dispensation to survive such a journey through the rarefied atmosphere of space, they come to the confines of Saturn. The amazing rings of that planet receive a certain measure of attention, but the true wonder to Jobson is that there can be life on such a distant world. The angel therefore points out that all of the planets have the power to sustain such life as God sees fit to put upon them; it is idle to say that one planet is uninhabitable because of heat, another planet because of cold, a third because of a lack of atmosphere.

The Saturnians are immense in size, with one eye in the front of their heads and the other in the back. Their fields and their livestock are fruitful and pleasing to the eye. The inhabitants have no laws; they live in a state of innocence, and after two hundred years are to be "translated to the Regions of Bliss, and are Spiritualiz'd to be Partakers of Transcendent Glories."

The last third of the pamphlet is a falling off from the imaginative force and humorous vigor of the earlier portion. Having left the outer planets, the angel and Jobson discuss the solar system and, after that, the fixed stars. Halley's Comet, due in 1758, whisks by (it actually appeared in 1759). The aerial travelers find themselves near the galaxy, "compos'd of an infinite Swarm of Suns and Systems, whose Orbits cut each other so frequently and exactly, that nothing but a Supreme Power can preserve them from Disorder and Confusion in their Miraculous Motions: Nay, it is even Astonishment to Angels, and Surpasses our Comprehension to account for all their Rotations." They enter one of the worlds in the Milky Way:

But how shall I describe this Fair, this Fragrant, this Charming Land of Love! the Delectable Vales and Flowery Lanes, the Myrtle Shades and Rosy Bowers, the Bright Cascades and Chrystial [sic] Rivulets, rolling over Orient Pearls and Sands of Gold, which have spread their silent Waves into broad Transparent Lakes, smooth as the Face of Heaven, and there break with rapid Force thro' Arching Rocks of Diamond and Purple Amethists!

Indeed, they now stand ready to explore the limits of creation; they are now on the very threshold of heaven. The mortal listener loses track of the general trend of his guide's discourse. A constant whizzing sound is explained as caused by the ceaseless journeyings of souls from all the worlds of creation up to the throne of God. And, at this critical moment, the angel regrets that he must leave Jobson for a time while he attends to his regular singing of anthems in praise of the Almighty.

Left thus alone, Jobson allows the steeds to bear him aimlessly along in the chariot. Paradise begins to open before him. But now the author can no longer be specific. He labors about in a lather of glittering poetic jargon of the neoclassical brand: there are "charming bowers," "lucid groves," "heavenly plains." The limitations of the exalted stylistic and phraseological clichés of the poetry of the time are too much for him, especially when he cramps himself further into his sometimes homely prose. The angel rejoins the Wanderer. Prodigious comets with blazing tails sport around the travelers, who seem to linger among them for a time. But when they return to the frontiers of our solar system, they plummet to earth within the space of a few minutes. And Jobson suddenly finds himself back on Penyghent Hill in the West Riding of Yorkshire. The angel disappears, after leaving the Wanderer with these solemn words:

Jobson, tho' neither Man nor Angel can tell the Time of your World's Dissolution, yet we suppose that both Men and Angels may take good Conjecture from the Completion of many Predictions ordain'd by the Supreme, to be Forerunners of that awful Day, most of which are already passed over. Tho' Wars, and Rumours of Wars, and Earthquakes[25] in divers Places, are sure Prognostications of this dreadful Event, yet many of you attribute those to natural Causes, not considering that natural Causes are only Instruments in the Hand of God. You have view'd your Solar System, had a Landscape of the Starry Regions, and a Prospect of Eternity; which may be an Inducement to arm you with Patience, to drudge in this Transitory Life till your System shall be destroy'd, and you absolved from your Pennance, by the Element of Fire, and arrive once more, (never to return) at those Blessed Abodes, not subject to Time or Chance.

Thus Israel Jobson, faced with the prospect of a tedious, dirty plodding on earth after a magnificent chariot ride through heavenly space, passes a disconsolate night on Penyghent Hill in gloomy prayer and contemplation. Then he arises and goes on his way until he reaches first Muscovy and then China, where, in conformity with the Wandering Jew's practice of using the language of the country in which he happens to be at a given time, he writes his memoirs in Chinese, dating the completion of his work August 10, 1719. And so Miles Wilson found them and transmitted them to an avid posterity.

This is a strange piece of writing—a mixture of popular astronomy, chiefly inaccurate except when it falls back upon the accepted concretion of traditional knowledge; some similarly accepted physiology and anatomy, in which Wilson preserves, nevertheless, a large amount of medieval belief;[26] a great deal of purely imaginative and clearly unscientific material; some expository paragraphs revealing a deistic turn of mind; still more paragraphs, however, of most platitudinous religiosity; some highly amusing seasoning of arrant ribaldry; some would-be lyricism. Medieval science and modern learning therefore elbow each other most rudely. Yet in all the enormous library of writings concerning the Wandering Jew there is nothing quite like it. It survives as an inspired chapbook. The obscure curate of Halton Gill remains the first to take Ahasuerus, alias Israel Jobson, the Wandering Jew, away from earth on a conducted tour of the celestial regions. For the first time, also, this Ahasuerus is a teacher of science.

Ahasuerus as Historian: The Beginnings

Usually, however, when Ahasuerus became a teacher, he gave instruction in history or geography. In the first of these fields, his province of special knowledge was nothing less than the survey of mankind. Now the itinerary of the Wandering Jew recited in the French *Histoire admirable* makes it clear that the author of that pamphlet had no coherent knowledge of geography and no interest in history. The version of the Legend in the *Turkish Spy* and in all accounts derived from that shows at least a sense of chronological consecutiveness. This sense had become fully developed by the middle of the eighteenth century. Thus even Uncle Toby, in Sterne's *Tristram Shandy* (1760-67), while he listens to Father's oration, recognizes the Wandering Jew not only as a world traveler but as something of a narrator of ancient events.[27]

In this respect, the first piece to be noted is an English broadside ballad, *The Wandering Jew's Chronicle,* from not later than 1714.[28] This is, however, little more than a catalogue in verse of the rulers of England from William the Conqueror to Anne. It is not until the last quarter of the century that one finds Ahasuerus engaged in an ambitious coverage of the history of the world; and the line of works engendered at this time sheds an influence which is not dissipated until the next century has passed. The new interest in historiography, evident in the latter half of the neoclassical age,[29] is reflected in the eventual appearance of some extensive surveys of mankind "from China to Peru," in which the figure of the Wandering Jew is the chief unifying element.

The earliest characteristic representative of what I call the Chronicle of the Wandering Jew, the evident progenitor of all later surveys of this type, is *Mémoires du juif errant,* which exists in an apparently single edition in the *Bibliothèque universelle des romans,* for July, 1777, published at Paris. The author is unknown.

The writer of the *Mémoires,* who could have been any one of the score and more of obscure contributors to the *Bibliothèque universelle des romans,* built upon the *Histoire admirable,* or at least upon that section of it that considered the life and wanderings of Ahasuerus.[30] He was obviously familiar with standard books of travel, both ancient and modern. On the other hand, much of the work is his own invention; certainly the arrangement and selection of details appear to be original. He has no political or social axes to grind. The *Mémoires* is, on the whole, a humdrum composition, but it would require extraordinary talent to make absorbing a book pitched on this particular intellectual level.

Four young men, a German, an Englishman, an Italian, and a Frenchman, meet the Wandering Jew at a fair in Leipzig. The date of the meeting is 1749. (This date advances in subsequent works derived from the *Mémoires* until it has neared the close of the 1780's.) Ahasuerus tells the youths of his many experiences, and the German transcribes the narrative. We are given an account of the major figures and events of world history from the time of the Crucifixion; the story ends with the reign of Louis XIV. Ahasuerus not only traverses Europe but also manages to make a tour of China and Africa. We hear of Prester John, of the wonders of Ethiopia and the Congo, of the principalities of Tartary. At the end of his rather long narrative, divided into chapters which correspond roughly with the centuries of the Christian calendar which have elapsed since the time of Christ, the Jew abruptly disappears, leaving the young men to ponder over his amazing career. (Emphasis is placed, in typical fashion, upon what the author wishes; he suppresses those details which seem to him unimportant or about which he has little knowledge. If we learn more than enough about Trajan and Zenobia, it is because the writer evidently knew more about those personages.)

In 1785 there appeared a free reworking in German of the *Mémoires*, entitled *Der ewige Jude: Geschicht oder Volksroman, wie man will*, published at Riga.[31] The author was Heinrich A. O. Reichard (1751-1828), a miscellaneous writer with particular interest in travelogues and descriptive geography, who had founded a *Bibliothek der Romane* in 1782 on the model of the French *Bibliothèque des romans*. It is true that his autobiography does not mention *Der ewige Jude*, but the work first appeared in the *Bibliothek der Romane* in installments between 1782 and 1785, and the separate publication unit of 1785 announces itself as a printing of the "Reichardschen" adaptation of the celebrated *Volksroman*. Furthermore, Reichard's obvious interest in travels and wanderings makes his choice of the Legend of the Wandering Jew a natural one. Yet the author seems to be throughout a trifle uncertain as to whether or not he should treat his subject in a learned manner; and so, as his subtitle indicates, he will leave it to the reader to accept the work as either history or popular tale. He goes over the same ground as the *Mémoires*, although in much more effective style. There is the same framework of the meeting of the four young men and Ahasuerus at the fair in Leipzig. The date of the meeting has been moved to 1780. The English youth is named—surprisingly enough—Smith; the Italian is Cambiaggi; the German and French representatives are unnamed. In general, the version is more sophisticated and given more definitely to topical allusion than the French *Mémoires*. Reichard's emphasis is an independent one: he cares little about Trajan but a great deal about Attila; he sees fit to mention Alfred the Great, whereas this king of Wessex is not deemed worthy to appear in the pages of the *Mémoires*.

One is justified, nevertheless, in considering the *Mémoires* and Reichard's adaptation as a duplex work. In both the Wandering Jew is an impressive figure. He is no ragged freak as he is in the German Ahasuerus-book. In fact, he is here a true citizen of the world—that is, the world of the eighteenth century. No longer is his glance humble and contrite;[32] no longer is he smitten with the consciousness of unforgiven sin. When he speaks, particularly in regard to his traditional woes, his tone is light: "Ich bin von Geburt ein Jude, und Jerusalem ist meine Vaterstadt; es werden ohngefehr tausend siebenhundert und fünfzig Jahre seyn, dasz ich sie verlassen habe, um einen Spaziergang durch die Welt zu thun, der noch dauert."[33] His promenade of some 1,750 years has been no great burden to him. He does not seem to be in the least worried about his fate. No longer is he much interested in seeing the marvels of the world through which he has traveled for so long; he is satisfied with it as it is. Although he never comes to the outright formula, "Whatever is, is right," he is peculiarly static in his outlook; and his rather neutral point of view imparts itself to the various sections of this work. In other words, this composite specimen of the genus Wandering Jew fits neatly into the background of the later years of the eighteenth century, when neoclassicism had entered into its decadent stage and had become tired and negative. The Wanderer's fate is to him as casual a thing as his view of life. From time to time he reminds the reader that he is in truth the Wandering Jew, and so gives somewhat perfunctory accounts of seventeen centuries of history; but for the present world of 1777-85 he cares little. At times, in fact, he has reached that stage of placidity where he is nothing more than a peg on which to hang extraneous material. Here we see emerging the essential weakness of the whole Legend—it can get only so far in an epic course, and then the spotlight of interest must turn to the things the Wanderer saw or the people he met rather than linger on the Wanderer himself.

The omniscience of this particular Ahasuerus, however, is at all times unquestioned. He has the unfailing ability to turn up wherever important events are taking place. With the typical refinement expected of a complete eighteenth-century man of the world he avoids violence and bloodshed, taking but little account of wars or even the rumors of wars. But he is always more than willing to engage in discussions. He will give the skeletal history of a whole nation and draw therefrom profound moral lessons. He loves to descant on personalities—princes, statesmen, poets, and philosophers—or on the net achievements of civilizations. Anecdotes and incidents of secondary importance fascinate him. In short, the duplex work is an honorable example of the curiosa which can attract any modern, supercultured mind. Thus the introduction of Byzantine and Levantine *objets d'art* and manuscripts is the subject of a protracted discourse; the innovation of glass panes and the growth of European drama invite Ahasuerus just as warmly to hold forth to the reader. Yet the whole Reformation is badly scanted; Luther is dismissed as an obstinate priest.

Moreover, for all the professed rationalism of the authors of these works, they are strangely unsystematic. The itineraries of the protagonist are disconnected; lands and peoples obtrude themselves unceremoniously. Clearly the authors have been impressed by the thought that "the race is not to the swift, nor the battle to the strong . . . but time and chance happeneth to them all." An irritating paradox in this duplex work, more obvious in Reichard's contribution than in the *Mémoires*, is the air of knowing observation which the authors bestow upon the Wanderer; Ahasuerus is on the whole a very tame critic and feeble satirist of human efforts. He is patronizing, as befits a rationalist, toward any swindles of credulous mankind, and yet he points out at some length the benefits that may accrue from "enthusiasm." The Crusades were folly, incomprehensible deceptions and hypocrisies, and yet they did some good. As to his own age, he concedes that, in spite of some forward steps in philosophy and world exploration, it is never free from intolerance, persecution, and the curse of faddism, from mob movements of all kinds, from mesmerism, from the pursuit of alchemy, from the conjuring up of ghosts, and from all the rest of the inanities and superstitions and prejudices which one could name, new Messiahs and what not.[34]

Still, the impression left by this double foundation-work to the Chronicle of the Wandering Jew is that it is a civilized performance, unfortunately too objective and not sufficiently acidulous to achieve memorable satire, too generally complacent and rational to touch or understand the deeper significance of the Legend of the Wandering Jew. Perhaps it is not fair to say that, beside Cyrano de Bergerac's voyager to the moon, beside Gulliver, or beside Candide, this Ahasuerus is the most neoclassical of neoclassical wanderers; but seldom has the Wandering Jew been given a more prosaic aura.

A Spanish translation and adaptation, with extensive concluding additions, of the *Mémoires* is the *Historia del Judío errante* (Madrid, 1819), by a certain Don Luis Fris Ducos. This is not a true Spanish name. Very likely Ducos (Duclos?) was a French expatriate, who managed to become a *comisario* of the Spanish Inquisition a few years before its dissolution and was also the *rector y administrador de la real iglesia-hospital de S. Luis rey de Francia*. In this translation the date of the meeting of the young men with the Jew is given as 1763. But the author adds to the original story much subjective comment on European history after 1789. The last third of the book degenerates into unabashed polemics, attacking the philosophers of the eighteenth century, whom Fris Ducos considers a pack of atheists, and Napoleon and his era. It is evident that the author was a Carlist. If we leave these polemics aside, we find only a few minor alterations of the material of the *Mémoires*. The Jew's name is given as Abasuero. He must proceed on a continuous narrative, for he can stay but three days, as in some versions of the folk tale; he therefore bids one of the four young men to keep awake and transcribe his story, which is told in relays. When he is finished there is an end—"al decir estas últimas palabras el Judéo errante se echó á andar, y anda todavia."

Similarly, Reichard's *Der ewige Jude* was translated and adapted in a Danish *Folksroman* under the title *Jerusalems Skomager* (1828).[35] This follows its original even more closely, if possible, than the Spanish book of Fris Ducos. It shies away from political controversy and exhibits very little of the author's personality. He himself remains unidentified. Since there is at this time nothing comparable in contemporary Swedish literature, where the Legend is still in the early *Volksbuch* stage, one may be permitted the opinion that the Danish treatment of the Legend had advanced more rapidly into a literary form than that of other Scandinavian countries—as is well substantiated by the appearance in the next literary generation of Hans Christian Andersen's *Ahasverus* and B. S. Ingemann's *Blade af Jerusalems Skomagers Lommebog* (pp. 221-22 and 224-25 below).

The Neoclassical Chronicle in Summation

The Chronicle is recorded in an important neoclassical document, *Briefe des ewigen Juden über die merkwürdigsten Begebenheiten seiner Zeit*, by W. F. Heller, in three volumes.[36] The first two volumes appeared in 1791, the third in 1801. The work is so rare as to be now virtually nonextant, especially the third volume, which has been seen by very few scholars. There was a second edition of volumes I and II in 1793, but volume III was not reprinted.

Heller's *Briefe* will be recognized immediately as utilizing a favorite literary device of eighteenth-century literature, whether fiction or expository critical writing. It will be recalled how admirably the *Turkish Spy* represented this epistolary category. Heller's *Briefe*, however, is a work of vast pretensions, particularly in the field of natural philosophy. It asserts confidently that it can teach the reader how to interpret precisely the significance of the most notable events about which the letters concern themselves. Its self-esteem is vainglorious. The author, we learn, has the power to look upon the course of world events in the large and to explain them, as far as mortal man is capable of so doing, in the only correct way. His method, however, is admittedly eclectic, for he has chosen only the most "interessante" events to interpret, and he will let the chaff fall to the ground and lie there. His stylus is to be sharp and pointed; his delineation is therefore certain to be keen and clear. We may as well say the worst about the work at the outset. The science and natural philosophy of the author are mostly accretions of hidebound beliefs, looking backward rather than forward. One may concede that he has been diligent.

There are sixty-four letters to carry the reader along the path of history from the beginning of the Christian era to the emergence of Napoleon Bonaparte. They are addressed, for the greater part, to erudite rabbis of antiquity who were roughly contemporaneous with the events referred to. In other words, the history of a given event is related in a letter to a wise man who lived at the time of the event or very soon thereafter. The first five letters, for example, are written to the eminent Jewish historian Josephus,[37] who appears in some derivative nineteenth-century versions of the Chronicle of the Wandering Jew (p. 156). Other noted recipients of the letters are the Spanish monk of the fifth century, Paulus Orosius,[38] and Saint Francis of Assisi.

Since the third volume of the *Briefe* is virtually unknown today, it deserves a little more attention than the first two, which are of no interest if one has read the *Mémoires* or Reichard's *Der ewige Jude*. It is given over almost entirely to an account of the French Revolution. First there is a rapid summary of the main events in the reigns of Louis XIV, Louis XV, and Maria Theresa. This is followed by a letter to each of these four: Catherine the Great, Gustavus III of Sweden, Voltaire, and Franklin. The last of these letters is an essay highly appreciative of its subject, considering Franklin as a sage and not as a politician, and including a German translation of the little allegory *The Whistle* written by Franklin in 1779. Nine remaining letters deal solely with the Revolution, which Heller approves in principle but against which he feels revulsion because of its excesses. The volume concludes with an excoriation of the Directory and of the rise to power of Napoleon.

Heller's conception of historiography is, in general, to give a bald narrative of actual happenings in brief scope. The author's claim to complete infallibility as a teacher of historical criticism and appreciation is belied in the very first letter. Reichard and the author of the *Mémoires* accomplished just as much as far as history is concerned, and they are better equipped as writers. Nevertheless, the three versions of the Chronicle afford good, fundamental examples of the panoramic survey of the world from the "pen" of the Wandering Jew. It is true that there is an over-all lack of comment by the Wanderer, save for some rather romantically slanted opening paragraphs in the first letter in each of Heller's three volumes, and this lack robs the works of any special connection with Ahasuerus himself: they remain primarily works of instruction in which the Wanderer is the co-ordinating element, merely longer and much more cosmopolitan in range than the trivial little broadside ballad of Queen Anne's time. Yet the framework furnished by these eighteenth-century tellings of the Chronicle influences all the writers about the Legend who follow. In time, Ahasuerus would assume Byronic garb and go strutting and posing amid a wild and fantastic landscape,[39] presaging the appearance of cholera,[40] fighting for the Jews against Titus and Vespasian,[41] observing in a spasm of revenge the fall of Constantinople,[42] sporting with Fénélon in the shade of the gardens of Versailles,[43] scowling at the excessive debauches of the court of Nero,[44] or disappearing under macabre circumstances from the monastery on the slopes of Mount Athos.[45]

Disregarding frameworks, digressions, and what little there may be in the way of subjective comment or special interpretation, we find that the following matters were considered important enough to be included in the eighteenth-century Chronicle of the Wandering Jew:

1. The Crucifixion and its sequel; in particular, the earthquake, the releasing of the many dead, the fall of the Temple, Joseph of Arimathea, the burial of Christ, the comment of the priests, and the Resurrection
2. The Pentecost and the conversion of Saul to Paul
3. The early missionary efforts of the various apostles; the rudimentary organization of the Church; the establishing of Christian priests and bishops
4. The reign of Nero, with a full account of the barbarities
5. The revolt of the Jews, Titus and Vespasian, the fall of Jerusalem, the collapse of the Temple of Solomon
6. The destruction of Pompeii and Herculaneum
7. The tyrannous emperors of Rome in the first century
8. Trajan and Hadrian, with special emphasis on the former
9. The building of Aelia Kapitolina; the unsuccessful rebellion of the Jews under Bar-Kashoba, put down by Severus and Musonius
10. Antoninus and Marcus Aurelius, especially the latter
11. The Romans in Britain
12. The spread of Christianity as a minority religion
13. Constantine and the conversion of the Empire
14. The controversy between Arius and Athanasius
15. The growth of Byzantium
16. The division of the Roman Empire and the Church
17. Ulfilas, the codifier of the Gothic language (This is to be found only in Heller's *Briefe*. In general, Heller is the most learned of the three chroniclers.)[46]
18. Alaric and the sack of Rome
19. Attila and the Huns
20. The migrations of the Vandals into Spain and Africa

21. The founding of the Venetian state

22. The Parthians and the "Neo-Persians"

23. Zenobia and her unfortunate fate

24. The rise of Mohammed

25. The virtues of the Germanic peoples (This subject is not mentioned in the *Mémoires,* and is touched upon only briefly by Reichard, but Heller devotes an entire letter to it and praises in particular the military spirit of the Germans.)

26. Clovis and the Franks, the Lombards, Charlemagne's empire

27. The mores of the early Church

28. Controversies as to the divinity of the Virgin

29. The matter of tithes, Purgatory, and the doctrine of atonement

30. Unfavorable comments on the despotism of the papacy in the Middle Ages (It has already been noted how the renaissance of the Legend in the seventeenth-century Ahasuerus-book owed some of its origin to the propaganda value of Ahasuerus as a follower of the Antichrist, that great adversary who included, according to some fanatical Protestants, the pope under his evil banners. It is, however, characteristic of the continuing strong Protestant bias in the German treatments of the Wandering Jew that Reichard and Heller, especially the latter, should note with satisfaction the coincidence of the highest power of the papacy with the lowest ebb of human knowledge and understanding. This point, needless to say, is not mentioned in the *Mémoires.*)

31. A summary of the Koran, an outline of the later Mohammedan dynasties, an account of the birth of the Crusades

32. The First Crusade in much detail (Heller had published a history of the Crusades in 1784.)

33. Saladin (The three works agree in recounting the episode first told in the *Turkish Spy* letters concerning Saladin and his poor shirt.)

34. The twelfth and thirteenth centuries in Europe, with particular attention to the worldly and spiritual dominance of Pope Innocent III

35. The importance to learning of the friars

36. The Crusade of St. Louis; the abortive insurrection of Manfred; the Sicilian Vespers; the great schism in the Church; the advent of the Knights Templars, Knights Hospitallers, and Knights of Malta; the Swiss Confederation

37. The awakening of interest in the Far East and Africa: the depredations of Genghis Khan, the travels of Marco Polo, the legendary activities and some early explorations of the travelers to the Nile and the Congo

38. The Hundred Years' War and Jeanne d'Arc (The English victories of Crécy, Poitiers, and Agincourt are ignored.)

39. The beginnings of the Reformation, dating from John Huss (Wycliffe is forgotten, and there is virtually no comment about the Reformation itself.)

40. The fall of Constantinople

41. The Inquisition in Spain (a subject later dear to every romantic writer who discusses the Wandering Jew in a Gothic novel), the voyages of Columbus and of Vasco da Gama, the wars of the Catholic League, the reign of Henry of Navarre, the persecution of the Huguenots (Little attention is given to the Massacre of St. Bartholomew.)

42. The Thirty Years' War, followed by the rise of Sweden under Charles XII and of Russia under Peter the Great

43. The eighteenth century in general (The spotlight is trained upon the four great figures of Voltaire, Frederick the Great, Rousseau, and Franklin.)

44. Catherine the Great, Gustavus III, Louis XIV and Louis XV, the French Revolution, and the advent of Napoleon.[47]

In these early recordings of the Chronicle of the Wandering Jew there are few important references to England. There is no mention of the Armada, the Revolution of 1688 and the Bill of Rights, Marlborough, or the growth of the British Empire. The English Civil War is disposed of in one line, the American Revolution in two. Indeed, save for a brief allusion to Alfred the Great, there is no significant concern with England after the time of the Roman occupation until we come to the younger Pitt, whose part in European power politics after 1795 cannot well be overlooked. Nor does the Dutch Republic have any appreciable standing in the scheme of things.

The Romantic Chronicle

Sooner or later, of course, the impact of the age of romanticism will make itself felt upon even the prosaic Chronicle of the Wandering Jew. A typical example is the work of "the Reverend T. Clark," the pseudonym of the rather obstreperous John Galt (1779-1839). He was an acquaintance of Byron, a would-be successor in popular fiction to Sir Walter Scott, and a writer of textbooks on history, geography, and travel—a generally colorful author of miscellaneous interests but of over-all mediocrity.[48] Masquerading as Clark, he brought out, in 1820, *The Wandering Jew: Or the Travels and Observations of Hareach the Prolonged*, of which there were three editions within the next three years. The second and third editions are entitled *The Travels and Observations of Hareach, the Wandering Jew*. The work evidently had a certain degree of initial success, which of course bespeaks the continuing interest in the Legend. Galt gave it some typically gratuitous advertising, presumably because sales had begun to decline. Under his own name he amassed a collection of curiosa and trivia called *The Bachelor's Wife*, in which he devoted several pages to *Hareach*, speaking of its virtues and hinting broadly that it was a valuable document, as he endeavors to demonstrate by excerpts.[49] His sources were obviously those earlier examples of the Chronicle of the Wandering Jew already noted; but, like Heller or Reichard before him, he emphasized events quite capriciously and furnished the Chronicle with a Gothic framework all his own. Furthermore, he explains that his purpose is not merely to entertain the reader; it is also to instruct him, and there is no better way to do this than to give the facts of history and tell what they mean.

As history, the pages of *Hareach* are extremely arid, and we have heard it all, or most of it, several times before. It is only the romantic decoration, in keeping with the fashion of the years between 1800 and 1840, that is in fact worth a second look. The story of Hareach the Prolonged begins with the arrival of the usual mysterious stranger at a Greek monastery on the slopes of Mount Athos. This stranger, surly, unsociable, and highly irreligious, cannot be persuaded to pay attention to the orderly life of the monastery. In fact, he is suddenly overcome by an acute attack of demoniacal hysteria:

One morning, he left his chamber at the dawn, and went into the garden, where he dug a hole like a grave, and continued all the day after sitting near it, making violent gestures, venting appalling sounds, and frequently bursting into tears. In the evening he came into the refectory, and having taken some refreshment, he called for a draught of wine, which when he had drank, he went to his own room; and, loading a pistol, returned and seated himself in the hollow which he had made in the earth.

In this situation he continued several hours, while the trembling friars, in great consternation, were at prayers in the chapel. What he did further, or what apparition rose to him, they never knew; but they heard the report of the pistol; and, soon after, the sound of his steps returning to his chamber. When they assembled in the refectory, he joined them, and partook of their supper with more cheerfulness than they had ever seen him assume; but it was remarked, that he had the pale and haggard look of a man exhausted by a great struggle.[50]

All this cheerfulness, however, is only temporary. He sacrilegiously kicks a picture of God presented to him by the superior, who is anxious to wrestle with his soul, and then disappears for a time. His room is searched, but the only object of note to be found is a huge volume in the center of the room. While they are looking at this, the stranger returns, looking like a decayed corpse; he falls into a violent convulsion, in which green and yellow hues overspread his body, and apparently stretches his limbs in death. They bury him in the grave he had already dug, but the body disappears during the night. It is all very strange, to say the least, but the consensus is that this has been the Wandering Jew. But whom or what did he shoot? Why had he died, and how? Indeed, had he died at all? Or, like the evangelist John, had he been rescued from the grave by powers too mighty to comprehend? One thing is clear: Galt omitted this charnel scene from the second and third editions. Presumably the meat was too strong even for Gothic tastes.

An English traveler, who comes to the monastery shortly afterwards, discovers that the huge volume is indeed nothing more sinister than a curious chronicle of the history of the world for the past eighteen hundred years. And so, while we hear no more of the stranger who was, perhaps, a walking dead man, Hareach (if it was truly he) nevertheless conducts us in this tome through a long and tiresome history. The rosy, romantic glow of the opening pages fades away into a gray expanse of obvious facts, in which the destruction of Jerusalem was a sad conclusion to a great dream, and Demonax, the Greek cynic philosopher, asks what five hundred million years are compared to what has been and is to be.

Hareach as a world observer is most prosaic, yet he cannot avoid romantic perambulations among venerable ruins. Thus, the remains of Babylon, seen at twilight, move his otherwise realistic imagination:

I sat down by a mass of earth by the side of the stream; and the spectre of ages passed before me. A feeling, to which no language can give utterance, rose in my heart. I was as a being placed between the world that is, and the world to be. The region of man seemed as at an immeasurable distance; and the events of yesterday, even of the day that had passed, were mingled with the earliest impressions of my memory and the traditions of the most remote antiquity, constituting as it were all the past into one dark, ponderous, and oppressive thought. The rushing of the river, as it rolled along, sounded in my ear like the passing of those mighty spirits which are continually going forth, without intermission, from the throne of heaven, to perform the tasks of Providence, and in giving being to the events of time.[51]

Other comparatively bright moments are the accounts of the sack of Constantinople in 1453, the execution of Mary Queen of Scots in 1587, and a stout and simple encomium of the English people.

Thus we may see that even the Chronicle of the Wandering Jew, fundamentally a neoclassical product, had become infused with the romantic by 1820, when such a flat-footed author as Galt can become excited about the past. In fact, all one needs to do to see clearly what has happened to some literary fashions between 1780 and 1820 is to place side by side *Hareach, the Wandering Jew* and the French *Mémoires*. Galt has given us another name for the Jew and is truly original in presenting him in an interestingly moribund condition, although I for one do not believe for a moment that Hareach really died.

But even if sprinkled with romantic perfume, Ahasuerus the teacher must travel and observe and comment. An obscure expatriate Italian nobleman, Count Pasero de Corneliano (1790-1852), who went through an extremely active four years of revolutionary pamphleteering between 1817 and 1821, sounded an original variation. His *Histoire du juif errant, écrite par lui-même* (1820) won sufficient recognition to be translated into German (1821).[52] The pamphlet promises "a quick and trustworthy sketch of his remarkable voyages for about eighteen centuries." At first glance it would seem to be no more than another telling of the Chronicle. It is furnished, however, with a battery of footnotes, most of which give merely the dates of the deaths of famous personages. The chronological progression is much more strict than in the eighteenth-century version of the Chronicle. Other differences soon begin to appear. The Wandering Jew has by now heard of Matthew Paris, Dom Augustin Calmet, Basnage, and other authorities who have gone into his case. Moreover, he is a French Ahasuerus—pleasant, insouciant, with a great deal of social aplomb which never deserts him under any circumstances. He admires Cassiodorus, the Renaissance, the Provençal troubadours; if he were not Ahasuerus, he would like to spend his days in an environment of arts and letters.

Occasionally Pasero de Corneliano strays away from accuracy, as when he associates King Edward III of England with the Round Table. But since Edward was the founder of the Order of the Garter, this mistake is not unpardonable. On the whole he does not err seriously as to general facts. He is, however, inveterately prone to gossip about the amours at the courts of Francis I and Louis XIV of France and of Charles II of England; for that matter, he enjoys little tidbits about Messalina, the queen of King Clovis of the Franks, Eleanor of Aquitaine, and others—"Go to Madrid, and watch Philip V in heavy dalliance with the Princesse des Ursins."[53] He inveighs against dueling; he deplores the censorship of Fénélon's writings, which is appropriate enough, for Pasero de Corneliano was greatly concerned about the restoration of the monarchy in France after the fall of Napoleon Bonaparte and had a volume of his works suppressed by the Bourbon censor in 1817. He was evidently a liberal, almost a democrat, and violently opposed to the Holy Alliance, which has been defined as a conspiracy to make the world safe for autocracy. But his pamphlet on the Wandering Jew stops with the outbreak of the French Revolution.

At least once, though, Ahasuerus fostered the Bourbon Restoration in France. A rare pamphlet, *Relation curieuse et intéressante de nouveau voyage du Juif-Errant: Son passage à l'Ile Sainte-Hélène*, is a royalist document of violent anti-Napoleonic animus. Champfleury, to whose pages I am indebted for any knowledge of this work, indicates that it was actually written at the time of the wedding of the Duc de Berry and Caroline Louise of Naples in 1816. The high spot of the pamphlet is the confession of Napoleon: "I am he who has surpassed in cruelty Nero, Caligula, and Tiberius!" Ahasuerus replies: "I was looking for a man and instead have found a monster!"[54]

For the record, the liveliest and most readable example of the Chronicle of the Wandering Jew before 1850, at least, remains the *Histoire du juif errant*, published at Paris without date but probably near 1830, and attributed to one Monsieur P. B. Its contribution is fresh, in that it mentions incidents not recorded earlier in the Chronicle and swings from the Sahara to the Arctic. In Constantinople the Jew offended the sensibilities of the Moslems and was sentenced to be beheaded, but we who know him know also that he is in the hands of Christ, and that such punishment cannot be carried out. The Arctic scenes of his wanderings are a real innovation. He is protected from packs of wolves by a friendly polar bear. Our old friend from the Ahasuerus-book, Paulus von Eitzen, now promoted in the hierarchy to Archbishop Eisen, is amazed to hear of the rigors of the dazzling white northland.

Once, as a matter of fact, Ahasuerus casually anticipated Peary by some three-quarters of a century when he reached the North Pole, but when he set his foot on it, he was held to the spot by concentrated magnetic force. Perhaps the magnetic pole is not the same as the geographical pole, but never mind the misleading geophysics. He liberated himself from this awkward situation by sliding (not lifting) his feet along the surface of the earth until he had moved a short distance south. Then, working his way down to Greenland, he took ship, only to suffer the inevitable shipwreck, for he is, as usual, the veriest Jonah. "But I was carried along by the waves without being submerged for an instant—dolphins, sharks, and other enormous fish came up to me and presented their yawning maws, but my glance alone was enough to make them flee."[55] Finally he reaches Scotland, which he found to be an inhospitable land, inhabited only by savage brigands given to the habit of stoning all strangers. Great was their astonishment when even the largest rocks bounced harmlessly off his hide, without even so much as bruising him. His arrival coincided with the ordeal of Mary Queen of Scots, and as a good romanticist he had no use for Elizabeth.

Next come the wars of the Catholic League and the Thirty Years' conflict. Once Ahasuerus was blown up by a mine but remained uninjured. He was in a city during a horrible earthquake. Doubtless P. B. was thinking of the Lisbon cataclysm of 1755, but he transposed the digits and asserted soberly that the disaster occurred in 1557. After all, he is telling this to Archbishop Eisen in 1633, and anachronisms cannot be tolerated (although, if we take into account the various dates of the Ahasuerus-book, it would seem that the Archbishop might be as much as two hundred years old). He leaves the reader with these solemn words, not unlike those which the guiding angel spoke to Israel Jobson in Miles Wilson's memorable pamphlet:

> My friends, do not seek for happiness at all on Earth: it lies in the bosom of God Himself; here below we must suffer everything in order to pay for the shadow of pleasure; it is simply that the true home of man is in the heart of the Eternal . . . My journey will doubtless last for a long time yet, before I can taste the peace of God. But my example should teach one never to stop revering Him who wrought all things.[56]

It is unfortunate that P. B. does not emerge more clearly as an identity; there are no less than fifty-two anonymous French writers of the period whose initials are "P. B." His is a colorful Chronicle, with the stress placed more on sheer adventure than on history. Still, he is given more than once to serious reflection upon the imperfect nature of man and his hopeless situation unless he can find some way of improving his moral stamina and his relations to his fellow men—an example of what is meant by social awareness. Moreover, his Ahasuerus is refreshingly free from the all-knowing cocksureness of most protagonists in the Chronicle, of whom perhaps the most blatant is that in S. E.'s *Almanach historique, polémique, et anecdotique du juif errant* (1845), which is propaganda directed against the bourgeois king of France, Louis Philippe.[57]

A more imposing contrast to P. B. is the case of Christian Kuffner (1780-1846), a Viennese man of letters, dabbler in the classics, and librettist for second-rate oratorio-writers, who wrote down two forms of the Chronicle, *Der ewige Jude* and *Die ewige Jüdin*, which appeared in 1846.[58] The second of these, the first "full-length" treatment of the Wandering Jewess, is a misnamed satirical fantasy, which I shall refer to later (p. 414). As to the other work, *Der ewige Jude*, it is a prosy, dull, chattering account of world events, illustrating all of the author's weaknesses in storytelling as well as his somewhat oppressive interest in the glories of ancient Greece and Rome. There is nothing in the work to detain us; but an excellent example of its singular lack of proportion—a fault which is hardly to be attributed to the archetypes of the Chronicle—is the glaring fact that the author devoted three-fourths of his work to the deeds of Ahasuerus during the Julian dynasty of the Roman Empire. There is a great deal of blood and thunder, for the Chronicle no longer is confined to a mere record of events recounted dispassionately. Ahasuerus is a sinful ally of Time and Death. They form a gruesome trio, wicked captains of the powers of darkness, a singular combination of traitors, murderers, blasphemers, and moralizers. Under the emperor Caligula, Ahasuerus is a keeper of the animals used in the gladiatorial arena, and for a time he walks about, Androcles-like, with a pet lion. Yet for all his ferocity, he tends the suffering victims of the disaster at Pompeii and Herculaneum. This lapse from evil eats into his wicked soul and eventually converts him, so that he becomes a willing Christian who aids Constantine some three centuries later. In his fight for the glory of the Cross, he is wounded, whereupon he stops to give a discourse on practical morality and social co-operation, and then abruptly vanishes.

Even more insipid is an anonymous German chapbook, *Ahasverus, des wahren ewigen Juden Wanderungen* (Regensburg, 1845),[59] which parrots the French *Mémoires* and is of interest only because it sprays contempt over the tales told about Isaac Laquedem and "Joseph Loquedant of Paris"—the latter a new name for the Jew, which originated with the author of the pamphlet. The work is inclined to wander off on the subject of impostors and charlatans. It is significant to observe how, as the nineteenth century advanced, the Chronicle could serve as a springboard for discourses on any and all matters. Thus the Dutch clergyman, O. G. Heldring, made use of the Jew's survey of history to illustrate a homily on right living and right thinking entitled *De nimmer rustender Israelit tot Rust gekommen* ("The Never-Resting Jew Come to Rest"), published at Amsterdam in 1839. The first part, that called "Het Verhaal den eeuwigen Jood," or "The Story of the Wandering Jew," considers the career of Ahasuerus (pp. 45-47 above). But the introduction of the Jew into the scene adds neither heat nor light to the discourse. Indeed, the periphery of the Chronicle is sometimes merely useless addenda. The important fact remains that any writer of the nineteenth or twentieth centuries who has anything to say about the Wandering Jew may give us the Chronicle in part or in full. After all, that is the natural way to treat a career that has lasted more than nineteen hundred years. If it is dull *in extenso*, it is only because the author spreads his butter too thin.

Hoffman's Contribution to the Chronicle

What may be called the climactic example of the Chronicle of the Wandering Jew is more often than not a freakish performance, one of the most troublesome of all literary monstrosities. This is the huge effort by David Hoffman, a retired jurist from Baltimore[60]—*Chronicles Selected from the Originals of Cartaphilus, the Wandering Jew, Embracing a Period of Nearly XIX Centuries.*[61] The work was to have been in two series of three volumes each. Hoffman died before the third volume of the first series was completed, yet he attained in this magnum opus the not unimposing total of almost seventeen hundred pages of exceedingly fine print. The sheer length of the work was almost enough to discourage any one from attempting later anything comparable. At any rate, after 1853-54, when it was published, only the twin works (pp. 359-60 and 360-66 below) of George Sylvester Viereck and Paul Eldridge—*My First Two Thousand Years* (1929) and *Salome, the Wandering Jewess* (1930)—bear any resemblance to the Chronicle of the Wandering Jew on a similar scale. Since the purpose of these is so different—to titillate rather than teach—they will be called merely imitations of the Chronicle, which use the device as a framework only, and will be considered separately.

It is extremely difficult to discuss Hoffman's work. Merely to describe it is arduous enough a task. Yet it contains, here and there, most felicitous passages and, every now and then, will give a twist to the Legend. At other times it is very dull. It opens with a dedicatory note explaining that "to the children of the dispersion, Jehovah's favored people, during so many ages—Christ's scattered flock, during as many more—these chronicles are affectionately inscribed, trusting that, under Providence, they may become a link, however small, in that mysterious but not invisible chain, that seems to be now drawing Israel's sad and long-enduring destiny to a speedy close—and Her to the only revealed and true faith." There is more to this preface, authored by none other than Cartaphilus himself, but it is merely typical of Hoffman's undeniable garrulity.

Passing over Hoffman's brief and very superficial essay on the Legend as it was known in 1850, we need only note that he chooses to name his protagonist Cartaphilus, for he seems to have in mind always the Awaiter rather than the Wanderer, and he certainly conceives of the Legend as an outgrowth of the Legend of St. John. Few readers of a book will ever be more overwhelmed by preliminary material than those who wade through the *Chronicles of Cartaphilus*. Following the dedicatory epistle and the essay on the Legend comes an even longer "Epistle of Cartaphilus to the Editor." In this the Eternal Awaiter explains that it is his "Polychronicon"—like that of the fourteenth-century English scholar Ralph Higden, whose *Polychronicon*, one of the most celebrated of medieval Latin chronicles, Cartaphilus knows well. Yet he, Cartaphilus, will not venture to tell all the events of history which have taken place during his more than eighteen hundred years of life, neither will he tell all his sins. And, in his consideration of the so-called Dark Ages, he brings himself into tune with twentieth-century historians, among whom the term is out of fashion:

Doubtless, the expression "Dark Ages" (from the Eighth to the Twelfth century) hath some just meaning; those centuries surely *were dark*, compared with some others that preceded and followed; but those Ages are yet much darker to all who fail to seek after the *lights* that actually belong to them: they are still far darker, from their prejudices—from the misrepresentations of indolent or sciolous authors—from their slovenly habit of yielding assent to traditional mistakes, or sheer falsehoods: and they are now again darker than once they were, from the fact of the loss of countless manuscripts, during a succession of fierce wars, of conflagrations, and of many accidents. But these greatly misrepresented Ages were not so dark *"in themselves"* (as a wise, and liberal, and very searching Protestant writer of the present day hath clearly proved—Maitland)[62]
—but that there were in them times in which the Church was *not dead*, but comparatively industrious, zealous, meritorious, and unorthodox—Ages that did much to preserve the stories of by-gone times, profane as well as sacred—rescuing no little of what we now possess from the grasp of heathen and barbarian ignorance—from the rude destruction of sectarian animosity and superstition: and, though possibly we have not remaining at this time the one thousandth part of the results of their unobtrusive toils and research, we still have quite sufficient to assure us that light, and piety, and good feeling, and burning eloquence and even good taste, were by no means extinguished in the Cloisters, or elsewhere![63]

In this "Epistle to the Editor," Cartaphilus narrates various incidents in his career which never get into his *Chronicles*. Perhaps Hoffman had never intended them to be there, or perhaps his purpose to include them was thwarted by his death before the *Chronicles* had been completed. At any rate, the Epistle mentions conversations which Cartaphilus had with many scholars in the medieval Church—such as Anselm, Berenger of Tours, and Peter Lombard—as well as with a learned Hebrew scholar, Moses Maimonides. He comments upon the characters of St. Bonaventure and Duns Scotus and Abelard as religious men and upon those of Petrarch and Matthew Paris as men of letters. He inveighs against the "incarnated folly and gross sensuousness" of Paracelsus, while praising the earlier Roger Bacon and two Lullys of France as sincere and able, though primitive, scientists.[64] It is his opinion that Albertus Magnus had "great merit mixed with the usual alloy, whereas

Lord Bacon's shining light dims not with age."

All in all, however, the most striking inclusion in this introductory matter is the story of Cornelius Agrippa and the Wandering Jew, derived straight from the versions told thirty years earlier by Henry Neele and William Aytoun, and told without any hint of acknowledgment. This tale can best be treated later (p. 216). It is not to be expected that Hoffman should give his sources any more than do Heller or Reichard or the author of the *Mémoires;* however, his plan is so pretentious and his genuine scholarship so specious-sounding that he often drops names in the most remarkable places. There is nothing of the *strengwissenschactliches* about his performance, and this is an understatement.

But to proceed to the main body of the *Chronicles of Cartaphilus,* the "author" has already indicated in the introductory matter that he will tell his story in a series of epistles between himself and famous personages of the many centuries through which he has lived, including theologians, scientists, poets, and philosophers—the same group of individuals with whom he had been hobnobbing in his "Epistle to the Editor." It is an interesting but perhaps minor point that most of these long and philosophical letters go to theologians both Christian and Hebrew. He warns explicitly, however, against believing anything told by a Jesuit.[65] As for the device chosen—the same epistolary plan followed in Heller's *Briefe* and Marana's *Turkish Spy*—it remains quaint and archaic but still effective, although it makes for a grand prolixity, which the passage quoted above will certify.

And so, in his opening letters to Rabbi Ben Ezra, at the time of the Crucifixion, Cartaphilus explains that he has been an orphan for some years, and that his maiden aunt has allowed him to lead the life of a scholar. He has come to the conclusion that, although Christ has done miracles, he must continue to remain skeptical about them. He is sure that Israel's star is setting. He recognizes the fact that he and the Rabbi are both Sadducees, and this gives him an opportunity to deliver a multiple blast against the Pharisees, or Separatists, in Israel; the Essenes, or the primitivist cult; the Samaritans, or idolators; the Nazarites, or ascetics; the Rechabites, or the uncircumcised; and the strange Karraites, or "phantasticists." The Sadducees do not believe in the Resurrection but adhere strictly to the Pentateuch.

Needless to say, the true meaning of the Crucifixion is lost on Cartaphilus, who in his distrust of Jesus has become the chamberlain of Pontius Pilate. His young friend, Artemas of Caesarea Philippi, writing to Rabbi Ben Ezra, relates the incidents of the Passion in greater detail. It is here that one reports the curse laid on Cartaphilus. As the familiar words, "Tarry till I come!" fell on his ears, he gave a wild cry and rushed away.

We must thread our way through the remainder of the work as best we can. There follows a long succession of letters to and from various personages. The historical events, as well as the legends, are multitudinous: among them the story of King Abgarus of Edessa, who offered his "small but noble state" to Jesus; the accounts of Saul of Tarsus and his conversion; the organization of the primitive Church at Caesarea Philippi, analyzed in full detail; and the voyages of Saul become Paul. Then the scene shifts to Rome under the emperor Nero, whom the wandering Cartaphilus begins by admiring and defending. His sojourn with Nero gives him an opportunity to express himself on a variety of subjects, whether germane or not, and to intensify all rumors—for this Cartaphilus is an inveterate gossip, with an approved "by-the-way" technique.

Cartaphilus attended Nero when he made an expedition into Greece, where the Emperor proclaimed himself "Master of the Universe," planned a canal through the Isthmus of Corinth, and thoroughly abused Greek hospitality. Thus the Wanderer made an extensive tour of the country, during which he visited all the famous places of Greek antiquity. The description of the Parthenon alone takes up twenty pages of the customary dense printing. Yet Cartaphilus is restive. He longs for the sacred mountains and lovely valleys of Judaea, the green banks of the Kedron, and the winsome heights of Olivet and Gihon. O Jerusalem, Jerusalem!

Now he is back in that city, where he finds that rebellion is about to reach the boiling point. He begins a friendship with the scholar and historian Flavius Josephus. After a long review of Jewish history from the death of Christ to the year 68, he tells of the siege and destruction of the Holy City by Titus and Vespasian, bringing us over most familiar ground. But this Cartaphilus is not positive enough to be a true Jewish patriot. In fact, he stays with the Roman army and takes up more time talking about their new battering-rams and catapults than about the merits of the Jewish cause. He visits an old flame, Rebecca, about whom we hear much in the early epistles, and finds her well. From her old mother, Priscilla, he learns of the singular resistance of the Ephesians to Christianity, of the visit of Paul to Ephesus, and of the first martyrdoms. Before she has finished, Cartaphilus has heard also of the twelve sources of hope and has learned much about the various cities of Asia Minor and their wise men and divines—especially Apollonius of Tyana, the sage who will appear later, in Dumas' *Isaac Laquedem* (pp. 262-64), as a pro tem. companion of the Wandering Jew. Once, Priscilla reports, Rebecca was saved from a grisly martyrdom through the magnanimity of the heathen king, Tiridates of Armenia.

Now, however, in this fateful year 70, Cartaphilus is bobbing back and forth between doomed Jerusalem and Edessa, where his former friend and companion, Artemas, now a grave elder, lives with his family. It is a time of desolation for Israel, but for Cartaphilus it is a time for musing on the funeral customs of the early Christians as well as their marriage ceremonies. Jerusalem falls while Cartaphilus is away, but he returns to voice his lamentation, viewing its melancholy state while others tell what happened, in both great and small detail.

Thereafter one Roman emperor follows another. As for Cartaphilus, in the meantime he is looking beyond the frontiers of Rome and Israel. For a while the religion of the Magi fascinates him. The sad story of Zenobia in Palmyra inspires him to extensive reflection. The eruption of Vesuvius and the destruction of Pompeii lead him to even more. Both events point up for him the transiency of life, while at the same time they urge him on to speculations about the unknown forces of nature—cosmic energy and animalculae. And why not? For it appears that he, Cartaphilus, was long buried under the ashes from Vesuvius. And lo! when he emerged from those ashes, he found himself a new man, young and strong as he was when Christ laid the curse upon him nearly a half-century before. Cartaphilus has symbolically undergone both a physical and a spiritual transformation—from vivisepulture he has returned again. Now he is no longer Cartaphilus, but Tacasulriph, the letters and elements mixed, but the soul the same.

This is only symptomatic, however, for the First Transformation of Cartaphilus is to come later—in 103, when all his former friends and companions are dead and buried, and a new era has begun. Actually he is now a hundred years old, and the old folk motif as it appeared in Roger of Wendover's version and elsewhere has now recurred. For the first time Hoffman takes Tacasulriph into strange and barbaric lands, where he labors among the Gauls, Helvetians, and Britons to bring before them the light of ancient culture. Another century goes by before he is aware of it, and he comes to the time for his Second Transformation, this time at Lugdunum (Lyons) in the year 203. The details of this transformation are not given, but as a newly revivified youth he finds himself interested in rabbinism, of which there was a great center at Lyons; and so with Rabbi Isaac he maintains a long and close friendship. In many conversations with him—by letter—he discusses free will, hope in divine benefits, and the nature and history of rabbinical lore—with many instances drawn from Oriental story, which are altogether irrelevant to his own tale. But evidently what this Cartaphilus-Tacasulriph sees in Rabbi Isaac is a semi-Christian conviction that such ecclesiastical tyrants as came during the patriarchate of Tiberias, whom Cartaphilus can liken only to the more depraved of Celtic Druids, can bring nothing but shame to the followers of Judaism. For the Wandering Jew, by the beginning of the second century, has begun to appreciate more than ever before the power and purity of early Christianity, however short its devotees may have fallen of the ideals they professed.

Rabbi Isaac is the narrator of most of the history of the second century. He is liberal and sympathetic toward such a great character as Marcus Aurelius. The story of the death of Marcus Aurelius is followed by one of a very long series of entries concerned with the careers of the decadent Roman emperors. Each century sees a transformation of Cartaphilus into a young man with a fresh outlook. The narrative epistles are addressed next to Tertullian and Heliogabalus. The letters to Tertullian begin around the year 225 and consider, in particular, the reign of the impious Caracalla, the luxuriousness of the Heliogabalus estate, and the comparatively orderly reign of Severus. Actually more interesting than the narratives is the series of discursive essays on the demoniac possession which leads to sin; the displaced condition of the Jews, suggested to Cartaphilus by a visit to Damascus and the holy places there; problems relating the millennium to the Hexameron, whereby a thousand years of human time represent only one of the six days devoted to the Creation. Cartaphilus becomes constantly more hopeful about the future of mankind, although he admits that he sees but darkly. In one letter to Tertullian, he comments on the oneness of God, the "spiritual or cogitative entity,"[66] in which oneness no chance can exist, for everything is God. It was, he believes, a fundamental error of Platonism that it did not sufficiently take into account the act of Creation. In another epistle to Tertullian he reports that he spoke with St. Hippolytus about the Deluge and discussed with him the analogies of this legend among other civilizations. He observes, indeed, that he once saw the remnants of Noah's Ark on Mount Baris, in remote Armenia. It would seem that Hoffman had once read Matthew Paris' *Historia Major*.

The Near East attracts him, as it does throughout the *Chronicles*—Ecbatana,

Babylon, Nineveh, Baalbec, and Persepolis—while Zenobia, whom he had unwittingly betrayed into the hands of the Romans, keeps him posted on affairs at Rome: the death of Longinus the stylist, the triumph of the emperor Aurelianus, and the advent of the notorious Diocletian. From Persepolis he goes to Thebes in Egypt and then back to Ephesus, where, standing by the famous Temple of Diana, he delivers a long monologue on Time, the mighty monster. While sailing between Ephesus and Crete he suffers shipwreck and is cast to the bottom of the sea, where, amid awe-awakening sights which no man had ever seen before, he undergoes his Third Transformation. When, as a strange new youth, he finally arrives in Crete, he receives an epistle from Zenobia informing him of the emergence of Constantine the Great.

Meanwhile, he has visited Diocletian and witnessed the martyrdom of Christian men, women, and children, which leaves him strangely unmoved. After the Council of Nicaea in 325 he goes to Byzantium with Constantine, but the successors of Constantine appall him—the sameness of their temporary success, their sins, and their deaths; the poverty of fame; the vanity of human wishes. He becomes interested in Julian the Apostate and exchanges letters with him; between them they try to rebuild the Temple of Jerusalem in 363 but are prevented from doing so by the intervention of Christian angels. Cartaphilus meditates upon the coming supremacy of the white race and of Christianity, the twin waves of the future.

After his Fourth Transformation, which takes place inside the glowing crater of Vesuvius, the gloomy procession of events begins again, with the Germanic invasions the most prominent. The Theodosian Code (A.D. 438) he considers a step forward for mankind; Attila and the Battle of Châlons (A.D. 451), great strides backward. He notes the beginnings of Venice in 452 and declines to serve on a commission to placate the Huns, whose menace was dissipated anyway after the death of Attila in 453. While Genseric is ravaging northern Africa, Cartaphilus visits Rome and holds a long conversation with Bishop Leo, who is about to assume the title of pope. Cartaphilus, as a legalistic scholar rather than as a Christian, argues successfully that no mere bishop, even the one at Rome, has the right to arrogate to himself the title of supreme pontiff. And, in the secular arm, what misfits are parading around under the name of emperor, from Anthenius to Odoacer! The melancholy of the Wanderer is lightened only by some heartening words with St. Augustine at Hippo.

In a cave on the island of Antiparos in the Aegean Sea, Cartaphilus or Tacasulriph goes through his Fifth Transformation, this one the most painful of all, for his body becomes petrified, and his soul must chip its way with the greatest difficulty out of the stone monument to assume its new garb of flesh and blood, this time as Ahasuerus, a "young relative" of the deceased Cartaphilus-Tacasulriph. The time has come for him to leave the Mediterranean world. He sets out for Britain. On the way he visits the emperor Theodoric the Great; Boethius, author of *On the Consolation of Philosophy;* Cassiodorus; and Clovis, king of the Franks. Back at Lyon he meets Rabbi Ben Joachim—the year is 516—who charges that he, Ahasuerus, has been seduced from Israel by the Nazarene and denounces him as a heretic when Ahasuerus foreshadows in his arguments the Copernican theory of the universe. This charge does not worry Ahasuerus much. He promptly attacks all rabbinical lore, for although he respects Ben Joachim as a reincarnation of his old friend Ben Isaac, he himself has been too far removed from Israel by centuries of living among Christians. A man without a spiritual country? Almost, but not quite.

When, in 517, he reaches London, he retraces the history of the Roman occupation of Britain and disputes with an Irish cleric about the date of the Nativity. Now, at the beginning of the last volume of this megalithic opus, Ahasuerus is in York in the year 586. He has been all over Britain; he has studied the Anglo-Saxon Heptarchy, the Druids, and Stonehenge; he has often been in danger, but his immortality has been confirmed through all perils. Now he tells us more about King Arthur, who had been mentioned briefly near the end of the preceding volume. Perhaps, between tomes, Hoffman had digested the substance of the story of Arthur to be found in the twelfth-century Geoffrey of Monmouth's *History of the Kings of Britain*. Now we are given to understand that Arthur lived from 446 to 542. Ahasuerus saw his tomb in Glastonbury and lamented over it, although it is known today that this "tomb" was not "located" until nearly 1200. More emotionally upsetting than the tomb, however, was Ahasuerus' experience with the two young British lovers, Cingetorix and Moina, who turned Christian and were in consequence cremated alive by the Druids in their notorious "Wicker-man," or wicker basket. The Druids were indeed a sadistic lot, yet Ahasuerus found the Anglo-Saxons to be but little better, especially because they should have been better, in view of their superiority over the Celts in both energy and capabilities. He visited King Ethelbert of Kent and his Christian queen, Bertha, but left at their request just before Augustine came from Pope Gregory the Great to convert the Anglo-Saxons to Roman rather than Irish Christianity in 597.

Once more on the Continent, he undergoes his Sixth Transformation in the Alps; this time he is crystallized rather than petrified. Now, as he pauses in the year 604, he has for the first time an inkling of another great religious force at work in the world, transmitted to him by a young Arab, Mohammed Abu-Talib, whom he meets in Smyrna. Mohammed is a descendant of Ishmael and hopes great things for the rising power of Islam. When young Mohammed unexpectedly dies, Ahasuerus takes his place as an adopted son of old Abu-Talib. Somewhat to our discomfiture, for the chronicle is very obscure at this point, Ahasuerus emerges from the transaction as the real historical Mohammed, the true prophet of God. None of the spectacular transformations of Ahasuerus quite equals that by which he emerges as the leader of a great religious movement.

At this point Hoffman's advancing age and ill health begin to get the better of him, for his chronology—never too solid—becomes badly scrambled, and his historical details become blurred. After writing a letter to Pope Gregory, reproaching him for assuming the title of *pontifex maximus*, Ahasuerus resumes the identity of Mohammed and in the year 611 has his famous vision in the cave at Hira; he encourages conversions and battles with his foes. Then come the Hegira in 622, the flight to Medina, and the Holy War against the Kuryesh. In various encounters he is always successful. Attempts to assassinate him inevitably fail. He captures Mecca in 630 and is proclaimed king. He proceeds at once to the purification of the sacred place, the Kaaba, destroying idols wholesale.

Since Mohammed, however, must die, as befits a mortal, Ahasuerus must return as the Wandering Jew. This time he is Josephus, and because as Mohammed he had harassed both Jews and Christians, he must bear the stigma of the number 611 (the Christian year of Mohammed's vision in the cave) imprinted on his neck in Egyptian numerals and on his chest two crescents with a miter between and a cross under each of the two crescents. This latter five-point design resembles the pattern of the five nails in the shoes of Ahasuerus, which leave their traditional telltale footprints. One thing is now clear: he can no longer have to do with Islam. A return trip to the cave at Hira convinces him that he should go back to his ancient Jewish faith. His Seventh Transformation, curiously delayed until after the Mohammed episode is over, twists him into a hideous cripple, condemned to witness in impotence the Caliphate Wars of the seventh century and the ravaging of Asia Minor and the sack of Alexandria by Othman in 643.

Hoffman was still working when death intervened. The remaining pages of the last volume are a mass of notes treating of the Caliph Harun-al-Raschid, Charlemagne, the Visigothic kings of Spain, and the Carolingian rulers of France. They are of no importance. It is irrelevant to say that it would have been better if the *Chronicles of Cartaphilus* had never been written or to wonder what could possess an intelligent man to attempt such an undertaking. Hoffman obviously had in mind what he described in his preface—a history of the world in the Christian era—and better men than he have failed in so vast a project. His work is actually a mine of nineteenth-century historiographic scholarship, thoroughly gentlemanly and pleasingly amateurish. As such, it scarcely deserves the comparative oblivion to which it has been consigned by students of the Legend. No doubt the reading of the work is a penitential achievement, which may be one good reason why it has been neglected. Another may be the fact that Cartaphilus in it assumes a bewildering number of names, characteristics, and intellectual and philosophical postures.

Yet, so far as Hoffman is concerned, his delineation of the protagonist has a certain consistency. Cartaphilus is throughout prejudiced against Christianity. Indeed, we may well believe that Hoffman is relieving himself of much relating to those aspects of Christianity which he dislikes. Although his Cartaphilus eventually comes to respect Christian ideals, and the emotional power and drive of early Christianity, he can never bring himself to accept them completely. Hoffman is essentially a monotheist and cannot be persuaded that the hierarchy and the elaborate organization of the Church constitute anything more than a thinly veiled and idolatrous polytheism. His whole attitude is summed up in his note about Charlemagne: here was a man regarded as one of the three great Christian Worthies of the World (along with Arthur and Godfrey of Bouillon), and yet, with all his virtues, how much better and greater he could have been. Hoffman's Cartaphilus, indeed, represents a range of man's intellectual and philosophical possibilities wider than that of any protagonist of the Chronicle of the Wandering Jew before him, and so it is only fitting that the *Chronicles of Cartaphilus* should be the capstone of this particular genre. Many other writers will find the chronological devices convenient, but they will be using them for altogether different purposes.

CHAPTER SEVEN

Early Examples of the Art Form of the Legend

To draw some sort of line of demarcation between a "popular" form and an "art" form of the Legend of the Wandering Jew is at best a difficult business and one which must depend upon an arbitrary judgment. Often the distinction is meaningless; yet it remains a fact that, within the past three hundred years, or from the middle of the seventeenth century to the present, the Legend has been treated in a manner varying greatly from one age to the next. It is a long distance from the *Kurtze Beschreibung* to Goethe, Byron, and Shelley, to say nothing of a writer in the 1950's. Moreover, such distances are not merely the result of the fact that Goethe, Byron, and Shelley had greater creative abilities than the unknown author of the *Kurtze Beschreibung*. Nor is it only a matter of chronology, either, for some of the earlier pieces have greater claim to the designation of "art form" than much of the stuff from second-rate authors in the nineteenth or twentieth centuries.

In a sense, the complacent writer in the *Hannoverische Beyträge* (p. 127 above) was right. We know more than our grandfathers. We should know more. It is no longer a question of believing or not believing; we all know what to think of legends. That is why they are called legends. We are no longer satisfied to hear that the Jew was seen in such and such a place and did thus and so. This was the weakness, from the point of view of any but the folklorist, of the popular tales and even of the Chronicle of the Wandering Jew, although Galt and particularly Hoffman gave us insight into the mind of the Wanderer. The objectivity of earlier accounts can awaken some interest, but this is no longer enough. The tendency becomes ever stronger to ask: What did the Jew think of his punishment? What were his sensibilities? What was his outlook upon his unending life, his hopes for the everlasting future? And so, more and more Ahasuerus is taken from the impersonal, objective world of folklore and is endowed with human tendencies toward emotional reactions. In this way the severity of his punishment tends to be sharpened and his larger significance heightened.

It is necessary, therefore, to consider as art forms all treatments of the Legend which present the Jew in a subjective manner or which tell what he thought and felt, as well as what the author thought and felt about the Jew. I have deliberately treated the Chronicle of the Wandering Jew, which is in some ways an art form, as something separate because it belongs to a distinctive genre—indeed, one of the very few distinctive genres in the mass of writings about Ahasuerus. Otherwise, however, I should include under the heading of "art form" all instances of the Legend in which the protagonist is treated knowingly as a symbol of moral or spiritual values, either positive or negative—for instance, Ahasuerus as a representative of souls in rebellion, as a symbol for the Jewish people, or, for that matter, as a grand symbol of all errant mankind or a substitute for the demonic. Such treatments of the Wandering Jew demand a greater artistic and intellectual sophistication than those which merely picture Malchus beating his head against a pillar or Ahasuerus shuddering at an oath. In brief, subjectivity and some degree of artistic *savoir-faire* should be the chief criteria of the art form of the Legend.

Very little of the folkloristic treatment of the Legend is anything other than objective. The tale of the Jew is stated as supposed fact; it is presented in direct narrative, with little or no comment or qualification. It may be epic in scope, but it remains very much dehumanized. The sufferings of Malchus in his prison may challenge the imagination; his torments may cause him to cry out in woe and anguish. Yet the authors of such accounts, thus far in our survey, have been content, in general, to state the facts as they have seen or heard them and to let it go at that. We have already seen how the Jew could be a synonym for long life and omniscience—and here we approach my concept of the art form—but his more complex qualities have not yet been emphasized. It is true also that he has been considered a miraculous creature, but all this miraculousness illustrates the infinite mercy of God, his glory, his tolerance, or what you will. Ahasuerus can hardly be termed, as yet, a real human being in the minds of his creators. He rides the midnight storm; he paces about the room in a lonely farmhouse; he prophesies doom and desolation. It is still difficult, however, to see him as a suffering man or to sympathize with his suffering.

When we experience this sympathy, and come to realize that here is a human being bearing his particular cross and not a mere figment, we are dealing with the art form. We shall find, of course, that this art form is usually being shaped by the hands of a writer of talent, for only such a writer can properly appreciate the awesome potentialities of the Legend. But individual talents vary so much, and pioneers are so often fumbling in their technique, that we may frequently meet very crude work hiding the original talent. In other words, the art form may often be poor art, and we must be prepared for it.

A final point, and by no means the least important, is the patent fact that the most complete expression of the subjective will be found in writers whose emotions and imaginations can work together; in terms of art and literature, this is likely to mean the so-called romantic artist or writer. Whatever the validity of this observation, it is certain that only in the nineteenth and twentieth centuries is the Wandering Jew the creation of authors who are interested primarily in portraying his inmost soul and in extracting from him all the possibilities of symbolic value. The seventeenth and eighteenth centuries were more likely to consider him a freakish showpiece.

The Complaintes

Nevertheless, we should return to the seventeenth century for the beginnings of the art form. One of the Dudulaeus pamphlets has, printed on the reverse of the title page, some sixteen lines of verse outlining the argument of the prose account. Daniel Sudermann of Schwankfeld expands this into over a hundred lines of what is virtually a written ballad (1621), the conclusion of which earnestly calls upon mankind to wonder at this tremendous miracle and to have pity for the deed.[1] At about this time, there arose the popular ballad in England (pp. 61-63).

Historically, however, the French *complaintes* are more productive than the ballad. They are a distinct contribution of the seventeenth century. The first of the surviving *complaintes* was printed at the conclusion of the *Discours véritable* (p. 54 above) of 1608 or 1609. The last important one to remain anonymous can be dated near 1800; it celebrates the alleged visit of the Wandering Jew to Brussels in 1774. Altogether some half-dozen *complaintes* have been preserved. We need concern ourselves with only one or two, which will illustrate how the genre proceeded from what was only a type of popular ballad to a true lyric— hoarse, crude, and perhaps too amateurish to receive critical attention, but still a lyric.

An example should be quoted in its entirety, and I have chosen the one from the *Discours véritable*. The musical setting of this *complainte* is designated as the sixteenth-century air "Dames d'honneur."

> Le bruit courant, ça et là par la France,
> Depuis six mois qu'on avait espérance
> Bien tost de voir un Juif qui est errant
> Parmy le monde pleurant et souspirant.
>
> Comme de fait en la rare campagne   5
> Deux gentils-hommes au pays de Champagne
> Le rencontrèrent tout seul en cheminant,
> Non pas vestu comme on est maintenant.
>
> De grandes chaussés il porte a la marine
> Et une jupe comme à la Florentine,   10
> Un manteau long jusques en terre trainant
> Comme un autre homme il est au demeurant.
>
> Ce que voyant lors ils l'interrogèrent
> D'ou il venoit et ils luy demandèrent
> Sa nation, le mestier qu'il menoit,   15
> Mais cependant tousiours il cheminoit.
>
> "Ie suis," dict-il, "Juif de ma naissance
> Et l'un de ceux qui par leur arrogance
> Crucifièrent le Sauveur des humains
> Lorsque Pilate en lava ses deux mains."   20
>
> Il dit aussi qu'il a bien souvenance
> Quand Iesus-Christ, à tort réceut sentence,
> Et qu'il le vit de sa croix bien chargé
> Et qu'à sa porte il s'étoit deschargé.
>
> Lors le Juif par couroux le répousse,   25
> L'iniuriant et plusieurs fois le pousse

En luy monstrant le supplice appreste
Pour mettre à mort sa haute Maiesté.

Nostre Seigneur bien ferme le régarde,
En luy disant: "A cecy prens bien garde,   30
Ie réposeray et tu chemineras,
Partant régarde à ce que tu feras."

Tout aussi tost le Juif meit à terre
Son petit fils, et s'encourut grand erre,
Mais il ne sceut iamais sa maison   35
Mettre les pieds en aucune saison.

Hiérusalem, le lieu de sa naissance,
Femme et enfans ne fust en sa puissance
Iamais de voir n'y pas un sien parent,
Et par le monde s'en va ainsi errant.   40

De son mestier cordonnier il dict estre,
Et à le voir il semble tout champestre.
Il boit et mange avec sobrieté,
Et est honneste selon la pauvreté.

Longtemps il fut au pays d'Arabie,   45
Et aux déserts de la triste Libie,
Et à la Chine, en l'Asie Mineur,
Iardin d'Eden et du monde l'honneur.

Comme en semblable en la stérile Afrique,
Au mont Liban, au Royaume Persique,   50
Et au pays de l'odoreux Lèvant,
Tousiours il va son chemin poursuyvant.

N'aguère estoit en la haute Allemagne,
En Saxonie, puis s'en va en Espagne,
Pour s'en aller les Anglois visiter   55
Et nostre France puis après habiter.

Pour estre à bout de son pélérinage,
Et accomplir son desiré voyage,
Il n'a plus rien qu'un tiers de l'Occident
Et quelques îles pour aller, Dieu aydant.   60

Tout cela le iugement faist attendre
Il faut de Dieu, et répentant se rendre
"Afin," dict-il, "qu'entre les réprouvez
Par nos mérites nous ne soyons trouvez."

"Je fay," dict-il, "icy bas pénitence,   65
Touché ie suis de vraye répentence,
Ie ne fay rien que d'aller tracassant,
De pays en autre demandant au passant.

"Quand l'univers ie regarde et contemple
Ie croy que Dieu me fait servir d'exemple 70
Pour tesmoigner sa Mort et Passion
En attendant la Résurrection."[2]

In lines 59-60, it will be noticed, the territory to be covered by the Wanderer has not yet included the whole earth. Lines 65-68 give at least the germ of the subjective, which blossoms in the later examples. Evidently this particular *complainte* had sufficient popularity to win for it a translation into Flemish. It is good to be able to report that the Wandering Jew was once in the Garden of Eden (1.48); this was the first time he had ever reached that pre-sinful spot.

Among the several offshoots of this first *complainte*, one, to the air of "Saint Eustache," attracted the attention of early editors, but calls for no special attention now. Between 1640 and 1650, however, appeared a French woodcut divided into an upper and a lower section; the upper depicts the Jew in shoemaker's costume being addressed by Christ, who is falling down under the weight of the Cross; the lower represents the Jew speaking to the two burgesses of Brussels. (In the *complainte* from the *Discours véritable*, the same device of having the Jew meet two solid citizens is used. We have seen that this is a definite motif in the Franco-Flemish treatments.) A note indicates that this woodcut was printed, with royal license, by a certain Le Blond, and a few verses explain who the Jew is; but both this and another *complainte* of about 1635 may be passed over. Somewhere between 1675 and 1710, there came into being a "Cantique spirituel sur les prédictions annoncées par les Juifs." This is a poem of nine six-line stanzas, beginning:

Venez, âmes fidèles,
Entendre maintenant
Les prédictions nouvelles
Du digne Juif-Errant,
Qui sont les nonpareilles
Depuis très-peu de temps.

Here the Wandering Jew is met, this time at Dijon, by the customary two upright citizens. He tells them who he is and how miserable he is because of his sin. There is no place in the world where he has not been, suffering bitter grief, without being able to pause in his wanderings, *fort attristé*. The personal note is much stronger here than in the preceding examples. It is possible that the "Cantique spirituel" had an origin contemporaneous with that of the first *complainte* but the extant version is obviously much later, as the language attests.[3]

Among the many alleged visits of the Wandering Jew, it may be recalled that he once paid his respects to Brussels (p. 115). The date was April 22, 1774; and, unlike other such visits, this one was timed at six o'clock in the evening. The alleged incident is negligible in itself, but it produced a *complainte* which has become easily the most celebrated of all the *complaintes* of the Wandering Jew. To some it has been known as the Brabantine ballad. It is, unfortunately, much too long to quote here, and yet a summary is essential. Most likely it was composed around 1800. After four stanzas of expository narrative, the poem resolves itself into a kind of Greek chorus, with the Wandering Jew as protagonist. Emotion is certainly in evidence; the Jew is miserable, and his respondents, the inevitable two bourgeois, are full of pity to the point of mawkishness. The opening lines are often quoted by other French writers on the subject:

Est-il rien sur la terre
Qui soit plus surprenant
Que la grande misère
Du pauvre Juif-Errant?
Que son sort malheureux
Paraît triste et facheux!—

set the tone for the whole.[4] The two citizens bid him enter the inn for refreshment; he accepts, but he cannot sit down. They ask him his age; he replies that old age oppresses him, and no wonder, for he is more than eighteen hundred years old. Yes, he is Isaac Laquedem (p. 59 above), and he has wearily traversed the world again and again. They hope God will pardon him, but he answers that he was bold and cruel and rebellious, and now he must be on his way—too much torment awaits him if he lingers too long. Some of the stanzas are suggestive of the image of the Jew in Gustave Doré's noted series of engravings in the mid-nineteenth century, much the best series of pictures of Ahasuerus yet done.[5] Beyond that, little more needs to be said about the Brabantine ballad, which for all its popularity is little short of doggerel. But its currency is a matter of record and it underwent translation into Flemish, Dutch, and Danish.

None of these *complaintes*, however, is very effective in literary accomplishment, nor does it have the strength of an eighteenth-century Danish poem, *Sandfaerdig Beretning om Jerusalems Skoemager, Ahasverus kaldet*, printed at Copenhagen without date.[6] This work, completely ignored by most scholars and antiquarians, may be perhaps as much narrative as lyric, but the total effect is certainly that of the *complainte*. Its outline of the story obviously comes from the Ahasuerus-book, but the itinerary of the Wanderer is made to include Baltic and Scandinavian lands also. Danzig, Stockholm, and Novedstaden supplement Cracow, Vienna, and Strasbourg. But the lyric emerges clearly enough in such stanzas as:

Mine Klaeder gamle ere,
  Over sytten hundred' Aar;
Penge maad jeg ikke baere,
  Af Guds Forsyn Føde faaer.
Jed fornøiet er i Gud,
Man min Synd vil slette ud,
  Og mig til sin Himmel tage
  Efter disse Jammerdage.[7]

Neoclassical Elements Persisting

For the greater part, however, we are still in the neoclassical aspect of Ahasuerus. The *complainte* indicates that he was looking for sympathy and getting it here and there, but in none of the *complaintes* and ballads has he any emotional fire. He is still a showpiece, a wonderful freak of nature who could be bent to satirical and comical purposes. We have already seen his potentialities as an agent of satire. As early as 1638, it will be remembered, he appeared with other comic characters in a French ballet concerning the marriage of Pierre de Provence and the fair Maguelonne, in which he delivered himself of some rather silly lines. Malone, in his *The Wandering Jew Telling Fortunes to Englishmen*, had considerable success in using his portrayal of the Jew as a medium for satirical thrusts at various members of society.[8] In the *Letters Writ by a Turkish Spy* (pp. 128-32 above), Michob Ader, the Wanderer, had some comments to make about the sorry side of human affairs.

Meantime, a few literary works, none of them important in itself, had begun to play with the satirical possibilities. The Spaniard Antonio Sigler de Huerta, in his play, *Las cinco blancas de Juan de Espera en Dios* (1669), presents the Jew in a comical light.[9] This play can best be judged by its plot, since Sigler de Huerta was not a master of either dialogue or characterization. Juan falls in love with Livia, daughter of no less a personage than the emperor Tiberius of Rome. His love is hopeless. Besides, to add to the disquiet of his soul, he is an incurable miser: avarice is his companion day and night. A miser, of course, is always fair game for the satirist. He is obliged to leave the court of Tiberius, and falls, for no good reason except that it seems to be required by the Legend, into the occupation of shoemaker. He then follows the path of the Wandering Jew, and his casual and unsystematic wanderings differ from those already described only in that Juan habitually uses a cloak of invisibility. Moreover, he is obliged to buy food and drink; but when he buys them, he pays first with his five little coins (already a familiar accessory) and then becomes visible. Farcical elements here are inevitable.

A somewhat different approach is that seen in the Fifth Satire of Claude d'Esternod's *L'Espadon satyrique*, a distinctly anticlerical poem. Here the Wanderer, an intimate participant in the satirical doings, mocks himself thus:

> Je me nomme le Iuif errant,
> Je vay deça de là courant,
> Mon logis est au bout du monde;
> Tantost je suis en Trébisonde,
> Et puis soudain chez le Valen;
> Ma teste aussi n'est pas de plomb;
> Car je suis né dessous la lune.
> Je vis au soir le Roy de Thune,
> Et aujourd'hui le Prestre Ian,
> Et il n'y a pas un quart d'an
> Que je vis le Roy de la Chine
> Qui portoit une capeline
> En guise de vostre couvrechef.[10]

Truly, in informal phrase, this *Juif errant* gets around, but it is the reader who is meant to do most of the mocking. The contempt in which Ahasuerus was held by critics and the learned of the age has already been described. A rather oblique comment on the skepticism expressing this contempt, however, receives its blessing from the distinguished French author Alain Le Sage, who in his *Le diable boiteux* (1707) tells of three booksellers, to each of whom an unscrupulous writer has sold a manuscript of the same play. The play must be palpably worthless and is therefore entitled *Le juif errant*.[11]

The world of the theater further insulted the Wandering Jew by condoning a mediocre comedy by Andrew Franklin, *The Wandering Jew: Or Love's Masquerade*, produced at the Drury Lane Theater in 1797.[12] A money-mad old father, Sir Solomon Swallow, has two daughters, Camilla and Lydia. They are being courted by two young adventurers, Atall and Marall, respectively. Sir Solomon bars the house to the two indigent swains, but they gain admittance by disguising themselves as the legendary Wandering Jew and his secretary, the master supposed to be fabulously rich and his secretary presumably wealthy also. When they spread the report that the Jew is seeking a wife, a commodity which his faithful secretary also wishes to purchase, Sir Solomon goes out of his way to bring them to his house, ostensibly to see his collection of paintings. Thus nature takes its course. The Jewish accent adopted by Atall in the guise of Ahasuerus is scarcely more convincing than that used by Moses in Sheridan's near-contemporary *School for Scandal*. In any event, this weak two-act dramatic effort ends on the moral note spoken by fatuous Sir Solomon, that "there is room for the old to reform as well as the young." The Wandering Jew is used as the sheerest kind of dramatic expedient and is nothing but a buffoon at that. Why the play should have been named after him is a mystery.

Another English work of about the same time, Richard Graves's[13] *The Spiritual Quixote: Or the Summer's Ramble of Mr. Geoffry Wildgoose* (1773), an anti-Methodist novel, recounts the adventures of a country squire who has become inflamed with Methodism and roams the countryside to spread his gospel. The Sancho Panza to this Quixote is Jeremias Tugwell, once a shoemaker, but now a mere patchwork cobbler, thanks to the confusing effects of alcohol. Jerry passes as a half-wit; he delights to talk of wondrous things and wondrous characters—including the Wandering Jew, in whose punishment he firmly believes. The point is, however, that the belief resides in the minds of crackpots and simpletons, and so we are once again in the world of the learned critics of the Legend. It is an amusing footnote to the whole attitude of the eighteenth century that John Jortin (1698-1770), in his *Remarks on Ecclesiastical History* (London, 1751-53), should refer to the protagonist as "the rambling Jew."[14]

Goethe and Schubart

And yet the imaginative potentialities of the Legend were still there, as always, and when artistic and literary fashions began to shift, around the middle of the eighteenth century, Ahasuerus would sooner or later attract the attention of those with a less intellectual approach. It is fitting in one way that this early in the development of the art form he should have wandered into the sphere of him whom many consider the greatest figure in nineteenth-century European romanticism, Johann Wolfgang von Goethe. But Goethe's contribution, while arresting in its originality and most promising in its basic concept, remains, unfortunately, a fragmentary work—so fragmentary, indeed, that if it were not for the author's own explanation, we would have difficulty in making much of the surviving piece. We certainly cannot judge fairly the value of his efforts.

In the first book of Goethe's *Dichtung und Wahrheit*, the author tells us that he became acquainted with the Legend through the Ahasuerus-book and other (unspecified) examples of popular journalism, precisely the sort of writing already considered. In his youth, between 1773 and 1775, while he was still fired with the enthusiasm and energy of a young romantic, he cast about for a fit subject on which to lavish some extensive creative endeavor, and so he fixed on Ahasuerus. His project was comprehensive in the extreme. He wished first of all to use the Legend as a canvas for certain events in the history of religion and the Church. He would transplant the shoemaker from Jerusalem to Dresden and make him a genial and helpful citizen. Here Christ would come, as he came to Jerusalem, and would receive counsel from the shoemaker. Ahasuerus, an average practical man, would disapprove of Christ's activities because they were politically disturbing and because he himself did not have the spirituality to understand Christ's higher message. Judas Iscariot would come into the picture as one who hoped that Christ would declare himself King of the Jews and rule the nation; the betrayal of Christ, in fact, was intended to hasten action on the part of the Saviour. But Jesus had ruined this scheme by allowing himself to be captured and led before the priesthood, who did not have the courage to back him up. The story of the Passion would then follow. When Jesus passes before the house of the shoemaker, however, the "common sense" of Ahasuerus prompts him to reproach Christ for his failure to save his nation. It is not until Veronica has covered the face of the Saviour and exhibited the imprint of his countenance that the shoemaker realizes the true divinity of Christ, and then it is too late; he has heard the fatal words and begun his wanderings, urged on by a consuming disquiet.

Goethe's fragmentary work was written in 1774 and 1775.[15] Its tone is satirical. The form of verse is a kind of sprightly short meter, ill-adapted to an epic of the nature which the poet originally had in mind, but it has a Hudibrastic quality admirably suited to the ironic and not too optimistic ideas of the text. The spirit, Goethe warns, prompted him to leap out of bed and write, but it is a spirit given to gibberish and cant, and the reader must beware. The Jew turns out to be an eighteenth-century German Jew. He is, for all his creator's plans about geniality, in the manner of Hans Sachs somewhat sanctimonious, with a theological viewpoint halfway between the Essenes and the Methodists—something of a Separatist, but actually a rather independent person. He expects too much. Daily he calls for signs and wanders, shaking his head at the daughters of Zion. His standards for mere mortal clergymen are far too high; even St. Paul, if he were to return to the priesthood, would not be without fault in the shoemaker's eyes. For, Goethe implies, no matter how zealous clergymen might have been as novices, once they get priestly charges, they wax fat and soft. "Woe to Babylon!" they may cry, but they are too self-indulgent and too willing to go the way of the world. Ahasuerus finds that in the eighteenth century the *ne plus ultra* was to blaspheme God and to find the mud comfortable. But why should the Jew worry?

The priests may cry that Judgment Day is at hand, but the Jew has heard that for a long time and is no longer fearful.

The scene then shifts to heaven. There God, sitting on his throne, calls for his Son. Christ comes "stumbling along over the stars." It appears that he has been on one of them helping a poor woman in childbirth. He is told to attend to the earth, which is in sad need of some kind of refurbishment. "Der Mensch is nur ein Tor!" Verily man is but a fool. Therefore Christ returns to earth, inevitably reminded of the treatment once given him on that obscure sphere. It makes him feel like a man returning to the bosom of a girl whom he had once loved but who has been faithless to him. Even the momentary thrill of recovered happiness is tempered by the thought that the earth has about it always the aura of tribulation and sorrow. A beautiful lyrical passage intervenes. As the Saviour alights on the hill where Satan once tempted him on earth, "the mother who bore me for the grave itself," and looks curiously about, he realizes that the world is indeed too much with us, that greed and the Devil are in the ascendant, that the rich shut themselves up within their castles while the poor go hungry, that the golden sign of Christ's own suffering hangs from the bosoms of those who in idleness and sloth wear it officially—and officiously. The country in which Christ first finds himself is Catholic; its ruler is a certain Louis XIV, and the covetousness prevailing there is the greed of the Catholic clergy. But when the Saviour, sore at heart, goes to a neighboring country which is Protestant—that is, Germany—he finds matters no better. In fact, it is difficult to see there any evidence of God at all. A paunchy minister sleeps with his fat wife, among many children, and has a good income from tithes. The minister guides Jesus about the city. At the city gates, he is asked by the military to give his name. When he replies that he is the Son of Man, it makes no impression. The sergeant casually notes that his father must have been named Mann. Efforts to get an audience with the senior pastor of the community come to nothing, for the cook innocently informs him that the pastor is in conference. At this point the fragment comes to an end.

Not till long after 1775 did Goethe abandon the idea of finishing his epic. Once, he informs us in Book XV of *Dichtung und Wahrheit*, he dallied with the idea of introducing the Wandering Jew to Spinoza, himself a Jew and a prophet of the philosophy of resignation. And in a salient passage from his *Italienische Reise*, under the date of October 27, 1786, he remarks, in reference to some striking scenery in Italy, that this would be a fit place to meet the Wandering Jew; yet, if that Jew should return, he would find things as Christ found them. And Christ, if he should return, would undoubtedly suffer a second crucifixion.

There seems to be a great gulf between Goethe's original plan, as he explained it, and the fragments. But, from the very fact that they are fragments, one must only speculate. As to the proposed outline, it is evident that it would have contained original stuff—original as to motivation and as to treatment. The Jew and Judas, for example, are both given a certain amount of justification. It is particularly interesting to see a political reason for Judas' betrayal of Christ. Moreover, the original personal affection of Ahasuerus for Christ as a man, when it leads to his offense against the Saviour, is a sound bit of psychology. It would seem that Goethe's ideas would have produced a work which would have been successful both as narrative and as drama. Considering the possibilities in the final scene between Judas and Ahasuerus, it might have turned out better as a drama than as an epic.

But in the fragments all is different. Satire has taken precedence over both epic and dramatic elements. Ahasuerus himself is shunted off the main track almost as soon as we begin. It is Christ who dominates the scene, and the poem seems to be shaping itself into an epic about the second coming of Christ. Undoubtedly several later writers to be met with on pages following must have taken the hint from the passages in *Dichtung und Wahrheit*. We shall see more than once this association of Ahasuerus and Judas as well as the friendship of Ahasuerus and Christ; and the twin magnets which draw these individuals, originally either separate or antagonistic in the Legend itself, into a close juxtaposition are, first, the motivation of political disagreement and, second, the disquieting thought that the world would be equally inhospitable to both, that neither the Jew nor the Saviour could derive hope from the contemplation of the miserable race of men.

Goethe's unfinished epic, incidentally, offers by implication some apt comment on the Legend as a whole. It is a curious fact that most attempts to give the Wandering Jew a central position in a long narrative have failed. The better writers seem to have recognized their difficulty and abandoned their projects. Goethe says that he dropped his planned epic because he lacked time to study the requisite details of background. Coming from one who possessed such enormous intellectual energy, this is the lamest of excuses. Perhaps he actually lost interest, but this hardly sounds like him. The real problem, of course, is always that the Legend lacks the dramatic tension needed to build up a cumulative narrative capable of holding, for an extended period, the interest of the reader. Once all the circumstances accompanying the Jew's wanderings have been told, and the protagonist has begun his peregrinations, there is little more to do than to give him adventures in a structure demanding only a stringing together of incidents, letting him bemoan his fate in the meantime; and such adventures and lamentations cannot be drawn out indefinitely. A writer with the power to carry the Jew ultimately, with increasing excitement, before the Great White Throne, where final disposition can be made of his case, would undoubtedly achieve a remarkable literary accomplishment. Yet only Edgar Quinet, in his *Ahasvérus*, a "modern mystery" which we shall meet later (pp. 202-7), has managed with some success to carry off such a tour de force; but his work, though brilliant, has many limitations.

Of all the authors of stature whose names are associated with the Legend, Goethe would have been the most capable of attempting the feat in question. In the fragments, however, he hardly got to the figure of Ahasuerus at all, and nearly all of the writers following him have been content to leave the Jew on earth. He was evidently wheeling into position for an attack upon the clergy of his time, but all we have are mere surface diggings. The fragments have considerable color and power, even some beauty, and there is no doubt that they contributed, at least through Goethe's own comments about them, to a diversity of treatment in the art form.

Of much more immediate impact, however, is the poem by the journalist, critic, poet, impresario, and general man of letters, Christian Friedrich Daniel Schubart (1739-1791), who, in 1783, delivered himself of something more than a hundred lines of verse, entitled, like nine-tenths of subsequent German works on the subject, "Der ewige Jude."[16] The subtitle, "Eine lyrische Rhapsodie," differentiates matters somewhat. Here is none of the suggestive vocabulary, the satiric thrust, the sophisticated implications, or the downright humor of Goethe's fragments. Schubart is simple, serious, and artistically sincere, uninspired, and highly important. He had no high-flown schemes for portraying world history; he wrote what is essentially a *complainte* of the Wandering Jew. It has been suggested that both Goethe and Schubart were moved to write on the Wandering Jew because they had known the Brabantine ballad. In Goethe's case this theory is impossible, for his fragments were begun in the very year that the Jew visited Brussels, and the Brabantine ballad must have been composed some time later—indeed, it may not have come into being until the end of the century. Schubart, on the other hand, might possibly have known of the ballad if it was in existence as early as 1783, which I very much doubt; but even if he knew it, he is too independent in his treatment for this knowledge to be at all important.

Schubart's Ahasuerus stands on Mount Carmel, in a thoroughly Byronic posture, although it is still a generation before Byron. He rolls skulls down the slopes of the mountain—those of his father, his wives, his children. All have died, but he cannot. He has thrown himself into Etna; he has rushed into battles and forest fires; he has cast himself into the raging ocean. But as he rises into a more and more hysterical mood—and Schubart changes then from blank verse into unrhymed and free dimeters—an angel assures the victim that God's wrath will not endure forever. There is a pardon awaiting him in some far-off age.

The theme hammered at throughout the poem is the fact that Ahasuerus constantly seeks death and does not find it. Nowhere before has this theme sounded so intensely as in Schubart's lines, although we shall certainly meet it often enough from now on. As a matter of fact, it had not been heard before so clearly except in the parallel of Chaucer's *Pardoner's Tale* (pp. 31-32 above). It lends special appropriateness to the German designation of the Jew as "eternal" rather than "wandering." For Schubart's Ahasuerus does no actual wandering in the poem; he never leaves Mount Carmel, even if he does begin by telling the reader of his wandering career. And for all the occasional ineptness of phrase, the arrant melodrama, and the fact that Schubart has a particular talent for showing how unmusical a language German can be in the wrong hands, the poem remains memorable, a fitting source for much ensuing romantic poetry dedicated to the theme of the immortal mortal, and one to bear watching as we proceed through the nineteenth-century literature of the Legend.

Yet despite a sense of completeness which Schubart's poem affords, it remains a fragment. The author had intended it as a part of a much longer work. But the same difficulty presented itself to him as to Goethe; the most he could envisage was a series of similar dramatic monologues, and the problem of integrating them was too much for him. These monologues were to present Ahasuerus on a mountaintop, surveying the "boundless ocean of time," presenting pictures of all the monstrous, spectacular upheavals of men and nature through which he had lived.

Among these scenes would have been the fall of the Colosseum at Rome, the Giant Apparition of the Papacy, the Reformation and its great Protestant heroes, the Thirty Years' War, Columbus and his voyages of discovery—in short, all the important experiences and events of the past eighteen hundred years. Schubart could not altogether resist the fascination of the Chronicle of the Wandering Jew, which was the best-known form of the Legend in 1783.

As the art form begins to take on shape and substance, the most important developments in the portrayal of Ahasuerus are the attaching of symbolism to his identity and the kind of romantic representation given him in Schubart's "Der ewige Jude." Since Goethe's fragments were not published until 1836 and were, besides, satirical in an age when satire was not strong or popular, it is easy to see why Schubart should be the more influential. As for the symbolism, it becomes, in its various aspects, the greatest single fact in the progress of the Legend, even though at first Ahasuerus was the symbol of omniscience, longevity, and ubiquitousness only. Schubart's poem was translated into English and then French. In either the original German or in translation it became known to the English romantic poets and to some not so romantic. Thus Coleridge read it in the original, as is evident from some of the details of his *Ancient Mariner*.[17] Shelley came upon the English translation quite accidentally and noted his discovery with typical naïveté. It was to him "some German work, whose title I have vainly endeavoured to discover. I picked it up, dirty and torn, some years ago, in Lincoln's-Inn Fields." In actual fact, the English translation, by one P. W., a cleric named Peter Will, was first printed in 1801 in the *German Museum*, a monthly periodical devoted to matters pertaining to German literature and civilization.[18] In the following year the translation appeared as a chapbook and circulated through the next few years with some success. Presumably, a copy of this was what Shelley acquired. The French translation, made about 1830 by Gerard de Nerval, appears in many French chapbooks of the nineteenth century, usually under the misleading title of "La mort du juif errant." About this same time there was printed, also, a rough prose translation into French, with the same title and substance.[19] The peaceful sleep promised Ahasuerus may be the end of it all, but it is not so described by Schubart. Few romantic writers, however, would ever ignore the possibility of a death.

Not the least significant factor in the success of Schubart's poem was the woodcut on the cover, which portrays Ahasuerus as a patriarchal Jew with flying beard and forbidding costume, almost a Woden-figure, hurling skulls down a mountainside. With such a picture before us, it requires but a touch to push Ahasuerus over into the realm of Gothic romance, which was flourishing in the 1780's and 1790's. The Gothic treatment of the Legend is therefore the next item on the docket.

CHAPTER EIGHT

Ahasuerus in the Romantic Heyday

As the romantic tide in literature and the arts began to rise in the latter part of the eighteenth century, to reach a peak in the earlier half of the nineteenth, the European imagination, as expressed in the various media, became less restrained, less disciplined, more excitable. It is, of course, an egregious error to assume that the neoclassical age suppressed the imagination. Such great representatives of its literature as *Gulliver's Travels, Candide,* and *The Rape of the Lock* have the true spark of genius so far as the imaginative process is concerned, and this is true without reference to their other manifest excellences. The same thing is true, on a lower plane, of a work like Miles Wilson's *The History of Israel Jobson.* In all these works, however, the imaginative elements are held in place by a series of rational checks and balances, which some may consider too binding and others essential. Thus Lemuel Gulliver stands to the Lilliputians as one foot to one inch, and this scale is applied throughout the story of Gulliver's first voyage; Candide and Pangloss, in spite of their eccentric peregrinations, observe and report and sharpen the critical scalpel of their versatile creator; Pope's imagination in his famous mock-epic is limited deliberately to the mentality of a belle at Hampton Court.

But to the romanticist in general and the Gothic-novel writer in particular, such checks and balances are to be rejected, not welcomed. In a chronological sequence, the Gothic romance is one of the earlier signs of a return to the romantic after the reign of the neoclassical. A genre dedicated primarily to the appeal of the terrible, the horrible, the grotesque, and the sensational, it emerged in rather tentative fashion during the 1750's and achieved its most noted effects within the eighteenth century. Among many writers of this type, there remained a sufficient residuum of the neoclassical to lead them to some sort of explanation of the customary presence of the supernatural in their works. In reality, however, the better Gothic romances are those which scorn such attempts to elucidate situations on a natural basis; their authors create these situations with the deliberate intent to evoke terror through the use of the supernatural *and* the mysterious. They throw themselves, so to speak, on the mercy of the reader. Let him first accept the real presence of devils, specters, witches, warlocks, and vampires, or even plain ghosts. Did not the poet Coleridge, himself no mean exemplar of the Gothic tradition, speak of "the willing suspension of disbelief"? The best ghost story is always that which is dominated by an unexplained spook, not by some apparition born of a magic lantern or of the wind whistling down the chimney.

The romantically inclined writers between 1750 and 1850 reveled, even wallowed, in the tale of terror, particularly in Germany and England, although the logical French were by no means immune, and America had her Charles Brockden Brown and Edgar Allan Poe. When the romantic imagination, infected by Gothicism, began to play also with the stuff of folklore, chaos indeed came again. Credulity and superstition, earmarks of the unsophisticated of all ages, can easily conquer the purely emotional individual; he usually has a considerable amount of native imagination which is not restrained by rational or cerebral processes of any kind, and is a natural propagator of folk tales. To put it in another way, we find that all authorities agree on the inherently romantic potential of folklore. As a corollary fact, one of the important characteristics of the romantic revival around 1750 was its affinity for the folkloristic.

Schiller's Geisterseher

It is time now to examine, in a chain of case histories, the various shifting conceptions of the Wandering Jew as the multitudinous and by no means brief works about him, written in the first half of the nineteenth century, pass before us. By the time this particular parade has passed, we shall be in a position to note the explicit and implicit possibilities in the sophisticated treatment of the Legend almost in their entirety, for the century between 1850 and 1950 has done little but follow in the footsteps of the early romantic writers when it undertakes to write about the Wandering Jew.

Let us first consider a fragmentary prose romance by Schiller, *Der Geisterseher* ("He who sees ghosts"), which appeared in the magazine *Thalia* between 1786 and 1789. Its composition therefore antedates in part the publication of Schubart's "Der ewige Jude" (1786), although the latter poem, as we have seen, was probably written as early as 1783. With that rather over-refined passion for the mysterious which permeates many a romance of this period, *Der Geisterseher*, drawing upon the papers of a Count O———, tells of the career of the Prince of ———. This prince is a wealthy fainéant of a brooding sort, who prefers to spend his time in Venice, living the life of a diffident, almost antisocial man, withdrawn from the world except for the company of a few intimates. A strange Armenian,[1] who can tell the Prince the exact hour when his near relative in a remote country will die—all without the benefit of any known means of communication—hovers over the first part of the romance. He bids fair to become a great force for good or evil in the life of the Prince, but one cannot be sure which, because he fades out of the picture. Present also is a Russian army officer, inscrutable and sinister, who is otherwise an undeveloped character. Let us not bother with the many adventures of the Prince of ———, if such they may be called. He falls in love, he becomes worldly, he loses his money. His inamorata is poisoned; he himself takes refuge in Mother Church. The Armenian bobs up at the end to sponsor the reform of the Prince.

But there is more to the business than this. The Armenian and the Russian officer merge into the same person, although this startling fact is never explicitly stated. The Prince and his friends, on a particular occasion, expose a Sicilian charlatan, who then evinces great terror upon seeing the Armenian-Russian stranger:

"But who is he? Whence comes he? Is he an Armenian or a Russian? Of the characters he assumes, which is the real one? . . ."

"He is nothing of what he appears to be. There are few conditions or countries of which he has not worn the mask. No person knows who he is, whence he comes, or whither he goes . . . Here we know him only by the name of the *Incomprehensible*. How old, for instance, do you suppose he is?"

"To judge from his appearance, he can scarcely have passed forty."

". . . There are several credible persons who remember having seen him, each at the same time, in different parts of the globe. No sword can wound, no poison can hurt, no fire can burn him; no vessel in which he embarks can be wrecked. Time itself seems to lose its power over him. Years do not affect his constitution, nor age whiten his hair. Never has he been seen to take any food. Never does he approach a woman. No sleep closes his eyes. Of the twenty-four hours in the day, there is only one which he cannot command, during which no person ever saw him, and during which he was never employed in any terrestrial occupation."

"And that hour is—?"

"The twelfth in the night. When the clock strikes twelve at midnight, he ceases to belong to the living. In whatever place he is, he must immediately be gone; whatever business he is engaged in, he must instantly leave it. The terrible sound of the hour of midnight tears him from the arms of friendship, wrests him from the altar, and would drag him away even in the agonies of death. Whither he then goes, or what he is then engaged in, is a secret to every one. No person ventures to interrogate, still less to follow him. His features at this dreadful hour assume a sternness of expression so gloomy and terrifying that no person has courage sufficient to look him in the face, or to speak a word to him. However lively the conversation may have been, a dead silence immediately succeeds it, and all around wait for his return in respectful silence, without venturing to quit their seats, or to open the door through which he has padded . . ."

"Does nothing extraordinary appear in his person when he returns?"

"Nothing, except that he seems pale and exhausted, like a man who has just suffered a painful operation, or received some disastrous intelligence. Some pretend to have seen drops of blood on his linen . . ."

"Did no person ever attempt to conceal the approach of this hour from him, or endeavor to preoccupy his mind in such a manner as to make him forget it?"

"Once only, it is said, he missed the appointed time. The company was numerous and remained together late in the night. All the clocks and watches were purposely set wrong, and the warmth of conversation carried him away. When the stated hour arrived, he suddenly became silent and motionless; his limbs continued in the position in which this instant had arrested them; his eyes were fixed; his pulse ceased to beat. All the means employed to awake him proved fruitless, and this situation endured till the hour had elapsed. He then revived on a sudden without any assistance, opened his eyes, and resumed his speech at the very syllable which he was pronouncing at the moment of interruption. The general consternation discovered to him what had happened, and he declared, with an awful solemnity, that they ought to think themselves happy in having escaped with the fright alone. The same night he quitted forever the city where this circumstance had occurred. The common opinion is that during this mysterious hour he converses with his genius. Some even suppose him to be one of the departed, who is allowed to pass twenty-three hours of the day among the living, and that in the twenty-fourth his soul is obliged to return to the infernal regions, to suffer its punishment. Some believe him . . . the disciple *John*, of whom it is said: 'He shall remain until the last Judgment.' "[2]

The Armenian is usually presented as wearing a mask. His appearance is always fascinating and sometimes frightening. The first description of the Russian officer gives him a passionless, wooden Slavic face with, however, the "calm, piercing look of one deeply versed in the knowledge of mankind," a look which abashes every one toward whom it is directed. This transfixing gaze is to be traced to the philosophy of hypnotism of Friedrich Mesmer, whose theory of animal magnetism was a source of the warmest discussion following its publication in 1775.[3]

As to the Sicilian charlatan, he contributes a tale-within-a-tale with the story about Lorenzo and Antonia, whose wedding feast was broken up by a stranger in the habit of a Franciscan friar, whose gaze proved fatal to Lorenzo. The Sicilian recognized in the friar the Armenian-Russian officer and implied that he was the Wandering Jew.

A few years later, Samuel Taylor Coleridge wrote a brilliant ballad about a mysterious stranger who halted one of the guests at a wedding feast, fixed him with a glittering eye, and told him an eerie tale that will never be forgotten. It is known that Coleridge was acquainted with Schiller's *Geisterseher*, Schubart's "Der ewige Jude," the English ballad, the *Letters Writ by a Turkish Spy*, and Dom Augustin Calmet's comments, and at one time contemplated a romance on the subject of the Wandering Jew.[4] He had near at hand the Gothic novel of Matthew Lewis, to be mentioned in a moment, and he was haunted for years by the specter of Ahasuerus, as was every romantic writer of note in the generation; but he finally wrote about a man who committed a different crime, although, like the Wandering Jew, he expiated it and moved from land to land and had strange powers of speech.

One cannot be sure what the role of Schiller's Armenian-Russian officer-seer was meant to be, but it was probably benevolent. His indestructibility derives as usual from the fact that Ahasuerus is not to die until Christ returns. At any rate, from this point on it will be easy to explain any subsequent appearance of Ahasuerus as an Armenian or as a Russian officer, for Schiller has remained a name to impress all romantic German writers. Very likely he got the idea of using an Armenian from the pages of Matthew Paris, but he might also have been struck by the adaptability of this detail to romantic Orientalism, of which the eighteenth century was fond. Indeed, the Russian officer may be another example of this Orientalism, for to a western European of the 1780's and 1790's, a Russian would be close enough to an Oriental to pass muster.

The double impact of Schubart and Schiller has wielded a powerful influence upon the whole nineteenth-century concept of Ahasuerus.

Monk Lewis, Godwin, and Southey

Again, the Wandering Jew appears in the subplot of Matthew Gregory Lewis' *The Monk* (London, 1796), where his portrayal owes much to Schubart—although even more, I think, to Lewis' lively and febrile Gothic imagination. In the subplot of "Raymond and Agnes, or the Bleeding Nun," Raymond, who has rescued the Baroness of Lindenberg from bandits, is invited by that grateful lady to spend some time as a guest at her castle. Here he meets and falls in love with her niece

Agnes, who has been affianced to the Church and is about to enter upon her novitiate. He persuades the girl to elope with him; it is arranged that the elopement shall take place during the night when the Bleeding Nun, a ghost who walks the castle of Lindenberg on stated occasions, shall make her next scheduled appearance. Agnes is to dress like the ghost in order to facilitate matters. Unfortunately the timing goes wrong. Raymond discovers that he has eloped with the ghost instead of with Agnes. Their carriage runs away with them; Raymond is thrown out and knocked unconscious. He is brought back to life by the peasants of a nearby village. The Bleeding Nun disappears but keeps returning later to Raymond, draining him of life, for it is evident that she is a vampire. The problem is complicated by the fact that she is invisible to all save Raymond. As he languishes hopelessly, attended only by his faithful servant Theodore, a stranger appears:

> One evening when I was lying upon my sofa, plunged in reflections very far from agreeable, Theodore amused himself by observing from the window a battle between two postillions, who were quarreling in the inn-yard.
> "Ha! ha!" cried he suddenly, "yonder is the Great Mogul."
> "Who?" said I.
> "Only a man who made me a strange speech in Munich."
> "What was the purport of it?"
> "Now you put me in mind of it, Segnor, it was a kind of message to you, but truly it was not worth delivering. I believe the fellow to be mad, for my part. When I came to Munich, in search of you, I found him living at 'The King of the Romans,' and the host gave me an odd account of him. By his accent he is supposed to be a foreigner, but of what country nobody can tell. He seemed to have no acquaintance in the town, spoke very seldom, and never was seen to smile. He had neither servants nor baggage, but his purse seemed well furnished, and he did much good in the town. Some supposed him to be an Arabian astrologer, others to be a traveling mountebank, and many declared that he was Dr. Faustus, whom the Devil had sent back to Germany. The landlord, however, told me that he had the best reasons to believe him to be the Great Mogul incognito."

The alleged Great Mogul then makes his appearance—a man of majestic personality, with an awe-inspiring glance. The feature of his costume, which is otherwise plain, is a band of black velvet which encircles his forehead. He assures Raymond that he can drive away the vampire which has been plaguing him. In speaking of himself, he virtually paraphrases Schubart:

> "No one . . . is adequate to comprehending the misery of my lot; Fate obliges me to be constantly in movement; I am not permitted to pass more than a fortnight in the same place. I have no friend in the world, and, from the restlessness of my destiny, I never can acquire one. Fain would I lay down my miserable life, for I envy those who enjoy the quiet of the grave; but death eludes me, and flies from my embrace. In vain do I throw myself in the way of danger. I plunge into the ocean; the waves throw me back with abhorrence upon the shore; I rush into fire; the flames recoil at my approach; I oppose myself to the fury of banditti; their swords become blunted and break against my breast. The hungry tiger shudders at my approach, and the alligator flies from a monster more horrible than itself. God has set his seal upon me, and all his creatures respect this fatal mark."

He put his hand to the velvet which was bound round his forehead. There was in his eyes an expression of fury, despair, and malevolence that struck horror to my very soul . . .

The stranger manages to exorcise the Bleeding Nun in an elaborate ritual which is of no importance here. But when the vampire resists his incantations:

He spoke in a commanding tone, and drew the sable band from his forehead. In spite of his injunctions to the contrary, curiosity would not suffer me to keep my eyes off his face. I raised them, and beheld a burning cross impressed upon his brow.[5]

The sight of this Mark of the Wandering Jew, as I shall call it, is too much for the vampire. The room is purged of her presence. Then the explanation: The apparition was the ghost of the wicked Beatrice de las Cisternas, great-aunt to Raymond's grandfather. Her bones lie unburied, and so she walks in torment until a decent interment can be provided for her remains. Raymond is naturally extremely grateful to the stranger and questions him about his origins. But the Great Mogul hesitates, saying that he will be better able to answer the questions in the morning. The next day Raymond finds that he has left. But Raymond's uncle, the Cardinal-Duke, states unequivocally that this stranger was the Wandering Jew.

What Lewis has given us deserves much attention, because it is, all things considered, the most complete portrait of the Wandering Jew drawn during the reign of Gothic romanticism. There are two features of this portrait which emerge at once. One is the now familiar piercing glance of the Jew, whose eyes are "large, black, and sparkling." The other is the flaming cross stamped on his forehead, which, in this instance, he hides from ordinary mankind by a band of black velvet. This Mark of the Wandering Jew is new to us. It is clearly analogous to the mark which the Lord placed upon Cain. I do not think we can credit its origin to Monk Lewis. He certainly made it famous, but this detail of contamination with the Legend of Cain may be much older than *The Monk*. It is clearly suggested in Reichard's *Der ewige Jude* (pp. 142-44 above), in passing, to be sure. Its being cruciform may have been suggested by the tradition alluded to in Pierre Bayle's famous *Dictionnaire historique et critique* (1697), which insisted that the Mark of Cain was also in the form of a cross. Curiously enough, an anonymous writer in *Bentley's Miscellany* for March, 1843, attributes the origin of the Mark to one Xeniola, "a Spanish priest." I have not been able to identify Xeniola, but it is altogether possible (though again I cannot find verification) that the Mark of the Wandering Jew originated in Spanish folklore.[6]

Very often Ahasuerus appears in nineteenth-century popular picturizations with this red cross gleaming or flaming on his forehead.[7] Whether this detail is due to the currency of Lewis' novel, which was long popular, or to an already established folkloristic tradition, must remain unanswered; I prefer the former explanation, but it is well to remember that it has not been mentioned in any of the folk tales cited thus far in the development of the Legend. In brief, since *The Monk* was read by many thousands, I am inclined to raise his importance over that of Xeniola, whoever he was.

The subplot of "Raymond and Agnes" had some popularity of its own. For example, it was condensed into a crude synopsis and published in an English chapbook of about 1800.[8] A ballet, *Raymond and Agnes*, was performed at Covent Garden as early as 1796; it was produced by an impresario named Farley, with incidental music by William Reeve.[9] A two-act play with the same title, by Henry W. Grosette, was put on in the minor theaters around London in 1809.[10] There is no definite report as to its success, but it is evident from the dramatis personae that the originally important role of the Wandering Jew has evaporated from the plot, and the emphasis has been placed upon the early career of Beatrice, the Bleeding Nun, which, it must be admitted, makes for spirited melodrama. Two other English dramatizations of the tale of Beatrice—an opera by E. J. Loder (1855) and a full-length play in five acts by James Boaden (1799)—were failures.[11]

For that matter, "Raymond and Agnes" was equally popular in France. Here again, however, the action was given over almost entirely to the story of the Bleeding Nun. Thus the obscure playwrights Cailleran and Coupilly concocted a tragicomedy in five acts entitled *La Nonne de Lindenberg* (1798), which enjoyed a long run.[12] A much better play was the adept Guilbert de Pixérécourt's "Le Moine, ou la victime de l'orgeuil," but I can find no record of its public performance.[13] In 1800 the Abbé Prévost essayed a dramatization of the French translation of *The Monk*, known as *Le Jacobin espagnol*, the success of which seems to have been only moderate.[14] During the 1830's there was an epidemic of revivals of the Monk Legend (for such we may well call it by that time), typified by L.-M. Fontan's *Le Moine*, a "drame fantastique en quatre actes et huit tableaux."[15] What a time this was in France for exhibitions of the fantastic, when Berlioz and Paganini were flourishing in music, and Gautier and young Victor Hugo in literature!

Other pieces, rather spectacular as to dramaturgy, were Fontan's *Le Dominicain* (1832) and Anicet Bourgeois's and Jules Maillan's *La nonne sanglante* (1835).[16] Later, in 1854, Gounod composed an opera based on the latter play, but he admitted in his *Mémoires d'un artiste* (1896) that it was at best a youthful indiscretion. It ran for only eleven nights, after which the director of the Paris Opera declared that there would be no more performances of "une pareille ordure"—and this despite the fact that the celebrated Eugène Scribe had had a hand in the brewing of the libretto.[17]

Yet for all this progeny of Lewis' *The Monk*, the parent work had much more to give to the Legend of the Wandering Jew than any of its children, even when some of its influence was only tangential. William Godwin's novel, *St. Leon* (1799), is a case in point.[18] This extremely long and dull affair tells of a man who is given the secret of the philosopher's stone by a dying stranger. In return for this tremendous gift, St. Leon must promise never to reveal the secret. In consequence he becomes a man of limitless and incomprehensible wealth, the source of which he must keep sealed from all mankind. Moreover, he has been bequeathed a chemical formula by the stranger, a recipe which will confer eternal youth and life. In any such novel dealing with the possession of the philosopher's stone, we see the alchemical phase of Rosicrucianism, and in the matter of eternal youth and life we have another legendary motif. But neither has to do in any actuality with the Legend of the Wandering Jew itself. It is true that St. Leon, whom Godwin no doubt endued with autobiographical significance, was a rebel under constant threat of restraint by Church and state, and therefore a wanderer of a sort. He possessed some characteristics of the Great Mogul, for Godwin had undoubtedly read *The Monk*. Once, at the beginning, St. Leon asked the stranger whence he came:

"That you shall never know. It makes no part of the confidence I design to repose in you. My name shall be buried with me in the grave; nor shall any one who has hitherto known me, know how, at what time, or on what spot of earth I shall terminate my existence. The cloud of oblivion shall shelter me from all human curiosity."[19]

Here the eloquent voice and transfixing glance of the stranger, or later of St. Leon, indicate simply that they have mesmeric personalities. On one occasion, in the course of his wanderings, St. Leon donned an "Armenian" costume for a disguise; but, quite apart from the probable influence of this detail in Schiller's *Der Geisterseher*, it must be remembered that Oriental disguises are very common in the fiction of the age.

On the other hand, a much more obvious borrowing from the Legend is that by Robert Southey in his epic, *The Curse of Kehama* (1810). A Promethean individual, Kehama, who is a kind of divine tyrant, has a son Arvalan, who, in an attempt to violate the maiden Kailyal, is mortally wounded by her father Ladurlad. In punishment Ladurlad is turned into an eternal wanderer who cannot die but, because of this immortality, cannot be destroyed even by Kehama. Tyranny, in short, creates conditions against which it cannot eventually prevail. The piece is turgid and unpoetic in the extreme, and an uglier set of proper names has seldom been bestowed upon a cast of characters.

The Major English Romanticists' Treatment of the Legend

As a matter of fact, most of the romantic poets of England at this time made some allusion, explicit or implicit, to the Wandering Jew, in proper recognition of the appeal of this legendary character to the emotional and imaginative instincts which were their stock in trade. Even George Crabbe, not usually noted for his exotic appeal, notes in his *The Parish Register* (1807) that in his village there is little knowledge of worldly affairs but that there are all kinds of books for all kinds of people, among them "the humbler works by pedlar's packs supplied," in which the ambulant Wandering Jew "has found his way to fame."[20] Such passing allusions, however, are so numerous among so many writers that it is impracticable to attempt to collect them; besides, they do little more than show that the writer had heard of the Wandering Jew.

But with some it is more than a matter of allusion. We have already seen how Coleridge had once contemplated a work on the Wandering Jew, although his ultimate debt to the Legend was worked off in the creation of a parallel legend of his own making.[21] In Wordsworth's play, *The Borderers* (written in 1796-97), which owes its plot and chief character to a composite of Goethe's *Götz von Berlichingen* (1773) and Schiller's *Die Räuber* (1781), we find a similar kind of parallelism. Here Marmaduke, leader of the Borderers, considers himself morally responsible for the death of the father of the woman he loves and resolves to expiate his guilt by wandering:

> No human ear shall ever hear me speak;
> No human dwelling ever give me food,
> Or sleep, or rest; but ever waste and wild,
> In search of nothing that this earth can give,
> But expiation, will I wander on—
> A Man by pain and thought compelled to live,
> Yet loathing life—till anger is appeased
> In Heaven, and Mercy gives me leave to die.[22]

Certainly an utterance typical of the Wandering Jew in the nineteenth century if there ever was one. Wordsworth also has a short "Song for the Wandering Jew" (1800), which emphasizes the ceaseless journeyings of Ahasuerus through beneficent nature.[23]

The analogous Legend of Cain inspired Byron to a major poetic drama, *Cain* (1821). This analogy is quite close, for, as we have seen, the example of Cain in the Scriptures may have suggested the creation of Ahasuerus outside the Scriptures. The flaming mark on the brow of the Wandering Jew is most likely a contamination with the Legend of Cain (p. 3). One curious little variant in Byron's treatment of his legend is worth passing note. When Cain, prompted by the satanic proddings of Lucifer, strikes down his brother Abel, he is visited with a curse, not from God, as in Genesis, but from the mother of him and his victim, Eve:

> . . . May all the curses
> Of life be on him! and his agonies
> Drive him forth over the wilderness, like us
> From Eden, till his children do by him
> As he did by his brother! May the swords
> And wings of fiery cherubim pursue him
> By day and night—snakes spring up in his path—
> Earth's fruits be ashes in his mouth—the leaves
> On which he lays his head to sleep be strew'd
> With scorpions! May his dreams be of his victim!
> His waking a continual dread of death!
> May the clear rivers turn to blood as he
> Stoops down to stain them with his raging lip!
> May every element shun or change to him!
> May he live in the pangs which others die with!
> And death itself wax something worse than death
> To him who first acquainted him with man!
> Hence, fratricide! henceforth that word is *Cain*.
> Through all the coming myriads of mankind,
> Who shall abhor thee though thou wert their sire!
> May the grass wither from thy feet! thy woods
> Deny thee shelter! earth a home! the dust
> A grave! the sun his light! and heaven her God![24]

Except for the fact that the true Ahasuerus would never live in fear of death, since he is usually hoping to die, the curse pronounced by Eve, however superheated in language, holds for the Wandering Jew as well as for Cain.

Byron's more earthly world traveler, Childe Harold, is one of the earliest great exponents of romantic *Weltschmerz*, as the "Song to Ines" in the first canto (1812) makes clear. Here there is a direct allusion to the "fabled Hebrew wanderer,"[25] an allusion which makes as one the melancholy of Harold and of Ahasuerus. This, however, is only a single example of the impress which Byron made upon Continental romantic literature. Thus the long line of German writers in the nineteenth century who felt compelled to write about Ahasuerus and to make him symbolic of the trials and sorrows of mankind, of the resolution to defy the universe, of the sinister and the sinful, of the arrogant world-shaker and blasphemous shrieker against God—all wrote as they did largely because Byron had created his Cain, his Childe Harold, and his Manfred.

Yet of all the major poets of this generation none showed keener interest in Ahasuerus than Shelley. Five of his works enter into our picture, and this fact takes no particular account of the poet's use of Gothic materials other than the Legend of the Wandering Jew. These five are: (1) his early Gothic romance, *St. Irvyne, or the Rosicrucian* (1811); (2) *Queen Mab* (1813); (3) *Hellas* (1822); and in particular two other works of his early years: (4) *The Wandering Jew* (ca. 1810), written in supposed collaboration with his friend Thomas Medwin; and (5) "The Wandering Jew's Soliloquy," composed about 1812 but not published until 1887. There is also a passing reference in *Alastor* (1816):

> . . . O, that God
> Profuse of poisons, would concede the chalice
> Which but one living man has drained, who now,
> Vessel of deathless wrath, a slave that feels
> No proud exemption in the blighting curse
> He bears, over the world wanders for ever,
> Lone as incarnate death! . . .[26]

As to *St. Irvyne*, it bears little more relation to the Legend than Godwin's *St. Leon*; whatever suggestion of the Jew there may be in the two chief male characters, Wolfstein and Ginotti, is owed to Monk Lewis. With the poetical works, however, it is different, and yet we can see that Shelley is greatly indebted to Schubart, a point that must be remembered a little later. In *Queen Mab* Ahasuerus is called up by the Spirit to argue to the Fairy that there is a God. Ahasuerus knows from sad experience that this is so. But this God is tyrannous. He begot a Son:

> . . . he shall arise
> In an unnoticed corner of the earth,
> And there shall die upon a cross, and purge
> The universal crime; so that the few
> On whom My grace descends, those who are marked
> As vessels to the honor of their God
> May credit this strange sacrifice, and save
> Their souls alive: millions shall live and die,
> Who ne'er shall call upon their Saviour's name
> But, unredeemed, go to the gaping grave.[27]

Ahasuerus has witnessed the Crucifixion and has seen all the subsequent human violence—battlefields and execution blocks:

> Thus have I stood—through a wild waste of years
> Struggling with whirlwinds of mad agony,
> Yet peaceful, and serene, and self-enshrined,
> Mocking my powerless Tyrant's horrible curse
> With stubborn and unalterable Will,
> Even as a giant oak, which Heaven's fierce flame
> Had scathed in the wilderness, to stand
> A monument of fadeless ruin there;
> Yet peacefully and movelessly it braves
> The midnight conflict of the wintry storm,
> As in the sunlight's calm it spreads
> Its worn and withered arms on high
> To meet the quiet of the summer's noon.[28]

The conclusion reached is reminiscent of that in Southey's *The Curse of Kehama*, but the poetry is a great deal better.

Brushing aside one or two minor deviations from the usual story, such as the detail that Shelley had Christ pronounce the curse from the Cross instead of from the *Via Crucis* and the rather sentimental fact that the poet takes a leaf from Schubart's book and adds macabre stuff about the dead children of Ahasuerus— we discover one distinct innovation: Ahasuerus is presented as a phantom "inessential," who does not cast a shadow. At the time he wrote *Queen Mab*, Shelley could not possibly have known the hero of Chamisso's extremely popular tale, *Peter Schlemihl*, which came out in 1814. It is simply to be noted that, according to folk tradition, supernatural creatures need not cast a shadow,[29] and both Shelley and Chamisso made use of the detail. Shelley employs it for descriptive and atmospheric purposes; Chamisso makes it an ingenious variant of the Legend of Faust, for Schlemihl sold his shadow to the Devil in return for wealth. But the chief importance of Ahasuerus in *Queen Mab* is not that he is a figure of Gothicism but rather a symbol of mortality accursed yet able to defy the oppressor who cursed him. Once a representation of the power and glory of God in his miraculous works, a humble awaiter of God's ultimate judgment, Ahasuerus is now in revolt, unbending and impious. The most defiant lines in this hyperdefiant poem are placed in the mouth of Ahasuerus, the "phantasmal portraiture of wandering human thought."

In like manner, Shelley's "The Wandering Jew's Soliloquy" is another statement of this perfervid defiance. Here Ahasuerus glories in the fact that he cannot be destroyed and therefore can fight the tyrant who created him. He will go where "dark Destruction" dwells and rouse the disruptive forces to combat. He dares God to crush him; and if he can, so much the better, for Ahasuerus can then thank him. The "Soliloquy," mocking and bitter in tone, is chiefly important as a supplement to the lines spoken by Ahasuerus in *Queen Mab*.

On the other hand, Shelley's *The Wandering Jew*, which is not to be confused with his "The Wandering Jew's Soliloquy," has had an obscure career and calls for some description. It is usually ascribed as a whole to Shelley, but the part played in its writing by Medwin is uncertain to this day.[30] The poem was first submitted to Ballantyne of Edinburgh in 1810 and was rejected in one of the most polite letters of rejection on record. Shelley had no better luck with a London firm, but eventually the poem was printed in the *Edinburgh Literary Journal*, in 1829,[31] after the poet's death. A second version was published as by Shelley, and with Mary Shelley's blessing, in *Fraser's Magazine* for July, 1831. The preface to the work in the *Edinburgh Literary Journal*, presumably by the editor, states that the poem was written entirely in Shelley's own hand. Medwin, an altogether unreliable biographer of Shelley, claimed at different times a varying portion of the work as his own—two-thirds, one-half, hardly less.

The matter of the authorship of *The Wandering Jew* is therefore a literary puzzle. G. E. Woodberry's comments seem to be the best summation of the problem. He classifies *The Wandering Jew* under the category of "Doubtful Poems" and observes, *inter alia:*

> The most plausible hypothesis is that Shelley worked with Medwin upon the subject in prose and in the first versification made of the poem; then he rewrote the whole, confined the poem to the story, and reserved the speculative part, which has never appeared, among those early materials out of which *Queen Mab* was written, in his eighteenth or nineteenth year, or 1809-10; but that *The Wandering Jew*, as we have it, is substantially the poem offered by him for publication in 1810, and that it was Shelley's work and not Medwin's, are statements as well supported by external and internal evidence as can be looked for in such cases.[32]

I might inject here, as a marginal note, the story that, according to Medwin, the poem was submitted to the minor romantic poet Thomas Campbell (1777-1844), who observed acidly that there were only two good lines in it.[33]

The introductory note in the *Edinburgh Literary Journal* is too long to quote here, but it must not be overlooked. It suggests that Shelley had at one time an ambitious poem in mind. He was not certain whether he should call his work simply *The Wandering Jew* or *The Victim of the Eternal Avenger*. The first of these titles is the one always given now; the second has become the subtitle. In a preface, which includes a dedication to Sir Francis Burdett (a member of Parliament who had made a name in attacking the law which required the imprisonment of delinquent debtors), "in consideration of the active virtue by which both his public and private life is so eminently distinguished," Shelley explains that he will avoid quoting the many authorities on the Legend and will "decline presenting to the public [anything] but the bare poem." Medwin observes that he and Shelley differed as to the handling of the subject, the most significant point of variance between them being that Medwin wished to put an end to the Wandering Jew, "a consummation which Shelley would by no means consent to." In other words, Shelley had more respect for the Legend.

The poem is far from bare, inasmuch as its four cantos of florid romantic verse are very much clogged by Shelley's heated lyricism. The actual plot is scarcely important. A novice, Rosa, about to take her vows, escapes from the attendants and faints in the arms of the inevitable mysterious stranger, who makes off with her. She yields herself to this sinister Paulo, and the effect is beneficial, at least to Paulo. In a more quiet moment, back at his castle, he confides to his friend Victorio, who wonders at his frequent travels, that he is the Wandering Jew. As proof he shows on his brow the mark of lambent flame. Victorio, who has fought on "ensanguined Wolga's strand," can scarcely brook the horror of the sight. Once in utter despair, explains Paulo, he decided to invoke all the spirits of hell, in the hope that they might be able to release him from the curse of Christ, but in vain. He suffered excruciating torments and ended where he had been before—on the march until Doomsday. Victorio proceeds to fall hopelessly but devotedly in love with Rosa, and when a witch promises him success with a love potion, he accepts the philter and unwittingly kills the girl. The poem ends with the heart-broken lament of Paulo, the Wandering Jew.

When romantic poets, even good ones, write bad poetry, the results are often much worse than the bad poetry written by any other kind of poet. Campbell was a good judge when he quenched the hopes of young Shelley and Medwin with liberal jugs of ice water. Yet uninspired as the tetrameter couplets of *The Wandering Jew* may be, it is debatable whether they are not preferable to the "German work" which Shelley names as his source. This, it will be recalled, was the dirty little chapbook he had picked up in Lincoln's Inn Fields. Printed in 1802, it is an English translation and paraphrase of Schubart's "Der ewige Jude," and Shelley included it in his notes to *Queen Mab*. It is indeed a purple effusion, as the following excerpt will show:

From cloud-encircled cliffs did I precipitate myself into the ocean; but the foaming billows cast me upon the shore, and the burning arrow of existence pierced my cold heart again. I leaped into Etna's flaming abyss, and roared with the giants for ten long months, polluting with my groans the Mount's sulphureous mouth—ah! ten long months! The volcano fermented, and in a fiery stream of lava cast me up. I lay torn by the torture-snakes of hell amid the glowing cinders, and yet continued to exist. A forest was on fire: I darted on the wings of fury and despair into the crackling wood. Fire dropped upon me from the trees, but the flames only singed my limbs; alas! it could not consume them. I now mixed with the butchers of mankind, and plunged in the tempest of the raging battle. I roared defiance to the infuriate Gaul, defiance to the victorious German; but arrows and spears rebounded in shivers from my body. The Saracen's flaming sword broke upon my skull; balls in vain hissed upon me; the lightnings of battles glared harmless against my loins; in vain did the elephant trample on me, in vain the iron hoof of the wrathful steed! The mine, big with destructive power, burst under me, and hurled me high in the air—I fell on heaps of smoking limbs, but was only singed. The giant's steel club rebounded from my body; the executioner's hand could not strangle me, the tiger's tooth could not pierce me, nor would the hungry lion in the circus devour me. I cohabited with poisonous snakes, and pinched the red crest of the dragon. The serpent stung but could not destroy me. The dragon tormented, but dared not to devour me. I now provoked the fury of tyrants: I said to Nero, "Thou art a bloodhound!" I said to Christiern, "Thou art a bloodhound!" I said to Muley Ismael, "Thou art a bloodhound!" The tyrants invented cruel torments, but did not kill me. . . .[34]

Shelley, however, admired all this in the year 1810. "I have endeavored to deviate as little as possible from the extreme sublimity of idea which the *style* of the German author, of which this is a translation, so forcibly impresses." It is, of course, superfluous to comment upon the fidelity with which the translator followed his original, except to say that he hardly does Schubart justice. The flaming mark which Paulo exhibits to the cowering Victorio seems to have come from Lewis' *The Monk,* to which Shelley is more than once obligated in his early work.

All things considered, Shelley's *The Wandering Jew,* the most extensive treatment of the Legend among his poems, does little more than emphasize the sufferings of the Jew, made poignant by the fact that the story of the harrowing experiences is told in the first person. The romantic affair of Paulo and Rosa is silly and badly handled. It is a great tribute to the poet's phenomenal growth as artist that in the *Queen Mab* passage and "The Wandering Jew's Soliloquy" the emphasis on mere sensation, sensationally expressed, should later have given way to a new emphasis on Ahasuerus as a symbol of God's tyranny and cruelty. For it is in Shelley's last imposing work, *Hellas* (1822), that Ahasuerus appears in truly impressive aspect.

Mahmud, the decadent Turkish potentate, anxious because of the ill omen of three gloomy visions, consults Hassan about the Jew "whose spirit is a chronicle of strange and secret and forgotten things." He would talk with this old Jew. Ahasuerus therefore comes to him from the sea cavern where he dwells, as in the old Sicilian folk tale concerning Malchus (p. 87 above). He proclaims himself to be no god, only a man and nothing more, but he knows the oneness of the eternal, which contains all things, even time, for "the coming Age is shadowed on the Past as on a glass." In many a line of fine blank verse he leads Mahmud to see in a vision his predecessor, Mahmud II, storming Constantinople to give the Turks their greatest military victory, then reminds him that this is all a dream which can bring Mahmud only the certainty of death. For the Turk is doomed. Hellas will arise as in the past: "The world's great age begins anew."

It is a remarkable change that Shelley has wrought through the successive concepts of the Wandering Jew—from the wild sufferer, Paulo, through the hectic Ahasuerus in *Queen Mab,* who kicks in bitter gloating against the pricks, to the calm, oracular old man in *Hellas,* to whom thought is all, transcending even time:

> ... Thought
> Alone, and its quick elements, Will, Passion,
> Reason, Imagination, cannot die;
> They are, what that which they regard appears,
> The stuff whence mutability can weave
> All that it hath dominion o'er: worlds, worms,
> Empires, and superstitions. What has Thought
> To do with time, or place, or circumstance.[35]

Nowhere, apart from *Hellas,* is Ahasuerus such a doughty exponent of the philosophy of the abstract ideal. No other writer of the romantic age, major or minor, has within the short span of a dozen years so transformed an important creature of his poetic imagination. It is almost possible to say that Shelley has laid down the basic framework within which move all of the later nineteenth-century aspects of the Wandering Jew. Beside his achievement in *Queen Mab* and *Hellas,* the vague and turgid poem of his officious friend Thomas Medwin, "Ahasuerus" (1823), is altogether undeserving of comment.[36] Moreover, it is possible to say, with or without apologies to Goethe and Schubart, that Shelley is the first successful creator of a worthy art form in which Ahasuerus is to appear.

Shortly after *Hellas*, another English work, this time a historical novel, from the pen of George Croly, achieved a far greater contemporary and later success than anything Shelley had written concerning the protagonist of the Legend. *Salathiel: A Story of the Past, the Present, and the Future* (1827), bearing the subtitle, *Tarry Thou Till I Come*, was enough of a hit to warrant translation into a foreign language.[37] It concentrates upon the Jew, here named Salathiel ("I asked from God") during the generation between the Crucifixion and the destruction of Jerusalem in the year 70. It is in all respects a typical performance of the school of Sir Walter Scott. For his background Salathiel, now a Jewish nationalist patriot, owes something to the *Histoire admirable*, for he comes from the tribe of Naphthali. Accompanied by his wife, two daughters, and a caravan of kinsmen, he leaves Jerusalem at the time of the Crucifixion. The curse has been pronounced upon him in the first sentence of the novel, yet he is unaware, at any point in the story, of the full import of the condemnation. He becomes the active head of the national Jewish opposition to the Romans and must contend not only against the might of Roman legions, with all their overwhelming resources, but also against the internal jealousies and treacheries of the various Jewish factions. The ultimate capture of Jerusalem by Titus and Vespasian, which serves as the climax of the novel, is therefore attributed not so much to Jewish military weakness, which is never noticeable, as to the lack of national unity and religious faith. It is idle to follow Salathiel through all his adventures. His daughters have intrigues with Roman soldiers; there are battles, disappearances, fires, imprisonments, murders, and supernatural calamities. After the sack of Jerusalem, the protagonist, often close to complete victory before the defeat, is left beaten down by circumstances and becomes the recognizable Wandering Jew. Here the novel quite appropriately ends.

In this lengthy work of three volumes and nearly a thousand pages, some new features of the Wandering Jew peer at us too steadily for us to ignore them. For instance, Salathiel is no longer in his traditional role of humble shoemaker. Now he shines as a man of means and social position, who has duties as a priest of the Temple in Jerusalem. He had long been opposed to Christ and what he stood for:

I had headed the multitude; where others shrank, I urged; where others pitied, I reviled and inflamed; I scoffed at the feeble malice of the priesthood; I scoffed at the tardy cruelty of the Romans; I swept away by menace and by scorn the humble reluctance of the few who dreaded to dip their hands in blood. Thinking to do God service, and substituting my passions for my God, I threw firebrands on the hearts of a rash, jealous, and bigoted people. I triumphed![38]

All this though his people were a race of oppressed slaves.

Unfortunately for Salathiel, it had been rumored in the city of Jerusalem that he had sold his soul in some kind of unholy compact, hence his success as a national leader. "There," thought I, "is the first inflection of the sentence that is to separate, to smite, to pursue me to the last hour of time. I instinctively put my hand to my brow, to feel if the mark of Cain were not already there."[39] Thus it follows that Salathiel must have one adventure after another—dreadful visions, imagined journeys through space, shipwrecks, hunger and thirst, violence of all kinds both real and imaginary. Not unnaturally, it begins to dawn on him that he is not as other men. For one thing, his immunity against injury is remarkable. The inviolability of his person, however, is not absolute. More than once he is cast into durance vile, and he must even undergo the awful condemnation of a sentence of death by the sadistic Nero. He is nevertheless rescued while Rome burns. And so he frustrates his enemies at every turn. Once he has given up the struggle for Jewish independence after the destruction of Jerusalem and has become in fact the Wandering Jew, as he does in the final pages, he inspires others to the defeat of Rome and, in a more positive way, still others to such achievements as the discovery of America and the introduction of printing. He knows that there is still much more to await, but since he has no prophetic powers he cannot tell what is to come.

It is a minor matter to note that Croly—"roly-poly Croly," as Byron called him —borrowed here and there from Lewis' *The Monk*, that he knew a fair amount of the popular literature about the Wandering Jew, and that he added a few details to the Chronicle of the Wandering Jew. But by this time there had come to be, as we have seen, something of an accumulation of material about Ahasuerus in England. While Croly was writing *Salathiel,* the legendary beturbaned Oriental youth was gliding about the Strand, book in hand, as a contributor to the *London Athenaeum* was to report years later (p. 119 above). Not very long before, the anonymous author of a naïve and dull piece of popular evangelism, *A New and True History of the Wandering Jew* (published in London without date, but probably about 1800), had identified the Jew with St. Paul. Original though its conclusion is, the little pamphlet is otherwise so manifestly tenth-rate that we may forget it. The point is that Croly was working in fruitful soil in his native England and produced an important increment to the art form of the Legend. For one thing, he gives us the first of many nineteenth-century works dealing with the fall of Jerusalem in which Ahasuerus is a prime defender of the city. For another, his protagonist is sympathetic, militarily brave, and generous—in most respects a normal man, whose manifold adventures are narrated with better than average skill. Finally, Croly makes Ahasuerus a true Jewish nationalist, fighting for the independence of Israel as a homeland—the first time the Wandering Jew has done this in the whole history of the Legend.

Salathiel was translated into German by Ludwig Storch in 1829 (*Der ewige Jude*), without acknowledgment of the English original.[40] Another translator, Rehberg-Worden (1913), is more gracious.[41] There was also a Dano-Norwegian translation as late as 1903 and, in 1901, an elaborate American edition.[42] The latter contained a foreword by General Lew Wallace, whose *The Prince of India* (1893), as we shall see, is a worthy representative of what we may call the Croly tradition or the Destruction-of-Jerusalem motif.

Less successful than *Salathiel,* as a piece of literature, is Charles Maturin's *Melmoth the Wanderer* (1820), which combines the legends of Faust and the Wandering Jew, for the Irishman Melmoth has sold his soul to the Devil for prolonged life. (The combination of these two legends which, one must insist, are separate and independent, is attempted more than once in the nineteenth century and seldom very attractively.) If Melmoth can find a mortal to exchange fates with him, he will be redeemed. But the resemblances between Melmoth and the romantic concept of Ahasuerus are not many. To be sure, Melmoth has the inevitable transfixing glance; he confronts thus a devout Spanish priest:

> Olavida rocked, reeled, grasped the arm of a page, and at last, closing his eyes for a moment, as if to escape the horrible fascination of that unearthly glare . . . exclaimed, "Who is among us?—Who?—I cannot utter a blessing while he is here."[43]

Melmoth hates God with a divine hate; he bears God's curse because of pride and presumption; and the curse is marked on his forehead. His love for the child of nature, Immalee, is closer to that of Faust and Gretchen than to, let us say, that of Ahasuerus and Rachel in Quinet's *Ahasvérus*, to be discussed later. Like Ahasuerus, his approach (in this instance heralded by delicious music) is a signal of potential misfortune, although we have already seen many instances in which the Wandering Jew was benevolent rather than malevolent. The end of Melmoth resembles the end of Faust in the Faust-book; he dies mysteriously in a lonely room in the midst of an unearthly tempest.

Maturin's novel is by no means dull; indeed, it is sometimes sprightly and even powerful. Its structure, however, is not inviting, for the separate stories are told by participants in a preceding story, so that the technique of a tale-within-a-tale-within-a-tale becomes both unwieldy and confusing.

The Art Form in Germany at the Death of Goethe

It is obvious by now that the English had much to do with the growth of the art form of the Legend at a crucial time, when a tale appealing to the fantastic and emotional elements of the human imagination was in high fashion. The best English contributions in this generation appear in the work of three men—Lewis, Shelley, and Croly; but the penumbra of the Legend affected Coleridge, Southey, Wordsworth, and Byron, and references to the Wandering Jew are many among other writers of importance, such as Crabbe and Dickens. It seems to be pushing matters a little far to see Ahasuerus in Carlyle's Teufelsdröckh of *Sartor Resartus* simply because he was "a Pilgrim and Traveller from a far Country," in whom "internal Unrest seemed his whole Guidance." Nor does Bulwer-Lytton's novel of Rosicrucian persuasion, *Zanoni* (1842), have a claim to inclusion among the art forms of the Legend merely because one of the themes of the novel is the matter of prodigious longevity.[44] We must concede, however, that *Zanoni* was a source of an important later work on the Wandering Jew, Max Haushofer's *Der ewige Jude* (1886), to be examined later.

There is, indeed, little reason for the comparative neglect which this English contribution has suffered. Yet the Legend did not creep into the bones of English writers, major or minor, as it did among the German. From about 1830 on, the story of the development of the Legend is largely the story of what German writers did for it.

Beginning with Schubart, in other words, the Germans had begun to work hard at the Legend, as they were to continue to do until well into the twentieth century; and the natural mode for most of their writing—thanks to the German artistic temperament—is the romantic. This is not to preclude occasional satirical treatments and a gradually increasing tendency toward social comment, the latter of which is characteristic of the whole century in the Western world. For the moment, however, let us confine ourselves to the writings before about 1850 in Germany and contiguous Germanic nations like Denmark and the Netherlands; in that first half of the nineteenth century all of the lineaments of the romantic concept of Ahasuerus are fixed.

One early piece, *Der ewige Jude: Eine komische Geschicht aus dem 18. Jahrhundert,* published at Leipzig in 1800, seems to have been lost, and so it is useless to speculate about it, although if one is to judge by its subtitle, it was probably satirical rather than romantic.[45] There is no uncertainty, however, about A. W. Schlegel's "Die Warnung," a ballad first printed in Schlegel and Tieck's *Musenalmanach* for 1802.[46] After reading it, one can surmise that Schlegel had had Chaucer's *Pardoner's Tale* in mind. The Jew stops at a little village inn for refreshment. There two roistering, "wilde, rohe Buben" are plying themselves with firewater. They are ready to push over the stars in the firmament, and a minor matter like the Crucifixion is the subject of ribald jest. The Cross, they believe, would have looked more picturesque if, instead of Christ, a pair of dead cats had been hanging from it. They accost the Jew with scurrilous remarks. The butt of their crude wit reproves them and tells them that nothing they can say or do can ever hurt him. He reviews his own experience and strikes the listeners dumb. The ballad ends with the heavily moralizing observation that the jesters did not live long thereafter.

In too many of the minor German romantic poets, however—and this stricture applies to most of the writers throughout the nineteenth century—the finished product is merely a description of the Jew's sufferings and of the landscape through which he passes. Wordsworth, in his "Song for the Wandering Jew," did this much better than most. A typical example is a lyric by Aloys Schreiber, first printed in a newspaper in 1807, and later published in his complete works (1817).[47] Occasional exceptions to the rule are welcome. In Switzerland Karl Witte revived the folk tale of Ahasuerus on the Grimsel (p. 83 above) with a ballad which first appeared in the *Alpenrosen* annual for 1820, "Der laufende Jude auf der Grimsel."[48] It will be remembered that Ahasuerus made the journey over the Grimsel three times. The first time he found there a vineyard, the second time a pine forest, and the third time a snow-clad waste. Now he reveals himself to the poet, who describes in adequate verse the terrifying beauty of the three scenes. This ballad, by no means inferior in quality, falls into three sections: the first, an allegro movement in which Ahasuerus savors the grapes of the vineyard; the second, an adagio mood evoked by the cool shadows of the pine forest—Ahasuerus sees in the pine tree, "brother of the cypress," a sleepless, passive waiting amid perennial shade; the third, in the tempo of allegro *con brio,* describes the glittering pinnacles of ice and snow, dazzling Ahasuerus, who still lives in the hope of ever-returning spring, for when the world awakens anew, released from the bonds of sin, he will enter the night of the grave and there find eternal rest.

Witte did better with his theme than J. J. L. ten Kate, whose *Ahasverus op den Grimsel* (1840) is inept as verse and tasteless in its combination of the more unattractive qualities of Schubart and Christian pietism. It does, however, contain a few small points of interest.[49] The protagonist is depicted as most horrible in appearance, a kind of travesty on the folkloristic picture of the graybeard with long mantle and patriarchal mien. He is unkempt and disheveled; he fingers nervously the flaming cross on his forehead. He complains that he has lost both wife and daughter. Christ, in the time of his miracles, could have brought the daughter back to life but did not. Therefore, out of revenge, when Ahasuerus heard the Saviour asking for water in the Via Dolorosa, he was only too glad to reject him, even if he did incur the fatal sentence. A chorus of guardian angels informs him that he must continue to wander, but gives him this solace: if his daughter had lived, hers would have been a life of suffering and despair, and as for him, some day the Saviour will unlock the gates of paradise, having forgiven Ahasuerus his sin. The Grimsel setting is rather pointless, for the author concentrates upon the third visit. If Ten Kate and others writing during these years had left Ahasuerus in his *Weltschmerz*, as did Byron and Shelley, they would have been far more successful, for they are all essentially romantic; but their Germanic pietism got in their way. As it stands, Witte and Ten Kate have some importance in that they allow the Wandering Jew the promise of death or death itself—Witte in his ballad, and Ten Kate in a slightly earlier work, *De Dood van Ahasverus den nimmer rustenden Israeliet: De Wandelende Jood tot rust gekomen*.[50] The latter is an unusually sentimental effort in which Ahasuerus comes for the second time to the place of his birth. He goes to the churchyard, to the graves of his parents, his wife, and his children. Tender feelings master him. A cross rises. He falls on his knees and hears a voice say, "You will be with me in paradise." Peace descends upon him and he dies.

This concession which allows Ahasuerus to die, however, has an earlier appearance than in either Witte or Ten Kate. The most important German work on the Legend in the first part of the century is Ludwig Achim von Arnim's *Halle und Jerusalem* (1809-10), a "Studentenspiel und Pilgerabenteuer."[51] One of Von Arnim's friends, Görres, had planned a medieval romance in which Ahasuerus was to be the protagonist, but he abandoned the idea because he thought that his primary source, the old Ahasuerus-book, was trash.[52] Not so with Von Arnim. Of this friend of Goethe and husband of Bettina Brentano, in whom Goethe showed at one time a more than passing interest, it may be said that he had a true lyric gift and all the sincerity that could be expected of any artist, but in other literary matters he had no sense of proportion. To put it bluntly, he was both disorganized and prolix.

I should call *Halle und Jerusalem* a two-headed closet drama which is in reality a novel in the form of a play. In *Halle,* the first section, Ahasuerus keeps well in the background. He is interested, however, in reckless, Byronic Cardenio, but there is little contact between the two. The heroine, Olympe, is a good girl whose modesty is such that she can hardly bear to undress in the dark. She has a suitor, one Lysander, who gets into her room by the old expedient of bribing the maid to admit him. When Olympe enters, he kisses her in the dark and thus compromises her with such finality that their marriage must be hastily solemnized. Olympe, however, who has nourished a chronic yearning for Cardenio, had cried out his name when Lysander kissed her. For a time, in fact, Cardenio is believed by gossip to have been the guilty man. At any rate, after the marriage of Olympe and Lysander, Cardenio shows a steady tendency not only to fall from social favor in the community but also to lose his moral stamina. He indulges in various affairs and eventually is captured by Celinde, whose passion for him sounds a trumpet before her. A courting parson who is wooing Celinde is killed by Cardenio. This is the conclusion of *Halle*, the "Studentenspiel." I take no account here of other incidents or of the enormous amount of chitchat and academic arguments among the students at the university. Ahasuerus has for his chief function in this first part the task of appearing while conversations are going on and of serving as a target for some not very brilliant witticisms. On one occasion, however, he separated a quarreling husband and wife, and on another he pleaded for the Christianization of all Jews.

In one of the few interchanges between Ahasuerus and Cardenio, the young man reveals a misanthropic bitterness of spirit, and Ahasuerus endeavors to comfort him by reminding him: "If ever you need me, you will always find me. See here how you can recognize me . . . In my beard, half-yellow in the center, there are some black hairs at the tip."[53] Foolish Cardenio, however, rejects him. He warns Cardenio that he, Ahasuerus, does not have forever. Soon all Jews must believe in Christ. Even so, he remains the willing whipping post against which Cardenio's feverish spirit keeps directing blows. Near the conclusion of *Halle*, Ahasuerus has a scene to himself. As a good illustration of the often fine lyric effects which Von Arnim could command, there comes the following passage (in reality a song, although this is not explicitly indicated) assigned to Ahasuerus, which no translation can render justly:

> Es weicht die dunkle Nacht,
> Die Welt wird frisch geschaffen,
> Doch wer die Nacht durchwacht,
> Der leidet fort die Strafen
> Der alten Sündenwelt,
> Dem löscht der Sonne Huld,
> Die Gottes Schoss entquellt,
> Noch nicht die alte Schuld.[54]

("Night has given way to morning, and the world begins anew, but whoever has watched through the night continues to suffer the punishments of this old world of sin; even the clemency of the sun, which springs from the Lord's bosom, cannot quench the old guilt.")

To Ahasuerus come Cardenio and Celinde, who, in nineteenth-century parlance, have sinned. Cardenio has killed the parson, and Celinde is pregnant with a child who will die. They are, however, sincerely repentant. Ahasuerus therefore advises a pilgrimage to Jerusalem and announces that he will come along with them, because they all need whatever absolution can be vouchsafed them.

Thereupon ensues the wild second part, the "Pilgerabenteuer," *Jerusalem*. All kinds of people, including British naval officers, are converging on the Holy City. Among them are Lysander and Olympe, for no good reason save their inherent religiosity, and Ahasuerus. One may assume, however, that it was part of his ancient curse that he should return to Jerusalem from time to time. After a ship-wreck, all the survivors, among them our trio, are cast up on the shores of Libya. Ahasuerus sits down from time to time and tells a sad tale of sinners; once, suddenly and without preamble, he reveals that Cardenio is his own son, "begotten in this very desert in lustful violence." The mother was a Greek pilgrim. She was later snatched from Ahasuerus by a band of Cossacks and was afterwards bought from the Russians by a "fine man," whom she married and by whom she became the mother of Olympe. Cardenio and Olympe are therefore half-brother and half-sister; Lysander had unwittingly saved them from Byronic incest.

The three arrive, in the course of their wanderings, in the neighborhood of the Holy Sepulcher. Ahasuerus is strangely exhausted. A group of Jews, incited by their rabbi, tries to set fire to the Sepulcher, but the flames will not catch. The three pilgrims frighten away the miscreants. Ahasuerus observes grimly that fire will overtake them for their attempted crime and then dies quite unexpectedly, with blessings on his lips for those who look upon the Lord. Shortly thereafter both Cardenio and Celinde die in the odor of sanctity, within the walls of the Church of the Holy Sepulcher.

This (1810) is the first time, at least in written literature, that the Wandering Jew has been able to die. In Galt's *Hareach* of 1820 he purportedly died, but it is rather difficult to believe it. Still later Witte and Ten Kate, as we have seen, allowed him to expire; and others after them. But Von Arnim is the first to kill off the protagonist, and the death is explicitly recorded. By doing so, he has achieved a certain measure of tragic catharsis and has shown some artistic courage and a proper sense of the finite in bringing Ahasuerus to the end of his interminable trail. This passing of the Jew, however, is only from earth. Doubtless he will be resurrected to stand trial at the Last Judgment. And then what? The author makes clear that the Lord has relented sufficiently to enable Ahasuerus, as his last act on earth, to preserve the holy burial place of Christ from the destroying hand of infidels; it is evident, therefore, that he has worked out his sentence and will go to heaven. His salvation has been effected by repentance on his part and the power to inspire repentance in others. Thus he stands as a symbol of both personal contrition and successful missionary efforts. For Cardenio and Celinde are themselves saved by turning to God, although they must first go through the preliminary agony of renouncing each other. It is unfortunate that this distinctive contribution of Von Arnim should be clothed in such an artistically monstrous dress. The work is lacking in structure, coherence, and dramatic impact, so that critical judgment is perhaps beside the point.

Now if Von Arnim thought of Ahasuerus as a repentant messenger of God bringing about salvation after sin, it was also possible to see in the Jew one who could forestall sin. Thus a piece in a little collection of narrative sketches and verse by S. W. Schiessler, *Monatrosen: Oder Scherz und Ernst* (1826), paints a more ominous picture than *Halle und Jerusalem*.[55] Schiessler himself was a pleasant individual with but few literary pretensions, but he was incurably romantic. His "Auch etwas vom ewigen Juden" tells how the once happy Engelbrecht, a refugee from the recently burned village of Lorchheim, is moping about in an out-of-the-way corner of the Black Forest. A wild autumnal storm is having its sport with the leaves and fallen branches of the forest, and owls are hooting dolefully. To Engelbrecht comes a mysterious saddle maker. In the ensuing conversation it is revealed that Engelbrecht has become a desperate beggar, for not only has his village been consumed, but his wife is critically ill, and his six children are starving. "Too bad!" says the saddle maker; but, after all, Engelbrecht has all his life been a good Christian and is therefore supposed to weather all such storms, be they what they may. The stranger suggests that Engelbrecht seek help from the dour Master of Mahrenwald, who is rumored to be in league with the Devil. Poor Engelbrecht is much tempted, but is dissuaded by a "tall, elderly man," who makes his appearance and tells his story—our familiar Legend. Engelbrecht is saved.

Von Arnim's brother-in-law evidently conceived of Ahasuerus as being somewhat different. There is a passing reference to the Jew in the attractive "Leiden des Herrn," from the famous collection of lyrics by Von Arnim and Clemens Brentano, *Des Knaben Wunderhorn* (Heidelberg, 1806-8);[56] but a more important item is Brentano's "Blätter aus dem Tagebuch der Ahnfrau" (1830). Here Ahasuerus enters and waves aside an offer of alms. What he really wants is rest:

> "Schön Dank! ich brauch' nicht Gut noch Geld,
> Mir fehlt, was ich versagt,
> Hab' Müden keinen Sitz gestellt,
> Werd' ruhlos umgejaget.
> Kömmt' je mit seinem Kreuz zu dir
> Ein müder Mann gegangen,
> Lass ruhen ihn und schenke mir
> Die Lieb', die er empfangen.
> Sitz' zu ihm, hör ihn an mit Huld',
> In ihm dem Herrn dies thue,
> Dann zählst du mild an meiner Schuld
> Und hilfst zu meiner Ruhe!"[57]

To paraphrase, if a tired man comes to you, let him rest, and you will thus be contributing to my eventual rest and helping in my redemption. Yet this Ahasuerus is querulous and irrational. Once the narrator met him on the road. This time he was calling himself Cartophilax, a pleasing variant of our old friend from the Middle Ages. He wept, shuddered, and winced noticeably at the word "rest" because he can never rest, not until all the shattered pieces of gems have been gathered together about the rejected cornerstone of the Temple. He is an exhausted man, who hastens away into the underbrush at the side of the road.

Brentano's style is rather muddy, but he makes it clear enough that Ahasuerus is on a new kind of quest. He emphasizes the point that while the Jew is constantly seeking rest—the most terrible aspect of his punishment is his exhaustion —still true rest can come only if he can reassemble the shattered jewels and find some fragment of the precious stone which was formed from the dust left over after Adam and Eve were created. Or perhaps it would suffice to find the shoulder clasp of Rebecca. These are references to interesting through obscure legends of extrascriptural nature. Their introduction into the sphere of the Legend of the Wandering Jew may be considered Brentano's part in the play, so to speak. Unfortunately for Ahasuerus, the nearer he gets to these precious fragments, the faster must be his wandering, and the more exhausted he becomes. A medieval increment, thrown in rather casually by Brentano, is the belief that one such piece of precious gem was imbedded in the Coronation Stone of the Scottish kings at Scone, whence it was carried away by King Edward I of England, to be preserved in Westminster Abbey.[58] Meanwhile the Jew continues to wander; his presence in the world is first, last, and always a witness to truth.

The best play to make use of the Legend during the Romantic Age is August Klingemann's *Ahasver* (1827).[59] Klingemann was a professional, who devoted most of his career to the Brunswick Theater. He had a good knowledge of the more famous Weimar stage and of the work of Schiller and Goethe. In the list of his dramas appear historical plays on such great figures as Cromwell, Columbus, Cortez, and Martin Luther. *Ahasver* is also to be considered, in part, a historical drama. The scene is Bohemia during the Thirty Years' War, and the death of King Gustavus Adolphus of Sweden at the Battle of Lützen, in 1632, is the chief motivating incident. It is recorded that *Ahasver* was performed four times in Berlin between September 5 and October 22, 1825, when it was presented as a "sidepiece" to *Faust*—another of Klingemann's plays, suggested by the first part of Goethe's *Faust*, with incidental music by F. L. Seidel.

In *Ahasver*, a stranger has been seen from time to time on the estate of Count von Warth in Bohemia. Twice he has rescued members of the Count's family from drowning in the stream which flows through the estate, yet his identity is still not known. The son of the family, Heinyn, has shocked every one by deserting from Wallenstein's army to go over to the Protestant forces under Gustavus Adolphus. The stranger suddenly walks up to the castle. The Count is urged to close the doors against him, although such an action would never have stopped the traditional Wandering Jew. The old servant Bartholomäus has heard of him. "He may not walk under roof or cell," he cries, "and nowhere can he rest longer than three days." The first of these restrictions is new to us; the second is familiar from as far back as the tale of Antonio di Francesco di Andrea. While they stand about deliberating, Ahasuerus enters unceremoniously. He is welcomed by the Count with reluctant hospitality, but he refuses to accept shelter, for he has no home on this earth, "nor do I anything for mankind, because evil walks by my side and penetrates within me, wherever I wander, without my will." "But you saved my life!" exclaims the Countess Maria. "On the contrary," replies Ahasuerus, "I was trying to drag you down into the whirlpool."[60] (Here is a hint, at least, of the old folk motif of the accursed man who can be redeemed only through the sacrificial death of a virtuous woman.)

The chaplain of the castle is reduced to incompetence whenever Ahasuerus is in his presence. The Jew, fixed in hatred against the Church, disappears into the woods, taking old Bartholomäus with him. Soon the old servant is found dead, with a look of ecstasy on his face, while Ahasuerus stands beside him staring straight ahead with eyes that might have been shedding bloody tears. At this dramatic juncture the son Heinyn arrives from the battle. He is in a sad mental state, with good reason. On the battlefield Ahasuerus had appeared before him and led him aside to a spot where the unfortunate Heinyn fell into a trance. While in a state of suspended awareness he shot King Gustavus Adolphus in the back. This outright murder of his commander in chief has evidently been suspected by the Swedish authorities, but for the moment there is no direct evidence of his guilt.

Meanwhile, the chaplain holds conversation with Ahasuerus. The Jew speaks of the great events of history. Heinyn continues to fry in his own conscience, behaving in a distraught manner and crying out in long monologues that he must fight. His wife can do nothing with him. He tries to inveigle Ahasuerus into a duel; the Jew only laughs bitterly. "I am Ahasuerus!" is all that he needs to say. Consider my example, he warns, as he tells his tale. Rest is what he desires above all else, and he can find none. (Here Klingemann borrows wholesale from Schubart the volcanoes which cannot devour, the lion which cannot kill, the sword which cannot pierce.) Then:

Thus have I wandered for centuries, and shall wander till the last day, lifeless yet living, the ghost of Time, who, without ill will, does evil and brings to chaos all that is about him. I hate none, yet can love none, because I must envy all in this monstrous God's-acre over which I must wander, a terrible monument. Time rolls by, one millennium after another in the somber book of history; my course takes me through all those pages. And even if I make myself known to a few only, still he trembles often in the quiet hours of midnight, the wicked man, at the picture of horror posed by the eternal Wanderer, who admonishes him never to slander the name of God.[61]

The strain of despair and terror in this speech is too much for Heinyn. He breaks down and confesses the murder of Gustavus Adolphus. When the Swedish Count Wasaburg, who has entered the scene as investigator, presents his sword to avenge the King's death, Heinyn falls upon it, finding the rest he desires; but Ahasuerus, giving the dead man a final blessing, reminds all present that he himself must still wander. The curtain descends.

Although the play creaks in its joints from sheer old age, it still can move, and there are many eloquent, if somewhat verbose, passages.[62] Its motivation, however, remains uncertain and its characterizations are sometimes blurred. Ahasuerus is a creature who believes he is evil, yet his actions save the lives of human beings (although Gustavus Adolphus is not so fortunate) and promote justice. If he is a would-be devil, it is not his destiny to succeed. He seems to be working out his own salvation in the drama, but there is still no assurance that he will eventually be redeemed. The only characters rescued are the insignificant mortals. In spite of Klingemann's intentions, expressed in his preface, to make Heinyn the real tragic hero, it is Ahasuerus who assumes tragic dimensions, frustrated to a degree too cosmic for mere flesh. Heinyn is only pathetic.

Another who had drunk deep from Schubart is Franz Horn, whose *Der ewige Jude* (1814) is a lugubrious and pedestrian novel laid, like Klingemann's play, in the Thirty Years' War.[63] A strange man in Oriental garb wanders through the battlefield at Prague and saves a young soldier, Leopold von Launingen, who in gratitude names his benefactor Christianus, since he refuses to give his name. He takes Christianus home with him, but the stranger is an apostle of gloom, talking constantly of the joys of death and the death wish. The family suffers misfortune, but Christianus continues to harp upon his theme of mortality. Leopold is constrained to fight a duel with Christianus, but his dagger breaks.[64] Christianus then reveals himself to be the Wandering Jew, telling his story pretty much as we know it. His animosity toward Christ arose from the disillusionment that came upon him after he had believed that Christ would indeed drive away earthly death. No wonder, then, that he could praise Death, the great Releaser. Leopold comes to realize that while life may be wonderful for those who wish to live only in the present, death is also sweet and more exalting.

Similar in most respects is Friedrich Laun's novel, *Der ewige Jude,* in which Ahasuerus interferes with abductions, reveals unsuspected enemies to each other, and spoils the thrust of the duelist's sword.[65] He can spring in the air—and makes his escape thus—or he can sink into the ground. But Laun complicates his story by having an adventurer pose as the Wandering Jew while the real Wandering Jew is there to baffle him and eventually to confront him. On the other hand, O. L. B. Wolff's "Der ewige Jude" (1829) does not scruple to allow Ahasuerus, a gigantic figure of superhuman strength, to rescue people from the horrors of a conflagration.[66]

These mournful tales, while typical of the age, were not swallowed whole by at least one contemporary. Wilhelm Hauff wrote a vigorous satire on life in Germany in *Mitteilungen aus den Memoiren des Satan* (Stuttgart, 1826-29).[67] The Devil, going about Europe somewhat in the manner of a preposterous French count of cheap fiction, ejaculating any number of *Ma foi's* and *Parbleu's,* encounters the Jew in the Berlin Tiergarten. For obvious reasons, the Jew is at first reluctant to converse with Satan; but he happens to be a singularly naïve Ahasuerus who, Satan believes, does not yet realize that the world has changed in the past eighty years since they last met. The ice is broken, however, when Ahasuerus mentions the fact that he is looking for an author whose initials are F. H. (Franz Horn), and who is responsible for a story "about me, with the stupid title of 'Der ewige Jude.'" This particular Ahasuerus, at least, does not like that word "eternal." The talk drifts off to other topics, including the far-ranging travels of the Jew, who describes with melancholy how he almost walked his feet off along the Great Wall of China. Then he suddenly breaks off to ask, "What time is it in Eternity?" Satan is much annoyed at this poetic whining. He encourages the Jew to stay in Berlin, to mingle in society, to frequent taverns. Ahasuerus takes his advice, is made a fool of in society, and is delighted with a foaming beaker. Hauff evidently believes that Ahasuerus would be improved by taking the world as he finds it—a good neoclassical principle for a belated neoclassical writer.

With all the defects of their works, the achievement of Von Arnim and Horn in establishing the Wandering Jew as a missionary of good works is important, for others were to follow the lead of these two men. A dialogue by Karl Rosenkranz, planned in the 1830's but never brought to completion, allowed the Jew to preach soul over body, faith over doubt, good will over malevolence, and independence over constraint.[68] A rather well-known work with the same didactic aim is the mediocre verse by L. Auerbacher in *Volksbüchlein* (Munich, 1827), which insipidly outlines the gradual conversion of Ahasuerus from doubter to believer.[69] Auerbacher's work may possibly have shed some influence of its own, notably on the epic by Hans Christian Andersen (pp. 221-22 below). Its emphasis upon the career of Ahasuerus at Rome in the first century after Christ is a frequently recurring theme for the literary generations following Auerbacher, as we shall see. Also apparent is a strong strand of the Chronicle of the Wandering Jew. But for the rest, we have heard it all before, particularly after reading Croly and Von Arnim.

To many, however, this conversion of Ahasuerus was an unconvincing business, as Jean Paul (Richter) put it in his "literary torso," *Plan zum Kometen* (Berlin, 1820-22).[70] To him the Wandering Jew was simply another Cain or Satan or Antichrist, and this attitude is not infrequent among some of the later students of the Legend. The attitude is embodied in an eccentric novel by the Freiherr von Maltitz, entitled *Gelasius, der graue Wanderer* (Leipzig, 1826), which takes its cue from the Legend and creates a fictional character analogous to the Wandering Jew whose chief desire is to be freed from a curse.[71] The work is similar to Maturin's *Melmoth the Wanderer*, in which a fundamentally different situation is made to resemble that of Ahasuerus by insisting that the protagonist live long and wander about. Von Maltitz' novel has a vague kind of relation to the revolutionary movement in Germany during the first half of the nineteenth century and is worth mention for that reason. More than that, it is unabashedly nationalistic, in the unpleasant sense that it assumes that all other nations beside Germany are as acorns beside the mighty oak, and that the oak must be kept free from parasitic growths. The title character Gelasius may have been suggested in part by Jan van den Tyden, or Juan de los Tiempos, the warrior at Charlemagne's court (p. 22 above). For the greater part, however, he is an abstraction. For example, one of the better scenes in the novel is a *Walpurgisnacht*, or witches' Sabbath, in which War, Sensuality, Sloth, Superstition, and Priest-Riddenness march past. The last two receive the prize as the most productive of evil in the body politic. The whole scene, nevertheless, seems to have been inspired by Goethe's *Faust*. Some other details are worth reporting. In one scene there is a plea for more civilized qualities among Germans, less beer and potatoes, and more stuff for the mind and soul; fewer financial obsessions and more food for the spirit. Gelasius is imprisoned in Judaea Nova (Europe), a region which cannot sympathize with his disinterested intellectual and moral nature. The anti-Semitic implications here are obvious. Von Maltitz incidentally shows some leanings toward the satirical but he fails to clarify them as Hauff had done.

Such satirists, however, are the exception rather than the rule in the years between 1800 and 1850. We could exchange them all for the fine little Sonnet 57 from Count August von Platen-Hallemünde's "Auf Golgotha" (1820), which sums up beautifully the futile regret of Ahasuerus for having uttered his fatal words and voices his philosophical hope for the future.[72] Perhaps even more poignant is the simple ballad, "Der ewige Jude" (1823), by Wilhelm Müller, a poet who owes at least some of his renown to the fact that many of his poems were set to music by Schubert.[73] In this particular poem, which is indebted to Wordsworth, Müller puts his finger unerringly upon that aspect of the punishment of Ahasuerus which the romantics found the most harrowing—inability to find rest. In all nature there is rest save only for the Wandering Jew, who begs mankind to pray for him before sleeping:

> O Mensch, der du den Lauf vollbracht
> Und gehest hin zur kühlen Nacht,

> Bet', eh' du thust die Augen zu,
> Für mich um eine Stunde Ruh'.

Another, in contrast, was pleased to think that he, like Ahasuerus, could travel. Zacharias Werner, better known as a playwright than as a lyric poet, once spent some time, like his great compatriot Goethe, in Italy: at Rome, on Saturday, June 12, 1813, about 11 P.M., he found inspiration for a little poem on the Wandering Jew.[74] It is not, however, to be taken very seriously. Werner remembers that he must go home to Germany, and the Jew traveled from Italy to Germany once long ago. Whether Werner realized that he was tracing the progress of the Legend with some degree of historical accuracy is unlikely. As we have seen, references to Ahasuerus are almost a matter *de rigueur* among romantic poets in this period, so that Werner's allusion, for it is little more, is to be thought of as a mere bibliographical item, like countless others.

Underneath some of this spirituality of concept, however, there occasionally runs an ugly current which is far from Christian. We have already noted how the spirit of anti-Semitism directed against the Wandering Jew came into being in the Germany of the Reformation and post-Reformation. Now, in 1821, there appeared a savage attack upon the Jews by Ludolf Holst (*Judenthum in allen dessen Theilen*).[75] This was a turgid, pretentious piece of prose, utterly valueless except as an example of the spirit of nationalistic bigotry. It had all the arrogant patriotism of Von Maltitz' *Gelasius* and combined it with a zeal for Jew-baiting. A blistering review by Ludwig Börne was an admirable reply. It bore the rather misleading title, "Der ewige Jude," but had little to do with the Legend; rather it discussed the "eternal" problem of the Jew in the Western world and made a noble plea for the clearing away of the "Pontine marshes" of anti-Semitism. Börne, who, like Heine, was endowed with one of the hardest-hitting satirical hammers of the nineteenth century, began his article with a magnificent comment on the German mind: "Germans, like apes, turn a nut over in their hands a hundred times before they crack it. They play with it so long that the kernel often eludes them, but they would rather lose the kernel than their own patience."[76] To any one familiar with German scholarship in the nineteenth century, this is the final word.

Caigniez and Quinet

We have already seen how French popular literature depicted the Wandering Jew. In the eighteenth century he had graduated from the class of Antichrist-like buffoon to be prophet of wind, weather, and farm problems. He could indulge in memoirs which portrayed him as a globe-trotter supreme. He could indulge also in *complaintes*. As a romantic creature, however, he was slow to develop in France, probably because the French themselves were slower than either the English or the Germans to accept a romantic attitude which, when all is said and done, remains somewhat alien to the French genius.

Indeed, Ahasuerus in France has always tended to be chatty, urbane, witty, and above all casual. A little jingle of 1805 entitled "Je donnerais tout mon quibus"[77] indicates that he had developed an occasional distaste for walking and preferred to ride an omnibus, although his five sous from his inexhaustible purse were not sufficient, since the fare was six sous! The early decades of the century in France were partial to the Jew on the stage of a theater. The flurry of dramatizations of Lewis' *The Monk*, or rather of the Raymond-and-Agnes subplot of *The Monk*, was the most convenient vehicle for the introduction of Ahasuerus to the Parisian theater. But these minor theatrical efforts pale into insignificance beside *Le juif errant*, a melodrama in three acts by Louis-Charles Caigniez, which was given a successful airing at the Théâtre de la Gaieté in 1812.[78] Caigniez's nickname of "the Corneille and Racine of the Boulevards" is hardly deserved. Actually he was too formidable a rival of the influential De Pixérécourt for the good of his own career. So far as the Legend is concerned, however, Caigniez achieved results and De Pixérécourt did not; *Le juif errant* is superior to the general run of similar plays with happy endings which besprinkled the period, whereas De Pixérécourt's "Ahasvérus" remained, as far as may be determined, on the author's desk.

The Wandering Jew in Caigniez's *Le juif errant* bears the unusual name of Samuel Iglouf, presumably derived from the German *Ich lauf'* ("I run"). He is a bringer of happiness to an impoverished noble family in Spain because he is back in his old folk-tale role of treasure finder. He can travel from Spain to Moscow and back in twenty-four hours because he can ride a whirlwind. He is a *bonhomme* of spirit, having an eye for pretty girls and the beauties of the landscape. He carries about with him a pleasing aroma of the supernatural, but there is little of terror in his comings and goings, nothing comparable to what a contemporaneous German writer might have evoked. He has no apparent aim in his immortal life other than the adjustment of family difficulties and the service of romantic lovers. He is not concerned with the souls of those he meets and does not bother to convert evildoers. In a word, he represents only entertaining diversion.

But we must not suppose that the French writers between 1800 and 1850 were unwilling to treat Ahasuerus with serious respect and sincere art or to endow him with mystery and *Weltschmerz*. Probably the masterpiece of French literature dealing with the Wandering Jew—certainly of all the writings about him in the first half of the nineteenth century—is the ambitious creation of the professor, scholar, and politician, Edgar Quinet. There are actually two works on the Wandering Jew from the pen of Quinet; they were published ten years apart and are utterly different—*Les tablettes du Juif-errant* (1823) and *Ahasvérus* (1833). From them we get ample opportunity to comprehend the author's mercurial mind, his love of rhetoric, his frequent grand bursts of poetry, his vagueness on the one hand and his witty satire on the other—a strange combination of Voltaire and Shelley, of *Candide* and *Prometheus Unbound*, without the brightness of the former or the pulsing idealism of the latter. That he wrote in prose instead of verse has led to the observation that he missed renown because he carved in wood instead of bronze, but such an objection is not so valid today as it was in the nineteenth century. By and large, Quinet is a romantic pessimistic poet who avoids running into morbidity and negation only by a last-minute application of the brakes. He shows, often, a bent for philosophical speculation more German than

French, which may be accounted for by the fact that he studied at Heidelberg, and this inclination becomes more pronounced as he grows older.

Les tablettes du Juif-errant consists of a half-dozen sketches, arranged in historical sequence, which are designed to demonstrate the negative of the proposition that this is the best of all possible worlds.[79] Such is the gist of Quinet's very salty Prologue. We can see that he, like every other romantic observer of the 1820's, was deeply absorbed in the spectacle of the Greek revolt against the Turks. His Wandering Jew began by attending the schools of the Greek philosophers during the Alexandrian period, and like Omar Khayyam, came out by the same door by which he entered—no more of an anachronism than the kind perpetuated by artists who portray Christ in modern French dress. Quinet's Gallic side also comes out in an episode in which the Jew consulted the priestess at Delphi: " 'What can I believe in?' 'Believe in a little winged god,' she answered, with a sweet glance at me . . . The next day, the same response, the same glance; but my heart beat hard—I was beginning to understand . . . The next day, the fair priestess threw herself into my arms, then dragged me through a secret door—and so I understood the oracle."[80] Unfortunately for *le juif*, he soon lost this mistress, Chryseis. She disappeared, only to be seen again as an old hag.

Time moves on. In the Middle Ages, the Jew finds that the Church, through the wickedness of its servants, has become utterly corrupt, indifferent to any and all human rights, interested only in perpetuating itself and its corruption "for the greater glory of God." A hypothetical exchange between the Jew and the reader follows: " 'Pardon me,' says the reader, 'your tale bores me; and besides, it is not fact.' 'Oh, isn't it?' I reply, 'Give me a little more time.' "[81] And so the Jew launches upon his experiences during one particular century of the Middle Ages. He wooed, by the conventional method of talking romantic talk and suiting actions to words, a princess of the *haut monde*, unfortunately penniless. She therefore had no other matrimonial prospects than the rather sinister figure of the Wandering Jew, and so she accepted him. The local baron exercised his right of the first night; she did not mind in the least—*au contraire*. The husband, our protagonist, passed those mortifying hours by calling off the watches of the night. But then the first night became a second night, the second a third. Finally the Jew, cuckolded beyond the letter of the *lex primae noctis*, departed in disgust. He joined a Crusade; his saintly companions-at-arms robbed him industriously. His wife? He looked for her patiently for two hundred years, and saw nothing but ignorant armies clashing by night. And that is how he has arrived at the present year, 1823, a time of inventions and constitutions and liberty. But *quel temps et quelles moeurs!* Two centuries from now he will be saying the same thing.

All this may sound frivolous, but it is in reality more trenchant than facetious. Meanwhile, Quinet was developing a profound, not to say mystical, cast of mind, which produces results in strange contrast to the satire of *Les tablettes du juif errant*. His *Ahasvérus* is a huge modern morality play couched in poetic prose; some of it is poetry of a high order, which can be now dramatic, now epic, now purely lyrical.[82] The ambitious vastness of Quinet's concept is typically romantic. It is impractical to trace here all the influences at work on the author, if indeed they can be traced. While there are obvious echoes of Goethe, Schubart,

Byron, Shelley, and Chateaubriand, the great bulk of the work seems to be Quinet's own creation. There is, in fact, nothing quite comparable to it in all the enormous mass of literature dealing with the Legend.

The four acts of the play correspond in general to four particular days in the history of the created world, but there are also a prologue and an epilogue. The Prologue, as was the fashion in medieval French mystery plays, is laid in heaven. The earth has ceased to exist; it has been more than three thousand years since Judgment Day, and the trumpets announcing it had long ago been sounded in the dismal Vale of Josaphat. This earth had been a wicked one; therefore God will attempt to create a new world which, he hopes, will be better. He thereby announces his plan to Thomas, Bonaventura, and Hubert, to whom he intends to entrust the new universe. He commands his archangels, however, to create once more, with a few representative characters, the old world and the evils of time past; lest the seraphim retrace this foul history for some six thousand years and play before his throne the bitter comedy of ages gone by. Let each epoch, each country, speak its own language; let lakes, rocks, and flowers find voices to reveal old earth's mysteries. The play begins; each age "shakes out the folds of its mantle, one after the other."

The first act, or *journée*, tells of the creation and the youth of the world, leading up to the advent of Christ. The lonely ocean cries out for creatures to dwell in it, and Leviathan, the bird Vinateyna, the serpent, and the fish Macar make their appearance. Giants and titans, receiving the breath of life, imagine themselves to be gods, only to be wiped out as unworthy by a new Deluge. On the world barely dry from the Flood, tribes arise, less crass and earthy. They seek God everywhere in nature, migrating hither and thither to find him. One tribe descends the valley of the Ganges, "shaded with fig trees and shaddocks"; another is guided by a griffin to Iran; a third follows the silent flight of the ibis, which "feeds in the plains where stone sphinxes build couches for themselves in the sands." One sphinx recounts the story of prehistoric ages and then the eloquent history of Egyptian Thebes, Nineveh, Persepolis, Palmyra, and Babylon, until Jerusalem enters and reveals that God has been born in a stable at Bethlehem.

Following this moving first act comes an intermezzo; in antithetical fashion it presents a chorus of devils who sneer at the new creation. Lucifer, Beelzebub, and Astaroth make merry at "the celestial comedy," aping and parodying all that has gone before, with Beelzebub getting in the climactic speech:

> Moreover, in everything the beginning is hard; and the Orient, which opens the human comedy, is a beginning by the Creator that deserves indulgence. Let us admit it; the hand of our divine Master shook as he fumbled for ideas, when he set millions of years to work for the molding of a nation, and when in Egypt and in India he wasted in the shade enough time to create four universes. How many centuries lost, in planting awkwardly two or three nations scorched in the sands along the Nile, stammering always the same ideas, in hieroglyphics, in chiseled stone, in murmuring villages—like a neophyte angel who stops in the midst of his song of praise, to count his syllables one by one, his fiddle-bow in his fingers![83]

The second *journée* brings the pageant of Christ, the Crucifixion, and Ahasuerus, as well as the inception of his Legend. When Ahasuerus has received the curse, he stands thunderstruck. Recovering a little from his daze, he enters his house and asks his sister Martha to sing him a song. He would drive out of his hearing the trumpetlike voice which uttered the curse. Barring his way, however, towers the archangel Michael, harbinger of misfortune, who is standing beside a black-maned horse which sweats blood. This is the steed Semehe, the first to be ridden by the Wandering Jew in the whole history of his Legend. Semehe too has been wandering, night and day, since the beginning of the world—the proper horse for the proper man. Ahasuerus must mount and leave before nightfall. He is allowed to embrace his father, his mother, his sister, and his little brothers. He is permitted to say farewell to his ancestral threshold. Then he starts on his first circuit of the world, his horse's hoofs kicking up dead leaves in the Vale of Josaphat.

Next, to avenge the death of the Saviour, other restless travelers, spurred on by God himself, clear the forests, the mountains, and the rivers of the earth. Goths, Huns, and Vandals rampage at will on their wild stallions, tearing to pieces the Roman cavalry sent against them. Almighty God hurls these packs of barbarians against Rome, just as he once hurled the waters of the Deluge against the ancient peoples of the East.

A second intermezzo follows. It is a song of battle, delivered in rhapsodic measures by the horsemen of Attila and the cavalry of Napoleon, pouring out contempt upon effete civilizations. The better parts of this second *journée*, however, stand out in isolated dramatic and poetic effects. For example, at the beginning the desert laments the coming Crucifixion:

> The mountain worships its shadow; the river worships its silt; the bark adores its anchorage. I have no shade, no silt to shape into an amulet. Jehovah is the idol which I hang about my neck; He is made like me; like me He is lonely; like me He walks in sand, without companionship; like me He looks at His road and sees no one, night or day, walking but Himself; His breath effaces the years better than I with my breath can wipe out the traces of the caravans with their jingling bells . . .[84]

The sardonic speeches of the crowd at the Crucifixion and in the streets of Jerusalem, with their mixture of sarcasm, awe, and superstition, are most remarkable. The soliloquy of Ahasuerus when confronted by the implacable archangel is bitter and eloquent, and the replies of Michael are powerful. The old father of Ahasuerus, Nathan, is a sympathetic figure—loving and bewildered yet hopeful, giving his son Polonius-like advice in simple and austere Biblical phrase. "Yes," replies Ahasuerus in despair, "I shall see once more the King of Sorrows, sleeping in my tears I shall see him, much later than the middle of the day!"[85] Finally, the scene in the Vale of Josaphat is not only melodramatically effective, it is poetically exciting as well.

But now in the third *journée*, laid in the Middle Ages, Earth has aged and is dying. The strange character called Mob (the world, the flesh, and the Devil) holds humanity in her clutches. She cannot, of course, touch the life of Ahasuerus, but she can freeze his heart, chill his faith, slay his ideals. She thrusts her hideous countenance into everything which should bring beauty and virtue to mankind. An angel has taken pity on the Wandering Jew and been cast out of heaven in consequence. This is the beautiful Rachel. She lives with Mob and is her servant. Although her reputation among the angels has been hopelessly besmirched, on earth she represents ideal love, eternal faith, all the better nature of humanity. She is consolation, hope, and love where Ahasuerus symbolizes doubt, materialism, and pain. She is the complement of Ahasuerus, an angel in human form, a being, like Christ, brought down from heaven to save humanity. It follows, then, that Mob is cruel to her, scoffing and sneering at every opportunity, and rejoicing in the thought that Rachel can never return to paradise.

Nevertheless, in spite of all Mob's efforts to prevent it, Ahasuerus and Rachel meet in the ancient German city of Worms. They fall immediately in love. As the Flying Dutchman comes to salvation through the undying love of a woman, so it may be with Ahasuerus. For Rachel continues to love him, disregarding a terrible moment when she saw the light of the damned in her lover's eyes, and her crucifix dripped gouts of blood. Not even Mob can break down the confidence inspired in Rachel by the touch of the hand of Ahasuerus. Finally, being a formalist of sorts, Mob comes to agree to the marriage of Rachel and Ahasuerus—indeed, she comes to demand it. She will be glad to assist at the nuptials, for she loves to be between two married people on their wedding couch. First, however, she wishes to take them on a witches' ride to the great cathedral at Strasbourg. There in the cathedral, a monument to the religious faith of man, a wild witches' Sabbath takes place, in which even St. Mark and Christ himself partake.

The third intermezzo is a gentle complaint by a Renaissance poet who is visiting the little church at Brou—not a great cathedral—and the tomb of Marguerite of Savoy. It is a delicate lyric in praise of human suffering, pitched in a mild minor key, in complete contrast to the harrowing climax of the third *journée*.

Throughout, the love of Ahasuerus for Rachel is beautifully portrayed, with no trace of false sentimentality. Rachel knows her lover only as Joseph—should we supply the name Cartaphilus? The terrible scene in Strasbourg Cathedral must have been, to the readers of the 1830's, revolutionary to the point of incomprehensibility. Goethe's *Walpurgisnacht* scene in *Faust* was enacted on the Brocken, a spot traditionally unhallowed, but Quinet laid his witches' Sabbath in one of the great European shrines of Christianity. But why not? The chorus of the dead who have burst from their tombs is explicit in its negation. "Christ has not risen, nor is he even with us. Leave us; there is no Christ!" "Then," says Ahasuerus, "no hell for me, either . . . Truly my day of joy has come."[86] The cataclysm at the end brings the whole scene to dust, while Mob gloats hysterically. "Fear not; I will cover over this night with my regal wings; have no fear."[87] The last lines of the act are chanted by the Cathedral itself, which sends forth this infernal message to all the saints, virgins, dragons, and gargoyles, from the crypts to the great bells in the towers, for all the world to hear.

The last *journée* is without doubt the boldest in conception of all. It is entitled "The Last Judgment," but it is very different from the doom portrayed, for example, in Revelation. In *Ahasvérus* the scene treats only of the future. Cities and men have already weakened before the incessant and tireless onslaughts of "Ocean," which in this last act is clearly the ocean of time. Even this ocean is growing old and weary. Skepticism and doubt have sapped its strength, as they have killed the strength of all created things—sun, stars, flowers, and all life. Mob has corrupted the world. Rachel alone has preserved her faith. The last hour of the world strikes at last. The entire creation has a rendezvous in the dread Vale of Josaphat. All great cities, from Babylon to Paris, keep the appointment. Albertus Magnus, who typifies the ascetic, scholarly recluse, is still looking for the secret of things and seems unaware of what is actually happening. The poet, on the other hand, is instantly alert to the fact that the crisis is imminent.

Now, at long last, the destinies of Ahasuerus and Rachel must be brought to consummation. Their love has bound them together for eternity, yet Ahasuerus is not satisfied. He wants heaven and rest, and in the light of these two things even Rachel is not enough. At the end they are the only ones left to stand before the Judge. All else in creation has received its doom. The Jew is asked by Christ who will follow him to where he wishes to go—to star dust, from world to world, from heaven to heaven, "to see the fountains whence spring the years of the ages." The voices of the universe refuse to follow Ahasuerus, but Rachel will follow. Her heart is not tired. "That voice has saved thee, Ahasuerus," says Christ. "I bless thee as the pilgrim of worlds to come. Give me the burden of the sorrows of the world. May thy foot be light."[88] And so the new world promised by the Almighty in the Prologue is created. The morality play as such is complete. There remain only the gentle harmonies of celestial voices and instruments singing in the New City.

Near the close of this fourth *journée*, a fine chorus of dead gods opposes the ancient orders of divinity to the omnipotence of God—in other words, the polytheistic against the monotheistic. "For men," they say, "it is hard to die; but for gods, the agony is a hundred times worse."[89] Change is inevitable, however; there is no turning back. God himself could not turn back to his Garden of Eden. Doomsday therefore proceeds ineluctably. The Lord resolves all the discords in the soul of Ahasuerus when he proclaims, just before the final chorus: "Ahasuerus is man eternal. All others are like him. Our judgment of him will serve for all. Now our labors are done, and the mystery as well. Our city gates are closed. Tomorrow we will create other worlds. Until that time let us rest beneath the trees of our forest, in our own eternity."[90]

Here Quinet might have ended, but his romantic imagination and melancholy required the Epilogue. It is short and powerful and, according to the author, created a sensation when it appeared, as well it might.[91] Now the New City has decayed; Mary is dead; all the Angels of God have folded their wings; and at last God himself has died—a most interesting early statement of the idea perhaps best known through Nietzsche's *Also Sprach Zarathustra*. The world, the firmament, the Sphinx, and oblivion itself are all swallowed up in eternity.

In this bitter, brutal scene, Quinet says his last word. It is unfortunate that his powers of expression were not always equal to his imagination; if he had possessed the genius of Milton or Dante, his *Ahasvérus* would certainly have been one of the great literary works of the nineteenth century. His brilliant prose dithyrambs, however, are more often effective than otherwise, and none can well deny the great strength of the work as a whole. It is easy to say that he was verbose; that he too often became enamored of the sound of his own words; that his vocabulary was repetitious, his imagery often uncertain, his poetic flights too long to be maintained. All such unfavorable comments are valid up to a point, but then will come a grand vision and an execution of design done with fidelity and an excellent sense of climax.

Whereas Von Arnim's Ahasuerus died, Quinet's comes to final judgment. In the fusion of Ahasuerus with Rachel, he, representing the active elements of life (while Rachel represents the passive), emerges as a symbol of mankind eternal, always searching and wandering and never satisfied, knowing the evil of the world but knowing also its beauty. No other writer who has treated the Wandering Jew has conceived such a vast panorama, placing his protagonist in the framework of a dissolving universe, and communicating to the reader such an overwhelming sense of the eternal and indestructible quality of the Wanderer. Other works may be livelier and more adventurous, but it is difficult for them to match the profundity of Quinet's mystery play. Even if one dislikes the vagueness of much of the work, or its predilection for clouds, meteors, and star dust, and speaking cathedrals and cities, there is no gainsaying the fact that the design of the whole is cosmic. It owes much to its age and to its literary environment, of course, and it unquestionably would have been greater if it had been given an appropriately lofty poetic form and style; but would it have been so human?

Minor Romantics

Quinet's masterpiece, however, remains a kind of leviathan. It is surrounded in its own day by a shoal of small fish, of which some of the most popular were those which continued to retail literary *complaintes* emphasizing the sorrows of Ahasuerus and disregarding philosophical or satirical overtones. These usually represent the sentimentality of second-rate romantic art and are even third-rate or worse in achievement, but they have a considerable degree of currency, and some stand out among the others.

The most famous of these is "Le juif errant" by Pierre-Jean de Béranger, first printed in the 1831 (Paris) edition of his *Chansons*. Not only was it immensely popular in France, and, through translations by Chamisso and Silbergleit, in Germany also, but it was well adapted to a musical setting. Béranger, intrinsically little more than an Edgar Guest of early nineteenth-century France, indicated that his verses were to be sung to the undistinguished tune, "L'air du chasseur rouge d'Amédée de Beauplan," but later generations have known it better through the vigorous baritone solo setting composed by Charles Gounod. The poem, based on the celebrated Brabantine ballad, which will be remembered as the most widely known of the traditional French *complaintes* of the Wandering Jew, is very far from being a great lyric, but it is an unabashed appeal for tears, depending heavily upon the pathetic, and it is rather embarrassingly melodramatic, though probably sincere enough as a creative effort. Perhaps it is sufficiently damning to call it cheaply romantic. Ahasuerus is in the tempest and the whirlwind, which hover about him in even his quieter moments, and the refrain "Toujours, toujours, toujours" indicates the pervading mood of hopelessness. Most significant of the trend, as the nineteenth century progresses, is Béranger's unmistakable implication that Ahasuerus is being tormented not so much for an offense against God as for his cruelty to a suffering human being—in brief, his crime is less against God and more against man. The effect is to render him more pathetic and sentimental.

A much finer poetic accomplishment is a series of thirteen-line "sonnets," entitled "Die Wanderungen des Ahasverus" (1839), by Johann Christoph Freiherr von Zedlitz; there are fifty of these moving little poems in the sequence, which is dedicated to the prime question, "How long, O Lord?"[92] The Wanderer is Byronic in nature, but rather restrained in his despairing thoughts on what has happened to the world from Caesar to Napoleon. Beside his terse and attractive eloquence the effusions of Antonio Bertani's "Il Giudeo Errante," in *Affetti e Rimembranze* (Parma, 1846), seem prosaically conventional as they depict the Jew's sufferings; and Isaac Rosenfeld's "Der ewige Jude" (1838)[93] barely manages to strike a spark of sympathy for the victim, although in fairness it must be granted that Rosenfeld's chief concern is to answer the anti-Semitic attitude of writers like Von Maltitz and Gutzkow (pp. 216-17 below). N. Martin, in *Sonnets et Chansons* (Paris, 1841), places the protagonist in a mood of melancholy retrospect upon his former Eden, much in the manner of Quinet, but without his ability. One new detail appears in L.-A. Gras's *Ahasvérus, juif errant* (Paris, 1842).[94] In this ballad-like *complainte* the Jew is squeezed, though not to death, by intertwining serpents in the manner of Laöcoön. Sometimes in these little poems Ahasuerus is visited by death, as he was in Von Arnim and Ten Kate; or the shadow of death may flicker over the verses, especially when they are in imitation of Schubart. So it is in a half-dozen poems of varying worth, though mostly mediocre: the anonymous "La dernière heure du juif-errant," published in the *Revue poétique de dix-neuvième siècle* (1839); F. Trautmann's little poem, "Ahasverus," from a fragment of a larger work, "Das Welt-ende" (1843);[95] A. Mugnerot's "Le juif errant," first printed in the *Receuil de poésies sacrées* (1846); the austere, macabre "Ahasver" (1850) by Adolph Strodtmann;[96] Johann Schoen's "Ahasverus der ewige Jude";[97] and the pleasingly straightforward ballad by F. Steinmann, "Der ewige Jude."[98]

The reader is swung back and forth between the narrative and lyrical elements of the Jew's lament, but, of these writers and their works, Trautmann and Strodtmann deserve a little more than passing attention. In Trautmann's poem, Ahasuerus is in a violently excited state when the world comes to an end, because while others—artists, princes, and lovers—can die, he cannot; but after much strenuous and rather sensational text he finds an angel on the spot where his offense was committed, and this angel gives him the kiss of death. God's love then envelops the twilight of the universe. In Strodtmann's case, the Wanderer sees the mutations wrought by time; as T. S. Eliot was aware of much the same thing a century later, he glimpses country-dances performed in ghostly wise on ancient wastelands and sees gallows erected on old trysting places and decay where once were dreams. Something of the same point is made by Nikolaus Stehling, in an extremely wordy epic, *Das jüngste Gericht* (Düsseldorf, 1841). Here mankind—a wicked king, a pious family, an old and feeble man, a betrothed pair, and a child—confronted by death, reacts in varying degrees of terror. But unlike humanity, Ahasuerus greets the prospect of death with ineffable joy.

No matter what the quality or nature of her poetry, we cannot afford to overlook Mrs. Caroline Norton, later Lady Stirling-Maxwell, and her *The Undying*

One, first printed in 1830 and then reprinted in several editions by 1860.[99] Mrs. Norton was the granddaughter of the playwright Richard Brinsley Sheridan; and she and her sister Lady Dufferin were considered leading poetesses of their generation. Indeed, Mrs. Norton fancied herself as the "female Byron," and with some appropriateness, for there is no doubt about her literary debt to the Pilgrim of Eternity. She has some of his sonority, his grasp of pathos and feeling, and his melodrama; all she lacks is his power to achieve that magic synthesis which produces true poetry. At that, however, she is no mean storyteller, and *The Undying One* is a succession of highly colored incidents which constitute one long lament. There is always plenty of action in the poem, although the total effect is hectic without the rather febrile virility of a more talented romantic poet.

Mrs. Norton has bestowed upon the Wandering Jew a new name—Isbal—for reasons known only to herself. He has brought death to various women whom he has loved down through the ages. To the most recent of his loves, Linda, he tells the melancholy stories of her unfortunate predecessors. He begins, of course, with the Crucifixion. Despite the intervening centuries, it all seems as yesterday. When the gaping crowd had departed from Calvary, Isbal was left alone, the Undying One. After this dark hour of agony, not an instant of fevered bliss could remain, but there was the sudden hope that he might be happy through half an immortality at least, and so he began to make "a guilty Paradise on earth." Yet his self-dedication to riotous living was useless. His gay life became empty, reminding him too often of the sad echoes of the past. Only those who have lived on when more than life itself has gone can understand him. The constant ever fades and changes, but he remains the same. He even goes through a tormented stage when he wishes that he might have the exquisite satisfaction of fawning and groveling before the one who will slay him. All avoid him, however, for his fearful tale of guilt has passed down from father to son. Therefore he flees from land to land, hunted and persecuted by mankind and by his shame as well. He moves among Mohammedans, Jews, and Christians, and only the last win any praise from him, for only they possess a social conscience. As to the women, only Edith, whom he once wooed in an English country churchyard, brought him any consolation or professed any permanent devotion—like Rachel in Quinet's *Ahasvérus* —and she died of fright when she learned his identity. (The weeping Linda, listening with gruesome fascination, clings to him like a burr, fearing that she may lose him and not realizing that the lightning will strike her in turn.)

Then there was Xarifa of Spain. On a beautiful spring day, by the banks of the Guadalquivir, she too died, having refused steadily to hear his story, lest she depart from him some day with a memory of him that "might not soar high." Their son, Abdullah, mourned her for the brief span of youthful sorrow, and Isbal cared for the boy until he was old enough for marriage. On Abdullah's wedding morning, a traveler brought to the assembling guests the tale of the Wandering Jew, and although Isbal publicly deprecated the story, his demeanor at last betrayed him to Abdullah, who repudiated him on the spot as a moral leper and the indirect slayer of his mother. Yet Isbal softened the young man and his bride sufficiently to be forgiven, but the next day they have disappeared without a trace, and Isbal must resume his wanderings.

He witnesses thereafter, a variety of personal suffering among many kinds of people, chiefly the pain of bereavement. In one case, however, it is a more abstract pang, when a young poet, dazed by care and poverty, bewails his failing poetic gifts. Isbal then rescues a babe from its Irish mother, who is bent on destroying it because she cannot feed it. The mother dies, perhaps of shock, when the little one is returned to her, but Isbal heeds her last wish and brings up the child as a lovely elfin girl who seems to foreshadow, in her spiritual precocity, disconcerting little Pearl in Hawthorne's *The Scarlet Letter*. They wander together through England, observing the persecution of the Jews under Richard Lion-Heart, and then pass on to Africa, for fey little Miriam seems to have a predilection for deserts. When Isbal tries to interest her in the world and humanity, she resists all efforts to make her an average atom of mankind. The trouble is that she has fallen in love with him. Sick at heart when he remembers what has happened to the other women who loved him, he struggles for a while with himself and then puts Miriam out of her misery by killing her. He is led to execution, but of course his death is impossible to contrive. The law is obliged to settle for a century-long imprisonment. (All this, nevertheless, fails to discourage the doting Linda. She persuades Ahasuerus to elope with her, whereupon her brother and her erstwhile suitor pursue them. Shipwreck follows, and all perish except the Undying One, who is now truly alone, at least until the next time. As we know, there will be an indefinite number of next times—the essential weakness of the Legend for narrative purposes.)

It is easy to see that, in spite of these tempestuous incidents, the epic that Mrs. Norton wrote is a Gargantuan *complainte*. She makes some minor concessions to the Chronicle of the Wandering Jew—as all writers about Ahasuerus must do if they are going to follow a chronological sequence—and she grants to the hero Isbal the privilege of fighting for freedom, a *sine qua non* for any romantic hero. Her plan to have a multiplicity of Byronic incidents is likewise obvious, but her poetic talent is weak and fitful, although she has a clear fluency which makes the reading of her verse not altogether a penance. Still, we could dispense with all the mournful chronicles of fatal loves for one scene between lovers comparable to that between Ahasuerus and Rachel in Quinet's *Ahasvérus*.

To mention Quinet again is to bring to mind a pretty little poem dedicated to him by Aglaé de Corday, "Ahasvérus" (Paris, 1837), and the dignified and pathetic "Der ewige Jude" (1848) by August Thieme.[100] Both poems partake in about equal proportions of autumnal romantic melancholy. Yet since sorrow is such a universal human experience, and the language of lamentation so circumscribed in even the greatest poets—thoughts of tears which do lie too deep for words—it is too much to expect minor poets to achieve true distinction when they try to picture only the suffering of Ahasuerus.

Thus, in his romantic bloom, Ahasuerus appears to us first of all as a sufferer. The accounts, largely subjective, of his pain, his remorse, his guilt-consciousness, his defiance, and his self-pity fill line after line of verse and prose by both major and minor writers. Such descriptions represent, for the most part, that phase of the romantic in art and literature which, justly or unjustly, we call Byronic, although it is clearly much older than Byron. So far as Ahasuerus is concerned, it might more properly be termed Schubartian. These sufferings of Ahasuerus may be attended by melodrama, the presence of the supernatural, the appeal to terror; or there may be tenderness of thought and reflectiveness which may lead through peace and quiet to a philosophical acceptance. All this is clearly intended to be taken seriously; here and there may appear a satirical rebuff to the Legend, but these are, for the moment, quite rare.

Usually the romantic Ahasuerus, when he can be jostled out of his egotism, is helpful to mankind; but he can be malevolent. Generally he will applaud the struggle for liberty. He moves through natural settings both awesome and idyllic, as the individual case may demand; but he cares about them only in so far as they reflect his mood and can stimulate him to utterance. All things considered, he is a figure of fantasy, but he is beginning to become a symbol—for suffering mankind, for the Jewish people (even a Jewish nation), for the rebel against tyranny (secular or divine), for the sinner either repentant or unrepentant. His symbolic value, however, is yet to be fully exploited. It remains now to continue to observe the variations on the complex romantic theme which the writers between 1800 and 1850 have stated.

CHAPTER NINE

Early Variations on Romantic Themes

To make the Wandering Jew into a symbol of this or that had become something of a literary fashion by 1850. For that matter, the nineteenth century always had a tendency to look in all directions for social symbols to express the obvious unrest of the age, the long and bitter uphill struggle for the rights of man and the just implementation of those rights. Of course, the details of this struggle are only indirectly our affair; but it is obvious that, ever since the days when the Legend came to be treated as something more than a mere folk tale, it is possible to trace in the artistic treatment of Ahasuerus the outlines of the literary and intellectual fads and fashions of the times. In the main, the Wandering Jew continues to stand out as a brave representative of sin, one who may be considered, as a sinner, in either a sympathetic or unsympathetic light. If unsympathetic, we must accept the attitude toward him as a manifestation of moral or religious conservatism. If sympathetic, he soon becomes, in his sinfulness, a symbol of the rebellious aspirations of a thinking man—thus he may stand for *Weltschmerz,* which is by no means the special property of the end of the nineteenth century; for the spirit of skepticism; for liberty and the libertarian; for revolution; for the Jewish people and perhaps a Jewish nation in Israel (Zionism); but quite generally for all mankind, groaning and travailing together against the cruel force of things as they are. For the next century and a half—down into the present day—Ahasuerus has invariably awakened interest because of his power to represent. Sometimes this representation is treated seriously, sometimes satirically, and often it is difficult to tell which.

At the same time, Ahasuerus may unexpectedly revert to some older role. Some of the minor variations of the Chronicle of the Wandering Jew are cases in point. Any critical reader would agree, for example, that Nathaniel Hawthorne, in "A Virtuoso's Collection" from *Mosses from an Old Manse* (1846)—where the Jew is a guide through a museum of antiquities and a commentator on historical personages—made more skillful use of the Chronicle device than most. It is appropriate to the 1840's that he should allow the Jew to be more interested in his living visitor than in his dead exhibits. To speak of Hawthorne, incidentally, is to recall that in "Ethan Brand," written in 1848 (though not printed until 1851), the seeker after the Unpardonable Sin, himself a wanderer, meets the Wandering Jew who, with his diorama, shows a series of scenes:

... outrageous scratchings and daubings ... Some purported to be cities, public edifices, and ruined castles in Europe; others represented Napoleon's battles and Nelson's seafights; and in the midst of these would be seen a gigantic, brown, hairy hand—which might have been mistaken for the Hand of Destiny, though, in truth, it was only the showman's—pointing its forefinger to various scenes of the conflict, while its owner gave historical illustrations.[1]

The Jew is tired of carrying his show box over the mountain, but it is evident that he must go on his appointed way; Ethan Brand, unpardonable sinner though he may be, has the privilege of throwing himself into the limekiln. His is an example, from a true literary artist, of an offender against the Deity who must wander in expiation. Yet, though his doom in life parallels that of the Wandering Jew, he is not Ahasuerus.

Again, such a figure as Ahasuerus the chronicler and world guide lends itself to parody. In general, however, although the burlesque Wandering Jew may be amusing enough, he is more interesting as an integrating figure in the portrayal of the civilization of a given age. Eduard von Schenck, the court poet of Ludwig I of Bavaria, and a dramatist of better than average ability, had in mind an epic which would describe the culture of the sixteenth century, the great age of the Reformation. Since Von Schenck was the protégé of a devout Catholic king, his proposed poem would have been no defense of Protestantism. Only three fragments of this epic, however, were ever published. These were: (1) a version of the Legend of St. George, in *Charitas* (1834); (2) "Albertus Magnus," in the *Deutscher Musenalmanach* for 1834; and (3) "Hi-Tong and Li-Song," in the same annual for 1836.[2] The plan was to have Ahasuerus, near the end of the seventeenth century, rest for a few days in a Benedictine monastery in southern Germany, there to entertain the monks with the story of his venerable and authoritative traversals of world history, with particular emphasis on the sixteenth century. The whole epic was to be called, not unreasonably, "Der ewige Jude." The fragments lead the reader nowhere in particular, but what was completed demonstrates that Von Schenck's talents were more dramatic than narrative or lyric. Passing over the banal treatment of the St. George story, we find in the "Albertus Magnus" fragment that two amateurs, desirous of wresting from their dead master the secret of life, and relying upon a magic ring for their information, are converted by the ghost of their master to a Christian outlook. In "Hi-Tong and Li-Song," Christian faith triumphs over non-Christian selfishness. Two young Chinese of aristocratic ancestry are made over into Christians and find solace in an artistic Shangri-La. On one occasion, the Wandering Jew rescues them when they have been thrown overboard by superstitious sailors—an echo from Von Arnim's *Halle und Jerusalem*. Ahasuerus, then, is back in his now familiar role of agent for good who works especially at promulgating faith in God; and his part as a chronicler remains in Von Schenck's design but not in his published product. When one remembers that in Quinet's play, *Ahasvérus*, Albertus Magnus was seen as a symbol of the futile scholar digging away on the Day of Doom for the elusive secret of life, one sees an interesting contrast between German pietism and French rationalism.

The old conception of Ahasuerus as a universal observer of human affairs accounts for the fact that *Le juif errant* is the name of a French periodical which ran through 1835 and 1836, and of another which had only five issues in 1848. These were gossipy journals of the old "town-topics" brand, with social notes from all over, though hardly scandalmongering. Such publications, in fact, were not unknown elsewhere at the time. As it happens, the most striking example was not French at all but German—the Augsburg *Ahasver* of 1831-32.

Random gleanings from *Ahasver* for 1831 will suffice to illustrate the nature of the publication. Fireworks on New Year's Eve roused the Wandering Jew, now a sober Augsburger of solid middle-class conservatism, to a high pitch of enthusiasm. So did the arrival of the carnival season. On the whole the right-wing tendencies of the editorial staff, headed by J. F. Bürgler, are tempered from time to time with innocent ribaldry—the atmosphere of the pub or *Bierstube*, with its gregarious mores, its songs of Bacchus, the "live and let live" spirit. Many pages are given over to the pleasures of rural life in the beautiful neighboring countryside—there was one spot in particular, a delightful scene of rolling country, fresh clean brooks, singing birds, and green everywhere—the most pleasant place in the world for a picnic. And the name of the place was Dachau.

Augsburg had its reckless drivers in 1831, and the condition of the streets frequently caused grief in the bosoms of the townspeople. The pride of Augsburg women, sad to relate, often preceded their fall; unlike the French periodicals, there are some incidents in the Augsburg *Ahasver* to raise eyebrows. A few pieces of art criticism are sprinkled through the journal. The provincial theater was commended in it as a matter of true civic duty. Patriotic verse abounded. Freedom, at least freedom of the press, was a very sensitive subject, but the censors in Augsburg evidently were liberal. The city aspired to become a resort; if only a Beau Nash would arise there to make the place another Bath, what glories might not redound to the prestige of all Bavaria. As for the Wandering Jew, he pops in and out of the pages as the peripatetic observer. The net impression left by the journal is that it was a rudimentary *New Yorker* (rather than a *Punch*); its humor and its local allusions, of course, are alike incomprehensible to an outsider, but between 1831 and 1832 it served its purpose, so far as one can now determine, to the satisfaction of a few Augsburgers. Yet its contribution to the Legend as such is in name only; its title is purely symbolic and nothing else.

Of some interest to the folklorist is the ballad by Wilhelm Smets, which, unlike the poems on an Ahasuerian folk tale by Witte and Ten Kate, who extracted a large amount of romantic juice from the Grimsel tale, is notably objective. Smets's "Ahasver" (1835) tells briefly the episode of the Wandering Jew at the Frankfurt fair (pp. 77-78 above), where he was revealed as the immortal Wanderer when he proffered a Roman coin from the reign of the emperor Tiberius.[3] The Baron de Reiffenberg, in *Souvenirs . . . en l'honneur de Schiller* (1839), explains how he once made a visit to Frankfurt and saw the very spot at the fair where the Jew showed the coin.[4] As a kind of footnote we may add a curious elaboration on the tendency of Ahasuerus to exhibit money, as described in the little article by Leo Vollländer-Riesberg in the *Kalander und Jahrbuch für Israeliten* for 1848.[5] According to this, Ahasuerus is a mendicant, yes; but he always has a gold louis of uncertain coinage, a definite piece of *Reisegeld*, which he can produce at any city gate in order to gain admittance, on the plea that he will have no need to beg. This is an evident deterioration of the theme of the Inexhaustible Purse.

Ahasuerus as Romantic Sinner

All these are comparatively minor matters. Let us return to Ahasuerus the Sinner, either to be granted pity and sympathy or to be reviled and degraded. Most of the moral cannonading directed against him comes from belated German romanticists, but there is never any national or racial monopoly on reactionism in morals and religion. The tradition with these writers is that Ahasuerus, a sinner because he abused Christ, maintains the power to corrupt and harm others. This is almost never convincing; the horrible example of his fate is scarcely likely to lead one to do the same as he did. The tradition is nevertheless there, and the villain sometimes succeeds. Thus, in a not impossible five-act drama, *Der ewige Jude* (Iserlohn, 1831), by Wilhelm Langewiesche ("Wilhelm Jemand"), Count Heinrich von Strahlen, a Crusader, is in an unfortunate hour rescued from the enemy by Ahasuerus, who proceeds to involve them both in a charge of heresy. Here it is, as usual, the mortal who is the actual victim. For Von Strahlen is condemned to death and executed, while Ahasuerus survives to wreak his evil powers on other unsuspecting persons. There is a resemblance to the basic situation in Franz Horn's "Der ewige Jude" (pp. 197-98 above), and some scenes in Langewiesche's play parallel, in a general way, some from Klingemann's *Ahasver* (pp. 196-97 above), for Von Strahlen is a weak reincarnation of Klingemann's tortured Heinyn. But while Heinyn is really guilty of murder, Von Strahlen can be charged with no such crime, and his punishment is altogether out of line with his offense. He has been most unfortunately contaminated—a case of guilt by association only. Ahasuerus has brought to a mortal, not the cholera or any such tangible pestilence, but a soul-sickness. The effect which he exerts on others, or on society as a whole, becomes more important than his own sufferings in the manner of a romantic hero.

It is usually sufficient, however, for these unsympathetic writers to label Ahasuerus a sinner and throw him onto the dunghill along with other egregious evildoers. Examples of this procedure make for tedious reading. Alois Jeitteles' *Moderne Walpurgisnacht* (Brünn, 1848), an extremely conservative anti-Polish tract, places Ahasuerus in unholy places along with Jesuits, Republicans, and Goethe. *Die Ahasveriade* (1838), a lugubrious epic fragment by F. F. Franke ("Ferdinand Hauthal"), pits Christianity against Islam and Jewry, and heaps infamy on the protagonist as an archskeptic.[6] E. Duller's *Der Antichrist* (1833), a queerly esoteric and nebulous fantasy, portrays Ahasuerus as a brutal, lecherous follower of Satan, who devises a wicked dance for his master's servants.[7] Friedrich Röse's lyric, "Ahasver" (1839), fancies Ahasuerus as one to spit contemptuously upon the efficacy of prayer.[8]

Perhaps the most diverting and readable of the various unsympathetic treatments of Ahasuerus at this time comes in Theodor Oelckers' *Prinzessin Marie von Oldenhof: Oder der ewige Jude* (Leipzig, 1844). Oelckers was a valiant liberal who took part in the German uprisings of 1848 and 1849, and was sufficiently active to win for himself a prison sentence and virtual exile from Germany after his release. Paradoxically, this longish novel, written in a rather erratic epistolary form, is interested hardly at all in the political implications of Ahasuerus the rebel. Instead, it is a literary throwback to the previous generation, the story of a curse laid upon a family because one of its members was sexually intimate with a descendant of the Wandering Jew. The work has its pages of interest in an old-fashioned manner; like the contemporary novels of G. P. R. James, it shows more than once a mysterious horseman riding over a lonely plain. Oelckers postulates for Ahasuerus a son in the seventeenth century. The mother is not identified. This son, according to the formula prescribed in many a Gothic romance, impregnates one Marie while she is sojourning in a nunnery. The child of this union is marked all his life by ill fortune of various kinds, and his children after him. The last chapters of the novel shift to the later generations of this family in the early nineteenth century. By this time the original virulence of the curse has begun to thin out. A legacy is divided among the clan, and Oskar happily marries his Rosamund. Another descendant, Rudolf, starts off to spend his share of the legacy doing missionary work among the infidels of India, but he is induced to marry a girl from Bombay and to set up a European tavern in that city. The anticlimax is painful. The Wandering Jew stalks in and out of the pages of the book, an antiquated but impressive individual with broad-brimmed hat and gray beard, a habitué of inns and taverns, with the unpleasant habit of appearing spookily and scaring people out of their wits. He is in general a symbol to remind us of original sin, but aside from begetting the son who started the family misfortunes, he contributes nothing important save the unmistakable and oft-repeated assertion that he is a terrible sinner.

In artistic contrast to *Prinzessin Marie von Oldenhof* is the neat little tale by Henry Neele, "The Magician's Visitor," which appeared in the London *Forget-Me-Not* for 1828—one of those innumerable annuals which pester antiquarians and literary historians long after their popularity among the general reading public has waned. Here the celebrated alchemist and necromancer, Cornelius Agrippa (1466-1535), is importuned by a stranger to reproduce the image of a deceased daughter of the visitor. Having begun his process of hocus-pocus, Agrippa is amazed to discover how far back in time he must go to evoke the requested image. But why not? For he eventually discovers that the stranger who made the request is none other than the Wandering Jew, who, confronted by the fact, promptly confesses that he is an unpardonable sinner and leaves in a huff. The same story fell into the hands of the Scotsman, William Edmondstoune Aytoun, who, in 1834, made it into a pleasant though rather flowery poem, with a flavor of Monk Lewis.[9] Hoffman retells it in the Introduction to his *Chronicles of Cartaphilus*.

These authors, from Langewiesche ("Jemand") to Aytoun, while they make plain that they consider Ahasuerus as a sinner of deepest dye, have at the same time been sympathetic enough to allow him a certain amount of dignity in hell. Others, however, are not so charitable. *Ahasuerus* (1842), by "a Virginian" (Robert Tyler, son of President John Tyler), is a turgid effusion in blank verse, now Shakespearean, now Miltonic, now Wordsworthian, now Byronic, now fustian, with all the worst qualities of each.[10] Its best passages undertake an account of the Crucifixion, and these at least contain traces of romantic vigor. It is the picture of the "sinful" Jew which recurs again and again; on him Tyler turns the fury of an American of Calvinistic persuasion, without Hawthorne's art and sympathy. Virtually the same harsh attitude edges into A. Cauvin's little ballad-like poem in the Paris *L'Aurore* for 1846.[11] It bursts into great bitterness in K. Gutzkow's "Plan eines Ahasvers" (1842), a verse fragment identifying the evil of the Wandering Jew with the evil attributes of all Judaism—the sneer on the lips of

Heine. Gutzkow is for letting all Jews utter their *Ahasverjammer*, for, he believes, they deserve their fate and what the Jews need to contribute is more accomplishment and less lamentation. Gutzkow, in his review of Julius Mosen's *Ahasver* (pp. 218-20 below), thrashes around in this dilemma: he wants emancipation for all Germans, including the Jews, but he is impatient with the claims of Judaism for sovereignty and is indeed more than a little contemptuous of Jews.[12]

An unidentified author in the Munich *Monatrosen* for 1842 is as vitriolic as Gutzkow, but he pours most of his venom on the person of Ahasuerus, whom he describes as a haughty, leering foe of the pretended King of the Jews:

About his big head hung his red hair, all tousled clear down to his neck; his beard curled about in matted ringlets over his chest; his sharply drawn features, brown of hue, were deeply worn. His clothes covered him only from breast to knee; his feet were bare and, like his hands, burned brown by toil and the heat of the sun.[13]

This Jew was present at the destruction of Jerusalem in A.D. 70. At the time the Temple was sacked, he came to see his future—nay more, the future of all mankind passed before him, and a grisly picture it was. Not without reason, therefore, does he echo Job asking why he was ever born. Thus we find ourselves back with Schubart's Ahasuerus. Neither fire and water nor earthquakes and the howling sandstorms of the desert can put an end to his woes.

Or again, Ahasuerus may be culpable because he is a crass materialist in conflict with idealism. This is the theme of Vacheslav Nebesky's long poem, *Protichudchi* ("The Antipodes"), published at Prague in 1844.[14] But whether or not he as a sinner is to be the object of pity or of condemnation, it is rare indeed when he is not sympathetic toward other sinners, whatever their stripe. In fact, it is often his consolation to see them go to their rest even if he himself cannot. If such a figure as Napoleon Bonaparte was evil, as many of the writers of the time considered him to be, he would still have Ahasuerus' support, for whatever it might be worth. This is the message of the anti-Christian speeches of the protagonist in "Ahasver und Bonaparte" (1838) by Alexander, Graf von Württemberg.[15] However unrepentant and uncontrite Ahasuerus may be, he has a fellow feeling for any other great rebel against the established order; but some writers cannot leave it at that, and so the Jew, by showing tolerance and understanding toward other sinners, comes to tread, imperceptibly at first, the path of righteousness and ends as a convert to Christianity, attaining a welcome death in all the bliss of repentance and forgiveness. This was how it appeared to O. G. Heldring, in his strange pamphlet, *De nimmer rustende Israeliet tot rust gekommen* (Amsterdam, 1839). A three-headed mongrel, it first gives a résumé of Franz Theremin's *Der ewige Jude* (1835)—a work it tends to popularize, in which Ahasuerus is presented as a rationalist and Epicurean, a worldling, whose only reality is reason and who entertains such great names as Lessing and Goethe with an account of his experiences.[16] The second part of Heldring's pamphlet is the story of Ahasuerus' last journey to his homeland. The third is a reprint of Ten Kate's *De Dood van Ahasverus den nimmer rustenden Israeliet* (p. 192 above). Heldring's main part in the history of the Legend is that of a minor editor, although the second section reflects subjectively upon the idea of even-handed justice. As for Theremin's work, it is much the best part of the pamphlet, being sprightly with a good many satirical overtones which gather about the behavior of the Jew, who is happy to see the spread of atheism in modern Germany.

Mosen

As for the *Weltschmerz*, the pain of it all, wherever Ahasuerus moves during the nineteenth century, he bears with him the capacity for disgust at the goings on in this world, a true *contemptus mundi*. Indeed, he is saved from believing that the world is always out of joint only by action, by direct interference in the lives of human beings, by agitating for political revolution, or by assuming the posture of a champion of liberty. Otherwise, he is likely to slump into profound dejection, a depression induced primarily by the contemplation of the follies of mankind and the remorseless alterations wrought by time.

Usually, however, the reactions are more complex. *Weltschmerz* is in effect the modern problem of Ahasuerus. It is given a strong early statement by the gifted German poet Julius Mosen, first in his short narrative poem, "Ritter Wahn" ("Knight Error") written in 1831, in which the sinister, restless Jew saves Error from death; and later in a much more distinguished achievement, the epic *Ahasver* (1838).[17] The form and doubtless some of the basic concepts of *Ahasver* derive from Dante's *Divine Comedy*. The poem is written in *terza rima*, and the advance from despair to the peace which comes from forgiveness reminds one of the journey from the Inferno to Paradise. At the outset the Jew is full of hate and bitterness. His wife has died; he is left to bring up his son Reuben and his daughter Leah. Pontius Pilate, hearing of his situation, offers to send the children to Rome for their education. Ahasuerus is grieved at the prospect of losing them, but, after all, Rome is Rome. Meanwhile, he holds a conversation with Christ, whom he has hitherto supported but who has offended him by prophesying that Jerusalem will be destroyed and that God will do nothing about it. The Jew's bitterness turns to complete despair. When a young Roman, sent by Pilate to convey the children to Rome, appears to be smitten by the budding charms of Leah, the Jew in a fit of rage slays both children. Then follows the story of the Crucifixion and the curse imposed upon Ahasuerus, who must wander until—through contrition, helpfulness, and obedience to the will of God—he finds salvation.

The first era of the Jew's wanderings is introduced by a scene between God and his bride, Nature, in which there is a brief review of pre-Christian history, when Jehovah, Brahma, and the Egyptian and Greek gods ruled. Ahasuerus, it appears, is only another such rebel against the true God. When we first see him, he is still festering in undiminished hatred against the world. His hair is not yet gray; his fist is as mighty as ever; his muscles still swell; but he cannot put down the inveterate restlessness which goes with the curse. His former companions are all dead. Another wife has died in the meantime, leaving him with another pair of children, also named Reuben and Leah. The Romans come to sack Jerusalem. (Mosen at this point is obviously indebted to Croly's *Salathiel*, presumably through Storch's translation.) Reuben II has a Christian friend, Matthias, who falls in love with Leah II and converts her to Christianity. The battle waxes bloody, and Jerusalem is sacked. Ahasuerus escapes to the seacoast and ultimately returns to find Leah II praying to a Christian God. In the absence of both Reuben II and Matthias, he persuades the girl to abjure her newly found faith. The remainder of this section is devoted to the destruction of Jerusalem, the parade of the victorious Romans, their desecration of the Holy of Holies, and the escape of Ahasuerus with his children, he having first denounced Matthias as a Christian and a Roman.

The second era continues the pattern of the first. The setting is now Rome in the days of Constantine and Julian the Apostate. Ahasuerus is still the hater, with a Reuben III and Leah III. Again it is Ahasuerus who seduces Julian into the renunciation of Christianity. When Jerusalem is to be rebuilt, it is decreed by the priests of Israel that the children of the oldest person present must be sacrificed to God, and since there can be no question as to who this may be, Ahasuerus flees in despair.

The third era brings Ahasuerus into the Middle Ages. In contrast to the rather pastoral tone of much of the second, the third is violent, with the Huns serving as fitting agents of destruction. The Vandals as well as the Franks appear, eventually accepting the faith of the Cross. Still Ahasuerus wanders, the serpent of bitterness gnawing at his heart. All nature conspires to ask him where his children are. He sees pass before him kings, pontiffs, rich men, and heroes, all led by Death, who alone seems to have an understanding with him. After talking with a Hebrew sage, he comes to believe that even the Jews love detested man more than they love their God. For a while he thinks he might do worse than associate himself with the Prophet of the Crescent, for the incursions of the Moslems hearten him greatly; and, after all, Allah is great. When the Mohammedans take Jerusalem, Ahasuerus is with them, surveying the famous city by moonlight in most Byronic fashion. "Like that moon, I too shall wander around the earth." In spite of himself, he begins to feel pity for humanity. For what do they but wander also, and in most ways as blindly as he? At the Holy Sepulcher pilgrims are praying. Ahasuerus, in the company of two Moslem youths, profanes the Sepulcher, and most of the pilgrims flee in terror; but two pilgrims continue to pray—Reuben and Leah (whether the third or a new pair is not clear, nor is it a material consideration since they are intended to symbolize the children of Ahasuerus in a timeless stage). Now Ahasuerus comes to realize that not only has he been truly despised and rejected of men, but he has made a fool of himself to boot. When his Mohammedan companions try to kill Reuben and Leah, he protects them with his invulnerable body. An angel intercedes and bears the children off to heaven; and although Ahasuerus, now overwhelmed by a sense of guilt, thinks that for him pardon is impossible, Christ appears in person. The issue is joined, and Ahasuerus is sentenced anew to continue his wandering, this time "in the service of mankind." At long last, he elects to follow the road to God.

Although Mosen agreed with Hegel that history develops through oppositions and contrasts, he clouds the idea with a large amount of rather unsatisfactory philosophical speculation. Ahasuerus, however, is not merely a passive spectator of world events, as he had been in the Chronicle of the Wandering Jew, nor a mere romantic sufferer. He is here an active, even heroic, participant, with both the strength and courage that become an epic hero. He wins from Christ the admiration bestowed upon a respected adversary. Consequently he is not crushed like a worm nor condemned to a meaningless wandering; rather he must grow into a kind of Prometheus, a being who rebels against God for the sake of humanity. The seed of such an idea has been planted during the early scene between God and his bride, Nature, to whom mankind is a beloved but perverse child. It is true that Mosen has left his poem without a definite conclusion. In one sense the career of his Ahasuerus has just begun. He is to leave aside his egoism, his overwhelming love for the Jewish people, and must become a co-operative citizen of the world. This vague ending, however, should not detract from the fire and power of Mosen's narrative passages. He is a better epic poet than a philosopher. Yet no single work in the earlier nineteenth century illustrates better the difference between the purely romantic concept of Schubart's Ahasuerus and the social consciousness of the image of the Wandering Jew after that century had advanced past 1830.

Ahasuerus Begins to Mix with Humanity

The next step would be the identification of Ahasuerus with all mankind through his sufferings, but at first this identification is wrapped up in a continuing preoccupation with the protagonist's *Weltschmerz*. A series of little poems by F. K. Joel-Jacoby, *Klagen eines Juden* (1835) and *Harfe und Lyra* (1837), actually anticipates the theme of Mosen's *Ahasver* by insisting that the Jew must forget himself as an individual in sorrow and assume instead the burden of the whole world. The poet here seems to be thinking in rather confusing manner of the whole Jewish people, for whom Ahasuerus is a focal point. His *Weltschmerz* is at least as much political as personal. "Die Welt ist zum ewigen Juden geworden, und deines Volkes Not und Qual wälzt sich rächend über die christlichen Nationen." These poems were roughly handled by Gutzkow, as might be expected, and by Nikolaus Lenau, who spoke disparagingly of attempts to found a paper Jerusalem.[18]

Lenau, however, was a superior poet, and his interpretation of Ahasuerus, while still pretty much in the sphere of the withdrawn romantic, is more effective than many. He wrote two poems on the Wandering Jew. The first, "Ahasver, der ewige Jude" (1832), originated during a sojourn in the United States. This is a useful contribution to the tradition of the pastoral elegy, not in memory of any individual celebrity but rather of a *pastor ignotus*. A shepherd youth lies dead. Ahasuerus comes to the sorrowing mourners, telling them not to weep, for death is a blessed rest. He gazes enviously at the coffin and the crucifix, and expresses himself eloquently in a passage which is more than an echo of Chaucer's moving lines in *The Pardoner's Tale* ("O leeve moder, lat me in!"):

> O mother Earth, behold thy forgotten son,
> Crush me and take me to thy stony heart.[19]

Effective as this may be, however, the poem is important chiefly because it typifies the *Weltschmerz* that Ahasuerus has felt and continues to feel.

But then in a later poem, "Der ewige Jude," from *Gestalten* (1834-38), Lenau draws a picture of Ahasuerus both more circumstantial and more melodramatic.

In a desolate landscape, in an atmosphere rainy and lowering, hovers a vulture, symbolic of the crassness of humanity. A nearby inn promises comfort and peace, but the restless spirit of the poet sees in mystic vision the Wandering Jew on Alpine heights, with the chamois and the eagle, and invulnerable to the bullet of the huntsman, for when he is shot, the pellet flattens out to assume the likeness of the Crucifixion. For this poet the problem of Ahasuerus can be settled only by religious faith. Christ has triumphed over Ahasuerus, and the *Weltschmerz* becomes by implication a lost cause, an altogether superfluous issue, overwhelmed by the soundness and solidity of the true believer.[20]

Yet religious feeling will not suffice unless there is true contrition in the heart of suffering Ahasuerus, as is made clear in an anonymous lyric outpouring called *Christliche Legenden* (1832),[21] where the total effect is merely boring, or in Guido Görres' overlong narrative poem, "Der ewige Jude" (1844),[22] where it is lively. The prevailingly heavy didactic tone of *Christliche Legenden*—a fair specimen of a depressingly common literary type in nineteenth-century Germany—could have been lightened by a little more attention to the folkloristic aspects of the story.

All such moralizing panaceas aside, the fact remains that one important element of *Weltschmerz* is skepticism, and who is better qualified to be skeptical than the Wandering Jew, whose very career is founded upon his willingness to deny? Besides, has he not traveled over the whole world more than once and been a perpetual witness to its follies and its failures? It is therefore appropriate that one of the more important works to treat of Ahasuerus in the mid-nineteenth century should play variations on the theme of the Wandering Jew as modern skeptic. This is Hans Christian Andersen's *Ahasverus* (1844), an epic poem of wide scope, partly a telling of the Chronicle of the Wandering Jew and partly a mystery play like Quinet's *Ahasvérus*; both of these works deal in abstractions such as winds, clouds, flora, fauna, and heavenly *daemones*. Ahasuerus is the living incarnation of Ahas, the angel of doubt, but Ahasuerus' origin in doubt means a ceaseless development leading to a hope of the divine, the first example of the theory of evolution which we have as yet met with in the Legend. To be sure, the hand of Goethe is behind the shaping of part of Andersen's design. Thus his Judas is, as Goethe had conceived him, a misguided patriot. Ahasuerus himself is a man of good intentions who doubts the divinity of Christ and for that reason is thrown into sharp contrast with the repentant Barabbas and the believing Veronica. His mother and sister had been slain in a massacre, a calamity which has turned him from anything less than revenge, and yet he is moved greatly when he hears Christ preaching in the waste places. He is finally disillusioned, however, when Jesus allows himself to be captured in the garden of Gethsemane.[23]

In his course through world history, such an Ahasuerus is now a familiar figure. He is the star of a gladiatorial combat, as in Croly's *Salathiel*. He supports the Hun Attila; he views with cynicism the Crusades on the one hand and the Reformation on the other, because he believes that neither of these two tremendous human endeavors can possibly represent the true spirit of religion. Are the execution of John Hus and the fulminations of Luther against Antichrist the true measure of Christianity? The voyage of Columbus to the New World, thus revealed, might of course be expected to bring some hope for times to come, but Andersen despondently observes that the spirit of Cain is everywhere, and that the skeptical and sardonic trail along right behind it. Such progress as mankind makes must be slow to the point of anguish, and although Andersen professes faith in its ultimate triumph, he prefers not to talk much about that achievement but rather to leave it to "some better bard." Yet the attractive blend of Platonism and positivism, as revealed in the letter to his friend Henriette Wulff (July 14, 1843), is typical of the intellectual temper of the decade in which he wrote *Ahasverus*.[24]

In spite of its carefully and skillfully chosen scenes, its underlying stubbornness of moral faith, its lyrical impulses, and its artistic design, Andersen's *Ahasverus* nevertheless contains only a few notable passages, for the plain fact is that the author was not in any sense of the word a first-rate poet. He lacks perception; he lacks power; he lacks even the proper intensity of poetic imagination to carry his bard's task to satisfactory completion. The large variety of verse forms used imparts merely a sense of artistic instability, which is not at all improved when he descends, as in more than one instance, to bald prose. Yet we must concede that few writers could have managed better in a work with such limitations to keep the reader in an atmosphere of sustained doubt—the curse or the blessing, as you will, of modern times—and few thoughtful persons can very well quarrel with Andersen's thesis that the evolutionary process is most painfully slow, so slow indeed as to be barely perceptible, and constantly liable to reversion. His is, in brief, a conscientious and capable attempt to state the abstract idea of evolution, as many others were doing in the 1840's, nearly a score of years before *The Origin of Species*. For the rest, his *Ahasverus* is only another example of the weakness of many a nineteenth-century writer for "serious" work when his real strength lay in less ambitious literary flights. The fairy tales of Andersen have given him literary immortality; his *Ahasverus* has not.

The Beginnings of Ahasuerus as Representative of Mankind

Skepticism makes for liberty of thought and conscience, and so Ahasuerus as an advocate of liberty comes to have many sides, as does any liberal. This point is stressed in an amusing essay, "Der ewige Jude," written as far back as 1819 by Johann Nepomuk Hartig ("Johannes Nariscus"),[25] and later, in a more serious vein, by Karl Beck, in his *Fantasien am Grabe Poniatowskys* (1838),[26] in which the remark is made that Ahasuerus, like liberty, is unable to stand still. Or to put it in another way, liberty is the new Ahasuerus. This interpretation of the Wandering Jew is very common during the 1830's and 1840's; after the revolutions of 1848 we hear less of it, although it continues to be endemic up to our present age.

It appears, for example, more than once in Ludwig Köhler's poem, *Der neue Ahasver* (Jena, 1841), which is dedicated to German youth and appeals frankly for new blood and new ideals in German life. Köhler manages a better than average presentation of the revolutionary symbol. At the outset, Christ has overcome Jehovah, a situation which leads to the likely possibility of successful revolution all over the world. While Köhler, however, is anxious to furnish his reader with a history of revolution as such, he is obliged to point out the disillusioning fact that not all revolutionary movements are either successful or laudable just because they are revolutions. As the poem proceeds, Ahasuerus becomes less and less an active participant and more and more an interested spectator, but he is induced to fight beside the sans-culottes against the Continental powers and with the Allies against Napoleon. He follows the Greeks in their war of independence against the Turks and strives mightily for the sake of Poniatowsky in Poland. Dictators and demagogues alike are repugnant to him. A liberal like Ludwig Börne he admires to such a degree that he is willing to set him up as a third Messiah, after Christ and Martin Luther; but, standing beside Börne's tomb in questionably melodramatic taste, he decides that his idol died an expatriate and therefore unappreciated. Messiahs must be both accepted and appreciated if they are to be true Messiahs.

To this point Köhler wrote a lively and rather moving poem, precisely suited to the intellectual and political turmoil of the 1840's; immediately thereafter, however, he allowed his work to decline into a loose and very tedious review of the history of oppression—a magnificent subject which should never be treated in a loose or tedious manner. He rewards the Spanish revolutionists of his generation with pats on the back. Liberty, he concludes, is, in the long run, like the famous treasure of the Nibelungs, which brought unhappiness and disaster to all those who laid hands on it. This pessimistic attitude—and in both Köhler's and Beck's work there is plenty of disillusionment—is a thread running through much of the contemporaneous literature of revolution and suggests at least one reason why the uprisings of 1848 did not more often succeed. At the end of Köhler's poem, Christ reminds Ahasuerus that liberty is not a matter of personal aggrandizement but rather a noble end in itself.

All in all, the chief interest of Köhler's *Der neue Ahasver*, aside from its occasional flashes of literary talent, is its remarks about contemporary European politics and the possibility of liberal reform. It is hardly a defense of democracy, however, because its note of disappointment is rather too loud. The theme that the world is out of joint is, of course, too familiar for further comment. But Johann Gabriel Seidl attacked the question in an original fashion. In his "Die beiden Ahasvere" (1836), he returned to the old duality of the Wandering Jew which had first appeared in some of the variant versions of the old German Ahasuerus-book.[27] He presents two distinct personalities. An old haggard fellow appears before some jeering carousers to lament the bad times and to upbraid the world for wasting its efforts in begging a deaf God for help. He is interrupted by a tall younger man, who claps a bony hand on his shoulder and warns him not to speak lightly of a curse, "whose weight I alone understand." The true Ahasuerus, who is the younger man, insists that one must turn away from the "poison of self-help," for the evil of the world lies in the fact that it is trying to help itself instead of awaiting salvation from God. The schizophrenic situation of two alleged Wandering Jews confronting each other in argument symbolizes the ancient contention between the idealist and the pessimist. Seidl, in addition to the Ahasuerus-book, may have had in mind also Laun's *Der ewige Jude*, in which, it will be recalled, there were two Wandering Jews, one real and the other pretended.

These writers, then, all seem to agree that liberty is not an easy achievement—

often, indeed, it is a painful one. And when it comes, what then? Is the whole Jewish race to profit by it? Some romanticists think so. Berthold Auerbach wrote a novel of romantic dimensions called *Spinoza* (1837), which is basically a historical treatment of the great Jewish philosopher of the seventeenth century, but Ahasuerus is one of its major characters.[28] Spinoza, as a revolutionary thinker, meets opposition from his companions in faith, who begin to turn away from him. In his discouragement he is visited at night by Ahasuerus, who wears over his heart an iron capsule containing a little scroll, the law of Jehovah. The capsule is attached to a cord around his neck, cutting deep into his flesh. As in George Herbert's distinguished poem "The Collar," the word of God is ever about the neck of a pronounced rebel. Ahasuerus explains his own doom to the listening Spinoza. He is, in effect, the embodiment of the Jewish people, and like them he must be without rest and yet uncomplaining. At the same time, he is deeply concerned with the liberty of all mankind, and ends by hailing Spinoza as a liberator of humanity, one who can rebuild a Jerusalem.

If Auerbach's Ahasuerus, assuming now the woes of a whole nation, could only be human, could only shed tears or wreak revenge on his enemies or, best of all, could only immolate himself on the swords of his foes, he would be happier. Since none of this can be, however, because of God's bidding, he must rely on a hope in the future. He looks forward to the time when he can see not only the spiritual but the physical rebuilding of Jerusalem and the return of the Jews to Zion, their promised home. If it had been possible for Auerbach to look from 1837 to 1947, what would have been his reaction? In 1837 he is convinced, to use the words of his Ahasuerus, that the time of the return to Zion will be a time "when Love and Faith can greet each other, Justice and Peace will exchange kisses, Truth will sprout from the earth, and Equity gaze steadfastly into the heavens." It is for Spinoza, the mortal Jewish philosopher, to break the trail forward to this blessed anticipated epoch. That Ahasuerus, a believer in Jehovah, should thus hail Spinoza, an unorthodox, even a heretic, as a Messiah of the new order of Zionism is illogical, and yet a closer reading of the novel will show that Auerbach is on the side of the freethinking rather than the orthodox Jew. As a matter of record, the young Zionists of the later nineteenth century were more interested in their revolutionism than in the consistency of their intellectual posture, which they might alter at will in their fight for independence. Revolution and logic are seldom compatible dwellers in the same house.

Apart from Auerbach, there are some traces in other writers of the desire not only for Jewish independence but for a Jewish homeland. For instance, Andersen's *Ahasverus* will show a few of them. In Gustav Pfizer's "Der ewige Jude" (1831), the protagonist is closely identified with his people, working and suffering with them.[29] He thinks that all Jews bear a curse; his is the duty, however, to take as much of this upon himself as he can, in order to lighten the burden for others, and in this respect he becomes symbolic of the sufferings of all his people. Yet the independence of a Jewish nation, if it can be called a nation, was in the mid-nineteenth century very far away, and this fact was duly recognized. In a collection of somewhat over eighty short "lyric-epic" poems by the Danish poet B. S. Ingemann, *Blade af Jerusalems Skomagers Lommebog* ("Leaves from the

Memorandum Book of the Shoemaker of Jerusalem"; Copenhagen, 1833), we can read a deeply felt lamentation for the fate of the Jewish race. The poems review the past of this "eternal people," the miseries of their everlasting and tedious pilgrimages, and the hopes for their uncertain future. The verse may not be noteworthy as verse, but it is sincere and competent. Ingemann does not have the assurance of Auerbach in *Spinoza,* nor the negative crabbedness of Gutzkow, and his collection of poems as a whole looks backward, rather than forward, affording a romantic glimpse of a remarkable past instead of any consolatory vision of a glorious time to come. Much the same attitude pervades the unimportant "Der ewige Jude" (1839) of Wilhelm Wackernagel.[30]

For a more realistic bit of portraiture, one should turn to H. von Levitschnigg's "Ahasver" (1842), which is an unusual delineation in verse of a modern Jewish banker and capitalist, a Rothschild instead of a Spinoza.[31] The twentieth-century reader will be more attracted to the work of Von Levitschnigg than to that of Ingemann. Even though it possesses less authentic value as poetry, Von Levitschnigg's work is unquestionably more important than Ingemann's in the development of the Legend, if only because of his early conception of the Wandering Jew as a contemporary businessman.

The clear impression remains, nonetheless, that the nationalistic consciousness of Jews in the years around 1850 was more emotional than realistic. This is shown, for example, in Ludwig Wihl's 1838 account of the Legend in the Nuremberg *Athenaeum,*[32] in *Na piaskach* ("On the Sands") by Michal Broch (Grodno, 1845), and in "Le juif errant" (Paris, 1859) by "P. L. Jacob" (Paul Lacroix).[33] The last of these works identifies the fate of Ahasuerus with the fate of the Jewish people, as did the others, but maintains further that the Jews all must wander because they were Christ-killers. Far superior are two independent works which can close out the list of those early writings which discuss Ahasuerus as representative of his people. L. H. Wolfram, known under the pseudonym of F. Marlow, wrote a very respectable dramatic poem, *Faust* (1839), which is undoubtedly the earliest and perhaps is the best work to bring together the actually separate legends of Faust and of the Wandering Jew.[34] Here Faust, who is obviously the protagonist of the poem, stands forth as the eternal doubter. He meets Ahasuerus, who personifies the eternal Jew. Neither doubter nor Jew can ever meet death; they remain immortal phenomena in human life. In spite of an occasional tendency to confuse Ahasuerus with the famous doctor, their legends are fundamentally dissimilar, and as antagonists they are excellent foils to one another. Wolfram's Ahasver, like Faust, has faced the horrors of modern civilization; but unlike him, he is comparatively smug and has adapted himself well to his new environment, as befits a practical man who would move at ease in Zion. And so he wishes to be "jung-Deutsch"—a German of the most recent generation in 1840, who will shave off his beard and comb his wild hair and dress as is fit and proper for the citizen of the highly civilized nineteenth century. In some respects he resembles the pragmatic Wandering Jew of the eighteenth-century Chronicle (pp. 142-44 above). Nevertheless, he is sobered by the thought that "to live is the most fearsome of the fears in a wanderer's eternity." The other independent work is a well-turned ballad, "Ahasver" (1839), written by Ritter Braun von Braunthal.[35] In the ballad a Byronic dandy at a society ball resents a remark by one of the company that the Wandering Jew is only a symbol. To confute this, the dandy not only insists that he is the real Wandering Jew but, to prove his assertion, turns into a decrepit old man before the fascinated eyes of the revelers; then, as a demon lover he seizes the daughter of the house and whirls her into the wildest of frenzied *Totentänzer*. The girl soon expires. The message is evidently that the Jew, symbol or not, will always be with us and will always be too much for mere mortals to compete with.

As a supernatural individual symbolizing the Jewish people, Ahasuerus was recognized as heroic enough, but also rather dangerous. After all, to interpret Zionistic aspirations in corporeal form was a narrow symbol. If he could represent a Jewish nation or the Jewish people as a whole, why not all humanity, which also must wander through the world for its assigned term, and which in the spiritual sense is as restless and unstable as Ahasuerus ever could be? There were many who caught early the magnificence of this larger symbol and portrayed the Jew accordingly. Unfortunately there were in the 1840's no Quinets or Mosens.

Among those who saw Ahasuerus in this light is L. C. Wittich, whose poem, "Ahasuerus" (1839), borrows from Mosen but is still original enough.[36] Here Ahasuerus appears as one troubled ceaselessly by the memory of a great sin, vague and undefined. But he is fitted into a human sort of framework; he can sleep, and though thoroughly unhappy most of the time, does not want to give up life. When confronted with twin chalices, one of death and the other of a miserable life, he chooses the latter. The poet insists that his choice was the right one. From that moment of choice, Ahasuerus is revivified. A mysterious voice (his intuition) informs him that he cannot attain his goal here below. That, however, is of little importance to him; the fact remains that he is still here below. In the joyous awareness of his revitalization, the memory of the past sweeps over him. He realizes that his life is going on within the boundaries of a fixed plan, undoubtedly divine, for it is a plan traced not by hate but by love. He cannot indeed hate Him who had bid us pray for our enemies. A tear drops from his eye; then a second, for he sees a tomb on which is written: "Here lies Hilda, fairest of women, who lived but sixteen springtimes." The allegory is plain enough: humanity, with all its sins, its hopes, its fears and misgivings, may often hate life; but it clings to life all the same, constantly finding regeneration, never quite rejecting the physical and materialistic in nature, and always giving ear to that mysterious instinctual voice, which shows the way to heaven, light, and love.

So much for this hopeful, sentimental, and rather banal message. Many a poet, similarly inclined, would not be quite so optimistic. Thus the play by Langewiesche, mentioned at the beginning of this chapter, can be taken as an allegory of mankind tainted by original sin, which is incarnate in Ahasuerus. Nor would Andersen's *Ahasverus*, if considered as a commentary on the state of humanity, yield any exhilarating sense of assured well-being. Besides, should not mankind be portrayed in terms of a given generation, as Pope had put it:

> His knowledge measured to his state and place;
> His time a moment, and a point his space?[37]

This was the belief of Adalbert von Chamisso, and his "Der neue Ahasverus" (1831) is the most lucid of such allegorical treatments during his own generation.[38] In telling the old tale of the Jew, Chamisso puts himself in the Wanderer's shoes, so to speak, and brings him to philosophize about his experiences. As he sees it, all mankind must suffer and work together; in a common denominator of affliction lies the essential unity of man—friends and brothers in woe. Humanity, as typified by Ahasuerus, is bound to its time and its particular environment. A man misunderstood and uncomprehending, Ahasuerus plods through one generation after another; yet his new experiences, the new ages through which he lives, the new people he encounters, and the new languages he learns are for him the most important considerations. He has only a dull memory of the past. A single incident from Chamisso's work will serve to bring his whole outlook into focus. In it Ahasuerus sees a crowd of pilgrims retracing their steps toward Jerusalem. His despair is deepened by the sight, but so also is his realization of the essential brotherhood of man.

Something of this same point of view, more muddily expressed, will be found in Karl Simrock's "Der ewige Jude" (1844),[39] but a more cogent footnote is added by a talented writer, Isaac Rosenfeld, who in his "Der ewige Jude" of 1838 had observed that all of us as individuals must bear our curse uncomplainingly and without respite; all of us must wander through a bewildering land; and any one who does this is truly the Wandering Jew.[40]

CHAPTER TEN

Mid-Century Satirists and Eugène Sue

In considering the symbolic potential of the figure of Ahasuerus, it is easy to overlook some of the more sprightly trivialities of the Legend before 1850, which are not only amusing but revealing. Many of these ephemeral pieces are unabashedly farcical; others may be serious enough in their main intent but unconsciously relegate Ahasuerus to a comic and undignified role or otherwise achieve unfortunate effects. A whole subchapter, for example, could be devoted to the appearance of the Wandering Jew in the Paris theaters between 1830 and 1850. Another subchapter, at least, could go into the account of the pictorial representations—some serious, some caricatures—of Ahasuerus the wanderer. Although mere froth, most of these minor efforts serve as necessary complements to the career of the Wandering Jew as a whole, and the very fact that they are minor is clear testimony to the continuing popularity of the Legend. Besides, the great number of ambitious works treating of Ahasuerus may lead us to forget that he could be a source of amusement.

A typical illustration of the kind of writing I have in mind is the work of an anonymous writer in *Petites misères de la vie humaine* (Paris, 1843). One of the pieces in this collection of humorous sketches is entitled "Old Nick et Granville," for the simple reason that neither name appears in the story. This is a bit of Gallic fluff telling how an ardent swain could have used the five sous in the purse of the Wandering Jew but did not have them and so lost his girl.

In other instances, the purpose of the author might even be grave, and yet his execution might be so unskillful that the result would be only bathetic. A Passion play is not exactly to be construed as farce, but in Friedrich Radewell's *Die Passion* (Weimar, 1840) we get a perverted choral effect which damns the play forever to the realm of the funny. Here Ahasuerus is a Jewish patriot, skeptical of Christ, whose temporizing he detests. He is much more violently against the Saviour than is Caiaphas; in fact, he almost succeeds in getting his hands on Christ as early as Palm Sunday, but Roman soldiers keep him off. One touch from this Palm Sunday scene should not soon be forgotten, and that is the disconcerting chorus of praise sung by sweet little children, who invoke incessantly a "Himmelentfliessender, Blumenbegiessender" blessing on the Lord. As far as hate is concerned, this Ahasuerus possesses a superfluity of the commodity, and the scenes between him and Judas degenerate into the vocabulary of drunken fishmongers: he calls Judas a "dirty scrub," and Judas retaliates by designating him as a "flatulent frog." The whole conclusion of the play is ineptly handled, so that the work, potentially important, becomes an unconscious burlesque of a sublime subject.[1]

It will be recalled that in the last years of the eighteenth century Andrew Franklin wrote a comedy, *The Wandering Jew: Or Love's Masquerade*, in which the Jew served as a vehicle for impersonation. A young man posed as the Wanderer in order to bring off a financially successful marriage. Claude Tillier, in *Mon oncle Benjamin* (1843), a comic novel of what the English might call the picaresque variety, resorts to much the same device for one of the incidents in his book.[2] This time Uncle Benjamin poses as the Wandering Jew as much out of sheer perversity as anything, for he is that kind of character. In the little village of Moulot, our red-faced, expansive, bibulous rascal of a Benjamin announces in the market place that he is indeed the Wandering Jew. His old mother interferes with his scene by asking him what he is doing there. He pretends not to know her:

"Monsieur Wandering Jew," said a peasant in whose mind still lingered some doubt, "who, then, is this lady who just shook her fist at you?"

"My good friend," answered my uncle, not at all disconcerted, "she is the Holy Virgin, whom God has ordered me to escort on a pilgrimage to Jerusalem on that little ass. She is really a good woman, but a little talkative; she is ill-humored this morning because she has lost her rosary."

"And why is not the infant Jesus with her?"

"God did not wish her to take Him along, because just now He has the smallpox."[3]

There are serious objections to this startling statement, but Uncle Benjamin parries them. The schoolmaster wants to know what has happened to the Wandering Jew's traditional beard. Benjamin explains that it got dirty too easily, and so he disposed of it. How could he shave, since he could never stop moving? God sent down the patron saint of barbers in the form of a butterfly, and he was shaved with the edge of its wing. There are more such embarrassing questions, but the fertility of Benjamin's imagination produces all the right answers. A pretty girl begs him to work a miracle by curing her invalid father. After bussing her heartily, Benjamin consents to try, saying that he expects to be canonized some day. Going to her house, he discovers that the father of the family, not a true invalid, has dislocated his jaw in trying to break a walnut with his teeth. With the aid of an iron spoon, the miracle is achieved, and Benjamin is on his way. It is all harmless horseplay and very well sustained.

The five sous of the traditional Wandering Jew puzzled many good people in Uncle Benjamin's village. For that matter, they puzzled also more serious thinkers with little information at their disposal, as J. B. Salques illustrates in his "Le juif errant" (*ca.*1820), which is much more speculation about the inexhaustible purse than about the Wandering Jew himself.[4] At least one humorist of the day, however, saw a good use for these ubiquitous sous. A diverting, anonymous little almanac and *apologie* for smokers, *La physiologie du fumeur* (Brussels, *ca.*1850), asserts with all the seriousness in the world that Ahasuerus always carried with him an ounce of tobacco, and his enjoyment of the precious weed was such that God, who did not approve of too much happiness, took the Jew out of circulation, lest one good custom should corrupt the world.[5]

Sometimes, however, the allegedly humorous treatment was downright silly, particularly when the Germans tried to be amusing. The prize absurdity of this kind is in *Der Erzähler,* an annual *Taschenbuch* or giftbook, which in its 1846 number explains that Ahasuerus, caught in the celebrated Prague fire, saved himself from a burning building by swathing himself in rubber garments and jumping out the window, whereupon he became a new kind of Wandering Jew, because his rubber clothing made him bounce so high that he is still bouncing.[6]

But to give the Germans their due, one of the most satirical as well as the most amusing of these farcical handlings of the Legend appeared in Eduard M. Dettinger's *Narrenalmanach* for 1845.[7] This entry was apparently influenced by Eugène Sue's novel and, like Bierglas' puppet play, discussed later, seems to have come into existence while the French novel was appearing in the pages of the Paris *Constitutionnel.* It belabors some of the prominent publishers of Leipzig and then launches into an account of the Wandering Jew as a *cursor mundi,* always looking for some way to end his wretched days. It quotes extensively from Schubart's poem, in which, it will be remembered, Ahasuerus tried to meet death and never succeeded. On one occasion, while he was poking around in Denmark,

He hit upon the capital idea of cutting his throat in two. As luck would have it, there was a razor lying near at hand, but no soapstone to sharpen it; still, a man who has traveled about as much as Ahasver would have a ready solution. He whetted the dull razor on the sole of his boot until he thought it was sharp enough; then with the greatest peace of spirit he cut right into the middle of his throat. But evidently the throat of the Wandering Jew must have been different from ours, for instantly it was healed over —and Ahasver remained alive. He shook his head and said only, "God damn!"

Most surprisingly, however, he one day finally achieved his desire. In Hamburg he was suffering from a mild indisposition, and against the advice of friends and acquaintances he sought the professional services of the famous Dr. Phips. The patient died in a remarkably short time; even his most pessimistic friends had not thought it could happen so quickly. Following this embarrassing business, there was a commotion in heaven:

Ahasver went straight to Paradise. When he arrived at the gates of Heaven, St. Peter drew a very frowning, thoughtful face, but, in view of his extremely advanced years, let him pass within.

The Wandering Jew moved through the great alley of poplars, where our Saviour, who was walking alone arm in arm with God the beloved Father, suddenly caught sight of him.

"Papa," said the Son to the Father, "there comes the Wandering Jew."

"*Mort de ma vie!* How did that fellow get in here?"

"Ask him."

"Jew," said the Eternal One, "how did you get in here? Did you really die?"

"Yes, dear God."

"Who treated you?"

"Herr Doktor Phips, in Hamburg."

"Well, my beloved Son, against such a man We cannot hope to prevail," said the Lord to the Saviour, and walked away.

And so the Wandering Jew was redeemed.

A Note on Ahasuerus in the Boulevard Theater

Meanwhile, Ahasuerus continued to make entrances and exits on the stage of Paris theaters. I leave aside from consideration here the dramatic pieces obligated to either Lewis' *The Monk* or Sue's *Le juif errant*. Even so, we still find the Jew entertaining audiences in the boulevard theaters, where he did little more than sing *complaintes* and serve as an occasion for fireworks. He had more substantial roles in the Théâtre Ambigu, so called because its list of offerings was of such great variety that no one could ever be sure what sort of play to expect there— whether, as Polonius puts it, "tragedy, comedy, history, pastoral, pastoral-comical, historical-pastoral, tragical-historical, tragical-comical-historical-pastoral, scene individable, or poem unlimited: Seneca cannot be too heavy nor Plautus too light."[8] As a matter of record, most of the plays at the Théâtre Ambigu between 1830 and 1850 were of the spectacular kind of fantasy, with often lurid stage effects, considerable melodrama, and quite a bit of purely farcical vaudeville. Indeed, Ahasuerus sometimes was useful in the plays of the Théâtre Ambigu by serving as a means of bringing together vaudeville and serious drama in the spirit of the fine arts. So it is in Dutertre de Veteuil's *Le Réveil de l'Ambigu* (Paris, 1841), which contains a song or two or three by the Wandering Jew, including the famous Brabantine ballad.

A good example of such fantasy is *Le juif errant* (Paris, 1834) by "Jacob."[9] It is a "morality play of the boulevards," which tells of a youth who is persuaded by his uncle that he must be Ahasuerus, for the uncle wishes to have the boy out of the running when it comes to dividing the family fortune. With the help of two friends, a chemist and an actress, the youth is enabled to have a vision of demons, archangels, and even the Seven Deadly Sins, thus confounding the scheming uncle. There is enough singing in the piece to qualify it as an operetta and some of the songs were gathered in the *Chansonnier du magasin théâtral* (Paris, 1835). A weird scene tying together the young man Isaac, an archangel, Lechery, and a balloonist who prophesies the air age to come, like the hero in Tennyson's *Locksley Hall* (not yet published), offers a remarkable quartet.

Sue and His Influence

What we have just examined has been light satire, without any great animus behind it—the humorous observation of mores with a special predilection for the fanciful or ludicrous. But there was one work of importance from this mid-nineteenth-century library on the Wandering Jew which carried a strong attack, not so much satirical as broadly propagandistic. This happens to be by all odds the most popular and influential of all the works of fiction treating of Ahasuerus. The author of the attack was Eugène Sue, who was at one time considered the equal, in respect to stories of adventure, of none other than Alexandre Dumas *père*. The object of the attack was the order of the Society of Jesus, expelled from France in 1765, suppressed by papal decree in 1773, restored to grace after the defeat of its enemy Napoleon in 1814, and dispersed once again after the popular revolution in France in 1830. Sue, who had developed during the 1830's a pronounced Socialist leaning, was even more of an opportunist than his contemporary, Charles

Dickens, when it came to riding to battle for a social cause. At the same time, he was no more of a leader in these causes than was Dickens, for his role was always that of an observer and reporter who knows what the public wants to think and is quick to exploit the taste of his readers. We are justified in calling him a literary soldier of fortune. He had drifted from medicine into writing, through Byronic and Gothic channels. He first ventured to turn out maritime novels in the manner of Frederick Marryat; then he traversed the field of the historical novel, and finally hit full stride in his long stories, picaresque in structure, of the underworld and the submerged masses. *Les mystères de Paris* (1842-43) and *Le juif errant* (1844-45) are highly colored, full of specious incident (which he nevertheless controlled with considerable skill), and spiced with the social messages in the air at the time. The structure and the variety of incidents in Sue's novels, as in so many nineteenth-century novels, were dictated in great measure by the fact that they came out in installments. Sue's name is, indeed, indelibly associated with the *roman feuilleton*, the novel running in newspapers; *Le juif errant*, for example, appeared first in the pages of the Paris *Constitutionnel*. His success was great; his artistic achievement, unfortunately, left much to be desired.[10]

Yet *Le juif errant* remains unquestionably the most celebrated single literary treatment of the Legend of the Wandering Jew. In more ways than one this is regrettable, because the novel is not one which can bear much critical scrutiny. In various details it challenges comparison with Victor Hugo's *Les Misérables* of about fifteen years later, but the challenge cannot be long maintained. From our particular point of view, Sue has done the Legend a disservice, because the title of the novel is misleading. The story is not primarily about the Wandering Jew at all. He is hardly to be considered a major character, although he is doubtless a kind of integrating element for a portion of the novel. Rather the narrative is concerned with the generally successful efforts of the Jesuits, who are guided by the fanatical, ruthless strategy of the villainous Rodin, to win for their order a fortune of millions of francs which would otherwise be assigned to the several heirs of the Huguenot family of Rennepont. These heirs must be in a certain house in Paris on a certain day at a certain hour, and Rodin does his best to prevent this. He is temporarily frustrated in his designs when the Wandering Jewess (see Appendix B) appears at the crucial moment as *dea ex machina* and shows that there is a codicil to the original Rennepont will which postpones matters for a few months. In the meantime, cholera rides Paris like a nightmare—the evil epidemic of 1832. There follow savage pictures of the Paris underworld dancing about on the graves of victims of the pestilence—riot, ribaldry, insane intoxication and desire, lynchings, violence of the most repellent kind; in short, a true sadistic as well as Gothic debauch. There are kidnappings, false arrests, robberies, murders, attempted deflowerings which stop just short of actual rape. There is never a dull moment in the novel, which concludes with all of the important characters either dead or dying, except for a few noble souls who want little here below and do not want that little for long.

From the ten octavo volumes in which Sue's *Le juif errant* was published (Paris, 1844-45) after it completed its course in the Paris *Constitutionnel*, there remain three scenes in which the Wandering Jew holds a dominant position on the stage.

The timely intervention of the Wandering Jewess, his sister, has already been mentioned. The first of these three scenes is a prologue to the novel. The setting is the Bering Straits between Asia and North America. The landscape is barren and desolate. The Wandering Jew is on the Siberian side; his sister on the American. His tracks in the snow are made by iron-shod shoes, from the soles of which protrude seven nails to form the figure of a cross. In silence the two figures confront each other across the miles of open water. If Sue intended to stress symbolism in the fact that the Jew is here discovered in the Old World looking toward the New, and the Jewess in the New World looking toward the Old—man looking toward the future and woman toward the traditional order of things—he takes little account of it thereafter. Instead, he proceeds at once to the year 1831 and introduces us to the first of the group of Rennepont claimants, who are journeying toward Paris in order to be there, at 3 rue St. François at high noon on February 13, 1832, to receive their shares of the princely patrimony. Then appear lion tamers, Napoleonic veterans, innocent little girls, independent young heiresses with advanced social ideas, the Assassins or Thugs of the East Indies, the Jesuits in Paris, any number of unsavory characters on the fringe of the underworld or within it, and, last but not least, a poor but honest hunchbacked virgin. We encounter shipwrecks, starvations, ambushes, and all the variety of treacheries of which the human imagination is capable. We collide head on with the grim specter of pestilence in pandemic form. Through most of this Ahasuerus remains a mere shadow; indeed, he is absent from the pages far more than he is present in them. Once he appears on a battlefield to encourage a badly wounded general. Again, he impresses a Thug with his inability to stay dead when killed and buried. But his assistance, obviously on the side of the Renneponts and against the Jesuits, is successful only in a negative way. He delays but cannot avert the murders. When the Jesuits have apparently won, he is able to burn the treasure and prevent it from getting into their hands. He broods long and well and gives a saintly aroma of the supernatural to some of the proceedings, but in all the long and hopelessly involved sequence of events he is seldom a participating character.

Still, when cholera appears in Paris, he has a second long scene. In his ancient function as a porter of pestilence—never exemplified so spectacularly as here—he is entitled to a few moments on the stage. In this dire social emergency, we discover for the first time that all the claimants to the Rennepont fortune are sprung from his sister's womb. No wonder the Jewess is involved:

> The history of this one family is the history of the whole human race!
> Passing through what innumerable generations, running through the veins of the poor and the rich, of the robber and the sovereign, of the sage and the idiot, of the hero and the dastard, of the saint and the atheist, has not my sister's blood been perpetuated in this very hour!
> ONWARD! ONWARD![11]

Now Ahasuerus reviews briefly the scene of his original misdeed. His fate is to follow the fortunes of the Renneponts and to aid them wherever and whenever possible. Yet even his supernatural help, to repeat, cannot suffice to prevent hardship and, ultimately, death for most of the seven major claimants. Later, before the gates of Paris during the epidemic, he repeats his monologue. This time, however, the Christian doctrine of the golden rule has impressed itself upon him, so that he begins to identify himself with humanity. But he cannot linger, for a voice draws him onward.

All in vain. For the cholera continues to rage, and many of the Rennepont descendants are struck down by it. Even Rodin, the Jesuit archvillain, is afflicted, but heroically brutal methods of treatment restore him to life at the last minute, and he proceeds to dispose of the progeny of the Wandering Jewess with inexorable success, in spite of all the prayers raised on high against him. The innocence, ignorance, stupidity, and general ineffectiveness of the Rennepont heirs can hardly be equaled elsewhere in fiction. It is hardly a surprise, therefore, to hear that the Jewess finds herself growing old; even death itself may be waiting for her in the offing.

Then, on a third occasion, when the postponed day of reckoning has arrived, when all but a few of the Rennepont claimants have died, and the fiendish Rodin has managed to delay the arrival of the survivors until the appointed hour has passed, only to fall dead of poison just as he is about to get his hands on the long-desired treasure and hand it over to his order, we have a sublime anticlimax. The fortune is consumed by a fire set by the mysterious caretaker of the house at 3 rue de St. François—the Wandering Jew. After that there is a glimpse four years into the future, where poor but worthy Agricol and his family, the sole survivors among the claimants, are living in idyllic peace and sufficiency, though still haunted by the misfortunes which have destroyed their relatives.

After the slaughter which concludes the main action of the novel, after those who had sought the treasure have been hurried along the way of all flesh, there is an epilogue in which the Wandering Jew and the Wandering Jewess, brother and sister, meet in an unspecified forest in an unnamed valley. Both have fulfilled their vague missions on earth and are ready to depart because their well-earned rest is at hand. From their dying speeches, we are correct in assuming that their sympathies had always been with the workers of the world. Indeed, throughout the novel they had been in rapport with Monsieur Hardy and his workers. In brief, they have been symbols of the champions of the oppressed of the world, male as well as female.

Sue finished *Le juif errant* only three years before Karl Marx published the *Communist Manifesto*. Meanwhile, throughout his generation, there had arisen various socialistic schemes in France and elsewhere, and nowhere more plentifully than in the United States. Most notable of these were those of François Charles Marie Fourier (1772-1837), whose arrangement of society into *phalanges*, or phalanxes, living in a communal establishment, or phalanstery, attracted wide attention from the liberals and a storm of abuse from the conservatives. The employees of Monsieur Hardy, in *Le juif errant*, lived in quarters and under a working regime which resembled the Fourieristic phalanstery. Throughout the novel come various attacks on British and Dutch imperialism, and on the tyrannical rich. There are diatribes against insufficient wages paid to laborers, and the distribution of medals to the undeserving. Sue gives also an ardent defense of the total establishment of trade-unionism and demands better living and working conditions for artisans, especially the female of the species. He adopts throughout a leftist viewpoint in politics. Whether or not he is sincere in this none can say for a certainty, but he clearly appealed to the liberal and radical segments of society at a time when unrest and rebellion were seething all over Europe, and the revolutions of 1848 were at hand. The same kind of literary opportunism, to take an uncharitable attitude, may be evident in Sue's championing of the cause of women, which attracted attention in radical circles at the time. It is probably because of this interest that we have the figure of the Wandering Jewess in this novel; never before had she been so articulate in word and action.

In all fairness to Sue, however, we should observe that his Wandering Jew tends to identify himself with the downtrodden multitude of laboring men and women. The descendants of his sister may have been defeated in their purpose, but he sees in the liberal program of an enlightened employer like Monsieur Hardy the hope for a brighter future for the workers. When that happy day shall have come, both he and his sister will be ready to die. In fact, they believe that things have progressed so far, by the time of the final scene, that they can begin preparations for their end. He has worked to help the wage slave, and she not only to help her descendants, but womankind in general. His sympathy for the worker lies partly in the fact that he was once himself a shoemaker, and partly in the development in him of a Christian spirit. He has so identified himself with the workingman, in fact, that Christ's curse has struck not only him but the workers also, through him. This is how it has been for centuries, but now a new day is coming, and with it the release of Ahasuerus.

The popularity of *Le juif errant* was enormous, not only in France but throughout Europe. The blood-and-thunder narrative was partly responsible, but the particular timing of the early editions was even more so. There had been a ground swell of anti-Jesuit feeling in western Europe, analogous to the anti-Masonic movements in the United States at about the same time—a tendency to make secret or mystical orders into scapegoats for the prevailing hard times. One sign of the popularity as well as the limitations of the novel is the way in which it lent itself to successful parody. The only one of these worth reading today, however, is that turned out by Charles Philipon and Louis Huart (1844), which was translated into German by F. C. Funke and anonymously into English in the very next year.[12]

For perhaps the best single criticism of Sue's work, it is advisable to turn to none other than Edgar Allan Poe, one of the world's greatest writers of the Gothic, who considered the supernatural elements in Sue's novel spurious, the introduction of Ahasuerus' sister, the Wandering Jewess, absurd, and puts his finger on the essential weakness of not using the Wandering Jew to positively further the plot.[13] What Poe does not stress sufficiently, however, are that the novel is so crammed with incident, held just enough under control, and the narrative action so fast-paced that it is not a work which a reader who has willingly suspended his disbelief will impatiently lay aside, once he has begun it. Moreover, all critical judgments aside, the fact remains that it was a large rock dropped in a pool, and the resulting splash and ripples were some years in subsiding, if indeed they have ever done so.

To return for a moment to the anti-Jesuit writing of the time, the most important act of aggression against the Society, that which triggered a noisy controversy, was the pamphlet against the Jesuits entitled *Des jésuites* (Paris, 1843), by that influential political and literary pair, Jules Michelet and Edgar Quinet.[14] Sue's novel did nothing to quell the controversy. The traditional sensitivity of the modern Catholic to any form of unfavorable criticism of the Church, to say nothing of unsolicited attack, is manifest in the pamphlets of rebuttal which appeared almost immediately. Thus the lively treatise by Victor Joly, *Des Jésuites, etc.* (1845), is a bustling exposition of the origins and purposes of the Society of Jesus and praises extravagantly the career of its founder, St. Ignatius of Loyola (1491-1556).[15] There is much heat and acrid smoke but very little fire and no light to speak of. An English translation of Joly, by J. Fairplay (obviously a pseudonymous creature), came out in 1845, and a German translation from Switzerland in that next year.[16] The English translation degenerates at times into a rather incoherent paraphrase, and yet it is the best written pamphlet in the group, even if it does conclude with the unexciting maxim that, "I have learned to judge with caution." The net result of a judicious examination by a truly impartial observer of the attitude in Sue's novel and also these pamphlets would be that in all of them the positions assumed are extreme and none is fair. For that matter, Sue's arch-Jesuit conspirator Rodin is one of the most tenacious and implacable melodramatic villains of any level of fiction, high or low.

One ambitious reply to Sue, however, just misses being a notable historical novel. This is J. Collin de Plancy's *Légende du Juif-Errant* (1847), based on the career of John of Leyden and the debacle of the Anabaptists of Münster in 1535.[17] The work has vigor and some real characterization, nor is it so long as to be wearisome. Its attitude, however, is so strongly pro-Catholic, or anti-Protestant, that it detracts from the integrity of the narrative. The strangely fanatical figure of John of Leyden comes through successfully, and his polygamous experiments are at least interesting, though the women involved are a singularly uniform group, fit only to be the brides of John of Leyden. They are submissive and stupid and ignorant. The Wandering Jew appears as both a spy for the Anabaptists and an intervener in a crisis. He holds back the hand about to strike with the avenging dagger; he reveals the plans of the Catholic leaders and so postpones the final day of reckoning for John of Leyden; he guides one of John's venturesome queens in her escape from the Catholic besiegers of Münster. As a novel, De Plancy's work is assuredly better than Sue's; it is comparatively tight and fast-moving in its narrative; it does not suffer from an overwhelming plot; it has both unity and climax.

Although it is very much of a belated example, Paul Féval's *La fille du juif errant* (Paris, 1878) remains an excellent example of Sue's influence. Féval, indeed, once wrote *Les mystères de Londres* to match Sue's *Les mystères de Paris,* and even late in life he retained Sue's naïveté of style and baldness of characterization. He, too, was once a writer of the *roman feuilleton.* Yet he gave an unusual twist to the Legend which has not since been imitated. According to him there are five Wandering Jews. First there is Ahasuerus (Isaac Laquedem), our old friend. Then there is Cataphilus (*sic*), the porter (*sic*) of Pontius Pilate. The third is one Ozer, the soldier who gave the dying Christ a sponge full of vinegar when he was thirsty on the Cross (Matthew 27:48). The fourth is the Pharisee Nathan, who allowed the money-changers to enter the Temple. The fifth is the servant of the high priest Caiaphas. Specifically he is called Caiaphas' valet, but he fills the slot ordinarily occupied by Malchus. Of these five the last two seem to be Féval's invention. Only the first three are significant in his novel. Ahasuerus is the only benevolent one. Cataphilus wishes him to be destroyed and tries unsuccessfully to do so. The truly vicious one, however, is Ozer, who is, in effect, a destructive spirit able, by the use of chemicals, to introduce himself into the body of a virtuous man and change him into an evildoer—having first exchanged souls with the victim, whose own spirit Ozer keeps in a little sealed test tube. In this way he can change a loving father into an abusive parent, or a silly Englishman into a soulless animal. Sooner or later his victims must slave away in a kind of limbo in a mine in the Hartz Mountains. Ozer has headquarters in Paris during the revolution of 1830. He lives in a sinister rooming house run by Potiphar's wife; there live, among others, Nathan the Pharisee and the servant of Caiaphas, Wandering Jews four and five.

Ahasuerus, as usual, intervenes at critical moments. For example, he manages to save from death in a burning house little Vicomte Paul, son of Count Roland. When the Count becomes one of Ozer's victims, Ahasuerus, in the company of his little daughter Ruthael, redeems Roland by interfering with the desperate machinations of Ozer, destroying the villain and also the entire menagerie of desperate spirits in the rooming house, and restoring to the Count his lost soul. Ruthael exists in double form: she is the beautiful adopted daughter of Count Roland who later marries Paul, but in spirit she is a ghostlike creature, not unlike a flickering flame, who accompanies her father Ahasuerus in all of his altruistic missions. Ahasuerus is not merely a final resource for good against evil, as he was in Sue's *Le juif errant*. He is also, as in Sue's novel, a supporter of liberty, who moves unwounded amid the barricades of 1830. Féval tries to convince us that Ahasuerus is a participant in the revolution on the side of the supporters of Louis-Philippe. But in aiding Vicomte Paul and his bewitched father Roland, Ahasuerus is also aiding the mother and wife, Louise, who is the goddaughter of the dethroned Louis XVIII; and so, by implication, he becomes a political as well as a social harmonizer. Here, however, there is nothing of the interest which Sue showed in Monsieur Hardy's phalansteries. The support given to the revolutionaries of 1830 is perfunctory. The author's intention, as he explains in his preface, is to write something "légère et même moqueuse." The light touch appears in some of the narrative, it is true, and the mocking references to things German are good-humored enough, considering how short a time it has been since the Franco-Prussian War. But of actual satire there is very little—a gossiping bourgeoise, a monomaniac psychiatrist who considers himself to be the true Wandering Jew. The rest is post-Romantic fantasy.

It is possible, though rather unlikely, that both Sue and Féval knew the anonymous farrago of adventure entitled *Der ewige Jude: Eine komische Geschichte*, first printed as early as 1800 but given a revision in 1840.[18] This is the tale of a greedy individual who is prevented by Ahasuerus from marrying young Melchem, whom the Jew places safely in the hands of her lover Wilhelm. The altruistic philosophy of Ahasuerus is maintained in a slyly humorous vein, but the main point is his position as a confirmed benefactor, which is maintained at all costs. It is hardly possible to determine whether an anonymous prose piece, *Ahasver, der ewige Jude der Urzeit* (Leipzig-Meissen, 1844), exerted an influence on Sue or not, but it is likely that the influence worked in reverse, for Sue's novel had already begun to appear in installments by 1844. In this pamphlet, at any rate, Ahasuerus is presented as a sage counselor of the downtrodden proletariat.

One of the most curious and inaccessible works inspired by Sue is *Der ewige Jude: Ein Berliner Puppenspiel,* published at Demmin in 1844, but listed in the bibliographies as of 1884. It must have been almost the first work to follow in Sue's tracks. Indeed, its author, one most pleasantly and appropriately named A. Bierglas (doubtless a pseudonym), must have picked up the incidents for his play from the early installments of Sue's novel in the *Constitutionnel* and rushed into production without waiting to see how the plot developed, for his work would seem to be a full year older at least than the last pages of *Le juif errant.* This trifle is a one-act skit, though whether it was meant to be played throughout by puppets or is only a puppet play within a play need not vex us further. Its main significance lies in its satire on such types of North German citizenry as would go to see a puppet play on the Wandering Jew. The owner of the theater greets his gathering audience, which comprises a dyspeptic grouch, a garrulous graybeard escaping temporarily from his wife, and an ineffable Prussian fool from Kolau with his stupid son, whose ears he boxes continually after the manner of a Prussian paterfamilias. The humor of the piece is broad, not to say low, based on wretched puns and misunderstood words, even malapropisms ("symphomanie" becomes "nymphomanie"). As to the puppet play finally presented to this collection of dolts, it consists of a prologue and two or three scenes which show us the Napoleonic veteran Dagobert, the animal trainer, and the two little girls (all four among the claimants to the Rennepont fortune) on their journey to Paris. These all had appeared in the early chapters of Sue's novel. The audience receives the entertainment most unfavorably, and the play ends in general disorder. Leidenberg, the proprietor, cannot see how such a masterpiece could have failed to please. He is sure that some kink in the production must have been to blame, but he cannot for the life of him determine what it could have been. He is deeply apologetic to the audience, but his remarks cannot still the tumultuous " 'Raus mit'n ewigen Juden!" and the scrimmage resulting therefrom. There is no suggestion that this playlet has any anti-Semitic purpose; on the contrary, the audience is such an idiotic, boorish assemblage that one might suspect "Bierglas" of being antinational. At any rate, he is not anti-Jesuit.

Since 1845, Sue's *Le juif errant* has appeared in over forty French reprints, over a dozen in England and America, and several in every language of western Europe. It can be found today in cheap paperback editions in American drugstores. It soon received its inevitable dramatizations—first by Montdidier and Saint-Ernest in 1849, then by D'Ennery, Dinaux, and Sue himself in 1850.[19] The 1849 play, with its happy ending, is a silly, sentimental, ranting effort, almost as outrageous to one familiar with the novel as it would be to hear that Hamlet and Ophelia were married and lived happily ever after. In Germany the French plays were anticipated by a stodgy drama by Carl Schmidt ("Carlschmidt"), *Der ewige Jude von Eugène Sue* (Darmstadt, 1846). Later, Leopold Lewis, George Lander, and T. G. Paulton concocted English versions (1894),[20] with scarcely better results. There was a French film version in 1926.[21] The essential difficulty with all of these plays is that the narrative material is simply too vast and sprawling to lend itself to a proper integration of dramatic forces. The possibilities of any such dramatization of *Le juif errant* were most cleverly parodied in Johann Nestroy's *Zwei ewige Juden und keiner*, produced in 1846 as a burlesque with music, under the title of *Der fliegende Holländer zu Fuss* ("The Flying Dutchman on Foot"). It was not published until the complete works of the author appeared in 1891.[22] There are here plenty of allusions to the Wandering Jew and some amusing sidelights on the problems of a stage director, but the play adds nothing of consequence to the Legend.

When we ponder Sue's ultimate contribution to the story of Ahasuerus, we see that Poe was right in most respects. The Jew serves only an external purpose in *Le juif errant*. He is a harbinger of pestilence and the ultimate destroyer of the long-sought-for treasure. His sister manages to delay matters at a critical moment and thus enables the novel to continue through another thirty chapters or so. Both the Jew and the Jewess are awaiting death at the end; this is at best an unorthodox conclusion (although it has happened before, as we have seen) and at worst sentimental melodrama. What is striking, however, is that Sue casts Ahasuerus as a champion of the workingman—the humble shoemaker of Jerusalem has become a spokesman for labor, and his protest against the fate of the laboring man is the protest of all workers against their oppressors, real or fancied, who in this novel are the rich, the idle, the arrogant, and the Jesuits. In spite of this significant detail, it is probably true that Sue has given many a wrong conception of the Legend, in the sense that most people know of the Legend only through Sue's novel.

Miscellaneous Satirical Writings

Apart from Sue and De Plancy one might easily get the general impression that, so far as the French of around 1850 were concerned, it was fashionable to think of Ahasuerus as did the author of the jingle of the early 1800's which depicted him as sorry that he did not have the bus fare to enable him to turn to vehicular transportation. Such is the tenor of the satirical verses in *Les accords enchanteurs*, a gift book of about 1850.[23] Some of this flippancy may be due to the unwillingness of the more discerning French readers to take Sue's novel seriously.

Such is certainly not typical, however, of the general treatment of Ahasuerus elsewhere at this time. Every now and then, for example, we will meet a hyperserious German treatment, for we can always depend upon a nineteenth-century German to wax philosophical. Perhaps, as has been said before, it was philosophy that kept nineteenth-century Germany together in one piece. Thus, at the very height of the Sue vogue, we have the case of J. Georg Köberle's *Der neue Thurm zu Babel: Oder Ahasverus und seine Gesellen* (Leipzig, 1847). The author was a Catholic priest. The date of the work is significant, for in page after page of the novel of two volumes there is sounded the note of social dissatisfaction, and an inference which will not be downed that the old order is corrupt and that the carrion should be removed from the scene. We meet Rudolf, a young and unstable libertarian. Under somewhat sinister circumstances he meets a Jew named Ahas, older brother to Ahasuerus, who typifies the wanderlust of mankind. Rudolf is an antisocial individual with patent Byronic inclinations and an incurable, distressing habit of breaking into commonplace song. He comes to a little German town, where he takes lodgings in the house of the town assessor Burgstaff, is impressed by Burgstaff's fair daughter Clothilde, and comes across an old acquaintance, the vagabond journalist Duderstein. Duderstein knows that Rudolf has an indefinite shady past—for his name is not Rudolf Horst but Ferdinand Torsten—and blackmails him to the extent of demanding odd lots of small change from time to time and blocking Rudolf's attempted love-making with Clothilde, in whom Duderstein is himself interested. One of the amusing passages in the earlier part of the novel comes in the picture of a small-town German "literary society," an organization hedged about with all sorts of little pettifogging rules and regulations. The meeting which Rudolf attends spends far more time on a discussion of the various grades of membership in the society than in any serious consideration of a literary or critical nature. One individual, Wellner the shoemaker's son, indulges in some pertinent reflections on Jewish authors, but Köberle observes acidly that his judgments are "exceedingly shallow." In fact, Wellner's literary standards, like those of the other members of the society, add up to a devastatingly apt description of the taste which prevails in any age:

Cries of joy from the masses were the utmost success after which he chased, in restless disregard of a nobler aim. Theatrical effects without psychological characterization; witty sallies and little coherence; empty love-stories without romance; highly colored treatment without motivation; and a superficial kind of dialogue without intelligence—these were the chief traits of his ideals in literature.[24]

One might expect the Wandering Jew to burst into such an assembly bringing with him a sulphurous atmosphere, and he does so. After delivering a few remarks, laden with brimstone, on the validity of the society's endeavors, he disappears in a cloud of dust, just as in Caigniez's comedy he rode away on a whirlwind. Later in the novel comes a rather deft attack on the local theater—the pompous, bumbling manager and producer; the feeble dramatic compositions of the local citizens, the torchbearers of general culture in the community. Knix, the manager, and Knax, the star actor, are indeed a silly pair. They are merged into a duplex character, Knix-Knax, and between them the dramatic aspirations of the town fall miserably to the ground.

Again Ahasuerus appears, this time to stand around and observe with apathy the various mix-ups in the lives of the characters. Eventually he bows to his immutable sentence and wanders away in an absurdly Byronic mood, through a landscape and atmosphere worthy of Childe Harold at his most febrile. Arriving in another town, he is promptly hustled into jail as an unauthorized stranger. Here he finds the mysterious Torsten, alias Rudolf—another unauthorized stranger —who becomes his friend. It appears now that the Jew has become "superior to his race," whatever that may mean, and has no use for Torsten's poetic laments and egotistical woe. Indeed, he is ready to break the poet's lyre and to suggest to him more strenuous consolation. This he does by introducing the bewildered young man to a Walpurgis Night scene, which is clearly borrowed from Goethe's *Faust*. Torsten thenceforth accompanies Ahasuerus as a student of mankind, covered by the traditional cloak of invisibility. Most of the conclusions he reaches are typical of romantic misanthropy, but a specific object of the scorn spewed out by both Ahasuerus and Torsten is stupid, hypocritical fondness for things French. Such a descent from the general and universal to the trivial and specific is too familiar a phenomenon of romantic literature to call for any observations.

Inevitably Ahasuerus develops into a Mephistopheles to Torsten's Faust. The young man's dramatic ambitions are thwarted through the combined pressures of Philistine clergymen and lawyers, and hostile, unsympathetic women. Although the content of Köberle's novel is most uneven, the work is not forbidding reading, and as a satire on the tastes of the literary world in mid-nineteenth-century Germany it comes off well. Its weakness lies in its Byronism—which is sometimes real and sometimes spurious, if not in effect a parody—and perhaps also in the fact that Köberle could never decide whether Torsten is to be Childe Harold or Don Juan. Even so, *Der neue Thurm zu Babel* is infinitely superior to Hermann Neumann's *Das letzte Menschenpaar* (Torgau, 1844), which owes a great debt to Quinet's *Ahasvérus*. Here the protagonist is no more than the stock figure we have already seen innumerable times. His contempt for mankind is bitter and comprehensive enough; but suddenly, at the eleventh hour and fifty-ninth minute of Doomsday, he turns Christian in the most mealymouthed manner. On the other hand, where Ahasuerus is an apostle of obscurantism, as in Friedrich Blaul's *Der ewige Jude und sein Liebling in München* (Munich, 1831), in this pamphlet of local political and intellectual satire he fails to impress as either a figure of satire or of anything else.

Moreover, in all of these primarily satirical pieces, the misanthropy of Ahasuerus may be balanced by an intellectual if not a physical exuberance; his scorn may amuse him with its infinite jest, even though it may sometimes depress him into despair. In the former case, the amusement may resolve itself into a parody of philosophy, a satire on the worldling with pretensions toward the metaphysical, as W. Hauff, in his *Memoirs of Satan* (p. 198 above), had pilloried the society of his time and place. A good example is Franz Theremin's *Der ewige Jude* (Berlin, 1835), a prose "legend" which was mentioned in the preceding chapter. It presents Ahasuerus as a lover of life who is determined to get what he can out of living, relying on intuition to invite opportunities for sensuality. The past, he thinks, is ridiculous; the very least he can do is to be sensible, as sensible a rationalist as Voltaire, Helvetius, or La Mettrie. At the same time, however, he seeks avidly the company of a great and versatile man like Goethe, with whom he spends much time in Weimar. Such an attitude removes him from the current intellectual vogue of Francophilism, which is attacked vigorously in a pseudonymous pamphlet, *Neueste Wanderungen, Umtriebe, und Abenteuer des ewigen Juden unter den Namen Börne, Heine, Saphir* (n.p., 1832),[25] fathered by one who called himself "Cruciger," and defended on the other hand by J. J. Hertel, in *Der Ausflug des ewigen Juden in malerische Auflage in die schönsten Gegenden des teutschen*

Vaterlands (Augsburg, 1822),[26] who believes that Ahasuerus, a conservative, would be much happier in Germany than in France, which has become altogether too liberal.

Satirists have always been conservative. A Tory viewpoint is as obvious among these later writers as it was in the works of Jonathan Swift. It follows, then, that they are inclined toward pessimism, since the world cannot be persuaded to linger in the good old days amid the good old ways. Their worlds are always crumbling beneath their feet. The purely satirical treatment of Ahasuerus therefore resolves itself into the attitude expressed in Hector de Jailly's "Ahasverus" in the conservative annual *Ikon Basilike* (1835).[27] Here the protagonist is an antirevolutionary, who recognizes all the sufferings engendered in the course of the struggle for liberty, equality, and fraternity, which, he believes, is energy expended on a chimera. He is happy when an angel grants him death and a release from this mad world of fools and wicked men.

The works which we have been surveying, from the important period between 1830 and 1850, wearyingly numerous as they are, and all too often unoriginal and jaded and repetitious, manage nevertheless to establish the Wandering Jew as a symbol of humanity in various aspects; and they take away from him some of the hopelessness that had sat, nightmare-like, on his shoulders since the romanticists first became aware of his existence. A philosophical writer like C. F. Göschel, in *Über Goethes Faust* (1824), had seen Ahasuerus as the symbol of eternity, of Jewry, of the Passion, and hence of all Christians, and had wound up by seeing him as the symbol also of death.[28] Now, ten to twenty years after Göschel wrote, it is a safe conclusion that Ahasuerus is progressing as a symbol of everything which humanity can suffer in life and of most to which it aspires. This enlarging concept of his poetic significance is well expressed in Johann Nepomuk Vogl's little four-page account, first printed in Edmund Duller's gift book, *Phönix*, at Frankfurt in 1835.[29] Ahasuerus, sick and weary, has a life-giving dream which lasts a full century. In this dream he comes by slow stages to a vision of Almighty God and of his ultimate salvation. He wakes from the dream, of course, in great disappointment—more than that, in desperate frustration. The vision, he knows with great regret, can never come true. But ever afterward, when he returns to the tree under which he had this dream, he finds there consolation, hope, and promise for the future. Let him therefore pause for a time under this tree.

Variations on Preceding Themes: 1850–1890

For another generation or so after 1850, Ahasuerus will continue to illustrate his romantic potentialities, but as time goes on he will be shedding most of his Byronic or Gothic integuments. He will become concerned with evolutionism and at times will be moved to linger in his wanderings and say something like "Onward, upward, and outward," referring not always to spiritual exaltation or a dissolution of the boundaries between the physical and metaphysical, but rather to a progressive development of body and soul which will be as far above ordinary man as ordinary man is above the apes. He will be giving recognition to a celebrated idea expressed in virtually those same words, late in the century, by Nietzsche—the idea of the superman, which had been growing in men's minds ever since the romantic revolution in the preceding century.[1] But this vision of "progress" he will see neither steadily nor whole. His vision will be clouded, much of the time, with that uncertainty voiced by Tennyson in a great poem published at the very mid-point of the nineteenth century:

> "Thou makest thine appeal to me:
> I bring to life, I bring to death;
> The spirit does but mean the breath:
> I know no more." . . .
>
> . . . .
>
> No more? A monster then, a dream,
> A discord. . . .[2]

Later, as we go past about 1875, we begin to hear of the dangerous and difficult phrase, *fin de siècle*, as if the approach of a new century meant misgivings about the age that was passing and a diminution of the joy of living in the face of disillusionment concerning one's accomplishments and aspirations. Actually, the years from about 1870 to 1900 in Europe were years of great material growth, with the spread of imperialism and apparent stability of the Occidental way of life. Germany and Italy finally achieved national unification, and Germany was on her way to challenging the whole world for supremacy. France, defeated by Germany in 1870-71, was determined to have revenge and to regain her lost prestige, and was building her fences against the day of retribution, when Alsace and Lorraine would return to the fold of the Republic. Britain was celebrating the peak achievement of the Victorian Empire. Russia was trying to keep the lid on its seething revolutionism. The United States was giving its energies to the expansion of frontiers and the amassing of riches for the barons of finance in the Gilded

Age. Soon she too would have a modest fling at imperialism. Over all nations was hovering the spirit of social reform, advancing rather rapidly and peaceably in the British Isles, much more slowly in America and France, backing and filling throughout Central Europe—where the dead hand of the Hapsburgs alone was sufficient to retard progress—and poised restively in Russia.

In the arts and literature, the once urgent forces of romanticism were locked in deadly combat with the many kinds of realism, with each side winning here and yielding there, so that the ultimate products were more often than not compounded of both, not so much in unions of love as of antipathy. The great intellectual fact during these decades was the dominance of German philosophy and scholarship; the great artistic phenomenon was the volatile originality of French arts and letters. The greatest social and political achievement was the tremendous expansion of the United States to become a world power.

It may be assumed that most of the changes in the Western world between 1850 and the turn of the century are reflected in the varying treatments of the Wandering Jew, but there are many writers who have preferred to follow in the tracks of those who had already written on the subject. Others, on the other hand, have shown much independence.

On the Fringes of the Folk Tale

Folklorists and antiquarians did much collecting, sifting, and studying of the popular accounts of Ahasuerus between 1850 and 1900, and the Legend began to be analyzed (see Appendix A) during that same period. The transmission of the folk tales in written form was, of course, a direct stimulus to knowledge of the Legend. We have already observed that the so-called art form of the Legend was well established by 1850 and was already both imaginative and inventive. When this art form concerned itself closely with the folk material, the fusion of the two led at times to so complete a blending that one cannot always know which will be uppermost in any given literary work. For example, the Grimsel tale, which we have seen treated romantically by Wittich and Ten Kate, reappears in a variant form in the poem, "Le juif errant," from *Les ombres blanches* by Jules Bertrand and Emile Colliot (Paris, 1853). But now it is filled not so much with romantic melancholy as with hope and trust in evolution. Ahasuerus returns to find the city a meadow only; then an arm of the sea; but, finally, another city fairer than the original. These authors, at least, believe that the course of events has moved not only onward but also upward. As if to cancel this hopeful trend, however, Jean-Gaston Romieux, in *Le juif errant, le remords, et le choléra* (Paris, 1858), reminds us of the old pestilence-bringing power of the Wandering Jew. Remorse is here a companion of Ahasuerus; Cholera taunts them with the reminder that he can leave the world, whereas Ahasuerus and Remorse must stay in it and can never be separated. The influence at work here is obvious, but it would be difficult for a Frenchman writing about the Wandering Jew in the 1850's to keep out of the looming shadow of Eugène Sue.

Sooner or later the border line between pure folk tale and literary imitation becomes no longer discernible. The analogy with the "popular" versus the "literary"

ballad is apparent. It is therefore difficult to classify Julie Dingern's "Zwei Legenden vom ewigen Juden," in *Märchen und Sagen der Jugend erzählt* (*ca.*1870).[3]
These appear to be pieces of original fiction; at least the stories had not been
printed before or been picked up from oral tradition by any students of the Legend. In any case, they have the virtues of good imitations, for they are told with
simplicity and economy. In the first and lesser legend, a grasping landlord, who
injures his leg while trying to kick a poor widow and must suffer amputation of
the limb, is fitted for an artificial leg by his tenant Abraham. When the landlord
demurs at paying a reasonable fee for this service, he is made to run perpetually
on this new prosthetic limb—a second Wandering Jew.

The second legend is an impressive short story of its kind. A Polish Jew is in-
sulted by a Christian, and the fair-minded judge requires that the Christian pay
the Jew five hundred gulden. The Jew goes back to his village, where, thanks to
his newly acquired capital, he prospers. He thus awakens the envy of another
Jew, Leib Chastid, who is very avaricious and burns to know the source of the
Jew's wealth. At first the Jew will tell him nothing, but finally, worn down by Leib
Chastid's importunities, he bids him go to the city and let himself be insulted.
Leib Chastid goes, but fortune is against him; he can find no one to insult him,
not even when he invites abuse and injury by blaspheming against the Christian
faith. Everyone he meets treats him with the most good-natured indulgence, and
he is therefore still looking for someone to kick him—a new kind of Polish Wandering Jew. The ironical humor and dry cynicism of these tales, quite apart from
the skill of their telling, are too much to expect of mere folk tales, and yet both
remind one of a medieval *exemplum*. They suggest analogues to the Legend rather
than a furthering of it.

This tendency to associate Ahasuerus with the protagonists of other legends,
to achieve the contamination inevitable whenever stories are circulating by word
of mouth only, is strong after 1850. Early examples immediately present themselves. A windy, sermon-like creation by Hermann Dalton, *Der ewige Jude und
der ewige Johannes* (St. Petersburg, 1867), attributes the Legend, quite inade-
quately, to the Legend of St. John, which as we have seen is only one of the
roots and not really the decisive one. Dalton would have been better advised to
have read Levin Schücking, who, in his short tale "Die drei Freier" in *Der Bauern-
fürst* (Leipzig, 1851), raises Ahasuerus to a position of equality beside two analogous characters, the Wild Huntsman and the Flying Dutchman. In fact, he does
more than that: he introduces Ahasuerus into the age-old Legend of the Demon
Lover. The three wanderers—Ahasuerus, the Wild Huntsman, and the Flying
Dutchman—meet at an inn in Augsburg in the year 1700. They assume leading
roles in the social life of the city as the young Armenian (*sic*) prince, Isaac Laquedem; the Master of Chase *en chef*, Herr von Rodenstein; and the Dutch admiral,
Van der Decken. All three try to win a certain young wife, who is something of
a misanthrope. When she remarks that she would like to do something new, to
endure some sort of ordeal or danger which posterity would agree that no human
being could undergo, Isaac Laquedem sees his opportunity. He persuades her to
follow him for a year. After that period, she is to follow each of the other two for
the same length of time. She agrees to follow the Wandering Jew first and sees the

handsome young prince turn into a musty-smelling graybeard, with a sinister companion (the Devil) always walking beside him. She tries to escape, but the now self-revealed Ahasuerus holds her in an iron grip. In utter despair she sells her soul to the Devil, who promises her deliverance if she will keep her promise to the Wild Huntsman. She will at least be spared the Flying Dutchman, or so she thinks. She has a harrowing ride through the air with the unspeakable Wild Huntsman, and to her horror discovers that the Flying Dutchman is now coming for her. Once more she appeals to the Devil, who jeeringly promises her safety if she will sell him also the soul of her child. This she refuses out of hand, preferring a voyage with the Flying Dutchman. Fortunately for her, the accursed Van der Decken relents, commenting that no man would have protected the soul of his child as did this woman. The next thing she knows she is in her room, awaking as from a dream, with her child peacefully sleeping beside her. Her beautiful blonde hair, however, has turned completely gray as a reminder of her horrible experience. The story is told with fine dramatic sense.

Goethe's association of Ahasuerus and Judas in his fragmentary epic, which he derived from some of the later variants of the Ahasuerus-book, is not without influence on later writers. An early example is Otto Franz's *Judas Iscarioth,* the second play in his dramatic trilogy *Der Messias* (Berlin, 1869). Since Ahasuerus is in this instance only a minor follower and friend of Judas and has little to do with the action, we need not consider this work further, particularly since in other pieces he is much more close to Judas and therefore much more important in the story.

A most interesting example of the mixture of legends is a ballad which appeared in the giftbook annual *Libussa* for the year 1852, published at Prague. In it are four poems entitled "Gedichte aus dem Böhmischen," which are translations into German of narrative verse by different writers of Czech and Polish nationality. The translator is T. Kral. The ballad in question is one of these; it is entitled by Kral "Die Silberlinge des Judas." Its author is Josef Jaroslav Kalina, and its Czech title is "Jidašův peniz"; the original was also published in 1852 in Prague, five years after Kalina's death. In slightly more than a hundred lines of simple ballad measure it tells how the Jew sinned and why he wandered. The earlier portion has been strongly influenced by Schubart. But instead of the inexhaustible purse, Ahasuerus has come by the thirty pieces of silver awarded to Judas for his betrayal of Christ. In Bohemia the Jew is received by a family and rewards them for their hospitality by acting like a good brownie (*Heintzelmann*) and leaving to the father of the house three of the accursed pieces of silver. The father at his death leaves the silver to his three sons as coheirs. The youngest is sent into town to get special food and drink for a celebration. The other two, staying at home, quarrel, and one kills the other. The youngest buys poison in town; when he returns he is greeted contemptuously by the surviving brother, who drinks the poison prepared for him by the youngest. In remorse the youngest then commits suicide. The Wandering Jew, returning, looks in the window at the corpses, laughs like Lucifer, and reclaims the silver.

This is a version of the celebrated Legend of the Accursed Treasure, of Oriental antecedents, best known to English-speaking readers through Chaucer's magnificent *Pardoner's Tale*. We have already observed how Chaucer introduced into this tale an old man who suggests the later figuration of Ahasuerus. The story survives, moreover, in analogues on the Continent, with two excellent examples from medieval Bohemia, as well as in an Italian morality play and in a sixteenth-century German play by Hans Sachs. Kalina, who was a dabbler in comparative literature, could have known Chaucer's work in or out of translation; he probably knew Hans Sachs's; and surely was acquainted with his native Bohemian folk tales, such as those associating the Jew with treasure—for example, the tale of Kokot the linen weaver (p. 115 above). Beyond that, he was also a young writer of more than ordinary imagination. The ballad is terse, dramatic, and enigmatic—altogether quite a literary find.[4]

The Purely Romantic Ahasuerus Continued

We have seen how Ahasuerus, in the various examples of the Chronicle of the Wandering Jew, observed all mankind in action over two thousand years. In romantic poetry, he could represent all mankind or be limited to the figure of Schubart's Ahasuerus atop Mount Carmel, seeking rest in death and not finding it, content to throw skulls down the mountainside. These concepts of the Wandering Jew continue, with occasional variations, into the twentieth century. The subjective sufferer, for instance, appears in J. B. Drouet's *Le juif errant* (Rheims, 1862) with virtually no change from the Schubartian image. Others, such as Adolf F. Graf von Schack, in "Der ewige Wanderer," from his *Gedichte* (1866), prefer to concentrate as before on the saddening spectacle of mortal ruin, in which the universe is brought to nothing, as Quinet had seen it a generation before.[5] And just as in Quinet's morality play, the passing away of the universe finds the Wandering Jew still on his feet, walking about in some ill-defined empyrean region, still seeking love in vain, and sympathy and laughter, still embittered because, even with the universe destroyed, his grief has not left him.

One of the more ambitious dramatic poems between 1850 and 1890 to present the Wandering Jew as a symbol of the world observer is *Ahasverus, den evige Jøde* (1853) by the Danish poet Paludan-Müller.[6] Disgusted by the followers of Antichrist, Ahasuerus takes refuge in a Christian churchyard where he is overtaken by Doomsday, for which the trumpets blare forth in terrifying cacophony. The initial weirdness of the scene, with the dead rising from their graves in this erstwhile peaceful cemetery, is dissipated by the fact that all mankind is involved. Misery loves company, or, to put it in classical terms, *commune naufragium dulce est*. And so, while the Wandering Jew lingers in the cemetery, various specimens of degenerate, frightened humanity pass before him. He witnesses a murder done for robbery—a matter of brutal violence and raw greed, because the murderers care nothing about the judgment soon to be visited upon them. The survivors of the victim appear—a wife, a child, and an old father, who in his day had been a free-thinking preacher, interpreting not the scriptures of old but new attitudes in new texts. Judgment Day reveals him with unbent knees and unbowed head: he will meet it as he has met everything else in life—standing straight and looking directly ahead. A pair of lovers utter sweet trivialities even in such gloomy eschatological circumstances, but they are mere innocent heralds, in their fleshliness, of Antichrist himself. And this is no ordinary Antichrist, no mere forerunner of the Day of Doom, no apocalyptic figure of mystery, but the very incarnation of modern culture. He prizes the arts and sciences, and defends tolerance to the last ditch. He is a true optimist of this earth, in contrast to Ahasuerus, who remains a passion-ridden pessimist, a man of the romantic supernatural, and who has mystic glimpses of the Divine Comforter, the Paraclete, whom he has come to recognize as a consolation in misery and a help in the ordeal of human suffering.

Once the trumpets of Judgment Day are silent, Antichrist vanishes, the dead arise, and the spirit of Pontius Pilate, granted a short respite, repeats his ancient question as to what constitutes truth. There is no answer. Pilate is led away to his doom; the universe dissolves in chaos, and only the Wandering Jew remains. A bell tolls. Ahasuerus enters into an open grave to rest for eternity, free from a universe which can no longer trouble him. He has been assured of the end both of this world and of his wanderings, and in this certainty he speaks the first and last words in the drama, if such it can be called.

There has been an obvious inclination, most annoying to students of the Legend, for the writers of the past hundred years to treat Ahasuerus as a subsidiary character only, sometimes as the merest shadow in the cast of characters. This happened occasionally before 1850, of course, but it is as if the later writers often considered him dramatically inadequate to carry a major role. For example, J. Schnell's *Das israelitische Recht in seinen Grundzügen dargestellt* (Basel, 1853) presents him merely as one of the several examples of the nomadic nature of the Jews. J. L. Chronik's *Ahasverus* (Zurich, 1855), a dramatic poem on the Book of Esther, alludes to him by name as one who is to assume the appellation of Ahasuerus (the Persian emperor Xerxes in the story) at a later date. Ernst Meier's *Deutsche Sagen, Sitten, und Gebräuche aus Schwaben* (Stuttgart, 1852) sees in Ahasuerus' story only a rude, modern (*sic*) parallel to the Legend of Faust.[7] Two other works, manifestly derived from Croly's *Salathiel*, cast out their dragnets and draw Ahasuerus into the group concerned with defending Jerusalem against Titus and Vespasian. The first, Leonhard Wohlmut's *Die Zerstörung von Jerusalem* (1857), a five-act tragedy of thick and muddy texture, at least enhances the part of Ahasuerus to the point where he stands as a proponent of an international and universal kingdom of a worldly Messiah.[8] The other, *Der Messias* (Berlin, 1869), by Otto Franz, is a dramatic trilogy. The first two plays, *Jesus von Nazareth* and *Judas Iscarioth*, may be passed over. In the third part, *Die Zerstörung von Jerusalem*, Ahasuerus fights, as usual, valiantly but to no purpose in the forefront of the battle against the besieging and pillaging Romans. The Wandering Jew is often to be found as a subordinate member of the dramatis personae in fiction, drama, and narrative poetry during the nineteenth and twentieth centuries.

From Sinning Jew to Agent of God

One theme, which has already appeared before 1850, tends to develop strongly during the remainder of the century. This is the use of Ahasuerus as a symbol of the Jewish people. At first there is little if any conscious nationalism in the idea, for Zionism had as yet not gathered force, although an awareness of Jewish political or national integrity may have appeared here and there in individual writers such as Croly or Ingemann. It seems to have been regarded at first as an eccentric dream rather than as a world movement. However, in the later decades of the century, about a dozen miscellaneous works show the Jew in this new light, if one allows a certain degree of latitude in interpretation. Thus Simonet's poem, *La malédiction* (Neufchâteau, 1886), explicitly identifies the Wandering Jew with the Jewish race—vital, indestructible, and original. In contrast, C. Kohlrusch, in his *Schweizerisches Sagenbuch* (Leipzig, 1854-56), while identifying him with his people, can think of him only as a Christ-killer.[9]

One can, of course, accept Ahasuerus as symbolic of his race and at the same time not like either him or his people. The purely political and social anti-Semitism, so rife in Germany in the past century, has its repercussions on the Legend and will be taken up later. It is enough to say here that in the process of unifying the German states into the German Empire, the Jew—either Ahasuerus or the Jewish people—was at best an alien element. A rather absurd expression of the chauvinism engendered by this Jewish question is C. J. Diepenbrock's *Germania* (1863), which is ostensibly a play in five acts, but is actually a fantastic, incoherent, dramatic poem. There are many scenes in these five acts, and each one introduces a new batch of characters, so that no shaping of the original plan is possible unless one accepts the work as a sprawling pageant. Ahasuerus speaks an epilogue in which he designates Christ as the perfect communist; in all of his appearances he is skeptical of nationalism and anticapitalistic. But, although this is one of the few times we shall ever see a Marxist Ahasuerus, Diepenbrock's work as a whole is not directly either for or against communism. His intent, rather, seems to be to start a parade of characters who typify the multifarious classes of society and the various ethnic elements which go to make up a great modern nation. Among these ethnic elements, according to Diepenbrock, the Jews do not deserve high rank. Taken *in toto*, the poem is a plea for integrating Germany politically and for spiritualizing German literature and making it independent. Its tone is arrogantly patriotic—one may as well call it jingoistic—and "Germania!" becomes almost as objectionable a cry as "Heil Hitler!"[10]

Diepenbrock makes clear that in his opinion the Jewish people as an entity can do little. This is also Ernst Ortlepp's belief in his *Israels Erhebung und der ewige Jude* (Constance, 1845), based on the fact that they have no homeland and no leader. Their higgling small-mindedness in their business dealings he concedes, but his poem is, in reality, pro-Semitic; the faults of the people he blames chiefly on the Christian intolerance that has surrounded them for centuries.[11]

Another Jewish trait which appeals to those who identify Ahasuerus with the Jewish people is his predilection for wandering. This fundamental restlessness is well expressed in Edouard Grenier's poem, *La mort du juif-errant* (Paris, 1857).[12] The opening scene is the Colosseum on a moonlight night, and Ahasuerus is in a mood of nostalgia. In a vision he sees a gentle manifestation of Christ. Thenceforth he leads a life of Christian reciprocity—loving where he is hated, blessing those who curse him. The final scene is a hut deep in snow-covered mountains. Christ enters, and the Wandering Jew bows in reverence before him, then washes his feet; he then is allowed to fall asleep, dies, and is buried by the poet. Ahasuerus has been a sinner because he never had possessed enough humanity until Christ taught him its full significance, and the reason for his deficiencies has been his essentially restless nature, which has been his heritage. All is forgiven in the end.

To look at the matter from another angle, this restlessness of the Wandering Jew is too fundamental a factor in the development of the Legend for any esoteric and symbolic interpretation to uproot it. And so, if there is to be an emphasis upon his symbolic value, it must stress his restlessness. A pure example of such an attitude is E. M. L. Heinen's "Der ewige Jude," in *Rheinische Glockentöne* for 1843.[13] This poem paints Ahasuerus as the infernal cause of all our frustration and lack of repose. He is identified with both almost as if he were a presiding genius of evil and controlled all the dissatisfaction of mankind toward life. If we could resist him successfully and ignore him when he appears before us, he would depart, and with him would go our unhappy instinct for wandering. We should then have peace for ourselves, and perhaps would help him to calm his own hectic spirit—although the poet is not sure of the last point.

From all this grows the mood which asks *"Wherefore, unsatisfied soul?"* and *"Whither, O mocking life?"* as Whitman phrases the questions in his "Passage to India." Only a few years before, Robert Hamerling of Vienna produced *Ahasver in Rom* (Hamburg, 1866), probably the best narrative poem on the Wandering Jew to appear in his generation.[14] It has action, color, characterization, poetic power, and an almost flawless exterior of form and style. Its six sections constitute a six-act drama in which Nero is the protagonist and Ahasuerus the deuteragonist. Within the vast range of the Chronicle of the Wandering Jew, Hamerling has concentrated on scenes which take place within the Roman Empire and lavished his talents on the portrayal of its decadence and cruelty, its pomp and splendor, its moral collapse, and its paradoxical promise of hope for the future. He does all this with such good dramatic and poetic effect that it is important to consider the epic in some detail.

Part I, entitled "The Gift of Locusta," is laid in a sordid tavern kept by the harridan Locusta. Nero arrives incognito, attended by the sage Seneca. He is insulted by the revelers, has spirited words with the republican shoemaker Saccus, and "marries" the beautiful little slave girl Actaea. There is brawling and ribaldry and carousing, but when things have quieted down, Ahasuerus enters, to brood over the rottenness of man. Nonetheless, Nero reappears in the dawn, as a bridegroom coming forth from the bridal chamber and rejoicing as a strong man to run a race; he invites the roisterers, now sodden in exhausted debauchery, to a Bacchanalia at his palace.

The greasy sensuality of Part I yields to the more refined yet grossly carnal profligacy of the Bacchanalia, with which Part II opens. The scene is a paradisical garden. The bacchanalian rout enters, with Nero himself assuming the role of Bacchus. His new bride, Actaea,[15] is enthroned as Ariadne, the repulsive Locusta as Hecate. It is a blasphemous orgy, for Nero would dethrone none other than

Jupiter himself. So confident is he of success, so insolent in his pride, that (speaking as Dionysus) he utters a full-throated defiance of the not yet defeated gods:

> "I will not bind you yet," cries Dionysus,
> "Nor cast you yet into dawning darkness;
>   You have yet to do with an exalted victor!
>   Indeed, you erst were known as merry little people,
>   And brought into this gloomy world of men
>   From heavenly heights the joyous message
>   Of beauty and of joy. And yet too proud
>   You were, too proud of birth, and far too envious!
>   Perhaps you wished mankind to be refreshed,
>   But not at your high table! Yet gladly
>   Did you descend to earth wherever you might spy
>   A lovely mortal to be ravished, though never
>   Did you endure it that the wretched mortal
>   Could even once come unto your Heaven . . .
>   All that is done now, all that is past,
>   For mine henceforth is now Olympus,
>   And all it may delight me to possess.
>   Sons of Chronos, your hour of doom has struck!
>   Give room! give room! and then depart in peace!"[16]

Thus insulted, the immortal gods must nevertheless have their way. Two sinister individuals enter, even while Nero is crying out his impudent defiance; one of these is Ahasuerus, who is playing for the moment the part of a sardonic spectator. The other is the beautiful goddess Roma, whose advent is the signal for Nero to abandon all other women, even his little bride Actaea, to center his attentions upon the bewitching newcomer. In the heart of a glamorous garden spot, Nero in private conversation confesses to her his infatuation, while boasting of his irresistible past conquests. He admits that although he has possessed the bodies of countless women he has never been able to possess a woman's soul. In a passage which would make an old Freudian's mouth water, he concludes that mother's love is the most satisfying of all. He remembers, however, that he is not only a mighty man but also an emperor, and so he bends all his efforts to the seduction of the goddess Roma. In the ensuing scuffle, the mask of the goddess is torn off, and he recognizes her as none other than his mother, Agrippina. The lady flees his embraces and escapes to her current lover, Paris, while the frustrated son plots her murder. Actaea accidentally falls beneath the feet of the bacchanalian rout, which tramples her to death and rushes thence to the burning of Rome.

Part III concerns itself with Agrippina. First there is the inevitable lush description of the voluptuous empress-mother, posed successfully against a drab background of bacchanalian orgy, seen in the gray dawn of the morning after. We are then transported to the deck of a gorgeous royal galley plowing the Tyrrhennian Sea. Thanks to the treachery of a rascally Moor, Tigellin, Agrippina, for all her beauty, is pushed into the cruel maw of the sea. Tigellin reports this to his royal master, Nero, and her corpse is washed up on the beach in the presence of some strayed revelers, who turn from their merriment to lamentation. Nero's gloating is interrupted by the news that Rome is afire. He is astounded, for he is certain that he did not himself kindle the conflagration.

Part IV is taken up with the burning of Rome. All the capacity of human beings for morbid excitement is embodied in psychopathic Nero and bestial Saccus. As Nero, in rising exhilaration, strokes his pet lion, the unspeakable Tigellin brings up a miserable band of Christians to be fed to the lions. Meanwhile, the flames have consumed the imperial menagerie, and all the wild animals are at large. Nero has his eye on a succulent Christian maiden, but the lion beats him in the race to her and devours her, to the great dismay of the Emperor, whose distaste is matched only by the curious revulsion of a pair of lions toward two grave and elderly Christians—Peter and Paul themselves. Here is an intensely dramatic moment in the poem—effete imperial Rome confronting the two great followers of Christ. To the credit of Roman courage, it is to be recorded that Nero does not shrink from ordering the two revered Christians to their deaths. Unfortunately for him, however, Ahasuerus, who has spent most of the scene rejoicing at the destruction all about him, interferes with the execution of the sentence. Nero puts up his loudest defiance, but Ahasuerus beats it down. In a long denunciatory speech, he informs Nero that the tyrant's little hour has passed, and that Ahasuerus himself is to attend to Nero's downfall. He tells Nero that he, Ahasuerus, has set the first burning brand to a Roman building and kindled the great fire, and that now Nero is himself to join the dead lying about in windrows. But although the Emperor is struck with terror, trembling from head to foot, he is not yet ready to give up. His tried henchman, Tigellin, rushes to a verbal defense of his master, but, when the Moor goes to lay violent hands on Ahasuerus, he touches a viper lurking on the pedestal of a statue of Augustus and perishes on the spot. Ahasuerus, satisfied temporarily with the death of the impious rascal who had killed Agrippina, withdraws, and the scene ends amid cinders and ashes.

The respite for Nero enables him to rebuild the city and spend time in retirement, brooding over all his cruelties and, particularly, his matricide. Part V is the beginning of the end. Nero is bored and filled with self-pity. He is no longer interested in his museum of relics, containing such glorious spangles of history as the clay out of which Prometheus shaped man, the whip of the emperor Xerxes of the Persians, the cup from which Socrates drank poison, the tooth of the she-wolf that suckled Romulus and Remus. In his desperate ennui he summons Seneca. His tutor and guide, however, can counsel only a return to republican virtues —no fit advice to give Nero, under the circumstances—and it is not surprising that the Emperor should "suggest" that Seneca kill himself. Sated with human understanding and all its petty limitations, Nero, like Faust, can imagine nothing more exciting than to knock on the gates of Hades. As if moved by the power of suggestion, Ahasuerus enters at this moment to propose that they both go to pay a visit to the noted Egyptian seer, Apollonius. But all that Apollonius can do is to parade before the Emperor the shades of those whom Nero has killed or who have perished in his service. This is too much for Nero. He falls in a faint, groveling at the feet of the Wandering Jew, who is delighted because it now appears that the slow abasement and punishment of Nero is proceeding apace according to some kind of divine plan.

It is unfortunate that the sixth and final section of *Ahasver in Rom* should be the weakest part of the poem. Nero, having returned to his abode, the Golden House, is continually prey to evil dreams. He hears of the revolt of Vindex in favor of Galba, but the senators who tell him this are contemptuously dismissed, even though there is no blinking the fact that Galba is at the gates of the city. He therefore flees with a German servant into a cave. This German servant has been deliberately used by Hamerling to insert propaganda in favor of the unification of Germany, as befitted the years 1865-1866, and also to add a pleasingly patriotic touch. More important to the narrative than this intrusive bit of special pleading is the melodramatic entrance of Ahasuerus in a flash of lightning. Nero, now frightened into incoherence, flees deeper into the cave, which has now been identified as the catacombs of Rome. Far within he meets a venerable man in prayer before an altar, a Christian refugee from the Colosseum. Nero falls into conversation with him about the Christian God of love. The Emperor is incapable of comprehending such a viewpoint as that implicit in the Christian faith, but he is impressed beyond measure, although he retains enough integrity to realize that he would always be outside the fold. It is his insane egotism which stands in the way, as he himself concedes. In a moment of sudden self-revelation he stabs himself with a sword lent him by his German servant. As he dies, he is committed to the gentle care of Death by Ahasuerus, who now stands forth as eternal, supremely old (*ururalt*), the first-born of the unborn, the first son of the first couple, the first human child, the first rebel, who brought into the world Death, which transcends mere Christianity. But he names no names, for he represents too enormous a concept to be held down by any single creed.

Ahasuerus ends as a gigantic figure, an embodiment of the mortality of man, while Nero represents the life-wish or urge to live. Ahasuerus here stands for the eternal in a conception of the Wandering Jew as impressive as any in the treatment of the Legend, with the exception, perhaps, of Quinet or Mosen. But Hamerling has made him into a kind of fanatical nemesis. There are inconsistencies in his portrayal—it is rather illogical, for instance, that he should blast Nero for murdering someone when Ahasuerus himself is such a herald of death. This, however, adds to the tension already engendered by the opposition of the vitality of Nero and the indestructibility of Ahasuerus. Besides, Hamerling has a precedent. Some ten years before, Otto Girndt, in his tragedy *Nero* (Berlin, 1856), had made Ahasuerus—for the most part only a minor character in the play, but filled with the death-wish—stand up as Nero's nemesis, as a thwarting spirit who seeks, if he can find it, the consolation of the Christian faith instead of barbaric bloodletting. To state the message of Hamerling's poem in another way, it presents the conflict between that which is permanent and that which is transitory, between that which is of the essence and that which is of the form only. All in all, it is Hamerling's best achievement, at times an exciting and even a noble work.

In smaller compass, J. G. Fischer's admirable little lyric, "Der ewige Jude" (1854), sets up the protagonist in bold relief as a Promethean individual who challenges God.[17] Like Hamerling's Ahasuerus, he has followed mankind along its course, but unlike him he has become a true befriender of humanity, who believes in the importance and pride of human reason. The colossus of the universe,

God, may spread his wings far and wide, but Ahasuerus has tasted His eternity to the point of satiety and is not impressed. Although he has been chained to a cliff, metaphorically speaking, like Prometheus, he still considers himself a free man. The irony of the situation is clear: the omniscience of the immortal Ahasuerus can pull down heaven itself. For not only is he immortal, he is all-knowing as well; he can look forward and backward upon the oneness of creation—a true monist, who admires and glorifies human reason and understanding in the Hegelian manner.

This rebelliousness of Ahasuerus may be tempered at the last moment by an unexpected repentance, although the artistic results are not too happy. Yet one powerful poem of the generation manages to overcome this handicap. Bernhard Giseke's *Ahasuerus, der ewige Jude* (Berlin, 1868), an epic poem in ten cantos, shows some more of this Hegelian passion for classification and systematizing. The subtitles of each of its ten sections lay bare the structure of the whole. Part I, "Der Fluch," contents itself with the genesis of the Legend. Ahasuerus is cursed; his wife and daughter die not long thereafter, and the Jew begins his ceaseless traveling immediately after their deaths. This is the story told by Quinet. The ensuing travels of Ahasuerus bear a few superficial resemblances to those which figure in the Chronicle of the Wandering Jew, but the author cuts short the wanderings of the Jew, insofar as we are permitted to follow him, with the Council of Nicaea in 325, when Western Catholicism, under the influence of Athanasius, is duly established for the Roman Empire of the West. Part II, "Der Fremde," brings Ahasuerus to Ephesus, where he wrangles long and loud with Paul, denying his preaching and hoping for a Messiah who will vindicate the Jewish faith. Then he sees Rome burning under the eyes of Nero and attributes the disaster to the intervention of Jehovah—as in Hamerling. But Giseke's Ahasuerus is more personal and sectarian than Hamerling's. He witnesses the martyrdom of sundry Christians in the Roman arena, including Peter's and Paul's; and, in spite of his prejudices against those who reject Jehovah, he is moved by the spectacle. In Part III, "Der Aufruhr," he returns to Jerusalem, where he finds the populace greatly inflamed against the Romans and ripe for revolution; and, although calm heads attempt to dissuade the people from such a suicidal insurrection, Ahasuerus pours oil on the flames. As a consequence, in Part IV, "Titus," the Romans go about suppressing the revolt and sacking the city. This sad event is preceded by an epic battle before Acre. Part V, "Der Hunger," recounts the famine within the city, as well as the heroic but vain sorties of the valiant garrison. The Jewish leaders are killed off one by one, but Ahasuerus obstinately refuses to intervene on the side of the Jews. In the meantime, cannibalism breaks out in the beleaguered city, and it is noteworthy that Miriam, a daughter begotten by Ahasuerus somewhere along the way, is involved in the grisly business. Part VI, "Zion," tells of the actual sacking of Jerusalem; it is one long lament, influenced on the one hand by the Book of Lamentations and on the other by Croly's *Salathiel*. In Part VII, "Masada," Ahasuerus escapes, first into a cave near the fallen city, along with some followers, most of whom die, and then to Masada on the Dead Sea, where Judaea makes its last stand. The usual difficulty presents itself: Ahasuerus cannot find death as do the other Jews. In Part VIII, "Der Zweifel," he wanders about in despair through a nameless forest, where he sees an old man beset by robbers. He rescues the intended victim and discovers that he is the apostle John, who manages to convert the brigands to Christianity but cannot convince Ahasuerus. Part IX, "Der Trotz," breaks away from the narrative into a moral romance, a reworking of the old medieval didactic Legend of Barlaam and Josaphat. In a sinister mountain region Ahasuerus comes upon a hut which houses a dead youth of singular beauty. This melancholy discovery enables Ahasuerus to explain to another youth, son of the local king, Avenius, what death really is. The young prince, Josaphat, greatly awed, is converted by the wise old hermit Barlaam, in spite of the strenuous objections of Avenius. Ahasuerus, having indirectly done Christianity a service, returns to Ephesus. Since it is the reign of the emperor Decius, he witnesses more tortures and martyrdoms of Christians, notably the ordeals of Saint Mary and Saint Barbara. Despite all he has seen, he remains skeptical of the teachings of Christ and in true rebellion against the Christian God. But when, in Part X, "Die Gewissheit," he beholds the glory of Byzantium and then hears Athanasius at the Council of Nicaea, he realizes that Jehovah has cast out his people and weeps bitterly at the thought that he is still Ahasuerus, a Jew born in Jerusalem. On this note of lament the poem ends. There is nothing Byronic or romantic, however, in Giseke's threnody; it is in many ways a realistic narrative, and its very flatness—its almost cold, remorseless objectivity of style —makes for dynamic writing.

Such repentance as Giseke's Ahasuerus experiences may be effected by more emotional means, as in Agnes H. Cleeman-Schindler's "Der ewige Jude," in her *Gesammelte Gedichte* (Greifenberg, 1854), where the protagonist is brought into church by a small child. Sentimental as it may be, this treatment is dramatically effective. With Giseke, on the other hand, the repentance strikes one as a bit mechanical, as if the author had wearied of the attitude of Ahasuerus and chosen an important date in the history of Christianity to bring his narrative to an end.

Also more dramatic than Giseke's epic is J. G. Rönnefahrt's *Der Tod Ahasvers, des ewigen Juden* (Tangermünde, 1855), a long narrative poem given partly in dramatic monologue and partly in multiple dramatic action. By these devices the author does his best to give some theatrical value to his basic epic treatment. That his attempt is not more successful is due to his shortcomings as a dramatist, for his material is good, and his narrative sense is at least satisfactory. Ahasuerus has been brought up to worship Jewish pre-eminence in civilization. He is present when his friend John the Baptist baptizes Christ, and is impressed. But his gnawing skepticism keeps asking him if this is truly the Messiah. Not without regret he answers himself in the negative. Such is his ardent, impatient temperament, however, that, as he watches the unfolding of Christ's career, the doubt in his bosom turns to active dislike and subsequently to outright hate. This hate is fostered by the fact that he, an erstwhile money-changer, was driven by Christ from the Temple, along with all the others of his occupation. Later, when he seeks support from Saul of Tarsus, he is disappointed when Saul is converted to Paul. When he sees Saladin defeat the Christians in the Crusades, he is disillusioned by both parties. Even when he thinks of the New World, he thinks of America; and America in 1855 still means slavery.

All of this, however, is by way of prologue. The multiple dramatic action of the work begins in a small German principality which remains unidentified, where Ahasuerus is lingering in the doldrums. Now a well-dressed stranger, he is no vagabond who prophesies. He is assumed by the tavern keeper to be the son of the newly arrived count, whom the tavern keeper has never seen, for the principality has long been ruled by a chronic invalid. Ahasuerus allows the mistake to pass uncorrected. He is withdrawn and suspicious of all save the children of the community. The man for whom Ahasuerus has been mistaken is young Rupprecht Pfaffenhut, who had once been driven to America, where he fought for freedom—in which war is not clear, but the American Revolution is the most likely possibility. This Pfaffenhut, however, has always been a shadowy individual. His wife has died in obscure circumstances, and he himself may have been a Rosicrucian. The Jew had once gone to the young Pfaffenhut's aid, when the latter was beset by bandits; the young man was killed, and Ahasuerus watched him die, regretting that he could not follow. In due course, Ahasuerus assumes the identity of Rupprecht Pfaffenhut, becomes the count, and leaves his Jewishness to dissipate itself to the four winds. He would rather be a local potentate than anything else; and since God allows it, he is content with his fortune. After much speechmaking, he yields to the inevitable, and with true resignation abandons himself to a life of ease and comfort, very much as the man rescued from exposure yelled to have brandy forced down his throat. Rönnefahrt obviously sees Ahasuerus as a symbol of resignation to the will of God. At the end Schiller and Schubart appear to speak to the Jew in soothing tones. The inference to be drawn is that the sleep of oblivion will some day overtake him, since it has become God's will that he should rest.

A much better illustration of the theme of resignation is the epic by the Russian V. A. Zhukovski, written in 1852 but not well known in western Europe until its translation into German in 1883 and into French in 1885.[18] The poem is a good example of the thesis that, all things else being equal, the Legend lends itself better to epic than to dramatic treatment. Zhukovski's Ahasuerus is at the outset a pitiable object: throughout the first few years following the Crucifixion he lives amid terror of death, constant and morbid, not realizing that death will never be his portion. His gradual success in readjusting himself to the fate which decrees that he shall be immortal constitutes by far the best part of the poem. At first he is the orphan of a divine storm. Jews and Gentiles alike reject him. And so he lives as a vagabond, miserable, aimless, tormented by thirst, hunger, cold, and poverty. Like Job, he curses his Creator as well as himself, the created. Then he retires to live among the dead and dying, the crippled and helpless. When in moments of complete despair he attempts suicide, he of course fails. Zhukovski, however, never stoops to sensationalize these efforts at self-slaughter; they are of value to him only because they represent one step along the way to Ahasuerus' full realization of his immortality. The beginning of his conversion to Christ comes when he fails to rescue Saint Ignatius from martyrdom in the arena, and although the road to this conversion is long and hard, it leads him to St. John on Patmos, who teaches him and baptizes him, sending him forth as missionary and ambassador of the Christian God.

In this guise he returns to his homeland, where the emotional side of his conversion is fulfilled. He stands before his old house, which is still resting on its foundations, and sees in his mind's eye the foreboding scene of that original Good Friday. He finds Golgotha lying peaceful in spring sunlight, all as it had been in his youth. The long-sought dream of the Jews of a Messiah all their own can no longer be his. Yet he is content with this new-found faith. He, once rejected and despised of men, abused, insulted, marked with the Mark of Cain on his forehead, has now become an affecting dispenser of the wisdom of God and a defender of Christ, who sends him each day a new reminder to keep his repentance verdant and flourishing. Henceforth Ahasuerus' aid to mankind will be spiritual, not material, and all his angry passions have subsided, to be replaced by a peace and calm approaching Nirvana.

One scene deserves special note, even if it is perhaps the most obvious of Zhukovski's achievement, simply because it descends from the sublime to the specific and topical, a weakness of even the best nineteenth-century writers. Ahasuerus confronts Napoleon at St. Helena, where he finds the onetime conqueror of Europe living in torment at the thought of his former glories crushed under the hopelessness of the future. The Little Corporal is even considering suicide. To console him under these circumstances is one of Ahasuerus' major accomplishments.

There is, unfortunately, no indication of Zhukovski's later plans for the poem, because it was cut short by his ill health and early death. What survives is sufficient to demonstrate that he was one of the most talented of all the writers who attempted to show the conversion of Ahasuerus from a miserable sinner to a devout and efficacious agent of the will of Christ—a transition brought about through a simple resignation to God's design.

Here, as elsewhere, there is agreement that Ahasuerus can attain this spirit of resignation only through the purgatory of suffering. So it is also in Ferdinand Stolte's dramatic poem in four parts, *Faust* (1869), the third part of which is entitled "Ahasverus."[19] This time the Jew is the illegitimate son of the high priest, Caiaphas; he is at first a narrow fanatic, embodying all that is undesirable in religious belief. He begins by hating Christians, but through his own suffering he comes to understand them and then to sympathize with them, and in so doing he turns against heathendom. On the other hand, Faust is fixed of purpose, even when in error, and this obstinacy contrasts with other traits of his character, for he is a doubter who can accomplish little. Ahasuerus and Mephisto engage in a struggle for Faust's soul. Ahasuerus wins when he is able to persuade Faust to make the most of his capabilities and enter on the right track, which will lead him to the furtherance of human civilization. When this victory has been won, Ahasuerus is able to retreat to an idyllic island, where he dies in blessedness and is received by Christ, who comes down to him as a flaming star.

Analogous to the function of Ahasuerus in Stolte's work, where he is, to be sure, only one of several important characters, is the part given him in Henry Peterson's poem, "The Wandering Jew," in his *Poems* (Philadelphia, 1863). This blank-verse monologue portrays Ahasuerus as being without rest and exceedingly old, yet with a spirit chastened through suffering; now ever youthful, doing whatever good he can; and looking forward with submission to a time when the whole universe will be at peace and his curse, symbolic of the curse of life which has been laid on all mankind, will have been removed.

In Kindness and Remorse

Once the Wandering Jew is placed among potential angels, he resumes his old activities as *deus ex machina*. This theatrical function is represented most characteristically in its natural place, the theater. There are two plays in this generation which, though by no means works of art, still were influential. The earlier of these is P. F. C. Merville and J. de Maillan's *Le Juif errant, drame fantastique en cinq actes, un épilogue avec choeurs nouveaux* (Paris, 1834). The play, which is one step beyond the boulevard theater presentations of the time, was first performed at the Théâtre de l'Ambigomique in Paris on July 31, 1834. In spite of its pyrotechnics, it has a good many effective dramatic moments.

Here Ahasuerus has a mother, Rachel; a wife, Noema; and a daughter, Esther. His devoted friend is Simon of Cyrene. For a time he believes in Jesus, who once cured him of blindness, but he later turns against him for reasons not made clear. When the time comes, the curse is pronounced not by Christ but by the Archangel Michael, who commands him in the harshest terms to begin walking. This detail, among others, indicates that the authors were influenced by Quinet. As soon as the Saviour yields up his spirit, Ahasuerus takes to his wandering. In the second act—the scene is Rome, twenty years later—Esther is about to be married to Simon's son, Manasse, but is abducted just before the wedding by soldiers of the emperor Claudius. There follows a general tumult, in the midst of which the Devil appears, to remark that this domestic misfortune is entirely the fault of Ahasuerus. The third act presents the Jew in France at the time of the Albigensian Crusade. Once more there is a great deal of milling about. Esther has been reincarnated, and the robber Barabbas also. She again attracts the unholy lust of soldiers, and in going to her immediate assistance, Ahasuerus becomes involved in a charge of heresy and is sent to the stake, but the fire is quenched. The fourth act takes the reader to Versailles in the days of Louis XV. Esther is now a nun, Ahasuerus a notorious impostor, the Comte de Saint Germain.[20] The ubiquitous sycophant Barabbas is the obsequious Neri. Esther wins for herself the unwelcome attentions of King Louis and kills herself to escape the terrible fate worse than death and a great deal more frequent. Satan claims the soul of the suicide. The final act takes place in hell. Ahasuerus comes to gamble with Satan for his daughter's soul. He wins it and hands it over to an archangel, who transports it to heaven. An additional scene, in the form of an epilogue, presents Judgment Day. Ahasuerus faces Barabbas. They begin to fight but, thanks to the intercession of the blessed damsel, Esther, Ahasuerus is redeemed and Barabbas damned. Merville and Maillan obviously owe something to Goethe as well as to Quinet, but they are slick professionals writing for the theater, not poets, and they succeed well, however banal the plot may sound in outline. To be noted are several interpolated musical numbers, chiefly choral. On one occasion Ahasuerus himself sings the old *complainte* beginning "Est-il rien sur la terre?"

About twenty years later came the opera, *Le Juif errant*, produced in Paris at the Académie royale de Musique in 1852, amid considerable social éclat. The libretto was by Eugène Scribe and M. de St. Georges, and the music by Jacques Halévy.[21] The music, of which more in a moment, is on the whole execrable, far below the standard of the same composer's *La Juive* (1835). The libretto is not of high caliber, either, being typical of Scribe's trickiness and meretricious melodramatic effects without some of his customary fluency. The work, however, while not spectacularly successful on the stage, had some popularity.

In the libretto, the Wandering Jew has two descendants, Théodora and Léon, living at Antwerp in 1190, when the Western world was getting ripe for one of its most sordid exhibitions of rapacity, the Fourth Crusade. Ahasuerus rescues from murder Irène, a daughter of the Countess of Flanders, and commits her to the care of Théodora. Irène grows to womanhood, wins the love of Léon, and is taken to Byzantium, where she has a libidinous effect upon the pretender to the imperial throne, Nicéphore. Ahasuerus not only protects the maiden from Nicéphore's embraces, but is able to get her installed as empress. At this point, while Irène is reigning in the imperial palace, in the presence of Théodora, Léon, and Nicéphore (whose love for Irène, as ardent as ever, has now become more "wholesome"), we must pause for the usual ballet required of all operas produced in Paris at that time; in this instance it is devoted to a silly sequence of shepherds and shepherdesses, birds and bees. At the conclusion of the ballet, Nicéphore proposes marriage to Irène and is refused, for, as the fourth act reveals, she is in love with Léon. Their love duet is overheard by Nicéphore. Egged on by the disappointed suitor, bandits attempt to kill Léon; again Ahasuerus intervenes, so that not even a terrifying destroying angel can bring about the young man's demise. Irène and Léon are united, and Ahasuerus expires peacefully, although his death is only an illusion. A violent epilogue, a dance of the damned angels in the Valley of Josaphat (reminiscent of Quinet), concludes with Ahasuerus once more on the march.

The music, as I have said, is altogether inferior, containing as it does almost every operatic cliché, but one may concede that Halévy made one contribution to musical tradition in writing a male quartet to be sung by four basses. Some sheet-music excerpts from the ballet evidently had some currency; "The Wandering Jew Mazurka," the "Valse du juif errant," and the "Polka of the Wandering Jew" survive. Scribe's use of Ahasuerus as a god from the machine is about as shameless as it well could be; by comparison Sue's Wandering Jew is a deft and discreet manipulator. A grotesque burlesque—apparently of the opera, although it pokes fun at some other tales about the Wandering Jew (particularly Sue's novel) —is H. van Peene's *De Wandelaer der Joden*, a "groote parodie" in five acts and ten scenes. Léon has become Leo; Irène, Hier-hinne ("hither and yon"); Nicéphore, Niets-Verdore ("not dried up"). Slapstick reigns amid many oblique digs at the influence of the French on the Flemish.[22] The work deserves to be forgotten, even though it gave the protagonist the unique name of Stapveurweerts ("step forward").

As a matter of fact, if we were to look for the most distinguished nonliterary presentation of the Wandering Jew in the nineteenth century, it would be not in musical forms but in the twelve remarkable engravings by Gustave Doré, which are based in tone upon the poem by Béranger and some new verses by Pierre Dupont, composed in collaboration with the artist. A handsome edition, containing both engravings and poetry, appeared in 1856, with a second edition in 1862. An English translation of the verses, reproducing the engravings, was published in London, probably in 1859.[23] These portrayals were in Doré's best manner highly imaginative, graphic, and finished performances like his illustrations of *The Divine Comedy*, *The Rime of the Ancient Mariner*, and *Paradise Lost*. They have remained something to be remembered by thousands of people during the last hundred years and have done much to make the popular image of the Wandering Jew what it is. Beyond all that, they have served as models for various imitators, particularly in Germany, who adorned the pages of literary and family magazines with derivative engravings—some good, some bad, and most indifferent.

We have by now seen many examples of Ahasuerus in restlessness, rebellion, complaint, and resignation. We shall see many more, but, meanwhile, we should observe how another emotion—remorse—tends to come into the foreground after the mid-century point. Works illustrating this are often nondescript, but they are symptomatic of a greater emphasis on remorse that is still to come. One of these, which is out of the ordinary, is A. D. Cohen's "Den evige Jøde in London."[24] It is the tale of John Mudley, actually a Jew from Smyrna, who posed as the Wandering Jew in London and indulged himself in sentimental, tear-inducing benevolence in order to calm the nostalgic regret which burned in his bosom. [The *London Athenaeum* for 1866 (p. 119 above) reported that at around this time a studious young man believed to be the Wandering Jew had been going about the streets of London, but this character was a peripatetic Oriental youth seen a generation and more earlier, not honest John Mudley.] Cohen's tale appears to be pure fiction, although it would be impossible to find a record of all the various legendary incidents current in popular fancy in a vast metropolis containing an infinite number of foreign elements. At any rate, the English themselves seem not to have noticed Mudley, and he appears to have been wished on England by an outlander, very much as Ahasuerus had been brought to London in 1694 (p. 109 above), when no Englishman knew anything about it.

Another work in this vein is an anonymous sonnet, "Le juif errant" (1866), a poem on the efficacy of remorse which names the plague, death in the gladiatorial arena, and huge conflagrations as benefactors of mankind because they have brought death to those who need it. Not surprisingly, this sonnet fails to come into logical focus. A far better statement is Gabrielle de Poligny's "Ahasvérus" (1857), a short, brilliant poem, in which Ahasuerus is pitied by a demon because he is afflicted with remorse. Is he not more regretful from the fact that he has such a long remembrance of things lost and gone?[25]

Thus Ahasuerus, whatever symbolic value he may have at a given moment or in a given work, can still strike with the full impact of the romantic, but he is assuredly less egocentric now, more closely in contact with the mass of humanity, and far more aware of society in general than he ever had been before.

Revivals of the Chronicle of the Wandering Jew

With all this nascent social awareness, Ahasuerus begins to look with more sympathy upon the world, even when he is only an observer. The old device of the Chronicle of the Wandering Jew, turning up as it does in each literary generation, remains a favorite technique, but the variations now being played upon it are many. One example is Seligmann Heller's *Die Wanderungen des Ahasver* (Vienna, 1865), a vigorous though overlong narrative poem in *terza rima* imitative of Mosen.[26] It is built on a structure of individual lays, forty in number, which carry the Wandering Jew from the time of Christ into the nineteenth century. As Heller has it, Jesus and Ahasuerus were once schoolmates in Jerusalem. Their relationship was close and friendly enough for Ahasuerus later to name his son after Jesus, but Ahasuerus could not tolerate what he considered to be politics in the Saviour's actions and became disillusioned about the pretensions of Christ, for he was a devout orthodox Jew. "Can He be the Redeemer . . . He who is Himself full of superstitious error?" He cannot reconcile Christ's social ideals with his apparent credulity. We pass briefly through the moving scene of the Last Supper. Then comes the Crucifixion, with the ugly, snarling crowd excellently sketched, as is the pale, fainting, but resolute figure of the Saviour. By the threshold of the house of Ahasuerus He falls, and the Jew's children rush in to tell their father that "a young man has fallen down out there; he looks much like our little brother Jesus!" When Ahasuerus spurns Christ with harsh abuse, he rises to his feet, transfigured, and pronounces his curse. Ahasuerus is on his way. Heller is indebted at this point to the prologue to Rönnefahrt's dramatic poem of eleven years before, to Croly's *Salathiel*, and in at least one passage to Browning's *A Death in the Desert*, published two years before. It is all familiar to us, especially the passages dealing with the destruction of Jerusalem.

When the Romans refuse to allow the rebuilding of the Temple, their stiff-necked policy kindles the rebellion of the Jews under Bar-Kashoba, which the emperor Hadrian suppresses. Heller devotes one and a half cantos to the ensuing lamentation of Israel, and this passage is one of the best in the poem. The whole melancholy story of this revolt serves to confirm the Jew in his Hebraism. All his previous qualms are allayed—qualms which had led him to argue with Christ and Paul and others. Now he can utter a proud affirmation of the Jewish faith, because he is convinced that Jehovah will ultimately overcome all foes.

Then, as if becoming aware of the romantic possibilities of his material, Heller allows Ahasuerus to indulge in a soliloquy, old-fashioned and Byronic, undistinguished and turgid, invoking blessings on the Holy Land and, as an afterthought, all that came out of it. Still, Holy Land or not, Ahasuerus must pause to recognize the actual presence in history of the Christian church and the church fathers, a new stimulus to asceticism of a kind which discredits the simple faith of the Jews. Yet he remains indifferent to the effect of these newcomers on his Hebrew faith; instead, he rhapsodizes on Platonic ideas in a vast, inchoate effusion, which is undoubtedly the weakest part of the poem. Our original parents were created by God: "in the Word of God our being was swallowed up; yet we have all turned

to our lusts, and our being has through its lusts pulled down the Word of God."
The problem of reconciling our dependence upon God with our appetites, however, is too difficult for Heller, and he returns to his history, into which the
poem spasmodically degenerates. In a section in which patristic doctrine is not
well digested, we are introduced to Origen and his new order; then we see once
more Christian martyrs in the arena. These miserable victims have had promise of
redemption, Ahasuerus notes; have they now anything more? There is no indication, in the days of Diocletian, of the *Gottesreich* which Ahasuerus seeks. But
Diocletian must pass, and we shall find in his place some day Constantine the
Great. The Devil gnashes his teeth at Constantine's very name, but Ahasuerus,
witnessing the first Council of Nicaea in 325, dismisses such affairs as mere *Zan-
kerei*.

Sooner or later Ahasuerus will meet the customary old sage who is both con-
genial and stimulating. It is not remarkable that in Heller's poem this should be
St. Anthony, whom many have considered the originator of the ascetic way of the
Church. To Ahasuerus the world-weary, Anthony preaches the virtues of rural
life, close to nature and not adulterated with the dross and sin of urban civilization. Ahasuerus agrees, saying that he lives ever in hope, although many past
events have impaired that hope, waiting always for the true favor of God—waiting like Cartaphilus, not necessarily wandering like Buttadeus. Anthony is sure
that, whatever else, he has helped Ahasuerus and is satisfied to die in the presence
of the Jew, who continues to await "the force of events, the call of the spirit."

It is idle to attempt a summary of the 15,500 lines of verse which Heller committed to paper. The farther one goes in this work, the muddier and more uninspired it becomes. It is evident that the poet has tried to portray the story of man
seeking to find himself. Man has debased the godhead from which he came;
but given enough opportunity, it seems possible that a new and perhaps even
greater godhead may come from man. Certainly Ahasuerus is intent upon finding this path between man and God, and he is willing to spend his wanderings in
this quest—in fact, he comes to believe that this was Christ's purpose in requir-
ing him to wander. If this be so, then the curse was not a curse but a blessing. He
is greatly impressed by Anthony's advice that man is at his best when he can be
reconciled "to work, to suffer, to love" (*wirken, leiden, lieben*). Ahasuerus also
has innumerable conversations with other great men—with Mohammed, Dante,
Newton, and particularly his idol, Goethe—and in the company of Faust he visits
America, a purely adventitious incident. It is unfortunate that Heller did not possess literary talent commensurate with the vastness of his plan. His characters
fail to coalesce; they are merely names. There are some good descriptive passages
here and there, but little movement in the narrative. The style is always too elaborate—with a sad overuse of the classical simile, which Heller allows to go on and
on and then fails to make vivid. In many ways the poem is the most spectacular
failure in the whole history of the art form of the Legend.

At the same time, Heller's is perhaps the most ambitious poem which attempts
between 1850 and 1875 to cast Ahasuerus as a symbol of patient humanity
against the background of the Chronicle of the Wandering Jew. The novel by

Alexandre Dumas *père, Isaac Laquedem* (Paris, 1853), is the most ambitious piece of contemporary prose fiction to make the same effort.[27] Here, however, the symbolism has been so incorrigibly romanticized as to be useless. The novel is assuredly one of the master fabricator's less inspired works. It is, in fact, unfinished, and for obvious reasons. In its first part, it is a colorful variation on the *Histoire admirable* of the seventeenth century, with Laquedem as the chronicler; in the second part, it is a romance of ancient Corinth in which Laquedem prevents the marriage of a mortal to a beauty of supernatural antecedents, who beneath her spell is a hideous old witch. This theme and its attendant situations are much better handled in Rider Haggard's popular *She* of a generation later.

In a lengthy prologue, Dumas presents Isaac Laquedem as a solitary pilgrim arriving in a city of the Italian Renaissance, where he exhibits his traditional ability to spy out treasure and demonstrates a superhuman capability as an archer. One may be reminded of the similar exploits of Robin Hood in *Ivanhoe,* but points of contact between Sir Walter Scott and Dumas are always easy to discern. The novel is readable enough up to this point. Then, however, Dumas decides to switch back to the Chronicle, garnished now with a great amount of excessively melodramatic seasoning, and the result is not happy. The events treated are military—the wars against Thebes, and the battles of Thermopylae and Pharsalus. On one occasion, Laquedem is the standard-bearer of the emperor Augustus. In his many wanderings he returns to the battlefield of Pharsalus, and there sees the ghosts of the combatants, including those of Caesar and Pompey, who must keep fighting after death because they were killed in a civil war. But this fine touch is immediately cheapened by the far too theatrical appearances of creatures of evil —among them harpies, Stymphalides, Gorgons, serpents, Chimeras, and other monsters of classical legend. Laquedem holds conversations with the shades of Achilles and the Sphinx; the latter tells him much about Cleopatra. He finally encounters the beautiful wraith of the old hag of Corinth. He squabbles with Prometheus over the secret of life and, to release the chained Titan, kindles a fire which consumes the old world and enables Laquedem to set himself up as a new Prometheus. He brings Cleopatra back to life, transports her to Rome, and sees her turn into Poppaea. Hamerling's *Ahasver in Rom* is in debt to this device in the scene in which the Goddess Roma is revealed as Agrippina.[28]

In fairness to Dumas, however, he should not be blamed for the inconclusive nature of his effort. The original scheme of *Isaac Laquedem* called for an immense romantic rendering of the Chronicle of the Wandering Jew in thirty volumes, covering more than fifteen hundred years, in the style of the *feuilleton* novel made famous by Eugène Sue. In fact, Dumas began publication of the work in the Paris *Constitutionnel,* but after enough material to fill two volumes had appeared, the censor stepped in. In his opinion, the incidents were bidding fair to become too scabrous; the tone, he thought, bordered upon the blasphemous; the thrusts at imperialism implicit in the pictures of the Roman Empire were, he insisted, much too keen to be tolerated by the still new regime of Napoleon III. There is a French ballad which was composed after the publication of the fragmentary *Isaac Laquedem* in book form. It may indeed have had the blessing of the Fourth Musketeer, as Dumas has been called. At any rate, it indicates that some marvelous things in the romantic line happened to Laquedem and promises more of the same—a promise which Dumas was never able to fulfill.[29]

Most of the attempts to romanticize the Chronicle of the Wandering Jew by selecting only certain melodramatic historical events have been unsuccessful. This kind of failure is what makes Paul Boiteau's tale in *Légendes pour les enfants* (Paris, 1857) a negligible item. Sometimes the chronicler, seeing Ahasuerus as representative of the omniscient man, takes advantage of the way in which historiography can lend itself easily to political discussion. For example, F. W. Gubitz, in the *Deutscher Volkskalender* (Leipzig, 1857), begins with a little essay on Ahasuerus himself, which is at first in a chronicling vein but ends with a querulous discourse on the lack of spirituality in the age, as illustrated particularly by the imperialism of Britain. As this was published only a few years before Germany entered the race for the so-called "place in the sun," it now makes for ironic reading. When Ahasuerus considers the sad prospect of the world in 1857, he repeats the hope that he may die soon, for if Christ were to come again, His redemption would be such that many Wandering Jews, instead of one, would be set a-wandering—a return to Goethe's fragmentary epic.

An American contribution, not distinguished for poetic talent, is Otway Curry's "Aaven" (1860), which introduces the Jew, now blessed with a Poe-like name, to a warder of the portals of history, with an "adamantine wand."[30] This warder reviews the ages for Aaven and conjures up spirits from the departed centuries. The situation is not original, since Neele, Aytoun, and others had allowed Ahasuerus to do this. But Aaven can at least join Isaac Laquedem, Hareach, Mr. Ferguson, Salathiel, and the others in the catalogue of aliases behind which the Wandering Jew can hide himself. More prosaically the Chronicle is related in the eighteenth-century manner in the anonymous *Ahasverus, des wahren ewigen Juden Wanderungen*. It was printed around 1845-50 but is probably much older, for it has about it the unmistakable flavor of the old German Ahasuerus-book, of which it is very likely a belated survival.[31] In this pamphlet Ahasuerus remains in the state of Kent in *King Lear:* "Not so young, sir, to love a woman for singing; nor so old to dote on her for anything: I have years on my back forty-eight." His actual age is a perennial forty-five. He is altogether cynical about women. The first part of the narrative concentrates upon Rome, beginning with the reign of Augustus, all events being dated from the building of the city (*anno urbis conditae*). Although pedestrian in style, it is entertaining. Ahasuerus, like Aeneas, sees the Sibylline leaves, a brief history of which is inserted. He is indignant at the realization that impostors are continually masquerading as the Wandering Jew and vents most of his wrath upon the unworthy figure of Joseph Loquedant (*sic*), whom we must consider identifiable with Isaac Laquedem. Ahasuerus has traveled much in France, but he can find little good to say about the French, which is inconsistent with the man-of-the-world tone of most of the pamphlet. One peculiarity of this Ahasuerus is that, like the White Queen in *Through the Looking Glass*, he can think into the future as well as into the past. On one occasion, for example, he traveled to imperial Rome and saw there both Claudius and Nero. And as he stood there and gazed at these tyrannous specimens, he realized that after them would appear Charlemagne, the first Holy Roman Emperor, and the entire caliphate of Bagdad. Then after Charlemagne would come the Carolingian succession, the Norman Conquest, the wars of the Guelphs and the Ghibellines, the Sicilian Vespers and the persecution of the Albigenses. But the virtuosity of the author hypnotizes him: the latter portion of the pamphlet, from around the year 1300 on is little more than a succession of names. Since the pamphlet, in its extant form, was written, I should guess, late in 1848, it is easy for Ahasuerus to prophesy the revolutions of that year. Hindsight is a wonderful thing: he does not come out so well when he foretells a fresh outbreak of the Black Death between 1848 and 1898.

Ahasuerus as a Vehicle for Satire

Now an entrenched symbol of mankind as a whole, Ahasuerus remains the butt of satirical attacks, for the sole target of satire is man in both broad and narrow aspects. After 1850 several lampooning items concerned with the Wandering Jew make their inevitable appearance. Some of these are fantastic, some trivial, some effective, and some incompetent. He also appears as a lover of nicotine in a quaint little French chapbook, the *Almanach du fumeur et du priseur* (1869), which is a miscellany in defense of nicotine, part of a not inconsiderable body of trivia in Occidental literature at this time. Many of the pieces in the *Almanach* were undoubtedly promoted by the tobacco interests; some, as were the *Reveries of a Bachelor* (New York, 1850) by the American Donald Grant Mitchell ("Ik Marvel"), or the early pieces of James Thomson ("B. V.") in England, were inspired by a romantic devotion to smoking. Then, between 1867 and 1870, the celebrated German humorous periodical *Kladderadatsch* presented a series of cartoons of a vaguely anti-Semitic nature in which Ahasuerus, typifying all Jews, appeared to serve as the object of jokes notable for their mastodonic heaviness.[32]

A most peculiar satirical work is the dramatic fantasy by Karl Koesting, *Shakespeare, ein Winternachtstraum* (Wiesbaden, 1864). In the prologue to this play Ahasuerus appears at Shakespeare's funeral to reprove the officiating Puritan pastor, Jeremias Himmelmann (the influence of Jonson's comedy of humors is evident here), for objecting publicly and in extremely bad taste to what he considered Shakespeare's worldliness. It is impossible to tell to what extent Koesting is to be taken seriously and to what extent he may be satirizing romantic idolatry of Shakespeare. At any rate five acts follow. In the first two, Shakespeare is in Stratford, a wild youth, who has been apprehended for poaching by Sir Lucy (*sic*). While in prison, he is repudiated successively by his father, his wife, and even his mother, but is visited and encouraged by the Wandering Jew. Acts III and IV take place in London. A British naval officer, answering to the most un-British name of Fortunio, says farewell to his lukewarm spouse, Amata (another Jonsonism), and departs for the wars. Ahasuerus, now posing as a rich cousin of Amata, gets her to go to the theater, where *Romeo and Juliet* is being performed. Shakespeare has been acting in the role of the Clown. After the performance many notables stand around vaguely—Marlowe, Nashe, Greene, Jonson, Henslowe, and Good Queen Bess herself. Koesting's knowledge of the Elizabethan theater, one must hasten to explain, was neither profound nor meticulous as to chronology.

Amata wins the eye of Shakespeare, but Ahasuerus interrupts this incipient romance by bringing on the scene the daughter of the playwright, Susannah, who awakens her father's better—that is to say, domestic—nature. Shakespeare is nevertheless so annoyed that he draws his rapier and runs the officious Ahasuerus through. Of course we know that the Jew is only feigning injury; Shakespeare, however, is conscience-stricken because he seems to have committed murder and returns in morbid gloom to Stratford, where the last act is laid. As a result of his deep depression, the poet is inspired to write superb tragedies. He also broods romantically in the Stratford graveyard. Ahasuerus, convinced that he has saved the soul of the poet, reveals to him that he is still alive and brings the desired reconciliation between Shakespeare and his family. And so the great dramatist is converted to his true callings, which are to be a builder of mighty tragedies and an exemplar of good family life. Ahasuerus, his work done in this bourgeois manner, embraces Shakespeare and fades from the scene.

The dedication of the play to Koesting's friend, the poet Friedrich Bodenstedt, explains how, in drinking powerful draughts of *German* wine—for the patriotic point can hardly be missed—Koesting was inspired by the concept of Ahasuerus as a doer of good, a creature with a loving, puckish countenance gently fanned by the breezes of peace, who smilingly belabors humanity until he can bring man to light out of darkness. This, then, is the objective which is aimed at in the play, but the total effect is one ranging from the gently amusing down to the outright silly.

Less effective because its satire is of the rather pithless kind associated with the ephemeral comedy of manners, but much better as an honest treatment of the Legend is A. Hartmann's "Baron Ahasver," which appeared in the periodical *Freya* in 1865 and then in a collection of the author's tales called *Schweizer-Novellen* (Berlin, 1877). This is a novelette whose action takes place mainly in a Swiss mountain resort. An unexplained arrival, dapper in clothes and manner, registers at the inn, incognito even to the management. He gets himself talked about by the other guests, a diverting group of the idle rich. People try to identify the stranger as someone seen before: one man met him hovering around the brink of the crater of Etna; another saw him on the banks of the River Ganges; another remembered how the stranger had once made a killing at the Casino in Monte Carlo; still another recalled that he had seen him on the Grimsel. Aside from the stranger's noteworthy appearance at the gaming table, Hartmann has taken care that the visitor is seen in all the usual places. As for the Grimsel affair, the stranger had reported that a party of travelers had been stranded far up in one of the more dangerous mountain passes, and so had been responsible for the rescue of many souls. The stranger can speak all known languages and is acquainted with the whole history of the Christian Era. His face, in spite of his only moderately mature years, is deeply lined. He carries a cane, which he handles in debonair fashion. When he finally leaves the resort, he leaves behind his calling cards, which reveal his true identity—Baron Ahasver. The picture presented by Hartmann is more French than German. It is about as inconsequential as that in the Parisian *Salmigondis* (*Revue de Salon*) for 1851, in which a pseudonymous

"Cham" furnishes an entertaining series of cartoons of the Wandering Jew in quasi-burlesque social comment.[33]

A comedy of Danish student and military life, Christian Hostrup's *Gjenboerne* (Copenhagen, 1847), introduces Ahasuerus in a brief part.[34] The author, a rather lively dramatist of the pre-Ibsen era, was acquainted with Schiller's fragmentary novel *Der Geisterseher*—for we may note in passing the presence of a Russian army officer, although this one has only a nominal relationship to Ahasuerus. In the play, a shoemaker complains bitterly of the shabby treatment accorded him by various people, paying his compliments in a loud tone of disrespect to several writers of note, particularly Hans Christian Andersen and Ingemann. The shoemaker is not named by name, but his identity is obvious.

But much more mordant than any of the satires yet mentioned is Eduard Grisebach's *Der neue Tannhäuser* (Berlin, 1869), a poem indebted to the Ahasuerus-book, as well as to Schubart and Goethe, but with many original turns.[35] The scene is Auerbach's cellar, made famous in *Faust*, where Ahasuerus is warning Faust not to throw away his soul for the sake of Helen. Life is hell-torture, and Faust, like Tannhäuser, may escape from the Venusberg too late, if he can ever escape at all. Ahasuerus has tried to poison himself with hemlock and belladonna, but they had no more effect upon him than wheat bread. Faust is a chronic hater and thinks of Ahasuerus as a "perpetual lover of sin," but the Jew denies this. Rather he hates life with all its stinking sins and diseases, where one can live a thousand years without laughing; he is therefore willing to go back and "thrash about some more in the thicket," since this is his fate. Grisebach is acid in his expression of the hopelessness of Ahasuerus, who is here the cynic of cynics—but it takes a cosmic satirist to deal Swiftian blows, and Grisebach is not that. In default of such endowment, he would have been better advised to have adopted a lighter touch, but this, too, seems beyond his capabilities.

On the other hand, it is just this lightness of touch that allows Gustav Sonnabend, in his *Das verlorene Manuscript: Ein Scherz* (Leipzig, 1865), to come out better than Grisebach. This is a comic short story which emphasizes the tiresome troubles of our complex modern society with more success than a much more ambitious effort by a more serious individual would have done. There was once a Julius Hirschbey of Leipzig, who wrote a play about Ahasuerus, who "died, after all." He tried to interest an impresario, a strangely effective work of caricature—a man who can barely finish any sentence he begins, but fool though he may be, can immediately detect a probable dramatic failure and so will not agree to produce the drama. Whereupon Hirschbey turns the play into a novel, which is a sensible thing to do, because the Legend is epic rather than dramatic. Yet he still cannot get the work published, and in the meantime is beginning to suffer Bohemian pangs of hunger. The brilliant idea comes to him to claim the manuscript as lost and then to sue the publishers for as much as the manuscript would have brought him if it had been accepted. The scheme fails; Hirschbey is obliged to admit at the trial that he himself had stolen the manuscript from the Cöthen railroad station, and is in consequence sentenced to two years in prison—where at least he does not starve. Sonnabend's humor is a queer combination of the naïve and the acerb, but the readability of his work shows that its ingenuous tone is more artful than otherwise. Be that as it may, his story and Grisebach's poem have much greater impact than two other satires on the Wandering Jew from the decade: Ludwig Eichrodt's poem, "Ahasver" (1869) and J. G. Saxe's ballad, "The Wandering Jew," in *Clever Stories of Many Nations* (1865). In Eichrodt's work, Ahasuerus is a sneering and vapid fop, mouthing a drinking song; in Saxe's he is merely silly, for the author tries too hard to be funny. Rudolf Baumbach's "Ahasver" (1878) has it that once the Wandering Jew soled some boots for Christ gratis and was granted a wish in payment: he chose to wander indefinitely, and, as Brother Straubinger, goes up and down the dusty country roads of Germany, observing mankind with all its foibles and enjoying the itinerant life of a friendly artisan. All the classic motivation for the wandering has been removed; the piece is pointless.[36]

Composites and Contaminations

In several instances, as we have seen, the Legend of the Wandering Jew has been contaminated with that of Faust. The works of "F. Marlow" (L. H. Wolfram), Seligmann Heller, and Grisebach are cases in point.[37] There will be more of these in the future, and contaminations with still other legends are always possible. The years between 1875 and 1900, in particular, afford some good examples which are diverting but necessarily mongrel in breed.

H. Rider Haggard's best sellers, *She* (London, 1887) and its sequels, may be dismissed because their theme is that of extreme longevity and therefore only cognate to the Legend of the Wandering Jew.[38] Besides, the heroine collapses into dust after the passing of a mere millennium or so. But the striking narrative poem by Emil von Schönaich-Carolath, *Don Juans Tod* (1883), presents Ahasuerus as a *prima causa*.[39] A ragged beggar, turned away by Christ, he meets Venus, who has been rejected by Christian society (there is an echo here of the old Legend of Beauty and the Beast). The affair of Ahasuerus and Venus is no vulgar bordello bout. It comes to fruition in the summer fields, between two beings dismissed from the Christian way of life. All of the efforts of Ahasuerus to celebrate the goddess of love, to seek her and to win her, are based in some measure upon the hope that he, like his kindred wanderer, the Flying Dutchman, can thus find redemption through the love of a woman. So long has he been deprived of intercourse with women that when he sees the fleeing goddess he overtakes and ravishes her:

> With furious lust he crushes to him
> The slim white limbs of warm divinity,
> The white though marble-cool-thighed goddess . . .

Venus, thus fructified, now comes to rule the world through her twin progeny—Don Juan and Faust, respectively the high priest of wine, women, and song, and the prince of human thought. Optimistically interpreted by Schönaich-Carolath, the union of Ahasuerus (restlessness) and Venus (beauty) is seen as having produced the ideals of body in Don Juan and of mind in Faust.

The core of the poem is taken up with Don Juan. He and Ahasuerus had been brought together on the same stage as far back as Auerbach in the late 1830's, but the unexpected parenthood of Ahasuerus and Venus are new details. For that matter, Venus has impinged on the Legend here for the first time. Having done so much to exalt the prowess of the Wandering Jew, Schönaich-Carolath regrettably descends, near the conclusion of the poem, to the most Junkerish kind of German nationalism, proclaiming Faust as the prince of the world of lofty thoughts of German men and women and of the spirit of German poetry. Not by any stretch of the imagination can *Don Juans Tod* be interpreted as a satire on nationalism. One must therefore conclude that the author was imbued with high opinions about the empire conceived and brought to birth by Bismarck. The lapse is perhaps forgivable; certainly it can be ascribed to *race, milieu, et moment*, a phrase which Hippolyte Taine made famous during this generation. It is better to pay tribute, where tribute is due, to the many fine passages in the poem.

Another writer who saw a connection between Ahasuerus and Faust takes a less sanguine view than Schönaich-Carolath. According to A. Schultz, in two articles published in 1866 and 1872, both Ahasuerus and Faust come from the kingdom of Satan, in which Ahasuerus represents Death and Faust the Devil.[40] But here, as elsewhere, one must insist that the essential partition dividing Ahasuerus and Faust as legendary figures must hold firm. They are not the same character in the same legend, although literary license may bring them together. Neither, for example, does Ahasuerus' appearance in A. T. von Grimm's dramatic poem *Meister Martin* (Wiesbaden, 1887) mean that the Legend of the Wandering Jew and that of Antichrist are the same legend. The two legends remain separate even though Ahasuerus appears in this dramatic poem in twelve scenes on Martin Luther as a prince of doubt and despair, a kind of cross between Antichrist and Mephistopheles (it is he against whom Luther hurls his inkpot at Ehrenbreitstein, not Satan nor any of the accepted lieutenants of the ruler of hell).

Thrusting itself up into all this talk of cognates and composites of the Legend is the monstrous specter of Max Haushofer's *Der ewige Jude* (Leipzig, 1886), by all odds the most ambitious single work on the subject from its decade, and a most annoying magnum opus.[41] It may be described as a dramatic composition in the form of a trilogy, embellished with a prologue and an epilogue. The trilogy comprises a "myth," a "tragedy," and a "fantastic comedy."

As for the "myth," it deals with the days of the breaking up of the Roman Empire. The Goths are attacking the city of Iuvavia (Salzburg). The outstanding characters are a Roman captain, a Gothic warrior (Walafried), a Christian priest, and, of course, the Wandering Jew. The Goths sack Iuvavia, and the leading characters take refuge, for one reason or another, in a neighboring mountain, the Untersberg. All of the men save the Wandering Jew are miraculously immured in the mountain for a thousand years. The leading genius in the operation of this miracle is the ancient Germanic goddess Perachta (Berchta), whose functions are similar to those of Venus and who works now for good and now for evil. Perachta and her handmaidens charm the walled-up Romans, Christians, and Goths, but the Wandering Jew is left howling without.

The "tragedy" is laid in seventeenth-century Austria, at the end of the thousand years. An alchemist-astrologer, Von Werth (suggested by Goethe's Faust), is seeking the elixir of eternal life. His adopted daughter Elsa, an unexplained descendant of the Wandering Jew, is seduced by a medical man, Thanatos ("Death"), becomes a prostitute, but finally returns to Von Werth for peace and quiet and a single bed at night. The villain Thanatos, however, hovers about, ruins Von Werth's lifework, and drives Elsa to suicide. Ahasuerus, knowing who she is, vainly attempts to follow her example.

The "myth" is difficult reading; the "tragedy" less so; but the "fantastic comedy" is prohibitively hard going, because Haushofer is gifted with a mercurial and at the same time a muddy mind. Yet the "fantastic comedy" is the best part of the work. It is connected directly to the Prologue at the beginning of the trilogy. In the Prologue, a Bohemian poet and his friends, among them a girl named Ada, are holding forth in the poet's studio about a tragic play on the subject of the Wandering Jew which is to be performed that day. It is the "tragedy" to which they are referring. The point is made that a man who never dies can hardly be a logical sacrifice in a tragedy, for a tragic hero must die to achieve immortality. This point is evidently Haushofer's reason for making a descendant of Ahasuerus rather than Ahasuerus himself the luckless victim of the "tragedy." Now, in the third section, the "fantastic comedy," the people in the studio reappear to hold the center of the stage, surrounded this time by countless others who make up a fine cross section of Viennese society in the 1880's. Kurt, the gay poet of the Prologue, is in love with Ada, but he fears a supposed curse which has been laid upon his ancestral domain in the Ardennes, and is diffident about declaring his love. After a great number of scenes with a plenitude of characters and a wide sweep of social panorama—which do not get very far except for some good epigrammatic wit—the entire group is transported to the Untersberg, where once more they will be immured for a thousand years. This time, however, the Wandering Jew, now a mysterious Marcus Schwartz, a suave and self-possessed urbanite, is permitted to enter with the others.

There follows a sequence of nine allegorical scenes—much in the manner of Dante, all laid within the Untersberg, a true land of illusion—culminating in an inferno or Walpurgis Night scene, where, amid a concourse of devils, there is a play within a play. This depicts the ruination of earth. The Last Man gives away his inheritance. But the Wandering Jew survives along with the Last Man, to discover that there is also a Last Woman. She is Minne ("Love"), an attendant of the goddess Perachta, who had appeared in the "myth." She hopes to mate with the Last Man, in order to create a new human race for a new world. Ahasuerus, however, jealous of Minne's love and, moreover, furious at this check to the hope that with the extinction of human beings he too could find death, blasts both Minne and the Last Man by revealing to them the hideous countenance of the destroying angel. Amid thunder and lightning the curtain falls on the play within a play.

In the Epilogue we find Schwartz, Kurt, and Ada passing a comfortable hour in a tavern. The "fantastic comedy" was, then, no more than a bad dream. Schwartz (the Wandering Jew), when about to leave, suddenly reveals to Kurt that his father was never insane, that there is in consequence no curse on his family, and that he can marry Ada with impunity.

Comment on Haushofer's work as a whole is difficult and thankless. German critical opinion seemed at one time to consider it, along with that of Mosen, as the leading German achievement in the art form of the Legend in the nineteenth century. Hamerling's epic was played down, and yet any impartial reading today would give it a place among the best of its genre. Haushofer has drunk deep of the second part of Goethe's *Faust* and been fascinated by the perennial problem of the eternal, for which he is in some measure indebted to the Rosicrucians in general and to Bulwer-Lytton's novel, *Zanoni* (1842) in particular. But while he has more literary talent than Bulwer-Lytton, he is no Goethe. He has the typical weakness of the second-class German writer for words and moralizing. The melodrama of the "tragedy" is good; the "myth," on the other hand, is static, clumsy, and not well related to the rest of the trilogy; the "fantastic comedy," while often effective in its wit and satire, is nebulous; its mystic values are at once vague and heavy-footed in a most incongruous mixture. In all this wide range of subject matter there are a few good scenes and many good lines—the laws of probability might account for this—yet here again, when the work invites comparison with Quinet's *Ahasvérus* and the comparison is ruthlessly made, Haushofer's work suffers.

There is little need to illustrate Haushofer's yearnings toward the infinite, for his gifts do not reach into the empyrean; they are more at home in melodrama. What should be remembered, however, in any criticism of Haushofer's work, is that it is a composite—a medley, as Tennyson called *The Princess*—and therefore, in spite of many apt sections, is almost sure to fail in the long run. It is by turns epic, lyric, dramatic, religious, satirical, philosophical, didactic, comic, gruesome, and ridiculous. It covers time with as much greedy appetite as Shaw's *Back to Methuselah* or Wilder's *The Skin of Our Teeth*, both of which are better achievements. Incidentally, there seems to be a curious anticipation, in the "fantastic comedy," of the technique and some of the effects of the Walpurgis Night scene in the hospital in Joyce's *Ulysses*.

One question hovers over the reader's mind throughout and is never fully answered, for it is doubtful whether Haushofer intended an answer to his riddle-like conclusion. What has Ahasuerus to do with all this? As in many works, such as Croly's *Salathiel* or Sue's *Le juif errant*, to take but two examples, Ahasuerus here has a personal interest in the destiny of humanity, since his race, to say nothing of his actual descendants, is involved in the action of the poem—Walafried in the "myth," Elsa in the "tragedy," and Wolfhart or Schwartz in the "fantastic comedy" and in the Prologue and Epilogue. Ahasuerus is to live through all the joys and sorrows of the Jews represented in the work and to show the feelings natural to an ancestor who sees what is happening to his progeny; in other words, he is himself a suffering human being. In the "tragedy" especially, he is neither Christian nor Jew. Throughout he is notably reticent about his history. Others may call him "a poor old man," but he avoids any such sentimentalizing about himself, although he complains from time to time of his weariness. Again, he may be a *geisterhafter Greis*, embodying thoughts of immortality in a changing world (which is typified by the general course of history). He considers himself on one occasion "a citizen of eternity, of that limitless condition of existence which confronts us all, young and old alike"—an example of Haushofer's occasional stuffy rodomontade. His appearance strikes more than one character in the poem with terror. On the other hand, particularly in the "fantastic comedy," he is the complete modern sophisticate, as compact as any man could be. His attitude toward earthly love can be cynical and faithless; he seems at times to have the instinct of a gallant. For the greater part he disdains the old-clothes, down-at-the-heel personality of the customary portrayals of the Wandering Jew. He craves death and cannot find it—an orthodox detail for an Ahasuerus of the nineteenth century. More or less reconciled to his unhappy situation, he sometimes treats his problem with a levity worthy of Heine. As a matter of fact, one may gather that Heine is the chief influence on Haushofer's lyrics. One may therefore expect irony in the attitude of this Ahasuerus, and it is there. At times it merges with the purely satirical, as in the comments on the life-giving elixir in the "tragedy." But this attitude is sometimes laid aside, as in the "fantastic comedy," where Ahasuerus, as Schwartz, is pictured as benevolent, good-humored, and tolerant. All in all, Haushofer has succeeded well in keeping what might have been a conventional Ahasuerus from following a stereotyped pattern.

As a philosopher, this Ahasuerus bears immortality upon his shoulders. He is prepared to discount the past; the present and the future are more important. The old romancers may be discredited, but Ahasuerus is not therefore dead. He is still living; he will always be living in some form. To know how Ahasuerus feels is to be Ahasuerus. If his independence leads him to break social molds to such an extent that he must visit a hospital for mental diseases, the superintendent of the institution may come to think that he himself is Ahasuerus, and the patient will be released.

What is eternity? Is it a closed ring? A current returning to its source? It is unfortunate that Haushofer is not as explicit in his questioning as he could have been. Perhaps it is best to interpret his work as a kind of dramatization of philosophy, in the sense that he tries to illustrate somewhere almost every conceivable type of philosophical attitude. He discusses immortality and the possibility of a future life, God and his attributes, and humanity living and loving. His God is a transcendentally great spirit, devoid of mercy. Mankind cannot be improved over what it is; all the changes are mere clothing; the longer one lives, the more one narrows living; the world is a madhouse; the Last Man is a fool. Yet life demands a purpose and labor—one will grow weary of joy sooner than of toil. Life is a short path to death, and only the ideals of art and love can enhance it.

Some have seen in the work not only a philosophical drama but also a history of civilization, a *Kulturgeschichte*. To them it is a great inclusive picture of life in late Roman times, in the late Renaissance, and in the contemporary era—life not so much of the religious as of the social thinker. With such an interpretation I find it difficult to agree, because nowhere in the work does one see an adequate representation of the society of the eras defined. This is one of the two long works by Haushofer and is a composite of the sources of his uneven inspiration. He was a teacher of economics as well as a poet; his son was Karl Haushofer, the noted exponent of geopolitics in Nazi Germany during the 1930's. Haushofer *père* was a well-read and intelligent connoisseur of literature; in consequence, his poem, although derivative in ideas and style, is not fully indebted to any one writer, unless to Goethe or Heine. Earlier writers about the Legend may have suggested a good deal to him—Quinet, Mosen, Croly, Andersen, and Seligmann Heller. Walafried's pilgrimage to Rome—indeed, the whole central arrangement of the "myth" —reminds one of the Legend of Tannhäuser. More diffuse, yet lending complete validity to the epithet "composite" as applied to his poem, are his debts to folk tales distinct from those of the Wandering Jew: for example, the tales of the Wild Huntsman, of Medea, of the Ancestral Mother, of Don Juan, of the Vampire, of the Man Who Has Death for a Guest, as well as those local legends associated with the Untersberg near Salzburg. The mixture of materials into often grotesque combinations shows a dangerous tendency to spread among the later writers about the Legend, as will soon be evident. It is as if the outlines of the Legend, simple enough as such legends go, were inadequate, and that only elaboration could bring originality and rescue the reader from the bareness of the Legend in its unadulterated state. To put it briefly, Haushofer has offered us a phantasmagoria on the Legend, based on the theory that modern life is itself a phantasmagoria.

Ahasuerus the Emerging Modern Man

Haushofer's "fantastic comedy" is enough to indicate that the satirical treatment of Ahasuerus, scattered about, as we have seen, over the preceding two hundred years, still appealed to perceptive writers, and it will become an invaluable vehicle for twentieth-century authors dealing with the Legend. Few satirical pieces on this subject between 1850 and 1890, however, can qualify as successful examples. Published in Leipzig in 1878, Fritz Mauthner's skit, *Der unbewusste Ahasverus, oder das Ding an sich als Wille und Vorstellung* ("The Unconscious Ahasuerus, or the Thing Itself as You Like It"), a "Festival Play about Trouble in Three Deals," is a whimsical attack on Richard Wagner's literary and musical style, his passion for alliteration and neologisms, his egomania, his megalomania, his leitmotifs, his institution at Bayreuth, and his not too tactful anti-Semitism. Ahasuerus is driven to drink by Wagner's *Ring* cycle and is finally given a lethal release from suffering by a particularly devastating leitmotif. In keeping with this idea, for sooner or later Ahasuerus in the nineteenth century must collide with the Wagnerian problem, there survives a student song of the times, attributed to Paul von Portheim and published at Dresden in 1884, which lustily assigns to the Wandering Jew, in good round goliardic verse, the role of Ahasuerus Dipsomanicus.[42]

In contrast is the pacifistic satire—if there is such a thing—in Albert Gehrke's "Ahasver," from his *Mit dem Diogeneslaterne* (Leipzig, 1889). It is unimportant enough in itself but interesting in its special appeal to Ahasuerus to avoid the intrigues of modern society and stand as spokesman for the purest Christian love for one's neighbor. It enjoins him to combat to the last stronghold all militant faiths, all lust for glory, all civil warfare, and, indeed, all liberty won through sword and slaughter. Apart from its blindness to the reality essential to good satire and its failure to recognize that liberty can result from bloodshed, the poem fails to impress because it gives Ahasuerus an illogical part to play. It insists that he, a Jew, must be the very quintessence of a Christian. Although we have seen him converted to Christianity more than once, it is always difficult to make him convincing in his new-found faith.

For that matter, Ahasuerus in these decades is more worthy of attention when he is concerned with Christianity only as a latter-day skeptic. He has derived comfort from Venus in Schönaich-Carolath's *Don Juans Tod* and from the goddess Perachta in Haushofer's *Der ewige Jude*. In the 1880's and 1890's, what they considered *fin de siècle* decadence sent the new generation scurrying after different gods, and revolt against older values and standards was everywhere. The powerful figure of Friedrich Nietzsche was proclaiming the gospel of the superman. In a poem in *Neue Dichtungen* (n.p., 1886), entitled "Der Trost," Richard Zoozmann introduces Ahasuerus to Woden, king of the Germanic gods, who assures the raging Jew that he will be released from his curse only when the reign of Christ on earth can be broken and the last Christian has ceased to believe, for no religion can outlive the god it worships. This anti-Christian sentiment is also developed successfully in Zoozmann's larger work, the narrative poem "Ahasver," in his *Seltsame Gedichten* (Zurich, 1890-91), which is described in its subtitle as a "mosaic of various ideas" (*Mosaik aus allerhand Einfällen*). It is in reality a hardheaded satire. Ahasuerus is now a "modern man," neither Christian nor Jew. The curse upon him has faded. He stands as a representative of struggling humanity who can never die. In almost Shavian fashion he becomes a dentist, who can extract anything except the *Zahn der Zeit*, by which we are to understand the ulcerated tooth of the age. This bumptious metaphor, also Shavian, is typical of Zoozmann's humor. The core of the poem is a scene in a luxurious railroad car. Ahasuerus, on a short trip to Babelsberg, falls into conversation with others in the car. He decries the trends in modern education, which he feels would be better if given over to the study of literature and natural history. He is arrogant in praise of modern inventions—a trifle blasé about them, too, but no wonder; after all, he feels himself to be older than Adam. Ahasuerus no longer wishes even to be called a Jew; it is, he believes, a distinct handicap in modern society. Here the anti-Semitic issue is uncovered, but Zoozmann deftly avoids the pitfall, and is satisfied to point out the handicap and then go on to other matters. Ahasuerus continues to talk informally and wittily about the social problems created by such dissimilar people as Moses and Cleopatra. For good measure he throws in disparaging remarks about Aspasia, for he does not think too well of brilliant women who run intellectual coteries. He believes that the chief riddle of present-day culture is the anomalous position of the Christian: it benefits the modern European man of the world to profess Christianity, yet the vast gulf between the teachings of Christ and the practice of assured Christians is sufficient to demonstrate the insanity of the whole situation. For the rest, Zoozmann's worldly Ahasuerus enjoys the technological age in which he is living and is especially proud of the great influence which his adopted native land, Germany, is exerting on it. About this he is jingoistic. There are other treatments of Ahasuerus which may turn him into a chauvinistic Hans, complete with dachshund and monocle, but Zoozmann's is one of the most insufferable of Wandering Jews and therefore most cutting in its satiric effect.

Another lively satire, altogether different from Zoozmann's, is Theobald Kerner's *Der neue Ahasver* (Weinsberg, 1885), a comedy of manners colored with a few dark hues. The scene is an inn high in the Bavarian Alps. A young Englishman believes himself to be Ahasuerus, although Cain would be a more appropriate delusion, because he has supposedly slain his father. Accompanied by the solicitous valet of English fiction and drama, he is trying to carry out his destiny by wandering—for the most part in comfortable places only. Near the inn he falls from a rock and is brought in for dead, but he survives, falls in love with the innkeeper's daughter, and is relieved of his guilt complex when his father walks in and explains all. The minor characters are of far greater interest than the young Englishman: a lovesick maiden worthy of Gilbert and Sullivan; a silly businessman from the north; and his daughter, who carries about with her, in an urn, the ashes of her deceased lap dog. In addition, there are the local schoolmaster—who talks incessantly and vaguely but is supposed to be at heart lovable, especially to the lovesick maiden—and the village preacher, whose anti-Semitism is so extreme that he cannot abide the mere thought of the Wandering Jew's presence.

Ahasuerus and the Judenfrage

One is justified in holding the spotlight a little longer than usual on this village pastor in Kerner's play, because the years from 1870 to 1890 were a time of especially powerful anti-Jewish sentiment in Germany, which has never been noted for its tolerance of the Jew. The upsweep of this particular wave of anti-Semitism began with the revolution of 1848 and reached a crest after the founding of the German Empire in 1871 and the consequent awareness of Germany that she was now a great world power. The Jews, by their very traditions and history, could not be narrowly nationalistic. They therefore came to be regarded by the more bigoted German patriots of the day as enemies of the state, along with the Freemasons, the Roman Catholics (sometimes referred to as the Black International), and the Social Democrats (the Red International). The most famous of the many Jew-baiters in the 1870's was Heinrich von Treitschke, whose catch phrase, "The Jews are our misfortune," served as a war cry for anti-Semites everywhere. August Rohling's *Der Talmudjude* (Berlin, 1871) set the seal of the infernal upon the traditions of the Talmud. One of the noisiest, as he was one of the most ignorant, of these vociferous teachers of *Judenhass* was Adolf Stöcker, a court preacher in Berlin, who, in 1878, founded the Christian Social Labor Party, which for all its brave title was indeed nothing more than an anti-Semitic faction made up of ultraconservatives in business and industry, and members of the lower middle class. Although Stöcker came to be repudiated by most fair-minded people, even among the anti-Semites—assuming that there were such—he nevertheless did great damage; the turmoil which he stirred up was never completely allayed and served as a strong emotional weapon in the hands of Adolf Hitler a half-century later. In Kerner's play, *Der neue Ahasver*, the fanatical village pastor was suggested by Stöcker. Kerner's contribution to the warfare was cleverly done and worked on the side of the Jews, but it was of little immediate weight.

We need not follow this line much farther, but since the name of Ahasuerus is bandied about among the disputants, we should know a few typical publications in this war. Some radical anti-Semites preached the extirpation of the whole Jewish race—genocide, in other words—so violently that W. Marr, originator of the term *Judenhass* and author of two strong diatribes—*Der Sieg des Judenthums über das Germanenthum* (Bern, 1879) and *Goldene Ratten und rothe Mäule* ("Gold Rats with Red Maws"; Chemnitz, 1880)—became disillusioned and moderated his tone in *Der Weg zum Siege des Germanthums über das Judenthum* (Berlin, 1880), in which he preached a patient assimilation of the "foreign" element. On the whole, however, the agitation at this time was bitter. The heavy anti-Jewish jokes which during these years were sprinkled through the pages of the leading German humorous periodical, *Kladderadatsch*, have already been noted in this chapter. Here, as elsewhere, Ahasuerus was a common representative of all Jewry. Throughout the generation Stöcker's *Das moderne Judenthum in Deutschland* (Berlin, 1880) was the Bible of the anti-Semites, right up to the publication of Hitler's *Mein Kampf* in 1933.

And there were many other pamphlets. Especially cruel was a pair of screeds by one "Germanicus": *Die Frankfurter Juden und die Aufsaugung des Volkswohlstandes* ("The Frankfurt Jews and Their Absorption of the National Wealth"; Leipzig, 1880) and *Der neueste Raub am deutschen Nationalwohlstand* ("The Latest Pillaging of German National Wealth"; Frankfurt, 1881).[43] The *Manifest* of the anti-Semitic congress, published at Dresden in 1882, makes rugged reading for all but the obtuse. Apparently there had been some incidents and a murder trial or two in which the accused were alleged to have committed the murders in the course of some obscene ritual—the veriest throwback to the Middle Ages. One affair seems to have been faked: the burning of a synagogue in Neustettin in 1884, the account of which resembles startlingly the story of the Reichstag fire of 1933. When a Prussian *Junker* entered the controversy, the ruthlessness of the point of view is sharpened, as in Alexander, Freiherr von Pawel-Rammingen's *Gedanken eines Cavaliers über Antisemitismus* (Berlin, 1886; 2nd ed.: Berlin, 1887). One of the more gory minds belonged to Egon Waldegg, who, in a pamphlet in 1879, defended the persecution of the Jews on the grounds of national necessity.[44] R. A. C. von Wedell, in *Vorurtheil oder berechtiger Hass?* (Berlin, 1880), may have thought himself impartial, but prejudice still seems to bulk larger in his mind than good honest hate. At least there is no mistaking his position. Others, more discreet, attempted to straddle the question, although their anti-Jewish bias would ultimately triumph. This is the case in Joseph Volkmann's *Die gesellschaftliche Stellung der Juden* ("The Social Status of the Jews"; Lobau, 1876), which is only mildly prejudiced.

All this, and more, forms a depressing library, especially in the light of what has happened since 1880. Nevertheless, the Jew had his defenders, not all from his own race either. Fritz Mauthner's novel, *Der neue Ahasver*, which I shall discuss in a moment, was one; and there were several minor counterblasts against Stöcker, much as Joly and others had rushed to the aid of the Jesuits against Eugène Sue in the 1840's. Some of these were overemotional, as was M. Baumgarten's *Wider Herrn Hofprediger Stöcker* (1881); or nebulous, like D. Paulus Cassel's *Ahasverus* (1885), whose strained, agonized theory that Ahasuerus and

Haman were the two beasts in Revelation was, he said, "a critical protest against
. . . Stöcker"; or eloquently humanitarian, as was Franz Delitzsch's article in *Saat
auf Hoffnung* for 1886; or grudging, like A. T. Hammer's *Juda und die deutsche
Gesellschaft* (Berlin, 1881), which cannot avoid the observation that Jews, for all
their good points, are responsible for a cheapening of German society.[45] One
sensible approach to the *Judenfrage* is Ernst Kelchner's *Wozu der Lärm?* (Frankfurt, 1881), which accepts the Jews as a fact of nature and waves the whole problem aside with the teasing question: "What's all the shooting for?" It is difficult
to appraise the pamphlet by S. Leon, *Unser heutiges Judenthum* (Berlin, 1890),
because it may be, and probably is, ironical, in which case it is malicious; but,
on the other hand, if taken at face value, it may be construed as a defense of the
Jews. In either case, we must conclude that Leon's contribution does not come
off. The highly sympathetic attitude toward Jews in Isidore Loeb's *Le Juif de
l'histoire et le Juif de la légende* (Paris, 1890) must be discounted to some extent
because of the author's race; yet it is a scholarly, dispassionate handling of the
question, and is important also because it points to the parallel anti-Semitism in
France, which was to boil over in the Dreyfus case only a few years later.

The fervidly nationalistic German historian Treitschke is ably answered in
two pamphlets by H. Naudh, *Israel im Heere* (Berlin, 1879) and *Professoren über
Israel: Von Treitschke und Bresslau* (Berlin, 1880). Both make the point that Jews
are not necessarily timid in the service of their country nor deserving of the bars
thrown against their advance in the learned professions. But of all the defenses
the one most worthy of survival is also the most inaccessible, for Moritz Rosenstock's article on the migration of the Jews into Europe and the consequences of
their wandering, especially in Germany, is buried in an annual of the Samsonschule in Wolfenbüttel (1878).[46] It is a warm, earnest, and urgent appeal for tol-
eration. So emotional is all this controversy, however, that attempts at impersonal discussion, such as H. K. Hugo Delff's *Judenthum und Christenthum*
(Husum, 1880) or C. F. Heman's *Die religiöse Weltstellung des jüdischen Volkes*
(Leipzig, 1882), seem now flat and dated.

The foregoing may seem to have little to do with the Legend, but actually the
Judenfrage hangs over many of the Continental treatments of Ahasuerus after
1830. A good case in point is Fritz Mauthner's novel, *Der neue Ahasver* (Leipzig-
Dresden, 1882). Mauthner had already associated the Wandering Jew with the
Germanic god Woden in his "Zur Geschichte der Sage vom ewigen Juden," in
Wochenblatt for 1878, as others, notably Zoozmann, had done. In this novel,
however, he is not thinking so much of the old folk tale as of the symbolism of
Ahasuerus as representative of a modern Jew. In August, 1789, old Ahasuerus
laid himself down in a grave, prepared to die; in fact, he was pronounced dead.
But his ghost arose and was reincarnated as another Wandering Jew, a little different, a little more worldly and "modern" than the original. In other words, this
new Ahasuerus came into being with the French Revolution. As in Auerbach's
Spinoza, he came to embody the persecuted Jewish people. But Mauthner's special originality lies in his insistence that this new Ahasuerus is the means by
which one can become aware of the burning Jewish question in the modern world
and of the part this problem must play in the development of modern Germany.

The plot of Mauthner's novel concerns a young Jewish doctor, Heinrich Wolf. Born in the Prague ghetto, by temperament a Christian rather than a Jew, he is prevented from marrying a highborn Christian woman because of the pressures of anti-Semitism and therefore turns to his own people, with results disastrous to himself and those about him. It matters not that he served his country well in the war of 1870; he is still a Jew—not the ragged, unkempt Ahasuerus of antiquity but a well-groomed, intelligent modern man, yet still a Jew. The novel is a powerful reply to the fanaticism and bigotry of the anti-Semitic circles of Mauthner's own time. As such, it is one of the more important satires in the art form of the Legend. Once its background is understood, of course, it becomes transparent enough, as is true of most good satire.

Central European Romantic Survivals

And all the while that this "new Ahasuerus" sweats and swinks amid the harsh realities confronting his race, a few poets offer him surcease from his sorrows or the sympathy which comes from an attempt to identify themselves with him. In a collection of attractive lyrics in Arno Holz's *Das Buch der Zeit* (Zurich, 1886), one little poem, "Ich Fuhr auf purpurner Galeere" (Phantasus 10), presents Ahasuerus as an earth-lover, rejoicing in its beauty and consoled by the loveliness of a garden on the island of Cytheros in the Cyclades. Karl Bleibtreu, in "Ahasver," from *Welt und Wille* (Dessau, 1886), revives the Jew as a romantic observer of mankind, wrapped in a Byronic integument but this time moving about in an Olympian atmosphere. The romanticism is heightened in another version of the same poem in the same book entitled "Ahasver auf den Trümmeln von Jerusalem." I am reminded of Carlyle's injunction, "Close thy Byron; open thy Goethe," for this is precisely what Bleibtreu has done. A new Ahasuerus arises, unfettered by gloomy reflections on the past.

Such dabbling with romantic motifs, of course, will continue to the present day. For example, Hubert Müller has taken more than a single leaf out of the book of Chateaubriand. His "Ahasver am Hudson" (1888) takes Ahasuerus from Russia to the state of New York, there to lament his conventional problem and to seek comfort from a hardy pioneer. I must regretfully report that the poem does not amount to much.[47] An anonymous sonnet cycle, *Le juif errant* (n.p., 1873), has Ahasuerus observe, in mediocre style, that life can be beautiful if one can escape from it—an illogical idea which is pure romantic yearning. But these poems go farther: they say that suicide is justified if no other escape from life is possible, for existence would be intolerable without an escape hatch. Such negative messages are consonant with those of Baudelaire and Rimbaud in contemporary French poetry. It is more appealing to hear Ahasuerus lamenting the death of his horse, which we have rarely heard of save in Quinet's *Ahasvérus*, in a pleasantly wrought little poem by the Bolivian poet Ricardo Bustamente, written some time near 1870.[48] When this useful means of transportation dies, as a mortal horse must, Ahasuerus wishes to die too. But of course he cannot—and so, Onward and upward!

In general, however, most of the older romantic themes sound passé even after the middle of the century. Yet it is in this romantic phase that Ahasuerus appeals to a few writers in Hungary during these years. I should observe, in passing, that Emeric Madách's good dramatic poem, *Az ember tragédiája* ("The Tragedy of Man"; Budapest, 1859), has for its protagonist Adam, who observes the passing of centuries much as Ahasuerus does in the Chronicle of the Wandering Jew. This parallelism is accounted for by Madách's indebtedness to Andersen's *Ahasuerus*. A fragmentary dramatic effort by Michael Vörösmarty, *Az örök zsidóból* ("From the Eternal Jew"; Budapest, 1850), presents the Jew as afraid to die but hopeful that he can stand upon the ruins of the universe. The desire of the poet to identify himself with Ahasuerus, which we have noted here and there, is accepted by the Hungarian writers more frequently than by others. Thus János Arany's lyric *Az örök zsidó* ("The Eternal Jew"; Budapest, 1860) equates his own sufferings with those of Ahasuerus; the influence here seems to be that of Béranger. Joseph Kiss on several occasions refers to himself in terms of Ahasuerus and his wanderings, both of body and soul, in quest of an abiding place. John Vajda identifies himself not only with Ahasuerus but with Prometheus, especially in his *Vegtelenseg* ("Infinity"; Budapest, 1875); and Julius Reviczky, in various poems, followed the example of Kiss and termed his life "the wanderings of Ahasuerus." In one of his most striking poems, *Az utolso költö* ("The Last Poet"; Budapest, 1889), he announces that it will be the duty of the last poet on earth to soothe the dying moments of Ahasuerus and then proclaim him happy when dead. Quinet had Ahasuerus outlast everything, even God; but Reviczky believes that it is poetry which is permanent. Haushofer, it will be recalled, tends to blast both. These various Hungarian contributions should not be regarded as isolated phenomena, although little attention has been paid them to date.[49] Rather, they seem to be belated strayers from the earlier part of the nineteenth century. It will be seen, however, that the twentieth-century treatments of Ahasuerus are represented by several valuable Hungarian variations (see Appendix C).

To others, Ahasuerus seems important only in his active moments, when he serves to unravel some knotty situation in the lives of men, as he has done many times before. But we should be thankful that a talented author like Adolf H. Povinelli of Vienna could rescue Ahasuerus from being a commonplace god from the machine. In his poem, *Ahasverus in Tyrol* (Vienna-Leipzig, 1890), he makes the Jew an embodiment of fate. In the Tyrol, at a time when witches were being persecuted, Ahasuerus manages to divert danger from the lovers Guntram and Hilde, saving the man when he was apparently mortally wounded and rescuing the girl from the stake. In the beginning it is explained that Ahasuerus, as one of Satan's spies, must wander until he has expiated his infernal sins through deeds of kindness and love. He shrinks violently from a demonstration of such Christian behavior, but cannot help himself because it is impossible for him to do what he wishes to do, try as he will. Phoenix-like, he resumes life whenever he thinks he is going to die, and each time he derives more spiritual satisfaction from his continuing existence. Povinelli has revived one detail from the old southern European folkloristic treatment of Ahasuerus. The old Wandering Jew had the inexhaustible purse of Fortunatus, but Fortunatus had also a cloak of invisibility, and Povinelli has borrowed the same for his Ahasuerus. The story is laid in fifteenth-century Austria. Ahasuerus is, of course, a rebel, but the year 1890 is so far removed in religious thought from the year 1450 that he can now be a rebel without having to be either flamboyant or melodramatic, and, in spite of the distaste which Ahasuerus has for the contrition required of him, Povinelli has not sacrificed good taste for modernity of religious thinking.

Ahasuerus Amid Suffering Humanity

This new Ahasuerus, as I believe we should think of him henceforth, is unregenerate in religious matters but assured of the spiritual independence which the later nineteenth century could grant him. He appears in many a work by 1890. One of these, *Ahasver: Ein Monolog* (Zurich, 1890), gives him an opportunity to cry a plague on all houses, theologically speaking. The author, who takes refuge behind the pseudonym "Ego," after calling upon Freemasonry to lay aside its absurd secrecy, allows Ahasuerus to undertake a brief survey of the history of religion. And a confused account it is, in truth. Christ comes in for harsh treatment, inasmuch as he, the "Son of Love," could preach love and yet curse those who turned against him as Ahasuerus did. Jesus called himself Truth and thereby put Jehovah in the wrong. Mohammed had many virtues, including singleness of purpose, yet he was a betrayer of God because his ideal was not Jehovah. As for John Huss, he, like Mohammed, would free the human soul and prophesy the white swan that would not be consumed, and yet he was himself burned at the stake. Obviously, then, he must have been a charlatan. Ahasuerus, says Ego, has been obliged to free his soul, also, in order to endure his unmitigated punishment; but he saw no swan, only a black raven, as black a raven as there ever was. Ego believes in Jehovah—that much cannot be doubted—and his Ahasuerus has virtue only when he can subscribe to the unifying figure of Jehovah and be his vicar on earth. Otherwise, Ahasuerus is only a lame and halting Prometheus, and must suffer the futility of all would-be redeemers of mankind who defy God.

We see in some of the portraits of Ahasuerus in these years reminders of Nietzsche's hero's statement: " 'Once blasphemy against God was the greatest blasphemy,' said Zarathustra, 'but God died, and therewith also these blasphemers.' " A little narrative poem written by Adolf Pichler in 1880, "Der ewige Jude," foreshadows this attitude, although its total effect is Christian.[50] On a Good Friday near the River Inn, the poet meets an old man who is lighting the lamp in a wayside shrine. The old man relates how once he saw a gigantic, hollow-eyed ancient, with withered arms, standing before the Cross, scornfully asking Christ why he keeps hanging there. His resurrection must have been a lie! Christ answers from the Cross that he must continue to hang there because man is still in need of redemption through sacrifice. Ahasuerus snarls his defiance of this and other matters, especially Christ's inability to deal with sin. After a futile exchange, he stalks away; the image of Christ is suffused with light, and roses grow about the crown of thorns, while the Saviour gives a sign of blessing to the retreating figure. The Schubartian titanism attributed to Ahasuerus here is notable; so also is the placing of Ahasuerus at the foot of the Cross, from which humble position he reviles Christ as did the impenitent thief, and in much stronger language.

Pichler was followed along this path by the only authentic royal member of the Association of Writers about the Wandering Jew. This was Elizabeth, queen of Romania, who, under the pen name of "Carmen Sylva," allowed Ahasuerus to steal the show in her epic, *Jehovah* (Leipzig, 1882). Here the Jew brings into focus all the romantic display of unbelief of which he is capable. He denies the divinity of Christ, remarking sardonically that *his* God would never bleed. "Am I to live when all else has passed away? Very well, then, I shall live until I come into God's presence!"[51] But then what? This Ahasuerus hopes to find God in solitude, in a whirlwind or an earthquake or some other shattering phenomena, or in love or money or war. Yet he cannot find him. Observing sourly that, if God existed, he would hate him because he has created only miserable man as the end product of his efforts, Ahasuerus nevertheless continues to search for him—by the Memnon Stone at Thebes on the banks of the Nile, in the Indies, across the desert, and on the battlefield. He tries to find him in song and poetry, through riches and worldly delights. Everywhere, however, Ahasuerus meets only the emptiness, the triviality, the downright worthlessness of earthly life. No wonder, then, that he should be brought to the point of negation. With this outlook, it is not surprising that the Inquisition should get him in its grasp, for he is willing to be both hero and martyr for his lack of faith. Yet all he gets from this is exquisite torture.

He goes to America, where, presumably in pre-Colonial days, he sets up what he hopes will be a happy, prosperous realm to be ruled by wisdom, peace, beauty, and wealth. But again in vain. His negative philosophy is too much for his subjects. Remarking bitterly that no god can satisfy the mass of men, he renounces his throne. He then goes to Florence, where he tries to become an artist extraordinary, hoping to find God in doing and thinking. Perhaps he himself can be such a god. His presumption, however, is his ruin. Yet unexpected little touches of nature stir within him an inkling of what God may be: for example, a mother nursing her child, a pair of lovers in springtime. He flees to an Alpine forest. In this pantheistic setting, which is romantic in the old style, he finds God in the mere fact of living:

> Im Werden da ist Gott,
> Gott ist ewig Werden.[52]

The discovery redeems him, enabling him to find comfort and death. The author's conception of Ahasuerus in his final development is a curious mixture of evolutionism and Hegelianism, and, at the conclusion, even what might be called Wordsworthianism. Elizabeth contributes little to the Legend that is new, but what she does is sound both in poetic style and artistic conception.

The full impact of Nietzsche on the Legend, however, was not felt until near the year 1900, though many of the speeches in both Pichler and Carmen Sylva are symptomatic of his unorthodox views. Meanwhile, another great philosophical influence of the nineteenth century, that of Karl Marx, was just beginning to affect the Legend in the 1880's. The socialism in Eugène Sue's novel, for example, is of a much earlier brand than Marx's. The first work to show a conscious Marxist trend is a reflective narrative poem, highly colored in style, "Le juif errant," in *Les Blasphèmes* (Paris, 1884; 2nd ed.: Paris, 1894), by Jean Richepin.[53] Ahasuerus here was never in sympathy with Christ, whose teachings he believed to be weak and ineffective. Therefore, when he saw the Saviour in the *Via Crucis*, he felt sorry for him; but, having a somewhat Nietzschean side, Ahasuerus hardened his heart against what he considered his pusillanimity. The curse upon him may have been unfortunate—who is to say that it was not?—but this Ahasuerus really does not care. He has seen all that the world has to offer, and a sorry sum total it represents. Nothing has disillusioned him more than to see how Christianity has been betrayed by the high and mighty princes of the earth. With them he will have no truck, for he wishes to identify himself—first, last, and always—with the uncountable proletariat, the great masses of humanity, who deny God and yet will be the masters of the world. Their ultimate victory is assured, and equally certain is the fact that when the last gun has been fired the proletariat will still be on its collectivistic feet. Under the circumstances Ahasuerus will be the last man on earth to die. The poem is assertive and cocksure to the point of bumptiousness; it might well have been written in the 1930's. But its convictions, inevitable in the 1880's, were a little too strong for some, who felt a reply to be in order. The most direct attempt at rebuttal was Alfred Dubout's "Le juif errant," in *Les Contre-Blasphèmes* (Paris, 1889). Dubout, however, was unable to write as boldly and impressively as the poet whom he was attempting to answer.

One additional point: Although Ahasuerus may not be willing to render unto God the things that are God's, he may render unto Caesar the things that are Caesar's. Ahasuerus can be irreligious but still patriotic. This is the message of Hans A. Herrig's dramatic poem, *Jerusalem* (Leipzig, 1874; 2nd ed.: Berlin, 1884), which owes much to Croly's *Salathiel*. Throughout this work Ahasuerus is a political agitator of a fanatical stripe, yet a hardheaded realist who cannot comprehend an ideal. He cannot take Christ seriously because he was not sufficiently a man of action. Ahasuerus fights in defense of the city against Titus and Vespasian, and preaches hatred for Christ, prophesying the eventual ascendancy of the banner of a united, independent Israel. He is actually an early Zionist, but Herrig does little more to anticipate twentieth-century Zionism than to turn the face of Ahasuerus in that direction from time to time.

To act upon this hint of nationalism is to give attention to a literary freak. In 1876 the International Centennial Exposition was held in Philadelphia, and in the wake of this celebration of a hundred years of American independence came one of the strangest occasional poems in existence, Julius Bruck's *Ahasver*, an epic of moderate length but of a most baffling architecture.[54] Bruck was a Silesian who had studied medicine in Breslau and Berlin; later he became a surgeon in the Prussian army, and still later emigrated to the United States, where he arrived in time to serve in a similar capacity in the Union army during the Civil War. He then settled as a practicing physician in Newark, New Jersey, where he wrote some poetry, including *Ahasver*, as an avocation. Unlike most German-Americans of this generation, however, he returned to Germany in 1889, where he died nine years later.

If we examine each of its sections separately, we can concede some merit to the narrative qualities of the poem, but not to its coherence. Ahasuerus represents mankind both errant and erring. We pass quickly over the original Good Friday scene and come upon Ahasuerus in Moravia, where a girl is mourning at the grave of her mother (the mother, Maria, and her lover, Wendelin—a kind of pale Eloise to an unprepossessing Abelard—had been separated by the wicked outlaw Bela Lajos). Ahasuerus comforts the girl and goes on his way. In a magical spot, savage and enchanted, he comes upon the girl's lover, Marcell. Having by this time become involved in complicated possibilities of plot, Bruck allows the reader a respite by introducing as an intermezzo a lusty chorus which sings patriotic, nationalistic songs glorifying the German *Vaterland* and a few songs of love and innocent merriment. None of the songs pleases Ahasuerus, however, and he urges Marcell to tell more of the girl, who has in the meantime disappeared. Marcell explains that the girl was mistaken in supposing that her mother made a good end; actually she passed away in shame, the victim of the lust of Bela Lajos. But all that is past; Marcell wishes only to find the daughter. Ahasuerus is happy to accompany him; searching, he remarks grimly, is his chief occupation.

The two go away together, and after much effort they find the girl, now named Lenore, a dancer in Paris. She is in a Poe-like mood, and after delivering herself of several gloomy speeches on death by pestilence, runs away again. Marcell and Ahasuerus resume their search, and Ahasuerus takes the opportunity to moralize over the bodies in the Paris catacombs. Suddenly the scene shifts from the catacombs to the charming Schoharie Valley in the state of New York. (An American milieu, already noted in Lenau, Hubert Müller, and Carmen Sylva, will be more frequent as time goes on.) The French and Indian Wars are in progress, and the scene is a widow's house not far from Albany. Ahasuerus—conversing with the widow's son, Eli—is contemptuous of such riffraff as the immigrants he encountered on shipboard on his way to America. Eli warns him that this is undemocratic talk and that in America one must learn to be democratic. Eli's wife, the lost Lenore, enters, worried by a belief that she is illegitimate. Her husband comforts her while he continues to upbraid Ahasuerus. The Jew departs in confusion. The curtain then falls for another century. In a sublime illustration of faulty continuity, Bruck indulges in another intermezzo, this time a centennial hymn entitled "Heil dir, Columbia!" Lady Columbia herself now materializes and scolds Ahasuerus without mercy, enjoining upon him love, not revenge, for love is the foundation of liberty, and liberty is America.

Bruck leaves us with the impression that, if Ahasuerus is to be identified with humanity, then humanity is decadent, unsatisfactory, and unworthy of preservation. Actually, for all its patriotic brouhaha, the atmosphere of the poem is as defeatist as that of Spengler's *Decline of the West* and Wagner's *Götterdämmerung*, in spite of the brass-band kind of uplift offered by Columbia. Far more inspiration is offered by the minor Czech Jewish poet Jaroslav Vrchlicky, who between 1874 and 1902 wrote three poems ["Jarní zpěv Ahasvera," "Kříž božetěchův," and "Smir Ahasverův" ("Spring Song for Ahasuerus," "Cross Divine," and "Ahasuerus the Trickster")], in which the Wandering Jew is the clear symbol of mankind rising *per aspera ad astra*.[55]

The idea that the Wandering Jew should represent the Jewish race only is not particularly frequent between 1850 and 1890. Perhaps the beginnings of Zionism were already strong enough to make such a legendary character seem too intangible to use even as a symbol. If we exclude Mauthners' *Der neue Ahasver*, there are few good examples of the individual Jew who portrays himself as a Wandering Jew. The occasional exceptions, however, may be arresting. One interesting phenomenon was a revival of interest in the Spanish Jewish poet Judah ha-Levi of the twelfth century. Judah ha-Levi's "Divan" was translated into German by A. Sulzbach in *Dichterklänge aus Spaniens besseren Tagen* (Frankfurt, 1873). Ha-Levi, a devout poet, trusts in his God as his only salvation: "Israel is the servant of God!" he declares, and, "Only in God is liberty." His poem on the Wandering Jew expresses the thoughts of a Jew expelled from Spain by Ferdinand and Isabella to wander wherever he can. His consolation derives from the reflection that throughout the wanderings of the Jews over the earth there is the fact of God's support. In a similar vein Moritz Rappaport's "Der ewige Jude," in a collection of poems entitled *Myrthen* (Berlin, 1885), identifies Ahasuerus with himself and the Jewish people by repeating the refrain:

> . . .O Israel, thou wretched Ahasver,
> Thou art like me, thyself art Ahasver!
> My wretched folk, art truly chosen of God?

He concludes with the thought that the people of Israel are a folk of torment, without rest.

Can Ahasuerus ever be free? It seemed possible to Wolfgang Kirchbach in his five-act drama, *Die letzten Menschen* (Dresden-Leipzig, 1890). Ahas, as he is called here, and Eve—the eternal wanderer and the eternal woman—are the last pair left on earth at the world's end. Ahas lusts after Eve in order to start a new human race, and Eve has the requisite *élan vital* to succumb to him, but Death reminds them of the failure of mortal humanity. Eve yields to Death; Ahas, still immortal, kneels beside her body and strikes off the chains of mortality. But, alas, Kirchbach's turgid poetry and foggy mysticism could well be sacrificed for the moving little poem by Catulle Mendès, "Ahasuerus," in *Le Parnasse contemporain* (Paris, 1869), in which the Wandering Jew, weary and without hope, sees a miserable beggar on a road in Norway and gives him his purse and cloak for protection. This simple act of unpremeditated charity gains liberation for the Jew. No German mystical yearnings are needed for Ahasuerus' release from his bondage, no profound lucubrations—simply obedience to the natural impulse to care for suffering humanity.

The same simple directness illuminates the pleasant tale by Aimé Giron, *Les Cinq sous d'Isaac Laquedem, le Juif errant* (Paris, 1883). Here the essential outline of the Legend is preserved, but the author does his best to excuse Laquedem on the grounds that he was drunk on that first Good Friday. Yet the archangel Michael sets the Wanderer on his way, as in Quinet. In the year 1724 Laquedem came to Brussels. As might be expected, he was in need of a cobbler. In an old shoemaker's shop he found an orphan girl, Gudule, and her three brothers, all destitute. He fills their chest with a steady stream of five sous from his inexhaustible purse, while the brothers go to work on his shoes. As a result of his charity,

Gudule is enabled to send her brothers to school, where they are a credit to her upbringing. All prosper: one becomes a master brewer and marries the daughter of his former employer; the second becomes a master shoemaker, cures the bunions of the governor of Brabant, and marries a rich widow; the third, a mousy little fellow, becomes a draper, and his aggressive, ambitious wife pushes him into the office of master draper. The sister Gudule, staying at home and managing the family affairs, continues to pray for the Wandering Jew. Fifty years later, Isaac Laquedem makes his famous visit to Brabant (1774), as the Brabantine ballad tells us. But Giron sees to it that he visits Gudule and finds her and all her brothers alive and happy. He can therefore return to Jerusalem, where, on the site of his original home, he is pardoned by Christ and allowed to die in blessedness. A more bourgeois interpretation of the Legend would be hard to find.

We have already seen Ahasuerus suffer to the point of satiety in innumerable works; we have also observed more than sufficiently his repentance, for which an author might or might not show sympathy. But it is rare to find so successful an effort to concentrate upon him within a framework of torment, while at the same time showing sympathy for his clear repentance, as in the account in George Macdonald's *Thomas Wingfold, Curate* (London-Boston, 1876), a novel which has hitherto been totally neglected. Macdonald introduces his version of the Legend through the manuscript of a brother of one of his characters and uses the Legend as an *exemplum* of how immortality can sometimes be a most undesirable thing. The writer of the manuscript never appears in the novel, for what prove to be obvious reasons. The brother, who reads the manuscript aloud, is a man resigned to the will of God, who helps to resolve some stormy religious doubts which contend in the bosoms of the hero (the curate) and the woman whom the hero has come to love. The Wandering Jew explains that he has recovered from a spell of madness, or so it seems, and that his mind is indelibly associated with England, where he is sure he spent much of his time before his insanity. However, since he is Ahasuerus, the Wandering Jew, he can no longer stay there. We soon discover that Polwarth, the man reading the manuscript, is none other than the brother of Ahasuerus.

In the pages following, Ahasuerus reviews his history. He had a grievance against Jesus, because he (Ahasuerus) was conservative and resented His attack upon the "great ones that administered the law," and because, when Christ cleared the Temple of the money-changers, His whip came down upon the Jew's uncle, "which truly hurt him not outwardly but stung him to the soul." His rebuff of Christ is therefore made in the spirit of revenge. He was present at the Crucifixion, where he stood near the women at the foot of the Cross. In his subsequent wanderings, he relates that he could never pass by a wayside cross without climbing upon it, "winding my arms about its arms and my feet about its stem," and hanging there "in the darkness of the moon, in rain or hail, in wind or snow or frost, until my sinews gave way and my body dropped, and I knew no more until I found myself lying at its foot in the morning. For ever in such case, I lay without sense until again the sun shone upon me."

More spectacular is the incident which took place in a large medieval city, where stood a great church with a great cross atop its spire. Ahasuerus entered the church, ascended the stairs into the steeple, and stood finally at the foot of the cross:

I scrambled up the pinnacles, and up on the carven stem of the cross, for my sinews were as steel, and my muscles had dried and hardened until they were as those of the tiger or the great serpent. So I climbed and lifted up myself until I reached the great arms of the cross and over them flung my arms, as was my wont, and entwined the stem with my legs, and there hung three hundred feet above the roofs of the houses. And as I hung, the moon rose and cast the shadow of me, Ahasuerus, upon the cross, up against the Pleiades [!] And as if dull Nature were offended thereat, nor understood the offering of my poor sacrifice, the clouds began to gather, like the vultures—no one could have told whence. From all sides around they rose, and the moon was blotted out, and they gathered and rose until they met right over the cross. And when they closed, then the lightning brake forth, and the thunder with it, and it flashed and thundered above and around and beneath me, so that I could not tell which voice belonged to which arrow, for all were mingled in one great confusion and uproar. And the people in the houses below heard the sound of the thunder, and they looked from their windows and they saw the storm raving and flashing about the spire, which stood in the heart of the agony, and they saw something hang there, even upon its cross, in the form of a man, and they came from their houses, and the whole space beneath was filled with people, who stood gazing up at the marvel. *A miracle! a miracle!* they cried; and truly it was no miracle, it was only me, Ahasuerus, the wanderer, taking thought concerning his crime against the Crucified. Then came a great light all around me, such light for shining as I had never before beheld, and indeed I saw it not all with my eyes, but the greater part with my soul, which surely is the light of the eyes themselves. And I said to myself, Doubtless the Lord is at hand, and He cometh to me as late to the blessed Saul of Tarsus, who was *not* the chief of sinners, but I—Ahasuerus the accursed. And the thunder burst like the bursting of a world in the furnace of the sun; and whether it was that the lightning struck me, or that I dropped, as was my custom, outwearied from the cross, I know not, but thereafter I lay at its foot among the pinnacles, and when the people looked again the miracle was over, and they returned to their houses and slept. And the next day, when I sought the comfort of the bath, I found upon my side the figure of a cross, and the form of a man hanging thereupon as I had hung, depainted in a dark color as of lead, plain upon the flesh of my side over my heart. Here was a miracle indeed![56]

The compulsion of Ahasuerus to hang upon a cross until he drops from exhaustion is a unique detail. The stigma on his flesh symbolizes the uniqueness. Two other features of Macdonald's treatment are the love for an orphan maid, duly requited, which brings Ahasuerus what nothing else can, and the unforgettable look cast by Christ upon the sinner at the time of the rebuff. Neither of these, of course, can be called new. This particular Ahasuerus, however, is proud of his indestructibility, for when he met Death in the desert, a shadow of a shadow against Orion's belt, he put the destroyer to flight by thinking of Christ's suffering eyes. He is fully aware of the fact that he will outlive the orphan girl who has followed him, that she will grow old, sicken, and die, while he tarries in eternal life. He leaves her for a while to brood in the crater of a volcano; in his defiance he walks over the fiery lava-flood safely enough, but when his beloved tries in her faith to follow him—successfully for a while—she suddenly falls below the surface and is incinerated. "And I laughed aloud in my madness, and the devils below heard me, and laughed yet again." Ahasuerus was so shocked that he went into a protracted siege of insanity.

As for the reproachful divine glance, it brings about an effective, original scene. Ahasuerus in his torment hopes that he will be pardoned if he can find God, but it seems an impossible quest, and he weeps:

And as I wept I heard a sound as of the falling of many tears, and I looked, and lo! a shower as from a watering-pot falling upon the lily! And I looked yet again, and I saw the watering-pot, and the hand that held it; and he whose hand held the pot stood by me and looked at me as he watered the lily. He was a man like the men of the world where such lilies grow, and was poorly dressed, and seemed like a gardener. And I looked up in his face, and lo—the eyes of the Lord Jesus! And my heart swelled until it filled my whole body and my head, and I gave a great cry, and for joy that turned into agony I could not rise, neither could I speak, but I crept on my hands and my knees to His feet, and there I fell down upon my face, and with my hands I lifted one of His feet and did place it upon my head, and then I found voice to cry "O master!" and therewith the life departed from me. And when I came to myself, the master sat under the tree, and I lay by His side, and He had lifted my head upon His knees. And behold, the world was jubilant around me, for Love was Love and Lord of all. The sea roared, and the fullness thereof was Love; and the purple and the gold and the blue and the green came straight from the hidden red heart of the Lord Jesus. And I closed my eyes for very bliss; nor had I yet bethought me of the time when first I began to be. But now when for very bliss I closed my eyes, my sin came back to me, and I remembered. And I rose up, and kneeled down before Him, and said, "O Lord, I am Ahasuerus, the Jew, the man who would not let Thee rest Thy Cross upon the stone before my workshop, but drave Thee from it." "Say no more of that," answered my Lord, "for truly I have myself rested in thy heart, Cross and all, until the thing thou didst in thy ignorance is better than forgotten, for it is remembered in love. Only see thou also make right excuse for my brethren who, like thee then, know not what they do. Come and I will bring thee to the woman who died for thee in the burning fire." And I said, "O Lord, leave me not, for although I would now in my turn right gladly die for her, yet would I not look upon that woman again if the love of her would make me love Thee one hair the less— Thou knowest." And the Lord smiled upon me and said, "Fear not, Ahasuerus; my love infolds and is the nest of all Love!" And I followed my Lord.[57]

It serves the purpose of Macdonald's novel that there should be this happy ending to the Legend, for the curate must persuade a murderer and his loving sister that even the greatest crime can be forgiven. Apart from this, however, it may be said that Macdonald's use of striking and colorful incident in his handling of the Legend belies some of the pedestrian quality of the novel itself: the Biblical nature of his style at this point—highly appropriate to the subject—comes off better than the self-torturing philosophizing of the protagonist, Thomas Wingfold, curate.

The Biblical simplicity of which I have spoken leads me to a rather useless generality: how much better it is to keep the Legend simple than to make it complex with interpretative padding—the curse of the treatment of Ahasuerus in the past century and a half. Except in rare instances, the nineteenth century could not let the simple alone. It was not content to allow the bare form to stand undraped. But one should not reproach the nineteenth century exclusively. The twentieth century, as we shall see, has allowed the Legend too often to be sicklied o'er with the pale cast of thought. As Ahasuerus moves up into our time, the abstract implications of his story become more and more important, and its folkloristic side more and more unconsidered.

Mark Twain and Van Nievelt

Two narratives, one pointing backward and the other forward, conclude this account of Ahasuerus' peregrinations between 1850 and 1890. The first is one of the best summaries of the Legend on a popular level of these decades. It is to be found in Mark Twain's *Innocents Abroad* (1869).[58] Ever since the tradition of the stations of the cross was initiated in the fourteenth century, pilgrims and tourists in Jerusalem have been entertained by local variations of the Legend, and Mark Twain's guide evidently contributed his share. The account in *Innocents Abroad* represents an inevitable concretion of details which have accrued through centuries of oral presentation—some of which, one suspects, are inventions of individual guides. Two or three increments appear here—the crashing, self-closing doors in the Temple when the Wandering Jew approaches; the lights of Jerusalem that turn blue in his presence; the building in the city which he owns and from which he periodically collects rent. Unusual also is the requirement that he report for duty, as it were, in Jerusalem every fifty years. There is also this puzzling detail:

> When the guide pointed out where the Wandering Jew had left his familiar mark upon a wall, I was filled with astonishment. It read:
> S. T.—1860—X.

I imagine that this was put there by one of those who scrawl their initials and a date in public places. On the other hand, it is conceivable that the initials may have a more esoteric significance—about which one's fancy may play, but should not play for too long. "S. T.," for instance, is a standard abbreviation for "Superintendent of Transportation"—almost too apt a title for the Wandering Jew. If the initials stood for *senza tempo* ("without time"), it would be highly appropriate for Ahasuerus, but too specialized within the field of music for one whose influence on music has been more baneful than otherwise. Finally, there is the ironic possibility that "S. T." stands for *Sancta Trinitas* because Ahasuerus is one whom the romantics have built up into an irreconcilable, to whom the Holy Trinity is a mockery.

Ahasuerus in the modern commercial role of landlord and rent collector is surprising, although he has gone into business several times during the past hundred years. As an absentee landlord he would be without a peer. His alleged interest in railroads, nostrums, and infernal machines bears the unmistakable stamp of the later nineteenth century. That he should pitch his tent upon the campground of Mohammed might be expected; indeed, we have seen that in Hoffman's *Chronicles of Cartaphilus* he was Mohammed himself in one of his incarnations, at least until the inevitability of the Prophet's death became apparent. That he should have courted death, however, by becoming a rebel against Islam is an unexpected turn. It is more than a slight exaggeration to say with Mark Twain that the Wandering Jew has been celebrated in song and story since the day of his calamitous transgression. But Mark Twain's guide is entitled to the right to add to an already good story, for that is the way the Legend can best be kept alive.

The other work to be mentioned at this point is later than *Innocents Abroad* and altogether different in nature. Mark Twain's version, for all its additions, maintains the basic outlines of the Legend as something preserved from the past. This is not the case in C. van Nievelt's *Ahasverus: Nieuwe Phantasieën* (Leiden, 1884), a collection of short stories which takes its name from the main character of the first, entitled "Baron von Goldstetten." Here the narrator, a man named Müller, puts up at an inn on the Grimsel one snowy night. This mountain and its pass have been heard of before; the old folk tale (p. 83) need not be rehearsed again. Also spending the night at the inn is a banker from Frankfurt named Baron von Goldstetten, who reveals that he is none other than the Wandering Jew, come to the Grimsel for a fourth visit to inspect the great glacier which, he had prophesied in the old folk tale, was to cover what had once been a prosperous town. But it appears that this prophecy had gone awry. After looking once more at the Grimsel Pass, the baron returns to the inn and then soon departs, leaving a note to the effect that his original prophecy had been only symbolic, induced by emotional stress. Later Müller visits Von Goldstetten in Frankfurt and learns that the baron considers himself the Wandering Jew because, although Ahasuerus had died not long after his third visit to the Grimsel, his tradition has been thoroughly respected among his many descendants, of whom Von Goldstetten is the current survivor. When he dies, his son will be the new Ahasuerus and a leader of the Jews. This rather feudal Messianic detail is for the moment unimportant, but when we shall meet with it again, it will bulk large. Von Goldstetten makes clear that the first thirty Ahasueruses must follow the curse imposed by Christ, but that the next ten will be human beings and free agents. Then he asks the pointed question: Are we not all Ahasueruses? Are we not all wanderers all our lives?

In short, there will always be a Wandering Jew, a symbol of universal nature from one generation to the next. There should therefore always be an individual who is a present-day incarnation of Ahasuerus; it is a kind of perpetual office to be occupied, as it were, in every age. I have heard of more than one person who has assumed the mantle and gone about his everyday business secure in the knowledge that he was the contemporary version of the Wandering Jew and that when he had died, his son, if he had one, would be the Ahasuerus of the next generation. Perhaps it is just as well that the present-day incumbent should never be identified officially, lest curiosity seekers beat too deep a path to his door. This is an innocent kind of megalomania, much safer for the world than the delusion that one is Napoleon.

CHAPTER TWELVE

Traditional Treatments of the Legend: 1890–1920

With the coming of the twentieth century, one could almost believe that everything vital had been extracted from the Legend and that as much had been said about the Wandering Jew as could be said. At least one could have wished that more writers had believed this, for the reading public would have been spared much mediocrity in the later contributions. But—granted that we get much repetition of treatment and that those who write about Ahasuerus seldom break out of a circle which takes them from perfervid romanticism to cold satire and back again—there are many notable twentieth-century deviations from the general run, and some of the restatements are acceptable. Analogies to the Legend present themselves in greater number. An occasional new way of telling the old story and sometimes a true work of art will demand attention.

Ahasuerus continues to exert a magnetic effect upon German-speaking writers. For example, the number of contributions from Germany and Austria between 1890 and 1920 increase, if anything, over the number in the preceding generation. Part of this increase, of course, is the result of the enormous growth in bulk of publication of all kinds, which has become a behemoth in the mid-twentieth century. But much of it is to be explained by the obvious romantic fascination which the Wandering Jew has always exerted upon Germans. In Germany, even before 1900, as we have seen, the name of Ahasuerus came to be a designation for all Jews, as well as a symbol of the human being who spends his time observing the actions of his fellow men. Ahasuerus has become an identifying name for the *Weltanschauer*, for one who goes everywhere and sees everything—an interesting point of revival in the role of the Wandering Jew in the late eighteenth century. He has now also become an embodiment of the target of German *Judenhass*.

In consequence there are many works of various kinds which borrow the name of the Wandering Jew without otherwise paying any attention to the Legend. I have already mentioned the German periodical of the 1830's in Augsburg called *Ahasver*, but this was at that time a rare instance. Now, by 1900, one will find many items whose titles indicate that they should be placed in a bibliography of the Legend, but which have only the veriest shred to connect them with the true Ahasuerus, and sometimes not even that.

Some Borderline Analogues

The analogues of the Legend noted during these years are for the greater part due to the deliberate contamination of the Legend with other legends, in the interest of imaginative writing. Few of them come about from mere ignorance, but confusions are likely when a Legend is first analyzed and studied, before the species has been distinguished from the genus. For example, a great deal of ink was consumed during the latter half of the nineteenth century in the comparative study of the legends of Faust, Tannhäuser, and the Wandering Jew. Yet it is obvious that these three characters are far from triune. Two or three works from near the end of the century will illustrate the problem.

We are fortunate in having Frank R. Stockton's *The Vizier of the Two-Horned Alexander* (New York, 1899), a light, amusing, altogether typical product of that whimsically eccentric author. It seems to be a turn-of-the-century sophisticate's version of the Chronicle of the Wandering Jew, but the protagonist is not the Wandering Jew, only an imitation. He is the Vizier of the Two-Horned Alexander, who first appears to us on an ocean liner during a transatlantic crossing. He is known as Mr. Crowder, a New York stockbroker with a Quaker wife. He has been everywhere and seen everything—or so it seems to a couple of his fellow passengers. He confirms their impression in a visit to their New York apartment. Here he explains that he lived originally in the days of the patriarch Abraham, and therefore had a distinct age-advantage over the Wandering Jew. Having drunk of the pool of immortality, he is in the world to stay, taking unto himself a wife in each generation, noting many of the events of history, but emphasizing the days of King Solomon and the Queen of Sheba, about whom he has some trenchant observations to make in Stockton's inimitable manner, and life in the Middle Ages. When it is remarked that he must be the Wandering Jew of whom the world has heard for a long time, he is properly contemptuous, for beside him Ahasuerus is a mere upstart. Anyway, he is at present a successful stockbroker with a charming (if somewhat sardonic) Quaker wife.

Then there is Louise Guiney's effective ballad, "Peter Rugg, the Bostonian" (1891), which retells the story of the legendary character created in the 1820's by William Austin—the man who tries to get back to his home in Middle Street, Boston, ahead of a violent thunderstorm. Yet this tale has no more relationship to our Legend than Andrew Lang's rather routine account of the eighteenth-century charlatan, the Comte de Saint-Germain, in *Historical Mysteries* (1904).[1] For the legendary Peter Rugg and the historical Saint-Germain—an authentic ghost and a spurious immortal, respectively—are neither of them Ahasuerus.

A creature who owes more to the Wandering Jew than any of the above, however, is the protagonist and title character in Edwin L. Arnold's *The Wonderful Adventures of Phra the Phoenician* (London, 1891). This post-romantic novel of adventure, which has a certain artistic affinity with Rider Haggard's *She* of some half-dozen years earlier, is by no means unreadable, although, from the very nature of its episodic structure, it is bound to end abruptly and unsatisfactorily. Phra, the immortal Phoenician, goes through many a career during a fifteen-hundred-year period, most of which is spent in Britain. The most important of his "lives" are: (1) in the time of Roman Britain, when his great love is Blodwen, a

British maiden who tends to reappear in subsequent reincarnations; (2) in Anglo-Saxon England at the Battle of Hastings; (3) in the days of Edward III before and after the Battle of Crécy; and (4) in the days of Elizabethan glory. In between his careers Phra slumbers in a cave or some other suitable hiding place (on one occasion in a tomb in a medieval church), usually for about three hundred years. His active "lives" do not last for more than thirty years at a time, at the end of which he falls asleep as an adult and awakens as a stripling. The number of these years corresponds roughly to a human generation. It will be recalled that as far back as the days of Roger of Wendover and his Cartaphilus the Eternal Wanderer resumed his youth at the age of thirty. Phra is impressive in both manner and appearance. He is also vulnerable, however, and, as it proves in the end, mortal, for he is eventually poisoned by a villainous Spanish steward in the Renaissance. The derivative nature of Arnold's novel need not detain us, but the work as a whole stands in interesting contrast to Stockton's fantasy, which has a more ingenious concept.

There are many works calculated to lure the serious student of the Legend into reading them, only for him to find that they have nothing to do with the matter in hand.[2] Ridgewell Cullum's *The Law of the Gun* (Philadelphia, 1918) is a story of the West in the old, approved manner of Zane Gray; it has a chapter entitled "The Trail of the Wandering Jew," yet it turns out that the reference is only to an outbreak of cholera in an Indian reservation—an allusion merely to the pestilence-carrying power that Ahasuerus sometimes showed.[3] Similarly, "In the Track of the Wandering Jew," an anonymous story in the *Cornhill Magazine* for 1895, is a Kiplingesque account of an army medical officer in India who is helping to fight a cholera epidemic.[4] Wilbur Bassett's *Wander-Ships* (Chicago, 1917) contains much material about legendary seacraft—"La Grande Chasse Foudre," "Méhul," and the Flying Dutchman's vessel—and refers only incidentally to the Wandering Jew, with but brief notes on him, and incorrect ones at that. Hans Zimmer's *Ein Ahasver der Liebe* (Weimar, *ca.*1910) tells of a lover who goes about continually from one love to another, an amoristic wanderer, as it were. Alfred Verreyn's "De Ahasverieden," in *Nieuwe Gids* for 1908, uses the immortality of Ahasuerus to lend an appropriate name to a society of students who are seeking eternal truth.[5] *Jesus und Judas in der Dichtung* (Hanau, 1910), by Arthur Luther, is apposite only because it mentions Goethe's concept of the returning Jesus in his fragmentary epic. Edward Shillito, in "The Disciple Whom Jesus Loved," from *The Omega and Other Poems* (Oxford, 1916), refers, of course, to John, whose legend was a headwater for the Legend of the Wandering Jew.

But all of these works are peripheral to the Legend and may well be ignored. More useful are those which are borderline analogues, to be included in or excluded from the discussion of the Legend at the whim of the investigator. In general they certainly owe their origin to the existence of the Legend. A rare example is Albert Eubule-Evans' *The Curse of Immortality* (London, 1873). The protagonist here is and is not the Wandering Jew. His name is Theudas; he has been condemned to immortality for insulting the Deity—a typical case of the Tedious Punishment—and he can be released from his doom if he can repent, but he will not. He renews his youth every forty years, turning from a decrepit old man to a handsome, gifted youth, a situation which naturally suggests complicated love affairs. Other elements of the supernatural intervene: angels and demons, for example, while the Aeons and the Intermedii (whoever or whatever they may be), appear as a chorus. The work is utterly inconclusive.

On the other hand, *Le secret du Juif-errant* (Paris, 1913), by Jean Drault, is more entertaining, but also unrelated to the Legend. It is a long novel under the unquestionable influence of Eugène Sue. Instead of attacking Jesuits, it attacks Jews and Freemasons together. The plot is concerned with the attempts of an international conspiracy of Jews (under Cerfbeer, with headquarters at Strasbourg) and of Masons (allied with a vague group of revolutionaries known as Illuminants, with their center at Ingolstadt). The purpose of the Jews is to kill Christ again, and that of the others is to establish universally the habits and institutions of the Masons, who are here synonymous with freethinkers and anarchists. There is a profusion of incidents and characters: we have a family of French military aristocrats, the De la Touches; a buried treasure left behind by the Knights Templars, which forms the core around which all the action centers; pleasing carnage in the French Revolution; the usual devoted old pensioner and the inevitable damsel in peril. Drault writes from the aristocratic and royalist point of view, and grudgingly concedes the victory of the Jewish financiers. In addition to Cerfbeer, the Rothschilds and Weishaupt appear as major figures. The Wandering Jew himself never comes into the story, the point being that the Rothschilds and their ilk are in reality Wandering Jews, moving all over Europe to gain their nefarious ends. The indestructible messenger Schnorrer (a kind of counterpart of Sue's Rodin) travels back and forth between Paris and Jerusalem in order to report to the cabal, which, it is finally revealed, is behind the attempted world upheaval.

Equally tangential to the Legend is *Bracke: Ein Eulenspiegelroman* (Berlin, 1918) by "Klabund" (A. Hentschke). In this episodic novelette which outlines the career of a village rebel, the Wandering Jew is identified with a Count Gapuzzi, an indigent absurdity of a fellow whose chief joy is music. It is finally revealed that Gapuzzi has been condemned because he refused Christ a drink of water—one of the very few intrusions of this secondary motif in the Legend. A much grimmer peripheral work is Georg Ruseler's "Ein neuer Ahasver," in *Helfe* (Berlin, n.d.), written about 1910. In this dramatic narrative, a good solid citizen—peaceful and well thought of in the community, and blessed with a good wife—is nevertheless obliged, through some sort of inner compulsion and because he is a Jew, to move on every six months or so. His faithful wife follows him without misgivings.

Ahasuerus and the Jewish People

Ruseler's story brings back the anti-Semitism which we can assume exists at any time in the twentieth century. I am reminded here of the curious little poem by "Roland von Berlin," entitled "Hebräische Melodie," in *Beiblatt zum General-Anzeiger für die gesammten Interessen des Judenthums* for April 15, 1906. The Wandering Jew is in Berlin at Eastertide, where he notes the forgiving spirit of the Germans and takes hope that a new era has come in with the new century. Unfortunately, a crowd of Jewish refugees from the 1905 rebellion in Russia disillusions him. Here the author is neatly balanced between pro- and anti-Semitism. A rather dispassionate consideration by J. Seidl, *Der Jude des neunzehnten Jahrhunderts, oder Warum sind wir antisemitisch?* (Graz, 1899), resumes discussion of the problem in Germany and is worth reading for its exposition of the subject; however, it does not bear upon the Legend in any but the obvious way, repeating once more the identification of the Wandering Jew with the Jewish people and setting him up as a symbol of the race. In more fervid terms, Josef Deckert's *Der ewige Jude, "Ahasver": Zur Abwehr eines philosemitischen Mahnrufes in der Judenfrage* (Vienna, 1894) puts it succinctly: Is Ahasuerus the symbol of all Jews? What to do about them? Is it the fate of Ahasuerus to wander? Are we to blame? Not too likely![6]

Many other works tend to clutter up the bibliographies of the Legend, although these works actually have little or nothing to do with the subject. At any rate, they testify to the vitality of the story. Some contain passing references to the Wandering Jew or to examples of the art form of the Legend and aspects of folklore contiguous to the Legend, as does Wilhelm Creizenach's "Zur Geschichte der Weihnachtsspiele und des Weihnachtsfesten," in the *Weinhold Festschrift* (Breslau, 1896). Otto Grauhoff's "Moritz von Schwind" (1905) is the tale of a painter who had some paintings of famous wanderers in which, however, a portrait of the Wandering Jew was *not* included.[7] Maxim Gorki's *Die Judenmassakre* (Vienna-Leipzig, 1904; translated by Sonja Werner) treats Ahasuerus only symbolically in reference to all Jews; it is concerned with a pogrom in Russia. A three-act play by Evgeni Nikolaevich Chirikov, *Die Juden* (Munich, 1904), deals with an anti-Jewish segment of Russia during another massacre of the Jews.[8] There are some overtones of Zionism in the drama, but the main action has to do with the love of Leah for the Gentile, Beresin, whom she renounces for the sake of her father. Beresin stays with her, however, and dies with the others in the pogrom.

This list could well be increased greatly, but for the moment it is better to dismiss what are largely peripheral pamphlets and linger over works in which Ahasuerus is identified with all Jews. Friedrich Bech's "Ahasver," in *Wesen des Lebens* (Zurich, 1908), is satisfied that the Jews, as represented by Ahasuerus, must wander until Judgment Day. This had been one of the ideas expressed in Chirikov's play, and two talented Jewish writers of the age also accepted it. Abraham Goldfaden's *Der ewige Jude* (Frankfurt, n.d.), written in the 1890's, is a poem in Yiddish, a lament for the pitiable condition of the Jews as a people. Perhaps repentance will bring relief to their souls. Back in the 1880's Moritz Rappaport had pleaded for virtue as a way for the Jews to be released from bondage. The piece was reprinted about 1900 in *Myrthen*, an anthology for Jewish family reading.

One of the most effective and socially significant works of the turn of the century to deal with this identification is Herman Heyermans' *Ahasverus* (1893), an excellent one-act play.[9] The Wandering Jew is now Karolik, a Russian Jew in the time of the pogroms. His son Peter, after having been pursued by the Cossacks, has taken refuge in a church and been converted to Christianity and baptized. On his return to his father's house, he cannot bring himself to take part in the Jewish Sabbath ritual. The Cossacks break in and maltreat and eventually expel Karolik and his intransigent wife—leaving the new Christian, Peter, to enjoy the dubious fruits of his conversion. The family is disrupted, but the father and mother—the older order—are unrepentant and cling hard to their Hebrew orthodoxy. Their unyielding faith, come what may, renders them symbolic of the eternal Jew. They are forced by intolerant Gentiles to break away from their home and move on.

Heyermans achieved a strong, economical dramatic effect in this play and wrought it with finesse. His purpose was serious and his manner almost severe. Although it makes many of the same points, Isaac M. Wise's *The Wandering Jew* (1899?)[10] forms a most remarkable contrast to Heyermans' play. Published in Cincinnati, where Wise was a rabbi for more than forty years, we may define *The Wandering Jew* as an elaborate lecture on the Legend. Its approach is at times facetious, and its scholarship is both cranky and individualistic. Wise believes that the Legend originated in Germany or Austria—at least in some German-speaking region—during the civil strife between Adolf of Nassau and Albert I of Austria: in other words, during the last decades of the thirteenth century, some fifty years and more after the Italo-Latin chronicle of 1223. In this strife there was a grand massacre of the Jews—according to Wise, a hundred thousand of them were slaughtered. But how and why the Legend began then is not demonstrated, and we should dismiss Wise's theory. Although the "lecture" degenerates into an emotional defense of the Jew's position in modern civilization, the author stays with his thesis that all Jews are wanderers and have been made so by the Gentiles. The Wandering Jew, then, is not so much a specific legendary individual as the embodiment of a general historical segment of the population of the world which must always be on the march.

If only these writers could find a single historical personage to serve as a focal point! The only successful effort to do so at this time is Richard Dehmel's "Eine Heine-Denkmal" (1901), an attractive piece in which various writers are introduced to pay tribute to Heinrich Heine as a representative of the Jewish genius and as a poet who understood the psychology of the Germans. Dehmel's view is that the Wandering Jew (at least the one of romantic persuasion, who seeks death as an end to his suffering) is confounded by the stable insight of Heine, despite the "living grave" in which the poet spent years of anguish. The piece chastises Ahasuerus the Byronic sufferer, yet it does not rule out such self-dramatizing torment as a part of the Hebraic temperament. It prefers to praise the courage and sanity of which the Jew—the eternal Jew of history—is capable.[11]

On this theme, as on others, the predilection of many German writers in the closing years of the century is for ambitious efforts whenever the name of Ahasuerus comes their way. Take as an example the three-act poetic drama by Johannes Lepsius, *Ahasver, der ewige Jude* (Leipzig, 1894). This is designated by its author a mystery play. The action takes place in a time now over-familiar to us—the days of the siege and destruction of Jerusalem in the year 70. The locale shifts: in the Prologue and one scene of the third act it is Mount Nebo; otherwise it is either the market place of Jerusalem or the portico of the Temple. The chief characters are Ahasuerus, his daughter Esther, his mother Miriam, and a host of spirits, ghosts, and miscellaneous personages (Moses, Elijah, High Priests, Romans, Hebrews, Christians, the Four Horsemen of the Apocalypse, and Death). It is clear that in his design Lepsius is indebted to Haushofer.

In the Prologue Ahasuerus dreads death. He would live at all costs. But Asmaveth, or Death, warns him that whoever has seen death must eventually die. God, however, has other plans for Ahasuerus. Although he has looked on death, yet:

> Without repose or rest he is to wander,
> Whithersoever his tireless feet may bear him,
> From one world's end on to another,
> Inconstant, fleeting, until Judgment Day.[12]

So runs God's will, as Moses and Elijah, emerging from a rocky cleft on Mount Nebo, make clear. Asmaveth, however, a Mephistophelian character of pronounced Goethean lineaments, sneers that if Ahasuerus is afraid of him, he will find ways to harass the old sinner most energetically and keep him from the ark of the covenant.

And so, in the first act, the story of sin of Ahasuerus is told by a priest and embellished by Simon, the head of the Christian community in Jerusalem, who is caring for the family of the Wandering Jew. As for the sinner, when he first appears, he is being importuned by a group of Jewish malcontents who wish to be free of Roman rule. They want him for their leader, their warrior, the prophet whom God promised for the salvation of Israel—in short, for their Messiah. He rejects the idea, scorning the rebels as a race of cowardly rabbits, but the folk insist on saluting him. In the next scene he is missing from their company, for his daughter Esther has disappeared. She has gone in search of her lover Abdias. The rebels quarrel among themselves. Ahasuerus, returning to them, is disgusted by their disagreements and counsels them to be lenient toward some Christian prisoners they have brought with them. He remembers his own youth and his once childlike acceptance of the sacred words of the prophets and wise teachings of his masters, "where the knee is ever bent before the one, the invisible God." Overcome by wild anger, he recalls the words of the rabbis as he had learned them. He repudiates them violently in an access of guilt-laden rebellion. Even the entrance of Abdias, his prospective son-in-law, cannot quench his anger. He curses all priests, whatever their religion: may they all be neglected and forgotten. He is now prepared to be hailed as the Messiah, and to bring to his people the ark of the covenant.

But Death continues to worry him, as he had vowed to do, refusing to give him any clue as to the whereabouts of the ark and spreading over the whole scene an atmosphere of skepticism by questioning the nature of the life substance of the soul and declaring that the soul, born of dust, must return to dust. No doubt Death will have to yield to Moses and Elijah, custodians of the ark, and Ahasuerus will be able to appear in Jerusalem with his precious covenant; but what good will the ark accomplish against the Romans or against famine? Be that as it may, the ark comes to Ahasuerus. He implores Jehovah to help him, and when his prayers are not immediately answered, he goes into another tantrum against God:

> Canst thunder only one kind of thunder, Sinai?
> Since thou deceiv'st my people, and bring'st me damnation,
> I'll shatter Thee here upon this marble pavement.[13]

Therefore he demolishes the tablets of the law. At this blasphemy the people rise against him, seize him to crucify him, and bring him to a cross, but are driven away by a crowd of fleeing Jews and victorious Romans. In the shock of the destruction of Jerusalem, Ahasuerus remembers the Passion of Christ. At the very threshold where he rebuffed the Saviour, there appear now the deceased, transfigured Esther and the Crucified One himself, who induce in the heart of Ahasuerus awe and true repentance. He begs that he not be cursed further. Esther's voice explains that he need not fear more damnation; he must continue to wander until Christ returns. For this Ahasuerus is grateful. With his acceptance, the play ends in the spirit of thankfulness on the part of Ahasuerus and in the hope that his sufferings will some day be ended and forgiveness will be his.

Whatever Lepsius intended by his portrayal of Ahasuerus as the spirit of rebellious man, he is most convincing when he associates the character with the post-Crucifixion Jew who was in search more of a true Messiah to bring him independence than of a transcendental ideal. As Christ had foretold, however, there were many false Messiahs, and the Jews were thwarted in their quest by the immanence of death, by the mortality of their would-be deliverers. The Ahasuerus of Lepsius' play symbolizes the mortal who, because of his sinfulness, is inadequate as a leader and in whose tragedy lies the tragedy of the whole Jewish people. Cowering on a cross, at the brink of death, Ahasuerus realizes that he must die to achieve the ideal of his race; but he cannot bring himself to undergo death, being all too grateful that he is allowed to live and wander. So much for the significance of this drama. It touches an interesting and moving point of history, but Lepsius is a mediocre artist, at his best only when he is deriving from Goethe and Haushofer; he is an immature poet and dramatist who conjured up a few good scenes and wrote a few good lines.

Beside this tragic concept of the inadequacy of Ahasuerus as a leader is the flamboyant tone of Ludwig Wihl's "Ahasvers Klage," in *Ost und West* for 1901.[14] Here the poet glories in the protagonist's Jewishness, breathing hot defiance on the anti-Semitic Occident: let it do its worst; he will go on wandering. Such defiance sometimes tapers off into a complacent sense of superiority, which tends to rationalize the political inferiority of the European Jew. This is the tendency in Nina Meyke's "Ahasver" (1900), which presents nothing new but emphasizes what might be called the egocentric predicament of the Jews.[15] The chief character in this novel is Ahasver Goldstern. His father had always insisted that the Jews were the greatest people on earth; his grandfather had maintained that the Jews were persecuted and despised by Christians because they had no political entity, no nation, being scattered as they were all over the earth. They had no sovereign ruler, and their God had brought this about in punishment for their sins. Indeed, the old man's preoccupation with sin and the necessity for right-doing reminds one of Matthew Arnold's definition of Hebraism. Goldstern

("Goldstar") personifies the struggle of his people for a place in the sun, to use the then current German political phrase. He desires very much the respect of the Christians. But in the whole course of his education, from primary school through the university, he is either ignored and snubbed or treated with unsympathetic jeers. His friend Grodizki explains that much of this anti-Semitism springs from pure religious nonsense, not to say bigotry, the kind of vicious intolerance which could punish a Saviour along with petty thieves in the same crucifixion. Religion, therefore, bears both a blessing and a curse: it is a two-edged thing. The consciousness of guilt, plus the undeniable fact that evil begets evil, means that the crucifixion of Christ cannot remain unavenged. Hence such a story as the Legend of the Wandering Jew. All of this adds up to the distressing truth that the Jews, represented by Ahasver Goldstern, are the scapegoats for Christian intolerance and cruelty. The story would have been more forceful if it had been written more incisively, but the point is well taken.

The same idea emerges from Adolph Rosée's *Der sterbende Ahasver* (1898), which stresses the sufferings of Ahasuerus.[16] Nina Meyke's Ahasver, Goldstern, was treated with indifference and resented it, but his father and grandfather had prepared him intellectually for such treatment. Rosée's protagonist, however, is the victim of a heart-devouring and brain-consuming torment, the anguish of the Jew who must bear this stone in his bosom because he is a Jew, although he has long since been assimilated into Western culture and cannot consider himself an Israelite. He must do what he can to clear the path for later generations of those who are born Jews but who grow up as cosmopolitans. Since this Ahasuerus is dying, the implication is that the task has been too difficult. Others are aware of what may be called the *Ahasvergefühl*—the sense of being the Eternal Wanderer. An example is Robert A. Jaffé's *Ahasver* (Berlin, 1900), a novel describing the career of Emil Zlotnicki, a victim of this particular form of *Weltschmerz*, and his efforts in the direction of Zionism. Although the work takes due notice of Ahasuerus as representing all Jews, it is not otherwise concerned with the Legend.

A little more than passing attention should be paid the collection of three one-act plays under the title *Ahasver: Einakterzyklus mit Prolog* (Bamberg, 1905), by Eduard Diener and Arthur Hesslein. In the Prologue there is a conversation between Ahasuerus and Death; and, unlike the similar scene in Lepsius' drama, Ahasuerus is established as the superior of Death. Why not, since according to tradition the Wandering Jew cannot die? The three plays that follow are connected by the part played in each by a Jew. In the first, "Johannes von Gischala," the Jew interferes in the love of a young Hebrew warrior and a rabbi's daughter, Sephora, at the fall of Jerusalem in the year 70, with the result that the play ends tragically for the lovers. In the second, "Der gelbe Ring," laid in medieval Germany, a young Jewish physician wins the love of the burgermaster's daughter, Johanna, and treats her ailing father; but when the old man unexpectedly dies, the two are engulfed in a wave of bigotry in concentrated anti-Semitic form. The climax is the burning of the local ghetto and the death of the principals. In the third, "Der vergoldete Löwe," a young Jew is rejected by a "modern" Gentile girl because she cannot "break her traditions." He commits suicide, but it was actually anti-Semitic prejudice that murdered him. The sympathy of the authors in all three plays is directed toward the victim or victims of the anti-Semitic blight, for the old Jew in the first play was doing merely what his orthodox faith had taught him to do. Diener wrote the Prologue and the first play; Hesslein the second; and the two collaborated on the third, which is the weakest. From the standpoint of dramatic effectiveness, the prize should go to the second.

But whether anti-Semitic or not, the spirit of the times made Ahasuerus and his people one. In Ferdinand Bronner's "Ahasver, der ewige Jude," from *Aus Zeit und Ewigkeit* (Leipzig) for 1893, when Ahasuerus beholds the state of his people, he can join them and Christ in one of the seven last words from the Cross: "My God, my God, why hast thou forsaken me?" The incongruity of the scene is somewhat diminished by the effectiveness of the poetic lament. It is this same identification which is implicit in the three novels of Jewish life by Israel Zangwill, which established a particular genre in modern fiction. In his *Children of the Ghetto* (Philadelphia, 1892), the Ansell family is "a typical group of Wandering Jews, straying from town to town in search of better things, from Poland to England to Chicago." They endure the "heartache of a hunted race," but take comfort in the thought that all over the world at the same hour of the day they look toward Jerusalem. In a sequel, *The Grandchildren of the Ghetto* (London-New York, 1894), one of the Ansells explains: "I figure the Jew as the eldest-born of Time, touching the creation and reaching forward into the Future, the true blasé of the Universe—the Wandering Jew who has been everywhere, seen everything, done everything, led everything, thought everything and—suffered everything." Finally, in his *The War for the World* (London-New York, 1916), subtitled *The Wandering Jew*, the accent is placed on the fate of the Jewish people, who have been wandering for twenty centuries; though they have had much to do with European politics and hence with the fate of nations (World War I is going on at the moment), they have as yet no nation of their own.[17]

At times this identification assumes whimsical forms. Georg Wilde's *Der ewige Jude* (Leipzig, 1914) tells how the author, a rabbi, once met the Wandering Jew in Egypt and persuaded him to come with him to Jerusalem. There Ahasuerus saw the self-renewing vitality of the Jewish people and the general air of health and contentment among them. He was delighted to see this because he now believed that his redemption was near, since God so loved the Jews. When last seen he was heading for the Mount of Olives, waiting to be released by death. "Der ewige Jude ist tot; das Judenthum lebt!" Then, there are four little poems by Arthur Silbergleit in the *Israelitisches Familienblatt* of March 7, 1912. (The first asks if the Jewish people are in need of new shoes to wander, as was Ahasuerus. In the second Ahasuerus finds consolation in nature; so must the Jewish people. In the third, in rustic, pastoral scenes, the Wandering Jew recalls the more dramatic moments of his career. The fourth asks if the Jews, like Ahasuerus, deserve their present-day situation—like him, have they sinned?) Finally, the name of the protagonist is the only point of contact with the Legend in L. Hersch's *Le juif errant d'aujourd'hui* (Paris, 1913), which is a study of Jewish immigration and emigration before World War I.[18]

I conclude this section with comment on a few minor works which follow the line so well laid down by Zangwill. P. H. van Moerkerken's "Ahasverus Graf" [first published in *Elezeviers geïllustrated Monatsschrift* for 1910 and later in *Dans des Levens* (Amsterdam, 1910)] is a story "expressive of the spirit of a people paying for its blindness." Ahasuerus is driven on by the terrible memory of Christ's supernatural glance. The Saviour has spoken no words of judgment; none are necessary. Only a look of infinite sadness, full of pity and divine love, is fixed upon the reviler. His wife and children die suddenly, and Ahasuerus' wanderings begin. He is to find rest only when the mystery of that profound glance is revealed. So, in the course of a single year, he goes to visit the two saddest graveyards in Europe: first the Jewish cemetery in Friesland, where an old peasant woman is mourning the people rejected by God; then the Hebrew graveyard in Prague. Yet even now he cannot rest; neither among the heathen who rage nor in the darkest corners of a modern metropolis will he find his grave. The same thought appears in Julius Sturm's "Ahasver" (1907),[19] which is insignificant, and in Alfred Steuer's *Galizische Ghettogeschichten* (Halle, 1891), which is more articulate: the Jews are a miserable, restless people always producing a new Ahasuerus who can never find rest. The treatment in both works is sympathetic to the Jews.

An out-of-the-way performance indeed is A. Commoda's "Drei Zwiegespräche," in the *Lasker-Liebknecht Beyschlag: Drei Zwiegespräche* (Stuttgart, 1902). The piece opens with a cursory sketch of the Legend, which is negligible. The first dialogue is between Ahasuerus and the German liberal statesman Lasker (1829-1883). Ahasuerus gives a brief sketch of his career, accompanied by enormous footnotes which contain a goodly amount of Talmudic lore. The discussion drifts toward anti-Semitism and the persecution of the Jews, and the point is made that the Jews were anti-Christian before the Christians were anti-Semitic. Ahasuerus recounts the troubles between Jew and Gentile in the Middle Ages, and calls attention to the deterioration of relations between them in modern Germany which has come about for financial reasons. The talk then turns to the problem of later nineteenth-century German anti-Semitism. Commoda insists that the Jews have never suffered as much as the Christians. He delivers a diatribe against war, while praising Jesus for his spirituality and his humanitarianism. As to the truth of death and resurrection, Ahasuerus saw it all long ago, the whole sad story of the arrest, trial, crucifixion, and rising of Christ, and he supports his narrative by calling attention to the evidence of the disciples and even of the enemies of Christ. The dialogue—unfortunately long-drawn-out and tedious—extols the superiority of Christ over Mohammed. About this the Wandering Jew remains to be convinced. He is willing to confess Christ and to be baptized, provided only that he then be allowed to die. Lasker, who has had very little to say up to this point, agrees. When he expresses a hope for mercy, Ahasuerus assures him that it will be forthcoming, for Lasker has loved truth, hated injustice, and died abroad. A further point in this dialogue is a challenge sometimes accepted by later writers—that perhaps a tempering of the twin cultures, Hebraic and Christian, in such a manner as to effect a blend or fusion might be the best solution of the interracial problem. [Oskar Waldeck's *Der ewige Jude* (Dresden, 1909)—a play in five acts, which, in spite of its title, does not concern itself with the Legend—argues that the merging of Jewish and Christian culture is necessary for a civilized future.]

All of the moderate writers of the time, of course, agree that anti-Semitism in any form is a bad thing. Having said this, they are inclined to sweep the rest under the rug. A freakishly inverted approach to the problem—in effect a conscious effort to turn the stocking inside out—is found in H. M. Bien's *Ben-Beor: A Story of the Anti-Messiah* (Baltimore, 1891). In this long prose performance in the tradition of the Chronicle of the Wandering Jew we have something analogous to a photographic negative: instead of the Wandering Jew there is a Wandering Gentile. The work is in two parts, the first entitled "The Man in the Moon," and the second "The Wandering Gentile." The author was a rabbi in Vicksburg, Mississippi.

In "The Man in the Moon," a series of "lunar intaglios," Balaam Ben-Beor, whose name is derived from Numbers 22:5, is enamored of Pharaoh's daughter, who had found Moses in the bulrushes. She is given the name Merris. She spurns him and marries Balak the Hebrew. And so begins Ben-Beor's career of revenge against all women and all Jews. After his death on earth he is transported to a kind of purgatory on the moon, where there is a spiritual Utopia. He succeeds, however, in becoming the evil genius of the place. Later the prophet Elijah, in the course of his ascent to heaven in his fiery chariot (II Kings 2:1), stops for a brief sojourn on the moon. Hearing the evil words of Ben-Beor, he throws him back to earth, under a malediction which will rest upon him until such time as God sees fit to lift it. Ben-Beor is to become a wanderer.[20]

The second part, "The Wandering Gentile," takes Ben-Beor through his travels on earth, ever lusting for revenge against the Jews. He is present at the destruction of Jerusalem and at the futile revolt of Simon Bar-Giora. At both Jewish defeats, so satisfactory to him, he shows himself to be a master intriguer. But he is nagged by the ever-present consciousness of some woman who is a reincarnation of Merris. In each instance he tries to win her and is always rejected, although he usually succeeds in bringing about either her humiliation or destruction. As he witnesses the gradual spread of Christianity throughout the Roman Empire, his favorite occupation is persecuting Christians. He sees Nero and the burning of Rome; he is present at the cataclysm of Pompeii. Then comes a pause. One hears of him next attending the birth of Islam, then visiting a primitive tribe of southern Russia. Next he meets Peter the Hermit and notes the wave of anti-Semitism which began with the Crusades. He is revealed as an inciter of the hatred for the Jews that established them as Christ-killers and led to their persecution by the Flagellants. He is at his cruel best during the Spanish Inquisition.

The advent of printing in western Europe, however, is a blow to his anti-Christian endeavors—that and the solid, sentimental character of the Germanic peoples. He tries to get the Holy Roman Emperor to act against the Hebrew writings; but in vain, thanks largely to Johannes Reuchlin, the celebrated German humanist (1455–1522). He attempts—in the person of the rebel Thomas Munzer, who broke with Luther and was a leader in the Peasants' War—to undermine the Reformation. We are to infer, although the point is subtle, that Munzer never really died in 1525 with his eight thousand Anabaptists; his body may have been destroyed, but as the Wandering Jew he was indestructible. That is to say, the Wandering Gentile, entering the body of Munzer, is the Wandering Jew. Therefore he continues his existence, observing and participating in the Thirty Years' War, and realizing its futility, so that he turns once more against the Christians. All this is in vain, however many beautiful females and strong men perish in the action. Finally, broken in spirit and baffled in mind, he visits the American colonies, hoping to start trouble there—only to be confounded by the obdurate individualism of the Americans. He is comforted in this winter of discontent, however, by the fact that, on the ship to America, he was visited by none other than Elijah himself, who told him that the curse had been lifted and that he would soon die. But there is still an ordeal for him to endure. After landing in Philadelphia on July 4, 1776, he heard the reading of the Declaration of Independence, and, utterly frustrated by the noble words of that document, fled into the wilderness of upper New York. There he became a recluse until liberated by an earthquake which caused his death on October 19, 1781, the day of Cornwallis' surrender. The death of this evil genius, in other words, coincides with the birth of a new era in a new world.

The style of this work is turgid, and its historiography is scrambled, but it is an original composition, for we have not heard of the Wandering Gentile before or since. It is an earnest plea for anti-anti-Semitism, and tucked away within its many pages is a stout defense of antialcoholism. I am sure that Rabbi Bien intended it as a defense of liberty and humanitarianism, which he elected to present in this inverted form. For all its peculiarities, it remains a readable kind of propagandistic extravaganza, written by a man of deep religious feeling. A member of one of the Jewish centers along the Mississippi, he was in the tradition of revolt against orthodox Judaism.

Ahasuerus and the Promethean Complex

Ahasuerus as a symbol of his race thus becomes an awakener of hate, for even when he is treated by a writer of anti-anti-Semitic persuasion, he may still be embroiled in bigotry and its consequences. On the other hand, many writings indicate the possibility that Ahasuerus, whether thought of primarily as a Jew or not, can be an inspiration to others. There are not so many, however, as one could hope for, perhaps because it is more interesting to write about evil than about good.

Ludwig Bund's charming poem, "Ahasver," appears in his *Gesammelte Gedichte* (Leipzig, *ca.*1900). In his boyhood the Legend had moved the poet deeply, because to him Ahasuerus represented long-suffering courage and stoicism. In later life Bund learned from him how to endure:

> I knew of men who suffered most exceedingly:
> An Ahasuerus merely complaining, courageless;
> Yet, Ahasuerus, I have come to know you,
> You human spirit, you wanderer eternal,
> You are the image that fire can ne'er consume,
> The pilgrim without rest or ceasing.

You are the light, that bright from sea to sea,
From land to land moves on with giant footsteps,
Yet never once in this sphere or another
Did find your peace or e'er your true abode.

You thirst—but who can offer you the chalice?
Who saw in sympathy your tear-exhausted eyes?
But some day for you the clouds will be dispelled,
And, Ahasuerus, to you will come redemption.

Bund's poem is sincere and serious. But one should expect the bathetic, farcical obverse to such true sympathy, and this is forthcoming in Ludwig Hopf's story, "Ahasver," published in, of all places, a collection of tales called *Neue medizinische und anthropologische Märchen* (Tübingen, 1903). Labeled by its author a "hygienic-dietetic" legend, it tells the lugubrious history of Alois Gerstinger, a rich young brewer's son in Munich, who is idle and overweight. He and a friend attend a vegetarian and temperance lecture given by a crank acquaintance. There he sees and falls in love with beautiful Anna, who rejects him because he is fat and useless. The despairing lover walks into the neighboring countryside, where he meets Ahasuerus, who tells him that there are two talismans which will help him: moderation in eating and drinking and hard work. Neither of these appeals to Alois, to be sure, but he has taken the rejection by Anna so much to heart that he is willing to follow the Wandering Jew's advice. He therefore avoids restaurants with their rich food and calorific beverages, goes to work in his father's brewery (where resisting the constant temptation to drink beer is good discipline), and reduces from 220 pounds to 180, whereupon Anna accepts him. Scarcely a lofty tale, but it shows what inspiration can do—whether the inspiration is Anna's love or the Wandering Jew's dietetic advice is immaterial, since the end of the story is happy.

Fortunately such a prostitution of the Legend is uncommon. If the Wandering Jew is to be an inspiration, it is only fit and proper that he should possess some spiritual force, because he was created in the first place as a kind of moral lesson. Bund's tribute to him is therefore more significant than Hopf's. It is seconded elsewhere, usually in weaker fashion, to be sure; but sometimes a simple, unpretentious poem can produce pleasing effects without shaking the earth. For example, there are the verses by Wilhelm Holzamer, "Der Wanderer," in *Avalun* (Berlin, 1911),[21] expressing the thrill of a spectator on seeing Ahasuerus go by, wearing his "Calabrian hat"—a detail from the southern European folkloristic treatments of the Legend—and the sense of loss after his departure.

Yes, Ahasuerus has won the affection of many. Hans Eschelbach, in a poem, "Ahasver," from *Wildwuchs* (Paderborn, 1896),[22] brings a despairing wanderer to meet the Jew, who directs him to the faith and peace of childhood. The verses are a little too melodramatic, for there is storm and tempest at the meeting, and the hopeless mortal has some Byronic posturing to do before receiving comfort. To him it is all lies and betrayal, and the soul of the poet sickens at the thought of it. But Ahasuerus reminds him that he himself once went through all that despair. He does not believe that man should seek God, when His curse can reduce man to nothing, as his own case demonstrates. But that is unimportant because there are still such things as faith, repentance, peace, and love. Eschelbach does not go more deeply into the relationship of Ahasuerus and his acquaintance.

In a similar poem by August Silberstein, *Der verwandelte Ahasver* (Leipzig, 1899), the touch is much lighter. Ahasuerus, indeed, exerts an undeniable charm, acting as a mere creature of fate who wanders into the St. Peter rathskeller in Salzburg. To the assembled revelers he explains how very often and in what ways he has sought death; there is no way to suicide that he has left unexplored —not even dynamite and nitroglycerine—but, of course, always in vain. Meanwhile, the inevitable revolutions of the wheel of fortune have brought him to various moods and situations. He considers himself not so much a wanderer as the editor of a chronicle or journal, and discourses at some length upon the problems of the editorial art. (Such an editor must seek the facts above all.) Ahasuerus sees in himself all aspects of humanity. His natural inclination is to wander, to find out what has happened, and to transmit this to humanity; and if humanity is properly aware, it can derive a great deal from what he has to say. Silberstein's verse is ragged, and his phraseology flippant, but it is obvious that he has something to tell, and he tells it amusingly, if not with great penetration.

The hazy expression of Eschelbach's poem is matched in a full-length drama by Carl Schottelius, *Sigmar* (Dresden, 1895), which also teaches that the innocence of childhood will bring ultimate resolution to the problem of despair. It presents the idea, however, through Faust instead of Ahasuerus. The patent truth is that neither Eschelbach nor Schottelius, for all their literary pretensions, comes as close to the human quality, the lovable potential in the character of Ahasuerus, as the quiet little pseudonymous poem by "Dolorosa" in *Confirmo te chrysmate* (Berlin, 1903), the lament of a woman who has loved the Wandering Jew. While Ahasuerus is sleeping in her arms, she mourns her inability to keep him, for it is his fate to wander. She is certain that, if her love were unhindered by worldly or religious considerations, she could redeem him.

Ahasuerus, then, may be useful to mankind sometimes for noble and sometimes for ignoble purposes. Again, he may be a virtual Prometheus, a symbol of leadership for the oppressed, the needy, the tortured—an incarnation of the desire to free them, to bring down fire from heaven, for their benefit. A good example of such a portrayal is Gustav Renner's *Ahasver: Eine Dichtung* (Leipzig, 1902). The ideas in this philosophical poem were foreshadowed, sometimes stated explicitly, in Renner's "Skizzen zu Ahasver," written in 1896-97.[23] Its derivation from these "sketches" may help to explain the formlessness of *Ahasver* and its diffused portrait of Ahasuerus, who fancies himself as the representative of the submerged working classes, striving to win for them happiness and justice. When they finally turn against him, he is bewildered and mutters that no doubt his fate must be consummated in himself alone; but he clings, all the same, to the hope that he will be able to embody their aspirations.

The "Skizzen" comprise seven scenes from history in which Ahasuerus plays an appropriate part. In some respects, then, they exemplify the Chronicle of the Wandering Jew. Both the "Skizzen" and *Ahasver* are given over to reflective contemplation, though they contain some epic and dramatic passages. Renner's sources are in particular Goethe, Mosen, and Lepsius. The author's choice of scenes betrays little originality, and there is a certain air of familiarity about his work. This Ahasuerus is no solid citizen; he is a beggar and an advocate of *Umsturz*, a discontented individual who wishes for a change in his own fortunes. He hates God and has no hope for the future, because it seems to him that Christ is a too passive deceiver. The individual touch which Renner does manage to give to the Legend is the willingness of Ahasuerus to swear to hatred of Christ to his dying day—a hatred which, evinced while He was on the Cross, led to the curse. While Ahasuerus wanders, he is a walking compound of bitter resentment, envy, and revenge. When Jerusalem is destroyed, his contempt for God is superseded by his denial of a God of any kind—else why should people suffer so? Therefore he turns to Mother Earth, who reminds him that his woe is the woe of all mankind, his fate the fate of all. "Very well, then," he replies, "let us break our bonds of slavery and bring happiness to the world." Yet he finds nothing to aid him in his crusade for freedom, either in heaven or hell, and frustration confirms him in his individualism, which tends to direct him more and more toward a pantheistic view of creation. Even nature and the elements, he discovers, are not free; he must stand alone if he hopes to bring his concept of justice to mankind. Needless to say, he fails. In the Babylonian captivity following the destruction of Jerusalem, he is taught by an old man that salvation comes from deeds rather than from words, and that it would be better for Ahasuerus if he came down to earth and lived out his days trying to benefit humanity in a way more practical than introspective brooding.

Ahasuerus is then shown some pictures of the future, of feudal society and the Peasants' War in Germany. When he asks who is leading the peasants in their struggle, he is told that it is he, Ahasuerus, whatever his name may then be. In the panorama of humanity suffering through the French Revolution, justice and happiness triumph, and the Wandering Jew plays an important part in the victory. Napoleon Bonaparte passes over the scene. Ahasuerus finds himself in the modern technological age, a partaker of death-in-life, speaking as a prophet of the proletariat in the days to come:

> I know it well, I stand at the turn of the times.
>
> . . . .
>
> O day of salvation! like unto the sunbursts
> In the bosom of the lightning I will descend
> And shatter forever all the ancient realm of darkness.[24]

His efforts succeed beyond his hopes. A new Nimrod builds a new Tower of Babel to celebrate the might of men. Man has become God; the old order of divinity is gone. In its place are love, peace, and helpfulness, and Ahasuerus is their high priest, a Messiah of social propensities. Now, with the adulation of the people to strengthen him, he can taunt the old God with the reminder that His curse was in truth a blessing. Meanwhile, the Furies are biding their time; when they see their opportunity they bring about the same fate for this new Messiah that befell Christ. The people call for action rather than words; more than that, they repudiate Ahasuerus as they repudiated Christ. He is seized and crucified as was

Christ. On either side of him is another victim, a young man and an old man. Even they turn away from him. There is no penitent thief to allay his bitterness as there was for Christ. In vast spiritual disgust, Ahasuerus groans that he is a very fool who tries to find salvation in truth and justice. He will not bow his head; perhaps he has been defeated but he cannot be broken and assuredly not killed. Some other time he will be a victor.

But though it is not possible for him to die, Ahasuerus has been rejected and is thrown back into his former lonely state. From this time on he proceeds as we have already seen him. He takes a wife, and she dies; he witnesses the death of his brother; he wanders apace, wishing ever for death. His significance becomes clear: he is the only creature in his life that is immortal. He has lost hope, desire, and the will to struggle, which means that happiness, peace, and love have been replaced within his sphere by pain, war, and hate. Yet when the Last Judgment comes bringing death, he will be forgiven, because the Scriptures reveal that he who loses his life shall find it, and he will be forever bound who never knew bonds. Or, to put it in another way, all things call to their opposites—pain and need are the road to joy and health; death is the road to life, and life the road to death.

All this is trite stuff, no doubt, but it depicts Ahasuerus as a Prometheus eager to help mankind whether or not it wants to be helped, only to discover that humanity is happiest when it is sweating and swinking in the usual course of events. It is a relief, after reading Renner's often turgid verse, to come upon a superior performance like Johanna and Gustav Wolff's *Ahasver* (Berlin, 1899), even if this closet drama is more closely related to Faust than to Ahasuerus. A prologue presents Lucifer in hell. He defines the issue between good and evil, for the struggle between light and darkness is continuous. God is about to descend to earth, there to defeat his enemies, who are threatening his reign. Then he will move against hell. Who will conduct its defense against Christ? None in hell is qualified. It therefore devolves upon Lucifer to find a man on earth endowed with all possible gifts—intelligence, wealth, and power—who is discontented with his lot. Ahasuerus is the chosen man. While Christ is turning men's minds away from earth to heaven, Ahasuerus preaches affirmation of life on earth and the enjoyment of the present rather than the future. It is a highly original kind of introduction, and the sole objection which the student of the Legend could raise is that this concept of Ahasuerus is atypical. Moreover, as one proceeds through the poem, one detects a similarity to scenes from the first part of Goethe's great work—a prologue in another world, a study-chamber, a festival in progress.

The Wolffs' Ahasuerus is a man of wealth. As a child he was cared for by Veronica—the only instance on record of the contamination of the legends of Veronica and of the Wandering Jew. She explains to him the teachings of Christ and the Christian way of life and brings him into the footsteps of the Saviour, whom he accepts for the nonce as the long-awaited Messiah. But deep within him lies the speck of doubt:

> For Doubt alone abides within our hearts
>
> .   .   .   .
>
> Whither the questions arising in my soul?
> Thou, O God, must give the answer,

I call to Thee deep in despair.

. . . .

What is mankind and what its goal?

. . . .

God is no hero; be silent concerning Him on high;
Let angels praise the Lord in Heaven,
On earth let it be a fighter among fighters.[25]

Under these circumstances, it is unlikely that when Christ is on his way to Golgotha and, bleeding and submissive, tries to rest for a moment before the house of Ahasuerus, the Jew would recognize a redeemer of the world. And so he curses Him.

Later, after he has begun his wanderings, Ahasuerus retires first into the wilderness, to seek God in either heaven or hell and to build the "golden house of the future," never to rest until he has found God on earth. He holds in his memory an old dream of peace and enlightenment, and meditates on the nature of things, on God and eternity, on life and human aspirations. He is seen in his study, like Faust, where he admits his inability to find the answers to the weighty questions which he has proposed for himself; but he must continue to seek, for in restless inquiry lies the ultimate wisdom, and each individual should make such inquiry his business in life. The professional philosophers, he believes, have never done that. Since life is at best the frailest of creations, it behooves one to bring it to an ever higher level, so that its worth and dignity will always be enhanced.

But from this point on the poem is more of Faust than Ahasuerus. A young female scholar, Atta—who has made a pact with the Devil (Feuro), in return for which her fate and that of her lover will be one—seeks out Ahasuerus as master. The latter, whose misogynism hitherto has been marked, observes that life is the worst of all evils, but that which is given us only once should be used for enjoyment and experience. Yet he cannot believe that women are capable of higher feelings or even of faithfulness, for their love, which is an undeniable attraction to men, is basically a belly-love. At first Ahasuerus is friendly to Atta out of pity, but he proceeds to fall in love with her and alters his views in consequence. He learns through her the beauties of nature and becomes persuaded that in the chivalric cult which grew up in the Middle Ages lay the solution of many a social problem.

In the final scenes Ahasuerus is the architect and overseer of labor in the building of a temple erected for the worship of life. Although this temple is destroyed through the powers of darkness, as he sees nature restoring itself amid the ruins, he thinks once more of the wonder of life, even among the small and weak. And so he goes to work once more to rear a more radiant temple, on the dome of which is to be a golden sun sending forth its beams, not the cross of renunciation and penitence. For earth is our true home; the temple of life is to be in our own hearts. Ahasuerus, his mission accomplished, sinks in death:

It was no curse, it was a blessing.
I felt long since its warmth within me,
I knew in many glorious ways
In life alone is worth and honor.[26]

It is clear that this is only a temporary death, a rest for a time from striving, and that Ahasuerus will return in some new person to stride again over the world. The Ahasuerus we see in this drama tries to consider mankind and its present needs, to build a foundation of faith in life—to be a Prometheus for man's spiritual and moral welfare. But he has not been released from his wanderings, if indeed he ever will be. Atta stands beside this fighter Ahasuerus, who bears the world on his shoulders, and remains true to him in childlike innocence. In this very constancy she frees herself from her compact with Feuro, the Mephistopheles of the play. She has served the world and mankind in her way, as Ahasuerus did in his.

Deriving from both Renner and the Wolffs, Josef L. Windholz' *Ahasver* (Vienna, 1909) is a "novelle" of the present time. The protagonist Matthias, called by his friends "Ahasver," is bitterly critical of the miseries of the age. His goal is to make the pent-up energy of the world more serviceable to man. He therefore begins to lay the foundations of a free socialism in Argentina, in order to establish a cryptic "horoscope of humanity." The work is not otherwise notable.

Apart from the inevitable shadow of Goethe, two influences seem to be working on these last few writers. One is the Nietzschean complex, and we find it in Ahasuerus' distrust of women and his *Herrenmoral*, which despises the weak. Atta, in the Wolffs' play, manages to counteract both of these beliefs, as well as the notion that God, who is dead, can no longer build a temple; it must be done by the hands of men. The second influence, which has a special interest to writers about the Legend, is Robert Hamerling's autobiography, *Stationen meiner Lebenspilgerfahrt* ("Stations in My Life's Pilgrimage"), which had gone into its third edition by 1889. Here Hamerling explains that the scheme for his *Ahasver in Rom* developed from the basic concept of a golden age for primitive man of happiness without intellect: when man began to think, he became unhappy, and it was not until he had freed himself from the traditional concepts of God and relied on himself that he came to have real worth.[27] In addition, all of these writers, especially the Wolffs, insist with Goethe on the necessity of the eternal feminine, on reliance on nature, instinct, and feelings. Their Ahasueri, in short, are concerned with man rather than with God.

To bring this new Prometheus out of the clouds of legend and down to earth is the purpose of *Ahasvera* (Berlin, 1910), a novel by "Hans von Kahlenberg" (Helene von Manbart). Written in the German Empire of the Hohenzollerns only a few years before the outbreak of World War I, it has for its protagonist an idealistic, antimilitaristic Jewish youth who baffles his mother with his apparent lack of German patriotism. Yet she applauds his bitter resentment of anti-Semitism and his overriding desire to work for the liberation of his people.[28] In effect, his striving constitutes the wandering of this Wandering Jew, and even though his efforts fall short of the goal, it is his Promethean spirit which is important. At the same time, one may wonder whether the story by Otto von Schaching, "Der ewige Jude" (1895), in which Ahasuerus is of service to some mountaineers in peril, is not more satisfyingly related to the Legend, even in this Promethean aspect, and more worthy of record than "Von Kahlenberg's" novel.[29]

If we do not take the Wolffs' drama into account, one of the next most attractive works on this Promethean theme is Viktor Rydberg's "Prometheus und

Ahasverus," in *Nord und Süd* for 1888.[30] This is a tale told partly in prose and partly in verse. Noah, after the Deluge had subsided, discovers Prometheus still chained to his rock, untouched by the flood and still in torment. He tells his sons of the punishment meted out to Prometheus, and they and their children remember it forever.

The parallel between Prometheus and Ahasverus, as Rydberg sees it, is obvious enough. Both suffer because they have offended a temporal deity. Prometheus, however, believes in an eternal God who will deliver him. The core of the work is the dialogue in verse between Prometheus and Ahasuerus. The latter is much more of a defeatist than Prometheus. He was once a promising industrialist in the shoe industry, but look at him now! In the course of the dialogue, Prometheus counsels hatred of all tyranny, including a temporal God; but Ahasuerus, on the other side, favors resigned acceptance, because, by acceptance, more can be done for humanity. At the end of the scene, the Messiah appears to both debaters. From the mere sight of the Saviour, whom he recognizes, the Wandering Jew derives more courage. Prometheus, however, does not recognize him. Besides, he does not really believe in him. He is comforted all the same by His visit, while he continues to undergo his perpetual torture. In the final appraisal Ahasuerus is more Promethean than Prometheus, for here Prometheus typifies mere defiance, whereas Ahasuerus represents service to mankind in compromise and practicality. The irony is well sustained throughout.

One of the ways by which mankind can be served is the important way of the artist. This is the theme of K. E. Knodt's "Auch ein Ahasver!" in *Ein Ton vom Tode* (Leipzig, 1905), a poem in which appears the observation that the artist is by his very nature a Wandering Jew. But one of the more remarkable early twentieth-century books to deal with this idea is Hans Georg Kühn's *Ahasver, ein Tagebuch* (Berlin-Leipzig, 1910). Edited by Ludwig Bär and published soon after Kühn's death by suicide in 1909, it is a moving human document rather than a specific contribution to the Legend. Kühn, a brilliant, eccentric young Viennese, was a belated *Sturm und Drang* romantic, a tremendous individualist and nonconformist. He was antidemocratic, anti-Wagnerian, antimaterialistic, and antipatriotic (quite a Nietzschean, at that!), and paid the usual price for nonconformity by being extremely unhappy most of the time. In all his unhappiness, however, he made some trenchant remarks in his journal. His enthusiasms in the artistic fields, leaving aside the usual pair of Goethe and Nietzsche, were the great classical composers from Bach to Schumann. At one time in his short life he had identified himself with the Wandering Jew and had planned a vast poem on Ahasuerus, of which there remains only a fragmentary sketch in his journal. It was doubtless this passion for the Wandering Jew, as well as the restless, vainly seeking spirit of the journal that prompted its editor to give it the title it bears.

This surviving fragment is a miniature one-act play, in which Ahasuerus attempts to persuade an ailing poet, Gumpert, who is handicapped by both illness and the weight of years of habit, to abandon his Philistine wife and follow the Wandering Jew. Gumpert cannot summon enough energy to make the necessary break and dies before Ahasuerus can get him away. The brief picture of Ahasuerus presented here, however, is striking. Kühn observes elsewhere in his jour-

nal that the versatility and universality of the Renaissance was ideal for the creation of Ahasuerus, who was intended by his original author (whoever he was) to
burn down, to extirpate the stuffy, materialistic *kultus* of the modern age. The
fragment is a pathetic and futile try at a good idea, and Kühn leaves an impression
on the reader all through his journal of a human being who would have been
worth saving, a cut branch that might have grown full straight.

The artist, of course, is never so completely accepted by society that it will not
prefer the man of action, and in his old role of god from the machine, Ahasuerus
continues to thrive in even a Promethean atmosphere. Unfortunately, the call for
a god from the machine is often an indication of a clumsily contrived plot or an
unconvincing piece of melodrama. Thus Wilhelm Herbert's *Der ewige Jude in
München* (printed without date or place of publication, although most likely
originating in the 1890's) is an incoherent novel involving horseplay, local scandal, and some murky philosophy, and with a theatrical ending altogether out of
keeping with the comic and satirical beginning and middle.[31] Somewhat better is
Willi Soendermann's *Ahasver, der ewige Jude* (Dresden-Leipzig, 1902), a tragedy
in five acts. Eberhardt, a young man who has entered monastic life, falls in love
with Ruth, daughter of a retainer of the feudal prince of Targowicz. It is no great
shock to learn that Ruth is coveted also by the prince. Ahasuerus comes in traditional costume and reveals to Eberhardt that Ruth loves him. He urges action
from the lethargic young man. The prince has Ruth abducted, and again Ahasuerus appears, this time to incite the people to insurrection. In the ensuing fracas
at the prince's castle, Eberhardt attempts to kill Ahasuerus, whom he is so misguided as to suspect of double-dealing. The only victim of his attack, however, is
Ruth, who receives the blow intended for the Wandering Jew. Eberhardt commits suicide, and the play ends with the destruction of the castle. In this instance,
at least, the well-meant manipulations of Ahasuerus have brought only calamity
—an echo of the ancient motif of disaster in the folk tales.

Among English-speaking people of the 1890's, the most popular presentation
of Ahasuerus as god from the machine was Lew[is] Wallace's *The Prince of India*
(New York, 1893), a full-length novel in the nineteenth-century sense of the
term, which means at least two substantial volumes.[32] It was the noble intention of
Wallace's Wandering Jew, an Oriental potentate who has been everywhere and
seen everything, to work for the integration of all religions. The central episode
is the capture of Constantinople by the Turks in 1453.

Wallace's Ahasuerus attained vast wealth when, some sixty years earlier, he
had plundered the tomb of Hiram, friend of Solomon the poet-king of Israel.
Thus Ahasuerus became a lavish, opulent Oriental prince, a brooding man who
at times could forget his curse in the quest for a solution of the problem arising
from his theory that faith is a natural instinct and that religion arises only when
there is a grain of doubt in that faith, for God is greater than any creed. Therefore Ahasuerus is a self-appointed discriminator among religions; his part in the
novel is to combine the best aspects of all of them into one universal faith, and
in this role he becomes a great manipulator.

Since the fanaticism of the Moslems holds no appeal for him, he travels to
Constantinople, a center of Christian culture which he thinks will be more con-

genial to his purpose than Islam. When questioned about his religious belief, he explains to the emperor Constantine and his assembled court and clerics that he is not a Hindu because he cannot believe that men can make their own gods; a Buddhist because he cannot believe that after death the soul departs into nothingness; nor a Confucian because he cannot make a ready interchange between philosophy and religion. Neither is he a Jew because he believes that God loves all men equally, nor a Moslem because he refuses to admit that a mortal man can stand between him and God when he wishes to pray, not even when that man is a prophet. He is not a Christian because he believes that God is God. He also rejects belief in the only begotten Son because he insists that God did not shed his love and his light over a particular people or a particular generation only once, but rather has poured them out continuously over all the sons of men.

In other words, he believes that all holy writings—the Bible of Jews and Christians, the Book of Avesta, the Book of Sutra, the King of Confucius, and the Koran of Mohammed—are all of equal worth, that the Spirit of God has resided to an equal degree in Moses, Elijah, Buddha, Zarathustra, Mohammed, Confucius, Christ, and all others who have led people toward the light. But, he reminds us, their inhabitation by the Spirit of God does not make them gods themselves. After all, our Father abides in heaven, not among mortals on earth.

When the Christians of Constantinople reject Ahasuerus' theories and try to imprison him, as the tradition of the Legend asserts itself, he escapes, to wreak revenge on the Christians by persuading the Sultan Mohammed to attack Constantinople. This human action lessens the stature of Wallace's Ahasuerus in his search for one world of divine love, and some of his other appearances in the novel hardly restore his lost dimensions. He is now an astrologer, now a philosopher, now a master intriguer. This variety of aspects to his character, however, makes for interesting incidents, which cannot all be summarized here, although they make *The Prince of India* good reading as late nineteenth-century historical fiction goes. As far as the Legend is concerned, it is to be noted that while he is in the throes of a wild spasm of revenge when Constantinople falls, Ahasuerus is taken with cramps and collapses, to discover, when he revives, that he has been rejuvenated. Perhaps Wallace had only the Matthew Paris version to draw upon for this detail; it is more likely, however, that he had read Hoffman's *Chronicles of Cartaphilus,* in which occur the most spectacular examples of such rejuvenation. In this case the youthful Ahasuerus finds his transformation an inconvenience: neither his former friends nor his much loved adopted daughter Lael recognize him, and he disappears from the novel, crushed by the impact of the curse which has foiled him in his laudable objective.

There are other characters in this novel who deserve attention, although we are justified in regarding the Prince of India as the protagonist. From what we know of the genesis of the novel, it is evident that Wallace had read widely in the histories of the Byzantine Empire before he began to write.[33] To these he is indebted for the portrayal of Princess Irene, beloved of both Constantine and Mohammed. He owes much also to Croly's *Salathiel* for the picture of Ahasuerus. The product of his reading is a novel not so rousing as his *Ben-Hur,* but full of vigorous episodes like the treasure hunt at Hiram's tomb, the pilgrimage to Mecca, and the storm on the Bosphorus—episodes typical of the romantic novels of nearly a century before, fiction rather than history, and fiction of an ephemeral quality.

The concept of Ahasuerus as the custodian, self-appointed or not, of world religion, or of any specific religion, is unusual and unconvincing. Thus when "Ben Israel," in "Der ewige Jude," from *Ost und West* for 1901, explains that Ahasuerus is sure of eventual salvation because he did a good deed for his faith (he saved the Torah from a ruined city and returned it safe), he seems to be crossing Christian and Hebraic traditions most awkwardly.[34]

At any rate, there are plenty of other works not so original. Paul Sonnenkalb's "Ahasver: Solospiel," written in 1895, is a dramatic monologue based on the concept of the Wandering Jew in Klingemann's drama created some seventy years earlier.[35] It is not notable in any respect. J. Horst made a dramatization of Hamerling's *Ahasver in Rom* which was actually produced at Hamburg in 1901, though not with much success. No wonder, for Hamerling's excellent narrative poem remains primarily epic. In both Sonnenkalb and Horst, Ahasuerus is a manipulator: in Klingemann's material, by inspiring Heinyn to murder Gustavus Adolphus; in Hamerling's, by confirming Nero in his will to suicide. And both of these manipulations are concerned with a religious problem.

Perhaps the most energetic role in which Ahasuerus has ever disported himself as a manipulator comes in a historical drama in six scenes by Albert Kachellek, *Ahasver und Bonaparte* (Dresden, 1904). Here he is a puppeteer who is complete master of the destiny of Napoleon and hopes, if the little Corsican can become the world figure he potentially is, for a comfortable generation in which to live. Perhaps, in such a golden era, Ahasuerus might find salvation. But, alas, like Beethoven he is disillusioned when Bonaparte proclaims himself emperor, and so Ahasuerus dedicates his efforts, as in Hamerling's poem, to the overthrow of the tyrant and the betterment of the oppressed. He therefore puts the torch to Moscow and gloats over Waterloo. A curious final scene at St. Helena presents the ghost of Queen Louise of Prussia before the dying Napoleon, speaking forgiveness to the repentant ravager of her kingdom and prophesying the future greatness of Prussia in the European scheme of things. Meantime, the Wandering Jew goes his appointed way. The play owes much to Schubart's "Der ewige Jude," even to the posing of Ahasuerus amid skulls (this time on St. Helena, not Mount Carmel), but derivative or not, it is a decided improvement on some of the other poetic dramas on the subject.

Ahasuerus the Defiant and Destructive

The attitude of the Promethean manipulator may lead to the spirit of defiance. Ahasuerus the defiant need not be in association with the powers of darkness, or skeptical, or malicious; rather he expresses an awareness that he is and should be mortal, not deathless. He therefore challenges God as Prometheus challenged Zeus. Many works around 1900 stress his defiance not only of the divine but of the human as well.

A vigorous little poem by Mathias Acher, "Ahasver an seine Widersacher" ("Ahasuerus to his Adversary"), in *Ost und West* for January, 1904, presents the Wandering Jew shouting bravely against those who would fight against him or otherwise bar his way. After all, he is invincible. Acher wrote more poems on the same subject; some of them were printed in *Ost und West* between 1902 and 1904; others remained in manuscript. They may be grouped under the title of *Ahasver-Gedichte*. For example, there is "Gott flucht Ahasver," a whimsical piece of near-doggerel which enumerates God's curses laid upon Ahasuerus (hunger, thirst, restlessness, defiance, and all that goes with them), but declares that from defiance will come strength as potent as the curse laid upon the victim. The burden of "Tröster Ahasver" ("Ahasuerus the Consoler") is that the consolation which a mortal experiences from contemplating the Wandering Jew lies in the defiance which Ahasuerus shows, as well as his never flagging courage. "Aus Träumen geweckt" ("Awakened from Dreams") is more personal. It does not mention the Jew by name, but takes its lesson from his immortality and from the fact that he is as eternal as the stars. "Im Walde" ("In the Forest") is a charming little poem expressing sympathy, even pity, for "Der Alte." In "Ahasver und Acher," a vision by the sea brings together the protagonist and the poet. Acher sees his image in the water; but no, it is not his reflection, it is that of Ahasuerus. He is the poet's other self, his *Doppelgänger*; the merging of Ahasuerus with mortality is complete. "Ihr und Ich," a poem addressed to the Jew, states much the same message: the poet had hated Ahasuerus for his sin, yet he came to love him, for he and Ahasuerus are actually one. Finally, there is "Ahasvers Sehnsucht" ("The Longing of Ahasuerus"), a poem in free verse which is the very soul of defiance. The protagonist yearns for neither death nor rest, which he holds in contempt, but for affection and understanding, even love. Taken as a whole, Acher's *Ahasver-Gedichte* give Ahasuerus precisely this kind of affection. They are terse little poems, expressed with beauty of an angular, reticent kind. They portray the Jew as a man of strength through suffering, of courage and independence won through difficulties. Even in his defiance he cannot hate God.[36]

O. J. Bierbaum's "Golgotha" (1901) is more explicit. It is a picture of the Crucifixion, a vision of Calvary and of Christ on the Cross, seen by Ahasuerus through a miasmic mist. Its conclusion is obvious:

> His death is for ever;
> His Love is dead, but I live
> And learn to hate; if only
> I might teach Him the same!
> Golgotha everywhere and hammer-blows on the Cross.[37]

According to Walther Nithack-Stahn's two-part dramatic poem, *Ahasver* (Halle, 1910), this corrosive defiance has a natural origin, for it began with the disobedience of Adam and Eve. Even before the crime of his son Cain, Adam had become a killer of animals, and so blood and death came into the world. With this primal tradition behind him, it is not surprising that Ahasuerus should feel some of these antidivine emotions. He is a realistic descendant of Adam and approves of nothing Christ ever said or did because, "He teaches one to hold in contempt that which is and to love that which is not." He is a creature of satanic mood who considers himself as much God as God, who put him into the world. Therefore exit laughing. Nithack-Stahn has, in effect, written a strong closet drama, which deserves to be better known. For example, when Pilate asks Ahasuerus what should be done with Christ, the Wandering Jew renders judgment against the Saviour, not because he hates him but because He is perpetuating falsehood. This Ahasuerus is a God-man with a vengeance. He encourages Judas to betray Jesus. Judas later commits suicide, and his mistress Miriam leaves to become a Christian. This acceptable moral ending, however, does not make up for the acid bitterness of Ahasuerus, who happens to be the protagonist.

Ahasuerus the God-man, real or imaginary—this is a common theme in the days of Nietzsche and his superman. The portrait of Ahasuerus in the poem by Nithack-Stahn was foreshadowed almost twenty years earlier in the turbid waters of Maurice Reinhold von Stern's philosophical narrative poem, *Die Insel Ahasvers* (Dresden-Leipzig, 1893). Here the Jew has survived a shipwreck. Despite his wish for death, he realizes that he must serve out the sentence imposed upon him and yield to his instinct for self-preservation. He is therefore thankful for a lonely island, where he can be his own master, at least for a time. On his first night on the island, he dreams a terrible dream of the conflict which mankind perpetually wages against itself. When he awakens, the experience of the dream has calmed him, for his essential misanthropy has been appeased. In his solitary state he thinks that he has won his greatest victory, that he is now his own law in his own little domain, and that the slave's chains which he had worn throughout his wanderings are dropping from him one by one. Now that he can build his own shelter he is happy. His feelings toward God are not inimical; they are even affectionate, but he does not stand in the least awe of the Almighty. He is not conscious of humility or fear or anger. He believes in God simply because he is himself godlike.

In time, however, his natural instinct asserts itself and brings him down from the spiritual mountaintop on which he has been resting. He would like to possess a woman, but he remembers the importance of self-denial and the need for a life of the soul. A strange passage of antialcoholic sentiment, for which the reader has been poorly prepared, illustrates the necessity for high thinking and simple living. Ahasuerus finds three tablets on which are inscribed who he was, what he is, and what he will be. He uses these tablets as a source of reflection, of philosophical rumination in three imaginary "portraits." In these portraits his soul speaks for itself, commenting upon the materialism of the masses, their blind stupidity and their soullessness. In his reflections, the development of personality is paramount. Cyclops, who typifies a base, blind, and impenetrable creature, is the subject of the second portrait, a disquisition on the lack of understanding of the masses. The third portrait deals with nothing less than the end of the world, or at least of civilization as man has built it. The effect of these visions, very well described, is to frighten Ahasuerus with his own loneliness. He becomes weary of himself alone:

> No longer will I suffer this silent torture;
> I must go back, a man among men,
> A heart, a heart in a warm and pulsing body;
> I cursed Him, but now desire a wife,
> Friendship, love, and trust . . .[38]

Vainly does he look, however, for a ship to rescue him, and so he casts himself into the sea, to bring to naught a life which he cannot endure. If Von Stern wishes to take liberties with the Legend, it is his poetic privilege, for he clearly wishes to paint Ahasuerus as a mortal man, not an immortal myth. But killing off his protagonist raises the question of why he should have selected Ahasuerus to expound his moral ideas. Any solitary person would have served better, for he would not have been bound by the Legend. For the rest, this Ahasuerus is an incarnation of the fierce, unilateral individualism preached by Nietzsche, and the solution offered is an attack upon Nietzsche's doctrine. Indeed, the idea that a man must take his place among men and live and love and die is a romantic idea that pervades the nineteenth century. It is one of the central ideas in the works of Tennyson and Goethe, to name but two major writers of the era. With Von Stern this message is more important than the Legend, and he is one of many writers at the turn of the century who made Ahasuerus into a vehicle for their ideas rather than the chief continuing figure in a continuing legend.

A further illustration of this point is August Schmitz's *Ahasverus, oder der Weg zur Versöhnung* (Leipzig, 1893). Schmitz, however, is handicapped in his writing of a dramatic poem by the patent fact that he is not a dramatic writer. His attempts to show allegorically "the road to expiation" cannot be termed successful. Better for him if he had essayed a philosophical poem and let it go at that, for the work is interesting only when Ahasuerus speaks—even if the direction of his reflections is uncertain. He is critical of the teachings of Christ, which are presented in a dialogue between a representative of Judaism and one of Christianity. Ahasuerus longs for a blessed rest. Humanus, whose significance is obvious, preaches that evil lies in arrogance (a sound medieval doctrine), while virtue lies in self-knowledge. Each individual has in him an ego and a portion of the over-all human, which are constantly at war with each other. It should be our goal to strive to balance these two contending elements of our nature so that we can become God-men. Where Ahasuerus emerges after this discussion is never clear, but at least he lifts himself up against God.

The general opinion seems to be that this defiance will bring trouble to the Wandering Jew (and to his family, if he has one) but not to the Jews as a whole, because they turn away from him when his challenge to God is too strong. One little facet should be noted here. When Ahasuerus is defiant, he is in his most sinful state and is most deserving of punishment because he is also most destructive. On this last point a small number of writers mention his pestilence-bringing property. An out-of-the-way contribution exemplifying this is Canadian. W. J. Wraith's *The Wandering Jew* (Lucknow, Ontario, 1917), tells, in seventy-four wretched stanzas, how the Wandering Jew met a traveler and stopped him, in the manner of the Ancient Mariner, to spill out his unfortunate story. He was with his bride at the time Christ cursed him and of course had to leave her—hence his malevolence toward the Saviour. At the moment the Wandering Jew is carrying desolation and plague to the next town he will visit. A rather gratuitous sonnet at the end begs ordinary mortals to pray for the undying one.

Fritz Lienhard's *Ahasver am Rhein* (Stuttgart, 1903) is difficult to categorize. It is a play in two scenes. The first, laid in Jerusalem, presents Ahasuerus as a fanatical upholder of the Mosaic law and hostile to Jesus. His two children, however, have been converted. One of them, Veronica, is the future saint. His friend Nicodemus also is sympathetic to Christ. The conflict is therefore between Ahasuerus the materialistic legalist and Nicodemus the idealistic humanist. (Ahasuerus has anachronistically sipped the Nietzschean beverage. His creed is power, and he has contempt for the humanist because he considers him weak, and he despises the weak.) The scene is interrupted by the events preceding the curse. Ahasuerus wanders away, leaving Nicodemus to care for the children. In the second scene, a community on the Rhine, a scientist of Faust-like countenance is looking for the secret of life; he is a dehumanized specimen, interested only in pure science. His son Erich, however, is an idealist, and so is his daughter-in-law, whose father had been a missionary. These two parallel the children of Ahasuerus in the first scene. Laban, the scientist's assistant, is exploiting, opportunistic, and dishonest. In an angry dialogue, Erich breaks with his father and exposes Laban, but the scientist is too stiff-necked to adjust himself to the apparent disaster. Instead, he commits suicide. An old friend, the parallel of Nicodemus, is left with the young couple at the end. The issue in both scenes is the same: the old traditional, conservative point of view against the Christian; the materialistic against the idealistic; the Old Testament against the New Testament; the ruthless against the merciful; the egocentric against the humanitarian; the destructive against the constructive. In this struggle Ahasuerus is a failure, along with what he represents. In short, the play uses the Wandering Jew as a symbol of unyielding conservatism, which must break because it cannot bend.

Lienhard published a reworking of the second scene of *Ahasver am Rhein* as *Ahasver: Tragödie* (Stuttgart, 1914), but the only significant innovation here is the fact that the scientist, the "professor," is lured to his death in the Rhine by none other than the Lorelei (the symbolist can make of this what he will). In its original form the tragic elements were not emphasized.

The foregoing will indicate that the line of demarcation between Ahasuerus the defiant and a villain of melodrama is often thinly drawn. In F. Marion Crawford's *A Roman Singer* (New York, 1883), the peasant boy Nino, adopted by an Italian professor and gifted with a magnificent operatic tenor voice, falls in love with Hedwig, the daughter of a stiff-spined German count. The father removes the girl to a castle in the hills, where she is courted by Count Ahasuerus Benoni, very rich and powerful, who appears to be the Wandering Jew. Nino, through the help of his adopted father, manages to elope with Hedwig, and the old German count is reconciled. Benoni, who had pursued the elopers with malice and devilish cunning, proves to be not the Wandering Jew but only a once wealthy banker of St. Petersburg and a lunatic to boot.

This feeble but not uninteresting story is of far less importance than some of the so-called minor pieces which adhere to the Legend in this period. Karl A. Esselborn's *Ahasver: Ein Gedicht* (Leipzig, 1890) shows the protagonist as embittered and defiant because he has been outraged by the heartless fanaticism of the Jewish priesthood. Hugo Köster's "Das Drama der Welt," in his *Kothuri und Leyer* (Leipzig, 1910), is a throwback to the old Byronic monologue, this time inspired by the ruins of Athens after the Goths have sacked the city. Oskar Ungnad's "Ahasver," in *Unsere Gesellschaft* for 1898 brings Ahasuerus back to the tavern, where he is a cynical alcoholic philosopher of imposing blasphemous propensities but meager stature.[39] In Vincent Cleerdin's "Ahasverus in den Paaschtijd," in *Paaschfantasien* (n.p., 1916), he is an ally of Satan and an evil propagandistic figure. Joseph Scheel's "Ahasver" (1914) is a longish baritone solo of mediocre musical value, whose text proclaims Ahasuerus to be defiant, frustrated, and unable to find rest, but with all eternity in which to wait, if need be.[40]

It is doubtful what to make of Felix Rutten's "Ahasverus," in *De Nieuwe Gids* for 1918.[41] This is a one-act play which, I am sure, is intended to be taken seriously. Late one evening, while a storm is screaming and rain is splashing on the windows, three travelers come to a little inn on the edge of a forest, where live the taverner and his daughter Martha. These travelers arouse in the simple country girl the desire for a more exciting life in town. Then Ahasuerus enters, travel-stained, soaked by the rain, in a gray habit with a broad-brimmed hat, a peddler's pack, and a staff. He asks for and obtains a lodging for the night. When Eigil, Martha's betrothed, comes to visit her during the evening, a discussion arises on the thesis that simplicity in life is something to be desired. So Eigil stoutly defends this thesis, while Ahasuerus stresses the joy of always pursuing, always being unsatisfied, always being able to flout conventions of religion and morality in the pursuit of these dissatisfactions. Martha takes Ahasuerus' side, and it is not long before she has been seduced by him (one of the more casual seductions in literature). Then comes a shot. Eigil falls, a suicide. Martha comes to her senses. Ahasuerus' laugh rings out bitingly. At any rate, he has been destructive.

Ahasuerus the Repentant but Unredeemed

Sooner or later someone will suggest that this destructive defiance on the part of Ahasuerus is a submerged love, an ambivalence, and that when he stands up against God he actually wishes to love him. This is the theme of the narrative by Rudolph Paulsen, *Christus und der Wanderer* (Cöthen, 1918). Ahasuerus, now a hermit, sees a crucifix on a mountaintop. He would destroy the image, but Christ himself intervenes, and the Jew realizes that his hate is really love in disguise. This is why there is an eternal conflict within him. In this moment of self-understanding, he takes the place of Christ on the cross, somewhat as in Macdonald's novel. He thus becomes symbolic of the eternal exchange of love and hate; each takes the place of the other—Ahasuerus on the cross, Christ mourning down below—and from this exchange comes redemption. This Wanderer, then, is less the Wandering Jew than a personification of the monistic blending of good and evil, which is beyond both. Here the Nietzschean influence is once more apparent.

Such an attempt to combine love and hate, or defiance and resignation, calls attention to the fact that many writers in these years stressed the awkward predicament of Ahasuerus as one who is repentant but not yet redeemed. In this situation he can exert much of his old charm, if only because in this in-between state he possesses a sense of responsibility in matters great and small. An attractive ballad by Lulu von Strauss und Torney, published in the family magazine *Daheim* for 1906, tells how she remembers, as a child in a small village on Christmas Eve, a stranger (the Wandering Jew, of course) who appeared before her. He was in such sorry straits that her family agreed to take him in on this holy night, but domestic peace and comfort on a cold winter evening cannot bring him quiet.

He disappears, and the child finds him later in the cattle pen, kneeling and appealing in a prayer of repentance beside the cattle—which, in conformity with an old Christian folk belief, kneel annually at midnight on Christmas Eve. Frightened at the sight, which is both touching and awesome, the child rushes back into the house. The next morning she sees his footprints leading away from her home. Where did he go? She can remember it as if it were yesterday.[42]

More ironical, and certainly a superior performance, is Edwin Arlington Robinson's "The Wandering Jew" (1920), which keeps the same sympathetic human attitude. The poet meets Ahasuerus, whom he recognizes from an old childhood image. Old and lonely as the Jew is, he looks like an Old Testament figure, who has not been fortunate enough to have been gathered to his forefathers along with his contemporaries. As the eyes of Ahasuerus meet those of the poet, they stir in the mortal beholder a twinge of compassion. But the poet wonders if this natural twinge of compassion is welcome, for pity can sometimes be offensive, and decides to let the Wanderer talk first about what is in his mind that baffles the human observer. Ahasuerus, however, seems lost in his own thoughts and inarticulate; "a dawning on the dust of years" stimulates his memories but distorts them into supposing that the past is more to be loved than the present. Once, perhaps, he had reviled this past and seen nothing good in life, "as he had seen no good come out of Nazareth." He continues to stand silent, with only the enigmatic gaze streaming from his eyes, as if he were in the presence of One who cannot be dismissed and who never dies. His pride, however, is still with him, stiff and intractable; and he has a right to it, for in all the centuries since his curse was pronounced he has seen many second comings come and go. The poet can only surmise that there may still be defiance mixed with this pride, struggling with repentance; but of this he cannot be sure, for the old unyielding eyes may flash, but they may also flinch and turn aside to look the other way. The poem is without question the finest American treatment of the subject.[43]

To deal thus subjectively with the Legend and to couch it simply and powerfully are unusual achievements among those who write of Ahasuerus. Too many are dedicated to the oblique, the indirect, the symbolic. Let others pray for peace and comfort to Ahasuerus, as Alfred Fleischmann did in a newspaper poem for August 2, 1906, for which I have seen only an unidentified clipping.[44] The result is not so convincing as Lulu von Strauss und Torney's ballad. Somewhere between them is Paul Bornstein's "Das Sonnenlied: Aus Ahasuerus," in *Neue litterarische Blätter* for 1895.[45] It is a hymn to the sun, the source of all healing and all hallowing, light, love, and longing. In the guise of Ahasuerus, the poet asks blessings for his mortal brothers, because the Wandering Jew bears all worldly sorrows. It is an effective though florid lyric.

An unusual performance is Adolf Frey's *Ahasvers Erwachung* (Leipzig, 1904), a dramatic poem set to music as a cantata by Friedrich Hegar.[46] The music is excellent, though greatly indebted to Richard Strauss; yet of all the instances where the Legend has impinged upon the realm of music, this is the best work from the standpoint of musicianship. Ahasuerus is asleep in a winter cave. Spring voices awaken him, and in rueful sadness he resumes his eternal march, wishing that he could die instead. We may call this a hibernation motif in the history of the Legend. It is worth noting that in Frey's libretto, as well as in Bornstein's lyric and Lulu von Strauss und Torney's ballad, Ahasuerus feels a sense of duty not only toward his allotted fate but also toward those with whom he comes in contact. He is conscious of enough love for them to pray for their well-being and indirectly for the salvation of all God's creatures. This idea also informs Oskar Lindemann's *Ahasvers Lieder* (Dresden, 1907), a group of poems in which the protagonist is a world vagabond working out a curse which he now admits he deserved, and adhering to the responsibilities of the task imposed upon him. If his restlessness is emphasized, that is in the nature of the curse itself, which he accepts and will continue to accept until redemption arrives.[47]

The most effective work to maintain this point of view is the novel by August Vermeylen, *De Wandelende Jood* (Brussels, 1906), which later received both French and German translations.[48] This is a clean-cut, eloquent tale of a shoemaker who dreamed of a new kingdom on earth, and for a while thought that Christ could establish it. However—and this is a point which has already been made often—when he understands that Christ is preaching a spiritual rather than a physical revolution as a basis for that kingdom, Ahasuerus is disillusioned and turns against Christ. For all that, Vermeylen's Ahasuerus is drawn by the Passion into vicarious suffering and despair. He knows that he will never again have rest, and so turns and flees without waiting to hear Christ's curse. Wandering about for an indefinite period, he witnesses massacres by armies and ignorant clashes by night; he travels over the whole world and even into fanciful regions like the Land of Cockaigne, where everything is made of good things to eat, and the rivers flow with milk and honey. But he can never forget the anguished expression on the face of Christ as he went to the Cross.

Vermeylen brings about an unusual contamination of the Legend with the folk tale of Undine, for his Ahasuerus has an affair with a water nymph—who promises him life and death but, unfortunately for the hopes of her lover, vanishes at the mere mention of Christ's name. Ahasuerus finds his surroundings growing murky and realizes that he is coming nearer and nearer to hell. The most terrible aspect of this Gehenna is a vision of the eyes of Christ weeping for the sinner that Ahasuerus knows himself to be, and the ultimate basis of all his suffering is that he must endure what he neither wants nor needs. This, with the inevitable frustration attending it, constitutes Ahasuerus' hell.

A tortured spasm ends in merciful unconsciousness. When he regains his senses, he is comforted by a simple, rustic hermit (a most effective use of an old narrative motif which goes back to the medieval romances in Europe and, before that, to the tales of ancient India). The recluse teaches Ahasuerus in direct fashion that God is the ineffable and imperishable Light of the world. Ahasuerus attains enough peace to be able to remain with the hermit for years. But as time goes on, and the hermit begins to sicken with old age, Ahasuerus catches from the dying man's thoughts and words some faint glimpses, perhaps presentiments, of Divinity. He still understands, however, that something he needs is missing. On one occasion he visits a tribe of gypsies, wanderers like himself; but although he sees another spark of the divine Light in the eyes of a newborn child, the gypsies are too earthy for him. He therefore returns to watch over the death of his friend, the hermit, and is awe-struck to see hierarchies of angels and a terrifying unknown light attending the departing soul of the aged man. Beneath this light are the shadows of this world, of mortality, to which Ahasuerus is returned, to his comfort and relief; for in contrast to the too rarefied atmosphere of the ineffable, the smell of nature is most refreshing.

He now joins a group of laborers, to find happiness in their hard physical work and close friendship. He concludes that one should never live alone. Nevertheless, like the gypsies, this company is too mundane. He is moved, of course, by their social oppression and tries without success to unionize them (if I may be permitted so prosaic a word), only to be dismissed from employment. When he meets a sympathetic peasant girl, who, like him, has been a "prisoner" of their employers, he runs away with her. Although he realizes that he must continue to wander, he is temporarily content. He knows that this short-lived surcease is all that he can expect until the day of his release has come to pass, but he is reconciled to the situation. Thus the novel ends—with no attempt to wrap Ahasuerus in a cloak of mystical significance, no moralizing, but with an unmistakable assurance that though he is not yet redeemed he has become repentant enough to be of some use to mankind.

The social implications of Vermeylen's novel may be absent in other works of the period. János Arany's poem "Az örök zsidó" (Budapest, 1860) was published in 1880 in a German translation as "Der ewige Jude."[49] It concentrates exclusively upon Ahasuerus' ceaseless, urgent wandering. The victim of the curse, thoroughly repentant, would like to stop and show regard for the world around him, but he cannot. L. Meilinger's "Der ewige Jude" (*ca.*1895) is a succinct poetic lament for the Wandering Jew, who is sorry for his act because he cannot forget the look on Christ's face when he pronounced the curse.[50] This, even for 1893, is trite stuff.

Others prefer to see Ahasuerus the repentant but unredeemed spending most of his time in contemplation. His thoughts in such instances are the long thoughts of the romantic brooders of long before, filtered into what many literary historians like to call post- or neo-romanticism. (The distinctions are quibbling; it would be a bold critic who would differentiate categorically between the romanticism of Hans Benzmann, for example, and that of H. Müller three-quarters of a century earlier.) The three poems by Benzmann which treat of the Legend in this manner are arresting. In the first, "Ahasver am Meer," in *Sommersonnenglück* ("The Joy of the Summer Sun"; Berlin-Leipzig, 1898), Ahasuerus reflects on how the sea has seen much and knows all; yet how peaceful to be beside it and fancy oneself into nothingness. But the world is like the sea, a chaos of woes and waves, shifting, subsiding, rising again—a mystery of mad striving and a symbol of the eternity of death. In the second, "Ahasver und Christus," in *Die Propyläen* (1904), the poet sees Ahasuerus on the beach at twilight. There is the sound of evening bells. Two churchmen, walking along the path to the beach, drive the visitor away. He merges into the twilight:

> His raiment shone afar like a white star,
> His head was limned with fire; his arms
> Stretched wide over the whole firmament . . .[51]

while above him is a vision of Christ raising his hand in blessing over land and sea. Ahasuerus, rejected by the Church on earth, may continue along his way with the hope of heaven, not yet attained, still before him. In the third poem, "Ahasvers Tod," in *Neue litterarische Blätter* for 1896, Ahasuerus' mother, who is Earth herself, nails the last nail into a black cross on which he is suspended. The pain of eternity is in her look as she does so, but she has given her son release.[52]

On the reverse side of the coin is an unusual, untitled lyric by Ferdinand Ave-narius in *Lebe!* (Leipzig, 1893), one of a series of little threnodies on a certain Gertrude. Ahasuerus appears in an autumnal setting of desolation and despair. In a landscape dominated by three fir trees, he stands as tall as they, with caw-ing crows circling about his head. He is silent in an attitude of contemplation; his eyes seem to be all-seeing, but sad—the very embodiment of lonely despera-tion.[53]

As usual, Ahasuerus in contemplation accents his weariness, part of which is to be traced to his remorse. If only he could rest and forget everything in a blessed repose, but people either upset him by shunning him or drive him onward if they meet him. This is the special point of Hermann von Gilm's lyric, "Ahasver," in his *Gedichte* (1894). Yet we know that Ahasuerus has been received hospitably by many. Indeed, Christian Federhold's "Ahasver," in *Alma Julia* for August 6, 1906, asks if it has not been helpful for him to have had such contacts with man and nature instead of having to brood constantly on death's release. Ahasuerus does not reply. After all, the prime consideration is still that he must wander.

A short poem by August Strindberg, "Ahasverus," in *Ordalek och Smakonst* ("Words and Crafts"; Stockholm, 1905), observes that in this modern world of confused uncertainty Ahasuerus has all that he can do to keep wandering. His mind must therefore be given to the things of the present—his irritations, weari-ness, aches and pains—rather than to either the past or the future. This point has seldom been emphasized before or since. It is one of the rare recognitions that the Wandering Jew is in the twentieth century—whose complexity (the "strange disease of modern life") threatens to overcome even the accursed of Christ.

At times, under these circumstances, there is the promised hope; at other times it is a discouraging prospect which lies before the Jew. On the whole, Ahasuerus has faith in his ultimate redemption. A much neglected little work by Charles Granville, *The Plaint of the Wandering Jew* (London, 1908), a "parable in prose," suggests some further implications. The narrator here is a hermit who meets the Wanderer "of the clan of the Wandering Jew" (the identity of the stranger is not more specific), who is awaiting the future: "Lord, I am weary awaiting Thee, and lo! Thy kingdom is more distant than before."[54] He intends to erase his impatience by interesting himself in the betterment of humanity, regardless of the conven-tions of social morality. He is not interested in the Church or even in a life of con-templation, unless either will benefit man. In short, he is willing to be antichurch and anti-intellectual when the need arises. The vein of revolt here is similar to the defiance already described.

Yet at other times Ahasuerus the repentant and the contemplative becomes nothing more than Ahasuerus the static. S. Weir Mitchell's "Barabbas" (New York, 1913), an out-of-the-way dramatic poem, transfers some of the attributes of Ahasuerus to the sinner Barabbas, who is led to recount his part in the story of the Crucifixion (thereby impressing an ignorant young Greek who is moved to belief). But this brief playlet is feeble and only tangential to the Legend.[55] In Friedrich Michel's "Vision" in his *Asraklänge* (Strasbourg, 1906) we are struck only by the seething sense of duty felt by Ahasuerus as he doggedly works out his sentence. Much thinner, though similar in substance, is Johannes Jörgensen's "Ahasverus" (1910); this is summer-night reflection, like the poems by Benzmann.[56] To attempt a description of the pain only is not sufficient to carry weight in a twentieth-century portrayal of the Jew. For this reason, Miek Janssen's "Na de Kruisiging" ("After the Crucifixion"), in *Schaduw van den Toren* ("Shadow of the Tower"; Amsterdam, 1916), and J. de Liefde's account of the Legend in *Fabelen, Vertellingen en Mythen* (Arnhem, 1917) may be ignored, although in the latter there is a Schubartian strain crossed with a detail from Sue in the protagonist's soliloquy by the Bering Straits. Anton Renk, in *Ins neue Land* (Basel, 1896), likewise makes use of Ahasuerus as a symbol of discontent and insufficiency, showing him as a member of Columbus' expedition.[57] But, as we have already seen, such secondary appearances of Ahasuerus are frequent in the literature of the past century; they should immediately be discounted. Another example is R. Ullman's *Feldpredigt* (Vienna, 1907), in which the Wandering Jew appears as old Botensepp, a hermit and minor philosopher. He utilizes the death of a crippled boy in mystic communion with earth as an allegory to teach the boy's cloddish father the meaning of Christ.

Instead of concerning ourselves with such trivialities, let us consider two works which sound the main chords in the motif of Ahasuerus the repentant but unredeemed in simple but effective cadence. René de Clercq's "Ahasver," in *XXe Eeuw* ("Twentieth Century") for 1907 (written in 1902) is a dramatic fragment of considerable power in which Ahasuerus is shown near the end of his career. Judgment Day is approaching. In the distance is a city which is apparently Jerusalem, where Antichrist is now ruling. Also near at hand are the conflagration of the world and Ahasuerus' own death. Tired and sad, he leans for a moment against a tree. A clap of thunder resounds, and a "crossman" appears, with a flaming rod in his hand. He points to a field blasted by lightning and bids Ahasuerus to get going. The latter obeys, for the curse is to remain upon him until the last possible moment. He must endure his pain to the full, even though the end may be in sight.

The other work is Gisella Banfi's *Ahasvers Traum: Eine Legende* (Leipzig, 1906).[58] This Ahasuerus is basically a human being and little more. Hence he is very tired, and all he desires is peace and sleep. For a while this sleep is allowed him. We have then a flashback to the day of the Crucifixion, when he was at home with his wife and children. When the crowd gathers, his wife Sara leaves the house to watch the dire event. Ahasuerus explains to some friends that he had always been skeptical of Christ as Messiah; He has brought trouble to Jerusalem, and Ahasuerus would rather have peace and quiet. The procession passes along the *Via Crucis*. Mary Magdalene and Veronica join the throng before Ahasuerus' house. When Christ asks to stop for rest, Ahasuerus rebuffs him, as the Legend demands, but one of his children hands the Saviour one of the colored eggs with which their mother had tried to entertain the children on that day. In gratitude for this small favor, Christ does not pronounce the curse, but it is implicit nonetheless, for Mary Magdalene warns Ahasuerus that he has driven peace away from his own doorstep. After Christ has passed by, Ahasuerus feels a compulsion to get away by himself. His wife, who has returned, and many friends try to hold him back, but he disappears in a tumult of wind and earthquake. He has aged greatly in the twinkling of an eye, and his wanderings have begun. Next we see him as at the beginning of the story, asleep. Then, on Easter morning, an angel awakens him and promises him a spiritual home someday. The particular virtue of this work is the simplicity of its narrative and the adeptness with which it catches the spirit of the original Legend.

Ahasuerus the Complex Sinner

Unlike Gisella Banfi, many who pondered the matter found Ahasuerus first and last a sinner. In some this attitude was tempered by sympathy, by the belief that he might be pardoned in the end. For others he remained unregenerate. The most elaborate work to treat of Ahasuerus *peccator* is dramatic in form, although it is hard to see what a theater could do with it. It is nothing less than a heptalogy, of which only the fourth and the seventh parts have to do with the Wandering Jew. The author is a Munich poet who takes refuge behind the pseudonym "M.E.S."[59] Its avowed purpose in casting such an extensive work in dramatic form is the naïve one of disseminating the gospel to as many as possible. The title of the whole heptalogy is *Kains Schuld und ihre Sühne: Eine Wort- und Ton-Dichtung* ("Cain's Sin and Its Expiation: A Word and Tone Poem"; Munich, 1896–98); but while enthusiasts might consider it a word-poem, the tone-poem element is missing, for no music for it survives. The seven parts are: "Kain" (1896), "Nimrud" (1897), "Moses" (1897), "Ahas" (1897), "Juda ben Salem" (1898), "Levi" (1898), and "Ahasvers Erlösung" (1898). There is also a prologue, "König Salomo im neuen Jerusalem" (1898).

The text of this multiple homily on sin (for such it is) lies in the major premise, expressed in the Prologue, that self-knowledge is the greatest achievement man can accomplish. Whoever turns away from this light to lead a life of darkness must remain in the depths until he can improve his attitude. (This message resembles that of Schmitz.) As a result of our failure to know ourselves, we have sin, beginning with Cain. When he killed Abel, Cain was cursed not only by God but also by his father Adam. The curse did not involve the sinner in physical torture but rather in an unsatisfied spiritual longing—for repentance and suffering alone can expiate the sins of the human will. The list of such sinners continues throughout the rest of the heptalogy: for example, Menu, son of the priest of the Parsees, who was unfaithful to his God because of Hela, the daughter of King Nimrod; and Korah, who abandoned Jehovah in favor of the Egyptian gods and was brought to heel by Moses.

Coming to the fourth part, "Ahas," which concerns us directly, we find that the title role is that of a tapestry weaver and carpetmaker, an uncle of Lazarus, Mary, and Martha. He is of the generation of David. To him Jesus is a dreamer, not a man of action; he believes that he cannot be the Saviour, for, according to the Jewish scriptures, the Messiah must be a man of might who will deliver the people from bondage. Ahas considers himself such a man and is arrogant and as culpable as the sinners of the three preceding parts. He heads a conspiracy against the Roman rulers in Jerusalem but realizes that he must win Christ to his side, for His following among the people cannot be ignored. In the meantime, Judas, who also has underestimated Christ's power, tries to perusade Ahas that he has no need of the Saviour, and so inflames the overweening pride filling the heart of the carpetmaker. It requires little self-searching for Ahas to abandon Christ and devote himself to the scribes and worshipers of Jehovah. But when the drama of the Crucifixion has played itself out, Ahas is not sure that he did the right thing. His doubt deepens to such an extent that he falls into despair, which in turn leads him to hate the memory of Christ. When he drove the Saviour away from his doorstep, he brought down on himself the curse; but more than that, the awful look which Jesus gave him has rendered him inarticulate.

In the folkloristic aspect of the Legend, we had analogues to the Wandering Jew in Cain or Al-Sameri or Pindola, among others. "M.E.S." has chosen to keep these sinners in a kind of spiritual genealogical line. He identifies the spirit of Cain with that of Ahasuerus; by implication he identifies Cain with Menu and Korah. In the latter parts of the heptalogy, therefore, we must understand that Cain (or Ahasuerus) is appearing in different dark forms seeking the light. Thus in the fifth part, "Juda ben Salem," the Sinner is the personal physician of Constantine the Great and the putative father of a certain Herodias. He hates all Christians and wishes them exterminated so that he can live once more as king of the Jews in Jerusalem. The emperor, he is sure, can bring this about. But Constantine takes a fancy to Herodias; and when the Sinner threatens to kill the girl to save her, Constantine swears to destroy the Christians as Juda ben Salem desires, in order to obtain Herodias. The maiden, however, pleads with Constantine to withdraw his oath and become a Christian, and caps her plea by stabbing the Sinner. Yet though the Sinner's body is destroyed, his soul proceeds immediately to inhabit one Levi, who is the chief character of the sixth part. (In medieval Germany, at a time of the persecution of Jews, Levi is a talebearer, a treacherous nuisance if not worse, who is nevertheless brought to sacrifice himself to save some of his people.) This is the weakest part of the heptalogy.

The final part, "Ahasvers Erlösung," is not related chronologically to the preceding play. The scene is laid in the indeterminate future. The Sinner now reigns as king in Zion, his pride undiminished. But, in spite of all his efforts, the people are turning to Christianity; he alone, with his children Israel and Rachel, remains true to Judaism. Ultimately he is obliged to flee with them to seek a new realm elsewhere, and in a mountain wilderness he encounters Melchior and Michael. To Melchior he appears not as the Wandering Jew, who has gone through one millennium after another, but as the spirit which struggles against the course of things. Still unregenerate, Ahasuerus hopes that his children, at least, can found a new dynasty. Rachel, however, falls in love with Michael and abandons her father for him. In a rage, Ahasuerus travels among the Brahmins, accompanied by his son Israel, but the young man falls in love with a Hindu girl. Without going into further details, I may report that the Jew is frustrated once more, and this time is borne down by the sheer force of numbers. The universality of love is too much for him; he recognizes his fault and in this way finds redemption.

In this heptalogy, Cain, Menu, Korah, Ahas, Juda ben Salem, Levi, Ahasuerus, and even Solomon in the Prologue are one and the same—the Sinner. Solomon is thus described only because he was obliged to learn and acknowledge his sins. When he achieves self-knowledge, he is forgiven. Ahasuerus reaches the same goal in the same way. The others, however, are more important for their exemplification of sin than for their achievement of redemption. The thesis of the Prologue—that the Sinner must aim for self-knowledge and purge himself of dark thoughts and actions before putting on the garment of love—is illustrated more than sufficiently. This is simply to say that a less pretentious kind of treatment can be just as effective as a heptalogy. The work of "M.E.S." should never be passed over hurriedly, but if one had to choose between it and that of Peter Merwin, one would probably prefer the latter, if only because it is more concentrated and less unwieldy.

Merwin's epic, *Der Tod des ewigen Juden* (Dresden-Leipzig, 1902), taking advantage of the natural superiority of narrative over dramatic treatment of the Legend, makes a fresh approach with some success. The author prefers to confine himself to three high points in the story of the Wandering Jew: the curse, the career, and the redemption. The protagonist is a simple-minded man, a humdrum follower of temple and throne, the sort of individual whom Paul had in mind when he observed that the letter killeth. For this Ahasuerus is an incurable literalist. His dislike of Christ is therefore natural, even inevitable. His petty shopkeeper's mind cannot rise above the trivial details of his business. He thinks that the crowd lining the road to Golgotha may be good for trade. When he drives Christ away from his doorstep, he is motivated as much by the fact that the Saviour would take up room and so drive away customers as by the fact that he dislikes Jesus. The Saviour does not curse him, only pierces him with the haunting look of reproach that is not to be forgotten.

And so, as Ahasuerus goes his way, he spends his time remembering that look, gradually losing hope to the point where he must deny God. Only the Wandering Jew is a reality to him. In his final section Merwin borrows a page from Goethe's book. The return of Christ to earth is a sad disillusionment for the Saviour, because none will recognize him or listen to him, and when he meets Ahasuerus, the latter observes that not all who call upon the Lord are willing to serve him. As they become comrades in misery, we are to understand that the troubles of both will not soon be over. As for Ahasuerus, however, his defiance has earned him not only respect but acceptance—he is a sinner not without honor. Merwin's poem is direct, uncomplicated, and effective, although his style remains gritty and uneven, and is not nearly so accomplished as that of "M.E.S."

It is likely that "M.E.S." knew Felix Weingartner's *"Die Erlösung"* (1895).[60] This sketch for a mystery play introduces Ahasuerus as one of a chain of eternal offenders against the divine, his evil soul having transmigrated from Cain and Judas Iscariot to the Wandering Jew. To be more specific, the traitorous spirit of

Judas entered into Ahasuerus as soon as the betrayer of Christ had committed suicide. But Weingartner's treatment is by no means so virulent as that of Hans Withalm in his collection of prose sketches, *Ecce Homines* (Strasbourg, 1904), where the Wandering Jew is identified with murderers, robbers, and lechers—returning thus to the folkloristic figure of the early seventeenth century who served in the ranks of Antichrist.[61]

This return, however, is only an isolated phenomenon, because, even when writers around 1900 link him with Antichrist, they extend to him the hope of some eventual redemption. A good illustration is Joseph Seeber's superior epic poem, *Der ewige Jude* (Freiburg, 1894), which devotes much attention to the approaching end of the Wandering Jew's career. In the beginning, Antichrist (here called Soter) is working to complete the conquest of Christendom and make Jerusalem the "Fabrikstadt" or the powerhouse city, his capital and the center of Jewry. Once the conquest is achieved:

> There it stands, a Unity grand and eternal,
> There my people have once more their home,
> Their king, their Messiah . . .[62]

Enoch and Elijah, the immortals, enter the city as secret missionaries to free wretched Christian slaves and to preach against this new Babel. As two who can never die, they are both invulnerable and invincible; Ahasuerus, also immortal, is their worthy adversary. In fact, the very core of Seeber's poem is the struggle between opponents who cannot die.

Hoping to become the true prophet of Antichrist and the manager of his worldly conquest, Ahasuerus does his best to expose these secret agents of the Lord Jehovah. In some excellent blank verse he meditates on the military expedition which he led against Europe. He also reviews the history of the world (a skillfully worded use of the tradition of the Chronicle of the Wandering Jew, this time in the manner of the historian Mommsen), pointing out that the Jews have always been a disorganizing, disruptive force in world annals. He defends the new post-Christian age and proclaims the victory of Antichrist as the inevitable outcome of the ineluctable conflict between Christ-hating Jewry and the Christian Church—inevitable in the light of the persecution and exile of the Jews in the past. The chancellor of Antichrist, Teitan, whose position Ahasuerus covets, complains to Antichrist about the frank speech of Ahasuerus and his careless disclosures to the people. Antichrist becomes disgusted with the flagrantly pro-Jewish propaganda put out by the Wandering Jew and decides to plow under this wretched pack of Hebrews. A particular Jew, Laban, whose daughter has been seduced and then abandoned by Teitan, observes that Antichrist must be merely having sport with Ahasuerus and the Jews.

In due time, Enoch and Elijah are captured and dragged into the market place of Jerusalem, there to be judged by Soter the Antichrist. They are defiant:

> But three days more are thine, but three days only,
> Then woe to thee and those who follow thee;
> But three days more, and then the awful God
> In the might of His wrath will pluck the weeds . . .[63]

Nevertheless, Soter the Antichrist, crowned victorious king of the world, announces that there is to be now but one god and his people, world without end. The scene turns into a gloating orgy, but Ahasuerus has gone away to the temple on Mount Moriah, there to ponder over the former destruction of the city by the Romans. He still hopes that Soter will exalt him over the currish Teitan, and that Israel will still be the people of the promised realm.

But it does not come out that way. Soter repeats, "There is but one god, and I am he," and chooses Teitan as his prophet. Ahasuerus has for his reward the privilege of offering the first sacrifice to the new deity. He is disappointed and resentful, and in an angry exchange with Soter comes to realize that, because of the curse originally laid upon him, he has never comprehended the misery of mankind nor heard its cries of lamentation. With Sara, the discredited daughter of Laban, as his guide, he departs. He represents the blind and she the sinful, but it is not necessary to labor the symbolism. They wander about in the mountains; and Sara, overcome with a sense of guilt, throws herself over a precipice. Ahasuerus mourns her fate, calls for death, and expresses his despair at the future of his people. Not only the world but death itself has deceived them.

Meanwhile, the victory of Antichrist has driven all Christians, even the pope, into an underground existence. Some of the survivors find Ahasuerus and lead him before the pontiff, who converts him with comparative ease. The ancient ark of the covenant is recovered. Ahasuerus is baptized as Paul in obvious imitation of the Saul-Paul incident from Acts. Many of the Jews follow the example of Ahasuerus and are martyred; others maintain their orthodox faith. Most turn to "Paul," to find peace with him. It is learned that Enoch and Elijah have been rescued by an earthquake, which buries the villainous Teitan under a crashing wall. Ahasuerus finds him still alive and vainly admonishes him to repentance. He then proceeds to a full program of counterconversion. One is either for Christ or for Antichrist (Soter); there is no middle way. Ahasuerus and Soter, in the manner of the Scholastics, hold a debate, and the issue narrows itself to the single question: "Who is like God?" Soter, although confounded by theological arguments, has recourse to his infernal powers, and disappears in a cloud. Ahasuerus lifts his hand; thunder and lightning follow:

> Behold, the cloudy curtain parts before us,
> The heavens rise; the Lord appears
> On His white steed, Prince of Eternity . . .
> The Lord's hand seizes upon Soter
> And crushes him to ground; the mountains
> Lift themselves up and split asunder;
> A fiery pool engulfs both him and Teitan,
> The infernal prophet, and the angel of the Lord
> Descends from heaven, and seals the abyss
> With the seal of God.[64]

Peace comes to earth, so that the Wandering Jew can now rest. He is the only survivor of the original troop of Antichrist, but he has seen the light and is entitled to repose. Although converted to Christianity, he still retains enough of his old

Jewish faith to contain within himself the essence of all Judaeo-Christian culture. In a sense he is the spokesman for all humanity:

> I too am God, eternally new-born, the ancient spirit
> Of Hebrew folk a thousand years ago,
> From whom He chose his only son as God,
> Whilst from his father-bosom he consigned
> The sons of other nations to misery.[65]

He will therefore never rest until all Israel has been redeemed; in short, he must wait long after Antichrist himself has been subdued.

The final pages of the poem take us into the distant future, to the last era in the history of the world. Until that time, one may assume that, despite his conversion, Ahasuerus is still linked with Antichrist, and is therefore a most important sinner. There is here some academic discussion as to exactly how long the period of the incarceration of Antichrist will be—whether the reign of the Messiah is to be a week, four hundred years, a thousand, or two thousand years. Seeber was something of a student of eschatology, but the point is not important. The poem insists that the followers of Antichrist are human, though of gigantic proportions (Teitan's name means titanic), and Antichrist is all too human. Ahasuerus was blinded in human fashion by his hatred of Christ and the Christians. Having seen the light, however, he has come to see God, and as Judgment Day approaches, we can see his redemption approaching also. Thus the poem ends. It is a vigorous story, somewhat slowed by the erudition of the author, but couched in language which is well wrought and in blank verse which is expertly handled. In many ways it is the most distinguished German work on the subject to come out of the 1890's.

It is indeed exceptional to find Ahasuerus associated, even for a brief period, with the demoniac, as he is in Seeber's poem. And Seeber in any case allows him to be converted, as do most contemporary writers. But in a novelette by Matthias Blank, *Ahasvers Brautfahrt* (Leipzig, 1910), Ahasuerus is certainly beyond the pale. Having just been married, he attempts to regain his much needed youth like a vampire, by sucking the lifeblood of his bride. The tale springs from the post-romantic liking for the horrible exemplified by Algernon Blackwood, Guy de Maupassant, Conan Doyle, and others; but the immediate analogue, if not the source, which leaps to mind is Bram Stoker's celebrated *Dracula*. Blank's effort can at least be said to stand in utter contrast to Seeber's religion-saturated epic.

Buchanan and Makeever

We may conclude this chapter with a consideration of two very different works which are both distinctive and unclassifiable. The first is a narrative poem by Robert Buchanan, *The Wandering Jew: A Christmas Carol* (London, 1893). Its title is even more misleading than that of Eugène Sue's novel, for the poem deliberately uses Ahasuerus and the Legend only as a means to an end. Nor is the subtitle, *A Christmas Carol*, applicable in any ordinary sense of the phrase. Buchanan was that curious type of writer who takes a perverse view and then admits that he has been wrong all along. Both the title and the subtitle make sense when it is realized that Buchanan is thinking of Christ and not Ahasuerus as the Wandering Jew, a concept which would be a logical development of Goethe's ideas back in 1774. As a matter of fact, Buchanan's poem was begun as early as 1866, and had been completed and ready for printing a few years before it was published.

The author seems to have entertained the superstitious notion that the printing of this poem would mean the end of his literary career, and there is no doubt that the point of view in the work is anti-Christian. The poet, wandering in the streets of London at Christmastide, meets the Wandering Jew, whom he first takes to be Ahasuerus but whom he soon discovers to be Christ himself. A vision of Christ brooding over the city on Christmas night follows, and then a reminiscence of the pageant of Golgotha, where Death itself was confounded. After this comes a startling picture of the indictment of Jesus by those who did not worship him, a long protest by various and sundry against the crimes and bloodshed on earth which have come about in his name. The archtraitor Judas and Ahasuerus appear against him, and so do Pilate, Nero, and many others—any one of whom might be considered Antichrist (for example, Julian the Apostate). Others less violent, such as Hypatia, and alien deities, such as Mohammed, Buddha, and Zoroaster, are included, along with minor detractors. On the other side, John the Baptist, Mary Magdalene, and Paul stand up in defense of Him. The host of His enemies, however, condemn him to renew his wanderings, for death is preferable to a half-starved soul, and pity, a gigantic failure, is not enough. In brief, then, the poem describes a trial of Jesus on the charge that he has deviated from the path of true Christianity.

Buchanan attempted to explain his purpose in an "interview" of himself he wrote for the London *Daily Chronicle:*

With what object did you write "The Wandering Jew"?

Because . . . I thought that only one subject remained to the modern singer—that of *fin-de-siècle* Christianity, and because, in my opinion, the legendary Christ of the Gospels was the one immortal spirit which had never been faithfully represented in poetry. All my life I had been haunted by the conception of a worn-out Saviour, snowed over with the sorrow of centuries, old, weary, despairing, yet indignant at the enormities committed in His name. . . .

Did you intend in the poem to satirize the progress of Christianity among the churches?

Well, not to satirize—the subject, I think, being too pitiful for satire—but to describe in a succession of vivid pictures how Christianity had been a cloak to cover an infinity of human wickedness; how Churchmen had juggled and cheated and lied in the name of Christ, and forgotten the real sweetness of His humanity. . . .

Why did you omit to describe such things as the cruelty of the Inquisition and the terrors of the Massacre of St. Bartholomew?

Because my book was to adumbrate the truth, not to support it by a mere catalogue of horrors. . . .

A series of letters followed in the same newspaper. In one of these letters, Buchanan wrote to a "kindly" critic that, "It is, as you say, a 'queer Carol,' but then life itself is queer, and among the queerest phenomena of life is literature . . ." In another he said:

My poem, "The Wandering Jew," was written to picture, not the nebulous Christ, "which is to be," but the living Christ which *is*, the Divine Antichrist, the revolutionary Dreamer, the Man who was martyred once by His own failure to realize the necessities, the conditions, and the laws of average human nature. He is with us; He is alive . . . His mission has failed. No ingenuities of explanation, no juggling with eternal truths can make us believe that He has essentially succeeded. His cry to the universe now is "Let Me sleep! Men are not worth saving!" . . . The whole thesis of my poem, then, is this: that the Spirit of Jesus, surviving on into the present generation, still stands apart from the strife and tumult of the human race, and most of all from Christianity.[66]

The inferences then are clear: Buchanan represents the spirit of the freethinker in regard to Christ, and his poem is a somber indictment of the professing Christian, an ironical Christmas carol indeed. It is a brave piece of writing, appropriate to the present age of doubt and denial, but in technique and as poetry a humdrum, irritating performance ("God help the Christ, that Christ may help us all"). And since it is the only piece I have been able to discover in which the Wandering Jew figures as Christ, its relation to the Legend is ambiguous.

The final item is one of those crackpot inventions without which no legend would be complete. This is John L. Makeever's *The Wandering Jew: A Tale of the Lost Tribes of Israel* (Osceola, Nebraska, 1891). A Jew by the name of Joseph Bar-Elim visits the author at his cabin in the Wind River Mountains of Wyoming on a stormy night. He is indignant when he is taken, not unnaturally, for a tramp. He informs the author that he was born in Pomerania on the eleventh of November, 1857. His parents were Jews, but he himself had become a religious backslider, although one with a deep religious instinct. After graduating from the University of Kolberg, he came to America to escape persecution as a Jew, made money there and then retired, a bachelor with a great interest in archaeology, especially where it pertained to the Ten Lost Tribes of Israel. He was rewarded when he came upon a community of cliff dwellers in Colorado who spoke Hebrew. The oldest of these cliff dwellers revealed himself to be none other than the prophet Elijah. This mighty man of God informed Bar-Elim that it was he who he led the Ten Tribes to America. He showed Bar-Elim the settlement where were the tombs of Abraham, Isaac, Jacob, and their wives—to say nothing of those of David, Bath-sheba, Esther, Xerxes, and Solomon. It so happened, moreover, that the Wandering Jew was about to pay them all a visit. Bar-Elim was so enchanted by this startling prospect that he burst into poetry and began to dream of Old Testament scenes.

Elijah conducted him farther into this amazing retreat. Bar-Elim found that the country bore a close resemblance to Palestine. Time had apparently stood still since Old Testament days, for the theocratic culture of ancient Israel still flourished. Bar-Elim joined a group of workers in the fields, meeting in this way a beautiful girl, Martha, and was taken to see the temple and the burning jewel which decorated its altar. He became acquainted with Jacob, son of Aram, and fell into conversation with him about the longevity of the patriarchs of the Old Testament and about the Wandering Jew, whom he was most anxious to meet.

His wish was gratified when he came upon a stranger haranguing a crowd. This was Ahasuerus, the Wandering Jew. An old man in peculiar garb, he announced that his lot was hopeless, for he could no longer look at a crucifix. He traced his own career back to the Legend of the Holy Cross (an unusual contamination with our Legend), describing how the three seeds were placed in Adam's mouth after his death and how from these seeds grew the three trees which were later made into the Cross. In his wanderings, he reported, he once met St. Helena, mother of Constantine the Great, who explained to him her part in the Legend of the Holy Cross. Continuing the account of his wanderings, he mentioned Paul and his conversion, and connected his own career with that of Nero (he actually had witnessed the martyrdom of Paul in Nero's amphitheater).

This Ahasuerus conventionally could never stay more than three days in a given locality. He had often been in London, Paris, and Alexandria. It is true that he had known Mohammed and was for a time attracted to the faith of the crescent, but his leanings through most of his career had been for Christianity. Of course he could not die—not even when a lion closed its jaws over his neck, as had once happened. He knew the proverbs of all lands, but was impressed especially by those of Normandy and Bohemia. In Bohemia, he remarked, there was the belief that, when a dog bays at the moon, he is baying at the Wandering Jew. He was also prepared to prophesy great events.

Meanwhile, the priests of Baal (for there were dissidents in even this mountain retreat) had become suspicious of Bar-Elim and put him in prison. The Wandering Jew persuaded Martha to effect his release, and she did so through the influence of Ahasuerus, who can always circumvent jailers. Martha took Bar-Elim to her home and sang to him love songs and such Hebrew songs as those of Miriam and Deborah, and about Joseph and Zuleika, Potiphar's wife.

Scattered all around the neighborhood were the remains of old pagan rites, including those of the vestal virgins and the worshipers of Ishtar and Ashtareth. Bar-Elim also saw the mummies of Solomon and Jephthah's daughter, and wished that he could revive the latter. On a sudden impulse, he looked for the amulet on Solomon's seal and found the Name Incommunicable written on it. Bravely invoking the spirit of love, and with the aid of the seal and the Name Incommunicable, he was able to bring the daughter of Jephthah back to life. Her name was Ada, and when she kissed him in grateful love, it awoke in him the feeling that he must have known her once before, in some previous incarnation. Unfortunately for him, however, the kiss awakened the jealousy of Martha, but although she kept handling a dagger in a businesslike manner, Ada and Bar-Elim continued to be interested in each other.

In fact, not even Martha's forthright confession of love for Bar-Elim nor her mother's putting the evil eye on Ada keeps these new lovers apart. On a trumped-up charge, Bar-Elim is thrown back into jail, where he is visited by Martha, who begs him to change his affections. But her efforts are useless. With the help again of the seal and the Name Incommunicable the young man is able to turn the bodies of the jailers to stone, and he and Ada steal away. A priest of Baal is discovered dead. Martha confesses the murder, attempting to justify herself on the grounds that she feared for Bar-Elim's life. She is sacrificed to Ashtareth, and her termagant mother with the evil eye is lynched by the followers of Elijah.

Ahasuerus now enters the picture once more, because the profanation of Solomon's body by Bar-Elim and the resurrection of Ada through the seal and the Name Incommunicable are fatal sins, particularly because they represent overweening pride, man's setting himself up against the Divine Will. Therefore Ahasuerus, dismayed at such recurring errors by a deluded mortal, must resume his wanderings to expiate the guilt of mankind. He grants personal forgiveness to Bar-Elim, who, however, can no longer have power over the seal. In his dismay at this loss, Bar-Elim rushes to the holy of holies and blasphemes by the Name Incommunicable. The consequences are an earthquake and the petrifaction of all save Bar-Elim (even Ada is turned to stone). Bar-Elim escapes, only too glad to flee from this sinister valley. But, as he hastens away, he is cursed by the Wandering Jew, who condemns him to live in perpetual fear of his memories. Bar-Elim had come to the author's cabin in the Wind River Mountains of Wyoming, because, like the Ancient Mariner, there are times when he must tell his story. Now, having told it, he departs—another Wandering Jew set in motion by the original one. In leaving he accidentally drops a roll of paper (a greeting to the witch Hilka from the rejected Martha) on which is inscribed a hymn of hate, which is perhaps the most eloquent feature of this eccentric novel.

It is easy to suggest that Makeever had been influenced by Rider Haggard or any one of a number of talented purveyors of sinister incident who flourished in the 1880's and 1890's. Much of the novel, however, is original, in spite of the author's familiarity with the traditional art-form material of the Legend—as shown by writing characteristic of the Chronicle of the Wandering Jew and the use of such details as the connections with Nero and Paul (best illustrated in Hamerling's *Ahasver in Rom*), and the flirtation with Islam. Although they are mentioned in the novel's subtitle the Ten Tribes of Israel cannot be said to bulk large in the novel, but Solomon's seal is another matter. Makeever's is the only extensive piece of writing to link the Legend with this peculiar esoteric tradition of neo-Hebraism, which many Jews consider spurious.

As we have seen, the literary output concerned with Ahasuerus, as the writers around the turn of the century poured it forth, can hardly be matched at any other time for variety. And this chapter has considered only a part of this output, for the scholarly treatments of the Legend will be discussed separately in Appendix A. To be sure, other periods of similar length may have produced a greater number of individual works, but their range has always been more limited, more conditioned by the artistic standards, vogues, and crotchets of the age. But around the year 1900, instead of being consistently romantic or satirical or folkloristic, Ahasuerus may be all three—singly or in combinations, some of which are complex indeed.

Along with the rise of Zionism, near the close of the nineteenth century, one finds Ahasuerus identified with all Jews deprived of their homeland; on the reverse side of the coin, because of this identification, he becomes a target at which the anti-Semitic element of the world's Gentile population can aim its missiles. And so Ahasuerus becomes a source of inspiration to many as a symbol of either love or hate. He represents, as before, the eternal sinner or even, in a few instances, Antichrist or some other devilish creation; he may also be a vampire or a bringer of calamitous pestilence. On the other hand, he may represent the defiant rebel against convention and orthodoxy. He is repentant, but seldom as yet redeemed because of this repentance; yet the idea persists that he will someday receive salvation. At times he may stand for the contemplative man. He is usually in a state of spiritual if not of bodily torment, but on occasion he may be complacent enough to satisfy the most confirmed Philistine. He may be completely withdrawn, hermit-like, from mankind; he may be a kindly ascetic or may partake of the lusts of the flesh. He can shine as a Prometheus, a helper of man in the individual or in the mass; he can be a grand manipulator when the occasion demands.

CHAPTER THIRTEEN

The Decline of the Romantic: 1890–1920

Serious scholarly attention to the Legend, including the collection of folk tales concerning it, began during the middle decades of the nineteenth century and has continued apace (see Appendix A). The full effect of this activity, however, can not well be assessed until the falling off of interest in the Legend which came with World War II. In the meantime, it is enough to say that such studies as Neubaur's multiple publications—which pay meticulous attention to the folkloristic aspects of the Legend and to what had been gathered between 1850 and 1920—and Gaston Paris's observations upon the spread of the Legend came to have a strong influence upon those writers who tried to imitate the folk tale or the Chronicle of the Wandering Jew. Conversely, certain other writers either parodied these imitations or turned them to their own satirical or humorous purposes. In the years between about 1890 and World War I, whatever the quality of the several contributions, we get some new ways of telling the old tale which do not always conform to the categories thus far observed.

Further Imitations of Folk Tale and Chronicle

For that matter, it is difficult to decide whether the purpose of a given writer is seriously to collect folk-tale material in the manner of an antiquarian or merely to write a good imitation. A case in point is Georg Scharrer-Schauenberg's *Ahasver, der ewige Jude* (Munich, *ca.*1890). It is sometimes like a folk tale, sometimes like the Chronicle, and sometimes like neither. The publisher has designed it as a handsome pamphlet, with illustrations and appropriate epigraphs at the beginning. As for the plot, it begins with Ahasuerus, having been cursed, skulking in a cave in the Lebanon Mountains. Finally breaking away from this passive existence, he goes to Rome and fights in the gladiatorial arena. The slave of a wealthy Roman, he delights in persecuting Christians. Yet in the long run their torments touch him, and he becomes a convert to their faith until he discovers that he cannot die a Christian martyr. He then repudiates Christianity and proceeds on his wanderings, preferably in regions which will remove him as far as possible from men. He constantly experiments with suicide, but to no avail. For a time he is tempted by Mohammed, but an angel appears to him with a celestial vision of hope if he will continue to wander, and he does, with a growing sense of humanity. He now goes everywhere, even to a submerged city in the vague northland, where he finds a surprising degree of peace among the waterlogged inhabitants. The piece ends with a retelling of the story of Paulus von Eitzen, followed by references to Hadek, the *Volksbuch*, Béranger, Sue, Dumas, Haushofer, and finally (oddly out of chronological order) Schubart. Having begun as if it were to be another telling of the Chronicle and having used some of the clichés of the Chronicle, Scharrer-Schauenberg suddenly deposits the reader on the doorstep of the Ahasuerus-book without sufficient preparation.

Somewhat similar, though supposedly more scholarly in intent, is the tale told in L. Frahm's *Norddeutsche Sagen von Schleswig-Holstein bis zum Hartz* (Altona-Leipzig, 1890), which differs from other such reports of the folkloristic Ahasuerus as have been noted before only in its literary embellishments.[1] It mentions Schubart's poem, the version told by Paulus von Eitzen, and a local legend associated with the visit of the Wandering Jew to Gravenstein in 1842 (p. 113 above), and ends with a quotation from Hamerling. Another such reference to the author of *Ahasver in Rom* is to be found in Peter Rosegger's "Ahasver an seinen verklärten Dichter," in his *Gedichte* (Vienna, 1891). Here Hamerling is greeted as Ahasuerus' brother-wanderer. In this sense the Wandering Jew is identified with humanity.

A much better instance of a blending of the folk tale with the Chronicle (amid much literary pretension) is the pseudonymous Ponzio Pilato's *La vera leggenda dell' Ebreo Errante (Isacco Lachedem)* (Milan, 1897). Again we begin with the Chronicle, this time in imitation of the *Mémoires*. The Wandering Jew meets some students of Heidelberg and tells them of his offense, punishment, and travels over the world. The ornamentation is spectacular. Instead of one cross on his forehead there are now three; in moments of crisis these stand out in flaming red, and the word "Golgotha" appears in the sky written in tongues of flame. The significance of the triad lies in the fact that, according to this account, the Wandering Jew repulsed Christ from his threshold three times. As he wanders, the archangel Michael goads the Jew on whenever he lags, and the Jew brings pestilence, earthquakes, famine, and in one instance a plague of locusts. This reciting of the Chronicle ends with the Napoleonic era. The author is indebted on various occasions to Quinet. It is a not inadequate representative of its genre, although obviously assembled by one who had come upon the old material and decided to elaborate.

Such imitations of folk tales are difficult to bring off, since the originals are too deceptively simple. Indeed, it is easier to write a ballad that sounds like a folk ballad than a convincing imitation of a folk tale, for the former has at least a characteristic metrical form. Yet some writers of this generation succeeded rather better than most. A short tale by V. Blasco Ibañez of about 1910 is a good example.[2] The Wandering Jew comes to a Spanish village. At first only his feet are visible, then his ankles, then his shins, until his whole body can be seen. When he is imprisoned as a suspicious vagrant, he gradually becomes invisible—first his head, then his torso, then his legs, and last of all his feet, which are seen walking away. I know of no other tale in any way similar to this. Blasco Ibañez may have adapted the material from an old Balearic tale, but it remains a gem of narrative writing.

Georges Fragerolle's fantasia of poetry and music, *Le Juif Errant*, a legend in eight tableaux (Paris, 1898), was actually performed at the Théâtre Antoine in Paris on April 7, 1898. It is a variant of the old folk tale (best known in the Grim-

sel version), in which Ahasuerus comes for a second or third time to a given locality and finds it greatly changed. Here he appears first as a new Cain in the
desert of Judea, then in an ancient city in that same place. Three hundred years
later, he finds only a plain there, on which herdsmen are letting their flocks graze.
After three hundred more years he finds the sea washing over the spot; in another three hundred years the sea has been replaced by a forest, in which lives a
hermit to whom the Wanderer goes for consolation; in still another three hundred years there is a modern city on the site. Ahasuerus now returns to Judea
and at Golgotha prays for forgiveness, which is granted him. Even more than the
text itself, which is colorless, the title-page portrait of Ahasuerus (in rags with a
long beard and staff) makes it clear that Fragerolle was attempting to imitate and
elaborate on the old folk tale.

A skillful, yet also more sentimental tale than Fragerolle's is Wilhelm Schmidtbonn's "Ahasver: Eine Legende" (1913).[3] It begins with many resemblances to a
folk tale. Ahasuerus comes to a village, exhausted and bestial from self-neglect
and lack of sleep. Yet he must continue to walk, for nothing—not hands nor
ropes nor chains—can keep him from walking. A sympathetic and innocent little
girl pursues him, although he insults her and finally pushes her so that she falls
down. She nonetheless catches up with him and sings him to sleep with a lullaby
she sings to her little brothers. She herself falls asleep. When she awakens, Ahasuerus has gone, and where he has had his rest there is a large moss-covered stump.
The little girl returns to her mother, and Ahasuerus is never seen there again.

A vivid little poem is Gustav Schüler's "Der ewige Jude," from his *Balladen*
(Leipzig, 1909). In Westphalia one Christmas Eve, Ahasuerus asks a farmer for
shelter and is assigned to the stable. But the animals, usually in a blessed state on
this holy night (as Lulu von Strauss und Torney had seen them in her poem), are
unhappy. The next morning, when the farmer goes out, he finds his visitor apparently lifeless. "Der ewige Jude ist tot!" But is he? Does Christmas remove the
curse forever or only temporarily? We are never told; one surmise is as good as
another.

Two tales quite different in nature round out this small sheaf of literary folk
tales. The first is a poem by Edmond Héraucourt, entitled "Satan's Money-Box"
(*ca*.1912), which has an authentic ring. The "heartless shoemaker" stands on the
edge of a chasm throwing five-franc pieces into the chasm at the rate of one every
second, so that the gulf becomes a monstrous money box. His supply is inexhaustible. The second is "A Simple Tale," a moving short story written by John
Galsworthy in 1914. A gentle old man, homeless in the streets of London, who
tries to sleep on doorsteps or in doorways, is always driven away, rejected by
those who might help him. Not unnaturally he thinks of himself as an Ahasuerus
in a modern metropolis, his position ironically substituted for that of the Saviour
on the way to the Cross. This is a beautifully told story, one of several that Galsworthy wrote about the mild, idealistic individual for whom there is no room in
present-day society.[4]

On the whole, these little tales are more successful than the attempts to perpetuate the tradition of the Chronicle. In the twentieth century such attempts have
become pretty much travesties on the original examples of the Chronicle, what-

ever the authors' intentions. Thus Hermann Conradi's latter-day phantasmagoria, "Ahasver im Karneval," in his *Gesammelte Schriften* (Munich, 1911), which begins with the narrator drunk in a tavern.[5] He tells how he saw the Jews in the desert seeking the Promised Land, and after them Alexander, Christ, Caesar, and Nero; then the Middle Ages, Columbus, and Frederick the Great—a true "Carnival of History." In the course of his story he holds a talk with Ahasuerus, who is "as old as God" and will not sleep until the "Great World Ash-Wednesday," which will not come until Lucifer and "Mademoiselle" Aphrodite have ceased their jealous contention that each is more deadly than the other. This Ahasuerus identifies himself and all mankind with "Doctor" Prometheus, whose wife is Time and whose children are the thoughts of God. A series of visions of varying degrees of ridiculousness follows—among them of Ahasuerus riding through the air in a gondola and Eve sitting under the tree of knowledge suckling the latest Hohenzollern. The protagonist weaves in and out of the narrative making such prophecies as that in the twenty-first century Sue, Ebers, Dumas, Dahn, Bebel, and Disraeli will all be canonized by the Greek Orthodox Church. Eventually he disappears, and the narrator "dies," to be awakened by the innkeeper's daughter. He reaches for her and is thus "returned to reality." All in all, it is a silly performance.

Nor do early twentieth-century versions of the Chronicle improve in dramatic form. There is no attempt to give an outline of all world history in Frido Grelle's *Ahasver, der ewige Kampf* (Zwickau, 1919), which may be called a play, but is a dramatic hash. Ahasuerus is here the immortal sinner who takes advantage of his immortality to stand from time to time as the ironic spectator of the eternal conflict between good and evil. We are furnished with a variety of scenes, of course— from the primal age, from the episode of Cain and Abel, and from the careers of Alexander the Great, Nero, and Pope Gregory VII. The inclusion of the Crucifixion must be taken for granted. The Chronicle is related up to the French Revolution, after some confused and confusing scenes based on important moments in the Reformation. At the conclusion Ahasuerus returns to Chaos, where the opening scene was laid, observing as he does so that this is all a part of the eternal scheme of things, according to which creatures and their Creator are harmoniously blended into one. It is fitting that Chaos should stand at the beginning and the end of the play, because it is a chaotic performance throughout, and some of the scenes—as, for instance, the important confrontation of Holy Roman Emperor Henry IV and Pope Gregory VII at Canossa—are downright grotesque.

Nor is an American contribution more satisfactory. Maxwell Sommerville's *A Wanderer's Legend* (Philadelphia, 1902) purports to be derived from a Coptic manuscript which the author discovered in an unlikely spot, the mountain resort of Darjeeling, in northeastern India. The narrative opens in 1529 with the Diet of Speyer, in the church of St. Sebald in Nuremberg, where the incipient Reformation was formally condemned. An aged man enters and introduces a tale obviously modeled after the *Kurtze Beschreibung*. Thenceforth, however, Sommerville seems to follow the *Histoire admirable* rather than the German Ahasuerusbook, for the story of Seth and the three seeds is followed by a telling of the

Legend of the Cross formed from the three trees that grew from the three seeds. Herod, in a brief appearance, supervises the Massacre of the Innocents, and there is an equally brief glimpse of Judas introducing the usual sequence of events having to do with the Crucifixion and the curse. Ahasuerus is shocked by the latter but for the peace of his family dares not show any sympathy for the Messiah. The wanderings then begin, as per formula.

The theologians at Speyer keep pumping this Ahasuerus for information about other lands and other times, and so we have to hear once more of his visits to Egypt and particularly Alexandria, where he tries to make much of the Moslem destruction of the famous library. The story of the early Church in Rome does not interest the author for long, and so back to Mohammed, who receives sympathetic treatment: "Your eminences," Ahasuerus tells the theologians, "with all respect to your denomination, I wish to say to you that the religion of Mohammed appealed directly to the souls of men, without the aid of such effigies, forms of worship, and reminders, as you employ in your Church."[6] Mention of Islam takes Ahasuerus far away, into Africa, with its horrid folkways and inhabitants, the most notable of the latter being a cannibalistic tribe of Amazons. And of course Africa includes Carthage, which is now described anachronistically. This flashback in time carries the reader all the way back to Greece, Crete, Minos, and Phoenicia. The work now begins to degenerate into scraps of trivial commentary. Even so staple a subject as Rome is discussed with strange errors of fact. Ahasuerus admires Constantine and deplores the schism between East and West. He looks with halfhearted interest on the Crusades. Before this, however, he had been in England at the time of the Danish conquest in 1014 and had become so interested in the Norsemen that he visited them in their original home, where he tried his best to freeze to death, though in the nature of things this is impossible. A happy chance enables him to discover that the worship of Baal was widespread in Denmark. Once, in Holland, at a village fair, he was insulted by a surly fellow, who accused him of striking Christ with a leather strap, as heartless men beat a fallen horse to make it rise and resume its toil. Just when this Dutch incident took place is not clear, for we are swept back to medieval France, where Ahasuerus joins the cause of the Avignon popes. Thence back to antiquity and forward again —Palmyra, Persia, China, Russia, America, Mexico, and parts west. This is the most naïvely scrambled of all the examples of the Chronicle.

The Skeptic Becomes the Jokester

The reappearance of Ahasuerus the eternal skeptic is appropriate at the end of the nineteenth century, yet it is less frequent than might be expected; nor is the treatment of him in the role distinguished at this time. There is no need to linger over the two works by Viktor Hardung—a play, *Die Kreuzigung Christi* (Paderborn, 1889), and a poem, *Ahasvera* (n.p., 1895). Both of these works are virtually inaccessible today, but since they are both mediocre, this is no great loss to literature. Essentially romantic in attitude, they present the Jew as one who assumed a hard shell of skepticism after overlong and overfrequent soaking in sentimental *Weltschmerz*.

There are other works not quite so negligible. Karl Landsteiner's novel, *Ein jünger Ahasverus* (Regensburg-Mainz, 1900), is the kind of semipietistic, semimetaphysical work that may appear in any age, but which had a peculiar flavor at the turn of the century. It may be described as the sort of novel a second-rate Mrs. Humphrey Ward might have written if she had been a German from the nest of Nietzsche. The work deals only superficially with the Legend per se. The protagonist is a skeptical individual, Columban, who is nevertheless a thirster after knowledge. He is a philosopher of "modern" outlook, without faith, who believes with Nietzsche that God has died, that theology is antiquated lore, and that man is only a link in the measureless chain of development which nature has set in motion. There is no explanation of the source of nature. As Columban contemplates himself, he realizes that he is a young Ahasuerus, whose denial of Christ has brought him face to face with truth. He finds no satisfaction, however, in this "modern" outlook, for it only weakens his energetic capabilities and alienates him from his beloved Helene, a deeply religious woman. An elderly uncle counsels resignation and acceptance of what is and what must be as the only remedy for the bitter pessimism which afflicts him. Restless beyond endurance (like Ahasuerus Columban must wander), he takes a steamer for Egypt on which he meets a member of a religious order who persuades him to try a pilgrimage to the Holy Land. Here he finds peace and a return to faith. When he finally comes home, he is reconciled spiritually with his youthful love, Helene, who enters a nunnery while he takes up a Christian life. The skeptic has been beaten into submission, and can be happy only when he eschews his skepticism. Not for him any longer the pleasant stimulation which comes from *Que sais-je?*

Another tale is one of those grotesque performances which do much to keep the Legend alive. Otto Bierbaum, whose poem, "Golgotha" (1901), is a forthright representation of Ahasuerus the defiant, is the author also of a short story, "Schmulius Caesar" (1908), in which, to a group of silly sophisticates chattering away about art and literature, the Wandering Jew appears, a symbol of old disbelief, "which is always wrong." A world-weary figure himself and a fantastic conjurer-up of such spirits of the past as the French encyclopedist Diderot and the amorist Casanova, he has, in fact, a predilection for eighteenth-century ghosts and needs only the portrait of an individual to bring him once more to life in the flesh. What has gone before, he observes, is "a pastel": modern colors applied to it are so much artistic poison. After performing some engaging parlor tricks for the assembled throng, he leaves with his parrot Schmulius Caesar, to wander until "the shadow of the Cross has disappeared from earth. . . . It cannot last much longer." A new order of modernity, he prophesies, will eclipse the Cross and bring an end to the Wandering Jew, who until now has been only a symbol anyway, and a quite superfluous symbol at that, of the old saying: *Alles vergeht; Juda besteht* ("All passes, but Judea remains").[7]

Skepticism may show Ahasuerus as a negativist of sorts, as in P. N. van Eyck's poem, "Door de legten" (1912), in which life is empty for him in a tragic way.[8] The same thought is voiced in the brief appearance of the Jew in Ferdinand Vetter's dramatic fragment, "Jezus," in his *Ernste Spiele* (1911).[9] The aimlessness of life in general and of the career of Ahasuerus in particular is the theme of

J. Schürmann's "Ahasverus" (1915), a sonnet of lament.[10] The punishment is meted out to the victim because he rejected much that was beautiful, doubting sinner that he was. Another sonnet by W. de Merode, "De eeuwige wandelende Jood" (1914), asks whether he is a true image of the original sinner, or whether he has deviated from his prototype with the passing of the centuries.[11] Such a question is resolved in obvious fashion in P. Heyse's "Das Weltende: Eine Phantasie" (1909).[12] The end of the world has begun. The sun has disappeared. Two brothers, Contentus and Contemptor, have fled in an airship (sic) into the Sahara, which already is covered with snow and ice. Contentus, as his name suggests, has been satisfied with life; Contemptor asks what it has meant. Ahasuerus appears, in good spirits; having been exhausted by his wanderings, he now rejoices at the coming end. He reproves Contemptor for asking such questions after all he has seen. He thinks it ill becomes human flies even to want to know the answer to the dark riddle of why God is not sympathetic and just toward mankind. Death is man's best friend, and now he is approaching with palm branches to be Ahasuerus' savior. In answer to the question, "What do we know?" comes the reply that it is best for us not to know what does not concern us in the grand design.

From such skepticism to satire is often only an imperceptible step. Of the various humorous and satirical uses of the figure of Ahasuerus at the turn of the century, it may be said that they have in them more than a little of the malicious; and when we bear in mind that most of the examples are in German, we must be prepared to find that a large number of them are anti-Semitic.

We have already seen that in the pages of *Kladderadatsch*, between the 1850's and the 1880's, Ahasuerus had been the butt of heavy-handed anti-Jewish jokes. As one follows the issues of this periodical after 1880, however, one will note a decline in the number of such squibs. On the other hand, the rival humorous periodical, *Fliegende Blätter*, published some anti-Semitic items after 1880, but they were more gentle in tone than before. In the volume for 1882 there was a short anonymous poem in which the Wandering Jew appeared before a certain Herr Schwabs to say that, although he is seeking death, nothing can kill him.[13] He cites an impressive list of methods of suicide which he had attempted at one time or another. Suddenly he falls ill and collapses. Three physicians are summoned, and by the various prescriptions they compound, manage to bring about his release through death. We are reminded of the spectacular success of Doctor Phipps of Hamburg, who killed Ahasuerus when all other agencies had failed (p. 230 above). The moral of both tales seems to be that doctors can settle anything. A contribution by Alois Modl to *Fliegende Blätter* for 1907 is obscure.[14] In these verses, entitled "Ahasvers Ende," the protagonist prays for death. He has tried it again and again, and has always failed. How is that? An echo, "Töff! Töff!" rebounds and kills him. This apparently local topical allusion eludes later readers.

On the other side of the Atlantic, in his *Overheard in a Garden* (New York, 1900), Oliver Herford made Ahasuerus into a traveling salesman, peddling a book entitled *The Wandering Jew* in which he himself appears in the title role. As this itinerant book agent, Ahasuerus admits that he is tired out from walking, but he has some subscriptions from famous ladies of antiquity to show for his peripatetics. The piece is a typical example of Herfordian fluff. Rudyard Kipling's

"The Wandering Jew," in *Life's Handicap* (London-New York, 1891), is more engaging. A rich man, who has inherited his wealth from a recently deceased uncle and wishes to enjoy it as long as possible, is encumbered by a great fear of death. Having taken to heart the old saying that every time you circumnavigate the globe going east you save a day, he travels incessantly around the world, spending his money as he goes. His relatives in general and his future heirs in particular resent his squandering his substance in this way and send a doctor to intercept him on one of his tours. The doctor, who finds him in Madras, persuades him to spend the rest of his life suspended from a perch while the world turns beneath him. Thus suspended, he can neither enjoy life nor use his money, but at least he can be economical of his time.

It is unusual to find Ahasuerus used as a peg on which to hang political satire. Nevertheless, we have an instance of this in Franz von Königsbrunn-Schaup's *Der ewige Jude in Monte Carlo: Ein Wintermärchen von der Riviera* (Dresden, 1892), which attacks the snobbery and tinsel pretensions of both the Prince of Monaco and King Milan I of Serbia. The force of its attack, however, is so weak and its target so restricted that it does not deserve special attention. Yet, if Ahasuerus can be made to typify an individual of some particular nationality, the result may be good comic satire. An excellent illustration is *Das goldene Kleeblat: Phantastische Komödie in einem Vorspiele und vier Akten* (Leipzig, 1894) by "Hector Sylvester" (Wilhelm Wölffert). Once more Faust and Ahasuerus are together, but this time their relationship is more or less farcical. One may ponder the significance of the fact that Ahasuerus is here a caricature, whereas the author treats Faust seriously and even bestows upon him a fair amount of characterization. Apparently Faust is to him no laughing matter, while Ahasuerus seems essentially ridiculous. At any rate, his Ahasuerus is a lackadaisical, bored, itinerant Englishman with a monocle (a typical stage Englishman, in fact) and he is in the company of Faust, Don Juan, and Mephisto (the scholar, the gallant, and the buffoon), the trio who form the golden trefoil which gives the work its name. Among these three Ahasuerus appears a morose, stupid chatterbox, who makes a spectacle of himself over women, all of whom are also abysmally stupid. The society in which he moves is chastised with almost abusive invective.

In contrast is the brisk little satire by Carry Brachvogel, "Die Wiedererstandenen" ("The Resurrected"), in his *Cäsaren-Legenden* (Berlin, 1900). As in the final play of Haushofer's trilogy, the leading character is a modern Jewish financial baron. Perhaps in the Legend he may once have been a simple shoemaker, but now he is at the head of an American corporation, a leather king. (Even in 1900 the millionaires were all in America.) He bears the fantastic name of Sam A. Hasveros. Once he was poor and friendless, except for his traditional five coins; now, through a long process of self-denial, he has become the richest man in the world, one who could put the Bank of England in his vest pocket. Once he was rejected, a martyr along with the rest of his unfortunate people; now he is a man for whom all doors stand open; emperors are proud to call him friend. He has come to terms with the effete Christian god of the eighteenth century and inspired the French Revolution, creating out of it a whole race of the privileged. In short, having repeatedly insulted the old divinity, he now stands ready to consummate his cosmic revenge on the God who cursed him. In this new incarnation he has daughters whom he can marry off to the highest nobility; one, in fact, has married an English peer and can call Queen Victoria "Auntie," and mix the accursed blood of the Wandering Jew with an ancient line of martyrs, crusaders, and inquisitors.

This energetic theme is elaborated in various incidents from the career of the protagonist. One that stands out is his night of love with a lady of the line of the imperial Roman Caesars, a line which had long persecuted him. Did not Messalina herself once spurn him with contemptuous laughter? Did not Theodora of Byzantium once have her myrmidons slit one of his ears? What about his treatment by Lucrezia Borgia, the daughter of a pope and the mistress of another, who once received as a gift from her lover the ashes of two thousand cremated Jews? What of the Marquise de Pompadour, who abducted the favorite daughter of the Wandering Jew (at least his favorite in the eighteenth century) and had Ahasuerus himself imprisoned for a time in the Bastille? Now at the end of the nineteenth century, however, things are different. The present incarnation of the desirable female is not a lady of the high nobility. There is no true high nobility anywhere any more. She is Theo de Riom, the most sought-after cocotte in Paris, who becomes his in return for a check for a million dollars.

The radical alteration of the traditional Ahasuerus into a sublime egotist of the dawning twentieth century, a maker of munitions and wars, is described with great skill. Having humbled the ladies of proud lineage, and, as he sees it, having adulterated their lineage beyond hope of remedy, he callously rejects them. In the last instance, his youngest daughter is to be married in the morning to the Duc de Montmorillon at the Madeleine in Paris. He says to his current mistress, "You understand, you never knew me, *mignonne.* After all, today there is a wedding . . . and I am the father of the bride."

Yet on the whole these satires are not usually so delicately sharp as Carry Brachvogel's. Some time around 1900, there appeared some jovial verses by Philo von Walde entitled "Ahasver," whose gist is that you will find Ahasuerus wherever a drink is forthcoming.[15] (The implication that all inebriates are wandering folk is too obvious for comment.) Virgile Josz's story "Le Juif-Errant," in *Revue politique et littéraire* for June 25 and July 2, 1898, tells of a Bonapartist refugee who returns and kills his rival in a duel. Later, at a country fair, he commits *lèse-majesté* and is arrested. But the charge of dueling, which is thrown at him for good measure, comes to nothing when it is discovered that the duel was witnessed by others who had no use for the victim. When the populace wishes to know what had happened, it is revealed by the police that the refugee was none other than the Wandering Jew. Hence it is futile to prosecute him for either the dueling or *lèse-majesté.* He is released, having served as both a political convenience for the Bonapartists and as a means for gauging the fickleness of the people.

For a writer to turn the Legend against those who write about Ahasuerus is perhaps a case of fouling one's own nest; yet it is done wittily in a manuscript poem by Olga Maier, wife of the noted collector of Ahasueriana.[16] In her verses, dated January 22, 1908, the Wandering Jew complains that he has become merely a victim of antiquarians, and that it has not been God so much as these men and women who have kept him going. Still, he is getting some measure of revenge from the endless stream of books about him and his woes.

These remarks of Frau Maier have special pertinence if one includes in the list the works which set up analogues to the Legend. For example, Ferdinand Fränkel's older *Ein neuer Ahasverus* (Munich, 1878) was a not unentertaining comedy of manners, whose title may have been suggested by the lively Augsburg periodical previously described (p. 213 above), in which the name of Ahasuerus represented the general observer of society. Otherwise there is no connection between Frankel's play and the Legend. As an example of the extreme negative, there is the poem by Alfred Nathan, "An Bacchus," in *Ebbe und Flut* (Fürth, 1906), which points out that the strayed reveler addressing the god of wine and merrymaking is *not* the Wandering Jew. (For that matter, no one had suggested that he was.)

Specific targets are set up in A. E. Dugaillon's *Echos du juif errant* (1845), which consists of three satirical poems: "Epitre à E. Sue," "A E. Sue: Une soeur d'Adrienne de Cardoville," and "Rodinade." While all three are of feeble compass and trivial import, the last—a jeremiad against the Jesuits—has the hardest bite:

> Napoléon disait, perçant la nuit des temps,
> "L'Europe de nos jours sera dans cinquante ans,
> Peuples, songez-y bien, cosaque ou république;
> Non, tu seras pour moi l'oracle si compliqué,
> Ou jésuite ou cosaque, il te reste le choix,
> Europe des marchands, Europe des bourgeois!"[17]

The German imperialistic push toward the east, the dream of Emperor William II for the Berlin to Bagdad railway, is the subject of Franz Wedekind's "Sommer, 1898," presumably written shortly after the turn of the century, and available only in his *Gesammelte Werke* (Munich-Leipzig, 1912-24). The junket of William to the Middle East is the occasion for some pointed questions. Is Jerusalem ready to recognize the German Emperor, since it had never been sure before, when the crusaders of the Middle Ages harried the Holy Land? Ahasuerus will remove himself to Canaan. Perhaps he can obtain favors from the new ruler; why not? For he is skeptical of the present-day effectiveness of his curse. The poem is a tragi-comic picture of a capricious observer of the contemporary scene. The protagonist has become one of those children of the world who can see only that which is immediately in front of them.

In spite of malicious thrusts, however, none of this satirical treatment of Ahasuerus, as the twentieth century comes in, is really savage. It remains for World War I to uncork the vials of disgust and hatred necessary to the brewing of powerful satire. In the interim before 1914, there continues some ironically humorous writing about the Jew. Probably the most interesting single item of this sort is "The Door of Unrest" by William Sydney Porter (O. Henry) in *Sixes and Sevens* (New York, 1911).[18] An editor of a small-town newspaper is visited by a seedy old stranger, who introduces himself as Father Time's younger brother, the Wandering Jew (actually a gentile, not a Jew). They hold conversations on predestination, Nero, the funeral of Tamerlane. Pilate's body is also discussed, and well it might be, for after the suicide of the Procurator of Judea his corpse was thrown into a lake, whence it emerges every Good Friday to wash its hands. The stranger is named Mike O'Bader, which is easily resolved into Michob Ader, the cognomen of the Wandering Jew in Marana's *Letters Writ by a Turkish Spy* of the seventeenth century. Ultimately the stranger is identified as a drunken shoemaker of a neighboring village, who has been in this condition ever since his daughter, having been run out of town as a suspected prostitute, had died shortly thereafter. Mike O'Bader is accompanied by the Seven Whistlers, birds which in English folklore were identified with the seven Jews who had arranged the Crucifixion. The tale is told with the deftness always associated with its author.

The Initial Impact of World War I

The years of World War I (and the year or two following Armistice Day) produced a handful of pungent works which are useful now for the light they throw upon the situation in Germany during that parlous period. One considerable work, however, was laid in wartime Britain, and this English work may as well be described first. It is Charles Brumm's *Ahasuerus* (London, 1916), which is primarily a propaganda novel, which should be appraised accordingly. Ahasuerus, led by a fey little fair-haired child (who remains invisible to all but a few privileged persons), is seen in the streets of Manchester. Brumm spares little detail in his portrayal of the squalor engendered by the materialism of this industrial city and in his description of various low-life characters to be encountered there. It is the time of Yom Kippur, and Ahasuerus enters a synagogue, looking contritely for love and forgiveness, but finding neither. The child, who is revealed as a symbol of loving hope, reappears to lead him away. But there is an accident; Ahasuerus is found lying in a street, attended by a repentant whore, who resents a policeman's statement that the victim is dead. His diagnosis is confirmed by a society doctor, but the Magdalen, whose name is Betsy, conveys the supposed corpse of Ahasuerus to a doctor with brilliant red hair and a black cat. This reputed charlatan, called Peter Burton, revives Ahasuerus with the aid of mysterious pills, injections, and electronic display. It is difficult to think that we are not back in the heyday of the Gothic romances of the mad scientists.

The reader is introduced next to the Five Fingers of Ainscoat—a physician, a lawyer, a musician, a journalist, and a priest, who form a kind of social and cultural oasis in the depths of the slums of the city. Ahasuerus' accident is brought to the attention of not only the Five Fingers but also of other influential people, including the magistrates of the courts, who are troubled by the evanescent child who led the Wandering Jew. Then Harry Smythe, Liberal M.P. enters, and there is an exhibition of his vulgarity. Interspersed throughout these pages are little essays which are anticlerical, antiplutocratic, and pro-proletarian. Why, Brumm asks, are there not more people in Manchester like the philanthropist John Rylands? The question could be asked of any city. Why are there such crude specimens as Harry Smythe in elected office? The same could be asked in any land where there are elective offices.

At long last Ahasuerus reappears, now an enormously rich diamond merchant. He goes to a solicitor and draws up a deed of gift, dividing one hundred thousand pounds among five beneficiaries: a church established to convert Jews to Christianity, a group working for the relief of foreign visitors in distress, to the Ainscoat Lighthouse, Dr. Peter Burton, and a mysterious Baron de Fer. There follow several pages satirizing church committees, business reactions, and the like. The church group spends all its share of twenty thousand pounds without converting a single Jew. Baron de Fer, who was supposed to spend his share paying the electioneering expenses of Jewish candidates for Parliament, refuses to handle the sum and frustrates the intention of Ahasuerus.

Meanwhile, Dr. Burton, who has taken a fancy to the repentant prostitute Betsy, sends her to his sister Lady Ashwell, who is noted for her courtly manners and her pet raven. The two women take a trip to Germany. At Hildesheim, on the day of Yom Kippur, Betsy encounters Ahasuerus in a vision. He greets her with a happy smile; then, while the shape of a cross emerges above him, his apparition slowly fades away. There is much anti-German, or rather anti-Prussian, propaganda in the next few pages, and much adverse criticism of the English political leaders of the 1910 decade. The scene shifts from Germany to Venice and Lake Como, then back to London. A Prince Artaxia of Armenia suddenly turns up to prophesy the fatal significance of June 28, 1914, the day of the incident at Sarajevo. This Armenian prince (shades of the chronicle of Roger of Wendover and Schiller) is the Wandering Jew, who now exhibits a weakness for chronicling world history. He is also a piano virtuoso and a hypnotist, who uses these gifts to extract money from British antiwar isolationists for charitable institutions. He relates his previous experiences in Manchester. There is a flash back to an incident in which, accompanied by the fair-haired child, he appeared to the verger of a church, the Cross hovering above him as he spoke (for it is his responsibility to carry the burden of crime and folly). Only when modern civilization has been destroyed will Christ and his faith reign. The world war which is to break out in 1914 will be Armageddon. Yet, as an opulent Armenian prince, he contributes vastly to the war chest and is privileged to attend conferences at 10 Downing Street.

It is indeed difficult to assign this fantastic piece of writing to any category except that of imitation Gothic. Its appeal is entirely meretricious, and whatever message it is intended to convey is perfunctory—almost as if Brumm had decided as an afterthought to add anti-German propaganda to the ill-digested ingredients of his book. There is little if any suggestion of the real impact of the war on Britain.

It is different with Hans Traugott Schorn's work, *Ahasver: Ein Sang aus der englischen Kriegsgefangenschaft* (Hamburg, 1920). This unimpressive philosophical poem is based upon the author's own experience as a prisoner of war on the Isle of Man. Here Ahasuerus adopts a consoling philosophical attitude toward adversity, appealing for the rebirth of greatness in Germany (a sadly depleted nation, morally and physically, in 1919) and preaching the omnipresence of Christ. Yet, in spite of everything, Schorn believes that the war was England's fault, and nothing can convince him otherwise.

A flash back to the Crucifixion and the curse starts us on our way. Ahasuerus laments his fate, which is accepted with joy by the devils in hell, who anticipate his ultimate presence among them. Their abode is a kind of classical Hades. The lament of the victim, however, has little substance when Ahasuerus prays in resignation to Christ and is comforted by the thought that Jerusalem, which nurtured him, may also be able to save him (how, is not made clear). The sections of the poem dealing with the Holy City are bookish and dull. The prayers to Christ avail to the extent that Ahasuerus can command an adjustment to his predicament. The influence of the Chronicle once more asserts itself: there is a special passage concerning Constantine and the Cross; Ahasuerus stands later in the presence of Dante, Beatrice, Giordano Bruno, and others in Florence; he chats with Michelangelo in the Sistine Chapel where he hears the great artist complaining about the inadequacies of his art (but on hearing the sad story of Ahasuerus, Michelangelo is inspired to his greatest achievements, the paintings in the Sistine Chapel).

Passing over many scenes in the Near East and a pilgrimage to the Holy City, where, always praying, he visits places important in the life of Christ, we find Ahasuerus suddenly transported to Paris during the French Revolution. The poet cannot find anything good to say about this great upheaval, and through the mouth of Ahasuerus, he denounces it in the tradition of Jeremiah. In another flash back, he wanders over Asia Minor as far as Mount Ararat in a Byronic survey of antiquity. He takes part in the Crusades and other holy wars, setting up a powerful contrast between the Paris of the Middle Ages and the Paris of today. He then reverses the picture by comparing modern Paris during the Commune of 1870-71 with Armenia during the struggle of its suffering inhabitants against the Turks. Yet, by this time, he has mellowed sufficiently to end this section with a prayer to the Trinity, offered up on the summit of Ararat.

But now to England in 1914. The notorious "Hymn of Hate," written in Germany during World War I, is now constantly on the poet's lips as well as on Ahasuerus'. In spite of the glamor of England's history, the Jew is repelled by the crass materialism of London, dramatized when he seals the eyes of a dead, poverty-stricken old woman. He is visited, in a vision, by that king of evil reputation, Richard III, who reminds him that Antichrist has always lived in London. To show Ahasuerus present evidence of this Richard takes him on a tour of the city which is so thorough that Ahasuerus is exhausted at its end. Is it possible that Byron and Shakespeare wrote in this hellhole? How much better it must have been in the days of Roman Britain! His remarks are overheard by a vigilant police constable on the alert for traitorous speech, and Scotland Yard asks him to leave. He was about to go anyway, for a visitation from Christ has assured him that he is now free from sin, and the *Erlösungswort*—the word bestowing redemption upon him—has been pronounced. This section ends in a farrago of anticlimactic nonsense, including an inexplicable visit to Egypt, largely of descriptive nature, and finally, with a hope for God's eternal light in heaven.

However, there is more to come—a leap into the future, to the year 3000. London, needless to say, is changed. Britain has become a principality dependent on the Continent. The caravanserai of diplomats and statesmen at Whitehall is vanished. Ahasuerus visits the battlefield of Waterloo, where Caesarism died. And so on to the Last Judgment, when he can witness the founding of a new heavenly kingdom, in which Britain is not. He is accepted as free from sin.

The poem is more interesting as a human document than as a contribution to the Legend, for most of the adventures undergone by Ahasuerus here have been told before. Its approximately five thousand lines express the hatred of England to be expected from a German prisoner of war in 1918. In contrast, Ernst Toller's *Die Wandlung* ("The Transformation"; Potsdam, 1920) is a dramatic piece told from the point of view of a Jew involved in the war. Its center of interest is the collision between the German's instinctive dislike of the Jews—a natural anti-Semitism, as it were—and the fact that countless Jews sacrificed their lives in the great conflict.[19] The protagonist Frederick suffers on the battlefield and later in the hospital. His Iron Cross, perfunctorily bestowed upon him to bolster his morale, means nothing to him. His misery renders him hostile to the reminder that he has earned full citizenship. Can a fatherland which exacts these sacrifices be divine? Frederick would rather wander restlessly with Ahasuerus than remain in such a Germany. He calls instead for a rebirth of mankind and joins the revolutionaries of postwar Germany. Even after the shock of defeat and consequent hysteria have died down, he remains alien. The play ends on this note.

Another dramatic piece, this time in verse, is Paul Mühsam's *Der ewige Jude* (Leipzig, 1924). Ahasuerus is hovering over a battlefield, gloomy not only because of the slaughter in no man's land but also because of the hopelessness of the future of the Jews. He is only too aware of the anti-Semitism which the war has done nothing to allay. He acknowledges himself to be a Jew—that has been his offense, and the thought that the world can believe this to be true is a reason for terror in the hearts of all Jews. To him Zionism is no solution, and the goal of the young Jews who cry for a fatherland of their own is a mere deception. The cry may be sincere, but the air of discouragement is so thick as to be palpable.

The most thoughtful work to concern itself with Ahasuerus and World War I, when all is said and done, is Gustav Meyrink's *Das grüne Gesicht* (Leipzig, 1917), a novel of special interest because it deals in some measure with the old Semitic legendary figure of Chidher (Al-Khadir), the regenerative spirit, whose "green face" is symbolic of immortality and ever-returning spring (see p. 11 above). More than the actual situation of the war, Meyrink is thinking of its aftereffects, for the peace treaty will signal a general twilight of civilization.

In his novel a congress has assembled in neutral Holland for the continuation of peace, while, among the formerly warring nations during this sick period of readjustment, the cold war between mystical, patriotic fanaticism and crass materialism is beginning to abate. The chief character of the novel is an engineer, Hauberrisser, who is certain that somehow, amid this senseless dance of phantom hopes, he can achieve a truly happy life. In the vast depression around him he finds a way to an inner truth, to the loneliness of the man who can rise above his own predicament. To him and to others like him the green face appears, a symbol of existence which has changed from the physical to the spiritual. Soon Hauberrisser's own aspect is altered, and various rumors circulate about him, one being that he is the Wandering Jew. Others think of him as Elijah; the faithful believe that he is John the Evangelist. But only those who dream mystical dreams see him as one to show the path to truth through misery. (If men really knew what they wanted, they would see the truth.)

Hauberrisser is first an old Jew given to prophecies, with a black band over his forehead and a countenance "now smooth, now furrowed," as the sea has deep swells "and is never puckered." Unlike an earlier Ahasuerus in Lewis' *The Monk*, however, he conceals under the band on his brow not the sign of God's curse, but the sign of a life of truth. His spirit animates all those to whom the world catastrophe of the war is only an empty dream.

Part of the novel takes place in Jewish circles. Most characteristic is an old man, Chasside Lazarus Eidotter, to whom Chidher appears as Elijah, in order to teach him how heart and brain can exchange places in the human scheme of things. Mysticism and magic elements run riot, particularly in the later chapters, and tend to obscure the clarity of the basic idea. But, throughout, the protagonist, an ageless spirit, keeps his dimension of greatness through his sincere but Nietzschean posture of being one who gazes on the downgoing and the uprising, who has forgotten weeping and has not as yet learned to smile. In this way he identifies himself with struggling mankind.

To be sure, this symbolic figure has the features of Ahasuerus in only one of his appearances. Elijah and Chidher were already parallel to each other in Arabic lore; now Ahasuerus can join them. It is clear, though, that Meyrink has in mind the struggle of Elijah and Enoch against the Antichrist and the defeat of the Devil as it is told in the medieval plays of Antichrist. The message of the novel may be somewhat opaque, but it is directed toward spiritual growth and is shot through with Buddhistic and theosophical ideas. It is a well-written, sometimes eloquent presentation of Ahasuerus in the borderland between earthly reality and the revealed world of the human soul.

Hints of Redemption

Among the usual assemblage of unclassifiable works from the years between 1890 and World War I, three or four deserve mention, if only because they tell the old story with new overtones. The best known of these is Adolf Wilbrandt's *Der Meister von Palmyra* (Stuttgart, 1889), which appeared at the threshold of the period of this chapter.[20] It is a rather long poem on the will of humanity to live, even under suffering. The symbol of this persistent clinging to existence is aptly named Zoe. At first a Christian maiden martyr who is loved by Apelles, the Master of Palmyra, she is later reincarnated in three successive scenes as Apelles' wives, Phoebe and Persida, and then as his son Nymphas. The theme of the poem is the idea that a soul's wandering will improve it to the point where it can renounce the animal. Thus Phoebe is a sensual Roman, Persida a pious woman, and Nymphas a brave idealist. The poem's theme comes close to that of Meyrink's later novel.

Among the many characters of contrasting nature in *Der Meister von Palmyra*, Apelles suggests the Wandering Jew, although he cannot be definitely so identified. He is allotted an indeterminate stay on earth—not, however, as a punishment for any heinous offense. It is merely his fate, or rather the will of the gods, that he should experience this longevity in order to deepen his spiritual perceptions. His wanderings are in time rather than in space, for he does not leave Palmyra. His ultimate death is a necessary manifestation of order, in keeping with the predominantly religious tone of the poem as a whole. The work is generally effective.

Unlike *Der Meister von Palmyra*, Charles E. Lawrence's "Spikenard," in the *Cornhill Magazine* for 1921, is in the familiar side current of the Legend which brings together Ahasuerus and Judas.[21] In this dramatic poem, the Wandering Jew, Judas, and Gestas (the impenitent thief at the Crucifixion) are all wanderers. They meet and wallow in self-pity, self-justification, and despair. When they come upon the repentant Mary Magdalene, she washes the feet of each with spikenard, bringing comfort to all three. In spite of unabashed sentimentality and traces of turgidity, the work is both original and appealing.

It is probable that David Pinski's one-act play, *Der ewige Jude* (1907), should be considered in any full study of the literary treatment of the Legend, and yet, in spite of its occasional points of correspondence, it is an alien work.[22] A stranger announces to a small Jewish village the fall of Jerusalem at the hands of the Romans, but declares in the same breath that a child was born that very day who will rebuild the Temple and re-establish the Jews in Jerusalem. Pending confirmation of these tidings, he is held in suspicion. A young woman enters, however, and acknowledges that she is the mother of the child in question. At the moment of rejoicing, the news comes that the child has been taken away in a high wind. The stranger sadly admits that he has sinned, and that this punishment of the Jews, for which there now seems to be no surcease, is due to his sin, for he had not lifted a hand to save Jerusalem. Therefore he must wander forever. The narrative is based upon an old Talmudic legend obviously analogous to that of the Wandering Jew, yet the sinner's offense is different, even though his punishment is similar.

There is no question, however, about A. T. Quiller-Couch's tale, "The Mystery of Joseph Laquedem," in *Old Fires and Profitable Ghosts* (London-New York, 1900), for it is a characteristic late romantic yarn derived from the Legend. The protagonist is a respectable business man who is also a smuggler on the Cornish coast. He meets a half-witted girl, Julia Constantine, whose soul he had known in a different body long ago in Byzantium. As he renews his love for her, she improves mentally while he declines physically. It appears that when he can be sure of her love for him it will be possible for him to be redeemed (the old folk motif of salvation through the love of a mortal woman). Eventually the law catches up with the smugglers. Joseph Laquedem is shot and falls into the ocean; Julia tries to rescue him by going after him in a boat, but when the officers of the law close in on them, she and the Jew have disappeared. Have they gone to the bottom of the sea? Or have they vanished into thin air? More likely the latter, for they were insubstantial to begin with. In spite of some rather obvious details, such as the Byzantine name of the girl and mysterious Byzantine coins in the possession of Joseph, the story is, as always with "Q," entertaining and directly to the author's purpose.

The most poetically effective of all these, written in the kind of cadenced prose so popular during the 1890's, is Eugene Field's "The Holy Cross" (1893), a short and eloquent tale of the days of the conquistadors.[23] A foraging band of Spaniards, attended by a priest, Father Miguel, is in a wild mountainous region. While the soldiers are off scouting, a ragged stranger comes to the camp and asks Father Miguel for food, drink, and shelter. It takes but little questioning to ascertain that he is the Wandering Jew. His story having been told in orthodox detail, he gets not only food and drink but also a prayer of intercession from Father Miguel. He rests, but sleeps badly, finally dreaming that he is back in Jerusalem, where, amid a confusion of scenes and voices, one clear voice assures him of redemption. Meanwhile, the soldiers return. When Father Miguel tells them of their visitor and his story, they are incensed and wish to drive the sinner away; but Father Miguel dissuades them. The Wandering Jew awakens, calm and hopeful, and goes on his way in comparative peace. Soon thereafter his dead body is discovered. Before burial is possible, a violent tempest, accompanied by an earthquake, drives all away in panic. When the storm is over, it is found that the body of the Wandering Jew has been completely isolated by great gulleys formed during the earthquake. A mountain has risen up; on it Ahasuerus—in a sequestered spot covered with flowers, with the image of the Cross above him—sleeps his sleep. And so Ahasuerus, who had turned away Christ when he had fallen under his Cross, will now sleep forever under the image of that Cross.

Ahasuerus Considered for Redemption

As we have seen, Ahasuerus can find redemption in the minds of those who wish him to be saved and do not group him with Antichrist or others less nefarious. Only a few, however, are willing to grant him salvation, although many hold out to him the promise of attaining his goal. Few works of real stature admit him to the blessed state.

The full-length drama in blank verse, *Ahasver* (Strasbourg, 1894), by Freiherr Heinrich Schilling von Canstatt is notably rare. It is in five scenes, all laid in fifteenth-century Europe. As to the work as a whole, it is turgid and stiff, and needs no extended comment. Ahasuerus wins redemption through the realization that his rejection of Christ has made him evil. It is true that he prevents Suleiman the Magnificent from invading Europe and not only saves the starving inhabitants of a medieval town through his inexhaustible largesse but also rallies them to repulse a robber baron. He is still rejected as evil. But when he brings together the lovers, Rando and Johanna, he is admitted to the presence of God. This is hardly an original motive, and, considering the rather dire actions that go on through most of the play, might be considered anticlimactic. The obvious point is that Ahasuerus, knowing himself to be wicked, has worked out his salvation through his own efforts.

Another much more effective work is the libretto for a music drama, although as far as can be discovered the music was never written. It is Heinrich Bulthaupt's *Ahasver* (1904), which consists of a prologue and three acts.[24] In the Prologue it is explained that Ahasuerus was friendly to Jesus as an individual but skeptical of him as the Messiah (the old detail which Goethe was the first to treat seriously). At the time of the Crucifixion Ahasuerus chooses to stay in the city rather than stand at the foot of the Cross. He is looking for the traitor Judas, who has been responsible for his withdrawing from Christ. The first act ("Hope") takes place during Nero's reign. Ahasuerus tries to incite the Jewish slaves in Rome to rebellion, but the great fire of Rome interferes with his conspiracy, and he only manages to get his would-be rebels and some betrayed Christians thrown into the flames—notably, Chloe the pagan maiden, Silas the Christian weaver, and Silas' mother Hanna. Ahasuerus, of course, survives, but his faintly glimpsed hope of doing good by rising against tyranny dies a-borning. The second act ("Faith") brings the reader to Rome again, this time near the year 1000, when Judgment Day is supposed to be imminent. The inhabitants are giving away their possessions and praying continually. Ahasuerus, ignorant of the reasons for all this, comes blundering into the scene. He sees the young Christian fanatic Andrea persuading many of the inevitable end. When midnight passes and the world is still spinning on its axis, a wave of relief and of revulsion against this sort of evangelical religion seizes the crowd, which sets upon Andrea and kills him. Ahasuerus only regrets that he cannot die in this way for a belief—any belief. The third act ("Love") is laid in a German town about the year 1525. Ahasuerus meets Maria, who is trying to help peasants who have been injured in the religious disturbances attendant upon the rise of Martin Luther. They are interrupted in their promising conversation by a turbulent mob led by the father of a little girl who had died despite the ministrations of Maria. Attacked by this mob, Ahasuerus is unhurt, but Maria is mortally wounded. Ahasuerus recognizes the fact that he had met Maria before, in some previous incarnation, and then remembers that she was present at Golgotha. This bond, this spiritual affinity, in addition to the prayers that Maria offers as she lies dying, enables Ahasuerus to call on Christ. He is forgiven and is granted the boon of death, expiring at Maria's side. Both are received by the angels. Until this third act, Ahasuerus had been a Jew consistent in his attitude toward Christ—nay more, a consistent hater of Christians—but love in some form conquers all, or so Bulthaupt would have it. It is interesting to speculate on what kind of an opera this libretto would have made, for the scenes are well drawn and the expression vigorous.

The favorite treatment of the redemption of Ahasuerus seems to have been dramatic. A rather ponderous specimen is Wolfgang Madjera's *Ahasver* (Vienna, 1903), a tragedy in five acts, which bears a slight resemblance to Schücking's "Die Drei Freier," inasmuch as the Wandering Jew and his analogue, the Flying Dutchman, are brought together—not physically but in descriptive attributes: black hair and beard, pale countenance, deep-set dark eyes, and a black mantle. Ahasuerus knows that he is damned until he has attained compassion and purity. The latter, indeed, approaches a renunciation of the flesh, and the condition is imposed because this Ahasuerus' perpetual youth keeps his animal passions at sufficient heat to produce carnal temptation. In order to achieve his salvation, therefore, he practices rigorously laws of moderation, even asceticism, and in consequence emerges as a mysterious eccentric who apparently subsists on no food and almost no drink. He can heal the sick and restore youth to the aged, but he preaches that the one true happiness which life can offer is death. When we hear of the dark and frightful sinner's thoughts which afflict him, we wonder that he has not long since been driven to despair.

Then he meets Maria, the pure and sympathetic, who had since childhood been absorbed in the story of the Wandering Jew and his sufferings (just as Senta in Wagner's *Der fliegende Holländer* was previously disposed to fall in love with the Flying Dutchman). Maria loves Ahasuerus completely, willingly, and idolatrously; but so innocently unsophisticated is the nature of her love that it fulfills the requirement of voluntary purity necessary to the salvation of her beloved. Slowly the messengers of peace come to Ahasuerus, the first friendly greetings of death: the silver hairs and the snapping tendons. Yet he remains lusty and lustful, and the faithless, skeptical, animal Eva seduces him. This, he remarks cynically, is his fate, the completion of his curse. At the same time, the probability of his ultimate redemption in his repentant return to Maria remains, and the tragedy is thereby lessened. This is a tedious business, however, for Madjera cannot make up his mind whether his play should be a morality play or a modern thesis drama, with the result that it is neither. If there is a moral, it is simply that redemption remains *in posse* rather than *in esse*.

Even so, Madjera has more human milk than P. Oosterlee, who in his critical essay, "Ahasverus" (1913), reveals himself as a dogmatic and pedantic Calvinist.[25] To Oosterlee the curse pronounced by Christ is a just punishment for the Wandering Jew's doubts about the validity of Christ's message. Ahasuerus and Judas are therefore bracketed, and the former is presented as "persecuted" by Christ's grace, in the manner of Francis Thompson's "Hound of Heaven." The ever-present theme of God's mercy leads Ahasuerus to waver in his hatred for the Saviour. Eventually he must heed the message in Matthew 11:28—"Come unto me, all ye that labor and are heavy laden, and I will give you rest." On Calvary, he must fall to his knees and stammer: "My Saviour, be merciful to me, a sinner!" Nevertheless, Oosterlee stresses the enormity of Ahasuerus' offense when he lifted his hand against Christ. In spite of all the evidence of Christ's divinity, he had not believed; therefore he was punished. He was not penitent until too late; for that reason he received his fitting reward.

It is probably correct to take the position that the treatment of the Legend after about 1900, in the main, falls off both in quantity and in quality, provided this stricture is limited to the usual romantic interpretation of the protagonist. To put this in another way: it is patent that the romantic appeal of Ahasuerus has worn off through overrepetition of the romantic concept. One indication of the decline is the nature of the minor miscellaneous works in which Ahasuerus plays some kind of part. These works must be mentioned, but as a rule they are interesting for only some one point or at most a very few.

In all of these early twentieth-century treatments, some aroma of the nineteenth century persists. Perhaps it persists in sentimental chauvinism colored by anti-Semitism, as in Adolf Graf von Westorp's poem "Ahasver," in *Herzblut: Neue deutsche Lieder* (Berlin, 1895), in which Ahasuerus represents all Jewish Germans, who, in spite of all the devotion which Germany has put into their education and welfare, remain foreigners. Or it may be evident in an overfamiliar picture of the follower of Antichrist, as in Margaret Szerviczky's extravagantly didactic narrative poem *Jézus* (1914), in which Ahasuerus fights against Rome, only to be captured, converted, and allowed to die.[26] On the other hand, the nineteenth-century aroma may persist in only another lament at the miserable nature of the times, with Ahasuerus seeing the evil of the present era (especially evil for those of his own race), and calling out in despair, "Lord, why hast Thou forsaken me?" This is the core of Ferdinand Bronner's poem, "Ahasuerus, der ewige Jude," in *Aus Zeit und Ewigkeit* (Leipzig, 1893). It may persist also in another attempt to put a new wrinkle in the old folk-tale cloth, as in Alexander Simonyi's short story, "Ahasver" (1912), in which Ahasuerus' curse can be lifted if three men will give him hospitality.[27]

The pressures of World War I may be noticed sometimes in these minor pieces, usually only in brief examples. Thus Thekla Skorra's unpublished poem contains the observation that the Jews may be good enough to fight and die for the Prussians but still cannot achieve their promised freedom in Germany, for all Jews are aliens there. Ahasuerus also represents the destiny of the Jewish people in both Michael Szabolcska's "Bolygó zsidó" ("The Wandering Jew," 1894) and Lewis Szabolcsi's "Ahasver" (1910).[28]

Seldom is this minor Ahasuerus bitter, although two dramatic fragments point out that Christ forgave all sins save that of Ahasuerus, and yet, though Christ repents the curse, he can do nothing to recall it. Such is the gist of poems by Hugo Salus (1917), and Coloman Harsányi (1910), both entitled "Ahasverus."[29] The poem by the Czech, K. H. Mácha, which Oskar Rosenfeld translated into German as "Der Ewige Wanderung" (1917), is a characteristic poetic lament, with some rather weak but pretty pictures of budding nature.[30] Repentance sometimes brings Ahasuerus a brief respite, as in Géza Szilágyi's *Ahasvér karácsonya* ("The Christmas of Ahasuerus"; Budapest, 1903), a little play in which the protagonist is permitted through Christ's grace to get a glimpse once more of his wife and child. Similarly, in Julius Dezsö's narrative poem "Ahasuerus" (1902), the conscience of the Jew is so troublesome that God pardons him.[31] We may note that, as in Zoozmann's work, Ahasuerus may be an up-to-date worldly citizen. He may, for instance, be a Jewish newspaperman, as in Francis Herczeg's poem, "A bolygó izraelita" ("The Wandering Israelite," 1895),[32] or a restless, suffering poet, as in Aladar Bán's poem, *Egyedül* ("Alone"; Budapest, 1898) and Andrew Ady's novel, *Sirisson meg* ("Mourn for Me"; Budapest, 1899). In all three of the foregoing cases the emphasis lies on restlessness—and many another beside Ahasuerus has been restless. Perhaps the logical extreme is reached by Lewis Bartók's "Ahasuerus" in his *Régi lant* ("Old Lute"; Budapest, 1891), a poem in which Ahasuerus calls for annihilation in order to take the curse of eternity with him. More to the point is Francis Szilágyi's dramatic fragment in his *Zsarátnok* ("Embers"; Budapest, 1902). When Jesus ultimately pardons Ahasuerus, He shows him poison. Although this might give the Jew the release he has sought, Ahasuerus prefers to go on living.

All this is to suggest that the writers of the nineteenth century had already extracted about as much essence from the Legend as there was to extract. But in the contributions to the Legend beween 1914 and 1920 of writers concerned with World War I, we may see some renewal of vitality in the story. The full effect of the war was delayed for a time. Because of the conflict, the world was not to be the same thereafter; nor would the Legend be exactly the same, either. In the new world after 1918, Ahasuerus would either remain the traditional figure we have now met time and again—or become a creation of the twentieth century. The creative aptitudes of this century have thus far not lent themselves easily to fostering a folk tale of the ancient supernatural, yet they have not exactly ignored Ahasuerus.

CHAPTER FOURTEEN

Within This Generation

World War I, as we have seen, brought the Wandering Jew into the foreground of a few writings, all but one of which were German. In the dreary years after the war—during the twenty-year armistice after November 11, 1918, when Germany was mired in disastrous economic and social problems which were resolved, as it proved, for the worse with the advent of Hitler—a few works were produced in which the ugly aspects of life in that country overlaid the figure of Ahasuerus. Again all but one of them were German.

We may as well treat the exception first. It is an English novelette, if such it may be called, a strong protest against the soulless leadership of Europe after the war. It presents a defense of a socialistic approach to government, because socialism "stands for a sort of recognition of immaterial rights." This was a familiar note in the 1930's but is interesting to find in 1923. The work in question is "Golgotha and Company" by Robert Nichols.[1] In it "Dr." Ahasuerus is an international Jewish magnate, a megalomaniac power unto himself. He is opposed by "Dr." Mammon, who is eager to push a program of muscular, materialistic Christianity. (The appellation of doctor is used here as sardonically as it was in those years by H. L. Mencken.) The third leading character is the "Protagonist," who is Christ. The world is awaiting the return of the Protagonist; but when he comes, it is only to be killed again by Ahasuerus who, in his infinite worldly power, issues a lethal denial of the Saviour. And so Christ, as in Goethe's fragment, is no more successful in his Second Coming than in his First.

Nichols takes much space in his story to describe the ways in which different nations prepare for the return of the Protagonist. Obviously they cannot be expected to present a united front. The bitterness engendered by the war breaks out when he comments on Germany:

> They achieved a federated Empire and, from considering themselves the Hamlets of thought, took to seeing themselves as the Hannibals of action, prated of "shining armor," "a destiny upon the seas," etc. Their earlier ethic had been idealistic and sentimental, now it became realist and cynical. In 1800 they had appeared to themselves as suffering martyrs; in 1850, with Lohengrin in place of Werther, they christened themselves conquering saints. In both roles they were characterized by a slavish suggestibility, witness of unsatisfied emotional cravings and incredible naïveté, the result of a racial preference for using the fact rather as the proof of subjective assertions than as a starting point for thought. Of these characteristics our Professor [Mammon] has known how to take full advantage.[2]

There is a distressing accuracy about this generalization made ten years before Hitler came to power; but Nichols is not unhappy in the part of prophet. The task of Ahasuerus, who is here identifiable with Antichrist, is formidable, and he knows it. "It takes more than a wombat to lick the late Jesus Christ." What breaks the Saviour's heart is the trenchant question of Ahasuerus: "Perceivest Thou not that behind today's knowledge of man's helplessness exists not regret, but the resolution to profit by it?" and his defiant "If Satan be, then Satan am I, and than Satan none is mightier—no, not even Thou! . . . None but Satan has the power to cast out Satan!"

A brief sketch of the Chronicle of the Wandering Jew is included in "Golgotha and Company," but it is of minor importance. At the end, Easter comes again, and Christ once more is risen, but Ahasuerus is still rebellious: "Once more we renew the eternal battle! Not yet, not yet is Thy kingdom come!" There are in this work many eloquent passages, as well as much balderdash. All in all, it represents fairly well the moral tone of its decade.

Like Zoozmann, Nichols portrays the Wandering Jew as a materialistic and sinister modern Jewish financier. But in the German works of this period there is a curious ambivalence, a hovering between the condemnatory and the idealistic. For example, in a novel by L. Audnal, *Ahasver* (Berlin, 1920), we are confronted with an idealistic, cosmopolitan young Jew whose marriage to a Belgian girl was prevented by the war. Its most interesting pages are those which describe Germany between 1914 and 1918. The unenviable position of Jewish Germans in an anti-Semitic milieu is stressed most effectively. As might be expected, the novel assails the disastrous consequences of too much nationalism at any time but especially in the powder-magazine Europe of 1914. At times the work is engrossing, but its structure is too weak for a proper pulling together at the end. Ahasuerus is here only the symbol of an unhappy quest for peace and happiness on the part of a young twentieth-century Jew, and arrives at the same hopeless kind of situation as prevailed in Mauthner's novel, *Der neuer Ahasver*, nearly forty years before.

Meanwhile, the anti-Semitism, which flared into the Nazi creed during the 1930's and cannot be discounted in any German work of the past century, obtains an angry outlet in Hans Hauptmann's propagandistic chronicle-novel, *Memoiren des Satans* (Munich, 1929). In it, the author has tied together Jews and Freemasons in the same package; both are anathema to the Fascist state. There is a long, detailed account of Satan's major activities after a pact signed between Masons and Jews at an alleged meeting in New York in 1829, and the novel is chiefly concerned with the damage wrought by this pact in the ensuing hundred years. The Wandering Jew—with a few of the traditional physical attributes, such as glittering eyes, strange mien, miraculous means of transportation (he is air-borne like Superman)—appears for the greater part as a messenger and informant, a subsidiary figure only. Satan himself is a strangely incompetent spectator of events. The whole course of European history after 1829, which culminated in World War I, is attributed to this international conspiracy of Jews and Masons. The defeat of Germany in 1918 is so obviously a result of this alliance, and the consequences so appalling, that Satan decides henceforth to confine his activities to keeping an orderly organization in hell. For it seems that not only was Germany never really defeated in the war—it was, rather, stabbed wantonly in the back by Jews and Masons—but all liberal movements stem from this same nefarious source. All this is consonant with the agitation led by many of the discredited army leaders, notably General von Ludendorf, which began about 1920. In spite of its wrongheadedness, the book is a sophisticated composition, but is dull in basic content; its more than a hundred thousand words make tedious reading. For what it may be worth, it may be reported that in this case the debacle of 1918 was too much for Ahasuerus. He is admitted in his distress to the brotherhood on Mount Athos, where he dies.

Whereas Meyrink dreamed of a better state in the future, in postwar German writers this hope quickly receded. For example, Wilhelm Gründler (in *Ahasuerus*, a five-act tragedy written during the war but not published until 1928) voiced in hoarse fashion a desire to love humanity in spite of its follies, the greatest of which is war. He saw the necessity for an association of peoples in a new context of spirituality, in which the soul may strive, however unsuccessfully, for survival:

> Das Vergehen und Werden
> Lässt uns keine Ruh'.[3]

His heart, however, is not in it, and the total effect is uncertain, reflecting his lack of conviction. Perhaps when the work was published he sensed the coming failure of the League of Nations. From his attitude emerges a concept of the Wandering Jew as a totally destructive agent in league with the Devil, who can be defeated, if at all, only by the integrity of a human soul—not by world associations.

A good example of this kind of skepticism is Max von Mallinckrodt's *Der Weg des Ahasvers* (Bonn, 1920), a dramatic poem. Ahasuerus is the persecutor of Gottschalk, a physician whose imperturbably scientific dedication is offensive to the Jew, who wishes to see him suffer and feel despair such as only the Jew has experienced. It is a large order, but it converts the physician into a new Job. His daughter dies of the plague because her father tries to conserve his limited store of a specific remedy in the interest of the whole community, which does not appreciate what seems to be a cold-blooded attitude if not outright murder. Even his wife is estranged by his ruthlessness. Gloating melodramatically, Ahasuerus carries her away into the mountains when she becomes sick to the point of death. Gottschalk nevertheless carries on under these mounting vicissitudes and maintains his integrity as scientist and man, finally dying in holiness at a refuge for incurables. Ahasuerus and Death are alike confounded. As we learn, Gottschalk has been comforted *in extremis* by the spirit of his deceased daughter Imagina. The poem could never be produced as a play, in spite of its elaborate stage directions, for it is extremely ponderous and turgid, with excessively long speeches.

Shorter and more readable is Otto Müller's *Götterdämmerung* (Berlin, 1926), a dramatic poem of Catholic *Weltanschauung* which presents in smooth-flowing iambics the conflict of light and darkness. In it Ahasuerus is a minor character on the side of the Devil, who occasionally exhibits moods of destructive rage. Such anger comes into high focus in Paul Baudisch's *Fragmente* (1920), in which the Wandering Jew is a tormented cynic seeking perverse novelty and driven along by boredom and sensation-seeking.[4] He is a breaker of systems and a father of revolutions. Catiline and the Marquis de Sade were his legitimate sons;

Napoleon his bastard. He is no longer an accursed man wrestling for his salvation, but a Nero with a compelling passion for mere sensation. In other ways, to be sure, he maintains a trace of the eternal, merely because he is the Wandering Jew. But Baudisch seems to believe that the disruptive in politics signifies the disruptive in society, a thesis he expounds in his "grotesque history" entitled *Catilina* (1921).[5]

Recent Examples of the Chronicle of the Wandering Jew

Examples of the Chronicle of the Wandering Jew since 1918 are not so numerous as before; and when they appear in more or less authentic form, they usually are meant to serve as illustrations of some primary thesis or as representations of some particular kind of search for something other than God. I am speaking here of works which give more than incidental attention to the Chronicle's historical settings or which emphasize the importance of consecutive historical events. One or two of these stand out in this category, and at least one of them is notorious.

Niels Henrik Thorald's *Tod dem Tode: Aus den Erinnerungen Ahasvers* (Magdeburg, 1919) is a disquisition on suicide, deeply penetrated by the gloom of postwar Germany. The novel is told for the greater part in the first person. The author, having lost wife and child, makes several attempts on his own life, but for one reason or another never succeeds and comes to think of himself as the Wandering Jew. He outlines the career of Ahasuerus, always identifying himself with the chief character. His Wandering Jew is an Armenian living in Jerusalem in the time of Christ. (This is the first appearance for a long time of the story of Roger of Wendover, supplemented by the version given by Schiller.) He suspects that Christ is not the Messiah, as many others in the twentieth century are inclined to do. He questions all thoughts of immortality, but the high priest in Jerusalem reminds him that the Jewish theory of immortality is always valid, inasmuch as one lives in one's children. After the curse is pronounced, there comes a change in Ahasuerus' attitude. His Schubartian lack of success in suicide convinces him that Christ may have been the Messiah after all. He therefore persuades himself to be a preacher and leader in attempts to convert others to his belief.

Yet the idea of suicide obsesses him, and he visits Seneca, who instructs him in how to die. He sympathizes with the thoughts of other Roman practitioners of suicide, but cannot stay long in Rome, because too many Christians who had once lived in Jerusalem recognize him. Nor do the Romans want him to stay. Before moving along, he gives an account of the troubles of the infant Church and of the early Christians in Rome, and discusses their individual attitudes, especially toward suicide until Augustine's explicit rejection of it.

From Rome, Ahasuerus, now known as Zerib, goes to Mecca to see Mohammed. Finding nothing in Islam to sustain him in his quest to justify suicide, he proceeds to Armenia, where he lives for some time as Joseph Cartaphilus. This was when Roger of Wendover heard of him. Ahasuerus' next sojourn is in Germany at the time of the Reformation. But he is discouraged by the confused thinking of these northern nations; he has arrived there too late: Christianity has spoiled them. He reports, however, on various manifestations of rebellion against the Christian code in the personalities and writings of Montaigne, More, and, especially, Donne, Hume, and Swift. Their attitude toward life, their distrust of excessive concern with the body, interest him greatly. He then goes on to report on suicide epidemics such as those brought on by romantic works like *Werther*, by Napoleon, and by other causes.

Finally—as a surprise to the reader, whom the author has done little to prepare for this—Ahasuerus begins to wonder how he could all this time have forgotten both love and duty. The novel ends in romantic fashion with a visit to the Colosseum by midnight, where, although the vanity of human wishes is manifest, he can think of no more to say than *Ora pro nobis*. Thorwald's work is pretentious and trite enough in the telling, but one little detail remains in the memory—an invention which is not to be found in folklore: "In London the people made fun of me and called me 'Mr. Between,' for in their museum they had a man who in the dim past (*aschgraue Zeit*) had been caught between two tree trunks and had been petrified along with them ever since."

A notorious example of the Chronicle of the Wandering Jew since 1918 is actually two works by the same partners in literary crime, George Sylvester Viereck and Paul Eldridge. One of these works deals with the Wandering Jew and the other in similar fashion deals with the Wandering Jewess. *My First Two Thousand Years* (1928) clearly meets the definition of the genre, but is more erotic than its predecessors, chiefly because of the presence of the Wandering Jewess (at the beginning Salome, but reappearing in various reincarnations).[6] John the Evangelist is the original Cartaphilus, but he is soon absorbed by the true Wandering Jew, who was once Isaac, a captain in Pilate's army. Throughout there is a strong stress upon reincarnation. This Wandering Jew is seeking neither Christ nor death, but sensation in the form of sexual enjoyment—or, as it is expressed in the only memorable phrase in the book, "unendurable pleasure infinitely prolonged." In deference to the principle of monogamy, it should be pointed out that the continual and continuous love affairs in which the Wandering Jew indulges are all with the same woman, the Wandering Jewess, in whatever guise she may appear. The moral idea, and I use the term loosely, is that for a well-rounded concept of humanity both masculine and feminine elements are essential. Others have said the same in a much less cheap and tawdry manner. In this work the Chronicle of the Wandering Jew is continued past World War I, to a very weak ending.

One may say, without much fear of being considered Pecksniffian, that it is difficult to see much excuse for the book except for its obvious sensational, quasi-pornographic qualities. But it is at least true to the spirit of the Chronicle: it keeps the concept of the Wandering Jew as a *parcoureur du monde*, as he was in the eighteenth century, and compounds this with the Goethean *ewigweibliche* thesis and the unmistakably twentieth-century creed of self-indulgence. Some of the historical figures encountered are stock in trade for the Chronicle—Charlemagne, Columbus, Luther, Spinoza, Rousseau, Frederick the Great—but others are more exotic personalities, such as Don Juan, Gilles du Retz, and, near the end, Nietzsche.

Curiously enough, the complementary work, *Salome . . . My First Two Thousand Years of Love* (1930), is a much more effective contribution.[7] It is a Chronicle of the Wandering Jewess which throws considerable light upon *My First Two Thousand Years;* and since it is also the fullest outline of the career of the Wandering Jewess, it calls for extended comment here. The protagonist, as I have said, is Salome, condemned to an eternal succession of lives on earth because she prompted the execution of John the Baptist. Her driving quest is to achieve superiority over men. She begins by arousing the love of Isaac, who appeared in the previous work as the Wandering Jew; but she is still adolescent, and the net result of this attraction is her vow to conquer the moon, which keeps women in biological bondage. After two quick and unhappy marriages, she leaves her home to wander in the desert. Here she meets Jokanaan, John the Baptist, who is preaching that he is Elijah. She is greatly impressed by him and manages to get him thrown into prison instead of being summarily executed as a heretic. When she tries to tempt him, he rejects her. She angrily causes his death in the manner described in the Gospel of Mark; but before he dies, Jokanaan says that she must continue to live for an eternity because she is "too vile for the grave."

Back in Jerusalem she meets Cartaphilus, whom she recognizes as the former Isaac, the cobbler's son who had first excited her. She takes no part in the Crucifixion, however, and so is ignorant of the curse imposed on the Wandering Jew. A century later we find her in Arabia, the wife of the king Hussein. She cannot have children by him because he is sterile, but she realizes that he may try to kill her to cover up the fact. His brothers prevent him from this deed by killing him, and then each brother marries her, but she remains barren.

She first learns of the Wandering Jew through the wise man Apollonius, her teacher, and expresses the hope that she may some day meet him. Resuming her wandering life, she meets the formidable Zenobia of Palmyra. The two try an experiment in female domination, in which Zenobia frees all of her female slaves and places women in important governmental positions. Zenobia, who vies in glory with her predecessor Cleopatra, insists that the defeat of the Serpent of the Nile by the Romans had come about not from the superiority of the Romans but from the physical handicaps of the female sex. Then Zenobia dies, and Salome retires temporarily to a quiet life on the Rhine, having meanwhile become enamored of an immortal turtle, Lakshmi, which is a symbol of women's revolt. At the first opportunity she and the turtle travel to the temple of Cartaphilus, who has by now become the God Ca-Ta-Pha. He is absent, and while awaiting his return, she proceeds to create a civilization in which the functions of men and women are turned around—an achievement which is weakened by the fact that she has worked with an extremely primitive people. When Cartaphilus returns, they find that they are still in love with each other, but decide that they should wait a few centuries for their love to ripen. Salome therefore continues to travel, learning many secrets from various cultures and falling in love with a young girl named Joan, who returns her love. By bribing all the chief authorities of the Church, in a manner not always specified, she manages to have Joan installed as pope, becoming herself a power behind the throne. For a time all goes well, but Joan is after all a woman and succumbs to an unnamed lover; she dies giving birth to a child in public, while wearing her papal robes.

Meanwhile, Cartaphilus and Salome have come together again, he always wallowing in sensuality in his search for unendurable pleasure infinitely prolonged. Centuries pass while Salome continues her adventures, sometimes dressed as a woman but more often as a man. She even manages to collect a harem. Finally, however, she concludes that the time has come for a female Christ to redeem womanhood. Her choice falls upon Joan of Arc and it is Salome's feats of ventriloquism which enable Joan to hear divine voices. After Joan's capture, Salome has the opportunity either to save her and expect her to succumb as the other Joan had done, or to let her become the great martyr womanhood needs. There could be only one choice.

Shaken by the incident, Salome retires to a convent, where, because of her heresies, she is condemned to the stake. By using magic she is able to substitute a dummy of flesh and bone and to escape to Elizabethan England, thence to Vienna, and finally to Tibet, where Cartaphilus had last been reported. In the process she sheds a husband or two, according to her usual custom. She decides that she is now fit to marry Cartaphilus, but he is too busy contemplating the final meaning of life. On his advice she becomes temporarily a nun and then returns to the Russia of Catherine the Great, who is called an old woman "impaled upon the phallus."[8] When her attempts to expose the worthlessness of Potemkin to his royal mistress prove disastrous, Salome is obliged to leave Russia for South America, where she attempts to found a race of lovers who can experience unendurable pleasure infinitely prolonged. After an attempt to interest Queen Victoria in the greatness of women fails (the Widow of Windsor will not even listen to talk about women's rights), Salome and Cartaphilus settle down in South America and marry. She contemplates the birth of Homuncula, one in whom unendurable pleasure can find infinite gratification. She herself, however, becomes less the revolutionary and more the lover. The book concludes with both Salome and Cartaphilus singing the praises of love.

These ridiculous books carry their own commentary. Fortunately, not all the works which resolve themselves into the Chronicle are quite so shoddy, so meretricious, so cynical, although they may never be so lively. Emile Bernard's epic poem, *Le juif errant* (Paris, 1927), is plodding and verbose, but it is serious in intent and not without merit as a narrative. Here Cartaphilus is the vindictive tool of the high priest, whose actions are motivated purely by envy. Mary accompanies Christ on the Via Dolorosa and shares the buffets of the crowd. At the time of the insult to Christ, Cartaphilus delivers a harangue of some two hundred lines, but is immediately ashamed and remorseful, recognizing the deserved curse as a purification. Yet when the angel appears with drawn sword (a detail which has appealed to French writers since Quinet), he protests that he has been a good Jew; however, he accepts his fate ("C'est vers la vie en Lui que Cartaphile sort"). In his wanderings he is enjoined by the angel from lingering over Jewish holy places. In Egypt and throughout the non-Christian world he sees false gods and their abominations. The superiority of Jesus begins to impress itself upon him. When he sees the eremites in the desert, he wonders whether they are holy men or fools. In the Acropolis at Athens he listens to the sophists. He hears Paul's Areopagitica, which, still unconvinced, Ahasuerus endeavors to controvert. He is in Rome at the time of the triumph over the fall of Jerusalem, with martyrdoms taking place everywhere, but he remains skeptical. He is shocked to see the unnatural crimes which take place in the Temple of Venus erected on the site of the Holy Sepulcher. The image of Christ appears before him, but he continues to repudiate the Saviour as he wanders.

At the time of the Crusades, Cartaphilus tries to stem the emotional flood by denying the divinity of Christ. But then he is obliged to reveal himself, which he does by assuming all the romantic characteristics of the Wandering Jew, already too familiar to us. He is literally overridden by the horsemen of the crusaders. Uninjured, of course, he repeats that all medieval churches, cathedrals, and the rituals held within them are folly. Having seen Christ as a suffering mortal, he cannot believe in his divinity. During the Reformation, in Wittenberg, he listens to a long debate between Luther and a voice (the Catholic Church). He sides with Luther, but an avenging angel condemns Luther as Antichrist and Cartaphilus as his henchman.

After this episode, there is a long leap ahead to the French Revolution and the year 1793. The execution of Louis XVI precipitates an angry squabble between radicals and moderates. It is made clear, however, that all order has been upset. Later, during the Consulate, two of the consuls are "sons of Luther" and the third a *philosophe*. At this point, the author's attitude is thoroughly reactionary, antirepublican, and Catholic. Everything is deteriorating rapidly (this pessimistic sentiment is placed, rather queerly, in the mouth of Napoleon Bonaparte). Another angel inveighs against the negative nature of all revolution. Lucifer has liberated Prometheus; Satan first emerged through the act of Cain. Prometheus and Satan will found the city of Cain, which is the modern industrial metropolis born out of revolution. The Wandering Jew, arriving here, concludes that he must be in hell. By contrast, the time of Jesus of Nazareth seems idyllic. In his repulsion, Cartaphilus can now believe in the Man-God, in spite of the despair about him. Indeed, many of the best lines of the poem are to be found in this Revolution episode, notably a chorus of despairing humans.

In a final flash back, Cartaphilus lives over again the original Good Friday. Now he no longer feels hatred for Christ, but rather love and remorse, and helps him as best he can, taking up part of the Cross on his own shoulder: "Le doute l'a quitté, la vérité l'inonde/ Il a trouvé Jésus en parcourant le monde."[9] In this recreation of the scene of the Crucifixion, Cartaphilus confesses to the apostle John that he now knows he had been mistaken in not accepting Christ as the true Messiah, for he had been deceived into thinking that he would come to earth in glory and not as a poor carpenter. After his repentance he turns back from Calvary. His experiences during his wanderings pass in review, especially those of the Midde Ages. He sees the Christian significance of all this—even of the French Revolution, which illustrates the folly of human self-dependence. Now Christ is always with him. But he must still wander; his redemption is not yet.

In the case of Albert Londres's *Le juif errant est arrivé* (Paris, 1930), we are dealing with a novel-like work, which appears superficially as a form of the Chronicle, but whose main purpose is to awaken interest in the Zionist movement. It regales the reader with lurid descriptions of ghettos and pogroms, especially Central European ones. The Wandering Jew has sojourned in many such

Jewries and now sees the Promised Land opening before him in the form of a state of Israel. Most of those whom he approaches, however, apathetically refuse to leave their miserable homes in the lands of their oppression. In spite of many vivid pages, the work as a whole is extremely flat.

In pleasing contrast, a work of smaller historical range, but superior in literary quality to any of the full-blown tellings of the Chronicle just cited, is Emil Lucka's *Heiligenrast* (1919).[10] It is a novel of the Middle Ages at the time of the Crusades. The opening section is an excellent description of a chivalric court of love in medieval France. These refined proceedings, however, are cut short by the sudden passion to win back Jerusalem from the infidels. The second part—the only one to concern us here—is the story of the conquest of Jerusalem and the founding of the kingdom of Jerusalem in 1099. A Jew crucifies his young son Joachim because he renounced Judaism in favor of Christianity. In battle the toll taken by the Saracens is frightful: most of the Crusaders are killed, but a few survive both the conflict itself and capture by pirates on their way home. They take refuge in a monastery (*Heiligenrast*), and while they are immured there the repentant and sorrowing father of Joachim appears in the aspect of Ahasuerus; but he is the Wandering Jew only in the sense that he is expiating his crime by wandering about in repentance. It is a hectic, strangely confused novel, but it contains some gripping pages, and the Chronicle portions are very well done.

In retrospect, it would seem that the best work in which the characteristics of the Chronicle are used is Ernest Temple Thurston's drama, *The Wandering Jew* (London, 1921), an eminently actable play which had something of a run in both London and New York.[11] The Prologue states the theme: "To each his destiny—to each his fate. We are all wanderers in a foreign land between the furrows and the stars." The acts, or "phases," follow a well-selected chronological plan. Phase I is the incident of the affront and the curse. The Wandering Jew is Matathias, who is jealous of the effect of Jesus upon his wife Judith (a new motive for the insult to Christ). When the affront has been offered, the curse received, and Matathias is on his way, Judith, who has long been tired of life, dies in blessedness, for she has in reality been dedicated to Christ. Phase II takes place on a battlefield near Antioch, in the time of the Crusades. The Wandering Jew is an unknown knight, who is an acknowledged champion in tournaments and a true Don Juan. He persuades his current love, Joanne de Beaudricourt, to his tent at night. But on discovering his identity, she turns away in abhorrence—the second of his loves lost because of the affront. In Phase III, in Sicily at the time of the expulsion of the Jews (1290), the protagonist, now known as Matteo Buttadeo, is a rich merchant of Palermo. He is urged to flee before the expulsion can be carried out, but his wife will not come with him, for she has secretly been converted to Christianity. All his riches are of no avail, and he suffers his third loss. Phase IV brings us to Seville during the height of the Spanish Inquisition, about the year 1560. The Wandering Jew is Matteos, a successful physician, but a freethinker and highly critical of the methods of contemporary Christians. He is deliberately betrayed to the Inquisition by a renegade Jew and innocently by a prostitute (Olalla). His willingness to forgive his betrayers, the emergence of his soul above the needs of his material life, make it possible for him to die at the stake and so to be released.

This is to say that in the first phase, Matathias is unrepentant and so loses the love of his wife; in the second, he is self-seeking, and so alienates the love of a woman who might otherwise have been his, a disaster which causes him to recognize the absence of spirituality in his being; in the third, he again loses his wife to Christ, but this time suffers deep anguish; in the fourth, he realizes his soul's potential and is redeemed through death. The play is dramatically strong and had the benefit of an excellent cast. Some years later (1934-35) a cinema version under the same title was produced in England.

In these days of the space age it is only fit and proper that the Chronicle (twentieth-century style) should be represented by a piece of pulp fiction that is nevertheless worth reading. Indeed, Nelson Bond's "The Castaway," in *Planet Stories* (New York, 1940), has not as yet been superseded.[12] The action takes place about the year 2200 in a space ship. The Wandering Jew is picked up, a castaway on an asteroid. He is known as Paul Moran, but admits later that he is really Joseph Cartaphilus. By profession a scientist, he had fled into space after having caused an employee's death by overwork. Actually he is still a desperate man who tries to wreck the space ship before it can return him to earth, where he expects to be punished. But when he is thwarted, he gloomily accepts it as the Lord's will and reveals his method for penetrating the "H-Layer" of the earth's atmosphere, the "Moran-H-Penetrant." In revealing his identity he gives a rapid but thorough account of his experiences in world history before he came to the unfortunate scientific encapsulation which the twentieth century seems to require. This is not the first journey of the Wandering Jew into space—there was the fascinating case of Israel Jobson in the eighteenth century and that of the protagonist in Schücking's tale "Die Drei Freier" in the nineteenth—but this is his first use thus far of a space ship.

This last work can be considered a telling of the Chronicle only by courtesy, for its framework is not respectful of chronology although the individual incidents in it are scattered in time through many centuries. The book is Emmet C. May's collection of tales, *White Bears and Gold* (Boston, 1931), in which the Wanderer bears the new name of Simon Malachus, "the Wandering Jew of traditional history . . . at all times a fascinating character . . . Germany calls him the Flying Dutchman [*sic*]." But Malachus is only a means to an end: the telling of miscellaneous tales, most of them pretty tall, in which he may or may not have much to do. They have much variety, however, and are of promising material; but the writing is bad and the printing worse, and the whole makes irritating reading. The attitude this Wandering Jew shows toward Christ is a common one in the twentieth century—that he turned against Jesus because he was disappointed in him. What happened on the first Good Friday is told simply and well enough.

The remaining nineteen tales in May's collection require only a thumbnail report. In China with Marco Polo in the year 1295, the Wandering Jew meets a khan who tells him of a marvelous drug which will make men wise and mature; but if they stop taking it, they will degenerate. In Brittany, in 1596, he takes advantage of the old belief that all the rocks go to the water to drink every hundred years; by watching for the right moment he is able to pick up treasure buried under the rocks. He is nearly crushed by the rocks returning from their drink but escapes on the stone statue of a horse, the Stone Horse of Plonhenik. Later, in the eighteenth century, he assists in the creation of an artificial man who functions perfectly, although he has no soul; mesmerism gives him just enough perception to obey commands. An unscrupulous assistant gets the artificial man to kill his creator, Doctor Klein, and then to destroy himself. The Wandering Jew is shaken, and no wonder. In the Middle Ages he finds a land of pigmy-like people in Africa, living in a subterranean country of peace and happiness; he describes this to Sir Walter Raleigh, who is awaiting execution in the Tower of London (the influence of H. G. Wells and perhaps Rider Haggard is manifest here). In 1511 he takes part, slapstick fashion, in the discovery of Florida by Ponce de Leon. The atrocities practiced by the Spanish Inquisition fascinate him, as do tortures in general; two of the tales are virtually essays on this unhappy topic. The same note is struck in his account of the last days of Peter and Paul during the reign of Nero.

One of the more ingenious tales—again reminiscent of H. G. Wells—describes Malachus' experimenting with radio as early as 1809, again as assistant to an erudite scientist. They recapture sound waves in space and hear again the tumultuous storming of the Bastille and, more marvelous yet, the preaching of Paul. The climax comes for the Wandering Jew when he hears his own fatal words to Christ. Subsequent probing of space brings them into contact with Mars; there is a fatal explosion from which only Simon Malachus escapes.

Most of the rest of the stories, however, are weak: of the judge who, when asked what kind of a man is most beneficial to mankind, decides in favor of him who "touches most the lives of others at needy times"; of blowpipes in Liberia; of a magic ring that burns the finger of evildoers; of the Indian rope trick. Twice, Simon confides to us, he was truly in love: the first time tragically, when his beloved is infected with vampirism after her death, and a stake must be driven through her heart; the second time happily, with Lillian Stewart, a female detective, who puts him through many jealous moments before she comes to him. It seems that Simon had always been a collector of antiques: he is the possessor of Aladdin's lamp; a magic carpet; a magic crystal, which reveals where anything is at a given moment; and an invincible sword, which can decapitate anyone against whom it has been directed. But, like all collectors, he becomes bored by overfamiliarity with even his most marvelous possession. The list is completed by stories of haunted houses, Indian fighting, and slaughtering polar bears in the Bering Straits. The last story accounts for the rather bizarre title of the collection, which is on the whole one of the shoddiest performances in our whole canon of works, although still not unreadable.

Latter-Day Ironists

Certain works, like those of Viereck and Eldredge, cannot be taken seriously, whatever their intention; and there are serious works which are nevertheless absurd. Deliberately humorous treatments of the Wandering Jew in the twentieth century, with only one or two exceptions, tend to be either light in touch or trivial in their approach. The essential irony to be squeezed out of the Legend as a whole can be illustrated in Hugo Salus' "Ahasverus," in *Das jüdische Prag* (1917).[13] Salus finds it ironical that a little shoemaker who offended a great God (who is said to forgive all) should be picked out for so dire a punishment! Salus also suggests an identification of this little shoemaker with all Jews.

Two treatments of the figure of Ahasuerus by Joseph Winckler engage us in what is virtually farce. In his *Irrgarten Gottes* (1922) the world is brought to an end through the outrageous behavior of Momus, the evil spirit of mockery who was exiled from Olympus.[14] Under these unusual circumstances Ahasuerus is allowed to come to rest, for there are now so many more unholy than he. His repose, however, is unenviable: he is homeless, without contentment, without love. The tone of the work is savage. In *Des verwegenen Chirurgus weltberühmbt Johann Andreas doctor Eisenbart . . . Tugenden und Laster* (Berlin, 1929), it is revealed that the restlessness of Ahasuerus' feet can be cured by cutting them off and throwing them into the fire.[15] But this is only a temporary respite, because the restlessness returns, forcing Ahasuerus to break off a couple of wagon beams and to use them as stilts, on which he makes off. The slapstick nature of the incident does not lessen its sadistic seasoning.

The Swiftian tone deepens and spreads most noticeably in Emil Szittya's *Klaps, oder Wie sich Ahasver als Saint Germain entpuppt* (Potsdam, 1924). The salient aspect of this pungent novel is the perverseness which permeates it. Ahasuerus stands for revolution; any revolution is a tragedy, says Szittya, in what would seem to be a classic statement of the conservatism of the true satirist. According to Szittya, Ahasuerus is a devil who first made it necessary for God to construct something new and who now always aspires himself to be the divine Father. Into a hurly-burly of fantasy, continually directed toward the destructive rather than the constructive, Ahasuerus stalks in his own person or as Paracelsus or Saint-Germain. He is an archetypal Jew, as the postwar German saw him, whose expert followers have been confusing mankind for thousands of years. Those who seek God are constantly being knocked about in infernal cruelty. This leitmotiv recurs with maddening insistence: all revolution is a breath from the Wandering Jew, whose course is bloody. This is not to deny that Ahasuerus is to others an inspiration to the finding of God, but to him the fulfillment of that inspiration is refused. Yet he goes on his way, and he has seen many a god perish by the wayside. This wayside is, of course, the path of world history, which can never be separated from a concept of God. Indeed, this Ahasuerus declares that through his wanderings he is related to God. In addition to this fundamental idea, various psychoanalytical observations are made, such as, "For Christ pain was a joy" and "Ahasuerus was suffering, and Christ was fulfillment." Moreover, Ahasuerus is here capable of a spiritual ache or hang-over (*Katzenjammer*), and wonders what is the use of always running away from himself. Nevertheless he must keep going, a contradictory Everlasting Nay, both constructive and destructive, a devil who continues to seek his divine Father. Szittya's Ahasuerus is a quester who has been perversely distorted by persecution. The important role of the Jew in the revolution in Europe after World War I and his peculiar adventures in the eighteenth century (when the charlatan Saint-Germain announced that he was the Wandering Jew) are used by the author to support the point of view that Ahasuerus is impelled as a matter of course by an urge toward abnormality.

Other ironical treatments of the Legend take the position that Ahasuerus cannot be merely perverse, but that he is representative of the polarities of life. For example, in the poem by Arnim T. Wegner, "Poeta Ahasverus," in *Die Strasse mit den tausend Zielen* (1924), it is ironically observed that he is a man of a hundred years old, wedded to a girl of seventeen.[16] Yet this absurd matrimonial packaging is only a wry example of the opposites Wegner is describing, such as light and shade, joy and sorrow, permanence and transiency. The polarities emerge again in Franz V. Werfel's amusing play, *Jacobowsky and the Colonel* (1944).[17] Jacobowsky is a Polish refugee, quite a wanderer for political reasons, but not the Wandering Jew. He is in Paris in June, 1940, having come from Russian Poland via Germany and way stations. He is a victim of ethnical as well as political persecution, always having to start life over again in some new place, always adaptable and cheerfully resourceful. Since an enormous flood of refugees is about to abandon Paris, one may presume that Jacobowsky is about to begin still another existence. He, in company with the Polish colonel (an intelligence officer seeking safety in Britain) and the colonel's inamorata, takes to the roads in a decrepit automobile. In the course of their flight they meet the real Wandering Jew. This Ahasuerus (labeled the Intellectual) is riding on a tandem bicycle with the Monk (St. Francis of Assisi), and is depicted as "a man of thirty-odd, lean, stooped, with high forehead, black curly hair, and the thick horn-rimmed glasses of an intellectual." He also is attempting an escape from the onrush of Hitler. The group meets in Bayonne, where the Intellectual is about to get away to America. He remarks that he is always trying to escape from catastrophes. When the colonel, a stiff-necked reactionary and by no means a Hebraphile, objects to the Jew's laughing with a "quivering mouth," he replies: "*You* try laughing at the same joke for two thousand years!" For that matter, why should not his mouth, or any other part of him, tremble? He has spent two years in Dachau, that pleasant Bavarian spot that was once a picnic ground. He and St. Francis, a striking polarity, get along very well, offering a prime example to Colonel Stjerbinsky and Jacobowsky, themselves polarities in character, who are always picking at each other. The play ends with the reconciliation of these two, in spite of the antipathies of the doctrinaire military and the humanistic citizen.

The gloomiest of such ironic considerations of the Legend is Rosa Mayreder's *Fabelein über göttliche und menschliche Dinge* (Leipzig-Vienna, 1921), an "Introduction" and a "Tale." The author explains that she is attempting to bring into harmony some of the contrarieties of life and to gain recognition for the relative importance of the ego in the world, as it relates to both the human and the divine; however, the seeking rather than the finding must continue forever. Her pretentious thesis is then illustrated by a well-told though gloomy *exemplum*. Unable to find their way back to their respective kingdoms, the Three Kings return to Bethlehem for directions. They meet a menacing figure, an old man with an evil look in his dark eyes. It is Ahasuerus, who breaks into scornful laughter at the fact that they, the believers, are lost and wandering about as ignorantly as the most benighted doubters. The realm of the future, he tells them, exists nowhere. Let the kings scurry around all over the world, and much good may it do them, because the world itself is wandering around without a goal. Here Ahasuerus is the image of the absolute negative, and little more than an image at that, since he is introduced into a story which takes place before the Crucifixion has set him upon his ceaseless course.

Folk-Tale Variants

Ahasuerus has continued to appear in subordinate, even trivial roles in folk tales from time to time until the present day. I have heard people from small towns in Italy and Austria and Germany remark on the periodic visits of the Wandering Jew to their communities. Now, however, no one can ever get near enough to him to lay a hand upon him. He appears and then is gone before one realizes it. This is all clearly the stuff of folk tales, but when he appears in the pages of a novel or drama, or in the lines of a poem, it is difficult to draw the distinction between legitimate folklore and mere association of Ahasuerus with some entirely different kind of narrative.

For example, there is Lion Feuchtwanger's *Jud Süss* (Munich, 1925), a lively historical novel laid in the Duchy of Württemberg in the early eighteenth century.[18] It recounts the rise and fall of Joseph Süss, a brilliant political and economic figure, an assured combination of Baron Rothschild, Father Joseph, and a grand vizier. At the summit of his power, on the death of Alexander, the sensual and tyrannical Duke, he is attacked by his enemies and imprisoned, tortured, and executed. The character who is more germane to the Legend, however, is Rabbi Gabriel, a kind of moral monitor to Joseph Süss. The alleged presence of the Wandering Jew, who is reported by hearsay in parts of Germany, gives potency, in an age of credulity and superstition, to the actions of Gabriel. Gabriel imitates the appearance and behavior of the Wandering Jew, but it is made clear that he is a cabalist and not Ahasuerus himself. In other words, the Wandering Jew is merely used as a device to give effective color to Gabriel. The report of the presence of Ahasuerus, however, is an excellent reproduction of such a folk tale as we have heard before (p. 71):

During these weeks the Wandering Jew had been seen in the Swabian districts, now in one place, now in another. In Tübingen it was reported by some that he had driven through the town in a private carriage; others would have it that they had seen him on foot on the highway, or in the stagecoach; the gatekeeper at Weinsberg told a tale of a queer stranger who gave a curious name and had an extraordinary appearance; and when he pressed him for identification papers, the uncanny visitant pierced him through and through with such a malevolent look that he was completely dazed and had to let him go, and he could still feel the effects of that diabolical look as a shooting pain in all his limbs. The rumors spread everywhere; children were warned to beware the stranger's eye; and Weil, the town where he had been last seen, gave its gatekeeper the strictest instructions.

A little later he appeared in Halle. At the town gate he declared boldly that he was Ahasuerus, the Wandering Jew. The Magistrate was sent for at once, and ordained that for the present he should be allowed into the suburbs. Anxious and curious crowds gathered. He looked like any peddling Jew, with a caftan and side-curls. He spoke freely, in a gurgling voice, often unintelligibly. Before the Crucifix he prostrated himself wailing and beating his breast. For the rest, he sold small wares, and disposed of many amulets and proved to be a swindler; brought before the Magistrate, he was flogged . . . But those who had seen him pointed out that he was certainly not the right one. . . . [For there was another claimant to the title of Wandering Jew.]

The other had had nothing remarkable in his garb; he was clad in a respectable Dutch coat like other people, a little old-fashioned in cut; he looked like a superior official or a comfortable citizen. It was only his face, and his general atmosphere, above all his eyes: in short, one felt immediately that he was the Wandering Jew. This was the story in which the most diverse people concurred, in all corners of the land.[19]

The line between the apparently authentic and the spurious, therefore, is not to be drawn with certainty. Whichever of the two one chooses, however, the fact remains that either description has its folkloristic merits.

Another contribution to the Legend by Feuchtwanger is as a whole unworthy of its author. "Wird Hill amnestiert?" in *Drei angelsächsischen Stücke* (Berlin, 1927) is a play in which a group of British businessmen and a crackpot woman sit about talking slangy German.[20] One of the men, H. B. Coogan, identified in the stage directions as the Wandering Jew, "who need not be known as such to the audience," and the ensuing events have nothing to do with the Legend. In fact, Coogan reveals himself as the Wandering Jew only by his handwriting, which appears to be ancient, and by constant amusing but irrelevant remarks about people whom he had known in previous centuries.

A rarity by the author of the old favorite, *Master Skylark*, is John Bennett's "The Death of the Wandering Jew," in *The Doctor to the Dead* (1946), a collection of folk tales and anecdotes set in Charleston, South Carolina.[21] Bennett gives first a brief sketch of the Legend, deriving it from Matthew Paris and the Ahasuerus-book. He then brings the protagonist to Charleston in 1845, and indicates that he will set down everything in true fashion, reminding us that miracles happen every day. The Wandering Jew is living in a savanna on the edge of the city, in a shed of twigs and tree trunks. He is said to have come from Russia or Poland, and is variously known as Cartaphilus, St. John, or the Wandering Jew, but he stubbornly refuses to give information about himself.

According to some, he was "an extraordinary being, formed in space, not born of woman, that comes and goes, unchangeable and undying, throughout the universe, as incomprehensible and unapproachable as are the immeasurable immensities of endless space." Characteristically, he was never seen to eat. The following picture of him combines traditional and novel details:

His grave face was worn and weary; his hair and beard were long and gray; his complexion was swarthy and beaten by wind and rain. He stooped as a wandering pedlar stoops who bears on his back a heavy pack. His feet were ordinarily bare, though at times he wore rough sandals. His toes were long and strong, like those of a great pedestrian, and the nails were thick, corrugose, and yellow as horn. His sandals, when he wore them, were of worn old rawhide, knotted across his feet with rawhide thongs. On his head at times he wore a blue skullcap, and for the more part he wore a long cloak of dark-blue coarse stuff, sunburned and rain-faded to a dull purple, and frayed into a long, irregular fringe of tatters at its edges. In his hand, wherever he went, he invariably carried a long, rough, unfinished staff; and, wherever he went, a wind went with him, tossing and tumbling his cloak about.

The wind is an interesting detail, for it will be recalled that in France he was in the howling wind and storm (p. 85 above). It is not an accident, perhaps, that this detail should appear in an area where there were many settlers of Huguenot origin:

This odd wind appeared to follow him and to enfold him like a fugitive cloud. It was not an ephemeral or casual wind, but a perpetual breeze like a breath from eternity, which, felt on one's face, brought that sense that it had followed him across the face of the earth for more than a thousand years. Of this queer wind remains still a singular remembrance. On summer mornings, just at sunrise, in Payne's Old Field, when calm rests on everything before the breeze turns landward from the sea, the trees suddenly toss their branches about and fling them to and fro; the little hard green leaves of the oak tapping together make a pattering sound like that of sandaled feet shuffling by . . . then the sound and the tossing end as suddenly as they began. This queer gust of wind, rushing down out of the blue pavilion of heaven, and as suddenly gone again, no man knows whither into the pathless air, has been for years known as "The Jew's blast."[22]

During his career in Charleston, the Wandering Jew lived, as we have seen, just outside the city limits, and after several years, it began to be noticeable that his strength was growing less. For the greater part he awoke both horror and sympathy among the common people, and he usually frightened children. Although it was an old custom to provide food and drink for the needy who appeared at one's front gate, provided they prayed or crossed themselves, the Wandering Jew never partook of this charity. He wrote warning texts from the Old Testament on the sidewalks in chalk, for which he was jeered and insulted, but he remained harmless and unharmed. Animals especially loved him. His favorite place to rest, when he could manage a moment's repose, was on the steps of St. Mary's Church; here he hoped to find the tomb of the Saviour, for wherever he roamed he thought he was in the Holy Land. In the Easter season, particularly on Good Friday, he was struck with the greatest anguish and would give money to the churches, although he never entered one, by throwing coins into the nave. On one horrifying occasion, fire broke out immediately afterward, destroying the building, while the Wandering Jew continued to pitch money calmly into the burning mass.

John Bennett's short story asserts that the Wandering Jew died during the Civil War. In the Da Costa cemetery for Jews the voice of Christ addressed him: "The Law endureth only so long as the World doth last. God's mercy endureth forever." The Wanderer confessed his life to be more difficult than death. Therefore Christ granted him the release of death in his little hut of twigs and branches. Two Jews, Solomon Scaiman and Nathan Kaune, carried the body next morning to another Jewish burial ground outside Charleston (Rykersville). There, beside the body of a girl who had committed suicide, the Wandering Jew still lies. When the cemetery was transferred to another place, no one could be found who would

venture to disturb either body. The railroad bought Rykersville. "The Lord scat-
tereth abroad the bones of them who have pleased themselves; but the bones of
those who have pleased Him shall rest forever in peace."

Bennett's style, as we can see, is poetic, and the treatment of his unusual material both graceful and moving. All things considered, it is perhaps the best account of Ahasuerus, in what we may call the folk-tale manner, to appear during
our generation combining authentic touches of the Legend and imaginative insight.

Of minor importance is a group of retellings of the Legend in simple form,
such as the Flemish *Echte wonderbare Historie van de Wandelende Jood* (Meche-
len, 1926) by A. Burssens; a Turkish version, J. Parijogi's "I gavene Juut," in
Jakusuküla poisid (1930);[23] and a French Canadian version which includes the
old Brabantine ballad, Paul A. W. Wallace's *Baptiste Larocque: Legends of French
Canada* (Toronto, 1923). The last-named also adds the hitherto unremarked detail that at the time of the Crucifixion the Jew was only twelve years old. As for
the *Schlesische Sagen* (1912) by Richard Kühnau, it is useful only because it includes some variants of the tale already told (p. 71).[24]

Ahasuerus in Passivity

Bennett's Wandering Jew was on the whole passive; although rejected by society
he was not inclined to fight back or even to thrust himself forward. This is his
character in several other contemporary works. Hermann von Gilm's "Ahasver,"
in his collected *Gedichte* (1894), presents the Jew as tired but apathetic in his
realization that rejection is his due in the world.[25] Equally tired, and bored as well,
he appears in the poem by Olaf Gynt, "Ahasuerus."[26] At other times he may accept his rejection as God's plan. In Leo Sternberg's poem, "Der Wanderer" (1921),
he is satisfied to be an averter of sin. A pair of postwar lovers desire suicide, but
he intervenes, counseling the lovers to go on living, lest they "disturb the
world."[27] He is satisfied to accept his curse as a favor, because through it he will
eventually come to know God and to spread his message. Still in passive mood,
though jovial at moments, he is used by Georg Asmussen, in "Der ewige Jude,"
from *Der Kranz* for 1920, to set up a comparison between himself and a tramp
who loves the freedom of the great outdoors.[28] In a curious piece of sheet music,
a "heroic ballad," called "The Wandering Jew" (New York, 1924) by P. M.
Raskin, he rouses himself enough to fight his way out of passivity, and, as a son
of martyrs, to defy the rack and the stake. This piece is pure balderdash from
both the literary and the musical point of view.

Such a passive Ahasuerus cannot be wholly effective, since he becomes only
a creature of two dimensions. It is more common to find in him the many polarities of life—light against shade, or joy against sorrow, or victory against defeat.
Two more works of considerable strength, one Dutch and another German, are
based upon this theme of contrasts. Jef Claes's allegory, *De geestelijke Bruiloft*
("The Spiritual Wedding"; 1929), introduces Saartje, the daughter of an antiquarian, Samuel Jonathan.[29] She is seeking truth hopefully although she finds
falsehood everywhere. She runs away to follow the "little bird of Truth" and
encounters the Wandering Jew, who is described as having great fascinating eyes,

a sharp hawk-nose, and a long white beard. Saartje enters into a spiritual marriage with him. He is strengthened by her love, and she by his wisdom. World War I ends their search for truth and happiness in domestic life. They go to a fabulous country, Astraland, where art and science comprise a twofold metropolis; but that too passes away. Finally they come to a new fatherland, where complete poverty prevails. Here Ahasuerus becomes minister of air transport and Saartje minister of women. The usual relative importance of husband and wife is soon reversed: Saartje advances to be a leader of the people, and Ahasuerus can do nothing to counter her enthusiastic rectitude. Under her guidance, Communism is triumphant. Furious quarrels break out between the two, until at last Ahasuerus chooses the better part of valor and takes to his heels. Doubt assails Saartje, but she overcomes it, allowing hope to enter her heart once more. Wisdom directs her toward the teachings of Christ, which go against the Communist grain. She is arrested as a traitor and sentenced to be shot, but the bullets have no effect upon her. She awakens in a hospital after a mental collapse and becomes finally convinced that "the purification of Man must be sought in self-sacrifice, in doing good." She allows herself to be baptized; Ahasuerus comes to jeer, but she remains steadfast to her newly found conviction.

In this work, Ahasuerus is the self-deceiver. He fails to overcome his skepticism toward Christianity, despite the fact that he has traveled all the paths of pleasure and sorrow, pain and joy, and has still found no rest. Obviously Saartje has found a better life. Ahasuerus appears externally much as he did in the Ahasuerus-book, save for the later mesmeric eye and a unique detail which Claes has furnished: he has spots on his back arranged in the form of a cross. The work is an interesting experiment at a time when straightforward allegory is uncommon, but it is wordy and a trifle precious. Ahasuerus is a technical means to an end—the assertion of the superiority of Christian peace over non-Christian restlessness.

Heinrich Nelson's *Ahasvers Wanderung und Wandlung,* written before World War I but not published until 1922, still serves as an index to *Kultur,* although its point of view must have seemed somewhat dated even by the time of its printing.[30] It is an arresting novel, however, and is in all respects an excellent summation of Ahasuerus the Rejected. At the beginning, the protagonist expounds the *Judenfrage* which has plagued Germany for centuries but particularly during the preceding hundred years. He speaks to an enthusiastic Zionist, asserting that Jewish teachings, like those of all religions, have become ossified, because life transcends all such intellectual forms. Himself a thoroughbred Jew who speaks Hebrew fluently, he understands that his curse had for its primary purpose not revenge but rather the redemption of all mankind. He is at the moment clothed in a dark impulse: "My destiny has become my profession, and my profession is to fulfill my destiny." He would become acquainted with a famous metropolis, and so visits the salon of a celebrated poet. We have here a parallel to the satire of Hauff's of more than a century before. The Jew's practical urge to live, however, renders him unsympathetic to esthetics and the progress of mankind; indeed, it makes him downright selfish and little else. He recounts to the Zionist his life history, telling how he lived through the assassination of Julius Caesar and the religious wars in Judea. He considers the Saviour a harmless visionary, whose martyrdom brought tears to his eyes. Having expected the people of Jerusalem to reject Christ the martyr, he had fled the heartless city.

To Nelson *der ewige Jude* is more an eternal man than an eternal Jew, let alone a wandering one. His Ahasuerus has not been cursed by God. Once more we find this rather necessary detail of the original Legend either omitted or allowed to remain only implicit in the writings of the present generation. In this work the omission explains both the practical, unspiritual way in which Ahasuerus accepts his fate and the fact that he does not wander much. He soon realizes that the man who died on the Cross has become deified. In Athens he meets Paul the preacher and decides that the God Paul speaks of was only an artful carpenter. Hearing that he does not accept Christ's divinity, Paul's followers drive him away. He runs into a temple to escape their intolerance. As an object of Christian bigotry he becomes, as the Wandering Jew often is, a true son of earth. After adventures in Rome and Ravenna he meets St. Boniface in the Alps—a hitherto undisclosed incident. Eternal unrest is prophesied for him, unless he can believe in Christ. But Christ remains in his eyes a gifted man, no more. So convinced, he tells Mohammed his adventures, and from these revelations is born Islam.

Ahasuerus sees that legends and myths rule the world everywhere. Has he himself not become the chief figure in a saga? The gifts by which he is able to do good make him appear as a magician. He rejoices in the Renaissance and has hopes for young America. In the French Revolution he is taken to be Voltaire redivivus. He makes a pilgrimage to Weimar, where Goethe discusses with him the spirit of the times and the advantages of endless experimentation. The poet believes that the time is ripe for the Last Judgment and is awaiting the second Crucifixion. On leaving, Ahasuerus hears Goethe express regret that they had not known each other sooner, before Goethe had written about him.

This may sound like another telling of the Chronicle, and of course the features of the Chronicle are an integral part of the work, but Nelson stresses so consistently the conflict between the would-be skeptic and the would-be believer that it is unlike any other form of the Chronicle. This polarity becomes most evident in the latter part of the book. Among some of the other adventures of Ahasuerus is a visit to the pope, who receives him as a visible wonder, but Ahasuerus expresses a desire never to see the Holy See again. He indulges in an unhappy love affair, as might be expected. Further studies in German universities do not encourage his faith in the ideals of German culture. Neither from the petrified Church nor from the one-sided social democracy of the age can he derive any satisfaction. He prefers therefore to build on the past, with a liberal outlook to guide him. He discusses possible new civilizations based upon harmonious human relationships and founds an extensive organization to bring them about. Church and state alike, however, band together against his radical plans. The pope pronounces him to be Antichrist. An attempt to establish himself as a teacher in Berlin fails, since his efforts are considered immoral to society and hostile to the state. His old doctor's diplomas from the University of Bologna in 1215 and from the University of Königsberg, where he studied under Kant, are no longer adequate, being utterly unsuited to modern times. Only a single professor stands up for him, likening his fate to that of Socrates. Rejected by the country of his choice, he accepts a professorship in China, but even there he doubts that he will ever reach his goal. The There never becomes the Here!

Ahasuerus Identified Anew with Humanity

Yet, on the other hand, if Ahasuerus is not to be rejected, then he must somehow be accepted, which means that he will become a part of society and symbolic of mankind in general. There are plateaus in this kind of progress, however. Sooner or later, as we have seen time and again, any treatment of Ahasuerus which considers his human plight will bring him some part of the way from complete rejection to complete identification with mankind. Not unexpectedly, then, the significant works dealing with him during the generation after World War I achieve some degree of identification. There is, however, no formula, for Ahasuerus can mean various things to various people.

For example, let us consider the tale by Rudolf Kassner, "Der ewige Jude," first printed in *Die Mythen der Seele* (1927) and again in *Der grösste Mensch* (1946).[31] Here the Jew Kirsch, a furrier, symbolizes the average man doing faithfully what it is his lot to do. He walks with energy and purpose (*mit Eifer und Willen*); his gait is his most noticeable attribute—no stick, no staff, only resolution. He attracts attention when he starts off in the morning, but none at all when he returns at night, weary from the day's work. It is a moving little tale of the progress from *Hoffnung* to *Hoffnungslosigkeit*—from hope to hopelessness, as youthful aspiration becomes mature exhaustion.

But nowhere is the sense of identification any stronger than in Edmond Fleg's *Jésus* (Paris, 1933).[32] This is essentially a biography of Christ told by the Wandering Jew, who in this case is the paralytic cured by Jesus according to Mark 2:1-12. In gratitude he becomes a follower and records the main events of the life of Christ and his words. In recording events, however, the Wandering Jew seems to represent the contrasting attitudes and opinions of the whole population of Palestine and the adjacent lands. The whole story is told in a dialogue between the author himself and the Wandering Jew, whom he has met in Jerusalem, on the supposed site of Gethsemane. Ahasuerus is both cicerone and historian.

The conversations among the disciples, particularly between the Wandering Jew and Judas, and the discussions among the Pharisees, the Sadducees, the Essenes, and others who would believe in Christ as the Messiah because they are oppressed by the Roman occupation of Judea are notable illustrations of the various attitudes recorded by the Wandering Jew. The two cousins of Ahasuerus, Baruch and Reuben, are prone to follow Jesus: the first becomes a Zealot, a man of action in favor of the overthrow of Roman rule and the violent accession of a Jewish ruler in Israel; the second becomes an Essene, an ascetic and withal Puritan who would live in the spirit rather than the flesh.

The career of the Saviour is outlined through a clever assembling of the sayings of Jesus by Fleg himself, in an order which does not correspond to the order in the Gospels. Indeed, the Wandering Jew insists that the evangelical order has been "doctored." Within these limitations, it is a powerful biography, although it is marred by annoying little stylistic tricks and particularly by some adventitious although eloquent statements of the position of the Jew in the modern world and descriptions of anti-Semitic movements from the time of Christ to czarist pogroms and Hitler's crusades.

At the same time, Fleg achieves an important biography of Ahasuerus during those crucial years before Calvary. In consequence, the book must be regarded as one of the important works since World War I to treat the figure of the Wandering Jew. Perhaps it does not yield any notably new fruit, yet it has many special points of interest. Thus, at the beginning, when Ahasuerus is showing the author around Jerusalem, and they come to the Martyrium, Fleg notes:

I saw his robe brush against the column in the wall that separated us from the Martyrium as he hastened in pursuit of his shadow, that fled before him across the square. As if they had been moved by an invisible spring, his legs mechanically carried him three times around the white dome beneath which the wood of the Cross is buried. Then, as if he had utterly forgotten me, or as if I had never existed, he strode past me with unseeing eyes, and hurried with frantic steps down the path by which we had ascended.[33]

Such a detail is new, but the inevitable amount of Chronicle material, which Fleg fortunately keeps to a minimum, is not. Another valuable detail is the author's insistence upon the Jewishness of Christ: "He was Jewish, sir, Jewish from head to foot, and if he could bless like our prophets, he could curse even as they."

This is not to say that one should do away with all of the occasional digressions or apparent irrelevancies in the biography. Some of the more trenchant of these are, in fact, very pertinent. Caiaphas says to the assembly: "If we let this Galilean alone, all men will believe in Him. The Romans will come with their armies, and destroy the Temple! Is it not more expedient for us that one man should die for the people rather than that the whole nation should perish?" Following this, Pilate turns Christ over to the soldiers, with a brutal, "Sell your garments and buy swords!" Ahasuerus thereupon meditates:

I remember those words today—today! I cannot fail to remember them now that Hitler, the Messiah of brute beasts, has restored the wheel and the branding-iron, torture by water, and the garotte! I cannot fail to remember them now that he has followed up the pogrom with a bloodless pogrom that starves us to death, body and brain![34]

He pointedly illustrates his thoughts with an anecdote about a stone statue of Christ on the Austro-Italian front in World War I, which was gradually shattered by artillery wielded by Christians.

Christ's harangues against the scribes and Pharisees in Jerusalem are likened to addresses before the League of Nations:

. . . all the seats are filled by the great ones of the earth. The representatives of every nation crowd into the semicircle of space by the receivers, through which they get translations of all the different languages of all the different speeches. The French delegate has proved that one army will be sufficient to make peace; the German delegate requires at least ten, provided they are German armies. The Soviet delegate has declared that a gun is a gun only when it is used against the proletariat; the English delegate that a shell kills only when it kills on land, for it never kills when it kills at sea. America has claimed: "No one will ever disarm the nations except by selling them an army." Italy: "We only prepare for war because of its beauty—we would never really make war, even if it were necessary." Last comes Japan: "War is only war when you call it war; you can do exactly the same thing if you call it peace." [Truly we are in modern times! At this stage of the biography, Ahasuerus is eloquent:] One nation shouts to the other: "You disarm first!" and the other shouts back: "After you!" But I, for my part, I exhort you: Jews, wherever you are, take the lead! The others will follow you! Urge disarmament wherever you are, as patriots in each country, as patriots of the world! Mankind will not secure peace unless it is ready to die for it! Be foremost in this, O Jews! for you will be working for the Kingdom! In saving your countries you will save the world![35]

So far as can be determined, this is the first time Ahasuerus has pleaded for disarmament—and before World War II at that, but of course he can always be a prophet when the vatic mood assails him.

Fleg has followed the nineteenth-century motif of the betrayal of Christ by Judas, who, at first an enthusiastic disciple, becomes disappointed at the lack of positive results from Christ's teachings and the failure of the alleged Messiah to bring the Kingdom of God to hand. Therefore he is persuaded that Christ must be handed over to the Romans and made an example of; otherwise he will be a menace to Israel. In short, Judas' motives are mainly patriotic, although he is painfully jealous of James and John, who, with Peter, are closer to Christ. And Christ not only knows of the betrayal ahead of time but also desires it, in order that his sacrifice may bring redemption to mankind. When the betrayal takes place, Ahasuerus, who has been the constant friend of Judas and is aware of what is happening, does nothing to prevent it, because he too wants mankind to be redeemed. But he acknowledges that he is guilty because he did nothing and because, when Christ was apprehended in the Garden, he was the young man who, seized by a Roman soldier, fled naked, leaving his cloak behind (Mark 14:51-52).

There is here a closer connection than usual between the Wandering Jew's immediate circle and the spectacle of sacrifice. For example, the relationship of his cousins Baruch and Reuben has been noted, but not the fact that they are part of the sad procession in the *Via Crucis*. They are the thieves crucified along with Jesus, Baruch the impenitent Zealot and Reuben the penitent Essene. When Christ begs for help in carrying the Cross, the fiancée of Ahasuerus, Dina, becomes the legendary Veronica and wipes the face of the Saviour with her handkerchief. This embroilment of his family is too much for Ahasuerus: he is only human, and so his rejection of Jesus on his doorstep is a natural gesture of desperate defiance. He hears Christ curse him, though none of those around him does. Beyond the few pages which recite the Chronicle there is little which tells his sufferings in detail, and, like the bumbling apostles—none of whom shows up well in the crisis—he benefits in part from the gifts of Christ:

Like them, I received the miracle of tongues! And like them, from that day forth, I have spoken in every tongue. I walk through the centuries, and I walk amongst the peoples, and in all the languages to all the peoples, during every century, I know what

Jesus would have said—the Jesus whom I myself saw and heard! And this Jesus, my Jesus, what would he have said today?[36]

The book ends with a plea for missionary zeal to save the world through disarmament. "But the world is not yet ready! Let it be ready . . . Blessed are those who die for peace, for they shall see God!" He pronounces a new Beatitude, just four years before Germany invades Poland.

By having Ahasuerus participate in the life of Christ (not just the Crucifixion), by making him the paralytic who was cured and the young man who fled from the Romans, Fleg has added greatly to both the vividness and the vitality of the Legend in its literary treatment. By filling in the antecedent spaces with material of his own invention, he has increased the dramatic tension among the disciples, has made the figure of Christ more real, and has offered logical explanations of the motives of both Judas and himself. While the literary accomplishments of the book are not the most commanding in the world, they at least make for drama, and the work as a whole is thought-provoking and mobile.

More obvious in its melodrama and far too traditional is a play by Hans W. Stein, *Ahasver: Eine Tragödie* (Halle, 1921). The play begins on Crucifixion Day, focusing its attention upon the relationship of Ahasuerus to the religio-political events going on about him. Here, however, he is the shoemaker squabbling with a Pharisee whose shoes are not ready on time. In a verbose soliloquy, Ahasuerus explains that he is fed up with shoemaking, restless with undefined desires, and perturbed at the thought of the coming execution of this strange prophet. It is not just, it should not be visited upon such a man. Ahasuerus is, in effect, already wandering, at least in spirit, and he is sensitive to the morbidity of the occasion. When another customer, a Sadducee, breathes his hatred of Christ, Ahasuerus goes into a panic. A woman of the neighborhood encourages him in his feeling of sympathy, and when Christ with the Cross falls before the Jew's house, it takes the combined proddings of the Pharisee and the Sadducee to get Ahasuerus to order Christ on his way. Yet this is an effective scene, and Christ's curse is unusual in its expression. He reminds Ahasuerus that He too is weak, and yet in spite of that He must curse him. "Ich bin der Mensch. Sollst ewig Menschen suchen." In short, Ahasuerus must spend his eternity seeking mankind, to which he does not now belong, and in seeking he must be always among men. Ahasuerus is almost immediately repentant, but it is too late. He prays for the Angel of Death, who appears and disobligingly rejects him. But Ahasuerus is learning fast. When Judas enters, in a state of hysterical remorse, he is rebuffed by all present except Ahasuerus, who recognizes and accepts him as an errant human being. This is the first step in his salvation.

In the second act, however, Ahasuerus has thus far found humanity to be a disappointment. He is in an idyllic Rome during the Empire on a coronation day, and he is lovingly received by young people. The villain of the drama emerges, a sardonic astrologer, who is the Sadducee of the first act. Astrolog's mission is to debase Ahasuerus. As part of this effort Astrolog tries to foment an insurrection of slaves and gladiators. The coronation ceremonies begin, with Astrolog, now playing the part of a soothsayer, entering and uttering dubieties: this stranger, this eternal Wandering Jew, must be bringing *Unheil*, for he has been observed before doing just that. A sibyl supports Astrolog's misgivings, saying that Ahasuerus can be recognized by a gray mark on his brow and that the people should flee from him. Ahasuerus appears and is confronted by Astro- log, but the suspicious emperor does not cordially receive the Sadducee, and when Ahasuerus defies Astrolog, the emperor makes the Jew an imperial coun- selor. Ahasuerus' first act as counselor is to suggest the remission of punishment for a particular recalcitrant slave.

A statue of Galatea is brought as a coronation present, but the new empress is dissatisfied with the sculpture. The approach of an unruly mob distracts all save Ahasuerus, who, in the confusion, apostrophizes Galatea and brings her to life. But she cannot love her Pygmalion. She tells him she is a statue, not a hu- man being, a taker and not a giver. Again the scene shifts to Astrolog and the rebellious slaves. While the insurrection mounts, Ahasuerus, in a monologue of 125 lines, announces his complete disappointment with love and with women, only through whom, seemingly, can he identify himself with humanity. When the rebellion finally breaks out, the emperor suspects Ahasuerus of causing it and tries to kill him, but his sword breaks on his intended victim's body. There is a general massacre, at the end of which Galatea, who has been announced as preg- nant by Ahasuerus, is smashed to pieces—she was truly only a statue.

The final act takes place in a Buddhist temple. The Sadducee, in the voice of Buddha, proclaims the vanity of human wishes. When a young woman is con- demned to suttee, Ahasuerus intervenes. He has now achieved a sympathetic feeling toward the human race which he intends to put into action, according to the laws of human rights. He rescues the woman, who is content to stay with him for the rest of her life. The statue of Buddha collapses. In spite of gloomy warnings from the Sadducee, love has conquered all.

Such a mere outline of this play shows its dramatic defects but fails to do jus- tice to its occasional flashes of poetic artfulness, as well as its humanitarian essence, which is presented with the greatest sincerity. The work as a whole, however, is old-fashioned, and in spite of its favorable reception in Germany, cannot compare in importance to the Legend with either Fleg's book or the work to appear next in the procession. S. R. Lysaght's *The Immortal Jew: A Drama* (London, 1931) is a distinctive poetic drama, most significant to the Legend. It deals with three generations of the Wandering Jew, beginning on Christmas Day in 1820, in the village of Rosenberg in Bohemia. In the opening scene, Am- brose, an artist, reveals his story to a priest, Father Marck. In his youth Ambrose had been betrayed by his wife and his good friend. He dismissed the wife and refused to let her see their child. She died soon thereafter. Eventually the lover lay on his deathbed and sent for Ambrose to ask forgiveness. But in his resent- ment Ambrose denounced him instead of forgiving him and prayed that the lover's punishment might be that of Judas. "The forgiveness you deny to me will be denied to you in your hour of judgment." Ambrose remembers with dis- may that in an earlier life he too had committed the same sin he is now refus- ing to forgive and as punishment has had to wander on earth, driven along by the memory of his previous incarnations.

In further conversation Ambrose reveals the Legend of the Wandering Jew as

Lysaght has interpreted it. The Wandering Jew does not live one unbroken life, but rather is born and dies, only to be reborn as his own son, grandson, or another of his race. There is no spontaneous rebirth, as in older versions of the Legend. He passes his days like other men until, at some critical moment of his life, after he has been given a choice between right and wrong and the desires of the self have prevailed, he awakens. He then remembers all his previous lives, which begin with the original ancestor—not Ahasuerus, but Judas Iscariot. Regardless of his age, he immediately grows old, burdened and bowed down by memories of the past. He becomes unable to bear his condition or to remain at home, and so wanders on earth for the time remaining until his next death. He says that all men are reborn, but only he can remember his former lives: it is his punishment to live eternally with his eternal self. The sins of the fathers of others are visited upon the children for three or four generations (although they are never known to the children) and may then be erased. Ambrose, however, must carry the sins of his former self forever.

In the second act it is twenty years later and the child, also called Ambrose, a brilliant young man, is haunted by the feeling that he has lived before. He is about to go away for a while, but it is clear that he will commit the same sins as his ancestors. He becomes the leader of a revolutionary movement. He has seduced Father Marck's niece Mila before her marriage to Karl, his best friend, and on his return from wandering for some years he is prepared to resume the relationship. The lovers elope, Ambrose having first betrayed the revolutionary movement to the authorities. At this point he is assailed by visions of himself as he lived in the fourteenth century. The Wandering Jew that he sees in these visions warns him that he must live until he finds the love that is not now in human hearts, and until he can sacrifice himself to save another.

Ambrose pursues these visions into a forest, where he is rescued by some peasants who consider him mad. After recuperating among them, he returns to Mila and tells her that he must leave her at once and forever. Overcome with the realization that she has forsaken God for Ambrose, she kills herself in his presence.

In the third act Ambrose's grandson Stefan, a poet and playwright of the year 1916, is represented as a man of great reputation, but like his ancestors of no faith, except in strength—a kind of Nietzschean incarnation. Like Lysaght's other Wandering Jews, he is not able to believe in God's love. He falls in love with Aneska, but does not speak because he realizes that she is still bound in the memory of her lost and supposedly dead lover, John Kollar. Kollar has in reality been exiled to Siberia, where he is working as a physician under grimly depressing circumstances. He is a foil to Stefan in that he believes in the heroism of man. To Kollar God is not one who sits securely above the miserable folly of his creatures but is a power in perpetual warfare against evil. Stefan and Aneska remain companionable for a while. Stefan does not yet reveal his love. She begins to alter his outlook on life, so that he tries, although unsuccessfully, to rewrite a happy ending to one of his gloomy plays. Inevitably he proposes marriage, and she accepts him. But a month before the wedding, he hears from Kollar. This is his moment of truth, and he resolves to have Aneska, defying reality in the name of love. They are married, but before consummation, Stefan, like his grandfather, is visited with visions of his past and taken away from Aneska, as Ambrose was alienated from Mila. He realizes that if he kills himself he will only be reborn; he has "forged his own chains." He is unable to accept his situation and decides to return to Aneska. But, when he remembers how Mila killed herself, he cannot face his wife.

Meanwhile, he has published anonymously the play with the happy ending that he had written for Aneska. Aneska is in the audience when it is produced. Instinctively she believes that Stefan must be still alive, and so she refuses to consider John Kollar, for she is deeply impressed by the great need she feels Stefan must have for her. In the hospital where Stefan is recovering from his visions, he performs a courageous rescue during a fire. His visions become less terrifying, and he persuades himself to return to Aneska. She accepts him as her husband, but when he realizes that the visions may return and trouble them both, he decides to make the sacrifice of their love and leave her once more. This is his essential step toward redemption.

He goes back to the church in Rosenberg on Christmas Day, praying that he may be relieved of memories of his past lives. A voice answers that what he is praying for is utter finality, beyond the imagination of any human being. He could better spend his life attempting to cure the evils of the world. Through rebirth he could prove himself worthy of the trust of others; he could also prove to Aneska that the Stefan she welcomed back was the great man she believed in, and not the scoundrel he had claimed to be. With this admonition, Stefan accepts life. The play ends with his catching a glimpse of Aneska from a concealed position in the church.

Lysaght's originality should be clear. There is no continuous life for the Wandering Jew, but a series of incarnations. Each generation is possessed of an Ahasuerus, who symbolizes any man, and the conflicts he must face represent those which all men must face during their lifetimes. Recurring trials relieved by periods of rest are man's lot. The interpretation of the Legend is presented in a lean, trenchant style in which the poetic element, often quite strong, is achieved more by indirection than by explicit statement. It is unquestionably a major contribution.

But many will consider the Roman Catholic Kees Meekel's excellent trilogy, *Ahasverus: Een Trilogie* (Amsterdam, 1923), as the true masterpiece of the generation. The work is far more moralistic than Lysaght's; indeed, it may seem rather oppressive to some, although some of this quality, which is undeniable, may be explained by the fact that the last member of the trilogy is rather unduly influenced by the harsh strictures on the Wandering Jew made by Oosterlee. Even so, this is certainly the most important contribution to the Legend from the Low Countries, following that of Vermeylen. Here, as with Fleg and Asch, there is an initial orientation toward the Legend of Judas. This Judas is spiritually *en rapport* with Ahasuerus. Both demand and expect from the Saviour the achievements of a successful earthly king. When they are disillusioned, it is Ahasuerus who takes the initiative in weakening the faith of Judas—to whose interest is not clear, though the results indicate that no one profited.

The first part of the trilogy, *Ahasverus in Jeruzalem*, is broken into three parts. The first is enacted in a room in the dwelling of the Jew. Unlike the situation in Stein's play, Ahasuerus is indeed a Pharisee, who condemns all that Christ has accomplished as "devil's work." His wife Rebecca is distressed, for her son Absalom has taken his crippled sister Naomi to Jesus to be healed. Ahasuerus enters, denouncing Christ as a troublemaker who cannot possibly be the Messiah. "Out of Nazareth? . . . A server from that village? . . . the Messiah?" All that Jesus has done is quackery, he confides to his friend Annas. When Absalom rushes in with his sister miraculously healed, however, a woman neighbor named Rachel is immediately converted.

Still Ahasuerus tries to wave it aside as a fearful delusion. Doubts nevertheless arise in him: "My powers of thought are slack! That is strange . . ." He suggests to Naomi that she has not really been cured. When the group is joined by Judas and Joseph of Arimathea, Ahasuerus exerts himself to show that Naomi's cure and other events have not come to pass through the influence of Christ. But he admits to himself that he is confused about Christ's identity:

> Thus says Ahasuerus to you, after much thought,
> That this death will none the less be useful,
> Though He may have said He was the Son of God.[37]

In a mood of hectic perturbation, they go to witness the death of the Saviour.

The second part takes place in a street or square in front of the flat-roofed house of Ahasuerus. The procession to the Cross draws near. Ahasuerus has arranged for an unruly mob to escort Christ on his way. At the traditional time, he spurns Christ. His daughter Naomi is a witness, however, and cries out: "O man, man, He is wholly innocent," running to the fallen Saviour to help him. But Ahasuerus comes up and gratuitously punches Christ in the loins: "Come, do a miracle, let the wood of the Cross bloom like Aaron's rod." "The slave of the Cross is saying something to him," observes a bystander.

From this point on there is no repose for Ahasuerus. The uproar of the ignorant crowd and the hardness Ahasuerus shows toward his wife Rebecca, who complains that Naomi may die of her affliction, serve to mask the doubt in the Jew's soul, which is to rob him of his possessions. Annas asks: "Has anything happened?" Ahasuerus can only answer evasively: "If only He would die! What would happen?" And again: "O Annas, if only His spirit might die! . . . His teaching! . . . His soul itself!" But the spirit of the Saviour has already entered the children Absalom and Naomi, and the unrest of the scene has cut into Judas' being.

The third section of the first part is played on the roof of the Jew's dwelling. Ahasuerus speaks now in wry tones, betraying the tumult of his spirit. Absalom has seen Christ resurrected. He bears witness to this against his father, even though he is cursed for it. Joseph of Arimathea has also seen Jesus. And now Ahasuerus himself comes to be convinced through the Word, although he does not wish to believe. The family cleavage is complete when Naomi curses her father because she wishes to crown Christ as the Messiah, and when his wife observes:

> We have lost Him amid insult. . .
> I feel the wounds of unrest burning within me,
> And Judas the same. Away! away!
> Death is best of all . . . [38]

At this point Annas remembers what Christ had said to Ahasuerus: "And you will walk and walk until I return." The tragedy of Ahasuerus' eternal wandering has been fixed. He attempts suicide by leaping from his own roof, but to no purpose. Gnashing his teeth, he runs out into the night.

In no other part of the entire trilogy does Ahasuerus seem so fully realized as a character as in this first part. Is it because here lies all of the true dramatic situation? Assuredly he is more the old-fashioned melodramatic stage villain than in any other work which springs to mind. Consider also, for example, the contrast between the domineering husband and the submissive wife. Ahasuerus throughout this part is earthbound: he fails to comprehend the spirituality of Christ and is filled with prejudice and warped judgment. He is more impressed by the "wisdom" of Annas than by the gift which Jesus bestowed upon Naomi—a gift which he would like to hide from his counselors. He expected the Messiah to be a strong, even military, leader; disappointed in this, he would destroy the whole image of Christ through hate. The weak spot in the whole work is that this hatred, a dominant driving force throughout, is not sufficiently motivated. For the rest, the learning Ahasuerus has derived from his books is not enough, and his doubts only increase the tensions within him. At his moment of apparent triumph he is defeated, although he cannot yield. "We have ignominiously lost."

So much for the first play of the trilogy. The second is a kind of literary montage comprising eighteen scenes in the history of the world from the death of Christ to the erection of a statue of Judas in Moscow with the advent of Stalin. In all of these eighteen scenes the Eternal Jew is in contention with the Eternal Christ. The first subpart, the enactment of the circumstances attending the Curse, is in effect a prologue. In the second subpart, the sense of the tragic is heightened ironically, because in his grim fight against the spirit of Christ Ahasuerus is unconsciously and repeatedly bearing witness to Christ. Bound in alliance with Satan, he would corrupt the world, but at times Ahasuerus is in doubt about the conquest. Thus one is slowly prepared for the third section of the trilogy, in which, after much fruitless strife, Ahasuerus throws himself down at the feet of Christ. The third play proceeds in seven scenes from our present time to the Last Judgment. Already unstable in much of the second play in his hatred of Jesus, Ahasuerus is led by the grace of God to conversion, repentance, and contrition.

It must be observed, moreover, that in the second play Ahasuerus, in league as he is with Satan, is struggling against the Church as well as against Christ. He becomes, therefore, the symbol of a man who will not bind himself permanently to anyone or anything. He represents also the obstinate sinner, while Satan and the Guardian Angel struggle over him as in a morality play. Normal earthly connections, such as a wife and family, disappear while the generalized figure of the Wanderer remains. All attempts to contravene God through imposing historical figures, such as Julian the Apostate or Attila, fail out of hand.

The eighteen scenes of the second play can be grouped into five types: the first three scenes take place in the mountains of Judea, in the Colosseum, and in Jerusalem at the time of Julian, respectively. In these the transition of Ahasuerus the man to Ahasuerus the Wanderer, unwilling to bow, is portrayed. Since he cannot die—from a lightning bolt, from the sword of a centurion, or from a fire in the foundations of the Temple—he remains an unwilling witness to God's power, identified though he may be with hate. The next three move him from a helper in hate to a reservoir of hate, threatening the Church. Scene iv places him in Attila's camp before Rome, where he incites the Hun to pillage and slaughter; scene v sets him down in Paris at the time of the *rois fainéants,* of whom he observes that "the heathen are preferable." In scene vi he tries in vain to prevent the conversion of a pagan at Charlemagne's court on Easter Day. In the next three scenes the intensity of hate, pestilence, starvation, and torture, none of which touch Ahasuerus, reaches a climax. He feels only intense frustration, as for instance, when his reincarnated son Absalom goes on a Crusade. Satan has his best opportunity here, yet he fails.

We may combine the remaining scenes into two masses. Scenes x-xiv deal with the concepts of liberty which are emerging; the proclaiming of freedom in the Middle Ages, the spirit of Protestantism, the French Revolution, the independence of the American cowboy. Ahasuerus prospers; one scene places him in the desk chair in the private office of a wealthy Jewish banker. Yet other Jews refuse to accept him because of his lack of service to Jehovah. The scorn shown him by his own people is one of his great vexations, together with an awareness that his warfare against Christ is useless. Gradually the germ of repentance grows within him as he sees how mankind revels in the materialistic. Not Ahasuerus but Nietzsche has won a victory. The final four scenes are meant to be an approach to the third play and a general picture of the moral disorganization of the times. In a madhouse Ahasuerus drinks poison in vain, while he hears the voice of the positivist spirit of modern science proclaiming plans for a superrace, which Ahasuerus loathes in principle. In the next scene, in Montmartre, an insipid dancing party brings him to the realization that all the revelry and debauchery of the age are merely expressions of self-infatuation. These prickings of repentance inform Satan that Ahasuerus has escaped him. He attempts to recapture the sinner with the news that a statue of Judas has been erected in godless Moscow. At first Ahasuerus rejects this as a lie. When he verifies the report in Moscow, he is disappointed. The statue speaks to him, whereupon he begs Judas to set him right, but there is no answer, for it is Satan talking, and Satan has no answer. All is confusion to Ahasuerus; this is the very acme of his disillusionment, yet he sobs out his defiance, in feeble voice but strong words.

Kees Meekel perhaps reveals his Catholic bias too much, but it would be difficult to disprove his thesis that our times are out of joint as a result of the Ahasuerus-Satan axis, or its rough equivalent. To an extent Satan and Ahasuerus have succeeded in their professed design, but the Jew can still help mankind and is doing so. Two things are in his favor: the erect probity of his moral constitution, and his recognition of the fatal uselessness of the conflict, even though he still hates Christ.

The third play of the trilogy is a look into the future and a summation of the other two plays. In it, Ahasuerus, representing sinful mankind, will receive the grace of God. The good powers, personified in Ahasuerus' wife Miriam, will overbalance the counterpowers of Satan. To be sure, at the confrontation of these powers, Ahasuerus will still be on Satan's side, but Miriam will fight successfully for her husband's soul. Ahasuerus (mankind) will be brought before the judgment of Antichrist and doomed, but this doom will be negated by the blood of martyrs (including Christ) and by Miriam's sacrificing spirit, which will prepare Ahasuerus for the final ordeal of God's judgment. It is obvious that the bond between Ahasuerus and Satan was a monstrous alliance which must be dissolved.

It would be difficult to find a more effective work portraying a chronic, intense hatred than Kees Meekel's trilogy, and it is a pity that the author's viewpoint makes it necessary for him to soften this animosity at the end of the work so that Ahasuerus may receive redemption. The romantics maintained that a great hate should be as abiding as a great love. The claim has been made by some that Kees Meekel has achieved the finest treatment of the Legend in the twentieth century, though, as to that, the same claim might well be made for the poem by Edwin Arlington Robinson that stands as an epigraph to the present book.[39] Such judgments, in a bibliography as vast and varied as Ahasuerus has necessitated, are at best subjective. One must concede Kees Meekel's scope and versatility and the skill with which he has represented the slow but remorseless transition from sublime hatred to utter contrition, even if the motivation for either is not too apparent, to say nothing of its being convincing. But it must be noted that in spite of its merits Kees Meekel's work lacks some of the shading that seems called for in the portrayal of a man driven by hate but eventually defeated by love.

The fixing of the features of Ahasuerus, not so much in the mask of hate as of bitterness, is the theme of a powerful but uneven poem by Howard Nemerov, "Ahasuerus," in *Mirrors and Windows* (Chicago, 1958).[40] The author alters the Legend slightly by having Ahasuerus hoary from the outset, in contrast to Christ's youth. But, having seen all history, he has also seen the atomic age. Come Judgment Day, when Christ gives him leave to drop his mask of suffering, he will find that this mask has hardened into the features of a race, "uncertain if it cares to bear Thy grace." The rift between him and Christ becomes unbridgeable; is it possible that he would have the courage, given a second opportunity, to commit again the same offense against Christ?

Two other works, far less revealing of talent, achieve nevertheless more of the desirable chiaroscuro. Joseph P. Widney's *Ahasuerus: A Race Tragedy* (Los Angeles, 1915) also contemplates the power of hate; indeed, this is the only notable achievement of this unwieldy and mediocre poem. There is the usual story and the by now usual motive: the Saviour was not the true Messiah, and so Ahasuerus hated him. He is rejected by all; Jerusalem is destroyed; the wife and children of Ahasuerus die. To himself the Wandering Jew poses the question: Did Christ ever hate? In his wanderings he once came into the camp of Attila, a bloodthirsty misanthrope. "But He did not hate." Once he saw in a vision the outcast Ishmael, now waxed fat and prosperous, his mother Hagar avenged. "Yet He did not hate."

Christ forgave the squalor of the ghettos, he reasons, and asks himself, did we Jews behave as we should have behaved? As he stands on Christmas Eve before a church, as carols ring out, his hatred is melted, and from that point on he can only pray for forgiveness—for himself and the whole Jewish race. "Let us go back to pastoral ways, for Israel is not dead."

Siegfried von der Trenck, in his long five-part epic poem, *Don Juan-Ahasver: Eine Passion der Erde* (Gotha, 1930),[41] presents Ahasuerus as a more complicated figure than did either Kees Meekel or Widney. It is, incidentally, the first work to bring together Ahasuerus and Don Juan since Schönaich-Carolath. Here Ahasuerus is an individual virtually shredded by inner conflict, a symbol of suffering hatred, hateful suffering, and constant change, an inspiration to the songs of Luther, the monk of Wittenberg. Like Don Juan, he is always acquisitive, "he of the flattering hands," always ambivalent, yet he is a devoted adherent of the scribes and a passionate adorer of mighty Jehovah. He takes particular pride in the fact that he belongs to the chosen people, for which reason he waits impatiently for the Messiah and for the re-establishment of the kingdom of Judea and the annihilation of the Romans. More than once he shows incipient sympathy for the new prophets, provided he can see in their messages the hope of fulfillment of his earthly mission. All the more grim is his anger, therefore, when the man who has claimed to be the Messiah collapses under the Cross. His beginning love turns at once to hate.

He assumes from the curse that he, Ahasuerus, must bear on his own shoulders all earthly pain. He is a seeker of the infinite good, inwardly at war with himself. He is the flight; in someone else must be the finding. Out of this situation love must grow. Through his inner conflict he feels close to mankind; and he believes his sufferings make him worthy of redemption. This message, as such, is trite, but its presentation is novel.

In the Don Juan Legend Doña Anna has a vision in which a kind of fresco of the human spirit floats before her eyes. Although it is described verbosely, this fresco remains obscure. In it, for better or worse, the ever-longing seeker, who moves about in the darkness of thought, is embodied in the "moth of love," Don Juan. This seeking spirit, however, dwells with equal ease in the indestructible soul of Ahasuerus, who is called here Juan Espera en Dios.

Ahasuerus does not appear much until the third part of the poem, when he has an impressively described meeting with Paulus von Eitzen. The presence of the ghostlike old man who acts as if he had with him the ark of the covenant, interferes with the bishop's sermon in church, and he is so annoyed at this spectral intrusion that he thinks unchristian thoughts. But in his imagination Von Eitzen can nevertheless picture the old house of the quondam industrious shoemaker of Jerusalem and hear the cynical wisdom of the populace: to know too much is to lose respect. Back in his church he hears from this terrible old man Ahasuerus, soon to be sixteen hundred years old, how he, as a true servant of Jehovah, drove the pale man with the cross away from his threshold.

In the last two parts, in which Ahasuerus figures, Von der Trenck for the most part relates the Chronicle. The episode in 1267, referred to in the Ahasuerus-book, when the Wandering Jew was said to have passed through Forli, serves as a bridge to a critical appreciation of Dante. Both the poet of the *Divine Comedy* and Ahasuerus are wanderers hurled hither and yon in the storm of human suffering, looking upon their souls' wounds as incurable. The mournful rhythm, Alighieri-Ahasuerus, breaks upon the ear. The urge to wander leads Ahasuerus back to Germany and along the eastern frontiers of Europe, and thence all over the world again. The passionate seeker wavers between enjoyment of the body and torture of the soul, and such figures of history as Adalbert of Prague (955-997), martyred priest and knight, or the Old Man of Königsberg, the superhumanly endowed Immanuel Kant, are encountered and honored.

Ultimately, Ahasuerus appears before the Great Wall of China. Lao-tse's words concerning the *Ur-All* and the *Ur-Ich* burn themselves into his mind; he accepts them as something for him to bequeath to posterity. His testament is the reason for the title of the last part of the poem: "Ahasvers Vermächtnis." He feels the greatest experience of his wandering has been the continual recurrence of human sympathy. Thus he assumes the features of all the spiritual wanderers whom he has met:

> From the Winter of Being blooms the Passing Away,
> Back into nothing surges the sea of creation.[42]

And so Ahasuerus can give himself up at last to blessed repose. In his jaded heart Don Juan can likewise await the coming dawn of the passing away. For both, restless thoughts have led to a clarity of vision and to rest; all burdens of mankind are only the pangs of being. There is no substitute for love, which enables creation to begin anew. Out of the confusion of our times emerges a knowledge that the restlessness of the world wanderer will lead to grace.

Von der Trenck's method is altogether explicit. On the other hand, the novel of Theodor Bogaerts, *Het oog up den Heuvel* ("The Eye on the Hill"; Amsterdam, 1928),[43] while it comes out at much the same point as Von der Trenck's work, is so close to surrealism that its moral ideas are blunted. It is basically the narrative of a cultural conflict, following the thesis that our refinement has progressed so far that one day men will dream that happiness and peace can actually be achieved along the path of life. So it will be also with the ambassador Peace, who will let time stand still in order to get ahead of war. The thesis is illustrated by the alchemist Alambik, who in his laboratory tells his assistants Pirewiet, Lowicke, and Ahasuerus the story of his love for his wife Anouschka. She represents love and serenity of heart. He has never yet been able to possess her wholly, although he takes comfort in the hope that time will mean nothing and that eternity will lie before them.

Alambik and his assistants go forth to strike blind the "eye on the hill," which may be interpreted as the "world too much with us," to make use of Wordsworth's convenient phrase. Worldly life in the modern metropolis brings about the destruction of the human soul; therefore the forces ("the eye") injurious to the soul must be destroyed. The eternity of opportunity in the career of Ahasuerus is the heavy artillery trained against them. Lowicke shoots the eye to pieces with the cannon of Ahasuerus. This destruction is necessary because the spirit of man must triumph in the long run. Man can no longer recognize his own civilization. His happiness lies, rather, in religious worship.

This is the idea which stirs Ahasuerus, for he has seen many generations and civilizations come and go. Now, however, he is submerged in the mystique of Christmas. Bowing his head, he knocks on his breast in humility, as in past ages the scribes and publicans had done. This is the beginning of the redemption and the end for the Wandering Jew, now identified as "the international cosmopolitan wanderer, with a hunger for both bread and love, and particularly for the supernatural, or at least metaphysical." It was in this hunger that Alambik had already found his happiness. And here too, Ahasuerus discovered his El Dorado. "The mystery of the masses had shot a golden arrow through his heart." He goes wandering again, now no longer in a negative way but to seek the happiness "of which in that sanctuary a honey-sweet foretaste had come to lie upon his tongue." On his knees in the snow he asks a priest for a crucifix and then goes on his way.

The novel is poorly constructed, and its expressionistic devices ridiculous, but at least we have here an original approach. Ahasuerus, shaped wholly in the imagination of Bogaerts, is a major figure beside Alambik. Foolish Lowicke brings the two together. Alambik finds nothing strange about the Wanderer, in spite of his redingote the worse for the wear and the long shoes which glide along awkwardly beneath his short legs, like rusty skis. On his side, Ahasuerus is patient enough to listen to the tale of Alambik's life. He wields a sobering control over the incidents in the novel; it is appropriate for him to expound the experience of the ages although he does not seem to have gained much from the experience; he is, in fact, rather unimaginative. He finds it silly that Lowicke grows flowers, although he understands that men must collect money; he can always comprehend a gesture toward the purse. He is skeptical of love: "Fair women . . . are hatchets which chop into life." Even so, his heart warms to the story of the pure love of Anouschka and Alambik. This moves him so deeply that he is prompted to bestow a gift on a poor woman and her newborn child on Christmas Day. This is, he thinks, his first act of pure love. Soon thereafter he is drawn to the beacon of faith, the Church.

In brief, Bogaerts' Ahasuerus is a symbol of the present-day international seeking and wandering spirit, who sees illustrated in Alambik's story the paradox that when omnipotent reason or science is triumphant, the victory converts reason to love, the traditional vanquisher of reason; then mankind begins its last wanderings toward belief. There is an absence of any reference to a curse, which has become something of a normal omission in the twentieth-century versions of the Legend.[44]

It is a welcome relief to come to the two excellent performances written by Pär Lagerkvist, *Sibyllan* (1956), and *Ahasuerus död* (1960), for their distinguished author combines a direct style with a powerful concept and manages to be readable while at the same time profound to the point of mysticism.[45] *The Sibyl* assigns Ahasuerus a secondary role, one that serves as a necessary counterbalance to that of the protagonist, the former Pythia at the Temple of Delphos, who has lost her position because she had a love affair with an ordinary mortal. The Wandering Jew has come to consult the Sibyl in her squalid retirement to ask about his future, to which she can give no satisfactory answer. By way of introduction he tells his own story. It is a remarkably succinct but eloquent narrative. He explains that he could not let this unknown "god," condemned to crucifixion as a criminal, rest his head against the house, partly because it was not in his aloof, unfriendly nature to allow it on general principles, and partly because it would bring bad luck to the house. The curse laid upon him—here Lagerkvist is explicit—operates by rendering him sexually impotent and blighting the lives of his attractive wife, who dies shortly after he has begun his wanderings, and of their child, who perishes in a plague. The main interest in this extended parable, however, lies in the Sibyl. She is living beyond the pale in a miserable goatherd's hut, tending her half-witted child, the son she had borne to the god, who in this instance seems to be Dionysus rather than Apollo. At the end of the story the son ascends to his father from an adjacent mountaintop, an obvious parallel to the Ascension of Christ.

There are many salient passages in this fine work, which, although it does not appear to deviate much from the original Legend, nevertheless introduces more than one new detail. For instance the Wandering Jew does not know anything about Christ before their confrontation. Unlike the Ahasuerus of Fleg and others, he has had nothing to do with the fisherman of Galilee. "I thought: if a condemned man, a man so unhappy leans against my house, he may bring ill fortune to it. So I told him to move on, and said I didn't want him there." It was just as simple as that, but then:

> Then he turned toward me, and when I saw his face I knew that this was no ordinary man—that there must be something special about him. But what it was that made me think so I could not have said. I believe that the look on his face was not usually angry at all, but gentle and submissive. But it was not so now: it was mighty and terrible in a way that I shall never forget. "Because I may not lean my head against your house your soul shall be unblessed forever," he said . . . "Because you denied me this, you shall suffer greater punishment than mine: you shall never die. You shall wander through this world to all eternity, and find no rest."[46]

The Wandering Jew admits that he had heard rumors that the followers of Christ proclaimed him to be God's son, but these were not at all reliable people, and what they said was unworthy of attention—the typical reaction of a typical conservative, well-established, and complacent member of society. The immediate effect of the curse, aside from the sexual failure referred to above, is a wild sense of regret. In looking for perhaps the last time on his wife and child, he knew that they were beautiful and deeply loved, "yet a sort of gray ash seemed to lie upon them, as it lay upon all I saw."

In traditional wise he proceeds to wander without halting, without rest, without a place to lay his head, through a world covered with this ash layer, powerfully symbolic of this desolate life-in-death. He becomes acutely conscious of evil, lovelessness, and homelessness and is saddened by the acrid realization that he is God-accursed. Not unnaturally there is bitterness in him, and searching questions as well:

> When it happened, I was a happy man, carefree and heartless, as is natural when one has nothing in particular on one's mind. Wicked perhaps, but not more so than others. Of his doctrine of love I know little—only enough to be sure that it's not for

me. And besides, is he really so loving? To those who love him he gives peace, they say, and he takes them up with him into heaven; but they say, too, that he hurls those who don't believe in him into hell. If this is true, then he seems to be exactly like ourselves, just as good and just as bad.[47]

It is characteristic that the word for the deity is never capitalized.

The Sibyl agrees with Ahasuerus that it is dangerous to meet a god—she of all people should know—but she asks why in the world Ahasuerus showed no sympathy. He replies that it is not in his nature. Indeed, he exhibits little repentance, rather a self-pity. The whole business in which he was involved illustrates to him Christ's vengeance on human happiness and on his elect. But he is willing to accept it all, if it is his fate: "Man's destiny is but one. When it is accomplished, nothing remains." The fact must be faced that Christ is merciless and therefore cannot be good—he is unpredictable, capricious, cruel even in his love, for all the severities of nature are his doing. And the Sibyl agrees with him, for experience with divinity has been equally catastrophic for her.

In the final scene, however, Ahasuerus begins to see the difference between the Christian and the pagan ascensions:

He reflected that the son of god who was the source of his own appalling fate—who had flung the frightful curse upon him—was said to have ascended into heaven from a mountain, too, and was received by the father-god in a cloud, if one were to believe those who worshipped and loved him. But he had first been crucified, which according to them made him extraordinary and his life full of every sort of meaning and significance for every age. Whereas this son of god seemed to have been born merely to sit at the dim entrance of a ruinous goat-hut and look out over the world and the breed of men and their many inventions, and his own magnificent temple, and laugh at it all.[48]

A difference, yes, but what did it amount to? God, whatever his kind, was still cruel and deserving of an immortal hatred. The reactions of Ahasuerus impress the Sybil, yet it is she who has the last word when she observes that even in her misery and her bereavement of her idiot son, it is still her god that is in her mind —there is nothing without him, now that she is old and alone:

"You want me to look into the future," she said. "I can't do that. But I know enough of the life of mankind and can glimpse enough of the road that lies before them to know that they can never escape the curse and the blessing that comes to them from god. Whatever they may think and do, whatever they may believe or disbelieve, their destiny will always be bound up with god."[49]

To this Ahasuerus must remain silent.

The second parable written by Lagerkvist, *The Death of Ahasuerus*, the most important recent treatment of the Wandering Jew, is more cloudy in thought and ambiguous in content. In many ways it is less successful than *The Sibyl*, but it is still a striking work. Three people—Tobias, Diana, and the Wandering Jew —are in a medieval inn for pilgrims in an unnamed country. They are on their way to the Holy Land. Tobias is an unconsciously repentant sinner, once a soldier, who does not know his reason for wishing to go on this pilgrimage except that he is sure it will redeem him. Once in a plague-desolated village he had come upon the body of a woman bearing the stigmata of Jesus, and this frightening experience had converted him at least partially. Diana, his former mistress, whom he had raped and then come to love during his war experiences, has come along with him. She is now a prostitute but still, although somewhat reluctantly, devoted to Tobias. The Wandering Jew is present for no discernible reason, either at the beginning or the end of the parable. After a storm has kept them housebound for a while, most of the pilgrims go on together, but the three remain behind for a time before following. Tobias, in spite of moments of reversion to his brutal state—he kills his faithful dog in a fit of temper—is now burning with a desire to get to the Holy Land. Diana is killed by a stray arrow presumably aimed at Tobias. Who shot the arrow? The author does not say. Perhaps, like the sinister figure in Frost's "The Draft Horse," it is an agent of something or someone that wishes to frustrate human beings. But Diana at least dies happy. Tobias and the Wandering Jew reach a port, only to discover that the pilgrims have already sailed away. Tobias manages to get transportation in an evil-looking boat manned by a rascally crew. Does he ever get to his destination? We are not told, but in any event he is last heard of headed, so he thinks, toward his goal. The Wandering Jew is suddenly stricken with illness and hurried to a nearby monastery, where he dies; but before this unusual event takes place, he utters a soliloquy in defiance of God, conceding at the same time that there is something we all seek even though we cannot know what it is.

It is reasonable to suppose that Tobias and Diana represent sinful men and women who nevertheless glimpse the possibilities of redemption, but what the Wandering Jew is doing in this picture is obscure. He is obviously no ordinary mortal, and yet he is mortal. Why should he die? What are we to gather from his death? Presumably he, like the others, has been seeking something—in this case, the surcease of death—and like them he has found it, or thinks he has.

As in *The Sibyl*, the anti-Christian tone of the speeches of Ahasuerus is notable:

You think you're the only one to endure your fate, your suffering, your crucifixion. But you know very well you're not. You're only one among many, in an endless procession. All mankind is crucified, like you; man himself is crucified; you're just the one they look up to when they think of their fate and their suffering, and of how they are victims of sacrifice; you're the one whom therefore they call the Son of Man. I understand this; I've discovered it at last: man lies forsaken, on his bed of torment in a desolate world, sacrificed and forsaken, stretched out upon a little straw, marked by the same wounds as yourself. Suffering and sacrifice are spread over the whole earth and throughout all time, though only you are called the Crucified—only you among all those who have been so; when one thinks of pain and anguish and injustice one thinks of you. [And of course it is God the Father who is responsible.] He sacrifices men! He demands continual sacrifice—human sacrifice, crucifixions! That's what he's like, if you would only listen to me. I know—I who have dragged my curse with me through the ages, dragged it as you dragged your cross, only much further than you. My curse as the enemy of god, the repudiator, the blasphemer, the rebel against god. For it was he who cursed men, not you. I know that: I've come to understand that at last. You just uttered what he prompted you to say. His was the power and the vengeance. What power had you? You yourself had been handed over, sacrificed, forsaken. Now I understand, you were my brother. He who pronounced the curse on me was my own brother, himself an unhappy, accursed man.[50]

With this comprehension comes to Ahasuerus also the realization that he has in reality triumphed over the one who was responsible for his curse, if not the one who actually cursed him. "I have lifted the curse from my own shoulders. I have delivered myself from my destiny and mastered it. Not with your help or any-one else's, but by my own strength. I have saved myself. I have conquered, I have conquered god."

Somehow it is a fitting costume which Ahasuerus wears in the year 1960.

Conclusion

After Lagerkvist's Ahasuerus has made his dying speech, there is little more that can be said, and yet people continue to say it. By and large, however, it is for the reader to judge whether a given work is germane to a study of the Legend or whether it has much, little, or nothing to do with the Wandering Jew. We have already seen in many works the presence of a Jew who wanders, yet who is not really the Wandering Jew. A classic example occurs in James Joyce's novel, *Ulysses* (1922).[51] Leopold Bloom, a Jew, wanders about Dublin throughout the day of June 16, 1904. Many have said that he must be the Wandering Jew, but is he? Has he insulted Christ and been cursed? Is he wandering about because of that curse—beyond the curse, that is, of mere existence or having to earn a living? Will he continue to wander on June 17, 1904, and every day thereafter? The fallacy here is similar to that which assumes that every man—even a crimi-nal—shot down by the authorities is a Christ-image, that every man rejected, as Falstaff was, is a Christian symbol.

For that matter, others have seen in Bloom a Christ-image, rejected by his wife and pushed about by society. If he is a Christ-image he cannot be the Wandering Jew: one cannot have it both ways, a Manichean gobbet that refuses to be swal-lowed. It is true that in one of the scenes, when Bloom passes between Buck Mulligan and Stephen Dedalus, and Mulligan looks at his retreating form, he observes: "[There goes] the Wandering Jew."[52] But is Mulligan a reliable witness? Can his wisecracking humor be taken seriously? It takes more than one point in common between two stories to make them the same.

An even more dubious example is Irving Feldman's "The Wandering Jew," in *Works and Days* (1961).[53] The poet gives us to understand that he himself is a Jew who wanders much in the contemporary scene. One is reminded of Thoreau, who traveled much—in Concord. But Feldman gives us an actual sequence of five poems entitled "The Wandering Jew," which identifies the real Ahasuerus briefly (especially in the first and last of the poems) with all mankind in general and with the Jews in particular. Such an extensive reference is the last word in the application of the Legend. The second and third poems are serious enough in intent but humorous in expression and imitative in style, with more than a slight suggestion of Ogden Nash. The ultimate message for all—whether Wandering Jews or just ordinary men and women—is that if you want something you must "screech/scratch/scritch" for it. The poems contain a high percentage of brash-ness, some eloquence, and not much that has not already been said by Feldman's predecessors.

On the other hand, a precise classification of James Branch Cabell's *Domnei*

(1920) is a problem.[54] This, one of the more readable of the author's neo-medieval romances, centers upon the cult of chivalric love. It is not advisable here to wade into these amoristic matters, except to observe with Cabell that this chivalric movement was a literary cult, a malady, and a religion quite inexplicably blended. The lady is Melicent and the lover is Perion, rumored to be a shady character in danger of his life. Melicent is, according to formula, betrothed to another— King Theodoret. She nevertheless helps Perion to escape, falling in love with him in the process. Perion is captured at sea by a heathen king, Demetrios, whose previous captives have all been consigned either to death or servitude except Ahasuerus, with whom (in view of the Jew's predicament) Demetrios, as a thoroughgoing enemy of Christ, can have no quarrel. Ahasuerus reports Perion's misfortune to Melicent, whereupon she goes to the kingdom of Demetrios to ransom the man she loves. Demetrios rejects her jewels and insists on the usual payment. When she refuses, he respects Perion's prior claim and leaves her alone but keeps her in captivity. Perion escapes, returns to Theodoret; and because he is a supreme warrior, and because Theodoret needs him, he is placed in command of the army which is to rescue Melicent. There is no need to go into details at this point. Perion is victorious over Demetrios, who on his deathbed assures Melicent that his conqueror is still her true lover. Meanwhile civil strife arises when a son of Demetrios, Orestes, proves a villain. Ahasuerus, employed by Orestes, buys Melicent from the new king and plots to trap Perion, but he too is struck by the depth of the love of Melicent and Perion and by the beauty of Melicent's soul, and so he betrays Orestes to Perion. This is the chief trait of Cabell's Ahasuerus—he betrays all with whom he comes in contact; he is the incarnation of evil, yet he is willing to hand Melicent over to Perion at long last with the sardonic words: "I that am Ahasuerus win for you all which righteousness and honor could not win." The novel, with this typical boast of the 1920's, ends like any self-respecting medieval romance, with the satisfaction of the lovers. It is perhaps safest to say that Ahasuerus is here a subordinate character.

At times, however, he is not even that, and yet a work may somehow be associated with him. A striking illustration of this is Shalom Asch's long novel, *The Nazarene* (1939), which immediately invites comparison with Fleg's *Jésus*, because both are biographies of Christ.[55] Both, particularly Asch's novel, give a great deal of attention to a setting in which the rich descriptive material, which attests magnificently to the studies which the authors must have put into their works, looms much greater than the actual narrative. But Asch handicapped himself with some awkward machinery. The life of Christ is told to a present-day young Jew by an evil but rich and influential old Polish Jew, who is a reincarnation (with memory) of the Roman governor of Jerusalem at the time of the Crucifixion. For a time the reader is led to believe that the old Jew is really the Wandering Jew, for he has had as many different lives. Much of the biography also depends upon a section called a fifth gospel—the gospel according to Judas. Both Asch and Fleg, but particularly Asch, make Judas an important figure. But the Wandering Jew as such does not appear, either in the account of the Crucifixion, which is quite detailed, or elsewhere.

There are, in addition, two works of parallel nature (so far as can be determined the parallelism is accidental) in which either Ahasuerus or the Wandering Jewess plays an important part. The first of these, which I have ignored until now although it is an older work, is William Sharp's (Fiona Macleod) *The Gypsy Christ* (1895);[56] the other, a much more substantial performance, is a long epic poem by Albrecht Schaeffer, *Parzival* (Leipzig, 1922). Both have to do with Wagner's *Parsifal*. According to Sharp, Wagner in his great religious musical drama did not draw correctly the character of Kundry. Sharp would make her into a figure of tragic symbolism, a gypsy woman of evil life who had mocked Christ on Golgotha and demanded of him a sign, and to whom he had said, "To thee and thine I bequeath the signs of my Passion, to be a shame and horror among thy people forevermore!"[57] Upon her hands and feet appear the stigmata, never to fade away. They are borne also by her descendants in every third generation. Many of these are crucified, and wherever the wanderers go on earth they bear these marks of horror. The curse will be lifted from them only when a Gypsy Christ should be born of a virgin. Then the Children of the Wind (not specifically identified) will be dispersed and will vanish from among men. In the last chapter, one Naomi prophesies that she will give birth to the Gypsy Christ. The novelette is written in a "poetical" style, with all the foggy imagery of most of the writings in the Celtic Renaissance.

Schaeffer, on the other hand, goes more directly to Wagner's libretto. The Master of Bayreuth had allowed Kundry to be acquainted with Ahasuerus in *Parsifal*, and permitted her moreover to mock Christ while he was carrying the Cross, for which she is condemned to vacillate eternally between lust and repentance. Schaeffer merely substitutes Ahasuerus for Kundry. After his first unproductive visit to the Temple of the Grail in Monsalvat, Parzival discovers in the den of Trevizent a half-decayed living skeleton with burning eyes. This is all that is left of Ahasuerus, who is awaiting salvation and rejuvenation from the one who can save the wounded king, Amfortas. He violently reproaches Parzival because he had neglected to ask the saving question, and he angrily assures him that the Grail is a delusion prepared by a cruel God. After time has passed, however, Parzival finds that the impotent rage of Ahasuerus has softened into a quiet madness: the victim is persuaded to believe in the Grail, because he has been fated to believe as soon as redemption comes out of all his torture. When Parzival then attains the Grail, he sees in the transfigured environment a rejuvenated Ahasuerus, a youth whose eyes now burn with faith.

Of Faustian flavor, but otherwise a conventional narrative, is Lambert Melissen's *Door Kristus vervolgd* ("Pursued by Christ"; n.p., 1929), in which the Wandering Jew makes an appearance. The action of the story is concerned with the struggle between God and the Devil for the possession of a human soul. The lesson is obvious: man follows God, but in return God follows man with his grace and his Cross, with which he earned the blessings he can bestow upon man. This conclusion is announced as early as the Prologue and is borne out by the interplay of two characters: Ahasuerus, who will not recognize God and flees him pursuing (but in whom God's love will win out in the long run); and Dismas, the penitent thief. The protagonist of the play, a pawnbroker, is similar in character to now one and now the other of these.

The same kind of subordination is accorded the Jew in Walter W. Miller's novel, *A Canticle for Leibowitz* (Philadelphia, 1960), where he is introduced in a curiously tentative manner. This novel is in part a narrative and in part a tract. It treats of a time some centuries hence, after civilization has been nearly destroyed by nuclear warfare and has been reorganized in an entirely different manner. In the new society the chief spiritual factor—indeed, the only one—is the Catholic Church. In spite of this, a final annihilating war is breaking out at the close of the novel, and missionaries are leaving for Alpha Centauri as the final pages are turned. Although it is ragged in concept, the novel is a powerful preachment against the state of things to be. As for the Wandering Jew, sometimes unnamed, sometimes Benjamin, sometimes Lazarus, he appears at odd moments—at the beginning to get things started, and sporadically elsewhere to no definite purpose, save as a symbol of weary but persisting mankind. His most obvious achievement is to turn the attention of a simple-minded novitiate, Francis, to some relics from the twentieth century (just before the nuclear deluge). He later buries Francis, after the latter has been murdered by savages. His general participation, however, is too uncertain to be significant, just as the whole novel is too formless to be satisfying.

As for David Mackinnon's *Ahasverus: A Persian Play* (London, 1920), it deals with the wrong Ahasuerus, for it is a poetic dramatization of the story of Esther and has nothing to do with the Legend.

I have heard of two moving pictures treating the Wandering Jew—the first a Jaffa Productions product in 1933, starring Jacob Ben-Ami, and the second an Italian film, *L'ebreo errante* (1948), made by Distributori Independenti, starring Vittorio Gassman. Its title was later changed to *Sablie del tempo*. And it is a matter of record that Ahasuerus has a walk-on role in the Passion Play of Oberammergau.

In so far as we are permitted to see him, Ahasuerus reached the end of the road when Lagerkvist witnessed his death. This is not to say that he will not be resurrected. He has died before and come back to life. If we take the Germans' word for it, he is still *ewig*; and it will be recalled that Quinet took his picture after God and the whole universe had passed away. He will always remain a symbol, but his terrestrial course has slowed markedly since the 1930's. And why not? Since that time thousands upon thousands of Jews have wandered in foreign lands, refugees from Nazi Germany, persons displaced by World War II, settlers in Israel—to say nothing of those who escaped Auschwitz and Dachau. For these there has been such a terrible reality about their wanderings that they have had no time for fiction or windy philosophizing. To those being overtaken by the rising tide of genocide, the Legend of Ahasuerus could not be even a child's diversion from tragedy.

But since mankind will always suffer, and since Ahasuerus is one obvious symbol of sinful mankind in suffering, it is not likely that this Legend will die out all at once. Perhaps the strict Christian might argue that this unchristian saga deserves to die, but facts remain facts. The Wandering Jew will still appear on Good Friday in some remote Italian village; at any moment he may appear on the streets of New York, where for years a self-appointed Ahasuerus wandered about (even on one occasion visiting the New York Public Library) when he was not plying his vocation of broker on Wall Street.[58] Perhaps it was he who rode the motorcycle on his way to America in Warfel's play. Whether he is still accompanied by St. Francis is not a matter of record. As might be expected, an Ahasuerus of the 1950's would never spurn the aid of an internal-combustion engine, which means that he may some time be encountered on an *Autobahn* or a cloverleaf interchange.

All facetiousness aside, one must nevertheless concede that the outlines of Ahasuerus are steadily becoming fainter. We have seen him walking his appointed course through the long stretches of the Middle Ages, blazing into special prominence during the Reformation and the Renaissance, traversing the world and all parts thereof through the eighteenth century, becoming the particular darling of the romantics of the nineteenth and later. He has all this time been comic and tragic, bathetic and pathetic, a lover and a hater, evil and saintly. He has withstood countless anti-Semitic agitations, thriving on persecution from nominal Christians who in their vengefulness once created him. Now, however, he is being pushed back, as in Fleg or Kees Meekel or Lagerkvist, more and more into the past. He has become a plaything for the academics, a topic for research, which means that sooner or later he will be put under glass and framed in a case like a dead beetle. He has come to resemble the organism which was so foolish as to develop a backbone, which scientists say means his eventual extinction. The critic rather than the creator has taken him over, and the godlessness of the twentieth century, now past mid-course, bids fair to annihilate him.

I cannot agree, however, that the study of a legend such as that of the Wandering Jew has no substance or significance in itself and can lead nowhere. On the contrary, it leads one everywhere, and as for substance and significance it should now be clear that it has something of both. It takes one all over the Western world, from Istanbul to Los Angeles, with stopovers all the way from the North Pole to the South, to the Near and Middle East, with even an overnight sojourn in the Far East, although it is true that the benighted inhabitants of Scotland, Ireland, Wales, and Central and South America need more education in the materials of the Legend. It surveys the whole history of the Western world from the time of Christ—nay even of Adam—to the days of Hitler and beyond. It brings one to close grips with folklore, one of the least understood, most disorganized, yet altogether absorbing of all the products of complex Homo sapiens. It is an almost infallible index of trends and fashions in literary history. For example, it draws one, however unwillingly, into the theology of the seventeenth century, or the astronomy of the eighteenth, or the political thought of the nineteenth; into the gossamer, sometimes meaningless intricacies of Kant and Hegel; into comparative linguistics; into French medical quackery of the 1830's and 1840's; into German humor since 1875; into most of the highways and byways of that which passes for human intelligence. Shall we say that this all is useless? If we do, let it not be considered a term of reproach. One should be a true believer in what is called the useless; without it civilization would indeed be bleak.

Alas, poor Ahasuerus! Although you are welcome to it, you do not need our pity. You have suffered as much as the cruel imagination of man can comprehend suffering. You have seen all of our Christian era; you have anticipated one of the great poets of the twentieth century by calling attention long ago to the rough beast that "slouches toward Bethlehem to be born"; you have seen kings and emperors go rolling by—Nero, Charlemagne, Richard Lion-Heart, Charles V and Philip II, Cromwell, Akbar the Great and Aurengzebe, Louis XVI and Napoleon, Victoria, Franz Josef, Wilhelm II and Hitler. And therefore you are not to be reproached if you are not impressed by Karl Marx and Lenin and are unperturbed by the mushroom cloud of a nuclear explosion. Perhaps from you we may learn something of the true meaning of the permanence of change.

Appendixes

A: Notes on the Study of the Legend

Nineteenth-Century Beginnings

Excluding the works, which have already been described, of the seventeenth and eighteenth centuries which preoccupy themselves with the credibility or noncredibility of Ahasuerus, we can begin the survey of studies of the Legend of the Wandering Jew shortly after 1800. Then, for the first time, the possible origins of the Legend, its manifestations in folklore, its symbolic values, and other germane matters become the materials for individual works. There are some preliminary monographs or briefer articles in longer encyclopedic works which pave the way, such as the anonymous *Unterhaltungen für die langen Winterabende* (Leipzig, 1822), or Ottmar F. H. Schönhuth's *Ahasverus, der ewige Jude* (1849),[1] the latter of which is important because it includes a modern German version of the *Kurtze Beschreibung,* the first "chapter" of the Ahasuerus-book. Others choose to discuss only individual aspects of the Legend, and so have been useful because they furnish the building blocks for future structures. Thus Paul Delasalle, in *La Bibliothèque bleu* (printed in 1840 in the *Revue de Calvados*),[2] touches upon the Breton *guerz* and the ballad linking the Wandering Jew with Bonhomme Misère. A *Notice historique et bibliographique sur la légende du juif-errant* (Paris, 1845) discusses the French *complaintes* but adds little beyond a cursory sketch. Its author, Gustave Brunet de Bordeaux ("G. B. de B."), however, is sometimes cited as an authority on the Legend.

Actually, the first significant pioneer study of the Legend is by Dr. V.-A.-J.-M. Coremans of Brussels, in his two-headed discussion of the Legends of the Unicorn and the Wandering Jew, *La Licorne et le Juif Errant* (Brussels, 1845). In the second of these two little monographs, he makes a true beginning of the folkloristic approach to the Legend. He discovers certain analogies, which seem more than doubtful, to both Legends among the Greeks; he sets up also as parallels Enoch, Elijah, and Frederick Barbarossa, as well as the analogue of Fadhila. He proceeds to Matthew Paris and then to the Renaissance, concluding by mentioning some contemporary titles, such as the play by Klingemann and the novel by Croly. He is wary of any definite pronouncement concerning the credibility or authenticity of the protagonist, although he suggests that Ahasuerus has not yet completed his pilgrimage. A few of his references, such as that to the appearance of Ahasuerus in Alsace at the end of the fifteenth century, have not been noted anywhere else, nor does he acknowledge his sources. His study, however, is an honest, successful innovation, if only because it attempts a detailed explanation of the Legend as the creation of the popular imagination and the natural inclination of the human mind in its untutored stage toward folklore. Moreover, Coremans usually buttresses his statements with acceptable authority. In this respect he is more helpful than the unknown author of a short sketch in *Bentley's Miscellany* for 1843, who discusses the Legend as a whole and then translates into English the well-known Brabantine ballad.[3] This is all very well, even though the outline is of the thinnest, but he mystifies later scholars when he observes that the mark on the Jew's forehead, as first seen in Lewis' *The Monk,* was placed there in the Legend by the Spanish monk Xeniola, who seems to have since been swallowed up in oblivion.

However unrevealing the remarks in *Bentley's Miscellany,* they are challenging when compared to the plodding account of the Legend by Ludwig Wihl in "Der Ahasver-Sage," in the *Athenaeum für Wissenschaft, Kunst, und Leben* for 1838, which is, in the light of even contemporaneous accounts, totally inadequate.[4] The critical writings resulting from the publication of Sue's *Le juif errant* are more stimulating, and there are many of them. Thus L.-L.-F. Bungener, in *Quelques mots au Juif errant* (Geneva, 1845), takes exception to the Fourierist social plan described in the novel and criticizes, in tepid terms perhaps, the plot, characterization, and general taste of the author, at the same time giving some attention to the work's tenuous relationship to the Legend. These criticisms, however, are concerned more with Sue than with the Legend. For example, the strongest attack comes in what is generally an accurate, thorough treatise on the *feuilleton* novel, Alfred Nettement's *Etudes critiques sur le feuilleton roman.*[5] This critique belabors the structure of the novel, its taste, its "Godlessness," its materialism, its anti-Jesuit bias, and its social radicalism. Indeed, it says almost nothing good about the work. At the same time it tells us virtually nothing about the Legend, nor how Sue used it.

Critical Works from 1850 to about 1875

From the outset we have assumed that the Legend throve in oral tradition, among those who are given to believing such tales. It was inevitable that scholars would collect and transcribe the many versions of folk tales. There are a number of such collections, appearing first about 1850 and continuing through the next generation or two. Rather than discuss them all, it is sufficient to enumerate a few of the landmarks and describe them briefly. It is to these works that we are indebted for our knowledge of folk tales described in chapter iv.

It is like meeting a familiar face to find that Franz Xaver von Schönwerth, in *Aus der Oberpfalz: Sitten und Sagen* (Augsburg, 1857-59), a book on the folkways of the Palatinate and southern Germany, mentions a particular boulder in the Black Mountains known as the "Judenstein," around which the Wandering Jew is accustomed to walk whenever he is in the vicinity. Such legends about particular locations appear so frequently among the German-speaking peoples as to be no longer notable. Similarly, C. Kohlrusch, in *Schweizerisches Sagebuch* (Leipzig, 1854-56), repeats the familiar tale of Ahasuerus on the Grimsel.[6] But both Schönwerth and Kohlrusch are drawing on what F. Nork had said in his important pioneer work, *Die Sitten und Gebräuche der Deutschen und ihrer Nachbarvölker* (Stuttgart, 1845), an imposing study of Central European folkways.[7] There is, however, this difference between Kohlrusch and Nork, and it indicates the progress of romantic folkloristic studies: Kohlrusch is not content merely to report the Legend as a folk tale; he must explain it as symbolic of the Jewish people, who have had imposed upon them the curse of being considered Christ-killers. The three visits of Ahasuerus to the Grimsel, where he sees first a fair meadow, then a town, then nothing but snow and ice, has become an allegory which indicates that the Jews were once a great people who, for the death of Christ, must be condemned to barren desolation. Also characteristic of the mythologists of the time is the explanation offered in Ernst Ludwig Rochholz' *Schweizersagen aus dem Aargau* (Aarau, 1856) that Ahasuerus is a defeated pagan god. Rochholz tries to identify Ahasuerus with either Woden or Buddha; since these two gods have little in common, to understate the fact, the author's efforts carry little weight.

At the same time, another kind of account of the Legend, which I term the family-journal or Sunday-supplement account, has developed everywhere since about 1850. The first few of these are not without value, for they give accounts of visits of Ahasuerus to particular places, but soon they degenerate into superficial epitomes that are superseded by some of the standard works on the subject noted below. In reading them one is reminded of the old theory of the individual epic lay, out of which the heroic epic was supposed to grow. There is nothing so tidy as that here, however. As a good example, we have an anonymous article in the *Illustriertes Familienjournal* for 1860 in which it is told how Ahasuerus appeared to a shepherd in Voigtland and was driven away as soon as the peasant, in mortal terror, uttered the name of Christ.[8] Such a craven Wandering Jew is of weaker mettle than him described by L. Otte in the *Bilder-Chronik*, No. 42 (1851),[9] who cursed a whole town in the Wallis, church and all, because the inhabitants had not offered him the hospitality to which he had been accustomed.[10]

Sometimes an antiquarian will mention older miscellaneous treatments of the Legend. Heinrich Döring's *Brittischer Balladenschatz* (1858)[11] offers a good German translation of the Elizabethan English ballad, *The Shoemaker of Jerusalem*. Charles Nisard's *Histoire des livres populaires* (1854) has an excellent description of the French *Histoire admirable*, although there is no reason to call even the French treatments of the Legend "a burlesque of the more sacred Christian mysteries."[12] Nisard, however, must take a distant second place behind Champfleury's admirable *Histoire de l'imagerie populaire* (1869), a complete collection of material particularly valuable for the light it throws upon the French *complaintes* and the picturization of the Jew in popular literature.[13] It has a later valuable companion piece in Emile H. van Heurck and G. J. Boekenoogen's *Histoire de l'imagerie populaire flamande* (1910).[14]

The identification of Ahasuerus with the Jewish people, suggested by Kohlrusch's comments and buttressed by the drama of Diepenbrock and the tract by Ortlepp, is reflected in contemporaneous scholarship. Ferdinand Bässler's *Über die Sage vom ewigen Juden* (Berlin, 1870) is a well-known extended study of the Legend, although it is actually a sketchy performance. Its sole value today lies in its eloquently expressed concept of Ahasuerus as the symbol of the *genus Judaicum*. G. W. Roeder's "Die Sage vom ewigen Juden," in *Deutsches Museum* for 1856, is also an elementary outline, and its simple identification of Ahasuerus with all Jews is unnecessarily verbose.[15] It suggests, however, that the Legend originated before the Fourth Lateran Council of 1215 passed favorably upon the tremendous regenerative power of baptism.

In passing I must remark that the Fourth Lateran Council is pointed up in a different way by E. Kurrein's article, "Die Ahasversage und Judenabziehungen," in *B'nai B'rith Mitteilungen für Oesterreich* (Vienna, n.d., perhaps about 1900), which holds that the mark on the Wandering Jew's brow was suggested not so much by the analogy of the Mark of Cain (although that is usually the explanation) as by the edict of Innocent III that the deicide Jews should be given some kind of distinctive mark.

Still, it is rare to find these early students of the Legend, who had as yet no inkling of its enormous complexity offering a single explanation of its origin, though some of them greatly stretch their points. Even the sober Nork sees too much in the fact that Ahasuerus is a foil to Christ—that is, he overemphasizes a contamination with the Legend of Antichrist. On the other hand, Rudolph Krickau, in *Die Sage vom ewigen Juden* (Teltow, 1867), generalizes to excess on insufficient grounds: he takes for granted that Ahasuerus is a German creation and therefore equates him with Woden, king of the gods, the Advancer and the Mover. Taking into account all that the mid-nineteenth-century writers did not know about the Legend, one must applaud the cautious judgment of Carl Paul Caspari in *Nogle Bemaerkninger angaaende Sagnet om den evigen Jøde* (Kristiania, 1863), who, after recognizing the Wandering Jew as a symbol of the nomadic Jewish people, contents himself with the theory that the Legend originated in the early Middle Ages.

To repeat, none of the treatments of the Legend as a legend, before 1875, can have more than historical interest today, although the study of pictorial representation, in Nisard and particularly in Champfleury, remains notable. The rest is so much pioneer digging. Thus as early as 1850 a German pamphlet, known today as *Volksbücher 52* (printed in Leipzig about 1850, although no publication date appears in the pamphlet), summarized the Legend briefly, attending especially to the seventeenth-century Ahasuerus-book, the pamphlets from the *Kurtze Beschreibung* of 1602 on; the work is acceptable even if the author seems to know little or nothing about the reprints after 1650. Too many lesser treatments are like Bruno Tideman's *Ahasverus* (Zwolle, 1870) —scanty and thin of content—which insists that the Legend must be Jewish. As if any people as proud as the Jews would invent a story of this sort about one of their own! Tideman believes that the Legend was brought to western Europe from the Saracens at the time of the early Crusades, which seems probable.[16] But like many others, Tideman confused the legends of various wanderers—the archetypal tale covering many different individuals who wander for various reasons—with the specific Legend of the Wandering Jew. More satisfactory is his discussion of Goethe's *Faust* and the Wandering Jew fragments and the position of the modern Jew in arts and letters, in which he casts the searchlight beam on Mendelssohn, Meyerbeer, and Offenbach.

This kind of skimming of the Legend perpetuates a grossly popularized treatment which is unsatisfactory, but the tendency is still to be noted in 1958 as much as in 1858. So it is with B. Rodiger's article in *Freya* for 1864;[17] or with S. J. Moscoviter's *Ahasverus* (Rotterdam, 1870), which, while maintaining the symbolism of Ahasuerus as the Jew living in the modern world, spends too much time differing with Tideman; or with the American A. J. Faust's *The Wandering Jew: A Mythical and Aesthetical Study* (Hartford, 1870), which wastes its efforts attacking the immoral modern French novels like those of Eugène Sue. The study of the Legend most quoted from these years, apart from Bässler, and the one with the most scholarly pretensions, is Johann Georg Theodor Grässe's *Der Tannhäuser und der Ewige Jude* (1844, rev. ed.; 1861), but this is more important for Tannhäuser than for Ahasuerus, if only because Grässe knew more about Tannhäuser.[18]

Yet, on particular details, the scholarship in the works of this period was sound, as in Gustav Hauff's comments on Goethe's concepts of the Legend in "Die Sage vom ewigen Juden und ihre characteristische Behandlung," in *Deutsches Museum* for 1867.[19]

From 1875 to about 1900

It was during the last quarter of the nineteenth century that the first truly comprehensive studies of the Legend began to appear. These were the years of the heyday of German scholarship in the humanities and social studies, characterized by sharpened research, a passion for the necessary minutiae, and analysis of what these minutiae represented. Between 1875 and 1900 comes the first powerful impact of the great syntheses wrought by the Germans in the study of language, folklore, civilization, and literature—what they themselves called *Philologie*—which the rest of Europe could for the time being only imitate.

So far as the Legend is concerned, however, it should be observed that the honors are not altogether on the side of the German tradition; there are some notable French and

Italian studies. More than forty special studies of the Legend came out between 1875 and 1900, in the form of books, monographs, and articles in learned journals and encyclopedias. If the Sunday supplement is included, the number is far greater. Of these forty and more, about a dozen still have value, in the sense that they are helpful to the student of the Legend. One or two of them, in fact, are indispensable.

The best work with which to begin this enumeration is a masterpiece. Leonhard Neubaur's *Die Sage vom ewigen Juden* had its original edition in Leipzig in 1884; but another one, much fuller, and accompanied by an excellent series of supplementary notes, the *Neue Mitteilungen*, appeared in 1893.[20] The general introduction includes copious notes; it moves with swift but sure steps over the Biblical clues to the origins of the Legend, although Neubaur is not yet aware of the pre-Roger-of-Wendover state of things. This knowledge comes later. Where his work shines is in his discussion of the growth of the Ahasuerus-book, his reprinting of the *Kurtze Beschreibung* and the Dudulaeus pamphlet, and his description of the title pages and contents, in summary, of a score of German *Volksbücher* of the seventeenth and early eighteenth centuries, as well as a close résumé of the *Histoire admirable*, in the Bruges version of about 1650. Even more impressive is his apparatus of explanatory and bibliographical notes, much the best that has ever been prepared to date for a study of the Legend. It is unfortunate, however, that the extensive bibliography was not printed in his book in either edition. Instead, it came out in a relatively inaccessible publication—the *Centralblatt für Bibliothekwesen*—in 1895.[21] Although this bibliography is now much too old and has been superseded by that of J. J. Gielen (1931), of whose work more later, Neubaur's study as a whole is a magnificent performance, and absolutely necessary to the study of the Legend before 1800—before the art form had snowballed into its vast nineteenth-century proportions. The work and the two additional articles—"Zur Geschichte der Sage vom ewigen Juden," in *Zeitschrift des Vereins für Volkskunde* for 1912,[22] and "Zur Geschichte und Bibliographie des Volksbuchs vom Ahasverus," in *Zeitschrift für Bücherfreunde* for 1914[23]—establish the author as the first great authority on the Ahasuerus-book and the folkloristic aspects of the Legend.

Yet Neubaur hardly does justice to the Legend in non-German-speaking countries, with the possible exception of France. This want is supplied, however, by two or three fine scholars in France and the western Mediterranean area. Even before Neubaur, Alessandro d'Ancona had contributed "La leggenda dell'Ebreo Errante" to the *Nuova Antologia* for 1880.[24] This is an able survey, helpful particularly to those who are confused by the merging of the Buttadeus and Malchus sublegends. D'Ancona had available the collected folk tales and folk songs of Sicily and southern Italy, assembled by Giuseppe Pitrè in 1875 and later.[25] He profited even more from the virtual collaboration of the great scholar Gaston Paris. Paris had published, also in 1880, a study of the Legend, "Le Juif errant," which appeared first in the *Encyclopédie des sciences religieuses* and then as a separate monograph.[26] With the usual willingness of a French investigator to divagate in an appropriate way, Paris sketches the Legend and other extrascriptural legends accruing to the story of the Crucifixion—those of Veronica, Longinus, and Judas—thus clearing the way for the individual Legend of Malchus, which, although originally separate, has become a sublegend in the cycle of the Legend of the Wandering Jew. Paris's monograph furnished the basis for his fine study, *Le Juif errant en Italie* (Paris, 1891).

A work published in the same year is Salomone Morpurgo's invaluable *L'Ebreo errante in Italia* (Florence, 1891), which prints in full the tale told by Antonio di Francesco di Andrea, without which, of course, no account of the Legend is complete, for it antedates by a full century the *Kurtze Beschreibung*. Even so, the Germans cannot be kept out of the picture, for Alfred Ruhemann gives an excellent summary of the Legend in Italy, "Die Sage vom ewigen Juden in Italien," in *Nord und Süd* for 1895.[27]

At about the same time the study of the Legend in the Iberian peninsula was initiated by Carolina Michaelis de Vasconcellos' "O Judeu errante em Portugal," in *Revista Lusitana* for 1887,[28] which introduces us to Juan Espera en Dios (João Espera em Dios) and remains until Maurice Bataillon's study (1941),[29] the best account of the Legend in that part of Europe.

The works by Neubaur, d'Ancona, Paris, Morpurgo, and Ruhemann are written by professional scholars, observant and meticulous in respect to detail. They are the intellectual descendants of Nork, Nisard, and Champfleury; they have no peers between 1875 and 1900. Another kind of student, however, must be given his due. He is among those who can be called honored amateurs, the antiquarians and collectors and littérateurs who are not satisfied merely to gather material but must describe it *in extenso*. Such students can be popularizers without being superficial dabblers; they must command respect as authorities on the gross anatomy of their subject. They are the general practitioners rather than the specialists and belong to a breed which the mid-twentieth century scarcely seems to understand. At their best they are valuable sources of reference; at their worst they are competent to write for general encyclopedias. Two of these toward the end of the nineteenth century stand out above the rest: Sabine Baring-Gould and Moncure Daniel Conway.

Baring-Gould's interest in the Legend, however, is incidental to his general interest in medieval stories and saints' lives. His study of the Wandering Jew takes up only a chapter in *Curious Myths of the Middle Ages*.[30] His contribution is to call particular attention to the analogue of the mysterious individual who periodically renews his youth in the tale of Vidförull in the *Bragda Magus Saga* of about 1500.

With Conway, on the other hand, the case is different, because if he had been able to see and follow the guide posts established since his *The Wandering Jew* first appeared in London in 1881, he might have become a definitive authority. As it is, he stops at the point where a thorough treatment must continue—at the art form, concerning which he is virtually indifferent, as Neubaur and Paris, writing contemporaneously, were also. Yet Conway is not only informative but readable as well. His book, to date the only full-length treatment of the Legend in English, has two obvious faults—one, a common contemporary tendency toward a nationalistic interpretation and emphasis, which results in an undue narrowing of his treatment to the manifestations among English-speaking people only; and the other, a weakness for unnecessary digression. These failings, however, are not evident in the opening chapters, for Conway does more than many others to explain the genus of which the Wandering Jew is a species: the immortal wanderers. And he has the imagination to fertilize his twenty chapters with many intelligent questions. Is Cain a Semitic Prometheus? Is there a connection between Al Sameri of the Koran and the island of that name in the Red Sea? Is Elijah analogous to the classical Aeolus, since both have to do with weather? At the same time, such virtuosity leads him to blur his legends. Antichrist, Nero, Cain, and Joseph of Arimathea tread too close on one another's heels. Sometimes, too, he wastes his energies in overgeneralizations, as in his wordy chapter, "The Jew in Theology." Or he may perpetuate a mystery, as when he assigns the mark on the brow of Ahasuerus to the as yet unidentified Xeniola, about whom we know no more, after reading his remarks, than we knew before, and that was nothing.[31]

Somewhat similar in its general objectives to Conway's work is Friedrich Helbig's *Die Sage vom "ewigen Juden"* (1874), but Helbig puts more stress on the art form than Conway.[32] Schubart, Schreiber, H. Müller, and Lenau (all Germans) pass in close review.

Helbig believes that the modern Ahasuerus derives from Lenau and Schopenhauer, but this is an untenable conclusion, although it may not have seemed so in the 1870's. He cares nothing for Schubart or Shelley, though he mentions Chamisso and Schlegel in an offhand way, but comes to rest for a while on Goethe, whose original linking of Ahasuerus and Judas he applauds. Then he moves forward once more through Schiller's *Geisterseher* to Mosen and Sue. He thinks a lot of Mosen and very little of Sue, although he concedes the great influence of Sue's novel. Back again in time he goes to Ludwig Köhler and Horn and Klingemann, and forward to Oelckers, Schücking, Von Zedlitz, and Andersen, ending with S. Heller and Hamerling. In Helbig it is easy to see where Conway got the material for his chapter on the "new" Ahasuerus in Germany. Helbig emphasizes Andersen's poem, although he makes a curious blunder in assuming that the German translation of the work (1865) was the original, whereas the poem was written in Danish and published in 1844. But at least one point in Helbig's study is still important: he was the first to show that the art form of the Legend is synchronized with an awareness of social development, which is a vital characteristic of the whole nineteenth century.

With all their omissions, and there are many, Conway's and Helbig's efforts are far more useful than the more brilliant performance of Charles Schoebel in *La Légende du Juif errant* (Paris, 1877), which itself wanders too much. Schoebel unquestionably knows this or that legend, yet he seems never to have heard of the German *Volksbücher*, and he assumes, on the basis of the French *complainte* of 1609, that the Legend is primarily a matter of "literary compositions." His scholarship, while versatile, is both erratic and inaccurate, and his bias too strong for the study to have any value today. He is determined to show a Germanic origin for the Legend (in spite of his inattention to the *Volksbücher*), even resorting to a wild derivation of "Buttadeus" from "fish of God," based on a nonexistent Germanic root. Besides, his theories of the origin of the Legend are not consistent. If it originates from purely literary compositions, then the Legend is false. If it derives from Woden, as he maintains on one occasion, then the Legend presents the type of wanderer associated with a solar or lunar myth. Perhaps the latter is so—such myths could account for *all* concepts of the wanderer. But then Schoebel suddenly identifies Woden with the Devil; and we are surprised to read that Ahasuerus is like St. Francis of Assisi, who was a Christian wanderer, or like John Wycliffe, who did not wander except in a theological sense, or like Lutterworth, the town in which Wycliffe served the Church and where he died, which, being a locality, could not be said to wander at all. Schoebel's comments on Luther and Hans Sachs are irrelevant and incorrect. His final genealogy of the Wandering Jew, who, he says, is identifiable with Christ—a most unlikely possibility—is not only confused but confusing. It is amazing that Schoebel should have commanded the attention he did, and it is no credit to other writers about the Legend that they should have cited him so often.

The Woden theory, as we have seen, crops up from time to time, and Schoebel is one of the first to exploit it, but readers interested in tracing this theory would do better to consult Karl Blind, whose "Woden, the Wild Huntsman, and the Wandering Jew," in *The Gentleman's Magazine* for 1880, is a more succinct statement.[33] Blind also assumes a Germanic origin for the Legend and indulges in etymological fantasies to establish his case. He writes persuasively but is not sufficiently informed. The earlier study of Bässler is today of more value than those of Schoebel and Blind combined.

The art of preparing encyclopedias, which developed greatly during the last quarter of the last century, resulted in a plethora of short articles about Ahasuerus. Most of these follow the same pattern: they go to such students of the Legend as Grässe, Bässler, Helbig, or Champfleury; or, if the article is late enough in time, to Neubaur,

Paris, or Conway. They are easily overshadowed by the achievements of the men who were their sources, and need not be named here. But some exceptions naturally occur. Conway himself did an excellent article for the *Encyclopaedia Britannica* (9th ed.; 1881),[34] and another good pair are those by Heinrich Joseph Wetzer and Benedict Welte in *Wetzer und Welte's Kirchenlexicon oder Encyklopädie der katholischen Theologie und ihrer Hülfswissenschaften* (1889)[35] and by J. H. Kruger in *La Grande Encyclopédie* (Paris, 1896).[36] One or two subsequent entries of this sort must be mentioned later.

Some of these articles for encyclopedias appear also in Slavic lands. Josef Hanuš', in Otto's *Slovník naučný* (1888) is one of the best in the Czech language.[37] In Poland there were a few of similar dimensions, such as that by Boleslav Czerwienski in the Helbig Festschrift, *Studyum wedlug Helbiga* (1874),[38] or the two monographs—Zygmunt Gawarecki's *Zyd wieczny tulacz* (Warsaw, 1865) or Adolf Dygasinski's monograph with the same title (Wedrowiec, 1887)[39]—but the best of these is Jan Karlowic's *Zyd wieczny tulacz* (Warsaw, 1873), which is one of the more forceful expressions of the idea that the Legend of the Wandering Jew, like that of Cain, is a solar myth. Alexander Wesselofsky's articles, published in Russian encyclopedias and in the *Archiv für slavische Philologie* for 1881, remain the only Russian contributions of importance until after 1900.[40] However, unless an encyclopedia article is capable of some special point —and almost all of them are necessarily too restricted in space to be so—it need be given no further attention.

Rather unclassifiable is the anonymous article, scholarly in tone, pleasant, and full of holes, in the *Revue des deux mondes* for 1883.[41] It is obligated to Gaston Paris, but has been pressed all out of shape. The freakish is always possible, of course. Even serious students of the Legend have sometimes flown off at a tangent and become so preoccupied with a particular essay in interpretation that they distort all their efforts. The strangest example of this is Paulus Cassel's *Ahasverus: Die Sage vom ewigen Juden* (1885).[42] The term "eccentric" is too mild to apply to it. Cassel believes that the Legend was originally suggested by the figure of Nero, and that Nero is so much the prototype of Ahasuerus that their names are linguistic relatives. The contortions of etymology by which he attempts to equate these two dissimilar names are remarkable. He proceeds to call attention to the famous beasts in the thirteenth chapter of Revelation. The second of these, one must remember, brings it about that the inhabitants of the world worship the first. Now, according to Cassel, we are to understand that the first beast was Nero. Of the second, it is said in the Scriptures that the number of his name is a human number and comes to 666. The prototype of this second beast, or dragon, as the text of Revelation calls it, is a composite of the king who plays an important part in the Book of Esther—that is, Ahasuerus—and his evil genius, Haman. (One can only protest feebly at the unfairness of springing on an avid reader a twofold kind of prototype.) It is on Haman that Cassel expends the greater part of his ingenuity. The letters of Haman's name, according to Hebrew spelling, when used as Hebrew numerals, make 5 plus 40 plus 50 plus 200 plus 300 plus 70 plus 1, or 666 as a grand total. Now, if one beast is Haman, the other could be Ahasuerus, that is, Nero. It matters not that this Ahasuerus is the Persian emperor Xerxes and not the Wandering Jew. A few years earlier Cassel had broached the same theory in *Thurm und Glocke* (Berlin, 1877), an idea at once fascinating and farfetched.

Another wild theory would reduce the Legend to the product of sheer neuroticism, or, to put it more romantically, the desire for unreality. In his *Le juif errant à la salpétrière* (Paris, 1893), Henry Meige imagined that the inventor of the Legend, who had observed "bearded Jewish vagabonds in bizarre costume and generally destitute," satisfied an abnormal craving for the supernatural or miraculous by substituting a fantasy, an idealistic conception of the Eternal Wanderer expiating his offense. The bearded Jewish vagabond, however, as we have seen, does not materialize before the seventeenth century.

Some attempted an approach to the Legend through the paths of comparative legendry, as Hirsch aus Lintorf tried in *Die drei grossen Volkssagen von Don Juan, vom ewigen Juden, und von Dr. Faust* (1875).[43] This method is difficult and not too well under control today. Amalgamations of this sort tend to degenerate into feats of individual imaginings, and so stories which were originally separate legends tend to become confused. We have seen where an author of a poem or novel may try the same method, nearly always with the same inconclusive result. A different kind of blending, with uncertain justification, is such probing as Ludwig Laistner performs in *Nebelsagen* (Stuttgart, 1879).[44] On a shaky common etymology of the Germanic words for "shoe" and "shadow"—both indicating a covering—Laistner rears a theory of the kinship between wandering and clouds, from which it is an easy step for him to relate Ahasuerus the Wanderer and clouds, which are personified in Germanic mythology as Woden. We have here, then, a variant of the solar myth. One does not need etymology, however, to show the relation between clouds and wandering; mere poetic imagination will suffice. Furthermore, only in Germanic can such an etymological relation be established. The student can best rely upon the scholarly treatments by Neubaur, Paris, D'Ancona, Morpurgo, Conway, De Vasconcellos, and Ruhemann, and to an extent upon Helbig's work. These will suffice for the period before 1900.

Other Minor Studies around the Turn of the Century

Following Neubaur's brilliant achievement, the most important scholarship concerning Ahasuerus was that which attempted to cage the formidable dragon of the art form. I shall discuss a half-dozen major works below. In the meantime, attention is due a few minor studies, in order to clear the way. Some of these tend to ride a particular theory into the ground, although none is quite so freakish as that of Cassel. For instance, Otto Henne-am-Rhyn is still hammering away at the Woden theory. In *Eine Reise durch das Reich des Aberglaubens* (Leipzig, 1893), an account of the general features and manifestations of superstition, he covers a mass of material concerning Woden the Wanderer, to which there cannot be any objection.[45] But his theory is that Christianity pushed aside this pagan deity and substituted Ahasuerus, or St. Martin, or St. Nicholas, or Pontius Pilate, all of whom in legend tend to wander into people's houses. By such substitution, he asserts, the Legend of the Wandering Jew grew in its own right. The fallacy here, as before, lies in Henne-am-Rhyn's unwillingness to listen to non-Germanic voices.

The predilection for jumping at conclusions in a blindly nationalistic spirit weakens most of the German studies. Take the case of Conrad Thümmel's "Mittelalterische Volkssagen als Ausdrück religiös-politischen Kämpfe," in the *Sammlung Wissenschaftlicher Vorträge* for 1898.[46] This otherwise useful study of medieval folk tales as expressions of religious and political conflict reviews the Legends of the Wandering Jew, Tannhäuser, and the Holy Grail, and in discussing Ahasuerus relies heavily upon the Woden theory. It considers the Legend itself, however, to be of English origin, on the basis of the accounts of Roger of Wendover and Matthew Paris. We have seen earlier appearances of the Legend in other places. Besides, one must never be naïve enough to assume that the first telling of a legend in writing must necessarily be its first appearance anywhere. Thümmel further believes that the Legend grew as a protest against Catholicism, whereas the probabilities are great that it was conceived in a vengeful spirit to illustrate the superiority of the Christian God as conceived by the Church.

Continuing in this chauvinistic vein is Eduard König's *Ahasver, der ewige Jude* (1907), which, in its only moderately satisfactory account, puts forth the statement that only with the 1602 *Kurtze Beschreibung* does the Legend bear "the clothing of an idea or ideal."[47] What König has in mind is that in this *Volksbuch* we see for the first time the sinner Ahasuerus in a repentant mood. Yet Juan Espera en Dios was repentant, and Cartaphilus before him, although not so melodramatically contrite as the individual whom Paulus von Eitzen saw in the church at Hamburg. Since most of the German scholars around 1900, however, with the exception of Neubaur and Ruhemann, speak as if they had never heard of Antonio di Francesco di Andrea, König's oversight is to be expected.

Or, for the sake of variety, the theorist may be moralistic, even a Calvinist. Thus Pieter Oosterlee, in *Legenden* (1913), asserts that the Legend arose from the desire to establish a moral tale, an *exemplum*, against doubt or skepticism.[48] Judas, having brought about the betrayal of Christ, immediately began to suffer misgivings because he had previously not been sure of the divinity of Christ. Similarly the Wandering Jew, another skeptic, did a terrible wrong to the Saviour by lifting his hand against him and must therefore suffer the inevitable penalty; hence the Legend. Oosterlee is a boring writer, and his explanation of the Legend is inadequate, but it is interesting to see how he links Judas and Ahasuerus, as the French *Histoire admirable* had done more than two centuries before, and as writers like Fleg and Asch were to do a generation later.

Another Legend sometimes connected to that of Ahasuerus is the Faust story, the reason being that both protagonists were striving to reach an unattainable objective, the paradoxical goals of an instinct for life on the one hand and a death wish on the other. So it is in Wilhelm Dworaczek's (Paul Wilhelm) *Aus Faust und Ahasver* (1894).[49] Such a thin common objective is hardly enough to make the two into one. If the ghost of Goethe is responsible for this particular contamination of legends, we must make the best of it. Incidentally, two of the best studies of Goethe's fragments concerning the Wandering Jew come from the early years of the century—J. Minor's *Goethes Fragmente vom ewigen Juden und vom wiederkehrenden Heiland* (Stuttgart-Berlin, 1904) and Robert Petsch's "Faust-Studien" in *Das Goethe Jahrbuch* for 1907.[50] The pseudonymous Dr. S.'s "Die Sage vom ewigen Juden," in *Deutsches Hausschatz in Wort und Bild*, comparing the two legends, is a study of the Sunday-supplement kind.[51]

Meanwhile, popularized versions of the study of the Legend continue. They may turn up sometimes as little more than journalistic fillers. The flagrant weakness of all of these, apart from their comparative ignorance, is their oversimplification, their unwillingness to do more than repeat material already published. An example is "Über die poetischen Bearbeitungen der Sage vom ewigen Juden," (1899) by Hans Eschelbach, who later wrote a passable lyric about Ahasuerus (pp. 303-4 above).[52] His exposition of the Legend is completely derivative. Similarly, Rudolph Fürst, in two articles in *Das literarische Echo*, gives a survey which tells little more than could be found in a reputable encyclopedia.[53] Here and there, of course, one may pick up a grain of value. Alphonse Levy's "Der ewige Jude—kein Jude," in *Im deutschen Reich* (*Zeitschrift des Centralvereins . . . Glauben*) for January, 1904, is quite right, for example, in its insistence that the Legend is not Jewish in origin.[54] It remains surprising, then as now, that so many have assumed that because the Legend treats of a Jew it is therefore Jewish. Another good example of this erroneous point of view is illustrated by C. Rosenkranz' "Die Ahasverus-Sage," in *Pädagogische Blätter* for 1894.[55]

The simplest and clearest of the popularizations of the Legend, generalized but free of undue expression of mere theory, is that by Hamilton Wright Mabie in *Legends That Every Child Should Know* (1906), which may be elementary but is at least accurate.[56]

More than passing attention is due Karl Hans Strohl's "Ahasver," in *Velhagen und Klassings Monatsschrift* for 1908.[57] Strohl takes the point of view that the Legend was a contamination of the old Moslem saga of Al-Khadir and the tale of the Wild Huntsman, or vice versa. Al-Khadir (Chidar, Chidire, Chadaire) is, according to tradition, an immortal; and from the meaning of his name ("the Green One"), he is to be associated with regeneration. He appears to be a Moslem version of Elijah, who was himself one who never tasted death. It is Strohl's contention that the Crusaders came to know the Legend of the immortal Al-Khadir and brought it back to Europe. Now the theme of regeneration or rejuvenation is universal in folklore; even so, such a polygenetic theme might have been transmitted to the case of the rejuvenation of Cartaphilus (in the Roger of Wendover version) in just this way. But why the Legend of Al-Khadir should then have been contaminated with the Legend of the Wild Huntsman —an extension of the myth of Woden—instead of the much better-known Legend of Cain, Strohl does not explain. At the same time, his is one of the first—and few— studies of the Legend to admit the probability that the Legend of the Wandering Jew may have had a composite source. As for Al-Khadir, it is likely that his story should be considered an analogue rather than a source.

One of the better accounts of the Legend which must remain, nevertheless, a minor study is "La leggenda dell'Ebreo Errante," in Rodolfo Renier's *Svaghi Critici* (1910)— minor only because it does little more than review the contributions of Neubaur, Paris, and Morpurgo.[58] But the exposition is both thorough and gracefully written. It tries to strike a balance between the folk tale and art form, but its disposition is to emphasize the latter at the expense of the former, or at least at the expense of the Ahasuerusbook as folk tale. Since it comprises only one of more than twenty literary essays, it must be restricted in scope, and as we have already seen, the Legend cannot be treated adequately in too restricted a scope.

Major Studies from Neubaur to Gielen

We come now to a few monographs which remain indispensable to the study of the Legend up to the day they were published, for we must, as usual, proceed on the premise that any study becomes dated as soon as it appears in print. But these works have no particular axe to grind; they are the ones which proceed on solid ground and give the reader a sense of having learned something about the Legend when he has finished reading them. Most wisely, none of them attempts to pin the Legend down to any one origin, for the ultimate answer is impossible.

Although it deals primarily with the Ahasuerus-book and is early in date, I should be inclined to place in the list of indispensables Franz Violet's "Die Sage vom ewigen Juden" in *Nord und Süd* for 1886.[59] It contains a very competent over-all sketch of the Legend and calls attention to some points generally overlooked in the more comprehensive works. One of these is the fact that the Ahasuerus of the *Volksbuch*, whether German, French, Flemish, or English, is a married man with a family, a bourgeois with most of the middle-class virtues. He is much more at home in the city than in the country, with a tendency to hover about market places, the centers of mercantile life. It must be understood that this point applies to the *Volksbuch* only, for in the folk tales Ahasuerus is usually seen in the country or in a small town.

But by and large, the twentieth century has produced six studies of major importance, the approximate chronology of which tends to coincide with their present usefulness. These are the works of Kappstein, Prost, Soergel, Schmidt, Zirus, and Gielen. A few works have appeared after Gielen, but they, for the most part, are restricted to consideration of a special topic concerned with the Legend, or a particular distribution thereof. These are important. One or two others are negligible because they are either derivative or ignorant or both.

Theodor Kappstein's *Ahasuer in der Weltpoesie* (1906) is competent and should always be read for the sake of its sound outline, but it is pietistic in tone and restricted in its range to a too small list of those authors necessary to consider in a survey of the art forms.[60] In other words, it is not at all "comprehensive." Its grasp of facts and knowledge of those facts is sound enough, but it remains the most old-fashioned of the six in the list.

Much more detailed, but still almost as selective in its range of authors discussed, is Johann Prost's *Die Sage vom ewigen Juden in der neueren deutschen Literatur* (Leipzig, 1905). Here the introduction is at least adequate, and the material on individual writers and their works from about 1850 on is full to the point of repletion, with long quotations from each important work and some trenchant criticism of them. It moves, however, too much in the world of German writers.

Although this same complaint can be directed against Albert Soergel's handsome accomplishment, *Ahasver-Dichtungen seit Goethe* (Leipzig, 1905), the actual fact is that it is a most useful book indeed, an excellent manual on the art form of the Legend, with the added attractiveness of being well written. Its careful introduction to the subject is admirable, although it makes no pretense to the severe bibliographical scholarship of Neubaur when it treats of the Ahasuerus-book. Yet the bibliography, arranged chronologically, is full and workable, although rather clumsily annotated on the given page. Its general treatment of the literary achievements in the field of the Legend and of the stirring-up of ideas in the nineteenth-century handling is better than anything up to its time.

The highly important monograph of Arno Schmidt, *Das Volksbuch vom ewigen Juden* (Danzig, 1927), brings into focus the importance of Danzig and the Marquis d'Orio in the publication of the *Kurtze Beschreibung*, and is therefore the most narrowly restricted of the six. Unfortunately, it has by now been all but forgotten and is virtually inaccessible. Its findings have deserved much more credit than they have as yet received.

Werner Zirus' contribution is in reality a double one: "Der ewige Jude in der Dichtung," which constitutes Number 162 of *Palaestra* (1928),[61] and "Ahasverus, der ewige Jude," volume VI of *Stoff- und Motivgeschichte der deutschen Literatur* (1930).[62] The first limits itself to German and English poetry (although dramatic works and even some prose pieces creep here and there into the fold), and the second is restricted, by the publication of which it is a part, to German literature alone, though Danish poets such as Andersen and Paludan-Müller may intrude. In some curious ways the second is a reworking of the first, and the author is not averse to plagiarizing from himself without scruples. Both works cover so much ground that their limitations of space require great condensation. In the bibliography of the second work, some attention is given to non-German works. The general approach to the subject is undertaken by a "history of ideas" route, which means an inevitable backing up and starting over again from time to time. All in all, however, it is the most comprehensive treatment of the art form alone.

There remains J. J. Gielen's *De Wandelende Jood* (1931), the last full discussion of the Legend to merit praise.[63] It does well with the folk material and is at least adequate on the subject of the art form, but its unwillingness to pay much attention to chronology makes it hard to trace any special development in the protagonist. He appears instead as a series of types somehow unrelated to the eras in which he is moving about. For example, it is difficult to see much difference here between the neoclassic and the romantic Ahasuerus, yet that difference is important. It is, however, the best book to treat the Dutch and Flemish handling of the Legend, which to most scholars has been terra incognita, but it gives both undue space and undue praise to these works, and inexcusably ignores the French art form. As to its bibliography, it is by far the most impressive part of the book, and probably the most useful so far as completeness goes, yet it is most disappointing from a mechanical point of view, for its cross references are seriously inaccurate. Nor is the typography without blemish. The fault here, however, lies with the proofreader rather than the author; at the same time, it makes working with the book a labor rather than a pleasure. But, with all these shortcomings, it is sound in its scholarship and helpful to the reader.

Miscellaneous Special Studies

For particular aspects of the Legend, however, special shorter works are necessary; some of these, indeed, are nearly as important as the fuller general surveys to comprehend the outlines of the Legend. For example, the article by Alice M. Killen, "L'évolution de la légende du Juif Errant," in *Revue de Littérature Comparée* for 1925, is an excellent introduction which stresses the origins of the Legend and observes the general spread of the saga over Europe, with particular reference to France, perhaps, but never unmindful of other contributions.[64] J. E. Gillet's "Traces of the Wandering Jew in Spain," in *Romanic Review* for 1931,[65] has been superseded by Marcel Bataillon's "Pérégrinations espagnoles du juif errant," in *Bulletin Hispanique* for 1941.[66] A little-studied aspect of the Legend—its currency in Slavic lands—is treated bibliographically in Avrahm Yarmolinsky's "The Wandering Jew," in *Studies in Jewish Bibliography and Related Subjects* (1929), a memorial volume for Abraham Freidus.[67] Similarly, Alexander Scheiber's "The Legend of the Wandering Jew in Hungary," in *Midwest Folklore* for 1954, opens up another hitherto dark corner.[68] The predilection of the English romantics about 1800 for the Legend is admirably treated in Eino Railo's *The Haunted Castle* (1927).[69] Here the Gothic elements of the Legend are emphasized, which is all very well, although I cannot accept with any confidence the extension of the Legend itself into Rosicrucianism, as in Bulwer-Lytton's *Zanoni* or similar tales. The best section of the book is that which discusses Monk Lewis, but in any case this, like all the studies cited in this paragraph, deserves complete respect.

George K. Anderson has published three articles on the Wandering Jew's folkloristic aspect in England—"The Wandering Jew Returns to England," in *Journal of English and Germanic Philology* for 1946;[70] "Popular Survivals of the Wandering Jew in England," in the same periodical for 1947;[71] and "The History of Israel Jobson," in *Philological Quarterly* for 1947.[72] The same author has discussed extensively the characteristic genre of the Legend in "The Neo-Classical Chronicle of the Wandering Jew," in *Publications of the Modern Language Association* for 1948.[73] A good brief survey of the whole Legend—depending too much, however, on Zirus—is chapter viii of Edgar Rosenberg's *From Shylock to Svengali* (Stanford, 1960).[74]

Finally, we should note that since 1900 some minor works have appeared which are acceptable enough within their limits. Others, however, have been a disservice to the comprehension of the Legend. The little group who see an Indian origin for the Legend should have their day in court. Albert J. Edmunds, in the first of two articles, sets up the Legend of Pindola (p. 4 above) to establish an analogue to the Wandering Jew and indicates his belief that *Buttadeus* derives from the Sicilian *Arributtadeu* (p. 87 above), which comes from *Arya Buddhadeva* ("Saint Buddha the God").[75] That is to say, here is a claim for a Buddhistic origin of the Legend. But why should the formulistic name of a deity be transferred to a sinner against the deity? The point seems important, because etymologies are treacherous as evidence of this sort. The other article by Edmunds, "The Wandering Jew: A Buddhist Parallel," in *The Open Court* for 1903, is a mere preliminary note.[76] On the other hand, P. Zondervan, in the *Nieuw theologisch Tijdschrift* for 1917, while suggesting that the Legend originated in the East, is not so specific.[77] He sees in it a thoroughly mixed mythological transmission of elements in the concepts of Baal, Moloch, Sol, and Saturn—altogether too much of a mélange to make much sense. B. Heller, also, in his article on the Wandering Jew in the *Encyclopaedia Judaica* for 1928, looks for origins in India, without much conviction, because 1) the name of Ahasuerus is much hated by Jews and 2) because the tale is patently anti-Semitic.[78] Perhaps his first point begs the question, but in any case no one can sensibly defend a Jewish origin, even granting that there are rabbinical legends about Jews who wander.

A rather freakish performance is a section of Arthur Heulhard's *La Sainte-Famille: Barrabas et les siens dans les mythes grecs de la Psyché et d'Apollonius et dans les Ecritures juives* (1914).[79] The author's initial statement is that the Legend arose from the desire of the medieval Church to have a witness, a Jew who had actually known Jesus. (This, of course, ignores any existence of the Legend before its appearance in western Europe.) "You shall wait . . . till I return" is the phrase used by Jesus in the Mehazeh of Corinthus, where it is applied to Simon Peter, not to John. Jesus is the carpenter of Nazareth. Ashafalsus (not yet Ahasuerus) is present during the flight to Egypt; at the spectacular death of Salome, who is decapitated by ice; at the miracle of the five loaves and two fishes; at the arrest of Jesus in the Garden; at the suicide of Judas. (But Judas is reincarnated as Juda Bar-Abba, a Jewish patriot, who was crucified by the Romans after the fall of Jerusalem in A.D. 70.) Ashafalsus then becomes Ahasuerus by name and wanders according to tradition. He spends much time in America and Japan, lest he witness human sacrifice. He is repelled by the tradition of couvade in an African tribe. Without realizing it, he witnesses the martyrdoms of Peter and Paul. His five coins are attached to a series of fives: the five vessels of the marriage feast in Cana, the five husbands of the woman of Samaria, the five porticos at the Pool of Siloam, the five pairs of oxen, the five loaves of bread, the five foolish virgins, the five brothers of man to whom Eleazar refused a drop of water. "What a lie!" concludes the author.

Although he does not get behind Roger of Wendover in time, Bram Stoker gives a helpful chapter on the Wandering Jew in his *Famous Impostors* (New York, 1910) and points to a few bibliographical items which other writers have usually ignored—for example, the printing of Matthew Paris' *Historia Major* in 1571 and especially the reprints of the work—at Zurich in 1589 and 1606 and in England in 1640 and 1684. He suggests a few analogues to the Cartaphilus aspect (actually the source) in the belief that John never died, that the aloe blooms only once in a hundred years.

The perennial theory that the Legend arose from a solar myth has been exploited again by Karl Jung in his "Wandlungen und Symbole der Libido" (1912).[80] Ahasuerus is the sun, which alternately raises itself from and submerges itself in the sea. Herein is a parallel to man's wavering amid his desires—his struggles between what he dreams and what he does. The Jungian approach seems already to be dated. The solar or lunar myth may lie behind the theory of all wandering; for that matter, it can represent all living. Like the sun, we all get up in the morning and go to bed at night, whether we are wandering Jews or sedentary Gentiles. In other words, such a theory is too general and at the same time too obvious to have much use.

The same inclination to see the Wandering Jew in any instance of long life or eternal suffering has damaged many of the shorter studies of the Legend, although parallels and analogous writings are always worthy of note. A good example is Corrado Ricci's "L'Ebreo errante" (1896-97), which sketches the Legend by citing the cases of Cain, Al Sameri, and Khareuti (unknown, but possibly the three-headed monster Geryon, slain by Hercules).[81] We have already perceived the relation of the first two of these to Ahasuerus. The sketch itself is not accurate, and in any event is interrupted by the Legend of Bengali, who lived in Cochin China to the age of three hundred eighty. (Longevity alone never made an Ahasuerus.) The work is nevertheless useful for its attention to the swarming adventurers and charlatans who were everywhere around and about in thirteenth-century Italy (and everywhere else in any place at any time, for that matter), and for its stout defense of Antonio di Francesco di Andrea.

It is unfortunate that the most recent longer treatment of the Legend, Joseph Gaer's *The Legend of the Wandering Jew* (New York, 1961), should be generally unsatisfactory. It does not distinguish properly between primary and secondary sources; it leaves gaps in the story of the development of the Legend, so that we do not see Ahasuerus changing with the times. No reader, having finished it, can have an adequate idea of the rich variety of works in which Ahasuerus appears, of the versatility of his roles nor their number, for the bibliography is inadequate. In spite of its easy, pleasant style, it illustrates amply the danger of overpopularization.

As to C. Jean Cordeau's *Ahasvérus* (Paris, 1951), one can only suppose that the author had read but a few books in the vast library on the subject.[82]

B: Notes on the Wandering Jewess

It was the *Kurtze Beschreibung* that first presented Ahasuerus with a wife and child. In most subsequent references to this unhappy family both wife and child (or children) die in the course of their natural lives. Sometimes their deaths are hastened by the fact of the curse which befell the husband and father. In some rare instances there is the possibility that wife and children may be reincarnated, at least for a few generations.

In the eighteenth century, it will be remembered, Frau Krüger saw Ahasuerus with a female companion who shared his wanderings. This, so far as I can determine, is the first appearance of the Wandering Jewess, since the earlier version which presented twin wanderers (in the seventeenth century) insisted that they were both male.[1] Frau Krüger's contribution went unnoticed. Nearly a century later Edgar Quinet invented Rachel, who became a constant companion for Ahasuerus, typifying, as we have seen, the transcendent power of human love which is capable of any sacrifice. Then, a few years later, Eugène Sue introduced the Wandering Jewess (Herodias) as a sister rather than a wife, a being who had communication with Ahasuerus only at stated intervals, but who was altogether capable of serving as a benevolent manipulator of human destiny.

The fact is, of course, that Sue's Wandering Jew and Wandering Jewess, Ahasuerus and Herodias, represented, among other things, a social conscience of humanity. In that sense they represented all humanity as well, just as in contemporary letters the concept of Ahasuerus as an embodiment of the Jewish race was extended to mean the embodiment of all mankind. A long "fantastic" novel by Christoph Kuffner, *Die ewige Jüdin und der Orang-Outang* (1846) identifies the Wandering Jew and the Wandering Jewess with all men and women.[2] But the title leads one completely astray, because the work concentrates on a man's attitude toward the world, with a woman chiming in but feebly. The novel has really nothing to do with the Legend. A gifted orangutan in Borneo holds conversations with a poet in a story within a story. In the course of his talk he covers, in ironic attitudes, the whole of western European society—its intellectual pretenses, its dress, the baneful influence of the New World (including the vogue for mint juleps, Italian opera, tarot cards, and the like). It is a vast harlequinade of nearly six hundred pages. Sometimes the orangutan yields the floor to others. Actually, the whole performance is a string of essays on social and literary matters—Greek drama, Shakespeare's plays, the salon fever of the mid-nineteenth century. The work finally ends with the announcement of the death of the author of the novel within a novel, and the inclusion of some random notes on how things would have come out. For one thing, the orangutan would have been betrayed into captivity in a zoo. Kuffner's ultimate purpose seems to have been to demonstrate that, whatever its defects, man needs a society in which he can participate. This, the author states cryptically, is the "heavenly constellation."

Let us return for a moment to Sue's Wandering Jewess. In her handling of the treasure box she has left her mark upon a long and tedious novel by Ceferino Tresserra, *La*

Judía Errante (Barcelona-Madrid, 1862), where she is extremely helpful in getting some important documents into the hands of the rightful relatives of the Renneponts. The chief interest in this novel, however, lies in the love story, in which the Jewess takes no important part.

Again, if we consider Hans von Kahlenberg's *Ahasvera*, we discover that the title is applicable only to the mother of the intelligent young Jew who is confronted with the problems of his race in an unfriendly environment. The same situation arises in the case of the play by Viktor Hardung, *Ahasvera* (n.p., 1895), in which the title role is assumed by a Jewish woman who is wrestling with the problem of woman's place in the world of the 1890's in Germany.

Obviously the work which gives to the Wandering Jewess her most sensational part is George Sylvester Viereck's and Paul Eldridge's *Salome*, which has already been described (pp. 359-60). But two earlier works had already placed her on the road to the dissolute supersophistication which she attains in *Salome*. Karl Gutzkow's "Die ewige Jüdin," in *Die schöneren Stunden* (Stuttgart, 1869), is in part a satire upon the cultural "literary society" of the nineteenth century.[3] At the final meeting of this particular salon's season a worthy but pedantic young man delivers a lecture on the Wandering Jewess. We learn that she was Salome, daughter of Herodias, duly certified in the sixth chapter of the Gospel of Mark. The effete background of both women prompts the speaker to lavish digressions. The entire lecture becomes a bore, yet in the interests of research we must report it. Salome was a spoiled brat who had learned to dance, her specialty being a kind of cancan. She is first amused and then attracted by John the Baptist, and his austere spurning of her attentions leads to her request for his head. In punishment she must dance forever. Some say that later Herod was transferred by the suspicious Roman emperor to a post in the Pyrenees, and Herodias and Salome with him. Here the dancer danced upon thin ice, fell in, and was decapitated by an icicle. Others, however, are sure that she never died. But whether in fleshly or ghostly wise, she has become a leader in the witches' Sabbath and rides in the forefront of the Wild Huntsman's chase.[4]

Salome was her Hebrew name; her Egyptian one was Pharaïldis, from which is derived the name of Frau Hülden or Frau Holle, the Hecate of Germanic tradition, whom we met in the first play, or *myth*, of Haushofer's trilogy. Again, this places her in the picture as the *bekannte wilde Jägerin*. Like the Ahasuerus of folk tales, she may occasionally rest on an oak stump or amid a stand of hazel trees. On the other hand, the French tradition identifies Pharaïldis with Fée Abonde, the good fairy of the *Märchen*, the bestower of good things. As either good or evil, or both, she comes in her versatility to be the representative of all women who have been disturbed by the contact of their humdrum lives with a great soul whom they admire or love. She stands for all restless women, all kindly women, and all women who have done harm to men. A comprehensive order, this! The lecture concludes with a longish catalogue of examples—Mary Stuart, the Empress Theodora, Diane de Poitiers, Christina of Sweden, Pauline Bonaparte, and Madame de Staël.

The lecturer then winds up his sixty-page discourse by attacking the narrow-mindedness of the clergy, and by being accepted in matrimony by the belle of the salon, whom he had been courting openly for a long time. No one present is surprised at this, nor is the reader.

Far different is Henry Champly's *La juive errante* (Paris, 1921). This salty Gallic novel is based upon the old Hebrew tradition that a widow should marry her oldest brother-in-law. The scene is the eastern Mediterranean at an indeterminate date; whether before or after the time of Christ is deliberately left obscure, though I should say that the

Messiah has not yet come. Beautiful little Nohomi, daughter of a Jewish innkeeper, is raped by Hakoub, a sensual brute. He is forced by her family to marry the girl. He dies soon after of apoplexy, and she travels to find his oldest brother, Theodore, a voluptuary and a worshiper of Baal. In Corinth, trying to experience the highest pleasure infinitely prolonged—as in Viereck's and Eldridge's novel—the couple give their souls to the goddess of evil. Nohomi, the hardy female, survives, but Theodore perishes. Next, the widow travels to Palestine, where she attaches herself, according to the law, to the miserly Enosch, to whom money is all. His basic indifference to the ordinary conjugal relationship leads her finally to kill him, or at least to let him die when he was seriously injured. Her wickedness, however, is well washed away in her fourth marriage, this time to Nahoum, an ascetic prophet who is not too ascetic, a shadow of John the Baptist or perhaps Christ himself, a worker of healing miracles and a champion of oppressed laborers. But the healing does not last, and the laborers turn against him and kill him. He is, then, no more than a false Messiah. Yet he did much to purge Nohomi of her evil angel. In her newly found virtue she will be able to finish the purgation. As she is being transported to the home of her next husband, a sinister enough figure, we are left with the belief that her spiritual and physical experiences have toughened her in such a way that she will always be able to cope with life in the spirit of tenacious femininity. To call her the Wandering Jewess, however, is rather misleading. She wanders from the embraces of one man to those of another, but she always wanders with a purpose and within the framework of the law of her people.

The dramatic trilogy by Joseph C. Heywood—*Antonius, Herodias,* and *Salome,* all published in 1867—is of little moment.[5] The first two parts are concerned with Salome's parents. In the last, Salome has become a Christian, has traveled about extensively, even in Britain, is pursued by various men, including the Wandering Jew as Kaliphilus (*sic*), and is finally betrayed into captivity and killed at the fall of Jerusalem in A.D. 70. The writing is wildly melodramatic, the speeches interminable, and fustian is all over the place. It is difficult to see any reason why this particular Salome should be promoted to the tenure of the Wandering Jewess. She is a Judaeo-Christian girl who traveled about with her parents and came to an unhappy end. As for Kaliphilus, he goes on his way at the end, pursued by Roman soldiery, but he will not die.

We see, then, that of the various treatments of this troublesome female, the Wandering Jewess, those of Gutzkow and Viereck-Eldridge come the nearest to forming a complete picture of her. The fact is that Salome, or Herodias, or Pharaïldis, or whoever she may be, is an excrescence, an annoyance, not important enough to require much attention, and yet too visible to be ignored. We should agree with the inhabitants of Luggnag in *Gulliver's Travels,* who, in granting the dissolution of marriage to the immortal Struldbrugs when they reached the age of eighty, observed that it was "a reasonable indulgence that those who are condemned to a perpetual continuance in the world should not have their misery doubled by the load of a wife." Let us leave the Wandering Jew lonely at the close as he was at the beginning.

C: A Note on Modern Hungarian Treatments of the Legend

We have seen that the Legend circulated to some extent in Hungary through folk tales (p. 99), although apparently not with the same degree of currency as it did in Germany. Indeed, some of these tales might be regarded as importations from Germany, just as many of the Slavic folk tales could be so regarded. Yet it remains a possibility that they were derived from the eastern branch of the folk tale as it came up from Greece and the Balkans. In any event, they bespeak a knowledge of the Legend in non-Germanic territory at a reasonably early date. In his valuable article, "The Legend of the Wandering Jew in Hungary," published in *Midwest Folklore* for 1954, Alexander Scheiber has called attention to ten Hungarian chapbooks printed in the nineteenth century.[1] I therefore do not need to repeat his information here, save to comment on the derivative nature of these publications as he describes them.

With the development of the art form of the Legend, as we have seen it throughout the nineteenth century, it may be said that the Hungarian writers, like the romantic writers of western Europe in the nineteenth century, may either content themselves with passing references or else deal with Ahasuerus on a major scale. We have seen this kind of thing, of course, outside Hungary. This or that poet likens himself to the Wandering Jew in this or that respect. To many, Ahasuerus is important because he stands for the Jewish race as a whole.[2] He must wander until he has learned the meaning of pain and suffering, and how they can draw him to perfection.[3] Unless one can find a way to make the world happy, there is no salvation for anybody.[4] If, on the other hand, he could have faith that he can help the world in any way, he might be released.[5]

One Hungarian author, at least, is willing to associate Ahasuerus with the anti-Semitism of the Fascist state. In Joseph Erdelyi's "Ahasver és a varázsfurulyás" ("Ahasuerus and the Magic Flutist," 1935), Ahasuerus is identified with Judas, the venal self-seeker.[6] He wanders with the incredible flutist, who represents divine faith. He must dance when the flutist plays, even against his will, and must pay his due to the musician to get him to stop. At the royal court both are in love with the king's daughter, who prefers the flutist. Ahasuerus accuses the latter of a crime and succeeds in bringing about his sentence of death, but the last wish of the condemned musician is to play his flute, and so Ahasuerus must dance. The people are entranced by the music, turn on Ahasuerus, destroy him, and bestow his fortune on the flutist. The allegory is obvious.

A different note resounds from Lewis Aprilly's effective "Ahasver," in *Rasmussen hajóján* ("Rasmussen's Ship"; Budapest, 1926).[7] Here a touching smile on the face of a dead child, rejoicing because he has died young, turns the Jew away in tears, to face another year. In repentance, Ahasuerus plays a part in a Passion play by Géza Voinovich, *Magyar passio* (Budapest, 1931), where he moves among a group of pilgrims at the foot of the Cross.[8] But, whereas Aprilly's performance is moving, Voinovich's is not. Even so, it may be better to have Ahasuerus in tears of contrition than in the guise of universal evil, a role which has never particularly suited him.[9]

The influence of Sue seems to be evident in Francis Hagymasy's "A bolygó zsidó engesztelo napja" ("The Wandering Jew's Yom Kippur"), in *Kisvàrda* (1929), for Ahasuerus and his "wife" (not his sister) have been wandering for two thousand years in the universe and in the worlds to come, meeting only occasionally, until Jesus finally pardons them. They have a last meeting and die. But perhaps the most vigorous of these later Hungarian versions is that in Bela Zsolt, "Legenda a jeruzsálemi vargáról" ("A Legend of the Jerusalem Shoemaker," 1923).[10] When Jesus enters Jerusalem, the hunchbacked shoemaker is a noisy member of the crowd welcoming him, but when Jesus approaches his home later, wearing his crown of thorns, the shoemaker receives him with an oak club, spits in his face, and yells out, "Crucify him!"

By and large, the Hungarian works in question are neither among the best of all treatments of the Legend, nor are they among the worst. Some of them exhibit some true originality. The important consideration remains that they are worthy representatives of the fact that Ahasuerus has achieved an international reputation in the Western world since the nineteenth century gave him full recognition.

Notes

Chapter One

1. Stith Thompson, *Motif-Index of Folk Literature* (rev. ed.; Bloomington, Ind., 1955-58); sec. Q contains a wealth of allusion. Other general studies, in alphabetical order, are William Andrews, *Bygone Punishments* (London, 1899); Harry E. Barnes, *The Story of Punishment* (Boston, 1930); Alice Morse Earle, *Curious Punishments of Bygone Days* (New York, 1922); George Ives, *A History of Penal Methods* (New York, 1914); and Georg Rusche and Otto Kirchheimer, *Punishment and Social Structure* (New York, 1939). Of these, Andrews and Earle are popular treatments; Ives and Rusche-Kirchheimer the most professional; and Barnes the best single introduction.

2. Cantos 9, 10.

3. See the list in Gertrude Jobes, *Dictionary of Mythology, Folklore, and Symbols* (New York, 1962), III, 367-69.

4. Eugène Burnouf, *Introduction à l'histoire du bouddhisme indien* (Paris, 1876), pp. 353-55.

5. That is, to the Cartaphilus phase; see pp. 18-21 below.

6. Fifth Day, Fourth Diversion ("The Golden Root"). A convenient translation is by Richard Burton (New York, 1927).

7. See Hans Plischke, *Die Sage vom wilden Heere im deutschen Volke* (Eilenburg, 1914); Valentin Schweda, *Die Sagen vom wilden Jäger und vom schlafenden Heer in der Provinz Posen* (Gniezno, 1915); and Otto Höfler, *Kultische Geheimbünde der Germanen: I. Das germanische Totenheer—Mythos und Kult* (Frankfurt, 1934). For Celtic parallels, see Tom Peete Cross, *Motif-Index of Early Irish Literature* (Bloomington, Ind., 1952), and his notes in *Béaloideas*, XXII (1951-52), 321. For other analogues, see Thompson, *Motif-Index*, Motif E 501.

8. The story is well told by the Anglo-Latin cleric Walter Map: see *Master Walter Map's Book, "De Nugis Curialium" (Courtiers' Trifles)*, trans. Frederick Tupper and Marbury B. Ogle (London, 1924), pp. 15-17, 223. There are some good older comments in Felix Liebrecht, *Zur Volkskunde* (Heilbronn, 1879), pp. 27-28.

9. As it appears in the great medieval story collection *Gesta Romanorum*; in Hermann Oesterley's edition (Berlin, 1872), Tale 190. See also J. L. Heiberg, "Theodorich vom den vilde Haeger," *Dania*, IX (1902), 239-40.

10. See Appendix B. The best study is Waldemar Kloss, "Herodias the Wild Huntress in the Legend of the Middle Ages," *Modern Language Notes*, XXIII (1908), 82-85, 100-2. See also Theodor Zachariae, "Abergläubische Meinungen und Gebräuche des Mittelalters in den Predigten Bernardinos von Siena," *Zeitschrift des Vereins für Volkskunde*, XXII (1912), 225-44, especially p. 238.

11. For these and other matters pertaining to the Wild Huntsman, see Thompson, *Motif-Index*, Motif E 501 with all variants.

12. He is referred to in Shakespeare's *The Merry Wives of Windsor*, IV, iv, 28-38, and V, v, 31-108; and in William Harrison Ainsworth's novel *Windsor Castle* (New York, 1843), pp. 281-96.

13. Thompson, *Motif-Index*, Motif E 501 with all variants.

14. A convenient modern edition is in *American Short Stories of the Nineteenth Century*, ed. John Cournos (Everyman's Library, No. 840; New York, 1955).

Chapter Two

1. One of these legends tells how the Gypsies, or more specifically a Gypsy woman, reviled Christ as he was bearing his cross. For this reason the Gypsies wander. The Gypsy woman appears in allusion in a few pieces of the late nineteenth and early twentieth centuries (p. 393). In another version from the Balkans in general and Romania in particular, the Gypsies made the nails to be used in the Crucifixion, and so were set to wandering. Their reply to the accusation was that they made the nails thin in order to save Christ some pain, but the excuse was deemed insufficient.

2. Beginning with Chrysostom's comments on John 18:10 in the fifth century and following

through Thomas Aquinas (*Catena aurea in quatuor evangelia*) of the thirteenth to various churchmen and writers of medieval drama of the fifteenth century, there persists the tradition that the servant of the high priest was in fact Malchus. See Leonhard Neubaur, *Die Sage vom ewigen Juden* (2d ed.; Leipzig, 1893), p. 4.

3. See *Le Pré spirituel,* a French translation by M. J. Rouët de Journel (Paris, 1946), pp. 70-71. A German version is offered in Leonhard Neubaur, "Zur Geschichte der Sage vom ewigen Juden," *Zeitschrift des Vereins für Volkskunde,* XXII (1912), 33-54, one of the more important brief articles on the Legend.

4. For this and similar matters pertaining to the Legend of St. John, see Richard A. Lipsius, *Die apokryphen Apostelgeschichten und Apostellegenden* (Brunswick, 1883-87), I, 348-592. The medieval version is well exemplified in Anton Hübner, "Eine altfranzösische Fassung der Johanneslegende," *Zeitschrift für romanische Philologie,* Suppl. 53 (1919).

5. On this point the article by John Chapman on Papias in the *Catholic Encyclopedia* is most illuminating.

6. Sulpicius Severus touches on this in his *Chronica,* and Tertullian in his *De Anima,* chap. l; see J. H. Waszink's edition of the latter (Amsterdam, 1947), p. 68. The Legend of St. John keeps reappearing later, of course—in the writings of the twelfth-century Theophylactus, archbishop of Bulgaria, and in the fifteenth-century George of Trevizond, among others—but the matter need not detain us longer.

7. First cited in V.-A.-J.-M. Coremans, *La Licorne et le Juif-Errant* (Brussels, 1845), p. 23. As is evident, this tale is connected with Elijah, a prophet concerned, *inter alia,* with weather and therefore with crops; the parallel of Elijah with the Wandering Jew is therefore not close, nor is the similar analogue of Al-Khadir (pp. 347, 409 below). J. J. Gielen gives a Dutch version of the tale of Fadhila in his *De wandelende Jood in Volkskunde en Letterkunde* (Amsterdam, 1931), p. 20, but further attention at this point is not necessary.

8. *The Chronicle of Ahimaaz,* ed. and trans. Marcus Salzman (New York, 1924), pp. 65-66.

9. Typical specimens of these are given in chap. iv.

10. The tale of Antonio di Francesco di Andrea; see pp. 25-26 below.

11. Edited by Augusto Gaudenzi at Naples in 1888. The Latin text of the relevant passage is given in Neubaur, "Zur Geschichte," p. 37.

12. See *Rogeri de Wendover liber qui dicitur Flores Historiarum,* ed. H. G. Hewlett (Rolls Series, No. 84; London, 1886-89), II, 352. There is an English translation by J. A. Giles: *Roger of Wendover's Flowers of History* (Bohn's Antiquarian Library; London, 1849), II, 512-14.

13. In the Italian chronicle, the Latin phrase is *iniuriose pepulerat;* it is still a question in my mind whether the Latin *pellere* necessarily means a physical blow. It can be so translated on occasion. In Roger of Wendover's account there is no question, for the blow is specific: "Pepulit eum pugno post tergum impie."

14. There has been general agreement on this etymology.

15. Matthew Paris, *Chronica Majora,* ed. H. R. Luard (Rolls Series, No. 57; London, 1872-83), III, 161. The entry for 1252 is to be found in V, 340. For an English translation by J. A. Giles, see Matthew Paris' *English History: From the Year 1235 to 1259* (Bohn's Antiquarian Library; London, 1889), II, 542.

16. Edited by Baron Frédéric-Auguste de Reiffenberg (Brussels, 1836-45), II, 491.

17. Listed in Avrahm Yarmolinsky, "The Wandering Jew," *Studies in Jewish Bibliography and Related Subjects* (New York, 1929), pp. 319-28; issued also as a separate pamphlet.

18. This etymology has now been accepted, but not until there had been some controversy. Older suggestions were that it came from a Hebrew word meaning "mother's breast" or "breast," and so could be applied to the disciple whom Jesus loved, who lay in his bosom—that is, John. This would immediately associate Buttadeus with Cartaphilus. Another suggestion is that *but* is a variant of the Hebrew *ben* ("son"); see Johann Georg Theodor Grässe, *Die Sage vom ewigen Juden* (rev. ed.; Dresden, 1861), p. 127. But the suggestion of "foster son" emerging is unsatisfactory. It was Gaston Paris who suggested the present etymology by deriving

the name from the Latin *batuere*, first in his ground-breaking article, "Le Juif errant," published first in the *Encyclopédie des sciences religieuses* in 1880 and then as a separate pamphlet at Florence in 1881; and later in *Romania*, X (1881), 212, he backed up his theory: "On serait tenté . . . d'y voir un composé de 'bouter' et de 'Dieu,' et le nom signifierait 'celui qui frappe, qui pousse Dieu.'" In the same issue of *Romania* (p. 214), Alessandro d'Ancona supported Paris. The proposed etymology has always seemed at once the simplest and least far-fetched.

19. The first edition is very rare; more accessible is that printed at Basel in 1550, in which see Part I, sec. 5.

20. For an account of this cognate legend, see Felix Liebrecht, *Zur Volkskunde* (Heilbronn, 1879), pp. 107-8.

21. Quoted in Salomone Morpurgo, *L'Ebreo errante in Italia* (Florence, 1891), p. 9.

22. *Ibid.*, pp. 9-10.

23. Cited in Gielen, *De wandelende Jood*, p. 22.

24. This is Book I, entitled *Le Livre de forme de plait* by Filippo de Novara (Philippe de Novaire), written between 1250 and 1255 and printed by Count Beugnot at Paris in 1841 as part of the *Recueil des Historiens des Croisades*. The germane passage is found on p. 570. See also Gaston Paris, *Le Juif errant en Italie* (Paris, 1891), p. 3.

25. "Rime inedite dei secoli XIII e XIV," ed. Tomaso Casini in *Il Propugnatore*, XV, Part II (1882), 335-39; the part dealing with the Legend specifically is printed again by Alessandro d'Ancona, *Romania*, XII (1883), 112. Gielen, *De wandelende Jood*, p. 22, refers to a poem of about 1275 of similar import. I can find no trace of this, and in view of Gielen's notorious bibliographical inaccuracies, I believe he is talking of the 1274 poem. In this case, his bibliographical reference is to a work which mentions the 1274 poem only.

26. Ermete Pierotti, *Jerusalem Explored*, trans. T. G. Bonney (London, 1864). But most of our information concerning these comes from the many studies of individual journals or accounts of travels from various pilgrims. Those which pertain to the Legend are enumerated in P. B. Bagatti, "The Wandering Jew," *Franciscan Studies*, IX (1949), 1-9, and notes.

27. Leonhard Neubaur, *Neue Mitteilungen über die Sage vom ewigen Juden* (Leipzig, 1893), p. 2, n. 5.

28. Edited by Canon Domenico Moreni (Florence, 1822), p. 29.

29. Alessandro d'Ancona, "Le Juif errant en Italie au XIIIe siècle," *Romania*, X (1881), 212-16.

30. Morpurgo, *L'Ebreo errante in Italia*, pp. 15-40. There is a French paraphrase in Gaston Paris's *Légendes du moyen âge* (Paris, 1903), pp. 230-45, and a translation in part in his *Le Juif errant en Italie*, pp. 4-29.

31. Morpurgo, *L'Ebreo errante in Italia*, pp. 45-47.

32. This, however, is a rare tradition, and I am inclined to believe that it represents a contamination of the Legend of Cain with that of the Wandering Jew. Or it may simply be an elaboration of the vagabond element in Cain's fate (see Genesis 4:12). It is first reported in Niccolò da Poggibonsi's fourteenth-century *Libro d'Oltramare*, ed. A. Bacchi della Lega (Bologna, 1881), II, 25.

33. For the motif of the inexhaustible purse, see Stith Thompson, *Motif-Index of Folk Literature* (rev. ed.; Bloomington, Ind., 1955-58), Motif D 1431. Although best known through German *Volksbücher*, it may very well have been in Spain that the inexhaustible purse, the cloak of invisibility, and the fabulous traveling garment were combined into the figure of Fortunatus.

34. In *El Criticón* (Huesca, 1653), Book II; in the edition of Julio Cejador y Frauca (Madrid, 1913-14), I, 287-89. For variations of the name of the protagonist in Spain, see also J. E. Gillet, "Traces of the Wandering Jew in Spain," *Romanic Review*, XXII (1931), 16-27.

35. Although the name appears in the sixteenth century, there is no satisfactory explanation of it until the nineteenth, when the folk tale was inserted in the pages of Fernán Caballero's novel *La Estrella de Vandalia* (Madrid, 1860), pp. 61-63. The standard edition is in Caballero's *Obras*

completas (Colección de escritores castellanos, CXXXI; Madrid, 1906), pp. 98-101.

36. Biblioteca económica de clásicos castellanos (Paris, 1912).

37. For all four, see the valuable early article by Carolina Michaelis de Vasconcellos, "O Judeu errante em Portugal," *Revista Lusitana*, I (1887-89), 34-45, and II (1893-95), 74-76.

38. The best single study of the Legend of Fortunatus remains H. Günther, *Zur Herkunft des Volksbuches von Fortunatus und seinen Söhnen* (Freiburg, 1914), but this tends to concentrate upon the German *Volksbuch* of 1509. The matter must remain a surmise only.

39. The two most useful studies, in order of importance, of the Legend in the Iberian peninsula are Gillet, "Traces," and Marcel Bataillon, "Pérégrinations espagnoles du juif errant," *Bulletin Hispanique*, XLIII (1941), 81-122.

40. See p. 24 above, and Gillet, "Traces," p. 23.

41. See Bataillon, "Pérégrinations," pp. 100-3.

42. As a matter of fact, the roles of Boutedieu or Malc are usually no more than walk-on parts, as if the author were not familiar with their participation in the Legend, or with the Legend itself. See Alice M. Killen, "L'évolution de la légende du Juif Errant," *Revue de Littérature Comparée*, V (1925), 5-37, especially p. 19; and particularly Hans Giese, *La Passion de Jésus Christ jouée à Valenciennes l'an 1547* (Greifswald, 1905).

43. Wilhelm Michael Anton Creizenach, *Geschichte des neueren Drama* (Halle, 1893-1916), I, 224.

44. Ed. Frances A. Foster (Early English Text Society, CXLVII; London, 1916), pp. 72-73.

45. Archer Taylor, "Notes on the Wandering Jew," *Modern Language Notes*, XXXIII (1918), 394.

46. Geoffrey Chaucer, *The Pardoner's Tale*, ll. 720-38, in *The Complete Works of Geoffrey Chaucer*, ed. F. N. Robinson (Cambridge, Mass., 1957). See in particular Nelson Sherwin Bushnell, "The Wandering Jew and the *Pardoner's Tale*," *Studies in Philology*, XXVIII (1931), 450-60.

47. This is not to say that there are not perpetual wanderers, but they are none of them the Wandering Jew. The distinction must be maintained.

48. See pp. 73-74 below.

49. See p. 115 below.

50. Sabine Baring-Gould, *Curious Myths of the Middle Ages* (rev. ed.; London, 1881), pp. 637-40; see also pp. 1-31.

51. Zuallardo and his *Devotissimo viaggio di Gerusalemme* (Rome, 1587), as well as Della Valle and his *Viaggi* (Rome, 1662), are discussed by Morpurgo, *L'Ebreo errante in Italia*, p. 12, n. 1. Agostino and his *Viaggio de Terra Santa e di Gerusalemme* (Tederici, 1886) and others appear in Alessandro d'Ancona, *Saggi di Letteratura popolare* (Liverno, 1913).

52. "Jan Baudewijn," ed. Emanuel Neefs, *Revue Catholique*, XXXV (1873), 577-79. This is a reprint of one of the several versions of Jan Aerts's narrative. The earliest extant is *Warachtige Beschryvunge der Jerusalemsche Reyse*, etc., printed at Leyden with no date but presumably during the sixteenth century; then *Coort Verhael eender heerlijcker Reysen*, etc. (Antwerp, 1595), and finally *Verscheyde Voyagien, ofte Reysen*, etc. (Dordrecht, 1652). The last named is less detailed and less vivid. There are also some minor variations in names and other details of no great importance for our general purposes.

53. *Fratris Felicis Fabri Evagatorium in Terrae Sanctae, Arabiae et Egypti peregrinationem*, ed. C. D. Hassler (Stuttgart, 1843).

54. *Reverendi patris, fratris Michaelis Menoti ordinis Franciscani Sermones*, etc. (Paris, 1525).

55. It was finally published by Alessandro d'Ancona under the title, "La leggenda dell'Ebreo errante," *Nuova Antologia*, Ser. 2, XXIII (1880), 418-20.

56. There is no extant original, but the story is told by several writers, notably by Father Quaresmi and Father Laffi. Pannalius' name, however, does not appear in the *Navis Peregrinorum*, a collection of the names of pilgrims in the guest registers of the Franciscans in Jerusa-

lem. This is described and printed in Bertrand Zimolong's edition (Cologne, 1938). See also Leonhard Lemmens' *Collectanea Terrae Sanctae* (Florence, 1933).

57. (Venice, 1881), II, 142.

58. (Bologna, 1683), p. 161.

59. Fr. Eugène Roger, in *La Terre Saincte* (Paris, 1664), p. 123, tells the same story, but from a later date.

60. See Neubaur, *Neue Mitteilungen*, p. 6, nn. 10-13. The Auberton material is reproduced by Emile Picot in *Revue Critique d'histoire et de littérature*, I (1884), 222-26. The probable identity of Auberton and Dauterlin is generally assumed; see Killen, "L'évolution," p. 20.

61. In his *Itinerarium breve Terrae Sanctae* (Florence, 1891), p. 161. There were other similar repetitions of the story which it is hardly practical to include here. I am much indebted, however, to Bagatti, "The Wandering Jew," pp. 1-9.

62. See pp. 288-89 below.

63. See especially Giuseppe Pitrè, *Fiabe, novelle e raconti popolari siciliani* (Palermo, 1875), pp. 131-38.

Chapter Three

1. Wilhelm Bousset, *The Antichrist Legend: A Chapter in Christian and Jewish Folklore*, trans. A. H. Keane (London, 1896). A most useful later treatment is Joshua Trachtenberg, *The Devil and the Jews* (New Haven, 1943), particularly for its relation of medieval belief to the Jewish question.

2. See Edmund K. Chambers, *The Mediaeval Stage* (reprint; Oxford, 1925), II, 62-64.

3. See David Strumpf, *Die Juden in der mittelalterlichen Mysterien-, Mirakel- und Moralitäten-Dichtung Frankreichs* (Ladenburg, 1920), p. 16; Oscar Frankl, *Der Jude in den deutschen Dichtunger des 15. 16. und 17. Jahrhunderts* (Leipzig, 1905), p. 27; Hans Preuss, *Die Vorstellungen von Antichrist im späteren Mittelalter* (Leipzig, 1906), p. 28; and especially Trachtenberg, *The Devil and the Jews*, chaps. vi-x.

4. See Preuss, *Die Vorstellungen*, pp. 5-10, 23-24, 41.

5. This motif appears in the Besançon Antichrist play and in various later French and German versions. See Preuss, *Die Vorstellungen*, p. 15, as well as *Handwörterbuch des deutschen Aberglaubens*, ed. Hanns Bächtold-Stäubli and Eduard Hoffmann-Krayer (Berlin, 1927-42), IV, 816, and J. E. Scherer, *Beiträge zur Geschichte des Judenrechtes im Mittelalter: I. Die Rechtsverhältnisse der Juden in den deutsch-österreichischen Ländern* (Leipzig, 1901), p. 433.

6. See Ludwig Geiger, "Die Juden und die deutsche Literatur des 16. Jahrhundert," *Zeitschrift für die Geschichte der Juden in Deutschland*, II (1888), 308-74; III (1889), 295-98.

7. (Paris, 1875-96), VII, 326; IX, 333-44.

8. Leonhard Neubaur, *Neue Mitteilungen über die Sage vom ewigen Juden* (Leipzig, 1893), p. 11, n. 40.

9. First printed at Barth (Pomerania) in 1597; see Leonhard Neubaur, *Die Sage vom ewigen Juden* (2d ed.; Leipzig, 1893), p. 113, n. 29. Note the resemblance to the medieval fifteen signs of doom.

10. The author is given as Nicolaus Raimarus; the title page is reproduced in Neubaur, *Die Sage*, p. 113, n. 30.

11. Jean Moreau, *Histoire de ce qui s'est passé en Bretagne durant les guerres de la Ligue et particulièrement dans le diocèse de Cornuaille* (Brest, 1836), pp. 347-49.

12. The great authority on the bibliography of the *Volksbuch* among the German-speaking peoples remains Leonhard Neubaur. The entire second part of his *Die Sage*, pp. 53-65, is devoted to the printing of the *Kurtze Beschreibung* and the Dudulaeus pamphlets. The third part of his work is given over to a discussion of the various editions of the *Kurtze Beschreibung*. J. J. Gielen, in the bibliography to his *De wandelende Jood in Volkskunde en Letterkunde* (Amsterdam, 1931), pp. 165-88, has listed the extant versions comprising the *Volksbuch* in Europe,

but it is a mere listing. Both works, however, entirely supersede Aaron Schaffer, "The *Ahasver-Volksbuch* of 1602," *Modern Philology*, XVII (1919-20), 597-604. The *Kurtze Beschreibung* has also been reprinted as Appendix A in George K. Anderson, "The Wandering Jew Returns to England," *Journal of English and Germanic Philology*, XLV (1946), 237-50; see particularly pp. 248-50 (this is the only American printing of the *Kurtze Beschreibung* in German).

13. Leonhard Neubaur, "Zur Geschichte der Sage vom ewigen Juden," *Zeitschrift des Vereins für Volkskunde*, XXII (1912), 39.

14. In his *Das Volksbuch vom ewigen Juden* (Danzig, 1927).

15. First suggested by Theodor Schiemann in his review of Neubaur's *Die Sage* in *Baltische Monatsschrift*, XXXI (1884), 619-24, especially pp. 621-23.

16. That is, on the basis of written literature before 1602. There is no way of telling about an oral tradition before that.

17. These and one or two other theories are found in Neubaur, "Zur Geschichte," p. 42.

18. See pp. 29-30 above.

19. Neubaur, "Zur Geschichte," p. 43, quotes both Waldis and Gruter.

20. An amusing corroboration of this concept is found in William Henderson, *Notes on the Folklore of the Northern Counties* (London, 1879), p. 82. An old shoemaker of Devonshire, on being reproved for his shiftlessness, observed: "Don't'ee be hard on me. We shoemakers are a poor slobbering race, and so have been ever since the curse that Jesus Christ laid on us." "And what was that?" she [who was chiding him] asked. "Why," said he, "when they were carrying Him to the cross they passed a shoemaker's bench, and the man looked up and spat at Him; and the Lord turned and said, 'A poor slobbering fellow shalt thou be, and all shoemakers after thee, for what thou hast done to Me.'"

21. The leading character in *The Shoemaker's Holiday* (1600), a comedy by Thomas Dekker. As for Hans Sachs, his fame as a mastersinger and poet should not blind us to the fact that he was also a shoemaker.

22. Rudolf Schwartz, *Esther im deutschen und neulateinischen Drama des Reformationszeitalters* (Leipzig, 1894).

23. This was broached by Albert Joseph Edmunds in "The Wandering Jew: His Probable Buddhist Origins," *Notes and Queries*, Ser. 11, VII (1913), 47.

24. The reference to this comes in a minor work, *Evangelia der Fest von Sontage durchs gantze Jahr*, etc., written by Paulus von Eitzen and published in Schleswig in 1590 and dedicated to Christine, daughter of Adolf of Schleswig and Holstein.

25. These also have been described by Neubaur, *Die Sage*, pp. 73-93; the one he considers the best representative of the 1602 series he prints, along with the *Kurtze Beschreibung*, on pp. 53-65. For the verse additions, see particularly Neubaur, "Zur Geschichte," p. 42.

26. These pamphlets occasionally broke into verses of varying lengths, the most striking being a kind of supplement to a version of the Dudulaeus pamphlets published in 1621 at Frankfurt. The author is Daniel Sudermann. The content comprises some scriptural justification for the circumstances, a description of the protagonist tallying with that in the *Volksbuch*, giving his name and explaining his predicament. The conclusion impresses upon the reader that the Jew is a living witness to what has gone before. But Sudermann's piece is more extensive than most, being of some hundred short lines in couplets. Most of the verse-comments are short. See Neubaur, "Zur Geschichte," p. 44.

27. Note particularly the description of this in Neubaur, *Die Sage*, pp. 79-81.

28. I choose to regard it as a printer's error; in any event it must not be taken seriously.

29. *Praxis Alchymiae* (Frankfurt, 1604). The passage which is germane is in the Supplement (*Additio*) to Book II, which has been edited by Karl Simrock in the periodical *Wolfs Zeitschrift*, I (1875), 435-36.

30. This particular tale was considered a good exemplum because the persons involved were seven Christian youths who took refuge in a cave from the persecutions of the emperor

Decius, fell asleep miraculously, and did not awaken until two or three centuries had brought Christianity to be the established religion of the Empire. It was a tale well suited for illustrating the miraculous power of God in preserving life.

31. P. 271.

32. XI, 385.

33. (Leyden, 1619), XIII, 357.

34. The first edition of Cayet's *Chronologie Septenaire* (Paris, 1605) is now very rare. In the more easily accessible third edition of 1607, the reference is to VII, 440-42.

35. *Mémoires-Journaux*, IX (April, 1609), 244.

36. *Histoire et antiquitez du diocèse de Beauvais* (Rouen, 1631-35), II, 677.

37. Versions of *Les rencontres faist* appeared as late as 1650. See Champfleury, *Histoire de l'imagerie populaire* (Paris, 1869), p. 80, and his "D'une nouvelle interprétation de la légende gothique du Juif-Errant," *Revue Germanique et Française*, XXX (1864), 299-325.

38. For the passages taken from the *Histoire admirable*, see particularly Neubaur, *Die Sage*, pp. 121-22, n. 74.

39. This is one of the very few examples of the impingement of the Legend of the Wandering Jew upon the Celtic world. There are also some Breton folk tales (pp. 85-86 below). The *guerz* (*gwerz, gwers, guers*) is a song-narrative in the nature of a *complainte*. The piece is given in Champfleury, *Histoire*, pp. 81-88.

40. Printed in *ibid.*, pp. 165-72. Curiously enough, there is a translation into German in Moritz Hartmann, *Bretonische Volkslieder* (Cologne, 1859), pp. 370-73.

41. Johann Georg Theodor Grässe, *Der Tannhäuser und der Ewige Jude* (2d ed.; Dresden, 1861), p. 127.

42. See Champfleury, *Histoire*, p. 33; Claude d'Esternod, *L'Espadon satyrique* (Cologne, 1680), V, 56.

43. First printed at Lübeck; there was a second edition, somewhat enlarged, in 1662.

44. First published at Leyden; his name also appears as Clüver or Cluwer.

45. See pp. 395-422 for germane material.

46. Edited by Johann Jacob Vogel (Leipzig, 1714); see p. 582.

47. *Memoryen ofte cort verhael der gedenck-weerdichste so kercklicke als worltlicke gheschiedenissen van Nederland, etc.* (Arnhem, 1624), Book VIII.

48. Canon Jean Cousin, *Histoire de Tournay* (Douai, 1619), IV, 367; the appropriate passages are cited by Baron Frédéric-Auguste de Reiffenberg in *Annuaire de la Bibliothèque royale de Belgique* (Brussels, 1840-50), pp. 201-2.

49. Noted by Gielen, *De wandelende Jood*, p. 177, n. 1 (under bibliographical item 218a).

50. These and other similar pictorial presentations are listed in *ibid.*, pp. 188-91; some are reproduced in Champfleury, *Histoire*, pp. 1-104, and in Pierre Louis Duchartre and René Saulnier, *L'imagerie populaire* (Paris, 1925), pp. 69, 321.

51. The issuance of these licenses was first noted in William Carew Hazlitt, *Second Series of Bibliographical Collections and Notes on Early English Literature, 1474-1700* (London, 1882), pp. 247, 316.

52. The collected *Roxburghe Ballads* (8 vols.) and the *Bagford Ballads* (2 vols.) have been published separately in London for the Ballad Society in 1868-95 and 1878, respectively. The ballad mentioned here appeared as No. 718 in the third part of the original Roxburghe collection and as No. 8 in the second part of the original Bagford collection.

53. II, 291-96.

54. John Ker Roxburghe, *Roxburghe Ballads* (London, 1868-95), VI, 693-94. The date of the original issue of the ballad is August 21, 1612, or October 9, 1620.

55. Unless it is the same as the 1620 ballad, the 1612 ballad has escaped previous notice.

56. Those which could have been available to an Englishman are mentioned on p. 54 above.

57. The transcription is literal, except for the paragraphing and minimal changes in the punctuation.

58. A seventeenth-century version of this turns up in Iceland.

59. Kristoffer Nyrop, *Fortids Sagn og Sange* (Copenhagen, 1907-9), II, 58; the ballad is discussed on p. 166 below, the chronicle on p. 144 below.

60. Gielen, *De wandelende Jood*, p. 186, has a bibliographical reference to an edition of 1776, which I cannot verify. The 1805 pamphlet was printed at Karlskrona.

61. Not noted by Gielen whose general list of chapbooks on the subject is usually comprehensive.

62. Printed in Turussa. A German version of the Finnish, *Der Schuster von Jerusalem*, appeared in Abo in 1822. There are a few late-nineteenth-century translations of the German into Estonian, and one in Polish (1852), listed in Gielen, *De wandelende Jood*, pp. 187-88.

63. Noted in Avrahm Yarmolinsky, "The Wandering Jew," *Studies in Jewish Bibliography and Related Subjects* (New York, 1929), pp. 319-28 (which is also issued as a separate pamphlet). This is much the best bibliographical aid to the preliminary study of the Legend in Slavic territory.

64. Alexander Scheiber, "The Legend of the Wandering Jew in Hungary," *Midwest Folklore*, IV (1954), 231-35.

65. Alfred Ruhemann, "Die Sage vom ewigen Juden in Italien," *Nord und Süd*, LXXV (1895), 67-84, particularly p. 71.

66. There is also a copy in the W. Easton Louttit, Jr., collection on the Legend of the Wandering Jew in the Brown University Library.

Chapter Four

1. J. J. Gielen, *De wandelende Jood in Volkskunde en Letterkunde* (Amsterdam, 1931), p. 3.

2. *Ibid.*

3. *Ibid.*

4. *Le folk-lore de Lesbos*, comp. and trans. G. Georgeakis and Léon Pineau (Paris, 1894), p. 345.

5. Gielen, *De wandelende Jood*, p. 4.

6. *Ibid.*

7. Avrahm Yarmolinsky, "The Wandering Jew," *Studies in Jewish Bibliography and Related Subjects* (New York, 1929), pp. 323–28.

8. A. Wesselofsky, "Der ewige Jude," *Archiv für slavische Philologie*, V (1881), 398-401.

9. *Ibid.*

10. P. B. Bagatti, "The Wandering Jew," *Franciscan Studies*, IX (1949), 6.

11. Yarmolinsky, "The Wandering Jew," pp. 326–27.

12. *Ibid.*, pp. 327-28.

13. *Ibid.*, p. 325.

14. Leonhard Neubaur, "Zur Geschichte des Sage vom ewigen Juden," *Zeitschrift des Vereins für Volkskunde*, XXII (1912), 46.

15. Ernst Meier, *Deutsche Sagen, Sitten und Gebräuche aus Schwaben* (Stuttgart, 1852), I, 116.

16. Adalbert Kuhn, *Sagen, Gebräuche, und Märchen aus Westfalen und einigen andern, besonders den angrenzenden Gegenden Norddeutschlands* (Leipzig, 1859), I, 115.

17. Ludwig Strackerjan, *Aberglaube und Sagen aus dem Herzogthum Oldenburg* (Oldenburg, 1867), II, 11.

18. Neubaur, "Zur Geschichte," p. 46.

19. Leonhard Neubaur, *Neue Mitteilungen über die Sage vom ewigen Juden* (Leipzig, 1893), p. 13.

20. *Ibid.*

21. *Deutsche Alpensagen*, ed. Johann Nepomuk von Alpenburg (Vienna, 1861), p. 17.

22. Baron Frédéric-Auguste de Reiffenberg, *Annuaire de la Bibliothèque royale de Belgique* (Brussels, 1840-50), pp. 171-77.

23. Georg Schambach and Wilhelm Müller, *Niedersächsische Sagen und Märchen* (Göttingen, 1855), p. 243.

24. Gielen, *De wandelende Jood*, p. 8.

25. Karl Mullenhoff, *Sagen, Märchen, und Lieder der Herzogthumer Schleswig, Holstein und Lauenburg* (Kiel, 1845), p. 160.

26. Neubaur, "Zur Geschichte," p. 45.

27. Otto Schell, *Bergische Sagen* (Elberfeld, 1897), p. 46.

28. Leonhard Neubaur, *Die Sage vom ewigen Juden* (2d ed.; Leipzig, 1893), p. 130.

29. Schell, *Bergische Sagen*, p. 33.

30. Neubaur, *Die Sage*, p. 46.

31. *Ibid.*

32. *Ibid.*

33. *Ibid.*

34. Ernst Ludwig Rochholz, *Schweizersagen aus dem Aargau* (Aarau, 1856), II, 306.

35. J. Rappold, *Sagen aus Kärnten* (Augsburg, 1887), pp. 211-15.

36. Theodor Vernaleken, *Alpensagen* (Vienna, 1858), pp. 52-53, and Franz Josef Vonbun, *Die Sagen Vorarlbergs* (Innsbruck, 1889), pp. 97-98.

37. Vernaleken, *Alpensagen*, p. 53.

38. *Deutsche Alpensagen*, ed. Von Alpenburg, p. 176. The same tale is told in the neighboring village of Imst.

39. Rappold, *Sagen aus Kärnten*, p. 53.

40. Neubaur, *Neue Mitteilungen*, p. 12.

41. *Ibid.*, p. 14. The best collection of tales from the neighborhood is Ignatz Zingerle, *Sagen aus Tirol* (Innsbruck, 1891); see especially pp. 18, 515, 532.

42. Josef Ferdinand Lentner, *Geschichten aus Tirol und Oberbaiern*, ed. D. K. Rosegger (4th ed.; Leipzig, 1881), pp. 120-22.

43. Rappold, *Sagen aus Kärnten*, p. 212.

44. Johann August Ernst Köhler, *Volksbrauch, Aberglaube, Sagen und andere alte Ueberlieferungen im Voigtlande, mit Berücksichtigung des Orlagaus und des Pleissenerlandes* (Leipzig, 1867), p. 568.

45. See the anonymous article, "Der ewige Jude zu Münnich Kirchen," *Zeitschrift für österreichische Volkskunde*, X (1860), 113.

46. Rappold, *Sagen aus Kärnten*, p. 213.

47. Eduard Osenbruggen, *Wanderstudien aus der Schweiz* (Schaffhausen, 1867), I, 256-57.

48. Vernaleken, *Alpensagen*, p. 13.

49. Heinrich Dubi, "Drei spätmittelalterliche Legenden in ihrer Wanderung aus Italien durch die Schweiz nach Deutschland," *Zeitschrift des Vereins für Volkskunde*, XVII (1907), 143-60.

50. Vernaleken, *Alpensagen*, p. 13.

51. *Ibid.*, and Dubi, "Drei spätmittelalterliche Legenden," pp. 143-60; see also *Deutsche Sagen*, ed. Heinrich Pröhle (Berlin, 1863), pp. 166-70.

52. *Deutsche Sagen*, ed. Pröhle, pp. 166-70, in particular.

53. *Deutsche Sagen*, ed. Jacob and Wilhelm Grimm (2d ed.; Berlin, 1865-66), p. 392; Rochholz, *Schweizersagen*, p. 307; *Walliser Sagen-Sitten* (Basel, 1872), p. 95, found also in Friedrich

Staub and Ludwig Tobler, *Schweizerischen Idiotiken*, I (1875), 609; Maria Savi-Lopez, *Alpensagen*, trans. Alfred Ruhemann (Stuttgart, 1893), p. 182.

54. *Taschenbuch für die vaterländische Geschichte*, ed. Joseph von Hormayr-Hortenburg (Munich, 1834), 216–17. See also Vernaleken, *Alpensagen*, p. 13.

55. Dubi, "Drei spätmittelalterliche Legenden," p. 149.

56. *Ibid.*, p. 155.

57. *Ibid.*, p. 143.

58. Otto Henne-am-Rhyn, *Die deutsche Volkssage*, comp. Joseph Anton Renne (Leipzig, 1874), pp. 378-79.

59. I quote from the third edition (Berlin, 1884), I, 82.

60. The Bern exhibit has been described by Heinrich Dubi in "Curiosa von Bern und der Stadtbibliothek in Bern," *Blätter für Bernische Geschichte, Kunst und Altertumskunde*, II (1906), 305, and XVII (1917), 157. Associated with the shoes was a mysterious banner. The whole thing can best be explained as an old exhibit of a shoemakers' guild. The Ulm exhibit, on the other hand, has been actually viewed by Neubaur and described by him, along with its history, in his "Zur Geschichte," p. 47, n. 3.

61. Henne-am-Rhyn, *Die deutsche Volkssage*, p. 379.

62. Vernaleken, *Alpensagen*, p. 13. Here we have a typical example of the Legend's running afoul of a local legend, with resulting contamination of both.

63. Neubaur, "Zur Geschichte," p. 50.

64. Paul Sébillot, *Le folk-lore de France* (Paris, 1904-7), I, 253.

65. Pierre Louis Duchartre and René Saulnier, *L'imagerie populaire* (Paris, 1925), pp. 69, 321, *et passim*.

66. Paul Sébillot, *Traditions et superstitions de la Haute-Bretagne* (Paris, 1882), I, 365.

67. *Ibid.*, p. 364.

68. The Legend of the Sunken City of Ys is one of the best-known stories of submerged cities. It is first mentioned in writing about 1500—that is to say, in Pierre Le Baud's *Histoire de Bretagne* (Paris, 1638; first published 133 years after the author's death)—which means that it originated in the later Middle Ages. See Sébillot, *Le folk-lore*, II, 55.

69. Sébillot, *Le folk-lore*, II, 55.

70. For a feeble parallel, see Ethel B. Parsons, "The Wandering Jew of Celtic Legend," *English Journal*, College Edition, XXII (1933), 676-78.

71. Marie de France, *Die Lais der Marie de France*, ed. Karl Warnke (3d ed.; Halle, 1925), pp. 225-55. There is an attractive English prose translation by Eugene Mason, *French Mediaeval Romances from the Lays of Marie de France* (Everyman's Library, No. 557; New York, 1932). A similar story, having to do with a certain King Herla, is told by Walter Map: see *Master Walter Map's Book, "De Nugis Curialum" (Courtiers' Trifles)*, trans. Frederick Tupper and Marbury B. Ogle (London, 1924), pp. 15-17, 223.

72. N. Gredt, *Sagenschatz des luxemburger Landes* (Luxemburg, 1883), p. 384.

73. Paul Sébillot, *Gargantua dans les traditions populaires* (Paris, 1883), pp. 117-76.

74. Alessandro d'Ancona, "Le Juif errant en Italie au XIIIᵉ siècle," *Romania*, X (1881), 212-16; Gielen, *De wandelende Jood*, p. 5.

75. For this and much of the matter pertaining to the folk tale in Italy, see Giuseppe Pitrè, *Fiabe, novelle e raconti popolari siciliani* (Palermo, 1875), I, 131-38. Also helpful is D'Ancona in "Le Juif errant," pp. 212-16, and in "La leggenda dell'Ebreo errante," *Nuova Antologia*, Ser. 2, XXIII (1880), 413-27. See also Alfred Ruhemann, "Die Sage vom ewigen Juden in Italien," *Nord und Süd*, LXXV (1895), 75.

76. D'Ancona, "Le Juif errant," p. 212.

77. An amusing but most incomplete list of such expressions is offered by Gielen, *De wandelende Jood*, p. 41. A full catalogue of proverbial or descriptive phrases is yet to be made; most of them would come directly from the folk tales themselves.

78. D'Ancona, "Le Juif errant," pp. 212-16.

79. *Ibid.*, and Pitrè, *Fiabe, novelle e raconti*, p. 131.

80. G. Pinoli, "L'Ebreo Errante nel Canavese," *Preludio: Revista di lettere, scienze, ed arti*, VII (1883), 266.

81. *Ibid.;* Neubaur, "Zur Geschichte," p. 52. I have myself heard many inhabitants of various villages in Italy and elsewhere tell me that the Wandering Jew used to appear, during their boyhood, in their native village on Good Friday morning. Apparently World War II drove him away. To speak seriously, however, there is plenty of oral evidence that the Legend still lingers on in isolated spots in Europe.

82. See Pitrè, *Fiabe, novelle e raconti*, p. 133.

83. See Ruhemann, "Die Sage," p. 76.

84. *Ibid.*, p. 77.

85. Bertha Ilg, "Maltesische Legenden und Schwänke," *Zeitschrift des Vereins für Volkskunde*, XIX (1909), 308. The name *Kumbu* is never explained by the editor; one may presume that it is the name of the protagonist in this particular tale. Its meaning is obscure.

86. Savi-Lopez, *Alpensagen*, p. 182.

87. Ruhemann, "Die Sage," p. 75.

88. George K. Anderson, "Popular Survivals of the Wandering Jew in England," *Journal of English and Germanic Philology*, XLVI (1947), 367-82.

89. Aubrey further remarks, "Doctor Gilbert Sheldon, since Archbishop of Canterbury, was then in the Moorlands, and justified the truth of this to Elias Ashmole, Esq., from whom I had this account, and he hath inserted it in some of his memoirs, which are in the Museum at Oxford" (p. 110).

90. In the Italian account—see p. 26 above and Salomone Morpurgo, *L'Ebreo errante in Italia* (Florence, 1891), sec. 2—the protagonist is something of a *bon vivant*. Sometimes in German folk tales he may permit himself a drink of schnapps (as in Tale 26) or wine for the sake of camaraderie; but he usually never touches liquor.

91. Victor T. Sternberg, "The Wandering Jew in England," *Notes and Queries*, Ser. 1, XII (1855), 503-4.

92. Pearson's story appeared first in "The Seven Whistlers," *Notes and Queries*, Ser. 4, VIII (1871), 268; later Moncure Daniel Conway incorporated it into *The Wandering Jew* (London, 1881), pp. 159-60. The "Gabriel-Hounds" of English folklore (cf. "Gabriel" in *A New English Dictionary on Historical Principles*, ed. James A. H. Murray, *et al.* [Oxford, 1888-1928]) may be, as usually explained, a flock of wild geese, but I believe them to represent the souls of the Jews who condemned Christ. They are clearly associated in the popular mind with the sinister or demoniac. But it would appear also that they are related more closely to the Legend of the Wild Huntsman than the Legend of the Wandering Jew. Note Wordsworth's "Though Narrow Be That Old Man's Cares," ll. 12-14:

> For overhead are sweeping Gabriel's Hounds
> Doomed, with their impious Lord, the flying Hart
> To chase for ever on aerial grounds!

Another deviation from the norm is the story told by William Henderson, *Notes on the Folklore of the Northern Counties* (London, 1879), p. 82: "An old woman of the North Riding once asked a friend of mine whether it was wrong to wash on Good Friday. 'I used to do so,' she said, 'and thought no harm of it, till once, when I was hanging out my clothes, a young woman passed by (a dressmaker she was, and a Methodist); and she reproved me, and told me this story. "While our Lord Jesus was being led to Calvary, they took Him past a woman who was washing, and the woman 'blirted' the thing she was washing in His face; on which he said, 'Cursed be every one who hereafter shall wash on this day!'" And never again,' added the old woman, 'have I washed on Good Friday.' "

93. It is most likely that the name "Wandering Jew" was applied to these plants during the age of romanticism, which pervaded the science of the early nineteenth century, when the protagonist of the Legend flourished in literally hundreds of European literary creations.

94. Marie Trevelyan, *Folk-Lore and Folk-Stories of Wales* (London, 1909), pp. 337-39. The author prefaces her accounts with the exasperating though understandable remark, "Stories of the Wandering Jew have been heard and chronicled in Pembrokeshire and Glamorgan, and both were connected with county families, whose names, for obvious reasons, were suppressed" (p. 338). It might be added that neither of these stories alters in any way my belief that the Legend is virtually neglected in Celtic tradition.

95. *Ibid.*, p. 339. Miss Trevelyan refers this to Pembrokeshire; it is told, however, by a Carmarthenshire squire.

96. Yarmolinsky, "The Wandering Jew," p. 324.

97. *Ibid.*, p. 327.

98. Gielen, *De wandelende Jood*, p. 42.

99. *Ibid.*, p. 16.

100. *Ibid.*, p. 17.

101. *Livische Märchen- und Sagenvarianten*, ed. Oskar Loorits, in *Folklore Fellows Communications*, LXVI (Helsinki, 1926), 150.

102. Gielen, *De wandelende Jood*, p. 14, n. 81.

103. Linda Kuusler's contribution, printed in *Eesti Rahvaluule Archiv*, III (1931), 32.

104. *Ibid.*

105. Gielen, *De wandelende Jood*, p. 15.

106. *Ibid.*

107. *Ibid.*, p. 13.

108. Alexander Scheiber, "The Legend of the Wandering Jew in Hungary," *Midwest Folklore*, IV (1954), 221-35. The ballad appears on p. 230.

109. A. E. Fife, "The Legend of the Three Nephites among the Mormons," *Journal of American Folk-Lore*, LIII (1940), 1-49. Nearly fifty tales have been collected in this important article.

110. (September 6, 1884), p. 151.

111. Just Matthias Thiele, *Danmarks Folkesagn* (Copenhagen, 1843-60), II, 313.

112. Gielen, *De wandelende Jood*, p. 9.

113. *Ibid.*, p. 17.

114. For this and several others of the same type in Lithuanian tradition, see *ibid.*, pp. 16-18.

115. For the Flemish tradition of the Legend, see especially Amaat Joos, *Vertelsels van het vlaamsche Volk* (Brussels, 1930), p. 52.

116. Strackerjan, *Aberglaube und Sagen*, II, 11.

Chapter Five

1. Marcel Bataillon, "Pérégrinations espagnoles du juif errant," *Bulletin Hispanique*, XLIII (1941), 81-122, particularly pp. 103-9.

2. The title page is given in Leonhard Neubaur, *Die Sage vom ewigen Juden* (2d ed.; Leipzig, 1893), p. 127, n. 111.

3. Reprinted in Tharsander's *Schau-platz vieler ungereimter Meynungen und Erzehlungen* (Berlin, 1742), III, 321-27.

4. II, 472.

5. She was a political refugee in England during the last dozen years of her life; she died there in 1699.

6. XIV, 723.

7. *Jüdische Merckwürdigkeiten, vorstellende was sich curieuses und denkwürdiges in den neueren Zeiten, etc.* (Frankfurt-Leipzig, 1714-18), IV, 488-512 (chap. xiii: "Von dem in aller Welt vermeinten umherlaufenden Juden *Ahasverus*").

8. Hermann Kurz, *Aus den Tagen der Schmach: Geschichtsbilder aus der Melacszeit* (Stuttgart, 1871), p. 108.

9. The incident is narrated in a chronicle of Ypres in the Ghent Library; it was first printed by Emile Varenbergh in *Messager des sciences historiques ou Archives des Arts et de Bibliographie de Belgique* (Ghent, 1870), pp. 505-8. There is a full summary in Leonhard Neubaur, *Neue Mitteilungen über die Sage vom ewigen Juden* (Leipzig, 1893), pp. 20-22.

10. Neubaur, *Neue Mitteilungen*, pp. 23-24.

11. *Chronologia* (Hamburg, 1615), p. 326.

12. J. S. Mitternacht, *Dissertationes de Johannis XXI* (Naumburg, 1665), pp. 395-422.

13. It is obviously impractical to include here every date of every reported visit in every reported locality. Those given here are taken from various source books, particularly from J. J. Gielen's *De wandelende Jood in Volkskunde en Letterkunde* (Amsterdam, 1931), and Neubaur, *Die Sage.*

14. Karl A. Reiser, *Sagen, Gebräuche und Sprichwörter des Allgäus* (Kemptem, 1895-98), I, 362-65.

15. *Ibid.*, 365.

16. Max Hippe, "Volkstümliches aus einem alten Breslauer Tagebuche," *Mitteilungen der Schlesischen Gesellschaft für Volkskunde*, VI (1910), 81-82.

17. *Taschenbuch für die vaterländische Geschichte*, ed. Joseph von Hormayr-Hortenburg (Munich, 1834), pp. 216-17.

18. Anton Birlinger, *Aus Schwaben. . . : Neue Sammlung* (Wiesbaden, 1874), I, 78.

19. *Das Apostel- und Missionarbuch* (4th ed.; Stuttgart, 1863), p. 400.

20. Emile H. van Heurck and G. J. Boekenoogen, *Histoire de l'imagerie populaire flamande* (Brussels, 1910), p. 586.

21. Johann Caspar Ulrich, *Sammlung Jüdischer Geschichten* (Basel, 1768), pp. 155-56. This is still another story about the English that the English know nothing about.

22. The tale is unusual in that it presents to us the Wandering Jew as a treasure hound, such as he had been in Italy in the Antonio version. It is, as usual, impossible to tell how old the tale really is, but it may well be earlier than most of the German folk tales stimulated by the *Volksbuch.* I believe it arrived in Bohemia from Italy via Austria rather than from Germany. It is, inconveniently, printed in an inaccessible periodical, *Der Gesellschafter* for 1845, No. 18, as "Kokot."

23. (London-Edinburgh, 1862-64), I, 534-45.

24. Leonhard Neubaur, "Zur Geschichte der Sage vom ewigen Juden," *Zeitschrift des Vereins für Volkskunde*, XXII (1912), 54.

25. The translation was printed at Jönköping in 1818; see Per Olof Bäckström's *Svenska folkböcker* (Stockholm, 1845-48), II, 107, and note.

26. (Rev. ed.; London, 1888-90), pp. 360-61.

27. Moncure Daniel Conway, *The Wandering Jew* (London, 1881), p. 143.

28. Printed in part and discussed in George K. Anderson, "Popular Survivals of the Wandering Jew in England," *Journal of English and Germanic Philology*, XLVI (1947), 367-82; see particularly pp. 374-75.

29. This may imply that the pamphlet was printed some thirty years or so after 1769; but later on it is stated specifically that the time from the birth of Christ to the pamphlet came to 1,769 years. In other words, the Jew is supposed to have started his wandering at the time of the birth of Christ instead of the Crucifixion, which is an obvious error.

30. *The Surprizing History of the Wandering JEW of Jerusalem with his Arrival at Dover This Year 1780, Attested: And His Removal in Order To Visit the Holy Island near Berwick, Confirmed by Three Ministers and an Attorney,* etc.

31. It might possibly be Overton in Hampshire, but there is no need to suppose so.

32. I have been unable to trace the authorship of this entry, which is little more than a space-filler. In some ways it is more authentic, from the folklorist's point of view, to hear merely that there was for a long time around Boston, Lincolnshire, "a belief concerning the exist-

ence of a person called the Wandering Jew." See Eliza Gutch and Mabel G. W. Peacock, *Examples of Printed Folk-Lore Concerning Lincolnshire* (London, 1908), p. 120.

33. *RELATION oder Kurtzer Bericht von zweyen Zeugen des Leydens vnsers geliebten Heylandes Jesu Christi Deren einer ein Heyde der andere ein Jude dasselbe zur Zeit da der HERR gekreutzigt worden angesehen vnd alle beyde noch heutiges Tages im Leben seyn sollen, etc.* (Amsterdam, 1660). See also Martinus Dröscher, *Dissertatio theologica de duobus testibus* (Jena, 1668), II, par. 14.

34. *L'Histoire et la religion des Juifs, depuis Jésus Christ jusqu'à présent* (Rotterdam, 1706-7), V, 1834-36.

35. Benito Gerónimo Feyjóo y Montenegro, "De El Judío Errante," *Cartas eruditas* (Clásicos castellanos, LXXXV; Madrid, 1928), p. 94. Feyjóo, however, devotes his comments to non-Spanish material; it is an extremely derivative study.

36. Printed in full in George K. Anderson, "Joseph Krantz, Twin of Ahasverus," *Germanic Review*, XXII (1947), 188-201; see in particular pp. 193-200.

37. On the semantics of Krantz, see Jacob and Wilhelm Grimm, *Deutsches Wörterbuch* (Leipzig, 1873), V, 2043.

38.
> Crantz to such brave loves will not be enthralled,
> But loves her only, who at Geneva is called
> Religion, plain, simple, sullen, young,
> Contemptuous, yet unhandsome; as among
> Lecherous humors, there is one that judges
> No wenches wholesome, but coarse country drudges.
> —"Third Satire," ll. 49-54.

39. *Dissertationes de Johannis XXI* (Naumburg, 1655), par. 22.

40. No place of publication is given for Hadeck's pamphlet. The name is sometimes spelled Hadek.

41. IV, 488-512.

42. III, 461.

43. *Praxis Alchymiae; hoc est, doctrina de artificiosa praeparatione praecipuorum medicamentorum Chymicorum* (Frankfurt, 1604). The appropriate material is in Book II.

44. (Tournai, 1619), IV, 367.

45. Christopher Schultz, *Dissertatio historica de Judaeo non mortali* (Königsberg, 1689).

46. *Joannis Sleidani de Statu religionis ac reipublicae continuatio* (Frankfurt, 1615-19), pp. 523-24.

47. Johann Cluverius, *Historiarum totius mundi epitome, a prima rerum origine usque ad annum Christi MDCXXX* (Leyden, 1637), pp. 713-15.

48. P. 713.

49. Cluverius, *Historiarum*, p. 714.

50. Nicolai is the putative author of the pamphlet whose title page reads: *D.O.M.A. / / PASSIONALIA / / Hoc est, / / DE / / PASSIONE Dom: & Salvatoris nostri IESU CHRIS- / / TI . . . / / . . . EXERCITATIO SCHOLASTICA / / singularis / / . . . / / AVTORE / / HENRICO NICOLAI. etc.*, (n.p., 1648); Johann Heinrich Hottinger, *Historiae Ecclesiasticae Novi Testamenti, trias* (Triguri, 1653), pp. 546-50; Erasmus Schmid, *Opus sacrum posthumum, in quo continentur versio Novi Testamenti nova, . . . ac animadversiones in idem* (Nuremberg, 1658), p. 245.

51. Johannes Lyserus, *Aphtharsia, sive de indeficientia animi dissertatio* (Leipzig, 1662).

52. (Nuremberg, 1686), chap. xiv.

53. (Nuremberg, 1698), II, 401-10.

54. *Physico-Theology: Or a Demonstration of the Being and Attributes of God from His Works of Creation . . . Being the Substance of XVI Sermons, Preached . . . at Mr. Boyle's Lectures* (London, 1713), p. 343. The German translation is *Physico-Theologie, oder Natur-Leitung zu Gott*; the translation is by Albert Fabricius (Hamburg, 1750), p. 344.

55. *Observationes miscellaneae, oder Vermischte Gedanken* (Göttingen, 1715), p. 616.

56. J. T. Jablonski, *Allgemeine Lexikon der Künste und Wissenschaften* (Königsberg-Leipzig, 1748), p. 715; in speaking of the Legend: "Es wird jetzt als ein Betrug oder als ein Mährlein angesehen."

57. Caspar Kildgaard, *Auspiciis D.O.M. et A.S.A. suffragiis contra Fabulam De Judaeo non mortali, etc.* (Copenhagen, 1733). The pamphlet seems to be the defense of a dissertation of 1713.

58. Gotthard Heidegger, *Acerra philologica nova, repurgata, aucta* (Zurich, 1735). There seems to have been an earlier edition in 1708, and another in 1730, but I have not been able to see either, if indeed they are still extant. See Gielen, *De wandelende Jood*, p. 235, and bibliographical note.

59. Mentioned by Gielen, *De wandelende Jood*, p. 149. I must take his word for it, for the pamphlet seems to be no longer extant.

60. (The Hague, 1744), III, 231.

61. (Leipzig, 1707); a second edition in the same year appeared in Dresden.

62. (Helmstedt, 1755), p. 48. There are, however, printings with the imprints of Berlin, Wolfenbüttel, Darmstadt, and Giessen, as well as a Danish translation of 1758.

63. A full account of this pamphlet is given in Neubaur, *Die Sage*, pp. 22-27.

64. *Erstes Supplement / zu der / ewigen Jüdinn / Marie Regine Krügerinn / geborne Rühlemanninn / Schreiben / an Herrn Professor Carl Anton / den ewigen Juden / betreffend* (Wolfenbüttel, 1756); see further Neubaur, *Die Sage*, p. 118, n. 55.

65. The original passage paraphrased here is cited in Neubaur, *Die Sage*, p. 27.

66. Gielen, *De wandelende Jood*, p. 151.

Chapter Six

1. George K. Anderson, "The Neo-Classical Chronicle of the Wandering Jew," *Publications of the Modern Language Association*, LXIII (1948), 199-213.

2. Material germane to the Wandering Jew is chiefly on pp. 176-81 of vol. II.

3. II, Book III, letter 1.

4. A common motif in the literary treatment of the Legend during the latter half of the nineteenth century.

5. VI, Book III, letter 3.

6. VII, Book IV, letter 8.

7. Pp. 12-16. The English translation by Stephen Whately (1733) is discussed by S. G. Andrews, "The Wandering Jew and 'The Travels and Adventures of James Massey,'" *Modern Language Notes*, LXXII (1957), 39-41; he makes the point that this is the first time Ahasuerus has been used to illustrate a theological point—the condition of the body in the afterlife. It is important to remember, however, that Tyssot de Patot's original work is more important than the translation in augmenting the conception of the Wandering Jew.

8. Champfleury, *Histoire de l'imagerie populaire* (Paris, 1869), pp. 1-104, and in Anderson, "The Neo-Classical Chronicle," p. 202.

9. The only known copy of the pamphlet is in the W. Easton Louttit, Jr., collection on the Legend of the Wandering Jew in the Brown University Library. See George K. Anderson, "The History of Israel Jobson," *Philological Quarterly*, XXV (1947), 303-20. Four basic background studies are important, all by Marjorie H. Nicolson: "The Microscope and English Imagination," *Smith College Studies in Modern Languages*, XVI, No. 4 (1935); "The Telescope and Imagination," *Modern Philology*, XXXII (1934), 233-60; "The 'New Astronomy' and English Literary Imagination," *Studies in Philology*, XXXII (1935), 428-62; and "Milton and the Telescope," *Journal of English Literary History*, II (1935), 1-32.

10. Thomas D. Whitaker, *The History and Antiquities of the Deanery of Craven in the County of York* (London, 1805; rev. eds., 1812 and 1878). I quote from the 1878 edition (with supplement by Alfred W. Morant), p. 586. Miles Wilson's name appears in the roll of curates

of the chapel at Halton Gill (p. 585). Whitaker's remarks are quoted in Thomas Allen, *A New and Complete History of the County of York* (London, 1828-31), III, 69, and note.

11. Whitaker, *The History and Antiquities*, acknowledges this, but in his outline of the work obviously confuses it with *The History of Israel Jobson*.

12. Another small village, now Horton-in-Ribblesdale, on the River Ribble, southwest of Halton Gill.

13. Found in Harry Speight, *The Craven and North-West Yorkshire Highlands* (London, 1892), 396-97. It is to be noted that neither Speight nor Allen, to say nothing of Whitaker, whose first edition of his history came out in 1804, has anything to say about *The History of Israel Jobson*.

14. After the first edition of this work in 1751, the name of Ralph Morris slips into limbo. Since the work, among other things, proposes a daring social expedient of a shipwrecked couple to people their island by inbreeding among their children, it is possible that Morris decided to disclaim responsibility; or perhaps the responsibility was disclaimed for him by the moral publishers of the reprints, which seem to have been many. See the best edition, published in *The Library of Impostors*, ed. Norman Mosley Penzer (London, 1926), I. For the moon incident, see p. 170 of this work, in particular.

15. It is not practicable to include here all the possible sources of information on which Wilson might have drawn. There is very little to suggest that he consulted authoritative works of science for his facts, although he probably knew Newton's *Principia* and perhaps some of Edmund Halley's papers in *Philosophical Transactions*. In regard to other works the bibliographical data in Miss Nicolson's "The Microscope," "The Telescope," "The 'New Astronomy,'" and "Milton and the Telescope" are invaluable. To appreciate the work of the real astronomers of Wilson's day, see Jean Baptiste Joseph Delambre, *Histoire de l'astronomie au dix-huitième siècle* (Paris, 1827); Henry S. Williams, *The Great Astronomers* (New York, 1930), pp. 193-221; and particularly John Hill, *Urania* (London, 1754), or John Keill, *An Introduction to the True Astronomy* (London, 1721), which ran through five editions before 1760. It is possible that Wilson learned his astronomy from the books by Hill and Keill.

16. Since the month Abib corresponds to the time of the vernal equinox, we may assume that it coincides in Wilson's mind with the time of the Crucifixion.

17. This detail appeared in some of the versions of the *Kurtze Beschreibung/Dudulaeus* pamphlets of the Ahasuerus-book (p. 47 above), but there is little likelihood that Wilson would have known these. He may have come across a French translation, which he might or might not have understood, but these translations do not mention the thickness of the soles. Presumably, then, Wilson's is an imaginative touch—a most natural one—which occurred to him independently.

18. As a matter of fact, the death of Aurengzebe, in 1707, heralded the rapid decline in power and prestige of the Great Moguls of India; certainly Shah Bahadur, who reigned from 1710 to 1712, was far from a resplendent figure. The historical detail is perhaps unimportant, but serves to illustrate Wilson's preference for the fictitious over the factual. Incidentally in Matthew Gregory Lewis' *The Monk* (London, 1796), which contributed some details to the Legend (pp. 177-81 below), the Wandering Jew appears as "the Grand Mogul."

19. One is reminded by this device, not of Dante, whom Wilson would not have known unless he could read Italian (which is unlikely), but of another excursus of the universe—Athanasius Kircher's *Itinerarium Exstaticum* (Rome, 1656), given in its second edition the title *Iter Exstaticum Coeleste* (Nuremberg, 1660). The purposes of this work and Wilson's, however, are vastly different. In Kircher, a certain Theodidactus is shown by an angel through the universe. Wilson may have known of this piece and also of Christian Huygen's *The Celestial Worlds Discovered* (London, 1698).

20. See Marjorie H. Nicolson, "A World in the Moon," *Smith College Studies in Modern Languages*, XVII, No. 2 (1936). Of the many "voyages to the moon," the most popular among the English-speaking peoples was John Wilkins' *The Discovery of a World in the Moone* (London, 1638), with another edition in 1640 under the title, *A Discourse Concerning a New*

World and Another Planet. This work went through several editions in England and was known in colonial America. In general, however, the most romantic of all these was Cyrano de Bergerac's *Histoire comique des états et empires de la lune* (Paris, 1685), translated by A. Lovell as *The Comical History of the States and Empires of the World of the Moon* (London, 1687). Lovell's translation came out in the same year as Newton's *Principia;* in the preceding year (1686) appeared in Paris the very influential work by Bertrand de Fontenelle, *Entretiens sur la pluralité des mondes,* translated by Mrs. Aphra Behn and also by John Glanvill—both in 1688, with other translations throughout the next century as late as 1783. The works by Ralph Morris (*The Life and Astonishing Adventures of John Daniel*) and Robert Paltock (*The Life and Adventures of Peter Wilkins*), both published in 1751, have already been mentioned.

21. William Whiston, *The Longitude Discovered by the Eclipses, Occultations, and Conjunctions of Jupiter's Planets* (London, 1738).

22. This is a good example of a northern English dialect form; there are many such in the pamphlet, for Wilson saw no reason to avoid occasional Yorkshirisms.

23. An illustration of Wilson's occasional lapses in grammar.

24. Compare *Gulliver's Travels,* Book II, chap. i: "But advancing forward towards (as I shall henceforth call him), his youngest son, who sat next him, an arch ten years old, took me up by the legs, and held me so high in the air that I limb; but his father snatched me from him, and at the same time gave him s the left ear as would have felled an European troop of horse to the earth, orde be taken from the table."

25. An echo, of course, of Matthew 34:6-8 or Mark 13:7-8. It is significant that Mil makes no specific reference to the great Lisbon earthquake of November 1, 1755, the greatest natural disasters ever to harm mankind. Would the news have reached Halton Gill even during the winter of 1755-56, while Wilson was composing his pamphl the fire," especially as he completed it, according to his own dating, as early as Ma 1756? Perhaps he includes the Lisbon earthquake under earthquakes in general "alrea passed over." If not, it is a superb piece of irony that such a calamity should have taken place while he was thinking some of the long thoughts which he expresses here. Likewise ignored is specific reference to the beginnings of the Seven Years' War, but Wilson nowhere gives any sign that he is at all interested in European politics.

26. For example, in addition to an enumeration of the various important organs of the body, Wilson mentions the natural, vital, and animal spirits—the natural spirits abiding in the liver, the vital spirits in the heart, and the animal spirits in the brain. Yet the principle of the circulation of the blood is well recognized, and the fact of blood pressure is implied: "Your blood flows thro' its various Channels, and at 16 Ounces in the Pound, passes thro' the Heart at least eight Times every Hour." (In 1733 Stephen Hales first measured blood pressure in an animal.)

27. Book V, chap. iii.

28. "Printed by T. Norris at the Looking Glass on London Bridge and sold by J. Walker." The subtitle reads: "A brief history of the remarkable passages from William Conqueror to this Present Reign."

29. By this I refer specifically to the historians of the later part of the Age of Reason, who practiced their art before the romanticists got their hands on it—in particular such works as Voltaire's *Siècle de Louis XIV* (Berlin, 1751); the Abbé Claude Fleury's *Histoire ecclésiastique* (Paris, 1691-1738); David Hume's *History of England, from the Invasion of Julius Caesar to the Revolution of 1688* (London, 1754-62); William Robertson's *The History of Scotland* (London, 1759), *History of the Reign of the Emperor Charles V* (London, 1769), and *The History of America* (London, 1777); Adam Ferguson's *The History of the Progress and Termination of the Roman Republic* (London, 1783); Edward Gibbon's *The Decline and Fall of the Roman Empire* (London, 1776-88); Johann Lorenz von Mosheim's *De Rebus christianorum ante Constantinum magnum commentarii* (Helmstedt, 1753); Johann Christoph Gatterer's *Versuch einer allgemeinen Weltgeschichte bis zur Entdeckung Amerikens* (Göttingen, 1792); August Ludwig von Schlözer's *Neuverändertes Russland* (Riga, 1767-69),

Allgemeine Nordische Geschichte (Halle, 1771-85), and *Weltgeschichte nach ihren Haupt-theilen im Ausguz und Zusammenhänge* (Göttingen, 1792). Of these, the German histories of Mosheim, Gatterer, and Von Schlözer represent the so-called Göttingen school, and from their tendency to "universal" history seem to have the closest connection with the Chronicle of the Wandering Jew. For the whole matter, see James Westfall Thompson and Bernard J. Holm, *A History of Historical Writing* (New York, 1942), II, 58-131.

30. As a matter of fact, the *Mémoires* purports to be merely a reprinting of the *Histoire admirable* issued at Rouen in 1751. But since none of the many surviving versions of the *Histoire admirable* gives the material found in the *Mémoires*, one may deduce that the *Mémoires* is not what it pretends to be. The author breaks down at the end and admits it: "Il ne nous reste plus qu'à demander excuse à nos Lecteurs de leur avoir donné, au lieu d'un extrait de la petite brochure bleue du Juif-errant [the *Histoire admirable*], qui ne contient pas 30 pages, & qui est bien un Roman, & même un misérable Roman, un volume entier, contenant 17 voyages autour de monde; mais cette fable nous a paru présenter un cadre si heureux, que nous n'avons pu nous empêcher de la remplir par différents tableaux, tous fidèlement & exactement tirés de l'Histoire." The author of the *Mémoires* has nothing to say about Judas Iscariot, the Tree of Life, or the Legend of the Cross. These independent sagas were combined with the Legend of the Wandering Jew in the French pamphlet.

31. The volume explains itself as "Ein Abdruck der Reichardschen Umarbeitung des bekannten Volksromans, welcher in einigen Bänden der Romanenbibliothek zerstreut stand, und nun, auf Verlangen mehrerer Leser, in Einem Band zusammengedruckt worden ist." See *H. A. O. Reichard*, ed. Hermann Uhde (Stuttgart, 1877).

32. The romanticists of the era, under the influence of the Mesmer vogue, were wont to dwell upon the transfixing power of the glance of the Wandering Jew.

33. Heinrich A. O. Reichard, *Der ewige Jude: Geschichte oder Volksroman, wie man will* (Riga, 1785), p. 9.

34. "Trotz einiger Schritte in der Philosophie und Aufklärung ist das 18. Jahrhundert nicht frei von Intoleranz, Taten des Verfolgungsgeistes, Gasznereyen, Mesmereyen, Alchymistereyen, Geisterseherehereyen, und wie die übrigen Krizen des Vorurtheils und des Aberglaubens weiter heiszen mögen, den neuen Messias und den Ziegenpropheten zue Berlin mit eingeschlossen" (p. 251).

35. Printed at Copenhagen in 1828. It is not to be confused with any one of several Danish translations of the German Ahasuerus-book which bear the same title.

36. The title page gives the author as "M. Heller" ("Monsieur Heller," perhaps?), but the work is entered in *Index locupletissimus librorum*, ed. Christian Gottlob Kayser, *et al.* (Leipzig, 1834-1911), III, 96, as Wilhelm Friedrich Heller's, who wrote also *Geschichte der Kreuzzüge nach dem heiligen Lande* (Frankfurt, 1784); *Kardonens Vermächtniss und Lieder von Selima zum Vorlesen für Mutter und Tochter* (Stuttgart, 1781); *Sokrates, Sohn des Sophroniskus* (Frankfurt, 1795); and three volumes of *Novellen* (Dresden-Leipzig, 1837-40). The imprints for vols. I and II are "Utopia, 1791"; for vol. III, "Germanien, 1801." A second edition of vols. I and II was printed in 1793. The author's having written a history of the Crusades may account for the emphasis placed upon these historical events in the *Briefe*.

37. His attitude toward Josephus is unusually respectful.

38. Paulus Oriosius, a historian and encyclopedist, is best known now because his *Historiarum libri vii adversus paganos* was one of the five books translated into English by King Alfred the Great as part of his educational program.

39. This is the general picture of Ahasuerus as an exponent of *Weltschmerz* in the Chronicle of the Wandering Jew; I have noted more than fifty such portraits of the protagonist in German poetry alone between 1820 and 1860. An unusually good example, from the artistic point of view, is Julius Mosen's epic, *Ahasver* (Leipzig, 1838; see pp. 218-20 below).

40. Eugène Sue, *Le juif errant* (Paris, 1844-45; see p. 232 below).

41. George Croly, *Salathiel* (London, 1827; see p. 188 below).

42. Lewis Wallace, *The Prince of India* (New York, 1893; see p. 311 below).

43. Pasero e Corneliano, *Histoire du juif errant écrite par lui-même* (Paris, 1820; see p. 150 below).

44. Robert Hamerling, *Ahasver in Rom* (Hamburg-Leipzig-Triest, 1866; see p. 251 below).

45. John Galt ("The Reverend T. Clark"), *The Travels and Observations of Hareach, the Wandering Jew* (London, 1821-23; see p. 149 below).

46. Heller's knowledge of Ulfilas seems to have been derived chiefly from W. Weingärtner, *Die Aussprache des Gothischen zur Zeit des Ulfilas* (Leipzig-Breslau, 1658), which was a reliable stand-by until Franz E. C. Dietrich's excellent early monograph, *Ueber die Aussprache des Gothischen waehrend der Zeit seines Bestehens* (Marburg, 1862).

47. References to Napoleon, of course, would come only in vol. III (1801) of Heller's *Briefe*. Most interesting in this long list is the matter excluded as well as that included.

48. See in particular Jennie W. Aberdein, *John Galt* (London, 1936), and Frank H. Lyell, *The Study of the Novels of John Galt* (Princeton, 1942).

49. Lyell, *A Study*, p. 112.

50. Galt, *The Travels and Observations*, p. 3.

51. *Ibid.*, p. 298.

52. The German translation is entitled *Geschichte des ewigen Juden, von ihm selbst geschrieben, etc.* [the translator's name is not given] (Gotha, 1821).

53. Pasero de Corneliano, *Histoire du juif errant*, p. 155.

54. Champfleury, *Histoire*, p. 29.

55. P. B., *Histoire du juif errant* (Paris, n.d.), pp. 75-76.

56. *Ibid.*, pp. 102-3.

57. Printed by Eduard Legrand at Paris in 1845. I have no record of its having been published in any other year as an annual. It contains also an advertising poster extolling the virtues of artificial teeth.

58. See Appendix B. Christian Kuffner, *Ahasver, der ewige Jude: Eine Wanderung durch Jahrhunderte* (Vienna, 1846), and *Die ewige Jüdin und der Orang-Outang; eine Reise auf, unter, und über der Erde* (Vienna, 1846), constituting vols. XVI-XVIII and XIX-XX, respectively, of his *Erzählende Schriften* (Vienna, 1843-47).

59. The pamphlet seems, however, to have been successful. There was a new printing in 1849.

60. *Dictionary of American Biography* (New York, 1928-58), IX, 111-12 ("David Hoffman").

61. The London edition is dated 1853-54; the American edition (Baltimore-New York) is dated 1858.

62. Not, of course, the well-known medieval historian, Frederic W. Maitland (1850-1906), but the Reverend Samuel R. Maitland (1792-1866), whose *The Dark Ages* (London, 1844) was for a time the authoritative work on the subject.

63. David Hoffman, *Chronicles Selected from the Originals of Cartaphilus, the Wandering Jew, Embracing a Period of Nearly XIX Centuries* (Baltimore-New York, 1858), I, xxviii.

64. The only Lully who would qualify for the term "scientist," loosely used, would be Raymond Lully (*ca.*1235-1315), a Spanish missionary and theologian, with a bent toward natural science, who was so prolific a writer that there was a common belief that he was more than one person.

65. After all, Hoffman's work was written less than ten years after the great splash caused by Eugène Sue's anti-Jesuit novel *Le juif errant*. It may be explained here that there were several anti-Jesuit movements in France and elsewhere during the nineteenth century; at times feeling against the Society ran as high as the feeling against Freemasonry.

Chapter Seven

1. See p. 426, n. 26.

2. Paul Lacroix, *Curiosités de l'histoire des croyances populaires au moyen âge* (Paris, 1859), pp. 105-41, prints both the lyric and the *Discours véritable* itself; Charles Schoebel, *La Légende*

du Juif errant (Paris, 1877), pp. 20-22; Charles Nisard, *Histoire des livres populaires ou de la littérature du colportage, etc.* (Paris, 1854), p. 563.

3. See Lacroix, *Curiosités*; Schoebel, *La Légende du Juif errant*; Nisard, *Histoire des livres populaires*; see also Alexis Socard, *Livres populaires* (Paris, 1865), p. 129.

4. See Lacroix, *Curiosités*, p. 129; B. Tideman, *Ahasverus* (Zwolle, 1870), p. 55; and Jean Weckerlin, *Chansons populaires du pays de France* (Paris, 1903), I, 225.

5. Actually, however, the direct inspiration for Doré's engravings is the poem by Pierre Dupont (1856); see p. 260 below.

6. But see the edition in Kristoffer Nyrop's *Fortids Sagn og Sange* (Copenhagen, 1907-9), II, 58 ("Den evige Jøde"), and the comments in Leonhard Neubaur, "Zur Geschichte der Sage vom ewigen Juden," *Zeitschrift des Vereins für Volkskunde*, XXII (1912), 48.

7. To paraphrase: "My clothes are old—more than seventeen hundred years; I carry no money with me; God's Providence takes care of me; I am content in God. He will wipe out my sin and after these days of woe bring me to his heaven." I have left the passage in Danish to preserve the original force of the lines.

8. There is a curious history to this work. Its putative author is W. Malone, otherwise unknown, and with its present title it was printed in 1640. But as early as 1609 it had appeared with slight differences as *The Man in the Moon, Telling Strange Fortunes*. The only edition of the work now left is that by James Orchard Halliwell-Phillips in *Books of Characters* (London, 1857), Part I. Malone, if he is the author, assures the reader that the book has been written for general edification. He once came to a house in London where he met a remarkable man: ". . . a cunning man, a sooth sayer or deviner, one that can tell fortunes." Having been invited to witness this man's skills, he accepts and watches a parade of miscellaneous characters—a drunkard, a tobacconist, a prodigal, a lewd woman, and others—come to this adviser (first called Fido, but in the 1640 version the Wandering Jew) who dispenses his sarcastic, ironical satire for the benefit rather of the reader than of those consulting him. The tone is remarkably vigorous in a Jonsonian vein. But it is obvious that Ahasuerus has nothing to do with all this, nor the book with Ahasuerus: he has been used simply as symbolic of unusual, not to say supernatural, powers of divination.

9. The play has been truly buried and forgotten, but see Ferdinand Wolf, "Beiträge zur spanischen Volkspoesie aus den Werken Fernán Caballeros," *Sitzungsberichte der philosophische-historische Klasse der Kaiserlichen Akademie der Wissenschaften* (Vienna), XXXI (1859), 188.

10. Claude d'Esternod (d'Esternaud), *L'Espadon satyrique* (Cologne, 1680), Satire V, p. 56.

11. Neubaur, "Zur Geschichte," p. 51.

12. There is no evidence to show that the play was in any way a hit. But see John L. Lowes, *The Road to Xanadu* (Boston, 1927), pp. 247-48, and 544, nn. 35-37.

13. Richard Graves (1715-1804) was also the author of religious reflections and meditations and some memoirs of the poet Shenstone.

14. For this reference I am indebted to Werner Zirus, "Der ewige Jude in der Dichtung, vornehmlich in der englischen und deutschen," *Palaestra* (Leipzig), CLXII (1928), p. 32.

15. The definitive study of it is J. Minor, *Goethes Fragmente vom ewigen Juden und vom wiederkehrenden Heiland* (Stuttgart-Berlin, 1904).

16. First printed in the *Schwäbischen Musenalmanach* for 1784, p. 173, but not well known until it was published in the author's collected works, *Sämmtliche Gedichte* (Frankfurt, 1786-87), II, 68-73.

17. Lowes, *The Road to Xanadu*, pp. 246-49.

18. The matter is discussed in Zirus, "Der ewige Jude in der Dichtung," p. 45. A most important contribution to the whole study of Shelley and the Legend is Manfred Eimer, "Zu Shelleys Dichtung, 'The Wandering Jew,'" *Anglia*, XXXVIII (1914), 432-76. The identity of "P. W." is considered on p. 470.

19. See Nisard, *Histoire des livres populaires*, p. 559. It is doubtful, however, that this chapbook had any influence on Shelley.

Chapter Eight

1. Schiller must have read Matthew Paris.

2. See the English translation in Schiller's *Works* (Bohn's Standard Library; London, 1853), IV, pp. 405-7. It is curious that all the writers of importance who have discussed the Legend of the Wandering Jew have neglected *Der Geisterseher*.

3. For this and other aspects of the romanticists' treatment of the Wandering Jew, see the illuminative and informative work by Eino Railo, *The Haunted Castle* (London, 1927), particularly the chapter entitled, "The Wandering Jew," pp. 194-243. The outline of the Legend by the author, however, pushes too far into analogous or parallel legends and tends to connect Ahasuerus with such legends when there is little basis for it. Another otherwise satisfactory brief treatment of the Legend, that in Edgar Rosenberg, *From Shylock to Svengali* (Stanford, 1960), especially chap. viii, does much the same thing. I am unwilling to concede that Svengali, for instance, is the Wandering Jew. He is, rather, a Jew who is closer to Mesmer than to Ahasuerus.

4. John L. Lowes, *The Road to Xanadu* (Boston, 1927), pp. 245-50.

5. Matthew Gregory Lewis, *The Monk* (London, 1796). I have used the edition of London, 1907, ed. E. A. Baker; see pp. 131-34, 136.

6. In any event, the mark comes about because of the analogy of the Legend of Cain.

7. The cross represents, of course, the Crucifixion: the Jew is being punished for the suffering inflicted on Christ, of which a cross is the obvious symbol.

8. Railo, *The Haunted Castle*, p. 347, n. 106. This gives a fairly complete list of the works adapted from *The Monk*, particularly from the Raymond and Agnes subplot.

9. *Ibid.* The name of the impresario is sometimes given as Forley.

10. This is apparently the play published in vol. XXXVIII of the series "Cumberland's British Theatre," which was published in London between 1826 and 1861. The full title is *Raymond and Agnes, the Travellers Benighted: Or the Bleeding Nun of Lindenberg.*

11. Railo, *The Haunted Castle*, p. 347.

12. Alice M. Killen, *Le roman terrifiant* (Paris, 1923), p. 110. In the same year a comedy(?) based on the novel by Lewis was concocted by Cammaille-Saint-Aubin.

13. For the general tone of this work, see Alexander Lacey, *Pixérécourt and the French Romantic Drama* (Toronto, 1928), chap. i. The reason that the play was not enacted was largely the oversupply of dramatic material on the same subject.

14. Killen, *Le roman terrifiant*, p. 112.

15. Published in 1831. There were many other minor dramatizations of all or part of *The Monk*, discussed at length by Killen, *Le roman terrifiant*, pp. 109-20, *et passim*.

16. L.-M. Fontan and A. Chevalier, *Le Dominicain, ou le Couvent de l'Annonciation* (Paris, 1832). The Bourgeois-Maillan play was also published in Paris.

17. This autobiographical collection of essays was most successful, going through six editions in one year (1896-97). It was translated into English by Annette E. Crocker as *Memoirs of an Artist* (Chicago-New York, 1896).

18. (London, 1799). A good reference book is Ford K. Brown, *The Life of William Godwin* (New York, 1926).

19. William Godwin, *St. Leon* (London, 1799). I quote from the 1850 edition, pp. 125-26.

20. Part I, l. 114.

21. Lowes, *The Road to Xanadu*, p. 249.

22. Unless otherwise specified, I have used the Oxford Standard Authors edition of all English major poets. The passage from *The Borderers* comprises ll. 2316-23.

23.
> Day and night my toils redouble
> Never nearer to the goal;
> Night and day I feel the trouble
> Of the Wanderer in my soul.

But the waterfall finds a comfortable bed in the valley. Clouds, springs, birds, and winds are always in movement; it is all in the nature of things.

24. Act III, scene i, ll. 421-43.

25. *Childe Harold's Pilgrimage*, Canto I, l. 854.

26. Ll. 675-81.

27. VII, ll. 136-45.

28. VII, ll. 254-66.

29. Stith Thompson, *Motif-Index of Folk Literature* (Bloomington, Ind., 1955-58), Motif F 1038; see also Ralph S. Boggs's notes in *Folklore Fellows Communications*, XC, No. 47 (1936), n. 325a.

30. A recent study of Medwin, Ernest James Lovell's *Captain Medwin* (Austin, Texas, 1962), tends to ignore the problem.

31. For June 27 and July 4, 1829.

32. *Shelley's Poetical Works* (centenary edition), ed. G. E. Woodberry (Boston-New York, 1892), pp. 339-40.

33. Thomas Medwin, *The Life of Percy Bysshe Shelley* (London, 1847). See for this remark the revised edition by H. Buxton Forman (London, 1913), p. 40.

34. Percy Bysshe Shelley, *The Complete Poetical Works* (Oxford, 1929), pp. 809-10.

35. Hellas, ll. 795-802. It was this passage in *Hellas* that made a profound impression upon William Butler Yeats; see his "The Trembling of the Veil" in *Autobiographies* (New York, 1927), pp. 211-18, 222.

36. See Lovell, *Captain Medwin*, pp. 140-41, *et passim*. Since this work is largely biographical, little is said concerning the actual content of the poem, but the specimens quoted (particularly on pp. 153-54) are sufficient to illustrate the tepid nature of the verse. The work was dedicated to Byron in memory of Shelley, and Byron was rather put out that the dedication was done without his permission.

37. Published in London in 1827, but apparently it ran into another edition early in 1828. The first edition seems to be quite rare.

38. George Croly, *Salathiel: A Story of the Past, the Present, and the Future* (2d ed.; London, 1828), I, 3.

39. *Ibid.*, II, 195.

40. *Der ewige Jude, eine historische Novelle der Vorzeit* (Stuttgart, 1829). Another translation, varying but little, is A. Kaiser, *Salathiel, oder Memoiren des ewigen Juden* (Leipzig, 1829).

41. *Ein neuer Ahasverus, von George Croly*, trans. A. Rehberg-Worden (Halle, 1913).

42. George Croly, *Tarry Thou Till I Come, or Salathiel the Wandering Jew* (New York-London, 1901). The Danish translator is not named; the version appears under the title *Salathiel* (Kristiania-Oslo, 1903).

43. There was another edition in London in 1892; more recently, an attractive edition with an introduction by William F. Axton was published by the University of Nebraska Press (Lincoln, 1961). The quotation is from p. 26 of the latter.

44. Railo, *The Haunted Castle*, pp. 209-15.

45. Cited in J. J. Gielen, *De wandelende Jood in Volkskunde en Letterkunde* (Amsterdam, 1931), p. 200. I have found no trace of this pamphlet. It may be a parody of the *Volksbuch*, as in Johannes Nariscus (Hartig), "Der ewige Jude" (Sulzbach, 1832), composed in 1819.

46. The poem was composed in 1801 and printed in the following year. It appears in his collected poems (Leipzig, 1846-47), I, 204-11.

47. *Poetische Werke* (Tübingen, 1817-18), I, 253.

48. I had available only the version printed in A. Nodnagel, *Deutsche Sagen aus dem Munde deutscher Dichter und Schriftsteller* (Dresden-Leipzig, 1836), pp. 154-55.

49. The first edition was published at Dordrecht in 1840; the second at Leiden in 1864.

50. First printed in his *Dramatische Poëzy* (Leiden, 1839).

51. Published at Berlin in two parts: the first part, *Halle,* in 1809; the second, *Jerusalem,* in the following year.

52. The plan for the romance is indicated in S. Reinhold Steig, "Joseph von Görres' Briefe an Achim von Arnim," *Neue Heidelberger Jahrbücher* (1901), pp. 203-5. Of particular interest is the letter dated April 25, 1811. His opinion of the old Ahasuerus-book appears in the anonymous *Deutschen Volksbücher* (Heidelberg, 1807), p. 203. He conceded the poetic worth of the subject, but found difficulties in setting up proper limits or purpose to such a work on such a subject.

53. Ludwig Achim von Arnim, *Halle und Jerusalem* (Berlin, 1809-10), p. 88.

54. *Ibid.,* pp. 166-67.

55. *Monatrosen* is a giftbook annual. Schiessler's contribution came out in the 1827 volume, p. 163.

56. I, 143; strophes 7-8, in particular.

57. *Gesammelte Schriften,* ed. Christian Brentano (Frankfurt, 1852-55), IV, 69-71; see also some notes in his second letter on "the new theater," IV, 449.

58. According to the Celtic tradition, the Stone was supposed to have been brought to Scotland from Tara in Ireland. In Tara the belief was that it was the stone on which Jacob rested his head at Bethel (Genesis 28:11).

59. *Ahasver: Trauerspiel in fünf Acten* (Brunswick, 1827). Some scenes had been printed as early as 1825 in *Zeitung für die elegante Welt.*

60. August Klingemann, *Ahasver: Trauerspiel in fünf Acten* (Brunswick, 1827), p. 45.

61. *Ibid.,* pp. 122-23.

62. Klingemann's play is dramatically the most effective of the theatrical representations of the Legend before 1850, but it is not the most ambitious. That honor must go to Nathaniel Bannister's "The Wandering Jew," in fifteen acts. Only two or three were presented on the New Orleans stage in 1837, and the play was never published, but it represented an honest attempt to dramatize the Chronicle of the Wandering Jew.

63. Franz Horn, *Der ewige Jude* (Berlin, 1819), was written as early as 1814, and was printed first in installments in Friedrich de la Motte Fouqué's *Frauentaschenbuch* for 1816. The complete version is in his collected *Novellen* (Berlin, 1819-20), I, 1-120.

64. This is a typical romantic contretemps; in the earlier part of the nineteenth century, Ahasuerus is invulnerable; in the latter part he may bleed quite freely, but only for the sake of gore.

65. In *Drei Erzählungen* (Leipzig, 1820), pp. 1-88.

66. "Der ewige Jude: Probegabe aus einer dramatischen Phantasie," *Zeitschrift für die elegante Welt* for August 4, 6-8, 11, 13-14, and 17, 1829. The piece is not complete.

67. The germane section is entitled "Unterhaltungen des Satans und des ewigen Juden in Berlin."

68. See his comments in his *Geschichte der deutschen Poesie im Mittelalter* (Halle, 1830), pp. 418-20.

69. The section on the Wandering Jew comprises pp. 1-24. An enlarged edition in 1835 expands his account of the Legend; see pp. 1-27, 267-75.

70. See Ferdinand J. Schneider, *Jean Pauls Altersdichtung Fibel und Komet* (Berlin, 1901), pp. 164, 242, 255, *et passim.*

71. G. A. Freiherr von Maltitz, *Gelasius, der graue Wanderer im neunzehnten Jahrhundert: Ein Spiegelbild unserer Zeit.* There is a good discussion of its salient ideas in Ludwig Börne's *Gesammelte Schriften* (Hamburg-Frankfurt, 1861-62), V, 328-41.

72. *Redliches,* I (1820), 516.

73. The ballad was composed in 1822 and first printed in a giftbook, *Taschenbuch zum geselligen Vergnügen auf das Jahr 1823.* Later it was placed among the *Wandernlieder* in Müller's *Lieder des Lebens und der Liebe* (Dessau, 1824).

74. *Sämmtliche Werke* (Grimma, 1840-44), pp. 79-80.

75. *Judenthum in allen dessen Theilen aus einem staatswissenschaftlichen Standpunkte betrachtet* (Mainz, 1821).

76. Ludwig Börne, "Der ewige Jude," *Gesammelte Schriften* (Hamburg-Frankfurt, 1861-62), VI, 3-68.

77. From vol. I of *Chants et chansons populaires de la France* (Paris, 1843), cited by Charles Schoebel in *La Légende du Juif errant* (Paris, 1877), p. 11. *Quibus* may be translated "wherewithal."

78. First printed in *Chefs d'oeuvre du répertoire des mélodrames joués à différents théâtres* (Paris, 1824), pp. 107-225. There is a translation into German by Theodor von Haupt (Theodor Peregrinus), *Ahasverus der nie Ruhende* (Mainz, 1825).

79. Written in 1822. See Edgar Quinet, *Oeuvres complètes* (Paris, 1857-58), VII, 409-41.

80. Edgar Quinet, *Les tablettes du Juif-errant* (Paris, 1823), p. 36.

81. *Ibid.*, pp. 98-100.

82. Edgar Quinet, *Ahasvérus, mystère* (Paris, 1833), printed also in his *Oeuvres complètes*, VII, 61-404. See also the essay by Charles Magnin, "De la nature du génie poétique," *Revue des Deux Mondes* (December 1, 1833), pp. 1-70, which is reprinted in Magnin's *Causeries et Méditations historiques et littéraires* (Paris, 1843), I, 89-258, and also in Quinet's *Oeuvres complètes*, VII, 5-60. An anonymous German translation appeared at Ludwigsburg in 1834.

83. Quinet, *Ahasvérus, mystère* (Paris, 1843), p. 75.

84. *Ibid.*, p. 82.

85. *Ibid.*, p. 109.

86. *Ibid.*, p. 246.

87. *Ibid.*, p. 253.

88. *Ibid.*, p. 380.

89. *Ibid.*, p. 342.

90. *Ibid.*, p. 383.

91. See also the comments of Richard Heath, *Edgar Quinet* (London, 1881), p. 178, and the editor's prefatory notes to *Ahasvérus, mystère* in Quinet's *Oeuvres complètes*, VII, 3-4. See also Georgette Vabre Pradal, *La Dimension historique de l'homme: La mythe du juif errant dans la pensée d'Edgar Quinet* (Paris, 1961).

92. At that, the collection represents a fragment of the author's original concept. The best edition is in Von Zedlitz' *Gedichte* (5th ed.; Stuttgart, 1855), pp. 417-71.

93. *Allgemeine Zeitung des Judenthums*, II (July 21, 1838), 87.

94. There was a reprinting in 1868.

95. In his *Proteus: Zwei Dichtungen* (Munich, 1843). "Ahasverus," pp. 66-68, is a portion of "Das Welt-Ende: Eine Phantasie," one of the two poems in the book.

96. In his *Lieder der Nacht* (Bonn, 1850), p. 72.

97. First published in *Archiv für Geschichte, Literatur, und Kunst*, LV (1826), 289.

98. Included in F. Bassman, *Die Romanzen und Balladen der neueren deutschen Dichter* (Leipzig, 1834), pp. 25-26.

99. Caroline Norton, *The Undying One* (London, 1830), reprinted in *The Undying One and Other Poems* (London, 1853), pp. 1-159. There are four editions intervening.

100. In his *Gedichte* (Berlin, 1848), p. 77.

Chapter Nine

1. *The Works of Nathaniel Hawthorne* (Riverside ed.; Boston, 1896), III, 490 (from *The Snow Image and Other Twice-Told Tales*). In *Mosses from an Old Manse*, like "A Virtuoso's Collection," "A Select Party" introduces the Wandering Jew as a member of an assemblage, but then observes: "This personage, however, had latterly grown so common by mingling in all sorts of society and appearing at the beck of every entertainer, that he could hardly be deemed a proper guest in a very exclusive circle. Besides, being covered with dust from his continual wanderings along the highways of the world, he really looked out of place in a

dress party; so that the host felt relieved of an incommodity when the restless individual in question, after a brief stay, took his departure on a ramble towards Oregon" (*ibid.*, II, 76).

2. Each fragment appeared under the title *Bruchstücke aus einem Epos*.

3. From Wilhelm Smets's *Kleinere epische Dichtungen* (Cologne, 1835), pp. 144-45.

4. Baron Frédéric-Auguste de Reiffenberg, unlike most others considered in this study, wrote more than one piece pertaining to the Legend. He was the editor also of Philippe Mouskes's *Chronique rimée* (see p. 21 above), which appeared in 1836-38; he has a simple telling of the Legend in a collection of such tales (*Le Dimanche*; Brussels, 1834, pp. 115-206). The item in question here is *Souvenirs d'un pèlerinage en l'honneur de Schiller* (Brussels-Leipzig, 1839), pp. 353-55.

5. The article is based primarily on the Frankfurt tale, derived from De Reiffenberg, *Souvenirs*, pp. 353-55.

6. *Die Ahasveriade: Des Christenthumes Kampf in der Weltgeschichte, oder Ahasvers Schicksal und Wanderungen* (Dresden, 1838). The original project called for six books and thirty cantos, of which some 112 pages were printed.

7. (Leipzig, 1833); Ahasuerus appears also as a subordinate figure in Duller's "Der Kettenschmidt," a novelette published in the Paris literary journal *Phoenix*, No. 216 (1835), p. 36.

8. In his *Gedichte* (Hamburg, 1839), pp. 18-19.

9. It was later published in Theodore Martin, *Memoir of W. E. Aytoun* (Edinburgh-London, 1867), pp. 50-56.

10. Tyler's literary efforts are confined generally to his youth—he was only twenty-six when *Ahasuerus* appeared. His later life was taken up with politics and business affairs. He was a pioneer in the development of the transcontinental railroad and served during the Civil War in the office of the Confederate Treasury.

11. This is rather unusual in a French treatment of the Legend.

12. Karl Gutzkow, "Plan eines Ahasvers, bei Besprechung von Mosens Ahasver," appeared in some miscellaneous writings, *Vermischte Schriften* (Leipzig, 1842), II, 158-60. For his comments on Mosen, see *ibid.*, II, 154-56. See also Elizabeth McConkey, *Karl Gutzkow as Literary Critic* (Chicago, 1941), which emphasizes his later career. Part of Gutzkow's difficulty as an early critic of his time lay in his involvement in a journalistic war with the *Allgemeine Zeitung des Judenthums*, whose counterblast against him in Nos. 114 and 117 for 1838 is typical; note Heinrich H. Houben, *Gutzkow-funde* (Berlin, 1901), pp. 144-280.

13. See *Monatrosen: Zeitschrift für Belehrung und Unterhaltung* (Munich), III (1842), 189-94.

14. See Jan Jakubec and Arne Novák, *Geschichte der čechischen Literatur* (2d ed.; Leipzig, 1913), p. 243. The piece is abstract and colorless in its positing of the struggle between idealism and materialism; it is too much Hegel and not enough Goethe.

15. In *Lieder des Sturms* (Stuttgart, 1838), pp. 216-19.

16. Franz Theremin, *Der ewige Jude: Eine Legende*. It was printed originally in *Abendstunden* (Berlin, 1835) and subsequently not only in Heldring (1839) but in a revised edition of *Abendstunden* (Berlin, 1841), pp. 285-326.

17. Julius Mosen, "Ritter Wahn," accessible most conveniently in his *Sämmtliche Werke* (Leipzig, 1871), II, 108-11. His *Ahasver: Episches Gedicht* (Dresden-Leipzig, 1838) was printed also in his *Sämmtliche Werke*, II, 149-321. It was the review in the *Zeitung für die elegante Welt* for June 16, 1838, that prompted the rather notorious comments by Gutzkow, *Vermischte Schriften*, II, 154-56.

18. Franz Karl Joel-Jacoby's *Klagen eines Juden* was written in 1835 but was not published until 1837, when it was amalgamated with *Religiöse Rhapsodien* and *Harfe und Lyra* into one volume (Berlin, 1837). The quotation is from *Klagen eines Juden*, pp. 81-82. The attack by Gutzkow came in *Telegraph für Deutschland*, II, No. 1 (1837), 1-3 and was reprinted in his miscellany, *Götter, Helden, Don Quixote* (Hamburg, 1838). Nikolaus Lenau's remarks will be found in "Der arme Jude," in Max Koch's edition of *Lenaus Werke* (Berlin-Stuttgart, 1888), I, 379.

19. One of his "Heidebilder." See Lenau, *Lenaus Werke*, I, 156-60.

20. *Ibid.*, I, 203-8. The dates given here are terminal dates between which the poem is believed to have been written. He also wrote a long dramatic poem, *Savanarola*, in which Ahasuerus is a subordinate figure; this work was published at Stuttgart in 1837; see Lenau, *Lenaus Werke*, II, 207-334.

21. *Christlich Legenden: Blumenlese religiös-moralischer Dichtungen*, by the editor of "Schule der Weisheit," who has thus far resisted identification. The appropriate material will be found on pp. 361-65. Actually, the piece is rather typical of the *complainte*.

22. In his *Gedichte* (Munich, 1844), p. 120.

23. Hans Christian Andersen, *Ahasverus* (Leipzig, 1844), included also in his *Gesammelte Werke* (Leipzig, 1847-52), XXIX-XXX. The disillusionment at Christ's refusing to make an earthly fight and allowing himself to be taken prisoner is a constantly recurring theme in the late nineteenth and particularly in the twentieth centuries. In other words, the collision between Christian submission and human resentment is too powerful; the human wins out over the idealistic. It is this same disillusionment that prompts Judas to betray Christ.

24. See A. Soergel, *Ahasver-Dichtungen seit Goethe* (Leipzig, 1905), pp. 50-52.

25. In his *Gesammelte Blätter* (Sulzbach, 1832), 169-90.

26. *Fantasien am Grabe Poniatowskys: Gepanzerte Lieder* (Leipzig, 1838); included in his *Gedichte* (Berlin, 1844), 26-29.

27. Published first in *Bifolien* for 1836, pp. 333-36; later in his *Gesammelte Schriften* (Vienna, 1877), II, 107-10.

28. *Spinoza: Ein Denkerleben* (Leipzig, 1837; rev. ed.: Mannheim, 1854).

29. In his *Gedichte* (Stuttgart, 1831), pp. 284-89.

30. In *Sieben Bücher* (n.p., 1839), p. 343.

31. In his *Gedichte* (Vienna, 1842), pp. 88-91.

32. The reference is to the October, 1838, issue of the *Athenaeum für Wissenschaft, Kunst, und Leben*, pp. 1-12. Reworked and somewhat fictionalized under the title "Ahasver," it serves as a kind of prologue to F. T. Wagenheim (A. A. Zeune), *Die Perle von Zion* (Leipzig, 1839), an uninspired novel in which Ahasuerus, a kind of glorified messenger, serves in a subordinate capacity.

33. In Paul Lacroix's *Curiosités de l'histoire des croyances populaires au moyen âge* (Paris, 1859), pp. 105-41; "Jacob" includes the *Discours véritable* (see p. 54 above), with its *complainte*, and a brief sketch of the Legend.

34. *Faust: Ein dramatisches Gedicht in drei Abtheilungen* (Leipzig, 1839); see especially pp. 189-95.

35. In his *Gedichte* (Nuremberg, 1839), pp. 20-21.

36. Wittich's poem appears in A. Nodnagel, *Sieben Bücher deutscher Sagen und Legenden* (Darmstadt, 1839), pp. 102-4.

37. *Essay on Man*, I, 71-72.

38. In his *Gedichte* (n.p., 1831), p. 123. The poem was composed in 1828. See in particular S. H. Tardel, "Ahasver-Gedichte," *Studien zur Lyrik Chamissos* (Bremen, 1902), VII, 42-50.

39. In his *Gedichte* (Leipzig, 1844), p. 429. Simrock later contributed a study of the Legend to the *Zeitschrift für deutsche Mythologie und Sittenkunde*, I (1853), 432-38, in which he pointed out the parallels between the Legend and the tradition of both the Wild Huntsman and the wanderings of the Gypsies (see pp. 5 and 421, n. 1 above).

40. *Allgemeine Zeitung der Judenthums*, No. 87 (July 21, 1838).

Chapter Ten

1. The piece was certainly serious in intent, however, for its subtitle defines it as a religious festival drama, "zur Stiftung eines Goetheums," a Goethe museum for the edification of the dramatic arts in Weimar. Note the recurrent theme of the impatience or disgust of Ahasuerus (Judas) at the lack of action in Christ.

2. Probably written about 1840, but I have seen no earlier edition than that given in Claude

Tillier, *Oeuvres* (Nevers, 1846). There are two translations into English, one by B. R. Tucker (Boston, 1890), and another, much the better of the two, by Marie Lorenz (New York, 1941), both under the title, *My Uncle Benjamin*.

3. Claude Tillier, *My Uncle Benjamin*, trans. Marie Lorenz (New York, 1941), p. 79.

4. In Salques's *Des erreurs et des préjugés répandus dans les diverses classes de la société* (3d ed.; Paris, 1823), II. "Le juif errant" comprises chap. iv. I have not been able to see an earlier edition.

5. Under "Le juif errant," pp. 105-7.

6. "Der ewige Jude Nummer Zwei," *Der Erzähler*, XI (1846), 170.

7. III (1845), 353. The short-lived periodical was a Leipzig publication.

8. *Hamlet*, II, ii, 416-20.

9. Not to be confused with the contribution to Paul Lacroix's *Curiosités de l'histoire des croyances populaires au moyen âge* (see p. 446, n. 33 above). "Jacob" is Victor Vincent Joly, a Belgian miscellaneous writer, who is best known for his reply to Sue's attack on the Jesuits (see n. 15 below).

10. The most recent work on Sue is Jean-Louis Bory, *Eugène Sue, le roi du roman populaire* (Paris, 1962). In reference to Sue's revolutionism, see particularly Pierre Chaunu, *Eugène Sue et la seconde république* (Paris, 1948). See also Nora Atkinson, *Eugène Sue et le roman-feuilleton* (Nemours, 1929).

11. Eugène Sue, *Le juif errant* (Paris, 1844-45). The quoted passage constitutes an epilogue to Part II.

12. *Parodie du juif errant* (Paris, 1844). It was then reprinted in Brussels (1845), translated into German (Frankfurt, 1845), into English (London, 1846; New York, 1847), and reprinted several times.

13. Unpublished MS review in the Henry E. Huntington Library, San Marino, Calif.

14. This pamphlet went through seven editions within the next two years.

15. *Des Jésuites et de quelques engouements littéraires à propos du "Juif errant"* (Brussels, 1845). There were some Dutch and Flemish repercussions also—the anonymous pamphlets *De wandelende Jood in een zothuis met den grooten advokaet der logie en kompe* (Brussels, 1845), and *De Wandelende Jezuït in 1845* (Amsterdam, 1845).

16. *Notes on the Wandering Jew, the Jesuits, and Their Opponents* (London, 1845); *Aufzeichnungen des ewigen Juden* (Schaffhausen, 1846).

17. (Paris-Lyon, 1847; 2d ed.: Paris, 1853). There is a Dutch translation by Henri Bogaerts, *De Wandelende Jood te Munster* (Amsterdam, 1872).

18. *Der ewige Jude: Eine komische Geschichte aus dem 18. Jahrhundert* (Leipzig, 1800).

19. *Le Juif Errant, drame en cinq actes et dix-sept tableaux, par Eugène Sue, mise en scène de Montdidier et Saint-Ernest; musique de Amédée Artus* (Paris, 1849; reissued, 1873); Adolphe d'Ennery, Eugène Sue, et Prosper Dinaux, *Le juif errant* (Paris, 1850).

20. There were also others. "Sue's novel was dramatized in 1849, and after its revival in 1873 . . . there was a glut of Wandering Jews on the English stage. Three, written respectively by Leopold Lewis, George Lander, and T. G. Paulton were produced at the Adelphi, April 14, 1894; Britannia, June 18th; and Marylebone, July 7th. These plays are crudely devised melodramas, sensational and spectacular, with combats, a carnival, and tableaux depicting the Jew in the Frozen North and impelled ever onward. For years the Jew wandered through the provincial theaters."—Dorothy Scarborough, *The Supernatural in Modern English Fiction* (New York-London, 1917), p. 175.

21. This film version by Jean Richard was derived from the D'Ennery-Sue-Dinaux combination.

22. *Gesammelte Werke* (Stuttgart, 1890-91), V, 127-72.

23. Neither place nor date of publication is given in the copy available to me.

24. J. Georg Köberle, *Der neue Thurm zu Babel: Oder Ahasverus und seine Gesellen* (Leipzig, 1847), p. 105.

25. Now an extremely rare pamphlet.

26. See pp. 6, 41.

27. Also published separately (Leipzig-Frankfurt, 1835).

28. This early work of Göschel bears no indication of place of publication.

29. "Der ewige wanderende Jude ging," *Phönix* (Frankfurt), No. 232 (1835), printed again in L. Karthäuser-Nelken's *Sagen und Legenden aus christlicher Vorzeit* (Vienna, 1845), pp. 16-20.

Chapter Eleven

1. See F. W. Nietzsche, *Thus Spake Zarathustra*, trans. A. Tille (Everyman's Library, No. 892; New York, 1933), "Discourse of the Superman and of the Last Man," especially sec. 3. The concept of the superman is, of course, but the natural outgrowth of the concept of the romantic hero, and the idea is treated in various ways by various writers, notably Byron and Shelley, Jean Paul (Richter), Carlyle, and Emerson.

2. *In Memoriam*, LVI, ll. 5-8, 21-22.

3. Presumably published around 1870, to judge by the format and the typography. I have been able to find no biographical material concerning the author; certain twists of phrase suggest that she was either Swiss or Tyrolean.

4. For a discussion of the whole work in relation to the Legend, see George K. Anderson, "*Die Silberlinge des Judas* and the Accursed Treasure," *Studies in Philology*, XLVIII (1951), 77-86. I am greatly indebted for my information concerning Kalina to the staff of the National and University Library of Prague (Národni a Universitní Knihovna v Praze). The poem was first published in Kalina's *Básnické spisy* ("Poetic Works") in 1852, but there was another edition in 1874. See Frederick Tupper, "The Pardoner's Tale," in *Sources and Analogues of Chaucer's "Canterbury Tales*," ed. William Frank Bryan and Germaine C. Dempster (Chicago, 1941), pp. 415-38, where both the Italian play and Sachs's are printed.

5. Most accessible in his *Gesammelte Werke* (Stuttgart, 1883), I, 447-49; also in his *Gedichte* (Leipzig, 1888), pp. 363-65.

6. It was written, according to the author, in 1853, but I have been able to see it only in the fourth edition of *Poetiske Skrifter* (Copenhagen, 1883), pp. 333-434. The poem is broken into six sections.

7. I, 167.

8. In his *Dramatische Werke* (Nuremberg, 1856-67), III.

9. Pp. 85-93.

10. See especially pp. 215-18.

11. See particularly "Die Rede des ewigen Juden," pp. 78-98.

12. Available also in Grenier's *Oeuvres* (Paris, 1895-1902), I, 1-59.

13. In particular, pp. 148-50.

14. There are numerous editions after the first (Hamburg, 1866); there were eight German editions by 1873 and have been many since, including a de luxe edition in 1885. There were two Dutch translations, both entitled *Ahasverus te Rome* and published in Amsterdam—the first by W. J. A. Huberts (1876) and the other by A. van Dissel (1893)—as well as an Italian version by Chiaffredo Hugues (Bologna, 1876).

15. Compare the treatment of this character in Carl Irmler's *Actäa* (Strasbourg, 1903).

16. Robert Hamerling, *Ahasver in Rom* (Hamburg, 1866), Part II, 11.

17. In his *Gedichte* (Stuttgart, 1854). I have been obliged to refer to the second edition (Stuttgart-Augsburg, 1858), pp. 188-91.

18. *Der ewige Jude, aus dem russischen Übersetzt* (Oppeln, 1883). The French translation, *Le juif errant*, came out in St. Petersburg (1885).

19. The first part, "Guttenberg," was printed at Leipzig in 1860, but the other three parts appeared in Hamburg in 1869.

20. A European adventurer of obscure origin who appeared at the court of Louis XV of

France about 1750 with a large fortune, most of which he dissipated in intrigues at the French court and elsewhere. He claimed to be several hundred years old and to have in his possession the elixir of eternal life. He died in Schleswig in 1780.

21. The libretto was published later in Eugène Scribe, *Théâtre* (Paris, 1857), pp. 261-311, and there is a German translation of the text by L. Rellstab (Mainz, 1852).

22. The work was produced in Ghent on February 10, 1853; later in the year it was printed in the same city. See J. J. Gielen, *De wandelende Jood in Volkskunde en Letterkunde* (Amsterdam, 1931), pp. 55-56.

23. Pierre Dupont, *La Légende du Juif-errant: Compositions et dessins par Gustave Doré* (Paris, 1856). The English version bears no date.

24. In his *Jødiske Noveller, Fortaellinger og Folkesagn* (Copenhagen, 1861), pp. 218-26.

25. The sonnet is available to me only in a newspaper clipping, on which the date of 1866 appears in the left-hand corner, above; the reverse side furnishes no further clue. "Ahasvérus" appeared in De Poligny's *Fleurs des Buissons* (n.p., 1857).

26. In the Leipzig, 1866, edition the title was changed to *Ahasverus: Ein Heldengedicht.*

27. A German translation appeared in the same year. Eventually an English translation by F. W. Reed was deposited in 1937 in the collection on the Legend of the Wandering Jew which W. Easton Louttit, Jr., has subsequently given to Brown University.

28. See F. W. Reed, "Dumas's Wandering Jew: Isaac Laquedem," *London Quarterly Review,* American edition (October, 1928), 207-10.

29. Arnold C. Bell, *Alexandre Dumas* (London, 1950), pp. 272-73.

30. In *Poets and Poetry of the West*, ed. William T. Coggeshall (Columbus, Ohio, 1860), p. 108. The poem was written at the request of a friend who wished some verses on the incident of Cornelius Agrippa and the Wandering Jew (as told in Aytoun's version and repeated in Hoffman's *Chronicles of Cartaphilus*).

31. *Ahasverus, des wahren ewigen Juden Wanderungen . . . nach einem alten Kloster-Manuscript beschrieben für die jetzige Zeit* (Regensburg, 1845). It appears to be an imitation of the *Volksbuch*, written perhaps about 1820.

32. In the *Almanach*, see p. 151. *Reveries of a Bachelor* went through sixteen editions by 1852; since then there have been thirteen additional ones, the last in 1931. I have not listed the *Kladderadatsch* cartoons because they have nothing in themselves to be connected with the Legend save the cant name Ahasuerus.

33. Yet this is, like the entries in *Kladderadatsch*, hardly germane to the Legend.

34. There were new editions in 1854 and 1918.

35. See particularly XVIII ("Faust und Ahasver"), 160-73.

36. Eichrodt's "Ahasver" is in *Lyrische Karikaturen* (n.p., 1869). Saxe's "The Wandering Jew" is in *Clever Stories of Many Nations* (Boston, 1865), pp. 141-49. Saxe has drawn chiefly on the Brabantine ballad and in a footnote has occasion to mention Lewis, Southey, and Croly. Baumbach's "Ahasver" is in his *Lieder eines fahrenden Gesellen* (Leipzig, 1878), pp. 85-93.

37. A writer may suddenly play tricks on the reader in disconcerting fashion. Thus Sylvester Judd, in *Philo* (Boston, 1850), writes a Christological dramatic poem with interlocutors human, angelic, and divine. In the mouth of the title character are put ideas and even phrases from the historical Philo (*ca.*20 B.C.-*ca.* A.D. 40), the Hellenistic Jewish philosopher of Alexandria. One of the scenes is a visit to the infernal regions and a rambling chat with the Devil, who is in high glee over the victims furnished by the Mexican War. It does not take long in this cumbersome interchange to discover that the Devil is simply an alias for the Wandering Jew.

38. *She and Allan* (London, 1887), and *The Return of She* (London-New York, 1905).

39. In *Dichtungen* (Stuttgart, 1883), pp. 127-29.

40. "Über die Volkssagen von Ahasverus und Faust im Licht ihrer Zeit," *Deutsches Museum,* I (1866), 193-210. "Rückblicke auf Dichtungen und Sagen des deutschen Mittelalters," *Bibliothek der gesammten deutschen National-Literatur*, II (1872), 85-105.

41. *Der ewige Jude: Ein dramatisches Gedicht in drei Theilen* (Leipzig, 1886). Another edition appeared in Leipzig in 1894.

42. See Mauthner's *Der unbewusste Ahasverus,* pp. 85-93. The song is in Von Portheim's *Silentium pro—,* pp. 87-88.

43. "Germanicus" is presumably Emil Richter, an incendiary editor whose headquarters were at Frankfurt am Main.

44. Egon Waldegg, *Die Judenfrage, etc.* (Dresden, 1879; 2d ed.: Dresden, 1880).

45. M. Baumgarten, *Wider Herrn Hofprediger Stöcker: Eine christliche Stimme über die Judenfrage* (Berlin, 1881). Paulus Cassel, *Ahasverus: Die Sage vom ewigen Juden . . . mit einem kritischen Protest wider E. von Hartmann und A. Stocker* (Berlin, 1885). *Saat auf Hoffnung: Zeitschrift für die Mission der Kirche an Israel,* XXIII (1886), 1-4.

46. "Die Völkerwanderung und ihre Folgen, etc.," *Jahresbericht der Samsonschule zu Wolfenbüttel, 1877-78* (Hannover, 1878).

47. In *Lieder eines ausgewanderten Kurmärker, 1888* (n.p., 1888); also in Müller's *Gedichte* (Berlin, 1892), pp. 60-61.

48. Published in his *Poesía* (La Paz, 1877).

49. I have limited myself to the more important considerations or approaches to the Legend. For others, see Alexander Scheiber, "The Legend of the Wandering Jew in Hungary," *Midwest Folklore,* IV (1954), 221-35, especially pp. 223-25. Emeric Madách, *Az ember tragédiája* (Budapest, 1859), is most easily available to English-speaking readers in the translation by William N. Loew (Imre Madach, *The Tragedy of Man;* New York, 1908). According to Scheiber, the first "literary" use of the Legend comes in the fragment of a drama by Michael Vörösmarty, *Az örök zsidóból* ("From the Eternal Jew"; Budapest, 1850)—Death laughs at the Jew, as he does at all.

50. Nietzsche, *Thus Spake Zarathustra,* sec. 3 of the Prologue. Pichler's poem was written in 1880, but is found only in his later collection, *Marksteine* (Munich, 1907), pp. 195-200.

51. Carmen Sylva (Elizabeth of Romania), *Jehovah* (Leipzig, 1882), p. 9.

52. *Ibid.,* p. 83.

53. There is a German translation by "Odoaker," *Der ewige Jude* (Geneva, 1905).

54. Julius Bruck, *Ahasver: Alter Sage, neue Deutung, zur hundertsten Jahresfeier der Unabhängigkeits-verklärung* (New York, 1876).

55. Cited by Avrahm Yarmolinsky, "The Wandering Jew," *Studies in Jewish Bibliography and Related Subjects* (New York, 1929), p. 320.

56. George Macdonald, *Thomas Wingfold, Curate* (Boston, 1876), pp. 516-17.

57. *Ibid.,* pp. 642-44.

58. In the two-volume edition, vol. II, chap. xxvii; in the one-volume edition, chap. liv.

Chapter Twelve

1. *Scribners Magazine,* X (December, 1891), 737-41; Andrew Lang, *Historical Mysteries* (London, 1904; 2d ed.: 1905), pp. 256-76.

2. Perhaps an exception might be made, among the works appropriate to this paragraph, for Joseph C. Heywood, *Antonius: A Dramatic Poem,* first published in New York in 1867 and again in 1904. Here the Wandering Jew appears briefly in Roman Gaul as Kaliphilus (*sic*).

3. Notably, of course, in Eugène Sue's *Le juif errant* (Paris, 1844-45).

4. New Ser., XXIV (1895), 164-81.

5. See also J. J. Gielen, *De wandelende Jood in Volkskunde en Letterkunde* (Amsterdam, 1931), pp. 68, 119.

6. Deckert is also the author of another interesting pamphlet, *Kann ein Katholik Antisemit sein?* (Dresden, 1893).

7. In *Die Kunst,* ed. Richard Muther (Berlin, 1905).

8. Trans. Georg Polonskij.

9. Herman Heyermans is a pseudonym for Ivan Jelakowitch. Originally in Russian, the play was translated into Dutch as *Ahasverus* (Amsterdam, 1893), and into German (1904).

10. No publication date is given, but a reference in the advertisements in the rear pages makes a date of 1899 likely.

11. In Dehmel's *Ausgewählte Gedichte* (Berlin, 1901), pp. 87-93.

12. Johannes Lepsius, *Ahasver, der ewige Jude* (Leipzig, 1894), pp. 5-22.

13. *Ibid.*, p. 141.

14. VIII (1901), 515.

15. In *Ahasver und andere Novellen* (Berlin, 1900).

16. *Der sterbende Ahasver: Ein Stück Gegenwart in vier Akten und einer Vorrede* (Berlin, 1898). The piece was largely written by 1890.

17. There were subsequent editions and a dramatization in 1899 of *Children of the Ghetto*. Three collections of short stories further exemplify Zangwill's point of view: *Dreamers of the Ghetto* (London-New York, 1898), *Ghetto Tragedies* (London-New York, 1893), and *Ghetto Comedies* (London-New York, 1907).

18. Indeed, this title is as misleading as the chapter in H. R. Fox-Bourne, *The Romance of Trade* (London, 1871), entitled "The Wandering Jew," which is actually a comment on the perpetual genius of the Jewish race for business, trade, and commerce.

19. *Euphorion*, XIV (1907), 617.

20. One is reminded inevitably of the voyage of Israel Jobson through space and of his comments upon the lunarians.

21. Reprinted in the Berlin, 1912, edition of his *Gedichte*.

22. I used the fourth edition (Paderborn, 1901), pp. 141-45.

23. First published in Renner's *Gedichte* (Berlin, 1904), pp. 114-21.

24. *Ibid.*, p. 118.

25. Johanna and Gustav Wolff, *Ahasver* (Berlin, 1899), pp. 22-24.

26. *Ibid.*, p. 100.

27. (3d ed.; Berlin, 1890), pp. 304-24.

28. The character of the mother in *Ahasvera* is such, however, that we may conceive of her as a latter-day Wandering Jewess: see Appendix B.

29. In Von Schaching's *Geschichte aus den Bergen* (Regensburg, 1895).

30. XLVIII (1888), 108-41.

31. My estimate of its approximate date is based chiefly upon the typography.

32. There was a second edition in the following year and a German translation, published at Freiburg, also in 1894. The novel was never so successful as the same author's *Ben-Hur*.

33. See Irving McKee, *"Ben-Hur" Wallace: The Life of General Lew Wallace* (Berkeley, Calif., 1947).

34. VIII (1901), 523.

35. In *Reclams Universal-Bibliothek*, No. 3416, ed. Carl F. Wittmann (Leipzig, 1895), pp. 5-12.

36. "Ahasver an seine Widersacher," *Ost und West*, XI (January, 1904), 58; "Gott flucht Ahasver," *ibid.*, IX (August, 1902), 575-76; "Tröster Ahasver," *ibid.*, pp. 577-78; "Aus Träumen geweckt," *ibid.*, pp. 515-16; "Im Walde," *ibid.*, p. 516; "Ihr und Ich," *ibid.* (September, 1902), pp. 635-36; "Ahasvers Sehnsucht," *ibid.* (June, 1902), pp. 389-90.

37. O. J. Bierbaum, "Golgotha," *Irrgarten der Liebe* (Berlin-Leipzig, 1901), pp. 221-26.

38. Pp. 60-61.

39. Oskar Ungnad, "Ahasver," *Unsere Gesellschaft*, VIII (1898), 316-17.

40. Joseph Scheel, "Ahasver: II Monolog," *Der Türmer*, XVI (June, 1914), 9. (I have been unable to locate the first monologue.)

41. Felix Rutten, "Ahasverus: Toneelspel in een bedrijf," *De Nieuwe Gids*, II (1918), 392-411.

42. *Daheim*, XLII (1906), 12. The poem is reprinted in her collected poems and ballads, *Reif steht die Saat* (Jena, 1929). Compare the cattle-pen episode in particular with Thomas Hardy's *The Oxen* (1913).

43. Edwin Arlington Robinson, "The Wandering Jew," *Collected Poems* (New York, 1930), pp. 456-59.

44. In the W. Easton Louttit, Jr., collection on the Legend of the Wandering Jew in the Brown University Library.

45. IV (October, 1895), 14-15.

46. The cantata was dedicated to the Basel Choral Society and was furnished with an English translation by Paul England, in addition to the German text.

47. See particularly pp. 23-25.

48. A French translation appeared in the *Mercure de France* for 1911, in three installments. The translation by Gaby Vermeylen was printed separately (Paris, 1925). A German version by Anton Kippenberg appeared at Leipzig in 1917. Vermeylen's work did rather well; it had reached a fourth edition by 1923.

49. Translated by Andor von Sponer in *Dichtungen von Johann Arany* (Leipzig, 1880), p. 171.

50. I can find no record of publication; the copy available to me is in the hand of Olga Maier (wife of the collector), who has written the poem out in an old copybook now in the W. Easton Louttit, Jr., collection on the Legend of the Wandering Jew in the Brown University Library.

51. I, No. 54 (April 19, 1904).

52. IV, 334.

53. I have seen only the fifth edition (Munich, 1904); the poem is on p. 14.

54. P. 3.

55. This poem is most easily accessible in S. Weir Mitchell, *Complete Poems* (New York, 1914), pp. 234-56.

56. *Udvalgt Vaerker* (Copenhagen, 1910), p. 26.

57. Also in his *Werke* (Munich, 1907), I, 3-27.

58. The subtitle indicates that it was written "automatically," but as automatic writing it is down-to-earth, pleasant reading.

59. I have been unable to get behind this pseudonym.

60. In *Die Lehre von der Wiedergeburt und das musikalische Drama nebst dem Entwurf eines Mysteriums "Die Erlösung"* (Kiel-Leipzig, 1895), pp. 101-400. There are three parts to *"Die Erlösung"*: "Kain, an einem Abend"; "Jesus von Nazareth, an zwei Abenden"; and "Ahasverus, an einem Abend."

61. P. 125.

62. Pp. 1-14. On this poem, see also Gielen, *De wandelende Jood*, p. 72, and Josef Gassner, *Seebers "Ewiger Jude"* (Frankfurt, 1896).

63. Josef Seeber, *Der ewige Jude* (Freiburg, 1894), p. 114.

64. *Ibid.*, p. 206.

65. *Ibid.*, pp. 208-11.

66. *Daily Chronicle* as quoted in Harriett Jay, *Robert Buchanan* (London, 1903), pp. 262-63, 268, 273.

Chapter Thirteen

1. Pp. 11-24.

2. I have been able to find this only in an English translation printed in *Golden Book Magazine*, XVIII (July, 1933), 103-11, as "The Wandering Jew."

3. In *Das neue Leben*, I (May 1, 1913), 439-44.

4. For Héraucourt's poem, see J. J. Gielen, *De wandelende Jood in Volkskunde en Letter-kunde* (Amsterdam, 1931), p. 216 (bibliographical item 983); "A Simple Tale" is in John Galsworthy's *Caravan* (London, 1925).

5. The story is printed also in his *Novellen und Skizzen* (*Zeitpsychologische*), published also at Munich in the same year.

6. P. 68.

7. "Golgotha" is in his *Irrgarten der Liebe* (Berlin-Leipzig, 1901), pp. 221-26; "Schmulius Caesar" is in his *Sonderbare Beschichten* (Munich, 1908), pp. 21-25; the quotation is from p. 25 of the latter.

8. In *De Nieuwe Gids*, I (1912), 884.

9. In his *Beiträge zur deutschen Bühnenkunst, etc.* (Leipzig, 1911). The project was for a set of trilogies, only one of which was completed.

10. In his *Uit de Stilte* (The Hague, 1915), p. 16.

11. In *Tijdschrift*, XIX (1914), 102.

12. In *Oesterreichische Rundschau*, XXI (October 1, 1909), p. 2.

13. "Ahasver," LXXVII, No. 1936 (1882), 73-74.

14. CXXVII, No. 3247 (1907).

15. The general tone of the piece, to say nothing of its typography, suggests that it was an item in *Fliegende Blätter*, but I have been unable to locate it there. I suspect that the author's name is a pseudonym.

16. In the copybook kept by Olga Maier in the W. Easton Louttit, Jr., collection on the Legend of the Wandering Jew in the Brown University Library.

17. *Echos du juif errant* (Paris, 1845), p. 50. The reprint available to me is probably near the turn of the century.

18. There have been two or three subsequent editions; I have used that of 1915, in which the story appears on pp. 117-32. See in addition Gerald Langford, *Alias O. Henry* (New York, 1957), p. 93.

19. This idea is not uncommon. Its most eloquent expression comes in Thekla Skorra's poem.

20. (2d ed.; Stuttgart, 1890). There is considerable discussion of the work in W. van Scholz, *Gedanken zum Drama* (Munich, 1905), pp. 94-112.

21. New Ser., L (1921), 413-20.

22. In *Unsere Hoffnung*, IV (1907), 26-42. Published in English as *The Stranger* in *Ten Plays by David Pinski* (New York, 1920).

23. In *The Holy Cross, and Other Tales* (Cambridge, Mass., 1893), pp. 13-35.

24. In *Die Musik*, III, No. 19 (1903), 23-38, and IV, No. 21 (1904), 187-210. Later the work was published in book form (Oldenburg, 1904).

25. In his *Legenden 3* (Nijmegen, 1913), pp. 7-22.

26. (Budapest, 1914), II, 5-55. In the second edition (Budapest, 1927), the appropriate pages are 165-201.

27. In *Szegedi Napló*, XXXV (1912), 21.

28. Skorra's poem, dated 1908, is in the W. Easton Louttit, Jr., collection on the Legend of the Wandering Jew in the Brown University Library. "Bolygó zsidó," is in Szabolcska's *Hangulatok* ("Moods"; Budapest, 1894), pp. 155-57; "Ahasver" is in *Egyenlöség*, XXIX (1910), 15.

29. In Salus' *Das Jüde-Prag* (Prague, 1917), and in Harsányi's *Páter Benedek* (Budapest, 1910), pp. 97-111.

30. K. H. Mácha, "Ewige Wanderung," trans. Oskar Rosenfeld, *Das Jüde-Prag* (Prague, 1917).

31. In his *Elbeszelö költemenyek* ("Narrative Poems"; Budapest, 1902), pp. 73-78.

32. In *Budapesti Hirlap*, XV (1895), 226.

Chapter Fourteen

1. In his *Fantastica: The Smile of the Sphinx and Other Tales of Imagination: I. Romances of Ideas* (London, 1923), pp. 176-515.

2. *Ibid.*, p. 360.

3. Wilhelm Gründler, *Ahasuerus*, ed. Herman Wendt (Berlin, 1928). "The past and the future leave us little rest." The date of composition seems to be 1915-16.

4. (Vienna, 1920; 2d ed.: 1930); see especially pp. 48-53.

5. Originally published as part of *Groteske Historien* (Dresden, 1921).

6. George Sylvester Viereck and Paul Eldridge, *My First Two Thousand Years: The Autobiography of the Wandering Jew* (New York, 1928). There have been a few cheap editions in paperbacks since that date. There is actually a sequel, very remote from the Wandering Jew, called *The Invincible Adam* (New York, 1932), which does not immediately concern us.

7. George Sylvester Viereck and Paul Eldridge, *Salome, the Wandering Jewess: My First Two Thousand Years of Love* (New York, 1930).

8. A good example of the scabrous and yet psychologically not inaccurate kind of characterization which both Viereck-Eldridge books afford.

9. Emile Bernard, *Le juif errant* (Paris, 1927); see especially pp. 277-87.

10. *Heiligenrast: Ein Roman aus alter Zeit* (Berlin, 1919).

11. The author's name, and to some extent the play, are the source of inspiration for a most engaging extended short story by Malcolm Lowry, "The Element Follows You Around, Sir!" in *Show Magazine*, IV (March, 1964), 45-51. In this fantasy a man, reminded of the final scene of Thurston's play where Ahasuerus is handed over to the stake by the Spanish Inquisition, is moved to think of someone named Thurston as the Wandering Jew, whose body was consumed by fire but whose external appurtenances were not. This Wandering Jew haunts him in the role of a firemaker, for wherever this man goes there are fires, ostensibly set by lightning. But we know better, of course.

12. This was even more poorly printed than most contemporaneous paperbacks and is no longer available. To the best of my knowledge it has not as yet been reprinted in any of the subsequent collections of the author's short stories.

13. Previously mentioned; see p. 353 above.

14. Joseph Winckler, *Irrgarten Gottes oder Die Komödie des Chaos* (Jena, 1922), chap. xxiv.

15. See especially chap. xxv.

16. (Dresden, 1924), pp. 104-5.

17. Franz V. Werfel, *Jakobowsky und der Oberst* (Stockholm, 1944), translated by Gustave O. Arlt (New York, 1944), and adapted for the American stage by S. N. Behrman (New York, 1944) under the title *Jacobowsky and the Colonel*. A second edition (Stockholm, 1945) bears the caption: "Made in the United States." The play was a definite success on the New York stage.

18. There is an English translation by Willa and Edwin Muir, *Jew Süss* (London, 1926), which was published in the United States under the title *Power* (New York, 1927), as well as a Spanish translation (Madrid, 1932). *Power* was dramatized by Ashley Dukes as *Jew Süss* (New York, 1930).

19. Lion Feuchtwanger, *Jew Süss*, trans. Willa and Edwin Muir (London, 1926), pp. 25-26.

20. The story is the last of the three.

21. John Bennett, *The Doctor to the Dead: Grotesque Legends and Folk Tales of Old Charleston* (New York-Toronto, 1946). See especially pp. 59-82.

22. *Ibid.*, pp. 68-69.

23. *Jakusuküla poisid* (Tartus), IX (1930), 89-95.

24. (Leipzig, 1912), III, 292.

25. (Innsbruck, n.d.), pp. 239-40.

26. In *Vild Hoede*, VIII (January, 1934), 92.

27. Leo Sternberg, "Der Wanderer: Scene," *O, seiet Menschen!* (Berlin-Leipzig, 1921), pp. 55-67.

28. *Der Kranz*, XVII (Berlin, 1920).

29. J. J. Gielen, *De wandelende Jood in Volkskunde en Letterkunde* (Amsterdam, 1931), p. 90.

30. Heinrich Nelson, *Ahasvers Wanderung und Wandlung: Ein Märchenroman* (Leipzig, 1922).

31. Rudolf Kassner, "Der ewige Jude: Eine Kinderheitserinnerung und physiognomische Studie," *Die Mythen der Seele* (Leipzig, 1927), p. 520; see also his *Der grösste Mensch* (Erlangen-Zurich, 1946), p. 212.

32. There is an English translation by Phyllis Mégroz (New York, 1935).

33. Edmond Fleg, *Jesus*, trans. Phyllis Mégroz (New York, 1935), p. 56.

34. *Ibid.*, p. 210.

35. *Ibid.*, pp. 234-37.

36. *Ibid.*, p. 311.

37. Kees Meekel, *Ahasverus: Een Trilogie* (Amsterdam, 1923), p. 31.

38. *Ibid.*, p. 47.

39. Edwin Arlington Robinson, *Collected Poems* (New York, 1920), pp. 456-59. The W. Easton Louttit, Jr., collection on the Legend of the Wandering Jew in the Brown University Library contains the original autograph manuscript, signed twice by the poet, and a separate printing of the poem (1936) with signed etching frontispiece of the author and a letter, dated December 2, 1931, by Robinson explaining the first appearance of the poem.

40. Pp. 43-49.

41. The five parts comprise: "Don Juans Aufbruch"; "Don Juans erste Verwandlung"; "Von Leib zu Leib"; "Ahasvers letzte Maske"; and "Ahasvers Vermachtnis."

42. Siegfried von der Trenck, *Don Juan-Ahasver: Eine Passion der Erde* (Gotha, 1930), p. 117.

43. For some minor but similar reflections, see A. van Atten, "Ahasverus," *Lezen en Voordragen*, III (1928), 133-37; and Jan Zeldenthuis, *Ahasverus in het allerlaatste jaar* (Amsterdam, 1927).

44. In fact the latest item of them all, in point of time, is a short story, "The Lost Leonardo," by J. C. Ballard, published in *Fantasy and Science Fiction* (March, 1964), 112-28. Here Ahasuerus is an international man of distinction who steals (or borrows) great paintings of the Crucifixion in order to alter those which portray him among the spectators in such a way that he will always appear as a sympathetic character. The painting is then "found." He rides around in a somewhat spectral automobile. But the author's tale is prefaced by a headnote which points out that Ahasuerus was a name never borne by a Jew but rather by a Persian (Xerxes). What obscure fate brought this Persian to Jerusalem on the day of the Crucifixion? It is an interesting deviation which Ballard has given, although our protagonist is too traditionally established by now as a shoemaker of Jerusalem to allow much room to an interloper. It is a pity that this story, quite direct and dramatic, should appear in this ephemeral medium; it is to be hoped that it can be reprinted in the future.

45. Pär Lagerkvist, *Sibyllan* (Stockholm, 1956), with English translation by Naomi Walford (New York-London, 1958); and *Ahasverus död* (Stockholm, 1960), with English translation by Naomi Walford (New York, 1962).

46. Pär Lagerkvist, *The Sibyl*, trans. Naomi Walford (New York-London, 1958), p. 12.

47. *Ibid.*, p. 25.

48. *Ibid.*, p. 146.

49. *Ibid.*, p. 152.

50. Pär Lagerkvist, *The Death of Ahasuerus*, trans. Naomi Walford (New York, 1962), pp. 110-11.

51. (Paris, 1922); there have been several subsequent printings.

52. James Joyce, *Ulysses* (Paris, 1922), p. 209. Joyce's choice of a Jewish background for his

protagonist is undoubtedly suggested by the history of the Jews as wanderers; another Semitic wanderer who is referred to is Sinbad the Sailor. See Richard Ellmann, *James Joyce* (New York, 1959), pp. 238-39; in referring to the original concept of *Ulysses* (1906-7): "Joyce's interest in the Jews was growing as he recognized his own place in Europe to be as ambiguous as theirs. He was interested in a Jewish divorce case in Dublin, in the fact that George Brandes was a Jew, and in Ferrero's theories of anti-Semitism." Although he made little progress at this time, "the figure of the cuckolded Jew did not leave him." There is no question, of course, that wandering is the main theme of *Ulysses*—its title alone is justification for that thesis. The choice of a Jew to represent the Greek here is complex and somewhat personal in Joyce's case. But the result is that we have a Jew who wanders, and this is not necessarily the Wandering Jew, as we have seen before. To make him automatically into Ahasuerus is to oversimplify.

53. Irving Feldman, "The Wandering Jew," comprising: "The Gates of Gaza," "The Face of God," "The Wailing Wall," "Assimilation," and "Scratch," *Works and Days* (Boston-Toronto, 1961), with annual reprinting since that year; see pp. 94-101 in particular. A work which recognizes the Jews as wanderers but which is even less applicable to a treatment of the Legend is Robert Nathan, *Road of Ages* (New York, 1935), a novel treating of the experiences of the Jews who make a trek from all over Europe to a designated spot in Central Asia, where they have been offered refuge.

54. (New York, 1920); published originally as *The Soul of Melicent* (New York, 1913).

55. Shalom Asch, *The Nazarene*, trans. Maurice Samuel (New York, 1939).

56. William Sharp, *The Gypsy Christ and Other Tales* (Chicago, 1895), pp. 3-43.

57. There is, in fact, more religious feeling in this scene than in most twentieth-century treatments, for the tendency seems to be to replace a religious attitude toward Ahasuerus and his curse with a sociological one which removes most of the dramatic tension.

58. See the issue of *The New Yorker*, XV (January 27, 1940), 35-36. The individual presented a calling card with the name "T. W. Jew." He was an insurance agent, "who does pretty well at his business under a more plausible name, when he's not thinking of himself as the Wandering Jew." But on Saturdays he hurries to the New York Public Library to read all the books he can find about Ahasuerus—he reads all languages—and refers to them as "my biography." I myself have been introduced, in the year 1948, to a Wall Street broker who considered himself Ahasuerus—perhaps he was the same one who visited the public library in 1940. It is good that these individuals are sure of themselves. Unlike the strange youth of 1866 (p. 119 above), they had to announce themselves; no one believed it for them.

Appendix A

1. Ottmar F. H. Schönhuth, *Ahasverus, der ewige Jude: Ein wunderbare und gar erbauliche Historie* (Reutlingen, 1849).

2. Paul Delasalle, "Le juif errant," *Revue de Calvados* (Paris, 1840), pp. 11-12.

3. XIII (1843), 48-52.

4. (October, 1838), pp. 1-12; see also the same author's "Ahasver," printed as prologue to A. A. Zeune (F. T. Wagenheim), *Die Perle von Zion* (Leipzig, 1839).

5. (Paris, 1845-46), pp. 57-228.

6. I, 93.

7. Pp. 427-52.

8. "Der ewige Jude im Voigtlande," *Illustriertes Familienjournal*, XII (1860), 254.

9. L. Otte, "Ahasver, eine Sage aus dem Wallis," *Bilder-Chronik* (Leipzig, 1851), p. 42; also in *Illustriertes Unterhaltungsblatt*, VIII, No. 8 (1851), 64.

10. See p. 82 above.

11. Heinrich Dörings, *Brittischer Balladenschatz in metrischer Uebersetzung mit beigefügtem Original* (Leipzig, 1858), p. 73.

12. Charles Nisard, *Histoire des livres populaires ou de la littérature de colportage, etc.* (Paris, 1854). There was a second edition in 1864. Nearly contemporary is a very useful compilation by Alexis Socard, *Livres populaires* (Paris, 1865). To these should be added, from a later date, Paul Sébillot, *L'Imagerie populaire* (Paris, 1888).

13. (Paris, 1869), pp. 1-104; see also, however, the interesting article by Champfleury, "D'une nouvelle interprétation de la légende gothique du Juif-Errant," *Revue Germanique et Française*, XXX (1864), 299-325.

14. (Brussels, 1910), pp. 99-102, *et passim.*

15. G. W. Roeder, "Die Sage vom ewigen Juden in mythischer, historischer, und ethischer Beziehung," *Deutsches Museum*, I (1856), 305-22.

16. Yet this is an oversimplification of statement. The Legend did not have a Saracen origin, but originated in lands which came later under Saracen domination and was transmitted to western Europe during this period of Moslem political rule.

17. B. Rodiger, "Der ewige Jude," *Freya: Illustrierte Blätter für die gebildete Welt*, IV (1864), 286.

18. Johann Georg Theodor Grässe, *Die Sage vom ewigen Juden* (Dresden-Leipzig, 1844); rev. ed., *Der Tannhäuser und Ewige Jude: Zwei deutsche Sagen in ihrer Entstehung und Entwicklung historisch, mythologisch und biographisch verfolgt und erklärt* (Dresden, 1861).

19. (1867), I, 72-82, 102-18.

20. Leonhard Neubaur, *Neue Mitteilungen über die Sage vom ewigen Juden* (Leipzig, 1893). The revised edition of his *Die Sage vom ewigen Juden* (Leipzig, 1884; rev. ed.: 1893) and the *Neue Mitteilungen* are printed together.

21. Leonhard Neubaur, "Bibliographie der Sage vom ewigen Juden," *Centralblatt für Bibliothekswesen*, X (1895), 249-67, 297-316.

22. XXII (1912), 33-54.

23. New Ser., V (1914), 211-23. Note should be made of Neubaur's "Noch Einmal die Sage von Ahasver," in *Zeitschrift des Vereins für Volkskunde*, XXII (1912), 411-12.

24. Alessandro d'Ancona, "La leggenda dell'Ebreo errante," *Nuova Antologia*, Ser. 2, XXIII (1880), 413-27. See also his article, "Le Juif errant en Italie au XIII° siècle," in *Romania*, X (1881), 212-16.

25. Giuseppe Pitrè, *Fiabe, novelle, e racconti popolari siciliani* (Palermo, 1875).

26. Gaston Paris, "Le Juif errant," *Encyclopédie des sciences religieuses publiée sous la direction de F. Lichtenberger* (Paris, 1880), VII, 498-514. The separate printing was not until 1892.

27. LXXV (1895), 67-84.

28. I (1887-89), 34-45, and II (1893-95), 74-76.

29. Maurice Bataillon, "Pérégrinations espagnoles du juif errant," *Bulletin Hispanique*, XLII (1941), 81-122. But the shorter study by J. E. Gillet, "Traces of the Wandering Jew in Spain," *Romanic Review*, XXII (1931), 16-27, is most useful.

30. (London, 1866; rev. eds.: 1873 and 1881). I have used the 1881 edition; see pp. 1-31, 637-40. See also his article, "The Wandering Jew," in *Publications of the Elzevir Library*, III (1884), 124.

31. *Bentley's Miscellany*, XIII (1843), 48-52.

32. Friedrich Helbig, *Die Sage vom "Ewigen Juden," ihre poetische Wandlung und Fortbildung* (Berlin, 1874).

33. CCXLVII (July, 1880), 32-48.

34. XIII, 673-75; this was replaced in the eleventh edition by an article by Joseph Jacobs, a little more up to date in detail though hardly more comprehensive in scope (XV, 362-63).

35. (2d ed.; Freiburg, 1889), V, 545-46.

36. XXI, 280.

37. Josef Hanuš, "Ahasver čili věčný žid," *Ottův Slovník naučný*, ed. J. Otto (Prague, 1888), I, 484.

38. Boleslav Czerwieński, "Żydzie wiecznym tulaczu," *Studyum wedlug Helbiga* (Lvov, 1874), pp. 27-28, 43-44, 59-60.

39. See especially pp. 537, 564.

40. The articles are listed in Avrahm Yarmolinsky, "The Wandering Jew," *Studies in Jewish Bibliography and Related Subjects* (New York, 1929), pp. 323-24. They are either reviews of such a basic work as Gaston Paris's "Le juif errant," or references to appropriate folk tales. The two articles entitled "Der ewige Jude," *Archiv für slavische Philologie*, V (1881), 398-401, and VIII (1885), 331-33, are more important.

41. LX (1883), 784.

42. Paulus Cassel, *Ahasverus: Die Sage vom ewigen Juden . . . mit einem kritischen Protest wider E. von Hartmann und A. Stocker* (Berlin, 1885); see especially pp. 34-36.

43. (Pfarrer) Hirsch aus Lintorf, *Die drei grossen Volkssagen von Don Juan, vom ewigen Juden, und von Dr. Faust, nach ihrer inneren Verwandtschaft und ihrer charakteristischen Verschiedenheit* (Frankfurt, 1875).

44. P. 291.

45. His earlier *Die deutsche Volkssage* (Leipzig, 1874) is of some value also; see p. 378.

46. (Hamburg, 1898), pp. 9-15, *et passim*.

47. Eduard König, *Ahasver, der ewige Jude, nach seinen ursprünglichen Idee und seiner literarischen Verwertung betrachtet* (Gütersloh, 1907). See also his controversial article against Leonhard Neubaur in *Zeitschrift des Vereins für Volkskunde*, XXII (1912), 300, and the reply by Neubaur on p. 411 of the same issue. He has some later comments, following the death of Neubaur: "Ahasver, der ewige Jude," *Neues Jahrbuch für das klassische Altertum*, XXIX (1927), 587-92; and a pedantic discussion as to whether the Legend should be called a saga or a myth: "Sage und Mythus in Bezug auf den 'ewigen Juden,'" *Nord und Süd*, XCII (1912), 217-21. To him it is a myth.

48. Pieter Oosterlee, "Ahasverus," *Legenden 3* (Nijmegen, 1913), pp. 7-22.

49. (Dresden-Leipzig, 1894); see particularly pp. 175-212.

50. XXVIII (1907), 105-33.

51. IV, No. 50 (n.d.).

52. *Judenthumes Literarische Studien* (Baden-Baden, 1899).

53. Rudolf Furst, "Ahasver-Dichtungen," *Das literarische Echo*, VI (1904), cols. 21-22; XI (1909), cols. 1467-77; and XII (1910), cols. 1539-49.

54. *Im deutschen Reich: Zeitschrift des Centralvereins deutscher Staatsbürger jüdischen Glaubens*, X, No. 1 (1904), 13-20; X, No. 2 (1904), 86-97.

55. XXIII (1894), 454-80.

56. (New York, 1906), pp. 152-55.

57. XXIII (1908), 531-38.

58. Rodolfo Renier, "La Leggenda dell'Ebreo Errante, nelle sue Propaggini Letterarie," *Svaghi Critici* (Bari, 1910), pp. 485-522.

59. XXXVII (1886), 230-47.

60. Theodor Kappstein, *Ahasuer in der Weltpoesie: Mit einem Anhang—Die Gestalt Jesu in der modernen Dichtung* (Berlin, 1906).

61. "Der ewige Jude in der Dichtung, vornehmlich in der englischen und deutschen," *Palaestra*, CLXII (1928).

62. *Stoff- und Motivgeschichte der deutschen Literatur*, ed. Paul Merker and Gerhard Ludtke, (Berlin-Leipzig, 1930), VI.

63. J. J. Gielen, *De wandelende Jood in Volkskunde en Letterkunde* (Amsterdam, 1931).

64. V (1925), 5-36.

65. XXII (1931), 16-27.

66. XLIII (1941), 81-122.

67. Pp. 319-28.

68. IV (1954), 221-35.

69. (London-New York, 1927), pp. 194-243.

70. XLV (1946), 237-50.

71. XLVI (1947), 367-82.

72. XXV (1947), 303-20.

73. LXIII (1948), 199-213; in reference to this type of writing about the Wandering Jew, see the valuable earlier article by H. Glaesener, "Le type d'Ahasvérus au XVIIIe et XIXe siècles," *Revue de Littérature Comparée*, XI (1931), 373-97.

74. Pp. 187-205.

75. Albert J. Edmunds, "The Wandering Jew," *Notes and Queries*, Ser. 11, VII (1913), 47.

76. XVII (1903), 755-56.

77. P. Zondervan, "Die Legende van den wandelende Jood," *Nieuw theologisch Tijdschrift*, VI (1917), 316.

78. In contrast, the article by Samuel Rappaport in the *Judisches Lexikon* (n.p., 1927), seems more orthodoxly contented with Matthew 16:28—"Verily I say unto you, There be some standing here, which shall not taste of death till they see the Son of man coming in his kingdom." In his article for the *Catholic Encyclopedia* (New York, 1910), IX, 126-27, A. F. J. Remy refers the Legend, I think rightly, to a Crucifixion cycle which sprang up in the vicinity of Jerusalem after the Crucifixion itself.

79. Arthur Heulhard, *La Sainte Famille: Barrabas et les siens dans les mythes grecs de la psyché et d'Apollonius et dans les écritures juives . . . avec l'explication de la pseudo-légende du Juif errant* (Paris, 1914).

80. Carl Jung, "Wandlungen und Symbole der Libido," *Jahrbuch für psycho-analytische und psycho-pathologische Forschungen*, IV (1912), 235, 253-55.

81. Corrado Ricci, "L'Ebreo errante," *Emporium: Rivista mensile illustrata d'arte, letteratura, scienze e varietà*, III (1896), 120, and IV (1897), 55-67.

82. In reference to both Cordeau and Gaer, I am reminded of the dialogue old Captain Horn had with Etheldrea Lewis, as reported by A. A. Horn in the *London Mercury*, XX (1929), 16-20. The trader once saw the Wandering Jew in Mozambique, a sad fellow, a wanderer, but then, "Isn't every Jew a Wandering Jew?" The remainder of the dialogue goes too far afield to be pertinent here, but in this one question Trader Horn came nearer to the philosophy of the Legend than many much more pretentious works.

Appendix B

1. See p. 108 above.

2. Christoff Kuffner, *Die ewige Jüdin und der Orang-Outang: Eine Reise auf, unter und über der Erde* (Vienna, 1846). This constitutes vols. XIX and XX of his *Erzählende Schriften*.

3. Pp. 96-163.

4. See p. 5 above.

5. Joseph C. Heywood, *Antonius: A Dramatic Poem* (New York, 1867); *Herodias: A Dramatic Poem* (New York, 1867); *Salome: A Dramatic Poem* (New York, 1867).

Appendix C

1. IV (1954), 221-35.

2. Andrew Peterdi, "Bolygó zsidó" ("The Wandering Jew"), *Egyenlöség*, LVI (1936), 18; Aladar Komlós, "Bolygó zsidó hazája" ("The Wandering Jew's Home"), *Himnusz a mosolyhoz* ("Hymn to a Smile"; Budapest, 1941), p. 28.

3. Henry Lenksi, "Ahasver," *Mult és Jövö*, VI (1916), 344.

4. Henry Lenksi, "Ahasver álma" ("The Dream of Ahasuerus"), *Isten tábora* ("God's Camp"; Budapest, 1931), pp. 127-39.

5. Marcel Benedek, "Äz örök zsidó" (MS play written in Budapest in 1916).

6. *Fegyver* ("Weapon"; Budapest, 1935), p. 1; see also his *Emlék* ("Souvenir"; Budapest, 1943), pp. 464-68.

7. P. 26.

8. Pp. 113-15, 125.

9. Francis Siliga, "A bolygó zsidó" (MS play written in Budapest in 1928).

10. *Igaz Könyv* ("A True Book"; Budapest, 1923), pp. 93-102.

Index

Index to Authors and Titles

Most works are indexed under the authors' or probable authors' names. Anonymous works are indexed under their titles. Cross references are made from the names of editors, translators, compilers, dramatists, etc., to authors. Cross references are also made from translated or revised titles to authors.

Short titles have been used for many works. Bold-face numerals indicate the main reference to works contributing directly to the formation of the Legend of the Wandering Jew. Numbers in parentheses following page numbers refer to notes. When there is a considerable lapse between the date of composition and the date of printing of a work, brackets indicate the date of printing.

Aberdein, Jennie W., *John Galt* (1936), 148(48)

Academy [London] (1884), 102

Accords enchanteurs (ca.1850), 239

Acher, Mathias
  "Ahasver an seine Widersacher" (1904), **312-13**
  "Ahasver und Acher" (n.d.), **313**
  "Ahasvers Sehnsucht" (1902), **313**
  "Aus Traumen geweckt" (1902), **313**
  "Gott flucht Ahasver" (1902), **313**
  "Ihr und Ich" (1902), **313**
  "Im Walde" (1902), **313**
  "Troster Ahasver" (1902), **313**

Açoka Avadana. See Divyavadana

Ady, Andrew, *Sirisson meg* (1899), **353**

Aerts van Mecheln, Jan, *Warachtige Beschryvunge der Jerusalemsche Reyse* (16th C.), rev. (*Coort Verhael eender heerlijcker Reysen*, 1595; *Verscheyde Voyagien, ofte Reysen*, 1652), reprint ("Jan Baudewijn," ed. Emanuel Neefs, 1873), **34**, 36, 87

Agostino, Ludovico degli, *Viaggio de Terra Santa e di Gerusalemme* (1886), 33

Ahasuerus-book (*Volksbuch*, German), 29(38), 30, 42(12), 45, 49, 51(26), **52-53,** 54, 55, 56, 57, 60, 63, 67, 68, 69, 70, 71, 73, 76, 85, 91, 105, 108, 113, 114, 115(22), 117, 120, 121, 122, 126, 128, 131, 135(17), 142, 144(35), 147, 151, 152, 166, 169, 191(45), 192, 223, 246, 264, 267, 334, 337, 369, 399, 402, 403, 409, 410
  See also *Berättelser om en Jude;*

Trenne nya och mycket märkwärdige Berättseler

Ahasuerus play (16th C.), 50

Ahasver [periodical], ed. J. F. Bürgler (1831-32), 213-14, 290

"Ahasver" (1882), **340**

Ahasver, der ewige Jude der Urzeit (1844), **238**

Ahasver: Tragödie. See Lienhard, Fritz, 316

Ahasverus. See Heller, Seligmann, 261

Ahasverus der nie Ruhende. See Caigniez, Louis-Charles, 201

Ahasverus, des wahren ewigen Juden Wanderungen (1845), 152-53, **264-65**

Ahasverus te Rome. See Hamerling, Robert, 250

Ainsworth, William Harrison, *Windsor Castle* (1843), 6(12)

Albertus Magnus, 38

Alcarotto, John Francis, *Viaggio in Terra Santa* (1595), 35

Alfred the Great. See Oriosius, Paulus

Allen, Thomas, *New and Complete History of the County of York* (1828-31), 133(10), 134(13)

Allgemeine Zeitung des Judenthums (1838), 217(12)

Almanach du fumeur et du priseur (1869), 265

Alpenburg, Johann Nepomuk von. See *Deutsche Alpensagen*

American Short Stories of the Nineteenth Century, ed. John Cournos (1955), 9(14)

Andersen, Hans Christian
  Ahasverus (1844), 144, 198, **221-22**, 224,
  226, 267, 273, 279, 405, 410
  letter to Henriette Wulff (1843), 222
Anderson, George K.
  "History of Israel Jobson" (1947),
  133(9), 411
  "Joseph Krantz, Twin of Ahasverus"
  (1947), 121(36)
  "Neo-Classical Chronicle of the Wander-
  ing Jew" (1948), 128(1), 133(8), 411
  "Popular Survivals of the Wandering
  Jew in England" (1947), 91(88), 117(28),
  411
  "*Silberlinge des Judas* and the Accursed
  Treasure" (1951), 247(4)
  "Wandering Jew Returns to England"
  (1946), 42(12), 411
Andrews, S. G., "Wandering Jew and 'The
  Travels and Adventures of James Mas-
  sey'" (1957), 133(7)
Andrews, William, *Bygone Punishments*
  (1899), 1(1)
Anhorn, Bartholomaeus, *Theatrum concio-
  num sacrarum topicum* (1691), 115
Annales Lipsienses, ed. Johann Jacob Vogel
  (1714), 59
Antichrist play, 39, 40(5)
Anton, Carl, *Lepidam fabulam de Judaeo
  immortali* (1755), 125-26
Antonio di Francesco di Andrea, version of
  Legend of Wandering Jew (*ca*.1450),
  17(10), **24-28**, 29, 33, 41, 47, 48, 67, 81-82,
  87, 92, 107, 196, 403, 408, 413
Apocalypse. See Revelation, Book of
Apostel- und Missionarbuch (1863),
  115(19)
Aprilly, Lewis, "Ahasver" (1926), 417
Arany, János, "Örök zsidó" (1860), trans.
  Andor von Sponer ("Ewige Jude," 1880),
  279, 320
Aristophanes, 49
Arlt, Gustave O. See Werfel, Franz V.
Arnim, Ludwig Achim von, *Halle und
  Jerusalem* (1809-10), **192-94**, 198, 199, 207,
  208, 213
Arnim, Ludwig Achim von, and Clemens
  Brentano, "Leiden des Herrn" (1806-8),
  195
Arnold, Edwin L., *Wonderful Adventures
  of Phra the Phoenician* (1891), 291-92
Asch, Shalom, *Nazarene*, trans. Maurice
  Samuel (1939), 380, 392, 408
Asmussen, Georg, "Ewige Jude" (1920), **371**
Atkinson, Nora, *Eugène Sue et le roman-
  feuilleton* (1929), 232(10)

Atten, A. van, "Ahasverus" (1928), 386(43)
Auberton, Friar, account of Legend of
  Wandering Jew (1623), 36
Aubrey, John, *Miscellanies* (1696), 91, 92,
  107
Audnal, L., *Ahasver* (1920), **356**
Auerbach, Berthold, *Spinoza* (1837), **224**,
  225, 269, 277
Auerbacher, L., *Volksbüchlein* (1827),
  198-99
Aufzeichnungen des ewigen Juden. See
  Joly, Victor: *Jésuites et de quelques
  engouements littéraires à propos du "Juif
  errant,"* 236
Aus Gallien chapbook (1589), 43-44
Austin, William, "Peter Rugg" (1824), 9, 10
Avenarius, Ferdinand, *Lebe!* (1893), **321**
Aytoun, William Edmondstoune, "Wander-
  ing Jew" (1834), 155, **216**, 264(30), 264

B., G. B. de. See Bordeaux, Gustave Brunet
  de
B., P., *Histoire du juif errant* (*ca*.1830),
  151-52
B. V. See Thomson, James
Bacchi della Lega, A. See Poggibonsi,
  Niccolò da
Bächtold-Stäubli, Hanns. See *Handwörter-
  buch des deutschen Aberglaubens*
Bäckström, Per Olof, *Svenska folkböcker*
  (1845-48), 116(25)
Bär, Ludwig. See Kühn, Hans Georg
Bässler, Ferdinand, *Über die Sage vom
  ewigen Juden* (1870), 401, 402, 405
Bagatti, P. B., "Wandering Jew" (1949),
  24(26), 36(61), 74(10)
Bagford, John, *Bagford Ballads* (1878), 61
Baker, E. A. See Lewis, Matthew Gregory
Ballad, after Dumas's *Isaac Laquedem*
  (*ca*.1853), 263-64
Ballad, from Dunkirk (*ca*.1775-1825), 60
Ballard, J. C., "Lost Leonardo" (1964),
  387(44)
Bán, Aladar, *Egyedül* (1898), **353**
Banfi, Gisella, *Ahasvers Traum* (1906),
  322-23
Bangert, Heinrich, *Commentatio de ortu
  vita et excessu coleri* (1644), **59**
Bannister, Nathaniel, "Wandering Jew"
  (1837), 197(62)
Baring-Gould, Sabine
  Curious Myths of the Middle Ages (1881),
  33(50), 404
  "Wandering Jew," (1884), 404
Barnes, Harry E., *Story of Punishment*
  (1930), 1(1)

Bartholinus, Thomas
  De Latere Christi aperto dissertatio
    (1646), 124
  Historiarum anatomicarum et medicarum
    (1654-61), 124
Bartók, Lewis, "Ahasuerus" (1891), **353**
Basile, Giovanni, *Pentamerone* (1674),
    trans. Richard Burton (1927), 5
Basnage, Jacques, *Histoire et la religion
    des Juifs* (1706-7), 121, 150
Bassett, Wilbur, *Wander-Ships* (1917), 292
Bassman, F., *Romanzen und Balladen der
    neueren deutschen Dichter* (1834), 208(98)
Bataillon, Marcel, "Pérégrinations espa-
    gnoles du juif errant" (1941), 29(39, 41),
    108(1), 404, 411
Baudaert, Willem, *Memoryen* (1624), 59-60
Baudelaire, Charles, 278
Baudisch, Paul
  Catilina (1921), 358
  Fragmente (1920), **357-58**
Baumbach, Rudolf, "Ahasver" (1878), **268**
Baumgarten, M., *Wider Herrn Hofprediger
    Stöcker* (1881), 276
Bayle, Pierre, *Dictionnaire historique et
    critique* (1697), 179
Bech, Friedrich, "Ahasver" (1908), **294**
Beck, Karl, *Fantasien am Grave Poniatow-
    skys* (1838), **222**, 223
Behn, Mrs. Aphra. See Fontenelle, Bertrand
    de
Behrman, S. N. See Werfel, Franz V.
Bell, Arnold C., *Alexandre Dumas* (1950),
    264(29)
Ben Israel, "Ewige Jude" (1901), **312**
Benedek, Marcel, "Örök zsidó" (1916),
    417(5)
Bennett, John
  "Death of the Wandering Jew" (1946),
    369-71
  Master Skylark (1897), 369
Bentley's Miscellany (1843), 179, 399-400,
    404(31)
Benzmann, Hans
  "Ahasver am Meer" (1898), **320**, 322
  "Ahasver und Christus" (1904), **320-21**,
    322
  "Ahasvers Tod" (1896), **321**, 322
Berättelser om en Jude (1823), 66-67
Béranger, Pierre-Jean de, "Juif errant"
    (1831), trans. Adalbert von Chamisso
    (1845); trans. Arthur Silbergleit (1845);
    music by Charles Gounod (1865), 115,
    207-8, 260, 279, 334
Bergerac, Cyrano de, *Histoire comique des*

états et empires de la lune (1685), trans. A.
    Lovell (*Comical History of the States and
    Empires of the World of the Moon*, 1687),
    136(20), 144
Berlin, Roland von, "Hebräische Melodie"
    (1906), **293-94**
Berlioz, Louis, 180
Bernard, Emile, *Juif errant* (1927), 361-62
Bertani, Antonio, "Il Giudeo Errante"
    (1846), **208**
Bertrand, Jules, and Emile Colliot, "Juif
    errant" (1853), 244
Beugnot, Count. See Novara, Filippo de, 23
Beyerlinck, L., *Afbeeldinghe ende corte
    beschrijvinghe van den dolenden Jode*
    (1620), 60, **66**
Bibliothèque universelle des romans, 141,
    142
Bien, H. M., *Ben-Beor* (1891), **301-2**
Bierbaum, O. J.
  "Golgotha" (1901), **313**, 339
  "Schmulius Caesar" (1908), **339**
Bierglas, A., *Ewige Jude* (1844), 230, **238**
Birlinger, Anton, *Aus Schwaben* (1874),
    114(18)
Blackwood, Algernon, 328
Blank, Matthias, *Ahasvers Brautfahrt*
    (1910), **328**
Blasco Ibáñez, V., "Wandering Jew" (1910
    [1933]), **335**
Blaul, Friedrich, *Ewige Jude und sein Lieb-
    ling in München* (1831), **241**
Bleibtreu, Karl
  "Ahasver" (1886), **278**
  "Ahasver auf den Trümmeln von Jerusa-
    lem" (1886), 278
Blind, Karl, "Woden, the Wild Huntsman,
    and the Wandering Jew" (1880), 405
Boaden, James, *Aurelio and Miranda* (1799),
    180
Boekenoogen, G. J., and Emile H. van
    Heurck, *Histoire de l'imagerie populaire
    flamande* (1910), 115(20), 401
Börne, Ludwig
  "Ewige Jude" (1861-62), 200
  Gesammelte Schriften (1861-62), 199(71)
Boethius, *Consolation of Philosophy*
    (*ca*.520), 158
Bogaerts, Henri. See Collin de Plancy, J.,
    236
Bogaerts, Theodor, *Oog up den Heuvel*
    (1928), **386-87**
Boggs, Ralph S., notes, in *Folklore Fellows
    Communications* (1936), 184(29)
Boiteau, Paul, *Légendes pour les enfants*
    (1857), **264**

Bonatti, Guido, *De Astronomia Tractatus X* (1491), **22-23,** 24, 26, 29, 41, 42, 43, 63, 65

Bond, Nelson, "Castaway" (1940), **364**

Bonney, T. G. See Pierotti, Ermete

Bordeaux, Gustave Brunet de (G. B. de B.), *Notice historique et bibliographique sur la légende du juif-errant* (1845), 399

Bornstein, Paul, "Sonnenlied" (1895), **318,** 319

Bory, Jean-Louis, *Eugène Sue, le roi du roman populaire* (1962), 232(10)

Boterius. See Boutrays, Raoul

Boulenger, Julius Caesar, *Historiarum sui temporis* (1619), 54, 120, **123-24**

Bourgeois, Anicet, and Jules Maillan, *Nonne sanglante* (1835), 180

Bousset, Wilhelm, *Antichrist Legend*, trans. A. H. Keane (1896), 39(1)

Boutrays (Boterius), Raoul, *De Rebus in Gallia* (1610), **53-54,** 59, 120, 123, 124

Brabantine ballad (*ca.*1800), 60, 115, 116, 163, **165-66,** 172, 207, 231, 268(36), 285, 399

Brachvogel, Carry, "Wiedererstandenen" (1900), **341-42**

Bradshaw, William. See Marana, Giovanni, 128

Bragda Magus Saga (*ca.*1500), 33, 404

Brand, John, *Observations on Popular Antiquities* (1777), 109, **116**

Braunthal, Carl Johann Braun von, "Ahasver" (1839), **225-26**

Brentano, Clemens, "Blätter aus dem Tagebuch der Ahnfrau" (1830), **195-96**

Brentano, Clemens, and Ludwig Achim von Arnim, "Leiden des Herrn" (1806-8), 195

Broch, Michal, *Na Piaskach* (1845), **225**

Bronner, Ferdinand, "Ahasver, der ewige Jude" (1893), **299, 353**

Brown, Charles Brockden, 175

Brown, Ford K., *Life of William Godwin* (1926), 180(18)

Browning, Robert, 32
  Death in the Desert (1863), 261

Bruck, Julius, *Ahasver* (1876), **282-83**

Brumm, Charles, *Ahasuerus* (1916), **344-45**

Bryan, William Frank. See Tupper, Frederick

Buchanan, Robert, *Wandering Jew* (1893), **328-30**

Bürgler, J. F. See *Ahasver*

Bulthaupt, Heinrich, *Ahasver* (1904), **350-51**

Bulwer-Lytton, Edward, *Zanoni* (1842), 190, 271, 411

Bund, Ludwig, "Ahasver" (*ca.*1900), **302-3**

Bungener, L.-L.-F., *Quelques mots au Juif errant* (1845), 400

Bunyan, John, *Pilgrim's Progress* (1678), 95

Burnouf, Eugène, *Introduction à l'histoire de bouddhisme indien* (1876), 4(4)

Burssens, A., *Wonderbare Historie van de Wandelende Jood* (1926), **371**

Burton, Richard. See Basile, Giovanni

Bushnell, Nelson Sherwin, "Wandering Jew and the *Pardoner's Tale*" (1931), 31(46)

Bustamente, Ricardo, "Judío errante" (1877), **278**

Byron, George Gordon, 148, 161, 187(36), 189, 190, 192, 203, 210, 243(1)
  Cain (1821), **182-83**
  Childe Harold's Pilgrimage (1812-18), **183,** 240, 241
  Don Juan (1819-24), 241
  "Manfred" (1817), 183

Caballero, Fernán, *Estrella de Vandalia* (1860), 28(35)

Cabell, James Branch, *Domnei* (1920), **391-92**

Caigniez, Louis-Charles, *Juif errant* (1812), trans. Theodor von Haupt (Theodor Peregrinus) (*Ahasverus der nie Ruhende,* 1825), **201,** 240

Cailleran and Coupilly, *Nonne de Lindenberg* (1798), 180

Calmet, Augustin, *Dictionnaire . . . de la Bible* (1722), **109-10,** 120, 132, 150, 177

Cammaille-Saint-Aubin, M. C., *Moine* (1798), 180(12)

Campbell, Thomas, 185, 186

"Cantique spirituel sur les prédictions annoncées par les Juifs" (*ca.*1675-1710), 165

Carlschmidt. See Schmidt, Carl

Carlyle, Thomas, *Sartor Resartus* (1833-34), 190, 243(1), 278

Carroll, Lewis, *Through the Looking Glass* (1871), 264

Casini, Tomaso. See "Rime inedite dei secoli XIII e XIV"

Caspari, Carl Paul, *Nogle Bemaerkninger angaaende Sagnet om den evigen Jøde* (1863), 401-2

Cassel, D. Paulus
  Ahasverus (1885), 276-77, 406, 407
  Thurm und Glocke (1877), 406

Cauvin, A., "Ahasvère" (1846), **216**

Cayet, P. V. P., *Chronologie Septenaire* (1605), **54,** 60, 63-64, 65, 66

Cejador y Frauca, Julio. See Gracian, Baltasar

Cervantes Saavedra, Miguel de, *Galatea* (*ca.*1583), 29

Cham, cartoons, in *Salmigondis* (*Revue de Salon*) (1851), 266-67

Chambers, Edmund K., *Mediaeval Stage* (1925), 39(2)

Chambers, Robert, *Book of Days* (1862-64), 115

Chamisso, Adalbert von
"Neue Ahasverus" (1831), **227**, 405
Peter Schlemihl (1814), 184
See Béranger, Pierre-Jean de, 207

Champfleury
Histoire de l'imagerie populaire (1869), 55(37), 58(39), 59(40, 42), 60(50), 133(8), 151, 401, 402, 404, 405
"Nouvelle interprétation de la légende gothique du Juif-Errant" (1864), 55(37), 401

Champly, Henry, *Juive errante* (1921), 415-16

Chansonnier du magasin théâtral (1835), 231

Chapman, John, in *Catholic Encyclopedia* (1910), 15(5)

Chateaubriand, François René de, 203, 278

Chaucer, Geoffrey, 61
Pardoner's Tale (ca.1393-1400), ed. F. N. Robinson (1957), **31-32**, 172, 191, 220, 246-47
Wife of Bath's Tale (ca.1393-1400), 32

Chaunu, Pierre, *Eugène Sue et la seconde république* (1948), 232(10)

Child, F. J., *English and Scottish Popular Ballads* (1861), 61

Chirikov, Evgeni Nikolaevich, *Juden*, trans. Georg Polonskij (1904), 294

Christiani, F. Albrecht, *Juden Glaube und Aberglaube* (1705), 125

Christliche Legenden (1832), **221**

Chronicle of Ahimaaz (ca.1055), ed. and trans. Marcus Salzman (1924), **15-16**

Chronicle of Ypres, 111(9)

Chronik, J. L., *Ahasverus* (1855), 248

Claes, Jef, *Geestelijke Bruiloft* (1929), **371-72**

Clark, Reverend T. See Galt, John

Cleeman-Schindler, Agnes H., "Ewige Jude" (1854), **255**

Cleerdin, Vincent, "Ahasverus in den Paaschtijd" (1916), **317**

Clemens, Samuel L. (Mark Twain), *Innocents Abroad* (1869), 36, 93, **288-89**

Clercq, René de, "Ahasver" (1902), **322**

Clüver. See Cluverius, Johann

Cluverius (Clüver, Cluwer), Johann, *Historiarum totius mundi epitome* (1637), **59**, 124

Cluwer. See Cluverius, Johann

Coffey, Charles, *Devil To Pay* (1731), 134-35

Coggeshall, William T.
Poets and Poetry of the West (1860), 264(30)
See Curry, Otway

Cohen, A. D., "Evige Jøde in London" (1861), **260**

Coleridge, Samuel Taylor, *Rime of the Ancient Mariner* (1798), 8, 10, 173, 174, 177, 181, 190, 260

Collin de Plancy, J., *Légende du Juif-Errant* (1847), trans. Henri Bogaerts (*Wandelende Jood te Munster*, 1872), **236**, 239

Colliot, Emile, and Jules Bertrand, "Juif errant" (1853), **244**

Comical History of the States and Empires of the World of the Moon. See Bergerac, Cyrano de, 136(60)

Commoda, A., "Drei Zwiegespräche" (1902), **300**

Complainte, 57-58, **163-66**, 200, 231, 399, 405
in *Discours véritable du juif errant* (ca.1608-9), 57-58, **163-65**, 225(33)
from Le Blond woodcut (ca.1640-50), 165
to air "Saint Eustache" (17th C.), 165

Conradi, Hermann, "Ahasver im Karneval" (1911), **337**

Constitutionnel [Paris], 230, 232, 238, 263

Conway, Moncure Daniel
in *Encyclopaedia Britannica* (1881), 406
Wandering Jew (1881), 93, 116(27), 404, 405, 407

Coort Verhael eender heerlijcker Reysen. See Aerts van Mecheln, Jan, 34

Corday, Aglaé de, "Ahasvérus" (1837), **210**

Cordeau, C. Jean, *Ahasvérus* (1951), 413

Coremans, V.-A.-J.-M., *Licorne et le Juif-Errant* (1845), 15(7), 399

Corneliano, Pasero de, *Histoire du juif errant, écrite par lui-même* (1820), trans. (*Geschichte des ewigen Juden, von ihm selbst geschrieben*, 1821), 146(43), **150-51**

Corte en de waerachtighe beschrijvinge van eenen Jode (ca.1610-12), 60

Coupilly and Cailleran, *Nonne de Lindenberg* (1798), 180

Cournos, John. See *American Short Stories of the Nineteenth Century*

Cousin, Jean, *Histoire de Tournay* (1916), 60, **123**

Crabbe, George, *Parish Register* (1807), 181, 190

Crawford, F. Marion, *Roman Singer* (1883), 316

Creizenach, Wilhelm Michael Anton
Geschichte des neueren Drama (1893-1916), 30(43)
"Zur Geschichte der Weihnachtsspiele und des Weihnachtsfesten" (1896), 294

Creutzer, Christoff, 42, 44

Crocker, Annette E. See Gounod, Charles: *Mémoires d'un artiste*

Croly, George, *Salathiel* (1827), rev. (*Tarry Thou Till I Come*, 1901), trans. A. Rehberg-Worden (*Neuer Ahasverus*, 1913), trans. Ludwig Storch (*Ewige Jude*, 1829), 146(41), **188-89,** 190, 199, 218, 221, 268(36), 248, 249, 254, 261, 264, 271, 273, 282, 311, 399

Cross, Tom Peete
Motif-Index of Early Irish Literature (1952), 5(7)
Notes in *Béaloideas* (1951-52), 5(7)

Cruciger, *Neueste Wanderungen, Umtriebe, und Abenteuer des ewigen Juden* (1832), 241

Cullum, Ridgewell, "Trail of the Wandering Jew" (1918), 292

Curry, Otway, "Aaven," ed. William T. Coggeshall (1860), **264**

Czerwienski, Boleslav, "Zydzio wiecznym tulaczcu" (1874), 406

Daily Chronicle [London] (*ca.*1893), 329

Dalton, Hermann, *Ewige Jude und der ewige Johannes* (1867), 245

D'Ancona, Alessandro, 404, 407
"Juif errant en Italie" (1883), 23(25)
"Juif errant en Italie au XIII⁰ siecle" (1881), 21(18), 24(29), 87(74, 75), 88(76), 403
"Leggenda dell'Ebreo errante" (1880), 35(55), 87(75), 403
Saggi di Letteratura populare (1913), 34(51)

D'Anglioieri, Cecco, sonnet (13th C.), 23

Dante, *Divine Comedy* (1300-14), 2, 22, 136(19), 206, 218, 260

Darwin, Charles, *Origin of Species*, 222

Dauterlin, account of Legend of Wandering Jew (17th C.), 36

Death of Ahasuerus. See Lagerkvist, Pär, 390

Deckert, Josef
Ewige Jude, "Ahasver" (1894), 294
Kann ein Katholik Antisemit sein? (1893), 294

Dehmel, Richard, "Heine-Denkmal" (1901), **295**

Dekker, Thomas, *Shoemaker's Holiday* (1600), 50(21)

Delambre, Jean Baptiste Joseph, *Histoire de l'astronomie au dix-huitième siècle* (1827), 135(15)

Delasalle, Paul, "Juif errant" (1840), 399

De l'Estoile, Pierre, *Mémoires-Journaux* (ca. 1601-9 [1875-96]), 40, 54, 57, 59, 120

Delff, H. K. Hugo, *Judenthum und Christenthum* (1880), 277

Delicado, Francisco, *Retrato de la Lozana Andaluza* (1528 [1912]), 28

Delitzsch, Franz, in *Saat auf Hoffnung* (1886), 277

Della Valle, Pietro, *Viaggi* (1662), 33

Deloney, Thomas, 63

Dempster, Germaine C. See Tupper, Frederick

D'Ennery, Adolphe. See Sue, Eugène, 238

Derham, William, *Physico-Theology* (1713), trans. Albert Fabricius (*Physico-Theologie, oder Natur-Leitung zu Gott*, 1750), 124

"Dernière heure du juif-errant" (1839), **208**

Deseret News [Salt Lake City] (1868), 101

D'Esternaud. See D'Esternod, Claude

D'Esternod (D'Esternaud), Claude, *Espadon satyrique* (1680), 59, **167**

Dettinger, Eduard M., "Ewige Jude" (1845), **230**

Deutsche Alpensagen, ed. Johann Nepomuk von Alpenburg (1861), 77(21), 81(38)

Deutsche Sagen, ed. Heinrich Pröhle (1863), 83(51, 52)

Deutsche Sagen, ed. Jacob and Wilhelm Grimm (1865-66), 83(53)

Deutschen Volksbücher (1807), 192(52)

Dezsö, Julius, "Ahasuerus" (1902), **353**

Dialogos beatae Mariae et Anselmi de passione Domini, 21

Dickens, Charles, 190, 231-32

Dictionary of American Biography (1928-58), 153(60)

Diener, Eduard, and Arthur Hesslein, *Ahasver* (1905), **298-99**

Diepenbrock, C. J., *Germania* (1863), **249,** 401

Dietrich, Franz E. C., *Ueber die Aussprache des Gothischen* (1862), 146(46)

Dinaux, Prosper. See Sue, Eugène, 238

Dingern, Julie, "Zwei Legenden vom ewigen Juden" (*ca.*1870), **245**

Discours véritable d'un juif errant (1603), **54,** 57, 58, 60, 63, 225(33)

Discourse Concerning a New World and Another Planet. See Wilkins, John

Dissel, A. van. See Hamerling, Robert: *Ahasver in Rom*, **280**

Divyavadana (*ca.*450), 4

Döring, Heinrich, *Brittischer Balladenschatz* (1858), 401

Dolorosa, "Ahasver" (1903), **304**

Donauschinger Passionsspiel (15th C.), 30

Donne, John, "Third Satire" (1633), 122

Doré, Gustave, engravings of Wandering Jew (*ca.*1850), 115, 166, **260**

Doyle, Conan, 328

Drault, Jean, *Secret du Juif-errant* (1913), 293

Dresdener gelehrte Anzeiger (1788), 127

Dröscher, Martinus, *Dissertatio theologica de duobus testibus* (1668), 121(33), 122-23

Drouet, J. B., *Juif errant* (1862), **247**

Dryden, John, 31

Dubi, Heinrich
 "Curiosa von Bern und der Stadtbibliothek in Bern" (1906, 1917), 84(60)
 "Drei spätmittelalterliche Legenden in ihrer Wanderung" (1907), 82(49), 83(51, 55, 56), 84(57)

Dubout, Alfred, "Juif errant" (1889), **282**

Duchartre, Pierre Louis, and René Saulnier, *Imagerie populaire* (1925), 60(50), 85(65)

Dudulaeus, Chrysostom Westphalus, 44, 52
 See also Dudulaeus pamphlets;
 Gründliche und Warhafftige Relation von einem Juden

Dudulaeus pamphlets (1602-19), 42(12), 44-45, **51-52**, 55, 59, 60, 65, 66, 67, 68, 69, 121, 127, 135(17), 162-63, 403
 See also Ahasuerus-book; *Jerusalems Skomager; Narrazione d'un Giudeo errante; Sandru Beskriffuelse*

Dufferin, Lady, 209

Dugaillon, A. E.
 "A. E. Sue" (1845), **343**
 "Epitre à E. Sue" (1845), **343**
 "Rodinade" (1845), **343**

Dukes, Ashley. See Feuchtwanger, Lion, 368

Duller, Edmund
 Antichrist (1833), **215**
 "Kettenschmidt" (1835), **215**
 See Vogl, Johann Nepomuk

Dumas, Alexandre *père, Isaac Laquedem* (1853), trans. F. W. Reed (1937), 156, 231, **262-64**, 334

Dunbar, William, *Flyting of Dunbar and Kennedy* (*ca.*1506), 31

Dupont, Pierre, *Légende du Juif-errant* (1856), 115, 166(5), **260**

Dworaczek, Wilhelm (Paul Wilhelm), *Aus Faust und Ahasver* (1894), 408

Dygasinski, Adolf, *Wieczny tulacz* (1887), 406

E., S., *Almanach historique, polémique, et anecdotique du juif errant* (1845), **152**

Earle, Alice Morse, *Curious Punishments of Bygone Days* (1922), 1(1)

Ebreo errante [motion picture] (1948), rev. (*Sablie del tempo*), 394

Edmunds, Albert
 "Wandering Jew: A Buddhist Parallel" (1903), 412
 "Wandering Jew: His Probable Buddhist Origins" (1913), 50(23), 411-12

Ego, *Ahasver* (1890), **280**

Eichrodt, Ludwig, "Ahasver" (1869), **268**

Eimer, Manfred, "Zu Shelleys Dichtung, 'The Wandering Jew' " (1914), 173(18)

Eitzen, Paulus von, *Evangelia der Fest von Sontage durchs gantze Jahr.* (1590), 50(24)

Eldridge, Paul, and George Sylvester Viereck
 My First Two Thousand Years (1929), 153, **359-60**, 365, 416
 Salome, the Wandering Jewess (1930), 153, **360-61**, 365, 416

Eliot, T. S., 208

Elizabeth of Romania (Carmen Sylva), *Jehovah* (1882), **281**, 283

Ellmann, Richard, *James Joyce* (1959), 391(52)

Emerson, Ralph Waldo, 243(1)

England, Paul. See Frey, Adolf, 318

English History. See Matthew Paris, 21

Erdelyi, Joseph, "Ahasver és a varázsfurulyás" (1935), 417

Erinnerung ("Reminder to the Christian Reader"), **51**, 52, 69, 121
 See also Dudulaeus pamphlets

Eschelbach, Hans
 "Ahasver" (1896), **303-4**, 408
 "Über die poetischen Bearbeitungen der Sage vom ewigen Juden" (1899), 408

Esselborn, Karl A., *Ahasver* (1890), **316**

Esther, Book of, 50, 248, 406

Eubule-Evans, Albert, *Curse of Immortality* (1873), **292-93**

Eucrates. See Moschos, Johannes

Evreux MS (*ca.*1325), 24, 29

Ewige Jude (1829). See Croly, George, 189

"Ewige Jude" (1880). See Arany, János, 320

Ewige Jude (1905). See Richepin, Jean, 281

Ewige Jude, aus dem russischen Übersetzt. See Zhukovski, V. A., 256

Ewige Jude: Eine komische Geschicht aus dem 18. Jahrhundert (1800), 191, **237-38**

"Ewige Jude im Voigtlande" (1860), 401

"Ewige Jude Nummer Zwei" (1846), **229-30**

Ewige Jude, von Eugène Sue. See Sue, Eugène, 238-39

"Ewige Jude zu Münnich Kirchen" (1860), 82(45)

Exodus, Book of, 3

Eyck, P. N. van, "Door de legten" (1912), **339**

Fabri, Felix, *Evagatorium in Terrae Sanctae* (ca.1480), ed. C. D. Hassler (1843), 34

Fabricius, Albert. See Derham, William

Fairplay, J. See Joly, Victor Vincent: *Jésuites et de quelques engouements littéraires à propos du "Juif errant,"* 236

Faust, A. J., *Wandering Jew* (1870), 402

Faust-book (1587), **41-42**, 45, 52, 190

Federhold, Christian, "Ahasver" (1906), **321**

Feldman, Irving, "Wandering Jew" (1961), **391**

Ferguson, Adam, *History of the Progress and Termination of the Roman Republic* (1783), 141(29)

Feuchtwanger, Lion
Jud Süss (1925), trans. Willa and Edwin Muir (*Jew Süss*, 1927; *Power*, 1927), dramatized Ashley Dukes (*Jew Süss*, 1930), **368-69**
"Wird Hill amnestiert?" (1927), **369**

Féval, Paul
Fille du juif errant (1878), **236-37**
Mystères de Londres (1849), 236

Feyjóo y Montenegro, Benito Gerónimo, "De El Judío Errante" (1781), 121

Field, Eugene, "Holy Cross" (1893), **349-50**

Fife, A. E., "Legend of the Three Nephites among the Mormons" (1940), 101(109)

Fischer, J. G., "Ewige Jude" (1854), **253-54**

Fleg, Edmond, *Jésus* (1933), trans. Phyllis Mégroz (*Jesus*, 1935), **374-77**, 378, 380, 388, 392, 395, 408

Fleischmann, Alfred, poem (1906), **318**

Fleury, Claude, *Histoire ecclésiastique* (1691-1738), 141(29)

Fliegende Blätter (ca.1880), 340, 342(15)

Fliegende Holländer zu Fuss. See Nestroy, Johann, 239

Flowers of History. See Roger of Wendover, 19

Folk-lore de Lesbos, comp. and trans. G. Georgeakis and Léon Pineau (1894), 72(4)

Fontan, L.-M.
Dominicain (1832), 180
Moine (1831), 180

Fontenelle, Bertrand de, *Entretiens sur la pluralité des mondes* (1686), trans. Mrs. Aphra Behn (1688) and John Glanvill (1688), 136(20)

Forman, H. Buxton. See Medwin, Thomas: *Life of Percy Bysshe Shelley*

Foster, Frances A. See *Northern Passion*

Fouqué, Friedrich de la Motte, *Frauentaschenbuch* (1816), 197(63)

Fox-Bourne, H. R., "Wandering Jew" (1871), 299(18)

Fränkel, Ferdinand, *Neuer Ahasverus* (1878), **343**

Fragerolle, Georges, *Juif Errant* (1898), **335-36**

Frahm, L., *Norddeutsche Sagen von Schleswig-Holstein bis zum Hartz* (1890), **335**

Francisci, Erasmus, *Lustigen Schau-Bühne vielerhand Curiositäten* (1698), 124

Franckenberg, Abraham von, *Relation oder Kurtzer Bericht von zweyen Zeugen des Leydens* (1647), **121**, 122

Franke, F. F. (Ferdinand Hauthal), *Ahasveriade* (1838), **215**

Frankl, Oscar, *Jude in den deutschen Dichtunger des 15. 16. und 17. Jahrhunderts* (1905), 39(3)

Franklin, Andrew, *Wandering Jew* (1797), **168**, 229

Franklin, Benjamin, *Whistle* (1779), 145

Franz, Otto
Jesus von Nazareth (1869), 248
Judas Iscarioth (1869), 246, 248
Zerstörung von Jerusalem (1869), **248**

French Mediaeval Romances from the Lays of Marie de France. See Marie de France: *Lais der Marie de France*

Frey, Adolf, *Ahasvers Erwachung*, trans. Paul England, music by Friedrich Hegar (1904), **318-19**

Fris Ducos, Luis. See *Mémoires du juif errant*, 144

Frost, Robert, "Draft Horse" (1962), 390

Fürst, Rudolf, "Ahasver-Dichtungen" (1904, 1910), 408

Funke, F. C. See Huart, Louis; Philipon, Charles

G. B. de B. See Bordeaux, Gustave Brunet de

Gaer, Joseph, *Legend of the Wandering Jew* (1961), 413

Galsworthy, John, "Simple Tale" (1914), **336**

Galt, John (Reverend T. Clark)
Bachelor's Wife (1824), 148
Wandering Jew (1820), rev. (*Travels and*

Observations of Hareach, the Wandering Jew, 1821-23), 146(45), **148-50,** 161, 194, 264

Gassner, Josef, *Seebers "Ewiger Jude,"* (1896), 326(62)

Gatterer, Johann Christoph, *Versuch einer allgemeinen Weltgeschichte* (1792), 141(29)

Gaudenzi, Augusto. See *Ignoti Monachi Cisterciensis S. Mariae de Ferraria Chronica*

Gautier, Théophile, 180

Gawarecki, Zygmunt, *Wieczny tulacz* (1865), 406

Gehrke, Albert, "Ahasver" (1889), **273-74**

Geiger, Ludwig, "Juden und die deutsche Literatur des 16. Jahrhundert" (1888-89), 40(6)

Genesis, Book of, 3, 27(32), 38, 182

Geoffrey of Monmouth, *History of the Kings of Britain* (ca.1150), 159

George of Trevizond, 15(6)

Georgeakis, G. See *Folk-lore de Lesbos*

Germanicus. See Richter, Emil

Geschichte des ewigen Juden, von ihm selbst geschrieben. See Corneliano, Pasero de, 150

Gesta Romanorum (ca.1500), ed. Hermann Oesterley (1872), 5(9)

Gibbon, Edward, *Decline and Fall of the Roman Empire* (1776-88), 141(29)

Gielen, J. J., *Wandelende Jood in Volks-kunde en Letterkunde* (1931), 15(7), 23(23, 25), 42(12), 60(49, 50), 66(60), 67(61, 62), 72(1, 2, 3), 73(5, 6), 78(24), 87(74), 88(77), 96(98, 99, 100), 97(102), 98(105, 106), 99(107), 103(112, 113), 104(114), 113(13), 125(58, 59), 127(66), 191(45), 259(22), 292(5), 326(62), 336(4), 371(29), 403, 410-11

Giese, Hans, *Passion de Jésus Christ jouée à Valenciennes l'an 1547* (1905), 30(42)

Gilbert, William Schwenck, 275

Gilbert, William Schwenck, and Arthur Seymour Sullivan, *Mikado* (1885), 53

Giles, J. A. See Matthew Paris, 21; Roger of Wendover, 19

Gillet, J. E., "Traces of the Wandering Jew in Spain" (1931), 28(34), 29(39, 40), 404(29), 411

Gilm, Hermann von, "Ahasver" (1894), **321,** 371

Girndt, Otto, *Nero* (1856), **253**

Giron, Aimé, *Cinq sous d'Isaac Laquedem, le Juif errant* (1883), **284-85**

Giseke, Bernhard, *Ahasuerus, der ewige Jude* (1868), **254-55**

Glaesener, H., "Type d'Ahasvérus au XVIIIᵉ et XIXᵉ siècles" (1931), 411(73)

Glanvill, John. See Fontenelle, Bertrand de

Godwin, William, *St. Leon* (1799), **180-81,** 183

Görres, Guido, "Ewige Jude" (1844), 192, **221**

Göschel, C. F., *Über Goethes Faust* (1824), 242

Goethe, Johann Wolfgang von, 161, 192, 196, 200, 202, 217(14), 217, 221, 258, 267, 273, 297, 305, 308, 309, 315, 325, 329, 350, 405, 408

Dichtung und Wahrheit (1811-33), 169, 170, 171

"Ewige Juden erstes Fetzen" [fragments on the Wandering Jew] (1774-75 [1836]), trans. Gerard de Nerval ("Mort du juif errant," ca.1830); Peter Will (P. W.) (in *German Museum*, 1801), **168-71,** 172, 173, 187, 246, 264, 292, 355, 402, 408

Faust (1808-33), 196, 199, 205, 241, 269, 271, 306

Götz von Berlichingen (1773), 181

Italienische Reise (1816-17), 170

Goldfaden, Abraham, *Ewige Jude* (ca.1890), 294

Goldsmith, Oliver, *Citizen of the World* (1762), 128

Gorki, Maxim, *Judenmassakre*, trans. Sonja Werner (1904), 294

Gounod, Charles

Mémoires d'un artiste (1896), trans. Annette E. Crocker (*Memoirs of an Artist*, 1896), 180

Nonne sanglante, libretto by Eugène Scribe (1854), 180

See Béranger, Pierre-Jean de, 207

Gracian, Baltasar, *Criticón* (1653), ed. Julio Cejador y Frauca (1913-14), 28

Grässe, Johann Georg Theodor, *Sage vom ewigen Juden* (1844), rev. (*Tannhäuser und der ewige Jude*, 1861), 21(18), 59(41), 402, 405

Grandes prophéties du Sieur de Montague, autrement nommé le juif errant (1722), 133

Granville, Charles, *Plaint of the Wandering Jew* (1908), **321**

Gras, L.-A., *Ahasvérus, juif errant* (1842), **208**

Grauhoff, Otto, "Moritz von Schwind," ed. Richard Muther (1905), 294

Graves, Richard, *Spiritual Quixote* (1773), **168**

Gray, Zane, 292

Gredt, N., *Sagenschatz des luxemburger Landes* (1883), 87(72)

Grelle, Frido, *Ahasver, der ewige Kampf* (1919), **337**

Grenier, Edouard, *Mort du juif-errant* (1857), **249-50**

Grimm, A. T. von, *Meister Martin* (1887), **269**

Grimm, Jacob. See *Deutsche Sagen* (1865-66)

Grimm, Jacob, and Wilhelm Grimm, *Deutsches Wörterbuch* (1873), 122(37)

Grimm, Wilhelm. See *Deutsche Sagen* (1865-66)

Grimm, Wilhelm, and Jacob Grimm, *Deutsches Wörterbuch* (1873), 122(37)

Grisebach, Eduard, *Neue Tannhäuser* (1869), **267**, 268

Grisman (Grismond), John, 61

Grismond. See Grisman, John

Grosette, Henry W., *Raymond and Agnes, the Travellers Benighted* (1809), 180

Gründler, Wilhelm, *Ahasuerus*, ed. Herman Wendt (1928), **357**

Gründliche und Warhafftige Relation von einem Juden (1634-35), **52**, 55, 66, 69, 128
See also Ahasuerus-book; *Trenne Trowärdiga Relationer*

Gruter, Janus, *Florilegium politicum* (1612), 49-50

Gualdo, Friderico, manuscript (*ca.*1700), 111

Gubitz, F. W., *Deutscher Volkskalender* (1857), 264

Günther, H., *Zur Herkunft des Volksbuches von Fortunatus und seinen Söhnen* (1914), 29(38)

Guerz [ballad] (*ca.*1650), 58, 86, 399

Guest, Edgar, 207

Guilbert de Pixérécourt, René-Charles
"Ahasvérus" (*ca.*1815-20), 201
"Moine, ou la victime de l'orgeuil" (*ca.*1815-20), 180

Guiney, Louise, "Peter Rugg, the Bostonian" (1891), 291

Gutch, Eliza, and Mabel G. W. Peacock, *Examples of Printed Folk-Lore Concerning Lincolnshire* (1908), 119(32)

Gutzkow, Karl
"Ewige Jüdin" (1869), 415, 416
Götter, Helden, Don Quixote (1838), 220
"Plan eines Ahasvers" (1842), 208, **216-17**, 225
in *Telegraph für Deutschland* (1837), 220

Gynt, Olaf, "Ahasuerus" (1934), **371**

Hadeck (Hadek), Georg, *Nathanelis Christiani Relation eines Wallbruders mit Nahmen Ahasverus* (1681), 123, 334

Hadek. See Hadeck, Georg

Haggard, H. Rider
Return of She (1905), 268
She (1887), 263, 268, 291, 332, 365
She and Allan (1887), 268

Hagymasy, Francis, "Bolygó zsidó engesztelo napja" (1929), 418

Hale, Edward Everett, *Man without a Country* (1863), 9-10

Halévy, Jacques
Juive (1835), 259
"Polka of the Wandering Jew" (1852), 259
"Valse du juif errant" (1852), 259
"Wandering Jew Mazurka" (1852), 259
See Scribe, Eugène; St. Georges, M. de

Halley, Edmund, in *Philosophical Transactions* (*ca.*1690), 135(15)

Halliwell-Phillips, James Orchard, *Books of Characters* (1857), 167(8)

Hamerling, Robert
Ahasver in Rom (1866), trans. W. J. A. Huberts (*Ahasverus te Rome*, 1876), trans. A. van Dissel (*Ahasverus te Rome*, 1893), trans. Chiaffredo Hugues (1876), dramatized J. Horst (1901), 146(44), **250-53**, 254, 263, 271, 308, 312, 332, 335, 405
Stationen meiner Lebenspilgerfahrt (1889), 308

Hammer, A. T., *Juda und die deutsche Gesellschaft* (1881), 277

Handwörterbuch des deutschen Aberglaubens, ed. Hanns Bächtold-Stäubli and Eduard Hoffmann-Krayer (1927-42), 40(5)

Hannoverische Beyträge zum Nutze und Vergnügen (1761), **127**, 161

Hanuš, Josef, "Ahasver čili věčný žid" (1888), 406

H. A. O. Reichard, ed. Hermann Uhde (1877), 142(31)

Hardung, Viktor
Ahasvera (1895), **338**, 415
Kreuzigung Christi (1889), **338**

Hardy, Thomas, *Oxen* (1913), 318(42)

Harsányi, Coloman, "Ahasverus" (1910), **353**

Hartig, Johann Nepomuk (Johannes Nariscus), "Ewige Jude" (1819), 191(45), **222**

Hartmann, A., "Baron Ahasver" (1865), **266**

Hartmann, Moritz, *Bretonische Volkslieder* (1859), 59(40)

Hassler, C. D. See Fabri, Felix

Hauff, Gustav, "Sage vom ewigen Juden und ihre characteristische Behandlung" (1867), 402

Hauff, Wilhelm, "Unterhaltungen des Satans und des ewigen Juden in Berlin" (1826-29), **198,** 199, 241

Haupt, Theodor von. See Caigniez, Louis-Charles, 201

Hauptmann, Hans, *Memoiren des Satans* (1929), **356-57**

Haushofer, Max, *Ewige Jude* (1886), 190, **269-73,** 274, 279, 297, 334, 341, 415

Hauthal, Ferdinand. See Franke, F. F.

Hawthorne, Nathaniel, 9, 216
"Ethan Brand" (1848), **212-13**
Scarlet Letter (1850), 210
"Select Party" (1846), **212**
"Virtuoso's Collection" (1846), **212**

Hazlitt, William Carew, *Bibliographical Collections and Notes on Early English Literature* (1882), 61(51)

Heath, Richard, *Edgar Quinet* (1881), 206(91)

Hegar, Friedrich. See Frey, Adolf, 318

Hegel, Georg Wilhelm Friedrich, 217(14), 219, 395

Heiberg, J. L., "Theodorich vom den vilde Haeger" (1902), 5(9)

Heidegger, Gotthard, *Acerra philologica nova* (1735), 125

Heine, Heinrich, 272, 273, 295

Heinen, E. M. L., "Ewige Jude" (1843), **250**

Heinsius, J. G., *Kurtze Fragen aus der Kirchen Historia des Neuen Testaments* (1725), 125

Helbig, Friedrich, *Sage vom "ewigen Juden"* (1874), 404-5, 407

Heldring, O. G., *Nimmer Rustender Israeliet tot Rust gekommen* (1839), 153, **217-18**

Heldvader, J. Nicolaus, *Sylva Chronologica* (1624), **53,** 121

Heller, B., in *Encyclopaedia Judaica* (1928), 412

Heller, Seligmann, *Wanderungen des Ahasver* (1865), rev. (*Ahasverus,* 1866), **261-62,** 268, 273, 405

Heller, Wilhelm Friedrich
Briefe des ewigen Juden (1791-1801), **144-46,** 147, 148, 155
Geschichte der Kreuzzüge nach dem heiligen Lande (1784), 144
Kardonens Vermächtniss und Lieder von Selima (1781), 144
Novellen (1837-40), 144
Sokrates, Sohn des Sophroniskus (1795), 144

Heman, C. F., *Religiöse Weltstellung des jüdischen Volkes* (1882), 277

Henderson, William, *Notes on the Folklore of the Northern Counties* (1879), 50(20), 93(92)

Henne-am-Rhyn, Otto
Deutsche Volkssage, comp. Joseph Anton Renne (1874), 84(58, 61), 407
Reise durch das Reich des Aberglaubens (1893), 407

Henry, O. See Porter, William Sydney

Hentschke, A. (Klabund), *Bracke* (1918), **293**

Héraucourt, Edmond, "Satan's Money-Box" (*ca.*1912), **336**

Herbert, George, "Collar" (1633), 224

Herbert, Wilhelm, *Ewige Jude in München* (*ca.*1890), **310**

Herczeg, Francis, "Bolygó izraelita" (1895), **353**

Herford, Oliver, *Overheard in a Garden* (1900), **340**

Herrig, Hans A., *Jerusalem* (1874), **282**

Hersch, L., *Juif errant d'aujourd'hui* (1913), 299

Hertel, J. J., *Ausflug des ewigen Juden in malerische Aufläge* (1822), 241-42

Hesslein, Arthur, and Eduard Diener, *Ahasver* (1905), **298-99**

Heulhard, Arthur, *Sainte-Famille* (1914), 412

Heurck, Emile H. van, and G. J. Boekenoogen, *Histoire de l'imagerie populaire flammande* (1910), 115(20), 401

Hewlett, H. G. See Roger of Wendover

Heyermans, Herman. See Jelakowitch, Ivan

Heyse, P., "Weltende" (1909), **340**

Heywood, Joseph C.
Antonius (1867), 292(2), 416
Herodias (1867), 416
Salome (1867), 416

Higden, Ralph, *Polychronicon* (*ca.*1350), 154

Hill, John, *Urania* (1754), 135(15)

Hippe, Max, "Volkstümliches aus einem alten Breslauer Tagebuch" (1910), 114(16)

Hippolytus, *De Antichristo* (3rd C.), 65

Hirsch aus Lintorf, Pfarrer, *Drei grossen volkssagen von Don Juan, vom ewigen Juden, und von Dr. Faust* (1875), 407

Histoire admirable du juif errant (*Volksbuch,* French) (*ca.*1650), **55-57,** 58, 59, 60, 66, 68, 70, 71, 86, 113, 128, 131, 141, 188, 263, 337, 401, 403, 408

Historia del Judío errante. See *Mémoires du juif errant,* 144

Historia Suidae, 69

Historie of a Wandringe Jewe (1620). See Shann, Richard

*Historische Nachricht von dem ewigen Ju-
den* (1723), 125, 127

Hitler, Adolf, *Mein Kampf* (1933), 276

Höfler, Otto, *Kultische Geheimbünde der
Germanen* (1934), 5(7)

Hoffman, David
  *Chronicles . . . of Cartaphilus, the
  Wandering Jew* (1853-54), **153-60**, 161,
  216, 264(30), 288, 311
  "Epistle of Cartaphilus to the Editor"
  (1853-54), **154-55**

Hoffmann-Krayer, Eduard. See *Handwörterbuch des deutschen Aberglaubens*

Holm, Bernard J., and James Westfall
  Thompson, *History of Historical Writing*
  (1942), 141(29)

Holst, Ludolf, *Judenthum in allen dessen
Theilen* (1821), 200

Holz, Arno, "Ich Fuhr auf purpurner
Galeere" (1886), **278**

Holzamer, Wilhelm, "Wanderer" (1911),
303

Hoornbeek, Joannes, *De convincendis et
convertendis Judaeis* (1655), 122, 124

Hopf, Ludwig, "Ahasver" (1903), **303**

Hormayr-Hortenburg, Joseph von. See
  *Taschenbuch für die vaterländische
  Geschichte*

Horn, A. A., in *London Mercury* (1929),
413(82)

Horn, Franz, *Ewige Jude* (1814), **197-98**,
215, 405

Horst, J. See Hamerling, Robert: *Ahasver
in Rom*, 312

Hostrup, Christian, *Gjenboerne* (1847), **267**

Hottinger, Johann Heinrich, *Historiae
Ecclesiasticae* (1653), 124

Houben, Heinrich H., *Gutzkow-funde*
(1901), 217(12)

Huart, Louis, and Charles Philipon, *Parodie
du juif errant* (1844), trans. F. C. Funke
(1845), **235**

Huberts, W. J. A. See Hamerling, Robert:
Ahasver in Rom, 280

Hübner, Anton, "Altfranzösische Fassung
der Johanneslegende" (1919), 14(4)

Hugo, Victor, 180
  Misérables (1862), 232

Hugues, Chiaffredo. See Hamerling, Robert:
Ahasver in Rom, 280

Hume, David, *History of England from the
Invasion of Julius Caesar to the Revolution of 1688* (1754-62), 141(29)

Huygen, Christian, *Celestial Worlds Discovered* (1698), 136(19)

*Ignoti Monachi Cisterciensis S. Mariae de
Ferraria Chronica* (781-1228), ed.
  Augusto Gaudenzi (1888), **18**, 19-20

Ilg, Bertha, "Maltesische Legenden und
Schwänke" (1909), 90(85)

"In the Track of the Wandering Jew"
(1895), 292

Index locupletissimus librorum, ed. Christian Gottlob Kayser, *et al.* (1834-1911),
144(36)

Ingemann, B. S., *Blade of Jerusalems
Skomagers Lommebog* (1833), 144, **224-25**,
249, 267

Irmler, Carl, *Actäa* (1903), 250(15)

Iter Exstaticum Coeleste. See Kircher,
Athanasius

Ives, George, *History of Penal Methods*
(1914), 1(1)

Jablonski, J. T., *Allgemeine Lexikon* (1748),
124

Jackson, Phoebe Dey, *History of the
Wandering Jew* (1898), 100

Jacob. See Joly, Victor Vincent: *Juif errant*

Jacob, P. L. See Lacroix, Paul: "Juif errant"

Jacobowsky and the Colonel. See Werfel,
Franz V., 367

Jaffé, Robert A., *Ahasver* (1900), 298

Jailly, Hector de, "Ahasverus" (1835), **242**

Jakubec, Jan, and Arne Novák, *Geschichte
der čecischen Literatur* (1913), 217(14)

James, G. P. R., 215

"Jan Baudewijn." See Aerts van Mecheln,
Jan, 34

Janssen, Miek, "Na de Kruisiging" (1916),
322

Jay, Harriett, *Robert Buchanan* (1903),
330(66)

"Je donnerais tout mon quibus" (1805),
200-1

Jeitteles, Alois, *Moderne Walpurgisnacht*
(1848), **215**

Jelakowitch, Ivan (Herman Heyermans),
Ahasverus (1893), **294-95**

Jemand, Wilhelm. See Langewiesche, Wilhelm

Jerusalemin suutari (1822), trans. (*Schuster
von Jerusalem*, 1822), 67

Jerusalems Skomager (1643), 66, 116

Jerusalems Skomager (1828). See Reichard,
Henrich A. O.: *Ewige Jude*, 66, 144

Jesus. See Fleg, Edmond, 375

Jew Süss. See Feuchtwanger, Lion, 368

Jobes, Gertrude, *Dictionary of Mythology,
Folklore, and Symbols* (1962), 2(3)

Joel-Jacoby, Franz Karl
  Harfe und Lyra (1837), **220**
  Klagen eines Juden (1835), **220**
  Religiöse Rhapsodien (1837), 220
Jörgensen, Johannes, "Ahasver" (1910), **322**
John
  First Epistle of, 15, 38
  Gospel of, 12, 13, 14, 15, 101, 123
  Second Epistle of, 15
  Third Epistle of, 15
John Chrysostom, 12(2)
Joly, Victor Vincent (Jacob)
  *Jésuites et de quelques engouements
    littéraires à propos du "Juif errant"*
    (1845), trans. J. Fairplay (*Notes on the
    Wandering Jew, the Jesuits, and Their
    Opponents,* 1845); trans. (*Aufzeichnun-
    gen des ewigen Juden,* 1846), 231(9),
    236, 276
  Juif errant (1834), **231**
Joos, Amaat, *Vertelsels van het vlaamsche
  Volk* (1930), 104(115)
Jortin, John, *Remarks on Ecclesiastical
  History* (1751-53), 168
Josz, Virgile, "Juif-Errant" (1898), **342**
Joyce, James, *Ulysses* (1922), 271, 391
Judah ha-Levi, "Divan" (12th C.), trans. A.
  Sulzbach (1873), **284**
Judd, Sylvester, in *Philo* (1850), 268(37)
Juif errant [periodical] (1835-36), 213
Juif errant [periodical] (1848), 213
"Juif errant" (1866), **260**
Juif errant (1873), **278**
Juif errant (1885). See Zhukovski, V. A.,
  256
Jung, Karl, "Wandlungen und Symbole der
  Libido" (1915), 412-13
Juvenal, 49

Kachellek, Albert, *Ahasver und Bonaparte*
  (1904), **312**
Kahlenberg, Hans von. See Manbart,
  Helene von
Kalina, Josef Jaroslav, "Jidašův peniz"
  (1852), trans. T. Kral ("Silberlinge des
  Judas," 1852), **246-47**
Kant, Immanuel, 395
Kappstein, Theodor, *Ahasuer in der Welt-
  poesie* (1906), 410
Karlowic, Jan, *Wieczny tulacz* (1873), 406
Kassner, Rudolf, "Ewige Jude" (1927), **374**
Kate, J. J. L. ten
  Ahasverus op den Grimsel (1840),
    191-92, 214, 244

*Dood van Ahasverus den nimmer rusten-
  den Israeliet* (1839), **192**, 208, 217
Kayser, Christian Gottlob, *et al.* See *Index
  locupletissimus librorum*
Keane, A. H. See Bousset, Wilhelm
Keill, John, *Introduction to the True As-
  tronomy* (1721), 135(15)
Kelchner, Ernst, *Wozu der Lärm?* (1881),
  277
Keller, Gottfried, *Grüne Heinrich* (1853),
  84
Kerner, Theobald, *Neue Ahasver* (1885),
  275
Kildgaard, Caspar, *De Judaeo non mortali*
  (1773), 124-25
Killen, Alice M.
  "Evolution de la légende du Juif Errant"
    (1925), 30(42), 36(60), 411
  Roman terrifiant (1923), 180(12, 14, 15)
King Horn (ca.1250-1300), 120
Kings, Second Book of, 301
Kipling, Rudyard, "Wandering Jew" (1891),
  340-41
Kippenberg, Anton. See Vermeylen, August,
  319
Kirchbach, Wolfgang, *Letzten Menschen*
  (1890), **284**
Kircher, Athanasius, *Itinerarium Exstaticum*
  (1656), rev. (*Iter Exstaticum Coeleste,*
  1660), 136(19)
Kirchheimer, Otto, and Georg Rusche,
  Punishment and Social Structure (1939),
  1(1)
Klabund. See Hentschke, A.
Kladderadatsch, cartoons (1867-70), 265,
  267(33), 276, 340
Klingemann, August
  Ahasver (1827), **196-97**, 215, 312, 399,
    405
  Faust (1815), music by F. L. Seidel, 196
Kloss, Waldemar, "Herodias the Wild
  Huntress in the Legend of the Middle
  Ages" (1908), 5(10)
Knodt, K. E., "Auch ein Ahasver!" (1905),
  309
Koch, J. C., *Observationes miscellaneae*
  (1715), 124
Koch, Max. See Lenau, Nikolaus: "Arme
  Jude"
Köberle, J. Georg, *Neue Thurm zu Babel*
  (1847), **239-41**
Köhler, Johann August Ernst, *Volksbrauch,
  Aberglaube, Sagen* (1867), 82(44)
Köhler, Ludwig, *Neue Ahasver* (1841), **222-
  23**, 405

König, Eduard
   Ahasver, der ewige Jude (1907), 408
   "Ahasver, der ewige Jude" (1927), 408
   Criticism of Leonhard Neubaur in
     Zeitschrift des Vereins für Volkskunde
     (1912), 408
   "Sage und Mythus in Bezug auf den
     'ewigen Juden' " (1912), 408
Königsbrunn-Schaup, Franz von, *Ewige Jude*
   in Monte Carlo (1892), **341**
Köster, Hugo, "Drama der Welt" (1910),
   316
Koesting, Karl, *Shakespeare, ein Winter-*
   nachtstraum (1864), **265-66**
Kohlrusch, C., *Schweizerisches Sagenbuch*
   (1854-56), 249, 400, 401
"Kokot" (1845), 115(22)
Komlós, Aladar, "Bolygó zsidó hazája"
   (1941), 417(2)
Koran, 3, 147
Kral, T. See Kalina, Josef Jaroslav, 246
Krickau, Rudolph, *Sage vom ewigen Juden*
   (1867), 401
Krüger, Maria
   Erstes Supplement zu der ewigen
     Jüddin (1756), **126-27**, 414
   Marien Reginen Krügerin . . . darinnen
     bewiesen wird dass es einen ewigen
     Juden gabe (Schreiben der Krügerin)
     (1756), **126**
Kruger, J. H., in *Grande Encyclopédie*
   (1896), 406
Kühn, Hans Georg, *Ahasver, ein Tagebuch*,
   ed. Ludwig Bär (1910), **309-10**
Kühnau, Richard, *Schlesische Sagen* (1912),
   371
Kuffner, Christian
   Ahasver, der ewige Jude (1846), **152**
   Ewige Jüdin und der Orang-Outang
     (1846), 152, **414**
Kuhn, Adalbert, *Sagen, Gebräuche, und*
   Märchen aus Westfalen (1859), 77(16)
Kuranty (1663), 67
Kurrein, E., "Ahasversage und Judenabzie-
   hungen" (*ca*.1900), 401
Kurtze Beschreibung und Erzehlung von
   einem Juden mit Namen Ahasverus (1602),
   42-53, 51(25), 55, 58, 59, 60, 64, 65, 68,
   70, 71, 86, 97(103), 98(104), 113, 116, 128,
   135(17), 161, 337, 399, 402, 403, 408, 410,
   414
   See also Ahasuerus-book; Cayet, P. V. P.,
     54; *Discours véritable d'un juif errant;*
     Dudulaeus pamphlets; Gründliche und
     Warhafftige Relation von einem Juden;
     Unruhiger Wall-Bruder aus dem

Jüdenthumb; Wunderbarlicher Bericht
   von einem Juden Ahasverus
Kurz, Hermann, *Aus den Tagen der*
   Schmach (1871), 111(8)
Kuusler, Linda, in *Eesti Rahvaluule Archiv*
   (1931), 97(103), 98(104)

Lacey, Alexander, *Pixérécourt and the*
   French Romantic Drama (1928), 180(13)
Lacroix, Paul (P. L. Jacob)
   Curiosités de l'histoire des croyances
     populaires au moyen âge (1859),
     165(2, 3), 166(4), 231(9)
   "Juif errant" (1859), **225**
Laffi, D., *Viaggio in Levante* (1683), 35(56),
   35
Lagerkvist, Pär, 395
   Ahasverus död (1960), trans. Naomi
     Walford (*Death of Ahasuerus*, 1962),
     387, **389-91**, 394
   Sibyllan (1956), trans. Naomi Walford
     (*Sibyl*, 1958), **387-89**, 390
Laistner, Ludwig, *Nebelsagen* (1879), 497
Lajos, Varga, *Ahasvérus vagy a Jézus által*
   megátkozott örökké élö zsidó (1894), 68
Lamentations, Book of, 254
La Motte-Fouqué, Friedrich de. See Fouqué,
   Friedrich de la Motte
Lander, George. See Sue, Eugène, 239
Landsteiner, Karl, *Jünger Ahasverus* (1900),
   339
Lang, Andrew, *Historical Mysteries* (1904),
   291
Langewiesche, Wilhelm (Wilhelm Jemand),
   Ewige Jude (1831), **215**, 216, 226
Langford, Gerald, *Alias O. Henry* (1957),
   343(18)
Laun, Friedrich, *Ewige Jude* (1820), **198,**
   223
Laurenberg, P., *Neue und vermehrte Acerra*
   Philologica (1708), 125
Lawrence, Charles E., "Spikenard" (1921),
   349
Le Baud, Pierre, *Histoire de Bretagne*
   (1638), 86(68)
Leicester, Lord, 45
Leloup, Pierre, "Vrai portrait du juif
   errant" (1784), 115
Lemmens, Leonhard, *Collectanea Terrae*
   Sanctae (1933), 35(56)
Lenau, Nikolaus, 404, 405
   "Ahasver, der ewige Jude" (1832), **220,**
   283
   "Arme Jude," ed. Max Koch (1888), 220
   "Ewige Jude" (1834-48), **220-21**
   Savanarola (1837), 221

Lenin, Nikolai, 396

Lenksi, Henry
"Ahasver" (1916), 417(3)
"Ahasver álma" (1931), 417(4)

Lentner, Josef Ferdinand, *Geschichten aus Tirol und Oberbaiern*, ed. D. K. Rosegger (1881), 81(42)

Leon, S., *Unser heutiges Judenthum* (1890), 277

Leonard of Clou, *Itinerarium breve Terrae Sanctae* (ca.1670 [1891]), **36**

Lepsius, Johannes, *Ahasver, der ewige Jude* (1894), **295-97**, 298, 305

Le Sage, Alain, *Diable boiteux* (1707), **168**

Lessing, Gotthold E., 217

Letters Writ by a Turkish Spy. See Marana, Giovanni, 128

Levitschnigg, H. von, "Ahasver" (1842), **225**

Levy, Alphonse, "Ewige Jude—kein Jude" (1904), 408

Lewis, Leopold. See Sue, Eugène, 239

Lewis, Matthew Gregory, *Monk* (1796), ed. E. A. Baker (1907), dramatized Abbé Prevost (*Jacobin espagnol*, 1800), 136(18), **177-80**, 181, 183, 187, 189, 190, 201, 216, 231, 268(36), 348, 400, 411

Libavius, *Praxis Alchymiae* (1604), ed. Karl Simrock (1875), 53, 123

Library of Impostors, ed. Norman Mosley Penzer (1926), 134(14)

Liebrecht, Felix, *Zur Volkskunde* (1879), 5(8), 22(20)

Liefde, J. de, *Fabelen, Vertellingen en Mythen* (1917), **322**

Lienhard, Fritz, *Ahasver am Rhein* (1903), rev. (*Ahasver: Tragödie*, 1914), **315-16**

Lignon, A. du, 127

Lindemann, Oskar, *Ahasvers Lieder* (1907), **319**

Lipsius, Richard A., *Apokryphen Apostel-geschichten und Apostellegenden* (1883-87), 14(4)

Livische Märchen- und Sagenvarianten, ed. Oskar Loorits (1926), 97(101)

Loder, E. J., *Raymond and Agnes* (1855), 180

Loeb, Isidore, *Juif de l'histoire et le Juif de la légende* (1890), 277

Loew, William N. See Madách, Emeric

London Athenaeum (1866), 119-20, 189, 260

Londres, Albert, *Juif errant est arrivé* (1930), **362-63**

Loorits, Oskar. See *Livische Märchen- und Sagenvarianten*

Lorenz, Marie. See Tillier, Claude

Louvet, Pierre, *Histoire et antiquitez du diocèse de Beauvais* (1631-35), **54**

Lovell, A. See Bergerac, Cyrano de, 136(60)

Lovell, Ernest James, *Captain Medwin* (1962), 185(30), 187(36)

Lowes, John L., *Road to Xanadu* (1927), 168(12), 173(17), 177(4), 181(21)

Lowry, Malcolm, "Element Follows You Around, Sir!" (1964), 363**(11)**

Luard, H. R. See Matthew Paris

Lucka, Emil, *Heiligenrast* (1919), 363

Ludus paschalis de adventu et interitu Antichristi (13th C.), 39

Luke, Gospel of, 12, 65

Lully, Raymond, 154(64)

Lundorpius, M. C., *Joannis Sleidani de Statu religionis ac reipublicae continuatio* (1615-19), 124

Luther, Arthur, *Jesus und Judas in der Dichtung* (1910), 292

Lyell, Frank H., *Study of the Novels of John Galt* (1942), 148(48, 49)

Lysaght, S. R., *Immortal Jew* (1931), **378-80**

Lyserus, Johannes, *Aphtharsia* (1662), 124

M. E. S. See S., M. E.

M. W. See Wilson, Miles

Mabie, Hamilton Wright, *Legends That Every Child Should Know* (1906), 408-9

McConkey, Elizabeth, *Karl Gutzkow as Literary Critic* (1941), 217(12)

Macdonald, George, *Thomas Wingfold, Curate* (1876), **285-87**, 317

Mácha, K. H., "Ewige Wanderung," trans. Oskar Rosenfeld (1917), **353**

McKee, Irving, "Ben-Hur" Wallace (1947), 311(33)

Mackinnon, David, *Ahasverus* (1920), 394

Macleod, Fiona. See Sharp, William

Madách, Emeric, *Ember tragédiája* (1859), trans. William N. Loew (*Tragedy of Man*, 1908), 279

Madjera, Wolfgang, *Ahasver* (1903), **351-52**

Magnin, Charles
Causeries et Méditations historiques et littéraires (1843), 202(82)
"De la nature du génie poétique" (1833), 202(82)

Maier, Olga, "Ahasvers Klagelied" (1908), **342-43**

Maillan, Jules, and Anicet Bourgeois, *Nonne sanglante* (1835), 180

Maillan, J. de, and P. F. C. Merville, *Juif errant, drame fantastique* (1834), **258**

Maitland, Frederic W., 154(62)

Maitland, Samuel R., *Dark Ages* (1844), 154

Major, Elias, diary (*ca.*1646), 114

Makeever, John L., *Wandering Jew* (1891), **330-32**

Mallinckrodt, Max von, *Weg des Ahasvers* (1920), **357**

Malone, W., *Man in the Moon Telling Strange Fortunes* (1609), rev. (*Wandering Jew Telling Fortunes to Englishmen,* 1640), **167**

Maltitz, G. A. von, *Gelasius, der graue Wanderer* (1826), 199, 200, 208

Manbart, Helene von (Hans von Kahlenberg), *Ahasvera* (1910), **308**, 415

Manifest, of anti-Semitic congress (1882), 276

Mannini, Salvestro di Giovanni, diary (*ca.*1416), 26-27, 107

Map, Walter, *Master Walter Map's Book "De Nugis Curalium"* (*ca.*1180-93), trans. Frederick Tupper and Marbury B. Ogle (1924), 5(8), 86(71)

Marana, Giovanni, *Espion du Grand-Seigneur* (1684), trans. William Bradshaw (*Letters Writ by a Turkish Spy,* 1686), 121, **128-32,** 141, 145, 147, 155, 167, 177, 344

Marchant, Edward, *Ballad Called "Wonderful Strange News out of Germanye of a Jewe"* (1612), 61

Mariage de Pierre de Provence et de la belle Maguelone (1638), 59, 167

Marie de France
    lai of *Guingamor* (*ca.*1200), 86
    Lais der Marie de France, ed. Karl Warnke (1925), trans. Eugene Mason (*French Mediaeval Romances from the Lays of Marie de France,* 1932), 86(71)

Mark, Gospel of, 12, 65, 140(25), 374, 376, 415

Marlow, F. See Wolfram, L. H.

Marr, W.
    Goldene Ratten und rothe Mäule (1880), 276
    Sieg des Judenthums über das Germanenthum (1879), 276
    Weg zum Siege des Germanthums über das Judenthum (1880), 276

Marriott, John, 61

Marryat, Frederick, *Phantom Ship* (1839), 8, 232

Martial, 49

Martin, N., *Sonnets et Chansons* (1841), **208**

Martin, Theodore, *Memoir of W. E. Aytoun* (1867), 216(9)

Marvel, Ik. See Mitchell, Donald Grant

Marx, Karl, 281, 396
    Communist Manifesto (1848), 234

Mason, Eugene. See Marie de France: *Lais der Marie de France*

Matthew, Gospel of, 12, 13-14, 38, 140(25), 352, 412(78)

Matthew Paris, *Chronica Majora* (*ca.*1235-59), ed. H. R. Luard (1872-83), trans. J. A. Giles (*English History,* 1889), **20-21,** 22, 29, 30, 32, 41, 42, 44, 47, 54, 60, 67, 106, 132, 150, 157, 175(1), 177, 311, 369, 399, 407, 412

Maturin, Charles, *Melmoth the Wanderer* (1820), **189-90,** 199

Maupassant, Guy de, 328

Mauthner, Fritz
    Neue Ahasver (1882), 276, **277-78,** 284, 356
    Unbewusste Ahasverus, oder das Ding an sich als Wille und Vorstellung (1878), **273**
    "Zur Geschichte der Sage vom ewigen Juden" (1878), 277

May, Emmet C., *White Bears and Gold* (1931), **364-65**

Mayreder, Rosa, *Fabelein über göttliche und menschliche Dinge* (1921), **367-68**

Mazarin, Madame de, letter to Madame de Bouillon (*ca.*1675-1700), **109-10,** 132

Medwin, Thomas, 185
    "Ahasuerus" (1823), 187
    Life of Percy Bysshe Shelley (1847), ed. H. Buxton Forman (1913), 185

Medwin, Thomas, and Percy Bysshe Shelley, *Wandering Jew* (*ca.*1810), 183, **184-87**

Meekel, Kees, *Ahasverus* (1923), **380-84,** 385, 395

Mégroz, Phyllis. See Fleg, Edmond, 374-75

Meier, Ernst, *Deutsche Sagen, Sitten und Gebräuche aus Schwaben* (1852), 76(15), **248**

Meige, Henry, *Juif errant à la salpétrière* (1893), 406-7

Meilinger, Lothar, "Ewige Jude" (*ca.*1895), **320**

Melissen, Lambert, *Door Kristus vervolgd* (1929), **393**

Mémoires du juif errant (1777), trans. Luis Fris Ducos (*Historia del Judío errante,* 1819), **141-44,** 145-46, 147, 150, 153, 155, 335
    See also Reichard, Heinrich A. O.

Memoirs of an Artist. See Gounod, Charles: *Mémoires d'un artiste*

Mencken, H. L., 355

Mendès, Catulle, "Ahasuerus" (1869), **284**

Menot, Michel, *Sermones* (1525), **34-35**, 87, 88

Merode, W. de, "Eeuwige wandelende Jood" (1914), **340**

Merville, P. F. C., and J. de Maillan, *Juif errant, drame fantastique* (1834), **258**

Merwin, Peter, *Tod des ewigen Juden* (1902), **325**

Mesmer, Friedrich, 177

Mexía, Pero, *Silva de Varia Lección* (1541), 29

Meyke, Nina, "Ahasver" (1900), **297-98**

Meyrink, Gustav, *Grüne Gesicht* (1917), **347-48**, 357

Michel, Friedrich, "Vision" (1906), **322**

Michelet, Jules, and Edgar Quinet, *Jésuites* (1843), 236

Miller, Walter W., *Canticle for Leibowitz* (1960), **394**

Milton, John, 206
    Paradise Lost (1667), 260

Minor, J., *Goethes Fragmente vom ewigen Juden und vom wiederkehrenden Heiland* (1904), 169(15), 408

Mitchell, Donald Grant (Ik Marvel), *Reveries of a Bachelor* (1850), 265

Mitchell, S. Weir, "Barabbas" (1913), 321-22

Mitternacht, Johann Sebastian, *Dissertationes de Johannis XXI* (1665), 59, 113(12), 122, 125

Modl, Alois, "Ahasvers Ende" (1907), **340**

Moerkerken, P. H. van, "Ahasverus Graf" (1910), **299-300**

Moller, Anton, 43

Moller, Johann, *Cimbria Literata* (1744), 125

Monatrosen (1842), **217**

Montdidier. See Sue, Eugène, 238

Montesquieu, Charles Louis, *Lettres persanes* (1721), 128

Moreau, Jean, *Histoire de ce qui s'est passé en Bretagne* (ca.1609 [1836]), **40-41**

Moreni, Domenico. See Siena, Mariano da

Mormon, Book of, 101

Morpurgo, Salomone, *Ebreo errante in Italia* (1891), 23(21, 22), 25(30), 27(31), 34(51), 92(90), 403, 404, 407, 409

Morris, Ralph, *Life and Astonishing Adventures of John Daniel* (1751), 134, 136(20), 136

"Mort du juif errant." See Goethe, Johann Wolfgang von: "Ewige Juden erstes Fetzen," 173

Moschos, Johannes (Eucrates), *Leimonarion* (ca.600), trans. M. J. Rouët de Journel (*Pré spirituel*, 1946), **13**, 16, 17, 18, 71

Moscoviter, S. J., *Ahasverus* (1870), 402

Mosen, Julius, 226, 253, 273, 305, 405
    Ahasver (1838), 146(39), 217, **218-19**, 261, 271
    "Ritter Wahn" (1831), **218**

Mosheim, Johann Lorenz von, *De Rebus christianorum ante Constantinum magnum commentarii* (1753), 141(29)

Mouskes (Mousket), Philippe, *Chronique rimée* (ca.1243), ed. Frédéric-Auguste de Reiffenberg (1836-45), 21, 22, 30, 32, 60, 214(4)

Mousket. See Mouskes, Philippe

Mühsam, Paul, *Ewige Jude* (1924), **347**

Müller, Hubert, "Ahasver am Hudson" (1888), **278**, 283, 320, 404

Müller, Otto, *Götterdämmerung* (1926), **357**

Müller, Wilhelm
    "Ewige Jude," music by Franz Schubert (1823), **199-200**
    Lieder des Lebens und der Liebe (1824), 199

Müller, Wilhelm, and Georg Schambach, *Niedersächsische Sagen und Märchen* (1855), 78(23)

Mugnerot, A., "Juif errant" (1846), **208**

Muir, Edwin. See Feuchtwanger, Lion, 368

Muir, Willa. See Feuchtwanger, Lion, 368

Mullenhoff, Karl, *Sagen, Märchen, und Lieder* (1845), 78(25)

Murray, James A. H., *et al.* See *New English Dictionary on Historical Principles*

Muther, Richard. See Grauhoff, Otto

My Uncle Benjamin. See Tillier, Claude, 229

Nachdenkliche Prophezeyungen, Visionen, und Träume (18th C.), **108-9**, 110, 260

Nariscus, Johannes. See Hartig, Johann Nepomuk

Narrazione dello Stato (1849), 68-69

Narrazione di quel servo (ca.1650), 68-69

Narrazione d'un Giudeo errante (ca.1650), 68-69
    See also *Narrazione di quel servo,* 69

Nash, Ogden, 391

Nathan, Alfred, "An Bacchus" (1906), **343**

Nathan, Robert, *Road of Ages* (1935), 391(53)

Naudh, H.
    Israel im Heere (1879), 277
    Professoren über Israel (1880), 277

Navis Peregrinorum (1561-1695), ed. Bertrand Zimolong (1938), 35(56)

Nebesky, Vacheslav, *Protichudchi* (1844), **217**

Neefs, Emanuel. See Aerts van Mecheln, Jan

Neele, Henry, "Magician's Visitor" (1828), 155, **216**, 264

Nelson, Heinrich, *Ahasvers Wanderung und Wandlung* (1922), **372-74**

Nemerov, Howard, "Ahasuerus" (1958), **384**

Nephi, Book of, 101

Nerval, Gerard de. See Goethe, Johann Wolfgang von: "Ewige Juden erstes Fetzen," 173

Nestroy, Johann, *Zwei ewige Juden und keiner*, trans. *Fliegende Hollander zu Fuss* (1846), 239

Nettement, Alfred, *Etudes critiques sur le feuilleton roman* (1845-46), 400

Neubaur, Leonhard, 49, 334, 404, 405, 407, 408, 409, 410
  "Bibliographie der Sage vom ewigen Juden" (1895), 403
  "Geschichte und Bibliographie des Volksbuchs vom Ahasverus" (1914), 403
  Neue Mitteilungen über die Sage vom ewigen Juden (1893), 24(27), 36(60), 40(8), 77(19, 20), 81(40, 41), 111(9), 112(10), 403
  reply to König, in *Zeitschrift des Vereins für Volkskunde* (1912), 408(47)
  Sage vom ewigen Juden (1893), 12(2), 40(9, 10), 42(12), 44(15), 51(25), 52(27), 57(38), 79(28, 30, 31, 32, 33), 108(2), 113(13), 126(63, 64), 127(65), 403
  "Zur Geschichte der Sage vom ewigen Juden" (1912), 13(3), 18(11), 42, 44, 45(17), 50(19), 51(25, 26), 76(14), 77(18), 78(26), 84(60), 85(63), 88(81), 116(24), 166(6), 168(11), 403

Neuer Ahasverus. See Croly, George, 189

Neumann, Hermann, *Letzte Menschenpaar* (1844), **241**

New and True History of the Wandering Jew (ca.1800), **189**

New English Dictionary on Historical Principles, ed. James A. H. Murray, et al. (1888-1928), 93(92)

New Yorker, 214
  (1940), 395(58)

Newe Zeytung—ein alter Prophet (1589), **49**

Newe Zeytung von den newgeborenen Antichrist (1579), 40

Newton, Sir Isaac, *Principia* (1687), 135(15), 136(20)

Nichols, Robert, "Golgotha and Company" (1923), **355-56**

Nicolai, Heinrich, *Passionalia* (1638), 124

Nicolson, Marjorie H.
  "Microscope and English Imagination" (1935), 133(9), 135(15)

"Milton and the Telescope" (1935), 133(9), 135(15)

" 'New Astronomy' and English Literary Imagination" (1935), 133(9), 135(15)

"Telescope and Imagination" (1934), 133(9), 135(15)

"World in the Moon" (1936), 136(20)

Nietzsche, Friedrich, 281, 309, 339
  Also Sprach Zarathustra (1883-84), trans. A. Tille (*Thus Spake Zarathustra*, 1933), 206, 243, 274, 280, 314, 315

Nievelt, C. van, *Ahasverus* (1884), **289**

Nisard, Charles, *Histoire des livres populaires ou de la littérature du colportage* (1854), 165(2, 3), 173(19), 401, 402, 404

Nithack-Stahn, Walther, *Ahasver* (1910), **313-14**

Nodnagel, A.
  Deutsche Sagen aus dem Munde deutscher Dichter und Schriftsteller (1836), 191(48)
  Sieben Bücher deutscher Sagen und Legenden (1839), 226(36)

Nork, F., *Sitten und Gebräuche der Deutschen und ihrer Nachbarvölker* (1845), 400, 401, 404

Northern Passion (ca.1300), ed. Frances A. Foster (1916), **30-31**, 61

Norton, Caroline (Lady Stirling-Maxwell), *Undying One* (1830), **208-10**

Notes on the Wandering Jew, the Jesuits, and Their Opponents. See Joly, Victor Vincent: *Jésuites et de quelques engouements littéraires à propos du "Juif errant,"* 236

Novaire, Philippe de. See Novara, Filippo de

Novák, Arne, and Jan Jakubec, *Geschichte der čechischen Literatur* (1913), 217(14)

Novara, Filippo de (Philippe de Novaire), *Assises de Jérusalem* (1250-55), ed. Count Beugnot (1841), **23**, 30

Numbers, Book of, 103, 301

Nyrop, Kristoffer, *Fortids Sagn og Sange* (1907-9), 66(59), 166(6)

Odoaker. See Richepin, Jean, 281

Oelckers, Theodor, *Prinzessin Marie von Oldenhof* (1844), **215-16**, 405

Oesterley, Hermann. See *Gesta Romanorum*

Ogle, Marbury B. See Map, Walter

"Old Nick and Granville" (1843), **228**

Oosterlee, P., "Ahasverus" (1913), 352, 380, 408

Oriosius, Paulus, *Historiarum libri vii adversus paganos* (ca.415), trans. Alfred the Great (ca.890), 145

Örökké való zsidó (ca.1848), 68

Örökké való zsidó (1861), 68
Ortlepp, Ernst, "Rede des ewigen Juden" (1845), 249, 401
Osenbruggen, Eduard, *Wanderstudien aus der Schweiz* (1867), 82(47)
Otte, L., "Ahasver, eine Sage aus dem Wallis" (1851), 401

P. B. See B., P.
P. W. See Will, Peter
Paganini, Niccolò, 180
Paltock, Robert, *Life and Adventures of Peter Wilkins* (1751), 134, 136(20)
Paludan-Müller, Frederik, *Ahasverus, den evige Jøde* (1853), 247-48, 410
Pannalius, Peter Brantius, account of Legend of Wandering Jew (16th C.), 35(56), 35
Papias, 15
Parijogi, J., "Gavene Juut" (1930), 371
Paris, Gaston, 334, 404, 406, 407, 409
    Juif errant (1881), 21(18)
    "Juif errant" (1880), 21(18), 403, 406(40)
    Juif errant en Italie (1891), 23(24), 25(30), 403
    Légendes du moyen âge (1903), 25(30)
    in *Romania* (1881), 21(18)
Parsons, Ethel B., "Wandering Jew of Celtic Legend" (1933), 86(70)
Passion play of Oberammergau, 394
Paul (Richter), Jean, *Plan zum Kometen* (1820-22), 199, 243(1)
Paulli, Oliger
    Bericht an alle Puisancen von Europaea (1704), 112
    document to Oberleutnant Neubaur and Father Hosmann, 113
Paulsen, Rudolph, *Christus und der Wanderer* (1918), 317
Paulton, T. G. See Sue, Eugène, 239
Pawel-Rammingen, Alexander von, *Gedanken eines Cavaliers über Antisemitismus* (1886), 276
Peacock, Mabel G. W., and Eliza Gutch, *Examples of Printed Folk-Lore Concerning Lincolnshire* (1908), 119(32)
Pearson, James, "Seven Whistlers" (1871), 93
Peck, Francis, *Academia Tertia Anglicana* (1727), 91-92, 107
Peene, H. van, *Wandelaer der Joden* (1853), 259
Penzer, Norman Mosley. See *Library of Impostors*
Pepys, Samuel, collections of ballads (17th C.), 61
Percy, Thomas, *Reliques of Ancient English Poetry* (1765), 61, 119
Peregrinus, Theodor. See Haupt, Theodor von
Peterdi, Andrew, "Bolygó zsidó" (1936), 417(2)
Peterson, Henry, "Wandering Jew" (1863), 257-58
Petsch, Robert, "Faust-Studien" (1907), 408
Pfeffinger, Johann Friedrich, *Merckwürdigkeiten des XVII. Jahrhunderts* (1706), 125
Pfizer, Gustav, "Ewige Jude" (1831), 224
Philipon, Charles, and Louis Huart, *Parodie du juif errant* (1844), trans. F. C. Funke (1845), 235
Physico-Theologie, oder Natur-Leitung zu Gott. See Derham, William
Physiologie du fumeur (ca.1850), 229
Pichler, Adolf, "Ewige Jude" (1880), 280-81
Picot, Emile, in *Revue Critique d'histoire et de littérature* (1884), 36(60)
Pierotti, Ermete, *Jerusalem Explored*, trans. T. G. Bonney (1864), 24(26)
Pilato, Ponzio, *Vera leggenda dell'Ebreo Errante (Isacco Lachedem)* (1897), 335
Pineau, Léon. See *Folk-lore de Lesbos*
Pinoli, G., "Ebreo Errante nel Canavese" (1883), 88(80, 81)
Pinski, David, *Ewige Jude* (1907), trans. (*Stranger*, 1920), 349
Pista, Karakoi, chapbook (1873), 68
Pitrè, Giuseppe, *Fiabe, novelle e raconti popolari siciliani* (1875), 37(63), 87(75), 88(79), 89(82), 403
Pitts, J., 117
Pixérécourt. See Guilbert de Pixérécourt, René-Charles
Platen-Hallemünde, August von, "Auf Golgotha" (1820), 199
Plato, 49
Plischke, Hans, *Sage vom wilden Heere im deutschen Volke* (1914), 5(7)
Poe, Edgar Allan, 9, 175
    criticism of Sue's *Juif errant*, 235, 239
Poggibonsi, Niccolò da, *Libro d'Oltramare*, ed. A. Bacchi della Lega (1881), 27(32)
Poligny, Gabrielle de, "Ahasvérus" (1857), 260
Polonskij, Georg. See Chirikov, Evgeni Nikolaevich
Polz, Hans, *Herzog von Burgund* (ca.1450), 39
Pope, Alexander
    Essay on Man (1732-34), 226
    Rape of the Lock (1714), 174
Porter, William Sydney (O. Henry), "Door of Unrest" (1911), 343-44
Portheim, Paul von, "Ahasver" (1884), 273

Povinelli, Adolf H., *Ahasverus in Tyrol* (1890), **279-80**

Power. See Feuchtwanger, Lion, 368

Pré spirituel. See Moschos, Johannes, 13

Prestos, Antonio, *Auto dos Dous Irmaos* (16th C.), 28

Preuss, Hans, *Vorstellungen von Antichrist im späteren Mittelalter* (1906), 39(3, 4), 40(5)

Prevost, Abbé. See Lewis, Matthew Gregory, 180

Pröhle, Heinrich. See *Deutsche Sagen* (1863)

Prost, Johann, *Sage vom ewigen Juden in der neueren deutschen Literatur* (1905), 410

Psalms, Book of, 20

Punch, 214

Quaresmi, Father, *Terrae Sanctae Elucidatio* (1616-26), 35(56), **35**

Quiller-Couch, A. T., "Mystery of Joseph Laquedem" (1900), **349**

Quinet, Edgar, 226, 253, 258, 273
 Ahasvérus (1833), 171, 190, 201, **202-7**, 208, 209, 210, 213, 221, 241, 247, 254, 259, 271, 278, 279, 284, 335, 361, 394, 414
 Tablettes du Juif-errant (1823), **201-2**

Quinet, Edgar, and Jules Michelet, *Jésuites* (1843), 236

Radewell, Friedrich, *Passion* (1840), **228**

Railo, Eino, *Haunted Castle* (1927), 177(3), 180(8, 9, 11), 190(44), 411

Raimarus, Nicolaus, *Chronoligische Gewisse* (1605), **40**

Ranzo (Soranzo), Carlo, account of Legend of Wandering Jew (16th C.), 35, 87, 88

Rappaport, Moritz, "Ewige Jude" (1885), **284**, 294

Rappaport, Samuel, in *Judisches Lexikon* (1927), 412(78)

Rappold, J., *Sagen aus Kärnten* (1887), 80(35), 81(39), 82(43, 46)

Raskin, P. M., "Wandering Jew" (1924), **371**

Raymond and Agnes, music by William Reeve (1796), 180

"Raymond and Agnes, or the Bleeding Nun" [subplot]. See Lewis, Matthew Gregory, **177-80**, 201

Reed, F. W.
 "Dumas's Wandering Jew" (1928), 263(28)
 See Dumas, Alexandre *père,* 263

Reeve, William. See *Raymond and Agnes*

Rehberg-Worden, A. See Croly, George, 189

Reichard, Heinrich A. O., 148, 155
 Bibliothek der Romane (1782), **142**

Ewige Jude (1785), trans. (*Jerusalems Skomager,* 1828), 66, **142-44**, 145-46, 147, 179
 See also *Mémoires du juif errant*

Reiffenberg, Frédéric-Auguste de
 Annuaire de la Bibliothèque royale de Belgique (1840-50), 60(48), 78(22)
 Dimanche (1834), **214**
 Souvenirs d'un pèlerinage en l'honneur de Schiller (1839), **214**
 See Mouskes, Philippe

Reiser, Karl A., *Sagen, Gebräuche und Sprichwörter des Allgaus* (1895-98), 114(114, 115)

Relation. See *Gründliche und Warhafftige Relation von einem Juden*

Relation curieuse et intéressante du nouveau voyage du Juif-Errant (1816), 151

Rellstab, L. See Scribe, Eugène; St. Georges, M. de

"Reminder to the Christian Reader." See *Erinnerung*

Remy, A. F. J., in *Catholic Encyclopedia* (1910), 412(78)

Rencontres faist ces jours passez du Juif-Errant (1615), 55, 66

Renier, Rodolfo, "Leggenda dell'Ebreo Errante" (1910), 409

Renk, Anton, *Ins neue Land* (1896), **322**

Renne, Joseph Anton. See Henne-am-Rhyn, Otto: *Deutsche Volkssage*

Renner, Gustav, 308
 Ahasver (1902), **304-6**
 "Skizzen zu Ahasver" (1896-97), **304-6**

Revelation, Book of, 15, 65, 205, 406

Reviczky, Julius, *Utolso költö* (1889), **279**

Revue des deux mondes (1883), 406

Rhode, Jakob, 43, 44, 49

Ricci, Corrado, "Ebreo errante" (1896-97), 413

Richard, Jean, motion picture based on Sue's *Juif errant* (1926), 239

Richepin, Jean, "Juif errant" (1884), trans. Odoaker (*Ewige Jude,* 1905), **281-82**

Richter, Emil (Germanicus)
 Frankfurter Juden und die Aufsaugung des Volkswohlstandes (1880), 276
 Neueste Raub am deutschen National-wohlstand (1881), 276

Richter. See Paul, Jean

Rimbaud, Arthur, 278

"Rime inedite dei secoli XIII e XIV," (1274), ed. Tomaso Casini (1882), 23

Robertson, William
 History of Scotland (1759), 141(29)
 History of the Reign of the Emperor Charles V (1769), 141(29)

History of America (1777), 141(29)

Robinson, Edwin Arlington, "Wandering Jew" (1920), **318**, 384

Robinson, F. N. See Chaucer, Geoffrey

Rochholz, Ernst Ludwig, *Schweizersagen aus dem Aargau* (1856), 80(34), 83(53), 400

Rodiger, B., "Ewige Jude" (1864), 402

Rodrigues Lobo, Francisco, *Corte ne Aldea* (1793), 28

Roeder, G. W., "Sage vom ewigen Juden" (1856), 401

Rönnefahrt, J. G., *Tod Ahasvers, des ewigen Juden* (1855), **255-56**, 261

Röse, Friedrich, "Ahasver" (1839), **215**

Roger, Eugène, *Terre Saincte* (1664), 36(59)

Roger of Wendover, *Flores Historiarum* (1228), ed. H. G. Hewlett (1886-89), trans. J. A. Giles (*Flowers of History*, 1849), **18-20**, 29, 30, 32, 33, 41, 47, 60, 67, 106, 157, 292, 345, 358, 407, 409, 412

Rohling, August, *Talmudjude* (1871), 275

Romieux, Jean-Gaston, *Juif errant, le remords, et le choléra* (1858), **244**

Rosée, Adolph, *Sterbende Ahasver* (1898), **298**

Rosegger, D. K. See Lentner, Josef Ferdinand

Rosegger, Peter, "Ahasver an seinen verklärten Dichter" (1891), 335

Rosenberg, Edgar, *From Shylock to Svengali* (1960), 177(3), 411

Rosenfeld, Isaac, "Ewige Jude" (1838), **208**, 227

Rosenfeld, Oskar. See Mácha, K. H.

Rosenkranz, C., "Ahasverus-Sage" (1894), 408

Rosenkranz, Karl, *Geschichte der deutschen Poesie im Mittelalter* (1830), 198

Rosenstock, Moritz, "Völkerwanderung und ihre Folgen" (1878), 277

Rossi, Nicolo de, 23

Rothen, Gottlieb (Gottlob), *Sogenannte unsterbliche Jude* (1706), 124

Rothen, Jakob, 42, 43

Rouët de Journel, M. J. See Moschos, Johannes, 13

Roxburghe, John Ker, *Roxburghe Ballads* (1868-95), 61, 63

Ruhemann, Alfred
  "Sage vom ewigen Juden in Italien" (1895), 69(65), 87(75), 89(83, 84), 90(87), 404, 407, 408
  See Savi-Lopez, Maria

Rulerius, Adrianus, 45

Rusche, Georg, and Otto Kirchheimer, *Punishment and Social Structure* (1939), 1(1)

Ruseler, Georg, "Neuer Ahasver" (*ca.*1910), 293

Rutten, Felix, "Ahasverus" (1918), **317**

Rydberg, Viktor, "Prometheus und Ahasverus" (1888), **308-9**

S., Dr., "Sage vom ewigen Juden" (n.d.), 408

S. E. See E., S.

S., M. E., *Kains Schuld und ihre Sühne* (1896-98), **323-25**

Sá de Miranda, Francisco de, *Vilhalpandos* (1560), 28

Sablie del tempo. See *Ebreo errante*

Sachs, Hans, 49, 50, 247, 405

Saint-Ernest. See Sue, Eugène, 238

St. Georges, M. de, and Eugène Scribe, *Juif errant* (1852), music by Jacques Halévy; trans. L. Rellstab (1852), **259**

Salazar, Eugenio de, 29

Salques, J. B., "Juif errant" (*ca.*1820), **229**

Salus, Hugo, "Ahasverus" (1917), 353, **366**

Salzman, Marcus. See *Chronicle of Ahimaaz*, 16

Samuel, Maurice. See Asch, Shalom, 392

Samyuktagama Sutra (*ca.*450), 4

Sandfaerdig Beretning om Jerusalems Skoemager, Ahasverus kaldet (n.d.), 166

Sandru Beskriffuelse (1621), 66

Saulnier, René, and Pierre Louis Duchartre, *Imagerie populaire* (1925), 60(50), 85(65)

Savi-Lopez, Maria, *Alpensagen*, trans. Alfred Ruhemann (1893), 83(53), 90(86)

Saxe, J. G., "Wandering Jew" (1865), **268**

Scarborough, Dorothy, *Supernatural in Modern English Fiction* (1917), 239(20)

Schaching, Otto von, "Ewige Jude" (1895), **308**

Schack, Adolf F. von, "Ewige Wanderer" (1866), **247**

Schaeffer, Albrecht, *Parzival* (1922), **392-93**

Schaffer, Aaron, "*Ahasver-Volksbuch* of 1602" (1919-20), 42(12)

Schambach, Georg, and Wilhelm Müller, *Niedersächsische Sagen und Märchen* (1855), 78(23)

Scharrer-Schauenberg, Georg, *Ahasver, der ewige Jude* (*ca.*1890), **334-35**

Scharschmidt, Carl, *Europaeischer Staats- und Kriegs-Saal* (1686), **124**

Scheel, Joseph, "Ahasver" (1914), **317**

Scheiber, Alexander, "Legend of the Wandering Jew in Hungary" (1954), 68(64), 99, 279(49), 411, 417

Schell, Otto, *Bergische Sagen* (1897), 79(27, 29)

Schenck, Eduard von
"Albertus Magnus" (1834), **213**
"Ewige Jude," 213
"Hi-Tong and Li-Song" (1836), **213**
version of Legend of St. George (1834), **213**

Scherer, J. E., *Beiträge zur Geschichte des Judenrechtes im Mittelalter* (1901), 40(5)

Schiemann, Theodor, review of Neubaur's *Sage vom ewigen Juden* (1884), 44(15)

Schiessler, S. W., "Auch etwas vom ewigen Juden" (1826), **194-95**

Schiller, J. C. F.
Geisterseher (1786-89), **175-77**, 181, 196, 267, 345, 358, 405
Räuber (1781), 181

Schilling von Canstatt, Heinrich, *Ahasver* (1894), **350**

Schlegel, A. W., "Warnung" (1802), **191,** 405

Schlözer, August Ludwig von
Allgemeine Nordische Geschichte (1771-85), 141(29)
Neuverändertes Russland (1767-69), 141(29)
Weltgeschichte nach ihren Haupttheilen (1792), 141(29)

Schmid, Erasmus, *Opus sacrum posthumum* (1658), 124

Schmidt, Arno, *Volksbuch vom ewigen Juden* (1927), 43-44, 49, 410

Schmidt, Carl. See Sue, Eugène, 238-39

Schmidtbonn, Wilhelm, "Ahasver" (1913), **336**

Schmitz, August, *Ahasverus, oder der Weg zur Versöhnung* (1893), **315, 323**

Schneider, Ferdinand J., *Jean Pauls Altersdichtung Fibel und Komet* (1901), 199(70)

Schnell, J., *Israelitische Recht in seinen Grundzügen dargestellt* (1853), 248

Schoebel, Charles, *Légende du Juif errant* (1877), 165(2, 3), 201(77), 405

Schoen, Johann, "Ahasverus der ewige Jude" (1826), 208

Schönaich-Carolath, Emil von, *Don Juans Tod* (1883), **268-69**, 274, 385

Schönhuth, Ottmar F. H., *Ahasverus, der ewige Jude* (1849), 399

Schönwerth, Franz Xaver von, *Aus der Oberpfalz* (1857-59), 400

Scholz, W. van, *Gedanken zum Drama* (1905), 348(20)

Schopenhauer, Arthur, 405

Schorn, Hans Traugott, *Ahasver* (1920), **345-47**

Schottelius, Carl, *Sigmar* (1895), **304**

Schreck, Valentin, 43, 45

Schreiber, Aloys, "Ewige Jude" (1807), **191,** 404

Schröter, Johannes, 42, 44

Schubart, Christian Friedrich Daniel, "Ewige Jude" (1783), 97, **171-73**, 175, 177, 178, 184, 186, 187, 190, 192, 197, 202, 208, 217, 220, 230, 246, 247, 267, 312, 335, 404, 405

Schubert, Franz. See Müller, Wilhelm: "Ewige Jude," 199

Schudt, Johann Jacob
Compendium historiae judaicae (1700), 123
Jüdische Merckwürdigkeiten (1714-18), 110-11, **123,** 125

Schücking, Levin, "Drei Freier" (1851), **245-46**, 351, 364, 405

Schüler, Gustav, "Ewige Jude" (1909), **336**

Schultz, A.
"Rückblicke auf Dichtungen und Sagen des deutschen Mittelalters" (1872), 269
"Über die Volkssagen van Ahasverus und Faust im Licht ihrer Zeit" (1866), 269

Schultz, Christopher, *Dissertatio historica de Judaeo non mortali* (1689), **123,** 125

Schurmann, J., "Ahasverus" (1915), **339-40**

Schuster von Jerusalem. See *Jerusalemin suutari*

Schwartz, Rudolf, *Esther im deutschen und neulateinischen Drama des Reformationszeitalters* (1894), 50(22)

Schweda, Valentin, *Sagen vom wilden Jäger* (1915), 5(7)

Scott, Walter, 148
Ivanhoe (1820), 263
Rokeby (1813), 8

Scribe, Eugène. See Gounod, Charles: *Nonne sanglante*

Scribe, Eugène, and M. de St. Georges, *Juif errant* (1852), music by Jacques Halévy; trans. L. Rellstab (1852), **259**

Sébillot, Paul
Folk-lore de France (1904-7), 85(64), 86(68, 69)
Gargantua dans les traditions populaires (1883), 87(73)
Imagerie populaire (1888), 401(12)
Traditions et superstitions de la Haute-Bretagne (1882), 86(66, 67)

Seeber, Joseph, *Ewige Jude* (1894), **326-28**

Seidl, F. L. See Klingemann, August: *Faust*

Seidl, J., *Jude des neunzehnten Jahrhunderts, oder Warum sind wir antisemitisch?* (1899), 294

Seidl, Johann Gabriel, "Beiden Ahasvere" (1836), **223**

Severus, Sulpicius, *Chronica* (*ca.*403), **15**

Shakespeare, William
Hamlet (*ca.*1600), 120, 231(8), 238
King Lear (*ca.*1605), 264
Merry Wives of Windsor (*ca.*1600), 6(12)

Shann, Richard, *Historie of a Wandringe Jewe* (1620), **63-66**, 117

Sharp, William (Fiona Macleod), *Gypsy Christ* (1895), 392-93

Shaw, George Bernard, *Back to Methuselah* (1921), 271

Shelley, Percy Bysshe, 161, 173, 187(36), 190, 192, 203, 243(1), 405
Alastor (1816), 183
Complete Poetical Works (1929), 186(34)
Hellas (1822), 183, **187-88**
Queen Mab (1813), **183-84**, 185, 186, 187
Prometheus Unbound (1820), 201
St. Irvyne, or the Rosicrucian (1811), **183**
"Wandering Jew's Soliloquy" (*ca.*1812 [1887]), 183, **184**, 187

Shelley, Percy Bysshe, and Thomas Medwin, *Wandering Jew* (*ca.*1810), 183, **184-87**

Shelley's Poetical Works, ed. G. E. Woodberry (1892), 185

Shenstone, William, 168(13)

Sheridan, Richard Brinsley, *School for Scandal* (1777), 168, 209

Shillito, Edward, "Disciple Whom Jesus Loved" (1916), 292

Sibyl. See Lagerkvist, Pär, 387

Siena, Mariano da, *Viaggio in Terra Santa* (1431), ed. Domenico Moreni (1822), **24**, 33

Sigler de Huerta, Antonio, *Cinco blancas de Juan de Espera en Dios* (1669), **167**

Silbergleit, Arthur
poems, in *Israelitisches Familienblatt* (1912), **299**
See Béranger, Pierre-Jean de, 207

Silberlinge des Judas. See Kalina, Josef Jaroslav, 246

Silberstein, August, *Verwandelte Ahasver* (1899), **304**

Siliga, Francis, "Bolygó zsidó" (1928), 417(9)

Simonet, E., *Malédiction* (1886), **249**

Simonyi, Alexander, "Ahasver" (1912), **353**

Simrock, Karl
"Ewige Jude" (1844), **227**
"Ewige Jude" (1853), 227
See Libavius

Skorra, Thekla, "Ahasverus" (1908), 347(19), **353**

Smets, Wilhelm, "Ahasver" (1835), **214**

Socard, Alexis, *Livres populaires* (1865), 165(3), 401(12)

Soendermann, Willi, *Ahasver, der ewige Jude* (1902), **310**

Soergel, Albert, *Ahasver-Dichtungen seit Goethe* (1905), 222(24), 410

Solinus, Christian, *Chronologia* (1615), **113**

Sommerville, Maxwell, *Wanderer's Legend* (1902), **337-38**

Song about Wandering Jew and Bonhomme Misère (*ca.*1700), **58-59**, 399

Sonnabend, Gustav, *Verlorene Manuscript* (1865), **267-68**

Sonnenkalb, Paul, "Ahasver," ed. Carl F. Wittmann (1895), 312

Soranzo. See Ranzo, Carlo

Southey, Robert, *Curse of Kehama* (1810), **181**, 184, 190, 268(36)

Speight, Harry, *Craven and North-West Yorkshire Highlands* (1892), 134(13)

Spengler, Oswald, *Decline of the West*, (1918), 283

Spinoza, Baruch, 170

Sponer, Andor von. See Arany, János, 320

Staub, Friedrich, and Ludwig Tobler, *Schweizerischen Idiotiken* (1875), 83(53)

Stefani, Bonifacius, *Liber de Perenni Cultu Terrae Sanctae* (*ca.*1552-64 [1875]), **35-36**, 74

Stehling, Nikolaus, *Jungste Gericht* (1841), **208**

Steig, S. Reinhold, "Joseph von Görres' Briefe an Achim von Arnim" (1901), 192(52)

Stein, Hans W., *Ahasver* (1921), **377-78**

Steinmann, F., "Ewige Jude" (1834), **208**

Stern, Maurice Reinhold von, *Insel Ahasvers* (1893), **314-15**

Sternberg, Leo, "Wanderer" (1921), **371**

Sternberg, Victor T., "Wandering Jew in England" (1855), **92**

Sterne, Laurence, *Tristram Shandy* (1760-67), **141**

Steuer, Alfred, *Galizische Ghettogeschichten* (1891), **300**

Stirling-Maxwell, Lady. See Norton, Caroline

Stockton, Frank R., *Vizier of the Two-Horned Alexander* (1899), **291**, 292

Stöcker, *Moderne Judenthum in Deutschland* (1880), 275, 276

Stoker, Bram
Dracula (1897), 328
Famous Impostors (1910), 412

Stolte, Ferdinand, *Faust* (1869), **257**

Storch, Ludwig. See Croly, George, 218

Strackerjan, Ludwig, *Aberglaube und Sagen aus dem Herzogthum Oldenburg* (1867), 77(17), 104(116)

Stranger. See Pinski, David

Strauss, Richard, 318

Strauss und Torney, Lulu von, "Ahasver" (1906), **317-18**, 319, 336

Strindberg, August, "Ahasverus" (1905), **321**

Strodtmann, Adolph, "Ahasver" (1850), **208**

Strohl, Karl Hans, "Ahasver" (1908), 409

Strumpf, David, *Juden in der mittelalterlichen Mysterien-, Mirakel- und Moralitäten-Dichtung Frankreichs* (1920), 39(3)

Sturm, Julius, "Ahasver" (1907), **300**

Suchnach, Wolffgang, 42

Suden, Hermann, *Gelehrte Criticus über curieuse Dubia* (1707), 125

Sudermann, Daniel, verse supplement to Dudulaeus pamphlets (1621), 51(26), 163

Sue, Eugène
  Juif errant (1844-45), dramatized Adolphe d'Ennery, Prosper Dinaux, Eugène Sue (1850); dramatized George Lander (1894); dramatized Leopold Lewis (1894); dramatized Montdidier and Saint-Ernest (1849); dramatized T. G. Paulton (1894); dramatized Carl Schmidt (Carlschmidt) (*Ewige Jude, von Eugène Sue*, 1846), 68, 146(40), 155(65), 230, **231-35**, 236, 237, 238-39, 244, 259, 263, 271, 276, 281, 292(3), 293, 322, 328, 334, 400, 402, 405, 414, 418
  Mystères de Paris (1842-43), **232**, 236

Sullivan, Arthur Seymour, 275

Sullivan, Arthur Seymour, and William Schwenck Gilbert, *Mikado* (1885), 53

Sulzbach, A. See Judah ha-Levi

Surprizing History of the Wandering Jew of Jerusalem (1780), **118-19**, 121

Svatovítský rukopis, 21, 32, 67

Swift, Jonathan, *Gulliver's Travels* (1726), 137, 138, 139(24), 144, 174, 242, 416

Sylva, Carmen. See Elizabeth of Romania

Sylvester, Hector. See Wölffert, Wilhelm

Szabolcsi, Lewis, "Ahasver" (1910), **353**

Szabolcska, Michael, "Bolygó zsidó" (1894), **353**

Szerviczky, Margaret, *Jézus* (1914), **352**

Szilágyi, Francis, "Ahasuerus" (1902), **353**

Szilágyi, Géza, *Ahasvér karácsonya* (1903), **353**

Szittya, Emil, *Klaps, oder Wie sich Ahasver als Saint Germain entpuppt* (1924), **366-67**

Tannhäuser und der ewige Jude. See Grässe, Johann Georg Theodor, 402

Tardel, S. H., "Ahasver-Gedichte" (1902), 227(38)

Tarry Thou Till I Come. See Croly, George, 189

Taschenbuch für die vaterländische Geschichte, ed. Joseph von Hormayr-Nortenburg (1834), 83(54), 114(17)

Taylor, Archer, "Notes on the Wandering Jew" (1918), 31(45)

Tennyson, Alfred, 315
  In Memoriam (1850), 243
  Locksley Hall (1842), 231
  Princess (1874), 271

Tertullian, Quintus Septimius Florens, *De Anima* (*ca*.202-8), ed. J. H. Waszink (1947), 15

Tharsander, *Schau-platz vieler ungereimter Meynungen und Erzehlungen* (1742), 109(3), **124**

Theatrum Europaeum (1702), **110**, 132

Theophylactus, 15(6)

Theremin, Franz, *Ewige Jude* (1835), 217-18, **241**

Thiele, Just Matthias, *Danmarks Folkesagn* (1843-60), 102(111)

Thieme, August, "Ewige Jude" (1848), **210**

Thilo, Gottfried, *Meletma historicum de Judaeo immortali* (1668), trans. (*Unsterbliche Jude*, 1702), 122

Thomas Aquinas, 38
  Catena aurea in quatuor evangelia (13th C.), 12(2)

Thompson, Francis, "Hound of Heaven" (1893), 352

Thompson, James Westfall, and Bernard J. Holm, *History of Historical Writing* (1942), 141(29)

Thompson, Stith, *Motif-Index of Folk Literature* (1955-58), 1(1), 5(7, 11), 7(13), 27(33), 184(29)

Thomson, James (B. V.), 265

Thorald, Niels Henrik, *Tod dem Tode* (1919), **358-59**

Thoreau, Henry David, 391

Thümmel, Conrad, "Mittelalterische Volkssagen als Ausdrück religios-politischen Kampfe" (1898), 407-8

Thurston, Ernest Temple, *Wandering Jew* (1921), **363-64**

Thus Spake Zarathustra. See Nietzsche, Friedrich, 243

Tideman, Bruno, *Ahasverus* (1870), 166(4), 402

Tille, A. See Nietzsche, Friedrich, 243

Tillier, Claude, *Mon oncle Benjamin* (1843), trans. B. R. Tucker (*My Uncle Benjamin*, 1890), trans. Marie Lorenz (*My Uncle Benjamin*, 1941), **229**

Tizio, Sigismondo, chronicle (1550), 24, 41, 42

Tobler, Ludwig, and Friedrich Staub, *Schweizerischen Idiotiken* (1875), 83(53)

Toller, Ernst, *Wandlung* (1920), 347

Trachtenberg, Joshua, *Devil and the Jews* (1943), 39(1, 3)

Tragedy of Man. See Madách, Emeric

Trautmann, F., "Ahasverus" (1843), **208**

Travels and Adventures of James Massey. See Tyssot de Patot, Simon, 132

Travels and Observations of Hareach, the Wandering Jew. See Galt, John, 146(45), 148

Travels of Sir John Mandeville (14th C.), 57

Treitschke, Heinrich von, 275, 277

Trenck, Siegfried von der, *Don Juan-Ahasver* (1930), **385-86**

Trenne nya och mycket märkwärdige Berättelser (1826), 67

Trenne Trowärdiga Relationer (1805), 66

Tresserra, Ceferino, *Judía Errante* (1862), 414-15

Trevelyan, Marie, *Folk-Lore and Folk-Stories of Wales* (1909), 94(94, 95)

Tucker, B. R. See Tillier, Claude

Tupper, Frederick
"Pardoner's Tale," ed. William Frank Bryan and Germaine C. Dempster (1941), 247(4)
See Map, Walter

Twain, Mark. See Clemens, Samuel L.

Tyler, Robert, *Ahasuerus* (1842), **216**

Tyssot de Patot, Simon, *Voyages et Aventures de Jacques Massé* (1710), trans. Stephen Whately (*Travels and Adventures of James Massey*, 1733), **132-33**

Uhde, Hermann. See *H. A. O. Reichard*

Ullman, R., *Feldpredigt* (1907), **322**

Ulrich, Johann Caspar, *Sammlung Jüdischer Geschichten* (1768), 115(21)

Ungnad, Oskar, "Ahasver" (1898), **316-17**

Unruhiger Wall-Bruder aus dem Jüdenthumb (1660), **52-53**
See also Ahasuerus-book

Unsterbliche Jude. See Thilo, Gottfried

Unterhaltungen für die langen Winterabend (1822), 399

V., B. See Thomson, James

Vajda, John, *Vegtelenseg* (1875), **279**

Vanegas, Alexo, *Agonía del Tránsito de la Muerte* (1537), 29

Vannozzo, Francesco, 23

Varenbergh, Emile, *Messager des sciences historiques* (1870), 111(9)

Vasconcellos, Carolina Michaelis de, "Judeu errante em Portugal" (1887-89, 1893-95), 28(37), 404

Vasconcellos, Jorge Ferreira de, *Eufrosina* (1561), 28, 407

Vermeylen, August, *Wandelende Jood* (1906), trans. Anton Kippenberg (1917); Gaby Vermeylen (1925), **319-20**, 380

Vermeylen, Gaby. See Vermeylen, August, 319

Vernaleken, Theodor, *Alpensagen* (1858), 80(36), 81(37), 82(48), 83(50, 51, 54), 84(62)

Verreyn, Alfred, "Ahasverieden" (1908), 292

Verscheyde Voyagien, ofte Reysen. See Aerts van Mecheln, Jan, 34

Vestovyia pisma (1663), 67

Veteuil, Dutertre de, *Réveil de l'Ambigu* (1841), **231**

Vetter, Ferdinand, "Jezus" (1911), **339**

Viereck, George Sylvester, 365, 416

Viereck, George Sylvester, and Paul Eldridge
My First Two Thousand Years (1928), 153, **359-60**
Salome, the Wandering Jewess (1930), 153, **360-61**, 415

Villalón, Cristobal de
Crotalon (ca.1557), **29-30**, 49, 53, 108
Viaje de Turquia (ca.1540), 29

Violet, Franz, "Sage vom ewigen Juden" (1886), 409

Vörösmarty, Michael, *Örök zsidóból* (1850), **279**

Vogel, Johann Jacob. See *Annales Lipsienses*

Vogl, Johann Nepomuk, "Ewige wanderende Jude ging," ed. Edmund Duller (1835), **242**

Voinovich, Géza, *Magyar passio* (1931), 417

Volkmann, Joseph, *Gesellschaftliche Stellung der Juden* (1876), 276

Volksbuch, French. See *Histoire admirable du juif errant*

Volksbuch, German. See Ahasuerus-book

Volksbücher 52 (ca.1850), 402

Volländer-Riesberg, in *Kalender und Jahrbuch für Israeliten* (1848), **214**

Voltaire
Candide (1759), 144, 174, 201

Siècle de Louis XIV (1751), 141(29)

Vonbun, Franz Josef, *Sagen Voralbergs* (1889), 80(36)

Vrchlicky, Jaroslav
"Jarní zpěv Ahasvera" (1878), **283**
"Kříž božetěchův" (1874), **283**
"Smir Ahasverův" (1902), **283**

W., M. See Wilson, Miles

Wackernagel, Wilhelm, "Ewige Jude" (1839), **225**

Waerachtight Bescrijvinghe van twee nieue Propheten (1616), **108**, 120

Wagenheim, F. T. See Zeune, A. A.

Wagner, Richard, 273
Fliegende Holländer (1843), 8, 352
Götterdämmerung (1874), 283
Parsifal (1877-82), 393

Wahre eigentliche Abildung desz unsterblichen Heydens Joseph Krantz (ca.1750), **121-22**, 132

Walde, Philo von, "Ahasver" (ca.1900), **342**

Waldeck, Oskar, *Ewige Jude* (1909), 300-1

Waldegg, Egon, *Judenfrage* (1879), 276

Waldis, Burkhard, fable (16th C.), 49

Walford, Naomi. See Lagerkvist, Pär: *Ahasuerus död*, 390; *Sibyllan*, 388

Wallace, Lewis
Ben Hur (1880), 310, 311
Prince of India (1893), 146(42), 189, **310-12**

Wallace, Paul A. W., *Baptiste Larocque* (1923), **371**

Wall-Bruder. See *Unruhiger Wall-Bruder aus dem Jüdenthumb*

Walliser Sagen-Sitten (1872), 83(53)

Wandelende Jezuït in 1845 (1845), 236(15)

Wandelende Jood in een zothuis met den grooten advokaet der logie en kompe (1845), 236(15)

Wandelende Jood te Munster. See Collin de Plancy, J., 236

Wandering Jew [motion picture] (1933), 394

Wandering Jew, or the Shoemaker of Jerusalem (ca.1769), **117-18**, 121

Wandering Jew: Or the Shooemaker of Jerusalem (1620), **61-63**, 66, 117, 119, 135, 163, 177, 401

Wandering Jew's Chronicle (ca.1714), 141

Wandering Jew Telling Fortunes to Englishmen. See Malone, W.

Ward, Mrs. Humphrey, 339

Warfel, 395

Warhafftige Contrafactur . . . von einem Juden (1614-19), **51-52**
See also Dudulaeus pamphlets

Warhafftige erschreckliche newe Zeitung und Geschicht (1597), **40**

Warnke, Karl. See Marie de France: *Lais der Marie de France*

Waszink, J. H. See Tertullian, Quintus Septimius Florens

Weckerlin, Jean, *Chansons populaires du pays de France* (1903), 166(4)

Wedekind, Franz, "Sommer, 1898" (ca.1900), **343**

Wedell, R. A. C. von, *Vorurtheil oder berechtiger Hass?* (1880), 276

Wegner, Arnim T., "Poeta Ahasverus" (1924), **367**

Weingärtner, W., *Aussprache des Gothischen zur Zeit des Ulfilas* (1658), 146(46)

Weingartner, Felix, *Lehre von der Wiedergeburt und das musikalische Drama . . . "Die Erlösung"* (1896), **325-26**

Wells, H. G., 365

Welsius, Dr., 43, 44

Welte, Benedict, and Heinrich Joseph Wetzer, in *Wetzer und Welte's Kirchenlexicon oder Encyklopädie der katholischen Theologie* (1889), 406

Wendt, Herman. See Gründler, Wilhelm

Werfel, Franz V., *Jakobowsky und der Oberst*, trans. Gustave O. Arlt (*Jacobowsky and the Colonel*), dramatized S. N. Behrman (*Jacobowsky and the Colonel*) (1944), **367**

Werner, Sonja. See Gorki, Maxim

Werner, Zacharias, "Ewige Jude" (1840-44), **200**

Wesselofsky, Alexander, "Ewige Jude" (1881, 1885), 74(8, 9), 406

Westorp, Adolf von, "Ahasver" (1895), **352**

Wetzer, Heinrich Joseph, and Benedict Welte, in *Wetzer und Welte's Kirchenlexicon oder Encyklopädie der katholischen Theologie* (1889), 406

Whately, Stephen. See Tyssot de Patot, Simon, 132

Whiston, William, *Longitude Discovered by the Eclipses, Occultations, and Conjunctions of Jupiter's Planets* (1738), 138(21)

Whitaker, Thomas D., *History and Antiquities of the Deanery of Craven* (1805), 133(10), 134(11, 13)

Whitman, Walt, *Passage to India* (1871), 250

Widney, Joseph P., *Ahasuerus* (1915), **384-85**

Wihl, Ludwig
"Ahasver" (1839), **225**, 400
"Ahasver-Sage" (1838), 400
"Ahasvers Klage" (1901), **297**

Wilbrandt, Adolf, *Meister von Palmyra* (1889), 348-49

Wilde, Georg, *Ewige Jude* (1914), **299**

Wilder, Thornton, *Skin of Our Teeth* (1942), 271

Wilhelm, Paul. See Dworaczek, Wilhelm

Wilkins, John, *Discovery of a World in the Moone* (1638), rev. (*Discourse Concerning a New World and Another Planet*, 1640), 136(20)

Will, Peter. See Goethe, Johann Wolfgang von: "Ewige Juden erstes Fetzen," 173

Williams, Henry S., *Great Astronomers* (1930), 135(15)

Wilson, Miles (M. W.)
    History of Israel Jobson, the Wandering Jew (1757), 133-34, **135-41**, 152, 174, 364
    Man in the Moon (ca.1752), 134-35, 136

Winckler, Joseph
    Irrgarten Gottes (1922), **366**
    Verwegenen Chirurgus weltberühmbt Johann Andraes doctor Eisenbart (1929), **366**

Windholz, Josef L., *Ahasver* (1909), **308**

Wise, Isaac M., *Wandering Jew* (ca.1899), 295

Withalm, Hans, *Ecce Homines* (1904), **326**

Witte, Karl, "Laufende Jude auf der Grimsel" (1820), **191**, 192, 194, 214

Wittich, L. C., "Ahasuerus" (1839), **226**, 244

Wittman, Carl F. See Sonnenkalb, Paul

Wölffert, Wilhelm (Hector Sylvester), *Goldene Kleeblat* (1894), **341**

Wohlmut, Leonhard, *Zerstörung von Jerusalem* (1857), **248**

Wolf, Ferdinand, "Beiträge zur spanischen Volkspoesie aus den Werken Fernán Caballeros" (1859), 167(9)

Wolff, Gustav, and Johanna Wolff, *Ahasver* (1899), **306-8**

Wolff, Johanna, and Gustav Wolff, *Ahasver* (1899), **306-8**

Wolff, O. L. B., "Ewige Jude" (1829), **198**

Wolfram, L. H. (F. Marlow), *Faust* (1839), **225**, 268

Woodberry, G. E. See *Shelley's Poetical Works*

Wordsworth, William, 190, 199
    Borderers (1796-97), **181-82**
    "Song for the Wandering Jew" (1800), **182**, 191
    "Though Narrow Be That Old Man's Cares" (1807), 93(92)

Wraith, W. J., *Wandering Jew* (1917), **315**

Wright, Edward, 61

Wunderbare Erzehlung von einen Juden Ahasverus (ca.1662), **69-70**, 128

Wunderbarlicher Bericht von einem Juden Ahasverus (1603), **44**

Wurttemberg, Alexander von, "Ahasver und Bonaparte" (1838), **217**

Yarmolinsky, Avrahm, "Wandering Jew" (1929), 21(17), 67(63), 74(7, 11), 75(12, 13), 95(96, 97), 283(55), 406(40), 411

Yeats, William Butler, "Trembling of the Veil" (1927), 187(35)

Zachariae, Theodor, "Abergläubische Meinungen und Gebräuche des Mittelalters" (1912), 5(10)

Zangwill, Israel
    Children of the Ghetto (1892), **299**
    Dreamers of the Ghetto (1898), **299**
    Ghetto Comedies (1907), **299**
    Ghetto Tragedies (1893), **299**
    Grandchildren of the Ghetto (1894), **299**
    War for the World (1916), **299**

Zedlitz, Johann Christoph von, "Wanderungen des Ahasverus" (1839), **208**, 405

Zeldenthuis, Jan, *Ahasverus in het allerlaatste jaar* (1927), 386(43)

Zeune, A. A. (F. T. Wagenheim), *Perle von Zion* (1839), 225(32)

Zhukovski, V. A., epic (1852), trans. (*Ewige Jude, aus dem russischen Übersetzt*, 1883; *Juif errant*, 1885), **256-57**

Zimmer, Hans, *Ahasver der Liebe* (ca.1910), **292**

Zimolong, Bertrand. See *Navis Peregrinorum*

Zingerle, Ignatz, *Sagen aus Tirol* (1891), 81(41)

Zirus, Werner
    "Ahasverus, der ewige Jude" (1930), 410, 411
    "Ewige Jude in der Dichtung" (1928), 168(14), 173(18), 410

Zondervan, P., "Legende van den wandelende Jood" (1917), 412

Zoozmann, Richard
    "Ahasver" (1890-91), **274-75**, 353, 356
    "Trost" (1886), **274**, 277

Zsolt, Bela, "Legenda a jeruzsálemi vargáról" (1923), **418**

Zuallardo, Giovanni, *Devotissimo viaggio di Gerusalemme* (1587), 33